PROGRAMMING IN VISUAL BASIC .NET

PROGRAMMING IN VISUAL BASIC .NET

Annotated Instructor's Edition

Julia Case Bradley
Mt. San Antonio College

Anita C. Millspaugh
Mt. San Antonio College

Boston   Burr Ridge, IL   Dubuque, IA   Madison, WI   New York   San Francisco   St. Louis
Bangkok   Bogotá   Caracas   Kuala Lumpur   Lisbon   London   Madrid   Mexico City
Milan   Montreal   New Delhi   Santiago   Seoul   Singapore   Sydney   Taipei   Toronto

McGraw-Hill Higher Education

A Division of The **McGraw-Hill** *Companies*

PROGRAMMING IN VISUAL BASIC .NET

Published by McGraw-Hill/Irwin, a business unit of The McGraw-Hill Companies, Inc., 1221 Avenue of the Americas, New York, NY, 10020. Copyright © 2003 by The McGraw-Hill Companies, Inc. All rights reserved. No part of this publication may be reproduced or distributed in any form or by any means, or stored in a database or retrieval system, without the prior written consent of The McGraw-Hill Companies, Inc., including, but not limited to, in any network or other electronic storage or transmission, or broadcast for distance learning.

Some ancillaries, including electronic and print components, may not be available to customers outside the United States.

This book is printed on acid-free paper.

domestic   1 2 3 4 5 6 7 8 9 0 QPD/QPD 0 9 8 7 6 5 4 3 2
international   1 2 3 4 5 6 7 8 9 0 QPD/QPD 0 9 8 7 6 5 4 3 2

ISBN 0-07-245903-4 (student edition)
ISBN 0-07-282650-9 (annotated instructor's edition)

Publisher: *George Werthman*
Sponsoring editor: *Steve Schuetz*
Developmental editor: *Craig S. Leonard*
Manager, Marketing and Sales: *Paul Murphy*
Media producer: *Greg Bates*
Project manager: *Destiny Rynne*
Production supervisor: *Rose Hepburn*
Coordinator freelance design: *Artemio Ortiz Jr.*
Senior supplement producer: *Rose M. Range*
Cover design: *Graphic Visions*
Interior design: *Artemio Ortiz, Jr.*
Typeface: *11/13 Bodoni*
Compositor: *GAC Indianapolis*
Printer: *Quebecor World Dubuque Inc.*

Library of Congress Cataloging-in-Publication Data

Bradley, Julia Case.
    Programming in Visual Basic .NET / Julia Case Bradley, Anita C. Millspaugh.—4th ed.
      p. cm.
    Includes index.
    ISBN 0-07-245903-4 (alk.paper)
    1. Microsoft Visual BASIC. 2. BASIC (Computer program language) I. Millspaugh,
A.C. (Anita C.) II. Title.
QA76.73.B3 B697 2003
005.13'3—dc21

                2002024411

INTERNATIONAL EDITION ISBN 0-07-112477-2
Copyright © 2003. Exclusive rights by The McGraw-Hill Companies, Inc. for manufacture and export. This book cannot be re-exported from the country to which it is sold by McGraw-Hill.
The International Edition is not available in North America.

www.mhhe.com

PREFACE

Visual Basic (VB) has become the most popular programming language for several reasons. VB is easy to learn, which makes it an excellent tool for understanding elementary programming concepts. In addition, it has evolved into such a powerful and popular product that skilled Visual Basic programmers are in demand in the job market.

Visual Basic .NET, the latest version of VB, is practically a new language. Microsoft has completely rewritten the language to be fully object oriented, compatible with many other languages using the new .NET Framework. This book incorporates the object-oriented concepts throughout, as well as the new syntax and terminology of the language.

Visual Basic .NET is designed to allow the programmer to develop applications that run under Windows and/or in a Web browser without the complexity generally associated with programming. With very little effort, the programmer can design a screen that holds standard elements such as buttons, check boxes, radio buttons, text boxes, and list boxes. Each of these objects operates as expected, producing a "standard" Windows or Web user interface.

About This Text

This textbook is intended for use in an introductory programming course, which assumes no prior knowledge of computer programming. The later chapters are also appropriate for professional programmers who are learning a new language to upgrade their skills.

This text assumes that the student is familiar with the Windows operating environment and can use an Internet browser application.

Approach

This text incorporates the basic concepts of programming, problem solving, programming logic, as well as the design techniques of an object-oriented, event-driven language.

Chapter topics are presented in a sequence that allows the programmer to learn how to deal with a visual interface while acquiring important programming skills such as creating projects with objects, decisions, loops, and data management.

A high priority is given to writing applications that are easy for the user to understand and to use. Students are presented with interface design guidelines throughout the text.

Features of This Text

Hands-On Programming Examples

These complete programming exercises guide students through the process of planning, writing, and executing Visual Basic programs.

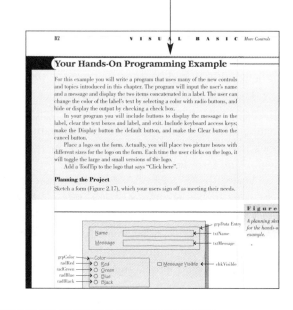

Introduction to Visual Basic .NET

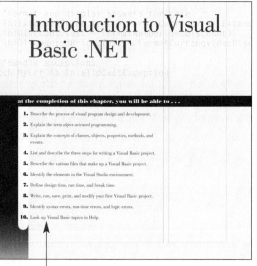

Learning Objectives

These specific objectives tell students what will be covered in the chapter and what they will be able to do after completing the chapter.

Feedback Questions

The Feedback Questions give students time to reflect on the current topic and to evaluate their understanding of the details.

TIPs

Tips in the margins help students avoid potential trouble spots in their programs and encourage them to develop good programming habits from the start.

Case Studies

The Case Studies provide continuing-theme exercises that may be used throughout the course.

Programming Exercises

The programming exercises test students' understanding of the programming skills covered in the chapter.

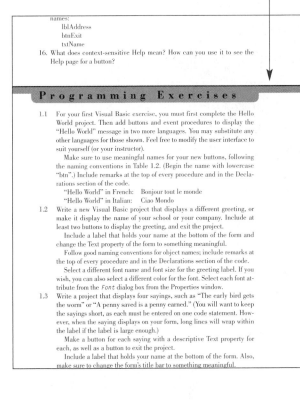

Changes in This Edition

This edition is a major revision of the text, reflecting the major revision of Visual Basic. The language is essentially new and now contains all of the features of a completely object-oriented language including inheritance and polymorphism. We have introduced object-oriented programming (OOP) in Chapter 1 and use its features in every chapter of the book.

Although all chapters have major changes, we have taken several steps to ease the transition. The new text follows essentially the same sequence as the previous editions. Instructors will appreciate the annotated edition, which shows the significant changes in the language. The code for all in-chapter projects is also available to instructors.

Features of This Text

Each chapter begins with identifiable objectives and a brief overview. Numerous coding examples as well as hands-on projects with guidance for the planning and coding appear throughout. Thought-provoking feedback questions give students time to reflect on the current topic and to evaluate their understanding of the details. The end-of-chapter items include a chapter review, questions, programming exercises, and four case studies.

Chapter 1, *"Introduction to Visual Basic .NET,"* introduces Microsoft's new Visual Studio integrated development environment (IDE). The single environment is now used for multiple languages. A step-by-step program gets students into programming very quickly (quicker than most books). The chapter introduces the OOP concepts of objects, properties, methods, and events. The elements of debugging and using the Help system are also introduced.

Chapter 2, *"More Controls,"* demonstrates techniques for good program design, including making the interface easy for users as well as guidelines for designing maintainable programs. Several controls are introduced, including text boxes, group boxes, check boxes, radio buttons, and picture boxes. Note that group boxes replace frames; radio buttons are renamed option buttons; and all of the controls have different properties than their VB 6 counterparts.

Chapter 3, *"Variables, Constants, and Calculations,"* presents the concepts of using data and declaring the data type. Some of the data types have changed, and VB .NET is much more particular about using the correct data type. Students learn to follow standards to indicate the data type and scope of variables and constants and to use the new `Option Strict`, which forces adherence to strong data typing.

Error handling has changed and is much improved. VB .NET now includes structured exception handling using the `Try/Catch/Finally` structure, which is introduced in this chapter along with calculations. The student learns to display error messages using the new MessageBox class and also learns about the OOP concept of overloaded constructors.

Chapter 4, *"Decisions and Conditions,"* introduces taking alternate actions based on conditions formed with the relational and logical operators. In addition to the If statement, this chapter uses functions to validate input data. The debugging features of the IDE are covered, including a step-by-step tutorial covering stepping through program statements and checking intermediate values during execution.

Chapter 5, "*Menus, Sub Procedures, and Functions,*" covers the new and greatly improved Menu Editor. Menus and context menus are now components that are added to a component tray (also new). Students learn to include both menus and context menus in projects, as well as to write general sub procedures and functions.

Chapter 6, "*OOP: Creating Object-Oriented Programs,*" explains more of the theory of object-oriented programming. Although we have been using OOP concepts since Chapter 1, in this chapter students learn the terminology and application of OOP. Inheritance is covered for visual objects (forms) and for extending existing classes. The samples are kept simple enough for an introductory class.

Chapter 7, "*Lists, Loops, and Printing,*" incorporates list boxes and combo boxes into projects, providing the opportunity to discuss looping procedures and printing lists of information. Many properties and methods for list controls have changed in VB .NET. Printing is totally different, using a graphics object and a callback event. The new printing controls also include a Print Preview, which should be a welcome addition for students and instructors, who can now view output without actually printing it.

Chapter 8, "*Arrays,*" introduces arrays, which follow logically from the lists covered in Chapter 7. Although the concept of arrays has not changed, arrays are declared differently in VB .NET than in VB 6. But the most significant change in this chapter is the Structure statement, which replaces user-defined types.

Chapter 9, "*Programming with Web Forms,*" is an all new chapter using the new Web Forms of VB .NET. Web Forms are used to create Web pages that execute in a browser application. Students learn to design and develop simple Web applications.

Chapter 10, "*Accessing Database Files,*" introduces ADO.NET, which is Microsoft's new technology for accessing data in a database. This chapter shows how to create connections, data adapters, and datasets. Programs include accessing data from both Windows Forms and Web Forms. Students learn to bind data tables to a data grid and bind individual data fields to controls such as labels and text boxes. Updating a dataset is also introduced.

Chapter 11, "*Saving Data and Objects in Files,*" presents the all-new techniques for data file handling. Students learn to save and read small amounts of data using streams. The StreamWriter and StreamReader objects are used to store and reload the contents of a combo box.

Object serialization is used to persist objects. The hands-on example includes both serialization (saving) and deserialization (restoring) objects.

Chapter 12, "*Graphics and Animation,*" covers the new classes and methods of GDI+. The chapter covers graphics objects, pens, and brushes for drawing shapes and lines. Animation is accomplished using the Timer control and the SetBounds method for moving controls.

Chapter 13, *"Additional Topics in Visual Basic,"* introduces some advanced VB topics. This final chapter covers multiple document interfaces (MDI), toolbars and status bars, and creating reports from databases using Crystal Reports. All of these topics are greatly changed from VB 6.

The appendices offer important additional material. Appendix A holds the answers to all Feedback questions. Appendix B covers methods and functions for math and string handling, which are totally different for VB .NET. In the new OOP style, most actions that were formerly done with functions are now accomplished with methods of the Math class and String class. Appendix C, on mastering the Visual Studio environment, is all new, based on the new IDE.

Resources for Instructors

Instructor's Manual   The Instructor's Manual is available on CD-ROM or on the book's Website. It contains the following features:

*   Objectives with built-in summaries for each chapter.

*   Teaching suggestions.

*   Answers to the Review Questions from the back of each chapter.

*   Chapter topics covered in the Programming Exercises.

Testbank   The Testbank provides questions that cover the terminology and concepts found in each chapter. The test questions appear in the form of true/false and multiple choice questions.

Diploma by Brownstone   Diploma is the most flexible, powerful, and easy-to-use computer-based testing system available for higher education. The Diploma system allows instructors to create an exam as a printed version, as a LAN-based online version, or as an Internet version. Diploma also includes grade book features, which automate the entire testing process.

PowerPoint Presentation   The PowerPoint presentation follows the outline of the Instructor's Manual and gives instructors a resource for presenting the text material to a classroom.

Figures from the Book   All of the illustrations, screenshots, and tables are available electronically for use in presentations, transparencies, or handouts.

Online Learning Center   (www.mhhe.com/cit/program/bradley/vbnet) Designed to provide a wide variety of learning opportunities for students, the Website includes additional Programming Exercises and Case Studies, Self-Quizzes for students, downloadable data files, and other great resources for both instructors and students.

Digital Solutions to Help You Manage Your Course

PageOut   PageOut is our Course Website Development Center that offers a syllabus page, URL, McGraw-Hill Online Learning Center content, online exercises and quizzes, gradebook, discussion board, and an area for student Web pages.

Available free with any McGraw-Hill/Irwin product, PageOut requires no prior knowledge of HTML, no long hours of coding, and a way for course coordinators and professors to provide a full-course Website. PageOut offers a series of templates—simply fill them with your course information and click on one of 16 designs. The process takes under an hour and leaves you with a professionally designed Website. We'll even get you started with sample Websites, or enter your syllabus for you! PageOut is so straightforward and intuitive, it's little wonder that more than 12,000 college professors are using it. For more information, visit the PageOut Website at www.pageout.net.

The Online Learning Center can be delivered through any of these platforms:

McGraw-Hill Learning Architecture (TopClass)
Blackboard.com
Ecollege.com (formerly Real Education)
WebCT (a product of Universal Learning Technology)

McGraw-Hill has partnerships with WebCT and Blackboard to make it even easier to take your course online. Now you can have McGraw-Hill content delivered through the leading Internet-based learning tool for higher education. At McGraw-Hill, we have the following service agreements with WebCT and Blackboard:

Instructor Advantage   Instructor Advantage is a special level of service McGraw-Hill offers in conjunction with WebCT designed to help you get up and running with your new course. A team of specialists will be immediately available to ensure everything runs smoothly through the life of your adoption.

Instructor Advantage Plus   Qualified McGraw-Hill adopters will be eligible for an even higher level of service. A certified WebCT or Blackboard specialist will provide a full day of on-site training for you and your staff. You will then have unlimited e-mail and phone support through the life of your adoption. Contact your local McGraw-Hill representative for more details.

Acknowledgments

Many people have worked very hard to design and produce this text. We would like to thank our editors, Steve Schuetz and Craig Leonard, and the publisher, George Werthman. Our thanks also to the many people who produced this text, including Destiny Rynne, Rose Hepburn, Rose Range, and Artemio Ortiz.

We greatly appreciate Robert Price of Antelope Valley Community College, Avram Malkin of DeVry College of Technology, Joann Cook of College of Du-Page, and Christy McCloskey of International Academy of Design and Technology, for their thorough technical reviews, constructive criticism, and many valuable suggestions. Many thanks to Laura Claytor for her helpful assistance. And most importantly, we are grateful to Dennis, Richard, Tricia, Eric, and Kenna for their support and understanding through the long days and busy phone lines.

The Authors

We have had fun teaching and writing about Visual Basic. We hope that this feeling is evident as you read this book and that you will enjoy learning or teaching this outstanding programming language.

Julia Case Bradley
Anita C. Millspaugh

To the Student

The best way to learn to program in Visual Basic is to do it. If you enter and run the sample projects, you will be on your way to writing applications. Reading the examples without trying to run them is like trying to learn a foreign language or mathematics by just reading about it. Enter the projects, look up your questions in the extensive MSDN Help files, and make those projects *run*.

Installing Visual Basic

For the programs in this text, you need to install IIS (Internet Information Services), the .NET Framework, Visual Basic, and the MSDN (Microsoft Developers Network) library, which contains all of Help and many instructive articles. You do not need to install C++ or C#.

You need IIS if you want to write any Web applications that run in a browser. All of the programs in Chapter 9 require IIS, as well as some programs in Chapter 10.

The order of installation is important. You must install IIS and the .NET Framework before installing VB.

Format Used for Visual Basic Statements

Visual Basic statements, methods, and functions are shown in `this font`. Any values that you must supply are in *`italics`*. Optional items are in [square brackets]. Braces and a vertical bar indicate that you must choose one or the other value {one | other}.
Examples:

```
Const Identifier [As Datatype] = Value
Do {While | Until} Condition
```

As you work your way through this textbook, note that you may see a subset of the available options for a Visual Basic statement or method. Generally, the options that are included reflect those covered in the chapter. If you want to see the complete format for any statement or all versions of a method, refer to Help.

Student Data Files

The student data files are located on the CD-ROM that accompanies the text and also on the text's Website. The following table lists the student data files.

Ch04Debug folder	Debugging Step-by-Step Tutorial.
DatabaseFiles folder	
Files for in-chapter examples and programming exercises	
Biblio.mdb	Small version from VB Version 4
RnRBooks.mdb	In-chapter examples
VBAuto.mdb	VB Auto case study
VBMail.mdb	VB Mail case study
VBVideo.mdb	Video Bonanza case study
VeryBoards.mdb	Very Very Boards case study
Graphics folder	
Graphics files for in-chapter examples and extras to use for exercises	
Books.gif	Extra graphic
Disgruntled.gif	Used for in-chapter Ch12AnimatedGif
DrinkMilk.gif	Extra animated graphic
Fish.gif	Extra animated graphic
Skateboard.gif	Graphic file for Very Very Boards case study
SteamEngine.gif	Used for in-chapter Ch12TimerAnimation
Train.gif	Extra animated graphic
trolley.gif	Extra animated graphic
Unicycle.gif	Extra animated graphic
Welcome.gif	Extra graphic

CONTENTS

CHAPTER

1

Introduction to Visual Basic .NET

at the completion of this chapter, you will be able to . . .

1. Describe the process of visual program design and development.

2. Explain the term *object-oriented programming*.

3. Explain the concepts of classes, objects, properties, methods, and events.

4. List and describe the three steps for writing a Visual Basic project.

5. Describe the various files that make up a Visual Basic project.

6. Identify the elements in the Visual Studio environment.

7. Define design time, run time, and break time.

8. Write, run, save, print, and modify your first Visual Basic project.

9. Identify syntax errors, run-time errors, and logic errors.

10. Look up Visual Basic topics in Help.

Writing Windows Applications with Visual Basic

Using this text, you will learn to write computer programs that run in the Microsoft Windows environment. Your projects will look and act like standard Windows programs. You will use the tools in Visual Basic .NET (VB) and Windows Forms to create windows with familiar elements such as labels, text boxes, buttons, radio buttons, check boxes, list boxes, menus, and scroll bars. Figure 1.1 shows some sample Windows user interfaces.

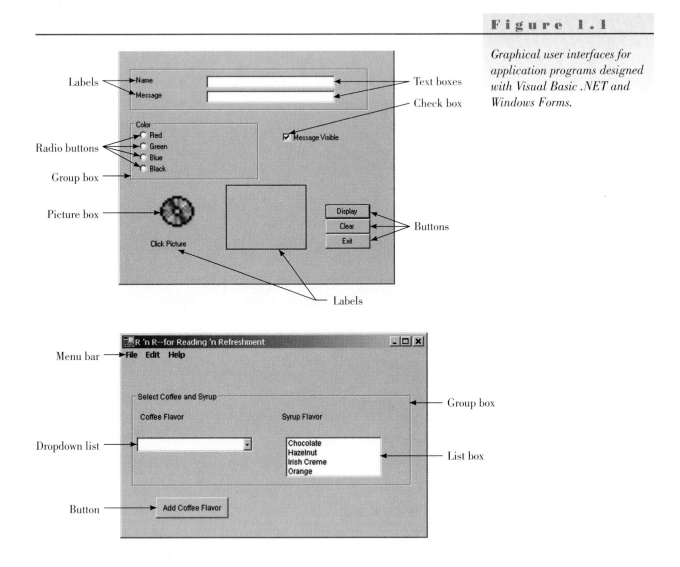

Figure 1.1

Graphical user interfaces for application programs designed with Visual Basic .NET and Windows Forms.

Beginning in Chapter 10, you will create programs using Web Forms. You can run Web Forms applications in a browser, such as Internet Explorer, on the Internet, or on a company intranet. Figure 1.2 shows a Web Form application.

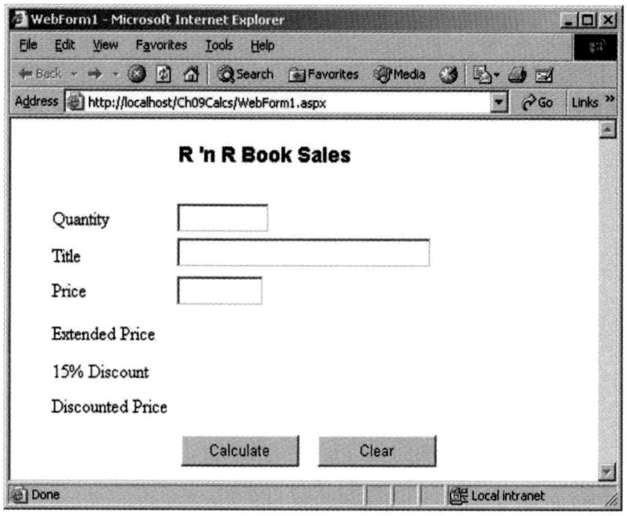

Figure 1.2

A Web Forms application created with Visual Basic .NET, running in a browser.

The Windows Graphical User Interface

Microsoft Windows uses a **graphical user interface,** or **GUI** (pronounced "gooey"). The Windows GUI defines how the various elements look and function. As a Visual Basic programmer, you have available a toolbox of these elements. You will create new windows, called *forms*. Then you will use the toolbox to add the various elements, called *controls*. The projects that you will write follow a relatively new type of programming, called *object-oriented programming*.

Programming Languages: Procedural, Event Driven, and Object Oriented

There are literally hundreds of programming languages. Each was developed to solve a particular type of problem. Most traditional languages, such as BASIC, C, COBOL, FORTRAN, PL/I, and Pascal, are considered *procedural languages*. That is, the program specifies the exact sequence of all operations. Program logic determines the next instruction to execute in response to conditions and user requests.

The newer programming languages, such as C++, Visual Basic .NET, and Java, use a different approach: **object-oriented programming (OOP).** Earlier versions of Visual Basic had many (but not all) elements of an object-oriented language. For that reason, Microsoft referred to Visual Basic 6.0 as an event-driven programming language, rather than an object-oriented language. But with the release of Visual Studio .NET, which includes Visual Basic .NET, VB is finally a true object-oriented language.

In the OOP model, programs are no longer procedural: They do not follow a sequential logic. You, as the programmer, do not take control and determine the sequence of execution. Instead, the user can press keys and click various buttons and boxes in a window. Each user action can cause an event to occur, which triggers a Basic procedure that you have written. For example, the user clicks on a button labeled Calculate. The clicking causes the button's Click event to occur, and the program automatically jumps to a procedure you have written to do the calculation.

The Object Model

In Visual Basic you will work with objects, which have properties, methods, and events. Each object is based on a class.

Objects

Think of an **object** as a thing, or a noun. Examples of objects are forms and controls. **Forms** are the windows and dialog boxes you place on the screen; **controls** are the components you place inside a form, such as text boxes, buttons, and list boxes.

Properties

Properties tell something about an object, such as its name, color, size, location, or how it will behave. You can think of properties as adjectives that describe objects.

When you refer to a property, you first name the object, add a period, and then name the property. For example, refer to the Text property of a form called Form1 as Form1.Text (pronounced "form1 dot text").

Methods

Actions associated with objects are called *methods*. **Methods** are the verbs of object-oriented programming. Some typical methods are `Move`, `Hide`, `Show`, and `Clear`.

You refer to methods as Object.Method ("object dot method"). For example, a `Show` method can apply to different objects. `Form1.Show` shows the form object called Form1; `btnExit.Show` shows the button object called btnExit.

Events

You can write procedures that execute when a particular event occurs. An **event** occurs when the user takes an action, such as clicking a button, pressing a key, scrolling, or closing a window. Events can also be triggered by actions of other objects, such as repainting a form or a timer reaching a preset point.

Classes

A **class** is a template or blueprint used to create a new object. Classes contain the definition of all available properties, methods, and events.

Each time that you create a new object, it must be based on a class. For example, you may decide to place three buttons on your form. Each button is based on the Button class and is considered one object, called an *instance* of the class. Each button (or instance) has its own set of properties, methods, and events. One button may be labeled "OK," one "Cancel," and one "Exit." When the user clicks the OK button, that button's Click event occurs; if the user clicks on the Exit button, that button's Click event occurs. And, of course, you have written different program instructions for each of the button's Click events.

An Analogy

If the concepts of classes, objects, properties, methods, and events are still a little unclear, maybe an analogy will help. Consider an Automobile class. When we say *automobile*, we are not referring to a particular auto, but we know that an automobile has a make and model, a color, an engine, and a number of doors. These elements are the *properties* of the Automobile class.

Each individual car is an object, or an instance of the Automobile class. Each Automobile object has its own settings for the available properties. For example, each object has a Color property, such as MyCar.Color = Blue and YourCar.Color = Red.

The methods, or actions, of the Automobile class might be `Start`, `SpeedUp`, `SlowDown`, and `Stop`. To refer to the methods of a specific object of the class, use `MyCar.Start` and `YourCar.Stop`.

The events of an Automobile class could be Arrive or Crash. In a VB program, you write procedures that specify the actions you want to take when a particular event occurs for an object. For example, you might write a procedure for the YourCar_Crash event. Note that you use an underscore between the object name and event, rather than a period.

Note: Chapter 6 presents object-oriented programming in greater depth.

Microsoft's Visual Studio .NET

The latest version of Microsoft's Visual Studio, called Visual Studio .NET, includes Visual Basic, Visual C++, the new language, C# ("C sharp"), and the .NET Framework. Visual Studio .NET, sometimes referred to as Version 7, is a major revision of the previous version. In fact, Visual Basic was completely rewritten from Version 6 to Version 7.

The .NET Framework

The programming languages in Visual Studio .NET run in the new .NET Framework. The Framework provides for easier development of Web-based and Windows-based applications, allows objects from different languages to operate together, and standardizes how the languages refer to data and objects. Several third-party vendors have announced versions of other languages to run in the .NET Framework, including .NET versions of FORTRAN, COBOL, and Java.

The .NET languages all compile to (are translated to) a common machine language, called Microsoft Intermediate Language (MSIL). The MSIL code, called *managed code*, runs in the Common Language Runtime (CLR), which is part of the .NET Framework.

Visual Basic .NET

Microsoft Visual Basic .NET comes with Visual Studio .NET. You also can purchase a Standard Edition of VB .NET by itself (without the other languages but *with* the .NET Framework). Visual Studio .NET is available in an **Academic Edition,** a **Professional Edition,** an **Enterprise Developer Edition,** and an **Enterprise Architect Edition.** Anyone planning to do professional application development that includes the advanced features of database management should use the Professional Edition or one of the Enterprise editions. You can find a matrix showing the features of each edition in Help.

This text is based on Visual Basic .NET, the current version. You cannot run the projects in this text in any earlier version of VB.

Writing Visual Basic Projects

When you write a Visual Basic application, you follow a three-step process for planning the project and then repeat the process for creating the project.

The Three-Step Process

The three steps for planning a Visual Basic application involve setting up the user interface, defining the properties, and then creating the code.

Planning

1. *Design the user interface*. When you plan the **user interface,** you draw a sketch of the screens the user will see when running your project. On your sketch, show the forms and all the controls that you plan to use. Indicate the names that you plan to give the form and each of the objects on the form. Refer to Figure 1.1 for examples of user interfaces.

   Before you proceed with any more steps, consult with your user and make sure that you both agree on the look and feel of the project.
2. *Plan the properties*. For each object, write down the properties that you plan to set or change during the design of the form.
3. *Plan the Basic code*. In this step you plan the procedures that will execute when your project runs. You will determine which events require action to be taken and then make a step-by-step plan for those actions.

Later, when you actually write the Visual Basic **code,** you must follow the language syntax rules. But during the planning stage, you will write out the actions using **pseudocode,** which is an English expression or comment that describes the action. For example, you must plan for the event that occurs when the user clicks on the Exit button. The pseudocode for the event could be *Terminate the project*.

Programming

After you have completed the planning steps and have approval from your user, you are ready to begin the actual construction of the project. Use the same three-step process that you used for planning.

1. *Define the user interface*. When you define the user interface, you create the forms and controls that you designed in the planning stage. Think of this step as defining the objects you will use in your application.
2. *Set the properties*. When you set the properties of the objects, you give each object a name and define such attributes as the contents of a label, the size of the text, and the words that appear on top of a button and in the form's title bar. You might think of this step as describing each object.
3. *Write the Basic code*. You will use Basic programming statements (called *Basic code*) to carry out the actions needed by your program. You will be surprised and pleased by how few statements you need to create a powerful Windows program. You can think of this third step as defining the actions of your program.

Visual Basic Application Files

A Visual Basic application, called a ***solution,*** can consist of one or more projects. Since all of the solutions in this text have only one project, you can think of one solution = one project. Each project can contain one or more form files. In Chapters 1 through 6, all projects have only one form, so you can think of one project = one form. Starting in Chapter 7, your projects will contain multiple forms and additional files. The HelloWorld application that you will create later in this chapter creates these files:

HelloWorld.sln	The **solution file.** A text file that holds information about the solution and the projects it contains. This is the primary file for the solution, the one that you open to work on or run your project.
HelloWorld.suo	Solution user options file. Stores information about the selected options, so that all customizations can be restored each time you open the solution.
frmHello.vb	A .vb file. Holds the definition of a form, its controls, and code procedures. This is a text file that you can open in any editor. *Warning*: You should not modify this file unless you are using the editor in the Visual Studio environment.
frmHello.resx	A resource file for the form. This text file defines all resources used by the form, including strings of text, numbers, and any graphics.
HelloWorld.vbproj	A **project file.** A text file that describes the project and lists the files that are included in the project.
HelloWorld.vbproj.user	The project user option file. This text file holds project option settings, so that the next time you open the project, all selected options will be restored.

After you run your project, you will find several more files created by the system. The only file that you will open directly is the .sln, or solution file.

• A Solution can contain multiple projects (all ours have only one). A Project can contain multiple forms (ours have only one form in Chapters 1–6). Forms, classes, and code files have an extension of .vb.

The Visual Studio Environment

The **Visual Studio environment** is where you create and test your projects. A development environment, such as Visual Studio, is called an ***integrated development environment* (IDE).** The IDE consists of various tools, including a form designer, which allows you to visually create a form; an editor, for entering and modifying program code; a compiler, for translating the Visual Basic statements into the intermediate machine code; a debugger, to help locate and correct program errors; an object browser, to view the available classes, objects, properties, methods, and events; and a Help facility.

In earlier versions of Visual Studio, each language had its own IDE. For example, to create a VB project you would use the VB IDE, and to create a C++ project you would use the C++ IDE. But in Visual Studio .NET, you use the one IDE to create projects in any of the .NET languages.

- Terminology changes:
  - VB IDE becomes the Visual Studio (VS) IDE.
  - Project Explorer becomes the Solution Explorer.
  - Document window has tabs to display various contents:
    - Form window becomes the Form Designer.
    - Code window becomes the Editor window or the VS editor.
    - Note that the tabbed display is the default but can be turned off in *Tools / Options / General / Tabbed Documents.*

The IDE Start Page

When you open the Visual Studio IDE, you see its Start Page (Figure 1.3). Recent projects appear on the list, which enable you to open an existing project, or you can select `New Project` to begin a new project.

Figure 1.3

The Visual Studio IDE Start Page.

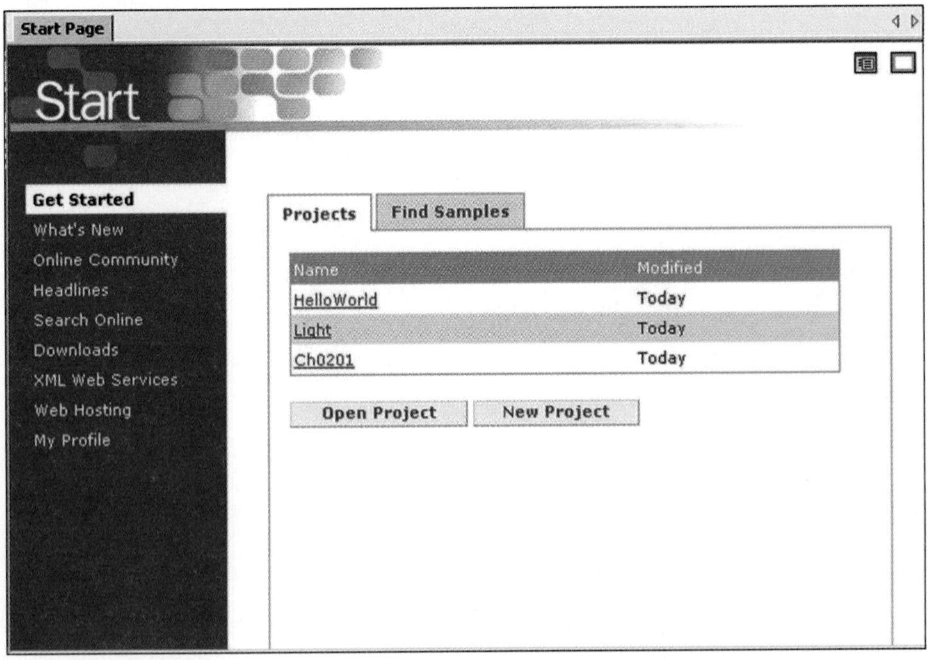

The New Project Dialog

You will create your first Visual Basic projects based on Windows Forms. In the *New Project* dialog (Figure 1.4) select *Visual Basic Projects* in the *Project Types* box and *Windows Application* in the *Templates* box. You also give the project a name and a path on this dialog box.

• The IDE automatically creates a new folder for each project. Do not create your own, or you will have a folder within a folder.

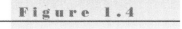

Figure 1.4

Begin a new VB .NET project using Windows Forms.

The IDE Main Window

Figure 1.5 shows the Visual Studio environment's main window and its various child windows. Note that each window can be moved, resized, opened, closed, and customized. Some windows have tabs that allow you to display different contents. Your screen may not look exactly like Figure 1.5; in all likelihood you will want to customize the placement of the various windows.

The IDE main window holds the Visual Studio menu bar and the toolbars.

Figure 1.5

The Visual Studio environment. Each window can be moved, resized, closed, or customized.

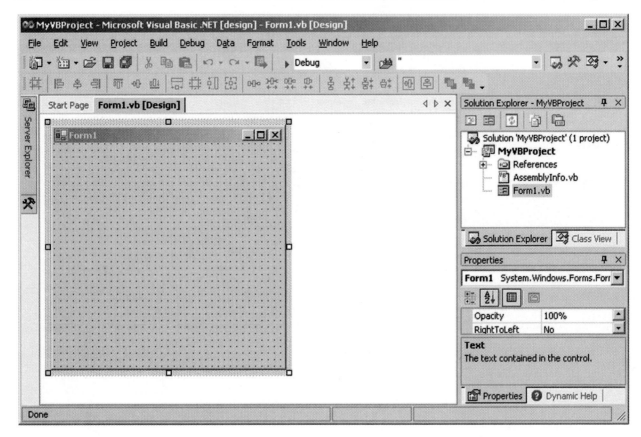

The Toolbars

You can use the buttons on the **toolbars** as shortcuts for frequently used operations. Each button represents a command that can also be selected from a menu. Figure 1.6*a* shows the toolbar buttons on the Standard toolbar, which displays in the main window of the IDE; Figure 1.6*b* shows the Layout toolbar, which displays in the Form Designer; and Figure 1.6*c* shows the Text Editor toolbar, which appears when the Editor window is displayed.

Figure 1.6

The Visual Studio toolbars contain buttons that are shortcuts for menu commands. You can display or hide each of the toolbars: a. *the Standard toolbar;* b. *the Layout toolbar; and* c. *the Text Editor toolbar.*

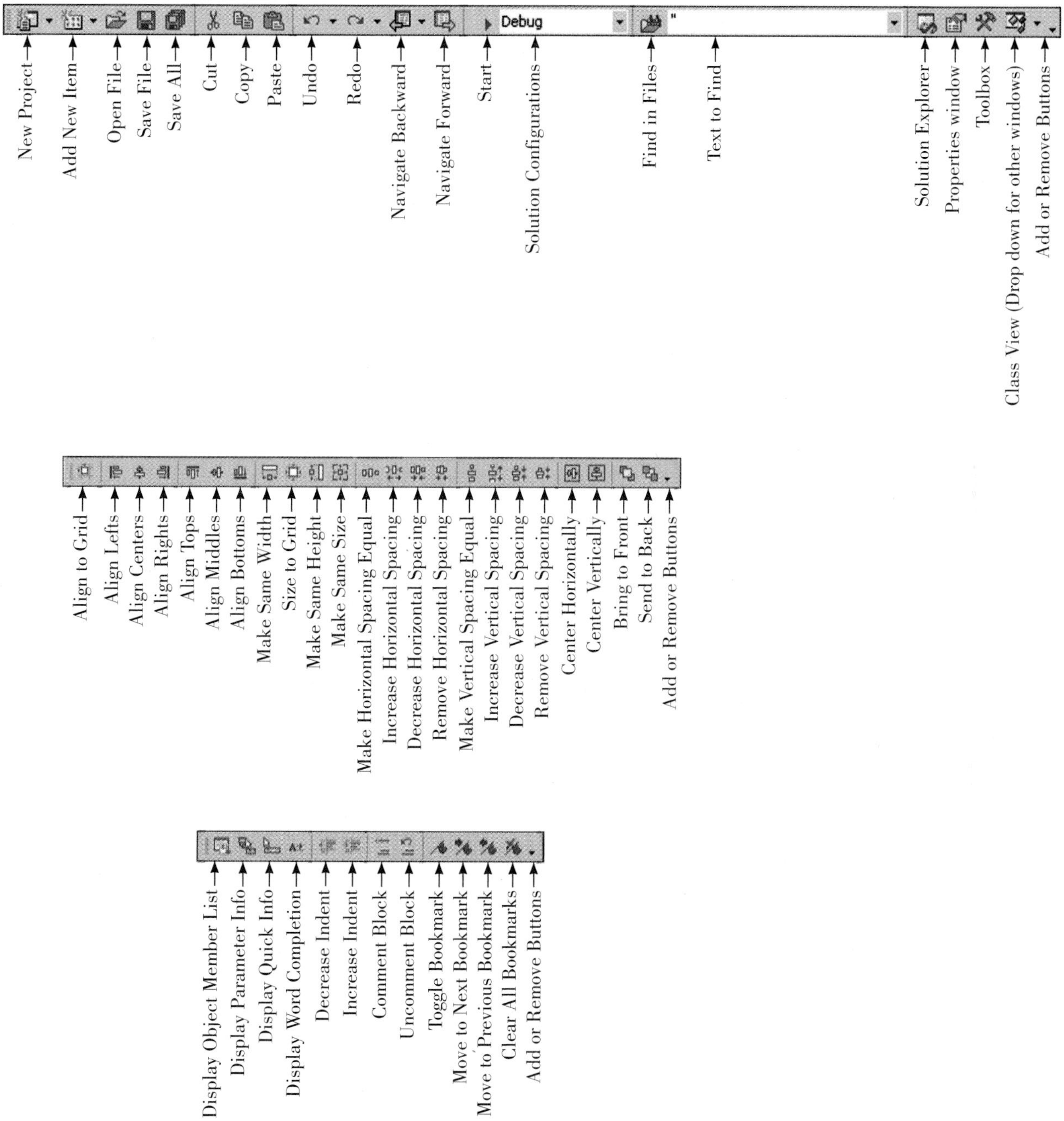

New Project
Add New Item
Open File
Save File
Save All
Cut
Copy
Paste
Undo
Redo
Navigate Backward
Navigate Forward
Start
Solution Configurations
Find in Files
Text to Find
Solution Explorer
Properties window
Toolbox
Class View (Drop down for other windows)
Add or Remove Buttons

Align to Grid
Align Lefts
Align Centers
Align Rights
Align Tops
Align Middles
Align Bottoms
Make Same Width
Size to Grid
Make Same Height
Make Same Size
Make Horizontal Spacing Equal
Increase Horizontal Spacing
Decrease Horizontal Spacing
Remove Horizontal Spacing
Make Vertical Spacing Equal
Increase Vertical Spacing
Decrease Vertical Spacing
Remove Vertical Spacing
Center Horizontally
Center Vertically
Bring to Front
Send to Back
Add or Remove Buttons

Display Object Member List
Display Parameter Info
Display Quick Info
Display Word Completion
Decrease Indent
Increase Indent
Comment Block
Uncomment Block
Toggle Bookmark
Move to Next Bookmark
Move to Previous Bookmark
Clear All Bookmarks
Add or Remove Buttons

The Document Window

The largest window in the center of the screen is the **Document window.** Notice the tabs across the top of the window, which allow you to switch between open documents. The items that display in the Document window include the Form Designer, the Code Editor, the Object Browser, and the pages of Help that you request.

You can switch from one tab to another, or close any of the documents using its Close button.

☑**TIP**

Use Ctrl + Tab to cycle through the open documents in the Documents window. ■

The Form Designer

The **Form Designer** is where you design a form that makes up your user interface. In Figure 1.5, the Form Designer for Form1 is currently displaying. You can drag the form's borders to change the size of the form.

When you begin a new Visual Basic Windows project, a new form is added to the project with the default name Form1. When you save the file, you should give it a new name.

The Solution Explorer Window

The **Solution Explorer window** holds the filenames for the files included in your project and a list of the classes it references. The window's title bar holds the name of your solution (.sln) file, which is WindowsApplication1 by default until you save it with a new name.

The Properties Window

You use the **Properties window** to set the properties for the objects in your project. See "Set Properties" later in this chapter for instructions on changing properties.

The Toolbox

The **toolbox** holds the tools you use to place controls on a form. You may have more or different tools in your toolbox, depending on the edition of Visual Basic you are using (Professional or Enterprise). Figure 1.7 shows the toolbox.

• The toolbox autohides by default. Click the push-pin icon to pin it open.

Figure 1.7

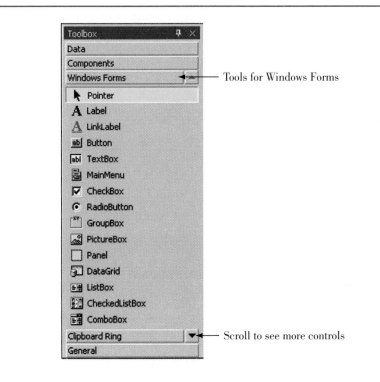

Tools for Windows Forms

Scroll to see more controls

The toolbox for Visual Studio Windows Forms. Your toolbox may have more or fewer tools, depending on the edition you are using.

Help

Visual Studio has an extensive **Help** feature that is greatly expanded for .NET. Help includes the Microsoft Developer Network library (MSDN), which contains reference materials for Visual Basic, C++, C#, and Visual Studio; several books; technical articles; and the Microsoft Knowledge Base, a database of frequently asked questions and their answers.

Help includes the entire reference manual, as well as many coding examples. See the topic "Visual Studio Help" later in this chapter for help on Help.

When you select `Contents`, `Index`, or `Search` from the `Help` menu, the requested item appears as another tabbed window on top of the Solution Explorer window. It's a good idea to set the `Filtered By` entry to `Visual Basic and Related`. Once you select a topic, the corresponding Help page appears in the main Document window.

In Figure 1.8, notice the tabs across the bottom of the Solution Explorer window and on the top of the Document window. The window for the Solution Explorer now shows the Help Index and the tabs allow you to switch between the Help Index, Help Contents, the Class View, and the Solution Explorer. Use the tabs on the Document window to switch back to the Form Designer (*Form1.vb [Design]**), the Code Editor (*Form1.vb**), or the Help topic (*Introduction t...s Label Control*).

F i g u r e   1 . 8

The Help Index displays on a tab in the Solution Explorer window and the Help text appears on a tab in the Document window.

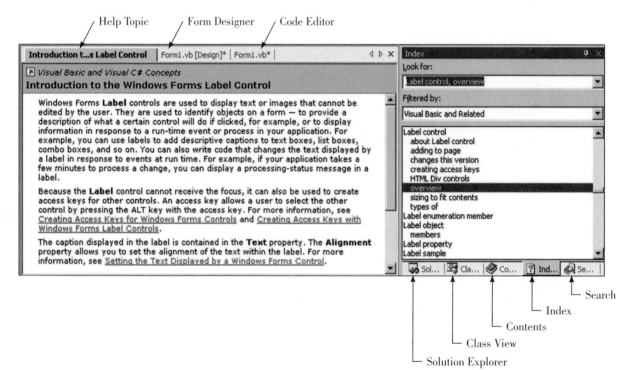

Design Time, Run Time, and Break Time

Visual Basic has three distinct modes. While you are designing the user interface and writing code, you are in **design time.** When you are testing and running your project, you are in **run time.** If you get a run-time error or pause project execution, you are in **break time.** The window title bar in Figure 1.5 indicates that the project is currently in design time.

Writing Your First Visual Basic Project

For your first VB project, you will create a form with three controls (see Figure 1.9). This simple project will display the message "Hello World" in a label when the user clicks the Push Me button and will terminate when the user clicks the Exit button.

F i g u r e   1 . 9

The Hello World form. The "Hello World" message will appear in the label when the user clicks on the Push Me button.

Set Up Your Workspace

Before you can begin a project, you must run the Visual Studio IDE. You also may need to customize your workspace.

Run Visual Studio

These instructions assume that Visual Studio .NET is installed in the default location. If you are running in a classroom or lab, the program may be installed in an alternate location, such as directly on the desktop.

STEP 1: Click on the Windows *Start* button and move the mouse pointer to *Programs*.

STEP 2: Locate *Microsoft Visual Studio .NET*.

STEP 3: In the submenu that pops up, select *Microsoft Visual Studio .NET*.
Visual Studio will start and display the Start Page (refer to Figure 1.3). *Note:* The VS IDE can be customized to not show the Start Page.

Start a New Project

STEP 1: Click on the New Project button. The *New Project* dialog box opens. (Refer to Figure 1.4.) Make sure that *Visual Basic Projects* is selected for *Project Types* and *Windows Application* is selected for *Templates*.

STEP 2: For *Location,* browse to select the path for your new project. *Note:* In this exercise we will use a diskette in the A: drive. You may use a path on the hard drive or network, if you prefer.

Do not create a new folder for your project; the VS IDE automatically creates a new folder for each new solution. If you create a folder yourself, you will have a folder within a folder.

STEP 3: Enter "HelloWorld" (without the quotes) for the name of the new project (Figure 1.10) and click on the OK button. The new project opens (Figure 1.11). *Note:* Your screen may look significantly different from the figure since the environment can be customized.

Figure 1.10

Select the path and enter the name for the new project.

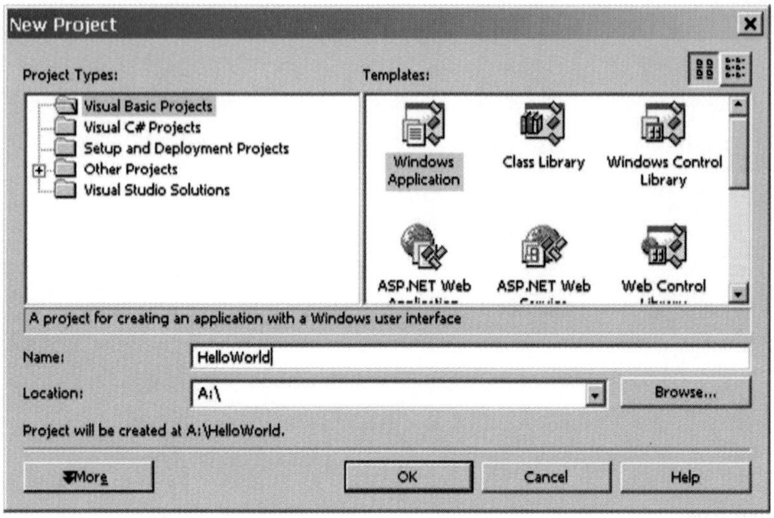

Figure 1.11

Begin a new project.

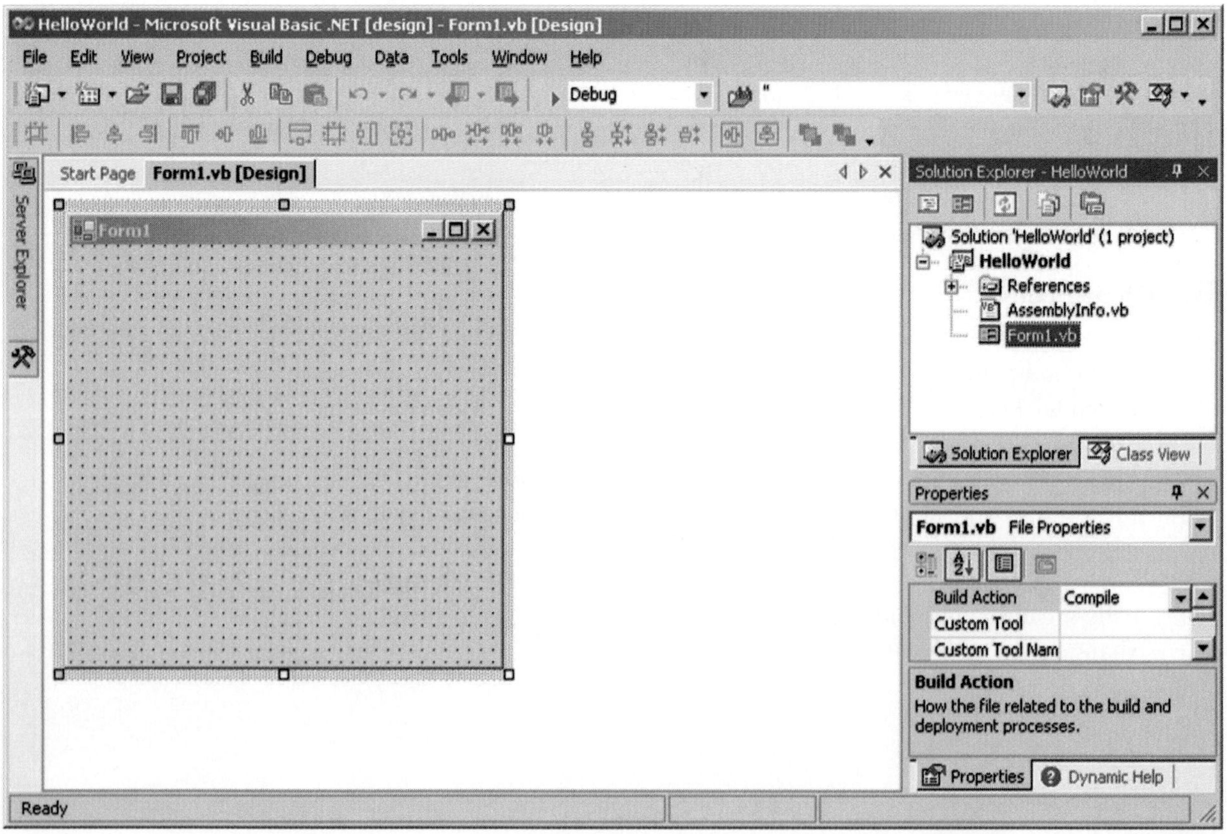

Set Up Your Environment

In this section you will customize the environment. For more information on customizing windows, floating and docking windows, and altering the location and contents of the various windows, see Appendix C.

STEP 1: Reset the IDE's default layout by choosing `Tools / Options / Environment / General / Reset Window Layout`; click OK on both dialogs.

The Server Explorer and toolbox are both set to AutoHide in the same location. You don't need the Server Explorer, but you do need the toolbox.

STEP 2: Point to the icon for the Server Explorer at the top of the hidden window's title bar (Figure 1.12). The Server Explorer will open.

——— Server Explorer Icon

——— Toolbox Icon

Figure 1.12

The title bar of the hidden window for the Server Explorer and the toolbox. Point to the correct icon to display the desired window.

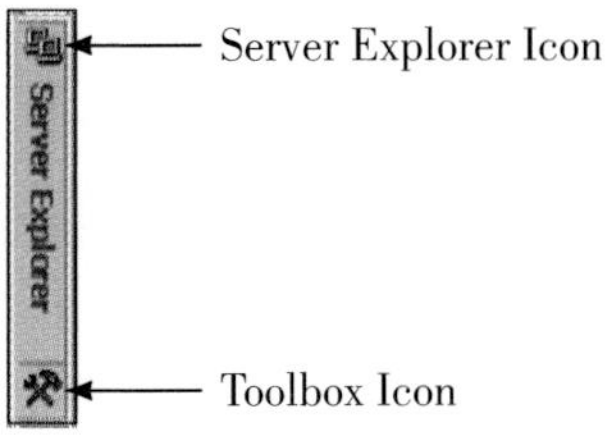

STEP 3: Point to the icon for the toolbox at the bottom of the window's title bar. The Toolbox window opens. Notice the push-pin icon at the top of the window (Figure 1.13); clicking this icon makes the window remain on the screen rather than AutoHide.

• The AutoHide behavior of the toolbox can be confusing. Use the push-pin icon at the top of the toolbox to fix it on the screen.

Figure 1.13

The Toolbox window.

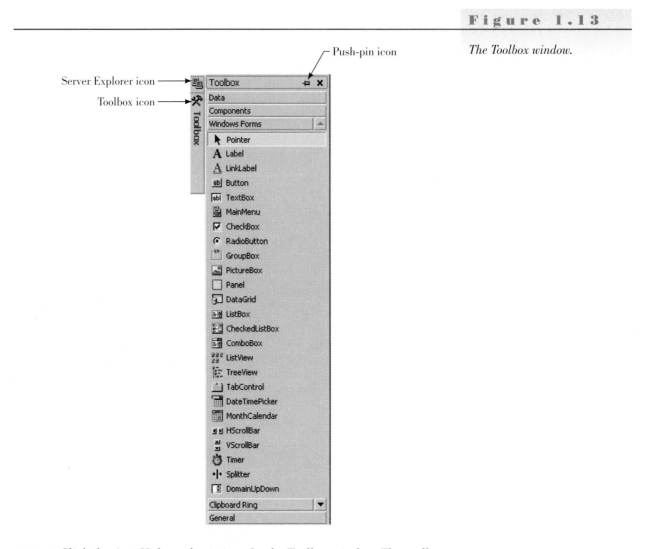

STEP 4: Click the AutoHide push-pin icon for the Toolbox window. The toolbox will remain open and tabs appear at the bottom of the window for the toolbox and the Server Explorer.

STEP 5: Click on the tab for the Server Explorer to make its window appear. Then click on the window's Close button to permanently close the window.

  Note: You can reopen the Server Explorer from the *View* menu, if you wish.

STEP 6: In the lower-right corner of the screen, click on the tab for *Dynamic Help* to bring its tabbed window to the top (Figure 1.14). Then click the window's Close button to close the Dynamic Help window. Later you can experiment with Dynamic Help turned on, but the feature slows the environment significantly.

Figure 1.14

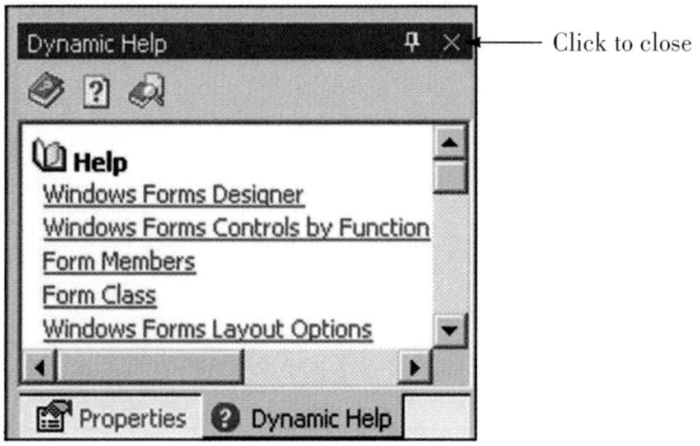

Click on the Close button to close the Dynamic Help window.

Click to close

Plan the Project

The first step in planning is to design the user interface. Figure 1.15 shows a sketch of the form that includes a label and two buttons. You will refer to the sketch as you create the project.

• The PrintForm method is no longer supported.

Figure 1.15

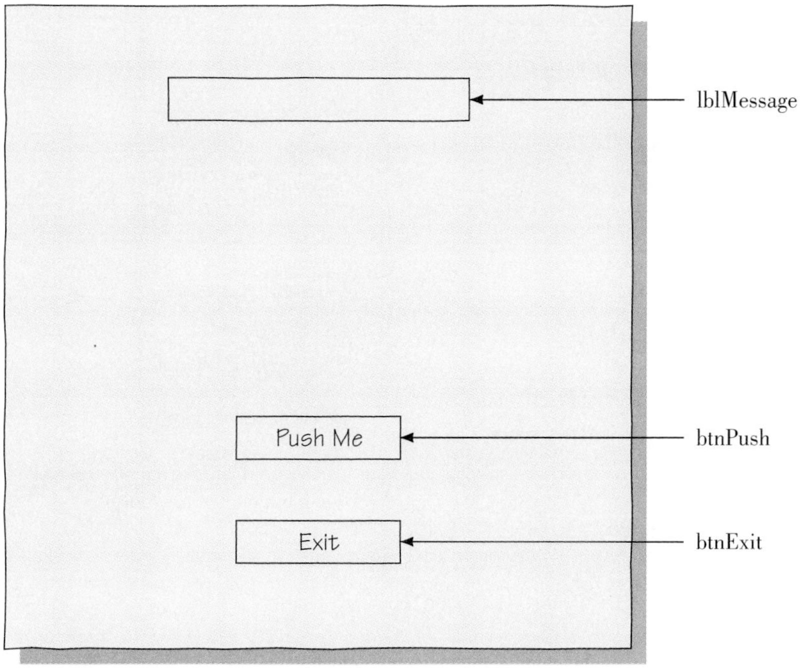

A sketch of the Hello World form for planning.

lblMessage

btnPush

btnExit

The next two steps, planning the properties and the code, have already been done for this first sample project. You will be given the values in the steps that follow.

Define the User Interface

Set Up the Form

Notice that the new form in the Document window has all the standard Windows features, such as a title bar, maximize and minimize buttons, and a close button. The grid of dots on the form is there to help you align the controls; the grid does not appear when you run the program.

STEP 1: Resize the form in the Document window: Drag the handle in the lower-right corner down and to the right (see Figure 1.16).

Figure 1.16

Make the form larger by dragging its lower-right handle diagonally. The handles disappear as you drag the corner of the form.

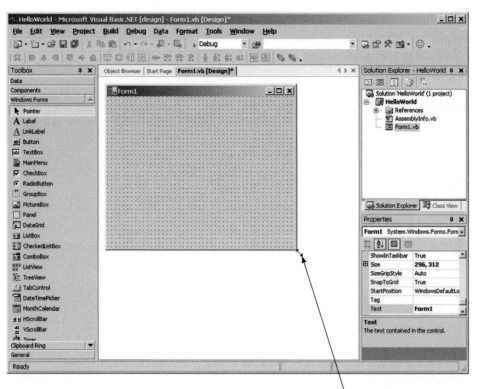

Drag handle to enlarge form

Place Controls on the Form

You are going to place three controls on the form's design: a **Label** and two **Buttons.**

STEP 1: Point to the Label tool in the toolbox and click. Then move the pointer over the form. Notice that the pointer becomes a crosshair with a big A, and the Label tool looks as if it has been pressed, indicating it is the active tool (Figure 1.17).

Figure 1.17

When you click on the Label tool in the toolbox, the tool's button is activated and the mouse pointer becomes a crosshair.

Crosshair pointer

Label tool
is activated

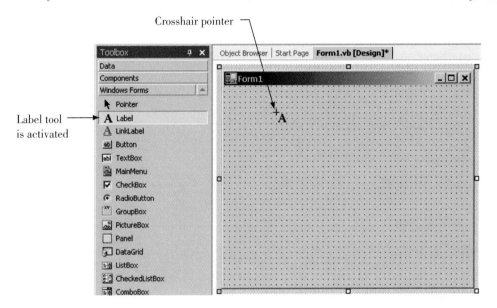

STEP 2: Point to a spot where you want one corner of the label, press the mouse button, and drag the pointer to the opposite corner (Figure 1.18). When you release the mouse button, the label and its default contents (Label1) will appear (Figure 1.19).

Figure 1.18

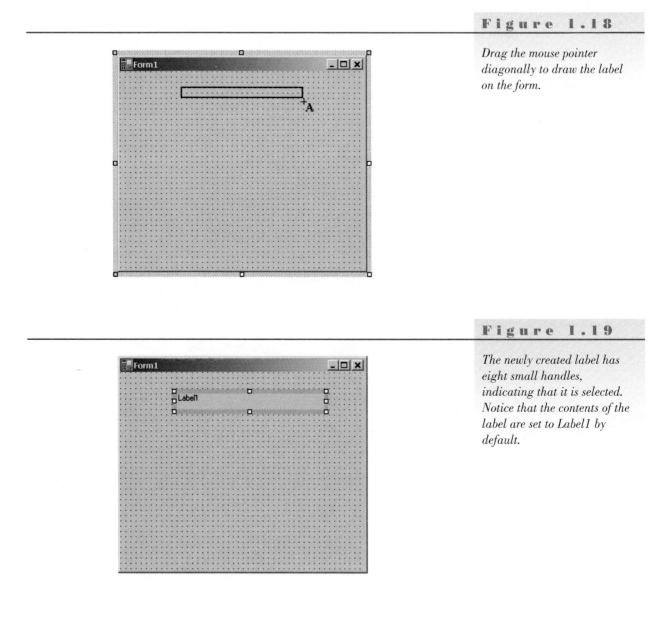

Drag the mouse pointer diagonally to draw the label on the form.

Figure 1.19

The newly created label has eight small handles, indicating that it is selected. Notice that the contents of the label are set to Label1 by default.

The label has eight small square **handles,** indicating that the control is currently selected. While a control is selected, you can delete it, resize it, or move it. Refer to Table 1.1 for instructions for selecting, deleting, resizing, and moving controls. Click outside of a control to deselect it.

Selecting, Deleting, Resizing, and Moving Controls on a Form

Select a control	Click on the control.
Delete a control	Select the control and then press the Delete key on the keyboard.
Move a control	Select the control, point inside the control (not on a handle), press the mouse button, and drag it to a new location.
Resize a control	Make sure the control is selected; then point to one of the handles, press the mouse button, and drag the handle. Drag a side handle to change the width, a bottom or top handle to change the height, or a corner handle to resize in two directions.

STEP 3: Draw a button on the form: Click on the Button tool in the toolbox, position the crosshair pointer for one corner of the button, and drag to the diagonally opposite corner (Figure 1.20). The new button should have selection handles.

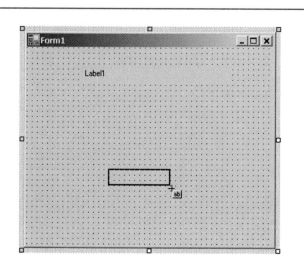

Figure 1.20

Select the Button tool and drag diagonally to create a new Button control.

STEP 4: Create another button using this alternative method: Point to the Button tool in the toolbox and double-click. A new button of the default size will appear on top of the last-drawn control (Figure 1.21).

Figure 1.21

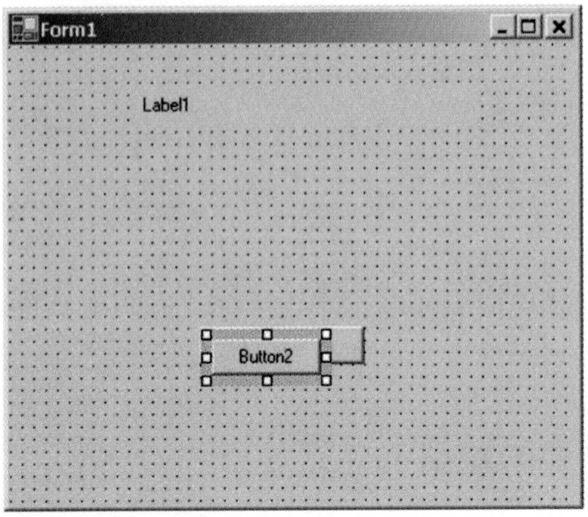

Place a new button on the form by double-clicking the Button tool in the toolbox. The new button appears on top of the previously selected control.

• Double-clicking a toolbox tool places the new default-sized control on top of the last-drawn control rather than in the center of the form. If no control is selected, the new control appears at the top-left of the form.

STEP 5: Keep the new button selected, point anywhere inside the button (not on a handle), and drag the button below your first button (Figure 1.22). As you drag the control, you see only its outline; when you release the mouse button, the control is actually moved to its new location.

☑TIP

If no control is selected when you double-click a tool, the new control is added to the upper-left corner of the form. ■

Figure 1.22

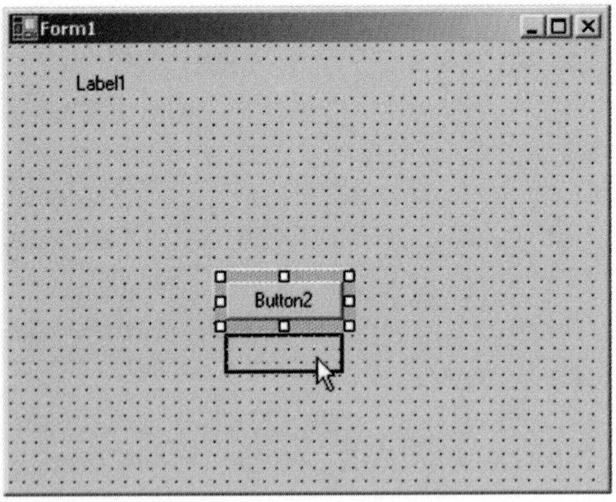

Drag the new button (Button2) below Button1. An outline of the control shows the new location for the control.

STEP 6: Select each control and move and resize the controls as necessary. Make the two buttons the same size and line them up.

STEP 7: Point to one of the controls and click the right mouse button to display a **context menu.** On the context menu, select *Lock Controls* (Figure 1.23). Locking prevents you from accidentally moving the controls. When your controls are locked, a selected control has no handles.

    Note: You can unlock the controls at any time if you wish to redesign the form. Just click again on *Lock Controls* on the context menu to deselect it.

F i g u r e   1 . 2 3

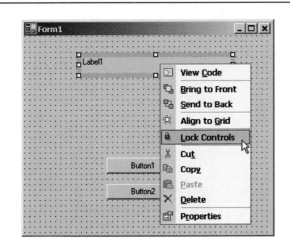

After the controls are placed into the desired location, lock them in place by selecting Lock Controls *from the context menu.*

    At this point you have designed the user interface and are ready to set the properties.

Set Properties

Set the Name and Text Properties for the Label

STEP 1: Click on the label you placed on the form; a shaded outline appears
around the control. Next click on the title bar of the Properties window
to make it the active window (Figure 1.24).

Figure 1.24

The currently selected control is shown in the Properties window.

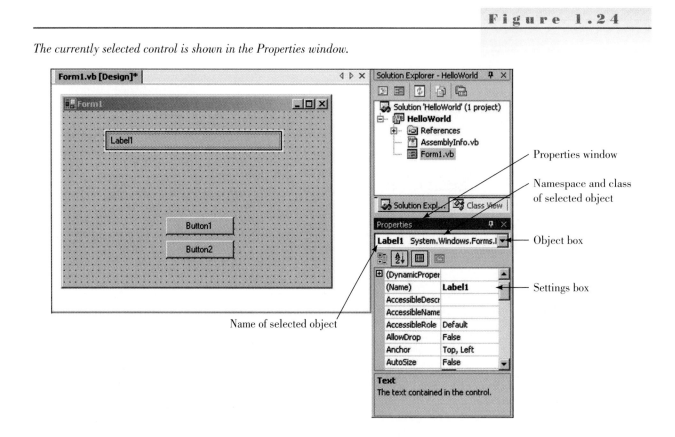

Notice that the Object box at the top of the Properties window is
showing `Label1` (the name of the object) and `System.Windows.`
`Forms.Label` as the class of the object. The actual class is Label;
System.Windows.Forms is called the **namespace,** or the hierarchy
used to locate the class.

STEP 2: Select the Name property. You may have to scroll up; Name is located near the top of the list. Click on (*Name*) and notice that the Settings box shows *Label1*, the default name of the label (Figure 1.25).

If the Properties window is not visible, you can press the F4 key to show it. ■

Figure 1.25

The Properties window. Click on the Name property to change the value in the Settings box.

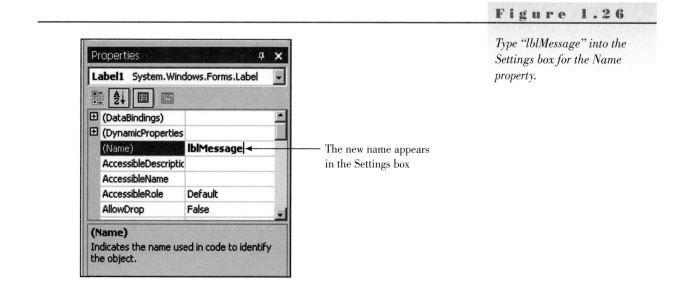

STEP 3: Type "lblMessage" (without the quotation marks). See Figure 1.26. After you change the name of the control, you can see the new name in the Object box's drop-down list.

Figure 1.26

Type "lblMessage" into the Settings box for the Name property.

STEP 4: Click on the Text property to select it. Scroll the list if necessary. Following the Name property, all properties are in alphabetic order.

    The **Text property** of a control determines what will be displayed on the form. Because nothing should display when the program begins, you must delete the value of the Text property (as described in the next two steps).

STEP 5: Double-click on *Label1* in the Settings box; the entry should appear selected (highlighted). See Figure 1.27.

- The Caption property of a form, label, and button changes to the Text property.

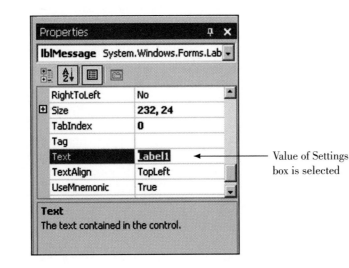

Figure 1.27

Double-click in the Settings box to select the entry.

                                        ← Value of Settings box is selected

STEP 6: Press the Delete key to delete the value of the Text property. Then press Enter and notice that the label on the form now appears empty (Figure 1.28). Changes do not appear until you press Enter or move to another property or control.

    As an alternate technique, you can double-click on the property name, which automatically selects the entry in the Settings box. Then you can press the Delete key or just begin typing to change the entry.

✓**TIP**

Don't confuse the Name property with the Text property. You use the Name property to refer to the control in your Basic code. The Text property tells what the user will see on the form. Visual Basic sets both of these properties to the same value by default, and it is easy to confuse them. ■

Figure 1.28

Delete the value for the Text property from the Settings box; the label on the form also appears empty.

Label is empty

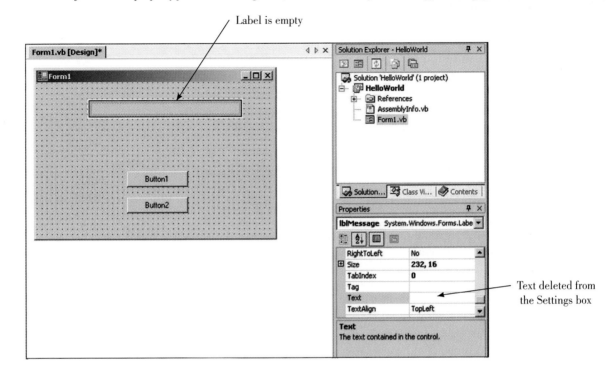

Text deleted from
the Settings box

Set the Name and Text Properties for the First Button

STEP 1: Click on the first button (Button1) to select it and then look at the Properties window. The Object box should show the name (*Button1*) and class (*System.Windows.Forms.Button*) of the button. See Figure 1.29.

Figure 1.29

Change the Text property for the first button.

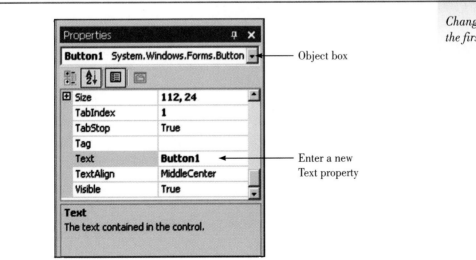

Object box

Enter a new
Text property

Problem? If you should double-click and code appears in the Document window, simply click on the *Form1.vb [Design]* tab at the top of the window.

STEP 2: Change the Name property of the button to "btnPush" (without the quotation marks).

Although the project would work fine without this step, we prefer to give this button a meaningful name, rather than use Button1, its default name. The guidelines for naming controls appear later in this chapter in the section "Naming Rules and Conventions for Objects."

STEP 3: Change the Text property to "Push Me" (without the quotation marks). This step changes the words that appear on top of the button.

Set the Name and Text Properties for the Second Button

STEP 1: Select Button2 and change its Name property to "btnExit".

STEP 2: Change the Text property to "Exit".

Change Properties of the Form

STEP 1: Click anywhere on the form, except on a control. The Properties window Object box should now show the form as the selected object (*Form1* as the object's name and *System.Windows.Forms.Form* as its class).

STEP 2: Change the Text property to "Hello World by Your Name" (again, no quotation marks).

The Text property of a form determines the text to appear in the title bar. Your screen should now look like Figure 1.30.

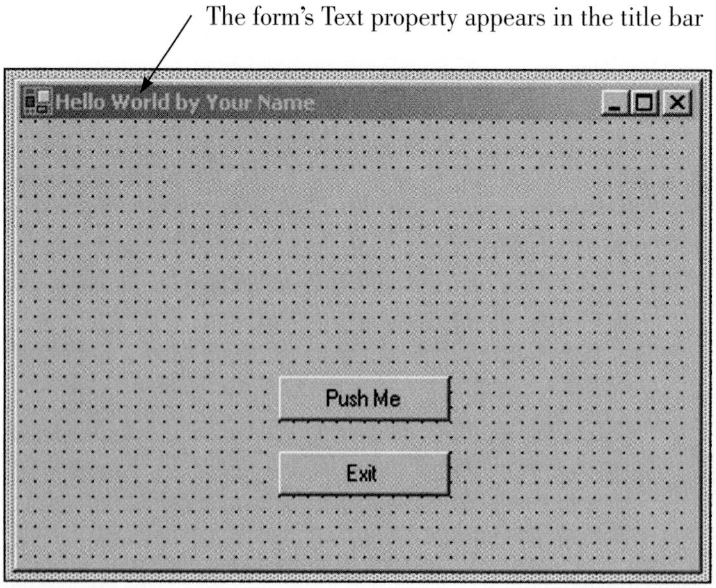

✓**TIP**

Always set the Name property of controls before writing code. ■

Figure 1.30

Change the form's Text property to set the text that appears in the form's title bar.

The form's Text property appears in the title bar

STEP 3: Click on the StartPosition property and notice the arrow on the property setting, indicating a drop-down list. Drop down the list and select *CenterScreen.* This will make your form appear in the center of the screen when the program runs.

STEP 4: Change the form's Name property to "frmHello". This step changes the name of the form's class, but not the name of the form's file, which is still Form1.

STEP 5: In the Solution Explorer, right-click on Form1.vb and choose *Rename* from the shortcut menu. Change the file name to "frmHello.vb", making sure to retain the .vb extension. Press Enter when finished. Now the form's class and its file should both be renamed (Figure 1.31).

- The IDE does not have a Form Layout window. Use the StartPosition property of the form.

- Changing the name of the form does not change the name of the form's file. Rename the file using the Solution Explorer to keep the project pointing to the correct filename.

Figure 1.31

Change the name of the form class and the name of the form's file.

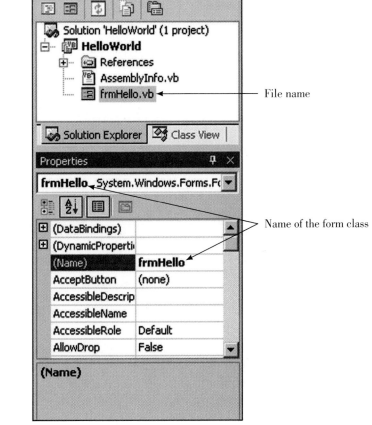

File name

Name of the form class

Set the Project's Startup Object

Whenever you change the name of the form, you must take one more step so that VB knows which form to run when the project begins. Each project has a Startup Object—the object with which to begin execution. By default, the Startup Object is Form1. If you change the name of the form, you must set the project's Startup Object property to the new name of the form.

- When you change the name of the startup form, VB does not automatically change the project's Startup Object. You must open the Project Properties dialog box and change it manually.

STEP 1: In the Solution Explorer, click on HelloWorld to select the project. Then you can either select *Project / Properties* or right-click on the project name in the Solution Explorer and select *Properties* from the shortcut menu. In the *Project Properties* dialog box, drop down the list for *Startup object* and select *frmHello* (Figure 1.32).

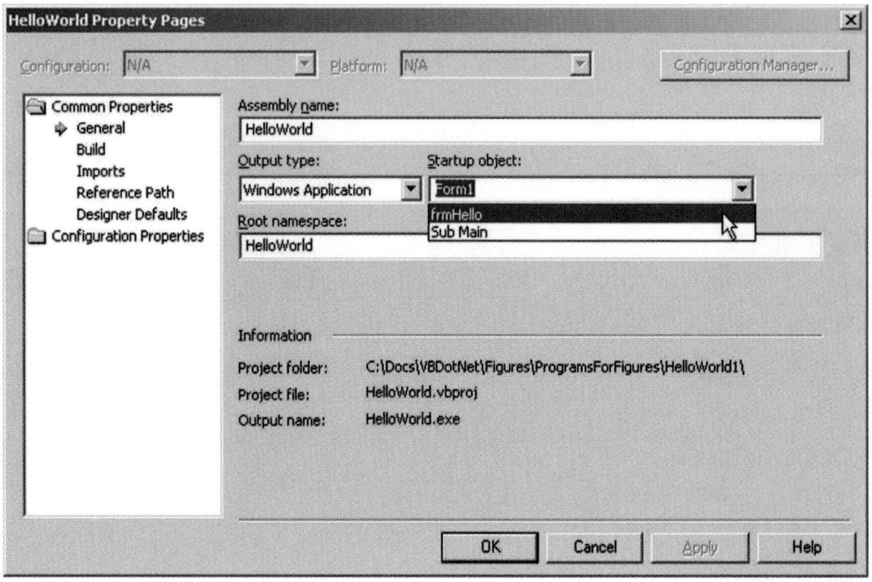

Figure 1.32

In the project's Property Pages *dialog box, drop down the list for* Startup object *and select the name of your form.*

If you ever receive an error message when you attempt to run a project telling you that it can't find Form1, you know that you have forgotten this step.

Write Code

Visual Basic Events

While your project is running, the user can do many things, such as move the mouse around; click on either button; move, resize, or close your form's window; or jump to another application. Each action by the user causes an event to occur in your Visual Basic project. Some events (like clicking on a button) you care about, and some events (like moving the mouse and resizing the window) you do not care about. If you write Basic code for a particular event, then Visual Basic will respond to the event and automatically execute your procedure. *VB ignores events for which no procedures are written.*

Visual Basic Event Procedures

You write code in Visual Basic in **procedures.** For now, each of your procedures will be a **sub procedure,** which begins with the words Private Sub and ends with End Sub. (Later you will also learn about other types of procedures.) Note that many programmers refer to sub procedures as subprograms or subroutines. Subprogram is acceptable; subroutine is not, because Basic actually has a different statement for a subroutine, which is not the same as a sub procedure.

Visual Basic automatically names your **event procedures.** The name consists of the object name, an underscore (_), and the name of the event. For example, the Click event for your button called btnPush will be btnPush_Click. For the sample project you are writing, you will have a btnPush_Click procedure and a btnExit_Click procedure.

Visual Basic Code Statements

This first project requires two Visual Basic statements: the remark and the assignment statement. You will also execute a method of an object.

The Remark Statement

Remark statements, sometimes called *comments*, are used for project documentation only. They are not considered "executable" and have no effect when the project runs. The purpose of remarks is to make the project more readable and understandable by the people who read it.

Good programming practices dictate that programmers include remarks to clarify their projects. Every sub procedure should begin with a remark that describes the purpose of the sub. Every project should have remarks that explain the purpose of the program and provide identifying information such as the name of the programmer and the date the program was written and/or modified. In addition, it is a good idea to place remarks within the logic of a project, especially if the purpose of any statements might be unclear. When you try to read someone else's code, or your own after a period of time, you will appreciate the generous use of remarks.

Visual Basic remarks begin with an apostrophe. Most of the time your remarks will be on a separate line that starts with an apostrophe. You can also add an apostrophe and a remark to the right end of a line of code.

The Remark Statement—Examples

```
'This project was written by Jonathon Edwards
'Exit the project
lblMessage.Text = "Hello World" 'Assign the message to the Text property
```

The Assignment Statement

The **assignment statement** assigns a value to a property or variable (you learn about variables in Chapter 3). Assignment statements operate from right to left; that is, the value appearing on the right side of the equal sign is assigned to the property named on the left of the equal sign. It is often helpful to read the equal sign as "is replaced by." For example, the assignment statement in the example would read "lblMessage.Text is replaced by Hello World."

The Assignment Statement—General Form

General Form

```
Object.Property = value
```

The value named on the right side of the equal sign is assigned to (or placed into) the property named on the left.

The Assignment Statement—Examples

Examples

```
lblTitle.Text = "A Snazzy Program"
lblAddress.Text = "1234 South North Street"
lblMessage.AutoSize = True
intNumber = 12
```

Notice that when the value to assign is some actual text (called a *literal*), it is enclosed in quotation marks. This convention allows you to type any combination of alpha and numeric characters. If the value is numeric, do not enclose it in quotation marks. And do not place quotation marks around the terms *True* and *False*, which Visual Basic recognizes as special key terms.

Ending a Program by Executing a Method

To execute a method of an object, you write:

```
Object.Method()
```

Notice that methods always have parentheses. Although this might seem like a bother, it's helpful to distinguish between properties and methods: Methods always have parentheses; properties don't.

• All method names require parentheses.

Examples

```
btnHello.Hide()
lblMessage.Show()
```

To execute a method of the current object (the form itself), you use the Me keyword for the object. And the method that terminates execution is the Close.

```
Me.Close()
```

In most cases, you will include Me.Close() in the sub procedure for an Exit button or an *Exit* menu choice.

Code the Event Procedures for Hello World

Code the Click Event for the Push Me Button

STEP 1: Double-click on the Push Me button. The Visual Studio editor opens with the first and last lines of your sub procedure already in place, with the insertion point indented inside the sub procedure (Figure 1.33). For now, you can ignore the extra lines of code that appear above your sub procedure.

• All references to the *Code window* are changed to the *Editor window* or just *editor*.

The Class list   The Method list

```
frmHello.vb [Design]*  frmHello.vb*                                    ◄ ▷ ✕
[frmHello]                              [btnPush_Click]              ▼

⊟ Public Class frmHello
      Inherits System.Windows.Forms.Form

  ⊞ │ Windows Form Designer generated code │

  ⊟     Private Sub btnPush_Click(ByVal sender As System.Object, By▼
            |
  └       End Sub
  └ End Class
```

Figure 1.33

The Editor window, showing the first and last lines of the btnPush_Click sub procedure.

STEP 2: Type this remark statement:

`'Display the Hello World message`

Notice that the editor automatically displays remarks in green (unless you or someone else has changed the color with the Environment option).

Follow good coding conventions and indent all lines between `Private Sub` and `End Sub`. The smart editor attempts to help you follow this convention. Also, always leave a blank line after the remarks at the top of a sub procedure.

STEP 3: Press Enter twice and then type this assignment statement:

`lblMessage.Text = "Hello World"`

Note: When you type the period after lblMessage, an IntelliSense list pops up showing the properties and methods available for a Label control. Although you can type the entire word *Text*, you can allow IntelliSense to help you. As soon as you type the *T*, the list automatically scrolls to the first word that begins with *T*. Type the next letter, *e*, and the property *Text* appears highlighted. You can press the spacebar to select the word and continue typing the rest of the statement.

✓TIP

Allow the editor and IntelliSense to help you. If the IntelliSense list does not pop up, you likely misspelled the name of the control. Don't worry about capitalization when you type the name of an object; if the name matches a defined object, the editor fixes the capitalization. ■

This assignment statement assigns the literal "Hello World" to the Text property of the control called lblMessage. Compare your screen to Figure 1.34.

Figure 1.34

Type the remark and assignment statement for the btnPush_Click event sub procedure.

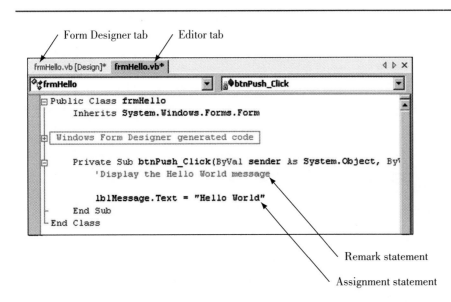

Form Designer tab   Editor tab

```
frmHello.vb [Design]*   frmHello.vb*                                    ◄ ▷ ×
frmHello                          ▼   btnPush_Click                          ▼
 Public Class frmHello
      Inherits System.Windows.Forms.Form

  Windows Form Designer generated code

      Private Sub btnPush_Click(ByVal sender As System.Object, ByV
           'Display the Hello World message

           lblMessage.Text = "Hello World"
      End Sub
 End Class
```

Remark statement

Assignment statement

STEP 4: Return to the form (Figure 1.30) by clicking on the *frmHello.vb [Design]* tab on the Document window (Figure 1.34).

Code the Click Event for the Exit Button

STEP 1: Double-click on the Exit button to open the editor for the btnExit_Click event.

STEP 2: Type this remark:

```
'Exit the project
```

STEP 3: Press Enter twice and type this Basic statement:

```
Me.Close()
```

Accept an entry from the Intelli-Sense pop-up list by typing the punctuation that follows the entry or by pressing the Enter key. You can also scroll the list and select the entry with your mouse. ■

STEP 4: Make sure your code looks like the code shown in Figure 1.35.

Figure 1.35

Type the code for the btnExit_Click event procedure.

```
frmHello.vb [Design]*   frmHello.vb*                              ◁ ▷ ✕
frmHello                          ▼    btnExit_Click              ▼
┌─ Public Class frmHello
│       Inherits System.Windows.Forms.Form
│  ┌────────────────────────────────────────┐
├  │ Windows Form Designer generated code    │
│  └────────────────────────────────────────┘
│       Private Sub btnPush_Click(ByVal sender As System.Object, By▼
├          'Display the Hello World message

            lblMessage.Text = "Hello World"
│       End Sub

│       Private Sub btnExit_Click(ByVal sender As System.Object, By▼
├          'Exit the project

            Me.Close()
│       End Sub
└─ End Class
```

Run the Project

After you have finished writing the code, you are ready to run the project. Use one of these three methods:

1. Open the *Debug* menu and choose *Start*.
2. Press the Start button on the toolbar.
3. Press F5, the shortcut key for the *Start* command.

Start the Project Running

STEP 1: Choose one of the three methods previously listed to start your project running.

    Problems? See "Finding and Fixing Errors" later in this chapter. You must correct any errors and restart the program.

If your form disappears during run time, click its button on the task bar. ■

If all went well, the Visual Studio title bar now indicates that you are in run time, and the grid dots have disappeared from your form (Figure 1.36). (The grid dots help you align the controls; you may turn them off if you prefer.)

F i g u r e   1 . 3 6

When you run the project, the form's grid dots disappear.

Click the Push Me Button

STEP 1: Click the Push Me button. Your "Hello World" message appears in the label (Figure 1.37).

F i g u r e   1 . 3 7

Click on the Push Me button and "Hello World" appears in the label.

Click the Exit Button

STEP 1: Click the Exit button. Your project terminates, and you return to design time.

Save Your Work

Of course, you must always save your work often. Except for a very small project like this one, you will usually save your work as you go along.

Save the Files

STEP 1: Open the Visual Studio *File* menu and choose *Save All*. This option saves the current form, project, and solution files. You already selected the path for the files when you first created the project.

Close the Project

STEP 1: Open the *File* menu and choose *Close*. If you haven't saved since your last change, you will be prompted to save.

After your project closes, you should again see the Visual Studio Start Page. This time you may see your project on the list.
Note: If the Start Page does not appear, display it with *Help/Show Start Page*.

Open the Project

Now is the time to test your save operation by opening the project from disk. You can choose one of three ways to open a saved project:

* If your project appears on the Start Page, you can open it by clicking on its name.

* Click on the Open Project button on the Start Page and browse to find your .sln file.

* Select *Open Solution* from the Visual Studio *File* menu and browse to find your .sln file.

Open the Project File

STEP 1: Open your project by choosing one of the previously listed methods. Remember that the file to open is the .sln file.

STEP 2: If you do not see your form on the screen, check the Solution Explorer window—it should say *HelloWorld* for both the solution and the project. Select the icon for your form: frmHello.vb. You can double-click the icon or single-click and click on the View Designer button at the top of the Solution Explorer (Figure 1.38); your form will appear in the Form Designer. Notice that you can also click on the View Code button to display your form's code in the Editor window.

Figure 1.38

To display the form layout, select the form name and click on the View Designer button, or double-click on the form name. Click on the View Code button to display the code in the editor.

View Code button

View Designer button

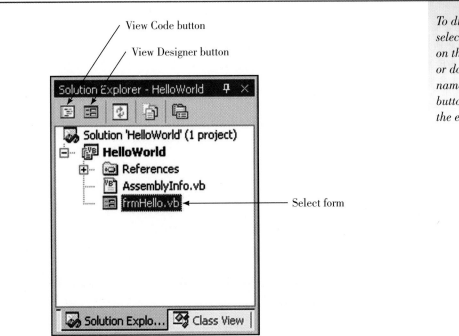

Select form

Modify the Project

Now it's time to make some changes to the project. We'll change the size of the "Hello World" message, display the message in two different languages, and display the programmer name (that's you) on the form.

Change the Size and Alignment of the Message

STEP 1: Right-click one of the form's controls to display the context menu. If your controls are currently locked, select *Lock Controls* to unlock the controls so that you can make changes.

STEP 2: Click on the label on your form, which will make selection handles appear. (If you see a dark border instead of selection handles, you must unlock the controls, as described in Step 1.)

STEP 3: Widen the label on both ends by dragging the handles wider. (Drag the right end farther right and the left end farther left.)

• Locked controls now have a dark border instead of selection handles. If no control is selected, the form has the dark border that indicates the controls are locked.

STEP 4: With the label still selected, scroll to the Font property. The Font property is actually a Font object that has a number of properties. To see the Font properties, click on the small plus sign on the left (Figure 1.39); the Font properties will appear showing the current values (Figure 1.40).

• The Font property changes to show the individual properties o the Font object.

Figure 1.39

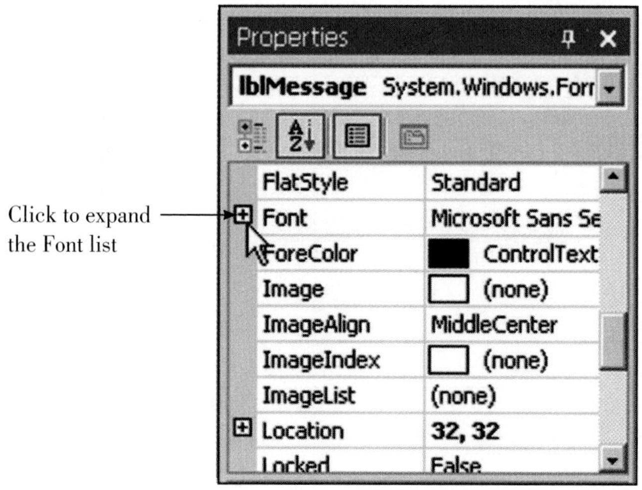

Click on the Font's plus sign to view the properties of the Font object.

Click to expand the Font list

Figure 1.40

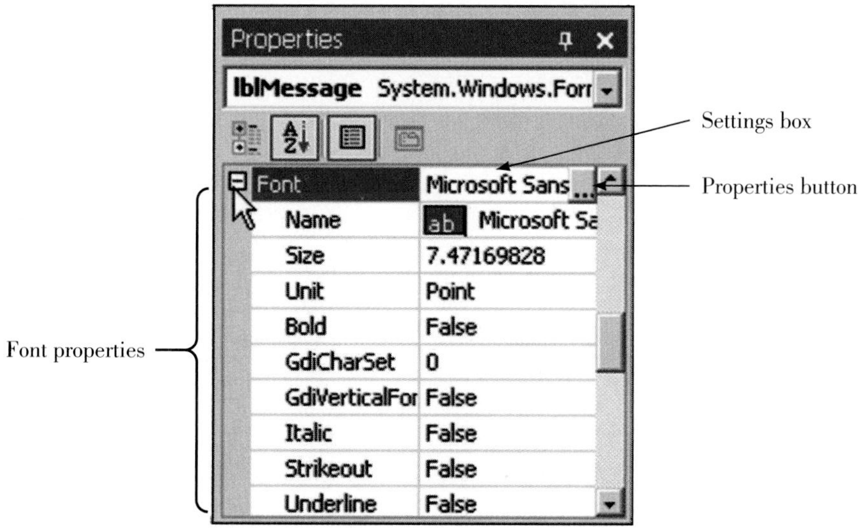

You can change the individual properties of the Font object.

Settings box

Properties button

Font properties

You can change any of the Font properties in the Properties window, such as setting the Font's Size, Bold, or Italic properties. You can also display the *Font* dialog box and make changes there.

To display the *Font* dialog box, click on the button with an ellipsis on top, which appears in the Settings box. The button is called the *Properties button* (sometimes the *Builder* button); the ellipsis indicates that clicking on the button will display a dialog box with choices.

STEP 5: Click on the Properties button to display the *Font* dialog box (Figure 1.41). Select 12 point if it is available. (If it isn't available, choose another number larger than the current setting.) Click OK to close the *Font* dialog box.

Choose 12 point from the Font dialog box.

—— Select 12 point

STEP 6: Select the TextAlign property. The Properties button that appears with the down-pointing arrow indicates a drop-down list of choices. Drop down the list (Figure 1.42) and choose the center box; the alignment property changes to *MiddleCenter*.

• The Alignment property becomes TextAlign.

Select the center box for the TextAlign property.

Add a New Label for Your Name

STEP 1: Click on the Label tool in the toolbox and create a new label along
the bottom edge of your form (Figure 1.43). (You can resize the form if
necessary.)

Figure 1.43

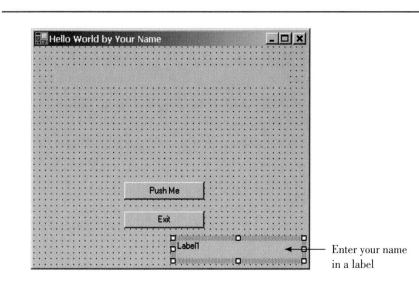

*Add a new label for your name
at the bottom of the form.*

← Enter your name
in a label

STEP 2: Change the label's Text property to "by Your Name". (Use your name
and omit the quotation marks.) *Note*: You do not need to name this
label because it will never be referred to in the code.

Change the Location and Text of the Push Me Button

Because we plan to display the message in one of two languages, we'll change
the text on the Push Me button to "English" and move the button to allow for a
second button.

STEP 1: Select the Push Me button and change its Text property to English.

STEP 2: Move the English button to the left to make room for a Spanish button (see Figure 1.44).

Move the English button to the left and add a Spanish button.

Add a Spanish Button

STEP 1: Add a new button. Move and resize it as necessary, referring to Figure 1.44.
STEP 2: Change the Name property of the new button to btnSpanish.
STEP 3: Change the Text property of the new button to Spanish.

Add an Event Procedure for the Spanish Button

STEP 1: Double-click on the Spanish button to open the editor for btnSpanish _Click.
STEP 2: Add a remark:

```
'Display the Hello World message in Spanish
```

STEP 3: Press Enter twice and type the following Basic code line:

```
lblMessage.Text = "Hola Mundo"
```

STEP 4: Return to design view.

Lock the Controls

STEP 1: When you are satisfied with the placement of the controls on the form, display the context menu and select *Lock Controls* again.

Save and Run the Project

STEP 1: Save your project again. You can use the *File/Save All* menu command or the Save All toolbar button.

STEP 2: Run your project again. Try clicking on the English button and the Spanish button.

> Problems? See "Finding and Fixing Errors" later in this chapter.

STEP 3: Click the Exit button to end program execution.

Add Remarks

Good documentation guidelines require some more remarks in the project. Always begin each procedure with remarks that tell the purpose of the procedure. In addition, each project file needs identifying remarks at the top.

The **Declarations section** at the top of the file is a good location for these remarks.

> • References to *General Declarations section* are changed to *Declarations section.*

STEP 1: Display the code in the editor and click in front of the first line (Public Class frmHello). Make sure that you have an insertion point; if the entire first line is selected, press the left arrow to set the insertion point.

> Press Enter to create a blank line.

> *Warning*: If you accidentally deleted the first line, click Undo (or press Ctrl + Z) and try again.

STEP 2: Move the insertion point up to the blank line and type the following remarks, one per line (Figure 1.45):

Figure 1.45

Enter remarks in the Declarations section of the form file.

```
'Project:       Hello World
'Programmer:    Your Name (Use your own name here.)
'Date:          (Fill in today's date.)
'Description:   This project will display a "Hello World"
'               message in two different languages.
```

> • The two list boxes at the top of the Editor window are called the *Class list* and the *Method list*. They work a little differently from the old lists. You must select from both lists to jump to a procedure. And to find the Form_Load procedures, select *(Base Class Events)* from the Class list and *Load* from the Method list.

Explore the Editor Window

STEP 1: Notice the two drop-down list boxes at the top of the Editor window, called the *Class list* and the *Method list*. You can use these lists to move to any procedure in your code.

STEP 2: Click on the left down-pointing arrow to view the Class list. Notice that every object in your form is listed there (Figure 1.46). At the top of the list, you see the name of your form and project: *frmHello.*

F i g u r e   1 . 4 6

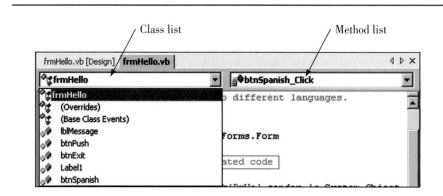

View the list of objects in this form by dropping down the Class list. Select an object from the list to display the sub procedures for that object.

STEP 3: Click on *frmHello* to select it. Then notice the Method list on the right, which says (*Declarations*). Clicking on (*Declarations*) is the quick way to jump to the Declarations section of a module.

STEP 4: Drop down the Class list (the left list) and select btnSpanish.

STEP 5: Drop down the Method list (the right list); it shows all possible events for a Button control. Notice that the Click event is bold and the rest are not. Any event for which you have written an event procedure appears in bold.

STEP 6: Select the Click event from the Method list; the insertion point jumps to the event procedure for btnSpanish. You are currently viewing the btnSpanish_Click event procedure.

    To write code for more than one event for an object, use the Method drop-down list. You can jump to another procedure by selecting its name from the list. Selecting a new event from the Method list causes the Editor to generate the Sub and End Sub lines for that procedure.

STEP 7: Select *frmHello* in the Class list and drop down the Method list. Notice that your event procedures are all listed. Try selecting *btnPush_Click* and *btnExit_Click* to jump to each of those procedures.

Finish Up

STEP 1: Save the project again.

Print the Code

Select the Printing Options

STEP 1: Make sure that the Editor window is open, showing your form's code. The *File/Print* command is disabled unless the code is displaying and its window selected.

STEP 2: Open the *File* menu and choose *Print.* Click OK.

• The IDE will print only code. It's no longer possible to print a form image or form text.

    If you want to have students turn in a printout of a form, have them press Alt + Print Screen while the program is running. This saves the current window to the Clipboard. Then have them paste the Clipboard contents into a Word document. You can instruct them to add their name and class info before printing.

    You can change an option to print or not print the heading line on the code printout.

Sample Printout

This output is produced when you print the form's code. Notice the ↙ symbol used to continue long lines on the printout. On the screen, those long lines are not split, but scroll off the right side of the screen.

If you are using a color printer, the colors on the screen will also appear on the printed output.

```
A:\HelloWorld\frmHello.vb                                                                     1
'Project:       Hello World
'Programmer:    Your Name
'Date:          Today's Date
'Description:   This project will display a "Hello World"
'               message in two different languages.

Public Class frmHello
  Inherits System.Windows.Forms.Form

Windows Form Designer generated code

  Private Sub btnPush_Click(ByVal sender As System.Object, ByVal e As System.EventArgs) ↙
  Handles btnPush.Click
    'Display the Hello World Message

    lblMessage.Text = "Hello World"
  End Sub

  Private Sub btnExit_Click(ByVal sender As System.Object, ByVal e As System.EventArgs) ↙
  Handles btnExit.Click
    'Exit the project

    Me.Close()
  End Sub

  Private Sub btnSpanish_Click(ByVal sender As System.Object, ByVal e As System. ↙
  EventArgs) Handles btnSpanish.Click
    'Display the Hello World message in Spanish

    lblMessage.Text = "Hola Mundo"
  End Sub
End Class
```

Finding and Fixing Errors

You already may have seen some errors as you entered the first sample project. Programming errors come in three varieties: syntax errors, run-time errors, and logic errors.

Syntax Errors

When you break VB's rules for punctuation, format, or spelling, you generate a **syntax error.** Fortunately, the smart editor finds most syntax errors and even corrects many of them for you. The syntax errors that the editor cannot identify are found and reported by the compiler as it attempts to convert the code into intermediate machine language. A compiler-reported syntax error may be referred to as a *compile error*.

The editor can correct some syntax errors by making assumptions and not even report the error to you. For example, if you type the opening quote of "Hello World" but forget the closing quote, the editor automatically adds the closing quote when you move to the next line. And if you forget the opening and closing parentheses after a method name, such as `Close()`, again the editor will add them for you when you move off the line. Of course, sometimes the editor will make a wrong assumption, but you will be watching, right?

The editor identifies syntax errors as you move off the offending line: A blue squiggly line appears under the part of the line that the editor cannot interpret, and a message appears in the Task list at the bottom of the screen (Figure 1.47). Notice also that the Task list shows the line number of the statement that caused the error. You can display line numbers on the source code (Figure 1.48) with `Tools/Options/Text Editor/Basic/Display/Line Numbers`. You can also pause the mouse pointer over the error line to pop up an error message (refer to Figure 1.48).

F i g u r e   1 . 4 7

The editor identifies a syntax error with a squiggly blue line and places a message in the Task list.

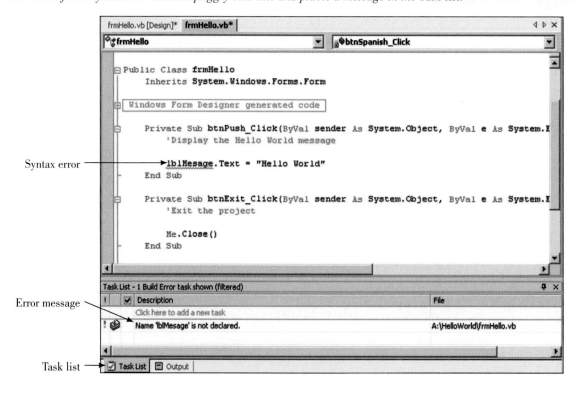

Figure 1.48

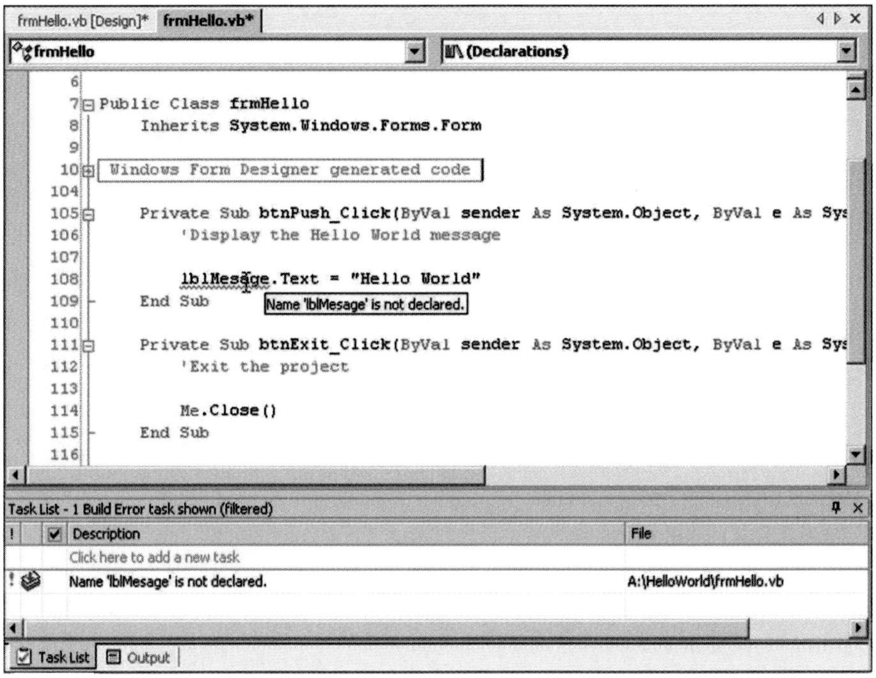

You can display line numbers in the source code to help identify the lines, and you can point to an error to pop up the error message.

Note: If the Task list does not appear, show it with *View/Other Windows/Task List.*

The quickest way to jump to an error line is to point to a message in the Task list and double-click. The line in error will display in the Editor window with the error highlighted (Figure 1.49).

Figure 1.49

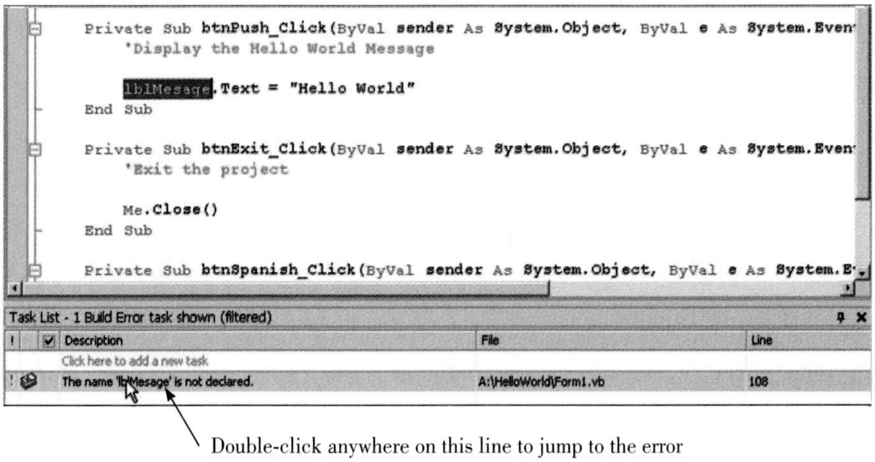

Quickly jump to the line in error by double-clicking on the error message in the Task list.

If a syntax error is found by the compiler, you will see the dialog box shown in Figure 1.50. Click No and return to the editor, correct your errors, and run the program again.

When the compiler identifies syntax errors, it cannot continue. Click No to return to the editor and correct the error.

Run-Time Errors

If your project halts during execution, it is called a **run-time error** or an *exception*. Visual Basic displays a dialog box and highlights the statement causing the problem.

Statements that cannot execute correctly cause run-time errors. The statements are correctly formed Basic statements that pass the syntax checking; however, the statements fail to execute. Run-time errors can be caused by attempting to do impossible arithmetic operations, such as calculate with nonnumeric data, divide by zero, or find the square root of a negative number.

In Chapter 3 you will learn to catch exceptions, so that the program does not come to a halt when an error occurs.

• No edit-and-continue as in VB 6. If you modify code during break time, you must restart the program. Attempting to continue from break time causes it to execute the "old" unchanged code. This behavior is due to the fact that VB must completely compile a program before running it.

Logic Errors

When your program contains **logic errors,** your project runs but produces incorrect results. Perhaps the results of a calculation are incorrect or the wrong text appears, or the text is OK but appears in the wrong location.

Beginning programmers often overlook their logic errors. If the project runs, it must be right—right? All too often, that statement is not correct. You may need to use a calculator to check the output. Check all aspects of the project output: computations, text, and spacing.

For example, the Hello World project in this chapter has event procedures for printing "Hello World" in English and in Spanish. If the contents of the two procedures were switched, the program would work but the results would be incorrect.

The following code does not give the proper instructions to display the message in Spanish:

```
Private Sub cmdSpanish_Click
    'Display the Hello World Message in Spanish

    lblMessage.Text = "Hello World"
End Sub
```

Project Debugging

If you talk to any computer programmer, you will learn that programs don't have errors but that programs get "bugs" in them. Finding and fixing these bugs is called **debugging.**

For syntax errors and run-time errors, your job is easier. Visual Basic displays the Editor window with the offending line highlighted. However, you must identify and locate logic errors yourself.

A Clean Compile

After you locate the problem and fix it, you must recompile the program and run it again. Each time you compile the program, you must have a **clean compile,** which means zero errors (Figure 1.51). You are looking for this line in the Output window:

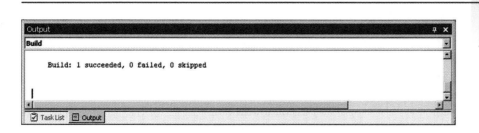

Figure 1.51

Zero build errors means that you have a clean compile.

```
Build: 1 succeeded, 0 failed, 0 skipped
```

You can confuse yourself if you try to run a program without first getting a clean compile. For example, say you *do* get a clean compile and run the program once; then you make some modifications to the program and tell it to run again. If you ignore the error message (refer to Figure 1.50) and attempt to run it anyway, you will actually be running the last cleanly compiled version, without the changes that you just made.

The Visual Studio IDE has some very helpful tools to aid in debugging your projects. The debugging tools are covered in Chapter 4.

Naming Rules and Conventions for Objects

Using good consistent names for objects can make a project easier to read and understand, as well as easier to debug. You *must* follow the Visual Basic rules for naming objects, procedures, and variables. In addition, conscientious programmers also follow certain naming conventions.

Most professional programming shops have a set of standards that their programmers must use. Those standards may differ from the ones you find in this book, but the most important point is this: *Good programmers follow standards. You should have a set of standards and always follow them.*

The Naming Rules

When you select a name for an object, Visual Basic requires the name to begin with a letter. The name can contain letters, digits, and underscores. An object name cannot include a space or punctuation mark.

The Naming Conventions

This text follows standard naming conventions, which help make projects more understandable. Always begin a name with a lowercase three-letter prefix, which identifies the object type (such as label, button, or form) and capitalize the first character after the prefix (the "real" name of the object). For names with multiple words, capitalize each word in the name. All names must be meaningful and indicate the purpose of the object.

Examples

```
lblMessage
btnExit
frmDataEntry
lblDiscountRate
```

Do not keep the default names assigned by Visual Basic, such as Button1 and Label3. Also, do not name your objects with numbers. The exception to this rule is for labels that never change during project execution. These labels usually hold items such as titles, instructions, and labels for other controls. Leaving these labels with their default names is perfectly acceptable and is practiced in this text.

Refer to Table 1.2 for the list of object prefixes.

• The maximum length for identifiers changes from 40 characters to 16,383—probably not a problem for most programmers. In the text we just omitted the statement concerning a maximum length.

Recommended Naming Conventions for Visual Basic Objects   **T a b l e   1 . 2**

Object Class	Prefix	Example
Form	frm	frmDataEntry
Button	btn	btnExit
TextBox	txt	txtPaymentAmount
Label	lbl	lblTotal
Radio button	rad	radBold
CheckBox	chk	chkPrintSummary
Horizontal scroll bar	hsb	hsbRate
Vertical scroll bar	vsb	vsbTemperature
PictureBox	pic	picLandscape
ComboBox	cbo	cboBookList
ListBox	lst	lstIngredients

Visual Studio Help

Visual Studio has an extensive Help facility, which contains lots more information than you will ever use. You can look up any Basic statement, object, property, method, or programming concept. Many coding examples are available, and you can copy and paste the examples into your own project, modifying them if you wish.

The VS Help facility is greatly changed and expanded in the .NET version. Help includes all of the Microsoft Developer Network library (MSDN), which contains several books, technical articles, and the Microsoft Knowledge Base, a database of frequently asked questions and their answers. MSDN includes reference materials for the VS IDE, the .NET Framework, Visual Basic, C#, and C++. You will want to filter the information to display only the VB and related information.

- Help is totally different. The Contents/Index/Search pops up in a new tabbed window in the Solution Explorer's space. A selected topic appears as a tabbed window in the Document window. And if several topics match the selected item in Contents/Index/Search, a new tabbed window appears at the bottom of the screen, docked with the Task List and Output window.

Installing and Running MSDN

You can run MSDN from a hard drive, from a network drive, from a CD, or from the Web. If you run from a CD, you must keep the CD in the drive while you develop programs, and, of course, if you plan to access MSDN from the Web, you must have a live Internet connection as you work.

When you install Visual Studio, by default MSDN is installed on the hard drive. If you don't want to install it there, you must specifically choose this option. You can access MSDN on the web at http://msdn.microsoft.com.

Or, if you want to go directly to VB documentation, add this link to your favorites:

http://msdn.microsoft.com/library/en-us/vblr7/html/vboriVBLangRefTopNode.asp

The expanded Help is a two-edged sword: You have available a wealth of materials, but it may take some time to find the topic you want.

Viewing Help Topics

You view the Help topics in various windows in the VS IDE. When you choose
Contents, Index, or *Search* from the *Help* menu, a new tabbed window
opens in the same location as the Solution Explorer (Figure 1.52). Select a topic
and the correct page appears in the Document window. Notice the new tab at
the top of the Document window in Figure 1.52.

F i g u r e　1 . 5 2

*The Help Index, Contents, and Search windows appear as tabs in the Solution Explorer window. Note that this window was
widened to show the text in the tabs.*

You can choose to filter the Help topics, so that you don't have to view topics for all of the languages when you search for a particular topic. Drop down the *Filtered By* list and choose *Visual Basic and Related* (Figure 1.53).

Figure 1.53

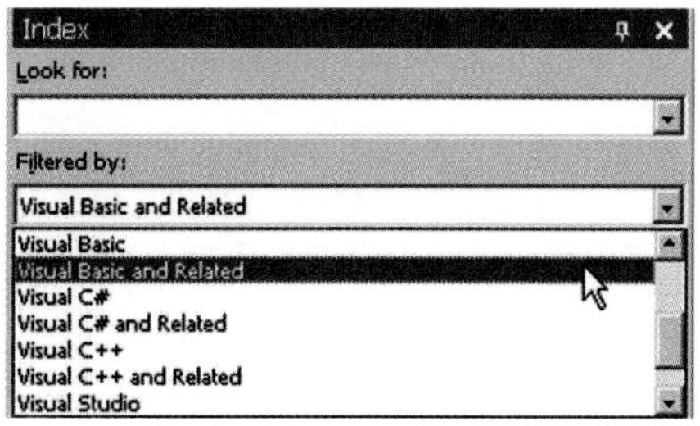

Filter the Help topics so that only Visual Basic topics appear.

Sometimes you may select a topic that has several pages from which to choose. When that happens, a new tabbed window opens in the Task List window (Figure 1.54). Double-click the topic you wish to view and the selected page appears in the Document window.

Figure 1.54

Multiple matching topics appear in a tabbed window at the bottom of the screen. Select a topic from the list and the corresponding page appears in the Document window.

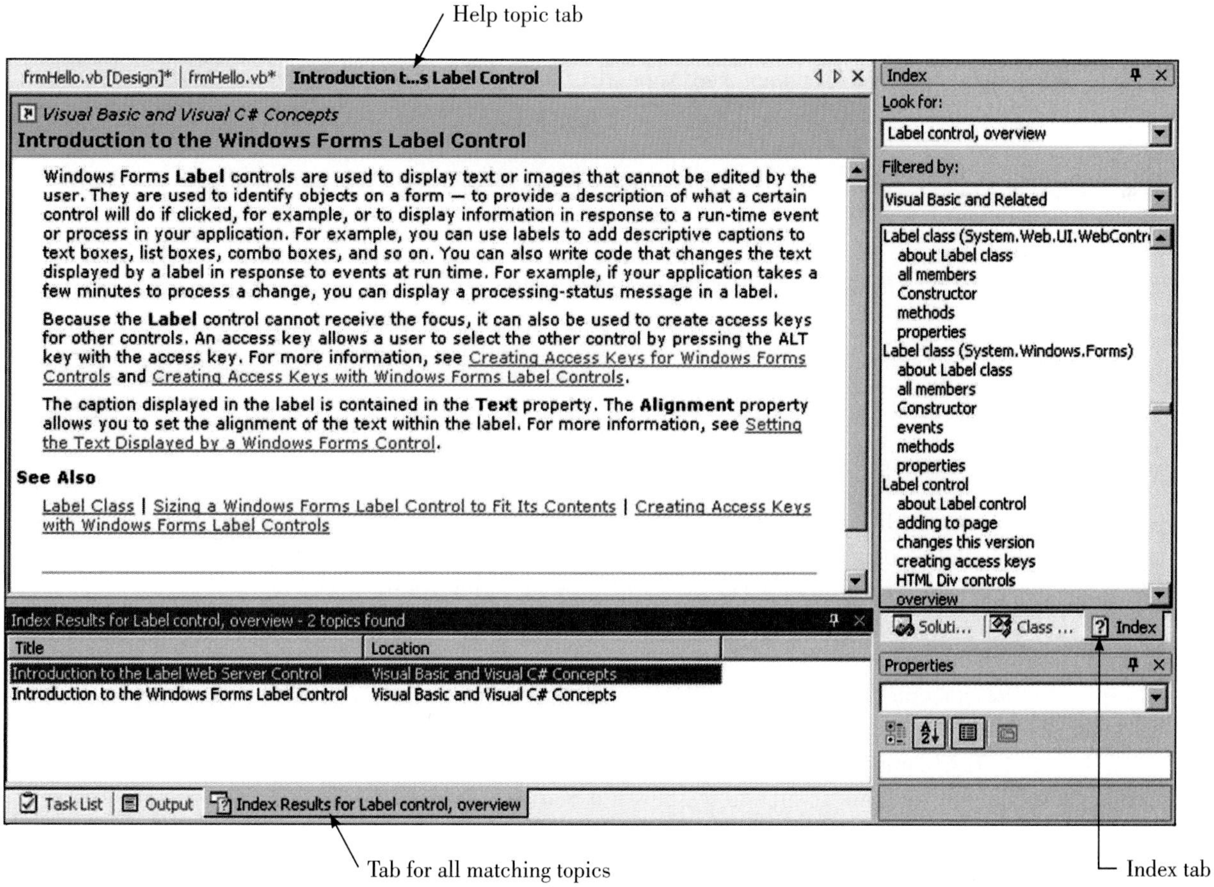

Many Help topics have entries for both Windows Forms and Web Forms. For now, always choose Windows Forms. Chapters 1 to 8 deal with Windows Forms exclusively; Web Forms are introduced in Chapter 9.

A good way to start using Help is to view the topics that demonstrate how to look up topics in Help. Select *Help/Contents* and choose *Visual Studio .NET/Getting Assistance/Using Help in Visual Studio .NET*.

Context-Sensitive Help

A quick way to view Help on any topic is to use **context-sensitive Help.** Select a VB object, such as a form or control, or place the insertion point in a word in the editor, and press F1. The corresponding Help topic will appear in the Document window, if possible, saving you a search. You can display context-sensitive Help about the environment by clicking in an area of the screen and pressing Shift + F1.

Managing Windows

At times you may have more windows and tabs open than you want. You can hide or close any window, or switch to a different window.

*   To close a window that is a part of a tabbed window, click the window's Close button. Only the top window will close.

*   To hide a window that is a part of a tabbed window, right-click the tab and select *Hide* from the context menu.

*   To switch to another window that is part of a tabbed window, click on its tab.

    For additional help with the environment, see Appendix C "Tips and Short-cuts for Mastering the Visual Studio Environment."

▶ Feedback 1.1

Note: Answers for Feedback questions appear in Appendix A.

1. Use the *Help* menu's *Index*, filter by *Visual Basic and Related*, and type "button control". In the Index list, notice that one heading covers Web Forms and another covers Windows Forms. Under *Button control (Windows Forms)* select *overview*. At the bottom of the screen, you should see a new tabbed window showing the two topics that Help found. Double-click on the "Button Control (Windows Forms)" entry; the corresponding page should appear in the Document window. Notice that additional links appear in the text in the Document window. You can click on a link to view another topic.
2. Display the Editor window of your Hello World project. Click on the *Close* method to place the insertion point. Press the F1 key to view context-sensitive help.
3. Display the *Help* menu and view all of the options. Try the *Contents, Index, Search, Index Results,* and *Search Results* options. Notice the *Next Topic* and *Previous Topic* items and the *Show Start Page* item; you can use this command to show the Start Page if its tab does not appear in the Document window.

Summary

1. Visual Basic is an object-oriented language used to write application programs that run in Windows or on the Internet using a graphical user interface (GUI).

2. In the OOP object model, classes are used to create objects that have properties, methods, and events.

3. The current release of Visual Basic (VB) is called .NET, which corresponds to Version 7. Visual Basic .NET is part of Visual Studio .NET. VS .NET has an Academic Edition, a Professional Edition, an Enterprise Developer Edition, and an Enterprise Architect Edition.

4. The .NET Framework provides an environment for the objects from many languages to interoperate. Each language compiles to Microsoft Intermediate Language (MSIL) and runs in the Common Language Runtime (CLR).

5. To plan a project, first sketch the user interface and then list the objects and properties needed. Then plan the necessary event procedures.

6. The three steps to creating a Visual Basic project are (1) define the user interface, (2) set the properties, and (3) write the Basic code.

7. A Visual Basic application is called a *solution*. Each solution can contain multiple projects, and each project may contain multiple forms and additional files. The solution file has an extension of .sln, a project file has an extension of .vbproj, form files and additional VB files have an extension of .vb. In addition, the Visual Studio environment and the VB compiler both create several more files.

8. The Visual Studio integrated development environment (IDE) consists of several tools, including a form designer, an editor, a compiler, a debugger, an object browser, and a Help facility.

9. VB has three modes: design time, run time, and break time.

10. You can customize the Visual Studio IDE and reset all customizations to their default state.

11. You create the user interface for an application by adding controls from the toolbox to a form. You can move, resize, and delete the controls.

12. The Name property of a control is used to refer to the control in code. The Text property holds the words that the user sees on the screen.

13. Visual Basic code is written in procedures. Sub procedures begin with the word `Sub` and end with `End Sub`.

14. Project remarks are used for documentation. Good programming practice requires remarks in every procedure and in the Declarations section of a file.

15. Assignment statements assign a value to a property or a variable. Assignment statements work from right to left, assigning the value on the right side of the equal sign to the property or variable named on the left side of the equal sign.

16. The `Me.Close` method terminates program execution.

17. Each event to which you want to respond requires an event procedure.

18. You can print out the Visual Basic code for documentation.

19. Three types of errors can occur in a Visual Basic project: syntax errors (violating the syntax rules of Basic statements), run-time errors (containing a statement that cannot execute properly), and logic errors (producing erroneous results).

20. Finding and fixing programming errors is called *debugging*.
21. You must have a clean compile each time you modify a program before you can run the program.
22. Following good naming conventions can help make a project easier to debug.
23. Visual Basic Help has very complete descriptions of all project elements and their uses. You can use the Contents, Index, Search, or context-sensitive Help.

Key Terms

Academic Edition   *5*
assignment statement   *33*
break time   *14*
Button   *21*
class   *4*
clean compile   *51*
code   *6*
context menu   *25*
context-sensitive Help   *56*
control   *4*
debugging   *51*
design time   *14*
Declarations section   *45*
Document window   *12*
Enterprise Architect Edition   *5*
Enterprise Developer Edition   *5*
event   *4*
event procedure   *33*
form   *4*
Form Designer   *12*
graphical user interface (GUI)   *3*
handle   *22*
Help   *13*
integrated development environment
   (IDE)   *8*
Label   *21*

logic error   *50*
method   *4*
namespace   *26*
object   *4*
object-oriented programming
   (OOP)   *3*
procedure   *32*
Professional Edition   *5*
project file   *7*
Properties window   *12*
property   *4*
pseudocode   *6*
remark statement   *33*
run time   *14*
run-time error   *50*
solution   *7*
Solution Explorer window   *12*
solution file   *7*
sub procedure   *32*
syntax error   *47*
Text property   *28*
toolbar   *10*
toolbox   *12*
user interface   *6*
Visual Studio environment   *8*

Review Questions

1. What are objects and properties? How are they related to each other?
2. What are the three steps for planning and creating Visual Basic projects? Describe what happens in each step.
3. What is the purpose of these Visual Basic file types: .sln, .suo, and .vb?
4. When is Visual Basic in design time? run time? break time?
5. What is the purpose of the Name property of a control?
6. Which property determines what appears on the form for a Label control?
7. What is the purpose of the Text property of a button? the Text property of a form?

8. What does btnPush_Click mean? To what does btnPush refer? To what does Click refer?

9. What is a Visual Basic event? Give some examples of events.

10. What property must be set to center text in a label? What should be the value of the property?

11. What is the Declarations section of a file? What belongs there?

12. What is a syntax error, when does it occur, and what might cause it?

13. What is a run-time error, when does it occur, and what might cause it?

14. What is a logic error, when does it occur, and what might cause it?

15. Tell the class of control and the likely purpose of each of these object names:

     lblAddress
     btnExit
     txtName

16. What does context-sensitive Help mean? How can you use it to see the Help page for a button?

Programming Exercises

1.1 For your first Visual Basic exercise, you must first complete the Hello World project. Then add buttons and event procedures to display the "Hello World" message in two more languages. You may substitute any other languages for those shown. Feel free to modify the user interface to suit yourself (or your instructor).

Make sure to use meaningful names for your new buttons, following the naming conventions in Table 1.2. (Begin the name with lowercase "btn".) Include remarks at the top of every procedure and in the Declarations section of the code.

    "Hello World" in French: Bonjour tout le monde
    "Hello World" in Italian: Ciao Mondo

1.2 Write a new Visual Basic project that displays a different greeting, or make it display the name of your school or your company. Include at least two buttons to display the greeting, and exit the project.

Include a label that holds your name at the bottom of the form and change the Text property of the form to something meaningful.

Follow good naming conventions for object names; include remarks at the top of every procedure and in the Declarations section of the code.

Select a different font name and font size for the greeting label. If you wish, you can also select a different color for the font. Select each font attribute from the *Font* dialog box from the Properties window.

1.3 Write a project that displays four sayings, such as "The early bird gets the worm" or "A penny saved is a penny earned." (You will want to keep the sayings short, as each must be entered on one code statement. However, when the saying displays on your form, long lines will wrap within the label if the label is large enough.)

Make a button for each saying with a descriptive Text property for each, as well as a button to exit the project.

Include a label that holds your name at the bottom of the form. Also, make sure to change the form's title bar to something meaningful.

You may change the Font properties of the large label to the font and size of your choice.

Make sure the label is large enough to display your longest saying and that the buttons are large enough to hold their entire Text properties.

Follow good naming conventions for object names; include remarks at the top of every procedure and in the Declarations section of the code.

1.4   Write a project to display company contact information. Include buttons and labels for contact person, department, and phone. When the user clicks on one of the buttons, display the contact information in the corresponding label. Include a button to exit.

Include a label that holds your name at the bottom of the form and change the title bar of the form to something meaningful.

You may change the Font properties of the labels to the font and size of your choice.

Follow good naming conventions for object names; include remarks at the top of every procedure and in the Declarations section of the code.

1.5   Create a project to display the daily specials for "your" diner. Make up a name for your diner and display it in a label at the top of the form. Add a label to display the appropriate special depending on the button that is pressed. The buttons should be "Soup of the Day," "Chef's Special," and "Daily Fish."

Also include an Exit button.

Sample Data: Dorothy's Diner is offering Tortilla Soup, a California Cobb Salad, and Hazelnut-Coated Mahi Mahi.

Case Studies

Very Busy (VB) Mail Order

If you don't have the time to look for all those hard-to-find items, tell us what you're looking for. We'll send you a catalog from the appropriate company or order for you. We can place an order and ship it to you. We also help with shopping for gifts; your order can be gift wrapped and sent anywhere you wish.

The company title will be shortened to "VB Mail Order". Include this name on the title bar of the first form of each project that you create for this case study.

Your first job is to create a project that will display the name and telephone number for the contact person for the customer relations, marketing, order processing, and shipping departments.

Include a button for each department. When the user clicks on the button for a department, display the name and telephone number for the contact person in two labels. Also include identifying labels with Text "Department Contact" and "Telephone Number".

Be sure to include a button for Exit.

Include a label at the bottom of the form that holds your name and give the form a meaningful title bar.

Test Data Department	Department Contact	Telephone Number
Customer Relations	Tricia Mills	500-1111
Marketing	Michelle Rigner	500-2222
Order Processing	Kenna DeVoss	500-3333
Shipping	Eric Andrews	500-4444

Valley Boulevard (VB) Auto Center

Valley Boulevard Auto Center will meet all of your automobile needs. The center has facilities with everything for your vehicles including sales and leasing for new and used cars and RVs, auto service and repair, detail shop, car wash, and auto parts.

The company title will be shortened to "VB Auto Center". This name should appear as the title bar on the first form of every project that you create throughout the text for this case study.

Your first job is to create a project that will display current notices.

Include four buttons labeled: "Auto Sales", "Service Center", "Detail Shop", and "Employment Opportunities". One Label will be used to display the information when the buttons are clicked. Be sure to include a button for Exit.

Include your name in a label at the bottom of the form.

Test Data	
Button	**Label Text**
Auto Sales	Family wagon, immaculate condition $12,995
Service Center	Lube, oil, filter $25.99
Detail Shop	Complete detail $79.95 for most cars
Employment Opportunities	Sales position, contact Mr. Mann 551-2134 x475

Video Bonanza

This neighborhood store is an independently owned video rental business. The owners would like to allow their customers to use the computer to look up the aisle number for movies by category.

Create a form with a button for each category. When the user clicks on a button, display the corresponding aisle number in a label. Include a button to exit.

Include a label that holds your name at the bottom of the form and change the title bar of the form to "Video Bonanza."

You may change the font properties of the labels to the font and size of your choice. Include additional categories, if you wish.

Follow good programming conventions for object names; include remarks at the top of every procedure and in the Declarations section of the code.

Test Data	
Button	**Location**
Comedy	Aisle 1
Drama	Aisle 2
Action	Aisle 3
Sci-Fi	Aisle 4
Horror	Aisle 5
New Releases	Back Wall

Very Very Boards

This chain of stores features a full line of clothing and equipment for snowboard and skateboard enthusiasts. Management wants a computer application to allow employees to display the address and hours for each of their branches.

Create a form with a button for each store branch. When the user clicks on a button, display the correct address and hours.

Include a label that holds your name at the bottom of the form, and change the title bar of the form to "Very Very Boards".

You may change the font properties of the labels to the font and size of your choice.

Follow good programming conventions for object names; include remarks at the top of every procedure and in the Declarations section of the code.

Store Branches: The three branches are Downtown, Mall, and Suburbs. Make up hours and locations for each.

CHAPTER

2

More Controls

at the completion of this chapter, you will be able to . . .

1. Use text boxes, group boxes, check boxes, radio buttons, and picture boxes effectively.

2. Set the BorderStyle property to make controls appear flat or three-dimensional.

3. Select multiple controls and move them, align them, and set common properties.

4. Make your projects easy for the user to understand and operate by defining access keys, setting a default and a cancel button, controlling the tab sequence, resetting the focus during program execution, and causing ToolTips to appear.

5. Clear the contents of text boxes and labels.

6. Change text color during program execution.

7. Code multiple statements for one control using the With and End With statements.

8. Concatenate (join) strings of text.

9. Make a control visible or invisible at run time by setting its Visible property.

Introducing More Controls

In Chapter 1 you learned to use labels and buttons. In this chapter you will learn to use several more control types: text boxes, group boxes, check boxes, radio buttons, and picture boxes. Figure 2.1 shows the toolbox with the tools for these controls labeled. Figure 2.2 shows some of these controls on a form.

Each class of controls has its own set of properties. To see a complete list of the properties for any class of control, you can (1) place a control on a form and examine the properties list or (2) click on a tool or a control and press F1 for context-sensitive Help. VB will display the Help page for that control, and you can view a list of the properties and an explanation of their use.

Figure 2.1

The toolbox showing the controls that are covered in this chapter.

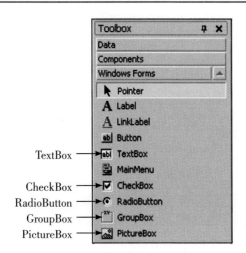

Figure 2.2

This form uses text boxes, a check box, radio buttons, group boxes, and a picture box.

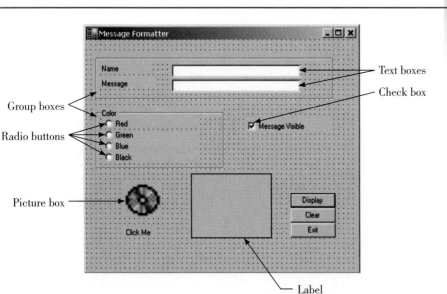

Text Boxes

Use a **text box** control when you want the user to type some input. The form in Figure 2.2 has two text boxes. The user can move from one box to the next, make corrections, cut and paste if desired, and click the Display button when finished. In your program code you can use the **Text property** of each text box.

Example

```
lblName.Text = txtName.Text
```

In this example whatever the user enters into the text box is assigned to the Text property of lblName. If you want to display some text in a text box during program execution, assign a literal to the Text property:

```
txtMessage.Text = "Watson, come here."
```

You can set the **TextAlign property** of text boxes to change the alignment of text within the box.

The values for the TextAlign property are

HorizontalAlignment.Left
HorizontalAlignment.Right
HorizontalAlignment.Center

- The Alignment property is now TextAlign, with a new set of constants for setting the alignment.

The three-letter prefix for naming a text box is "txt".

Examples

```
txtTitle
txtCompany
```

Group Boxes

Group boxes are used as containers for other controls. Usually, groups of radio buttons or check boxes are placed in group boxes. Using group boxes to group controls makes your forms easier to understand.

Set a group box's Text property to the words you want to appear on the top edge of the group box. The three-letter prefix for naming a group box is "grp".

- Group boxes replace frames; the class name is GroupBox and the prefix is "grp".

Examples

```
grpColor
grpStyle
```

Check Boxes

Check boxes allow the user to select (or deselect) an option. In any group of check boxes, any number can be selected. The **Checked property** of a check box is set to False if unchecked or True if checked.

> • The new Boolean Checked property of check boxes replaces the Value property. The event to use for change of state is CheckChanged.

You can write an event procedure for the CheckChanged event, which executes when the user clicks in the box. In Chapter 4, when you learn about If statements, you can take one action when the box is checked and another action when it is unchecked.

Use the Text property of a check box for the text you want to appear next to the box. The three-letter prefix for naming a check box is "chk".

Examples

```
chkBold
chkItalic
```

Radio Buttons

Use **radio buttons** when only one button of a group may be selected. Any radio buttons that you place directly on the form (not in a group box) function as a group. A group of radio buttons inside a group box function together. The best method is to first create a group box and then create each radio button inside the group box.

> • Option button are now radio button; the prefix is "rad."
>
> • The Change event for radio buttons is now CheckChanged.

The Checked property of a radio button is set to True if selected or to False if unselected. You can write an event procedure to execute when the user selects a radio button using the control's CheckChanged event. In Chapter 4 you will learn to determine in your code whether or not a button is selected.

Set a radio button's Text property to the text you want to appear next to the button. The three-letter prefix for naming a radio button is "rad".

Examples

```
radRed
radBlue
```

Picture Boxes

A **PictureBox control** can hold an image. You can set a picture box's **Image property** to a graphic file with an extension of .bmp, .gif, .jpg, .png, .ico, .emf, or .wmf. First place the PictureBox control on a form and then select its Image property in the Properties window. Click on the Properties button (Figure 2.3) to display an Open dialog box where you can select a filename (Figure 2.4).

Note: It's a good idea to place the graphic file into the folder with your project before you assign it to your picture box. However, the picture is actually saved in the form's .resx file.

- Image controls no longer exist, use the PictureBox control.

- Picture boxes can display more graphic formats than the old Image controls, including animated .gif files.

Figure 2.3

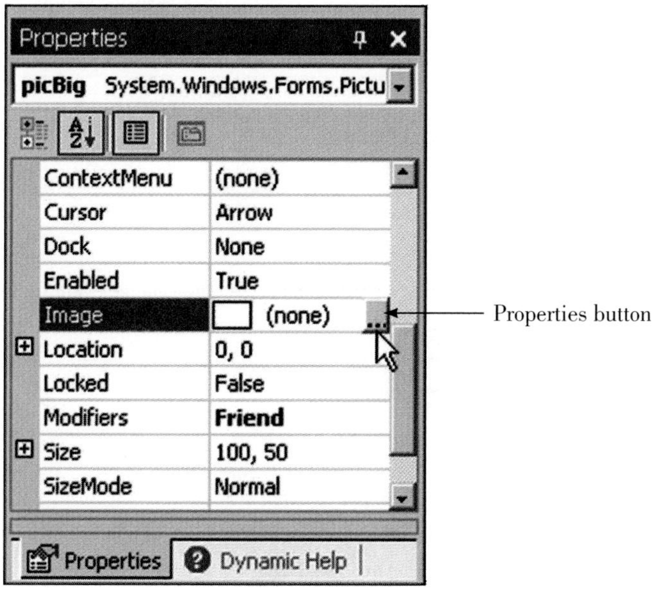

Click on the Image property for a PictureBox control, and a Properties button appears. Click on the Properties button to view the Open dialog box.

Properties button

Figure 2.4

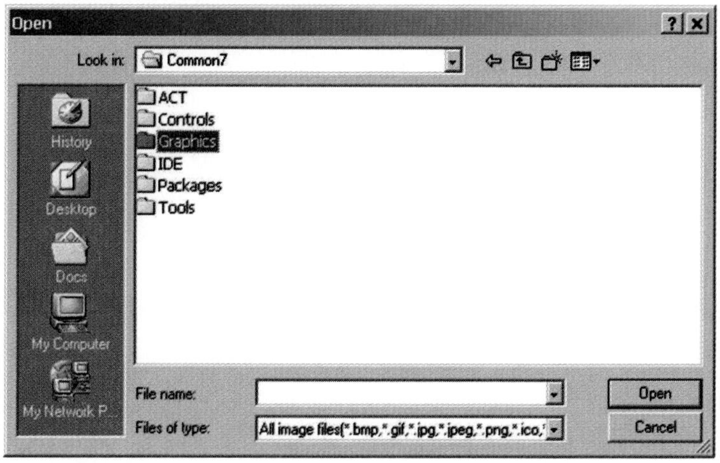

The Open dialog box. Make your selection here for the graphic file you want to appear in the PictureBox control.

You can use any graphic file (with the proper format) that you have available. You will find many icon files included with Visual Basic. This is the default location (Figure 2.5):

```
Program Files
    Microsoft Visual Studio .NET
        Common7
            Graphics
                Icons
```

✓**TIP**

To use the VB icon files, you must install them when you install VB. If you don't have the files, reinstall VB and choose to install the graphics files. ■

Figure 2.5

Find the Visual Basic icon files in several folders beneath the Microsoft Visual Studio .NET \ Common7 \ Graphics \ Icons folder.

PictureBox controls have several useful properties that you can set at design time or run time. For example, set the **SizeMode property** to **Stretch-Image** to make the picture enlarge to fill the control. You can set the **Visible property** to False to make the picture box disappear. To make a picture box invisible at run time, use this code statement:

```
picLogo.Visible = False
```

The three-letter prefix for naming a picture box is "pic".

• The Stretch property is gone; use SizeMode set to StretchImage.

Setting a Border and Style

Most controls can appear to be three-dimensional (refer to Figure 2.2) or flat. Labels, text boxes, and picture boxes all have a **BorderStyle property** with choices of *None*, *FixedSingle*, or *Fixed3D*. Text boxes default to Fixed3D; labels and picture boxes default to None. Of course, you can change the property to the style of your choice.

• If you change the BorderStyle property in code, you must include the enumeration's prefix: BorderStyle.Fixed3D.

> **Feedback 2.1**

Create a picture box control that displays an enlarged icon and appears in a 3D box. Make up a name that conforms to this textbook's naming convention.

Property	Setting
Name	
BorderStyle	
SizeMode	
Visible	

Drawing a Line

You can draw a line on a form by using the Label control. You may want to include lines when creating a logo, or you may simply want to divide the screen by drawing a line. To create the look of a line, set the Text property of your label to blank, set the BorderStyle to None, and change the Backcolor to the color you want for the line. You can control the size of the line with the Width and Height properties.

• There are no more Line or Shape controls. A label can be used to display a line.

You can also draw a line on the form using the graphics methods. Drawing graphics is covered in Chapter 12.

Working with Multiple Controls

You can select more than one control at a time, which means that you can move the controls as a group, set similar properties for the group, and align the controls.

Selecting Multiple Controls

There are several methods of selecting multiple controls. If the controls are near each other, the easiest method is to use the mouse to drag a selection box around the controls. Point to one corner of a box surrounding the controls, press the mouse button, and drag to the opposite corner (Figure 2.6). When you release the mouse button, each control will have selection handles (Figure 2.7).

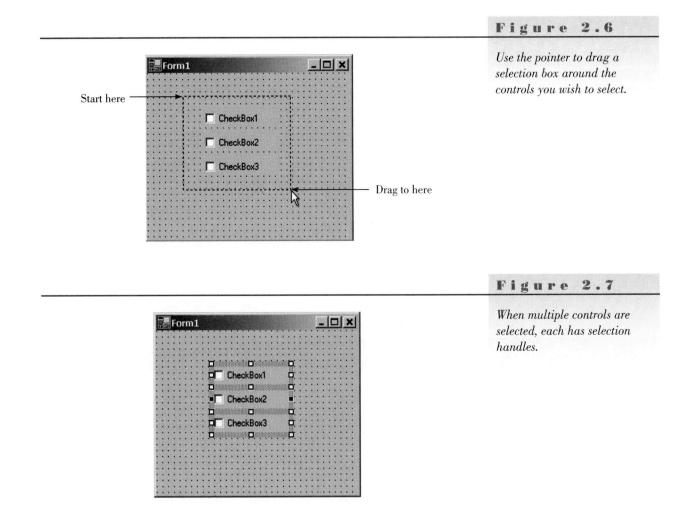

Figure 2.6

Use the pointer to drag a selection box around the controls you wish to select.

Figure 2.7

When multiple controls are selected, each has selection handles.

You can also select multiple controls, one at a time. Click on one control to select it, hold down the Ctrl key or the Shift key, and click on the next control. You can keep the Ctrl or Shift key down and continue clicking on controls you wish to select. Ctrl-click (or Shift-click) on a control a second time to deselect it without changing the rest of the group.

When you want to select most of the controls on the form, use a combination of the two methods. Drag a selection box around all of the controls to select them, and then Ctrl-click on the ones you want to deselect. You can also select all of the controls using the *Select All* option on the *Edit* menu or its keyboard shortcut: Ctrl + A.

Deselecting a Group of Controls

When you are finished working with a group of controls, it's easy to deselect them. Just click anywhere on the form (not on a control) or select another previously unselected control.

Moving Controls as a Group

After selecting multiple controls, you can move them as a group. To do this, point inside one of the selected controls, press the mouse button, and drag the entire group to a new location (Figure 2.8). As you drag the mouse pointer, an outline of the controls moves. When you release the mouse button, the controls move to their new location.

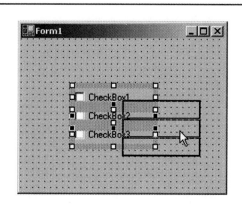

Figure 2.8

Drag a group of selected controls. An outline of the controls moves as you drag, and then the group moves when you release the mouse button.

Setting Properties for Multiple Controls

You can set some common properties for groups of controls. After selecting the group, check the Properties window. Any properties that appear in the window are shared by all of the controls and can be changed all at once. For example, you may want to set the BorderStyle property for all your controls to three-dimensional or change the font used for a group of labels. Some properties appear empty; those cannot be set for multiple controls.

Aligning Controls

After you select a group of controls, it is easy to resize and align them using the buttons on the Layout toolbar (Figure 2.9) or the corresponding items on the *Format* menu. Select your group of controls and choose any of the resizing buttons; these can make the controls equal in width, height, or both. Then select another button to align the tops, bottoms, or centers of the controls. You can also move the entire group to a new location.

Figure 2.9

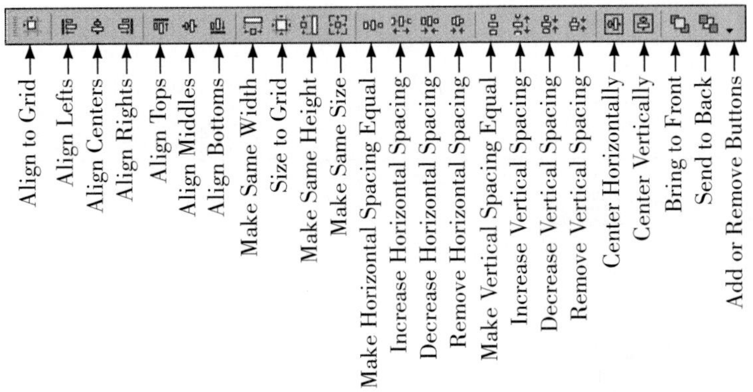

Resize and align multiple controls using the Layout *menu.*

To set the spacing between controls, use the buttons for horizontal and/or vertical spacing. These buttons enable you to create equal spacing between controls or to increase or decrease the space between controls.

Designing Your Applications for User Convenience

One of the goals of good programming is to create programs that are easy to use. Your user interface should be clear and consistent. One school of thought says that if users misuse a program, it's the fault of the programmer, not the users. Because most of your users will already know how to operate Windows programs, you should strive to make your programs look and behave like other Windows programs. Some of the ways to accomplish this are to make the controls operate in the standard way, define keyboard access keys, set a default button, and make the Tab key work correctly. You can also define ToolTips, which are those small labels that pop up when the user pauses the mouse pointer over a control.

Designing the User Interface

The design of the screen should be easy to understand and "comfortable" for the user. The best way that we can accomplish these goals is to follow industry standards for the color, size, and placement of controls. Once users become accustomed to a screen design, they will expect (and feel more familiar with) applications that follow the same design criteria.

You should design your applications to match other Windows applications. Microsoft has done extensive program testing with users of different ages, genders, nationalities, and disabilities. We should take advantage of this research and follow their guidelines. Take some time to examine the screens and dialog boxes in Microsoft Office as well as those in Visual Basic.

One recommendation about interface design concerns color. You have probably noticed that Windows applications are predominantly gray. A reason for this choice is that many people are color blind. Also, gray is easiest for the majority of users. Although you may personally prefer brighter colors, you will stick with gray, or the system palette the user chooses, if you want your applications to look professional.

Colors can indicate to the user what is expected. Use a white background for text boxes to indicate that the user should input information. Use a gray background for labels, which the user cannot change. Labels that will display a message or the result of a calculation should have a border around them; labels that provide text on the screen should have no border (the default).

Group your controls on the form to aid the user. A good practice is to create group boxes to hold related items, especially those controls that require user input. This visual aid helps the user understand the information that is being presented or requested.

Use a sans serif font on your forms, such as the default MS Sans Serif, and do not make them boldface. Limit large font sizes to a few items, such as the company name.

Defining Keyboard Access Keys

Many people prefer to use the keyboard, rather than a mouse, for most operations. Windows is set up so that most functions can be done with either the keyboard or a mouse. You can make your projects respond to the keyboard by defining **access keys**, also called *hot keys*. For example, in Figure 2.10 you can select the OK button with Alt + o and the Exit button with Alt + x.

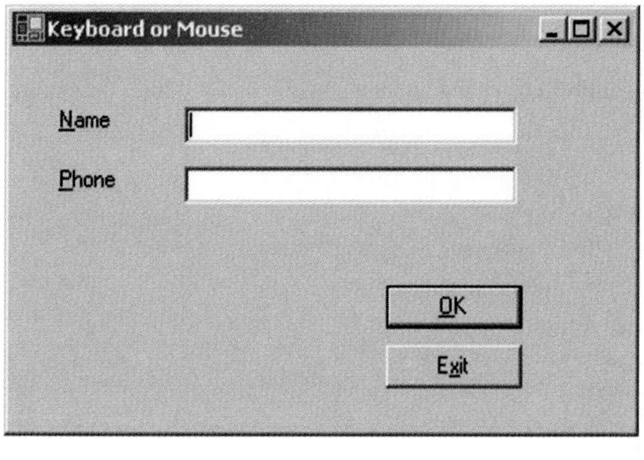

Figure 2.10

The underlined character defines an access key. The user can select the OK button by pressing Alt + o and the Exit button with Alt + x.

You can set access keys for buttons, radio buttons, and check boxes when you define their Text properties. Type an ampersand (&) in front of the character you want for the access key; Visual Basic underlines the character. You can also set an access key for a label; see "Setting the Tab Sequence" later in this chapter.

For examples of access keys on buttons, type the following for the button's Text property:

```
&OK      for OK
E&xit    for Exit
```

When you define access keys, you need to watch for several pitfalls. First, try to use the Windows-standard keys whenever possible. For example, use the *x* of Exit and the *S* of Save. Second, make sure you don't give two controls the same access key: It confuses the user and doesn't work correctly. Only the first control is activated when the user presses the access key.

Note: To view the access keys on controls or menus in Windows 2000 or XP, you may have to press the Alt key, depending on your system settings.

Setting the Default and Cancel Properties of Buttons

Are you a keyboard user? If so, do you mind having to pick up the mouse and click a button after typing text into a text box? Once a person's fingers are on the keyboard, most people prefer to press the Enter key rather than to click the mouse. If one of the buttons on the form is the default button, pressing Enter is the same as clicking the button. You can always identify the default button on a form by its darker outline. In Figure 2.10, the default is the OK button.

You can make one of your buttons the default button by setting the **AcceptButton property** of the form to the button name. When the user presses Enter, that button is automatically selected.

You can also select a *cancel button*. The cancel button is the button that is selected when the user presses the Esc key. You can make a button the cancel button by setting the form's **CancelButton property**. An example of a good time to set the CancelButton property is on a form with OK and Cancel buttons. You may want to set the form's AcceptButton to btnOK and the CancelButton property to btnCancel.

> • AcceptButton and CancelButton are properties of the form, rather than properties of the buttons themselves.

Setting the Tab Order for Controls

In Windows programs one control on the form always has the **focus**. You can see the focus change as you Tab from control to control. For controls such as buttons, the focus appears as a light dotted line. For text boxes, the insertion point (also called the *cursor*) appears inside the box.

Some controls can receive the focus; others cannot. For example, text boxes and buttons can receive the focus, but labels and picture boxes cannot.

The Tab Order

Two properties determine whether the focus stops on a control and the order in which the focus moves. Controls that are capable of receiving focus have a **TabStop property,** which you can set to True or False. If you do not want the focus to stop on a control when the user presses the Tab key, set the TabStop property to False.

The **TabIndex property** determines the order the focus moves as the Tab key is pressed. As you create controls on your form, Visual Basic assigns the TabIndex property in sequence. Most of the time that order is correct, but if you want to Tab in some other sequence or if you add controls later, you will need to modify the TabIndex properties of your controls.

When your program begins running, the focus is on the control with the lowest TabIndex (usually 0). Since you generally want the insertion point to appear in the first control on the form, its TabIndex should be set to 0. The next control should be set to 1; the next to 2; and so forth.

You may be puzzled by the properties of labels, which have a TabIndex property but not a TabStop. A label cannot receive focus, but it has a location in the tab sequence. This fact allows you to create keyboard access keys for text boxes. When the user types an access key, such as Alt + N, the focus jumps to the first TabIndex following the label. See Figure 2.11.

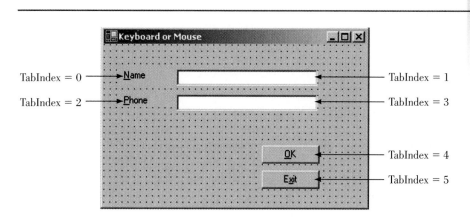

Figure 2.11

To use keyboard access keys for a text box, the TabIndex of the label must precede the TabIndex of the text box.

By default, buttons and text boxes have their TabStop property set to True, but radio buttons have their TabStop property set to False. If you want the tab sequence to include radio buttons, you must set their TabStop property to True. Be aware that the behavior of radio buttons in the tab sequence is different from other controls: The Tab key takes you only to one radio button in a group, even though all buttons in the group have their TabStop and TabIndex properties set. If you are using the keyboard to select radio buttons, you must tab to the group and then use your Up and Down arrow keys to select the correct button.

✔**TIP**

Make sure you do not have duplicate numbers for the TabIndex properties or duplicate keyboard access keys. You may hear a "ding" at run time if there is duplication. ■

Setting the Tab Order

To set the tab order for controls, you can set each control's TabIndex property in the Properties window. Or, you can use VB's great new feature that helps you set TabIndexes automatically. To use this new feature, make sure that the Design window is active and select *View / Tab Order.* (The *Tab Order* item does not appear on the menu unless the Design window is active.) Small numbers appear in the upper-left corner of each control; these are the current TabIndex properties of the controls. Click first in the control that you want to

• The new feature for setting the tab order is *wonderful*. Be sure to check it out.

be TabIndex zero, then click on the control for TabIndex one, then click on the next control until you have set the TabIndex for all controls (Figure 2.12).

Figure 2.12

Click on each control, in sequence, to set the TabIndex property of the controls automatically.

When you have finished setting the TabIndex for all controls, select *View / Tab Order* again to hide the sequence numbers. If you make a mistake and want to change the tab order, turn the option off and on again, and start over with TabIndex zero again.

Setting the Form's Location on the Screen

When your project runs, the form appears in the upper-left corner of the screen by default. You can set the form's screen position by setting the **StartPosition property** of the form. Figure 2.13 shows your choices for the property setting. To center your form on the user's screen, set the StartPosition property to *Center Screen.*

- Unfortunately the Form Layout window is no longer in the IDE. Set the form's initial position by setting the StartPosition property of the form.

Figure 2.13

Set the StartupPosition property of the form to CenterScreen *to make the form appear in the center of the user's screen when the program runs.*

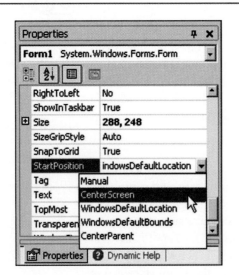

Creating ToolTips

If you are a Windows user, you probably appreciate and rely on **ToolTips**, those small labels that pop up when you pause your pointer over a toolbar button or control. You can easily add ToolTips to your projects by adding a **ToolTip control** to a form. After you add the control to your form, each of the form's controls has a new property: **ToolTip on ToolTip1,** assuming that you keep the default name, ToolTip1, for the control.

To define ToolTips, select the ToolTip control from the toolbox (Figure 2.14) and click anywhere on the form. The new control appears in a new pane that opens at the bottom of the Form Designer (Figure 2.15). This pane, called the ***component tray,*** holds controls that do not have a visual representation at run time. You will see more controls that use the component tray later in this text.

- ToolTips are done differently. Individual controls do not have a ToolTip property unless you add a ToolTip control to the form. Then each control has a new ToolTip on ToolTip1 property (assuming that the ToolTip control is named ToolTip1).

- Nondisplay controls added to a form are shown in a new panel under the form; the panel is called the *component tray*. Other controls that will appear there later in this text are the common dialog components, the timer, the printer controls, and database access components.

Figure 2.14

Add a ToolTip control to your form; each of the form's controls will have a new property to hold the text of the ToolTip.

Figure 2.15

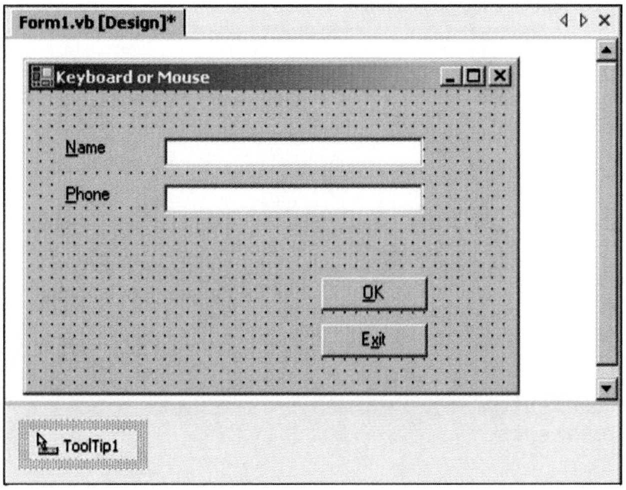

The new ToolTip control goes in the component tray at the bottom of the Form Designer window.

After you add the ToolTip control, examine the properties list for other controls on the form, such as buttons, text boxes, labels, radio buttons, check boxes, and even the form itself. Each has a new ToolTip on ToolTip1 property.

Try this example: Add a new button to a form and add a ToolTip control. Change the button's Text property to Exit and set its ToolTip on ToolTip1 property to "Close and Exit the program". Now run the project, point to the Exit button and pause; the ToolTip will appear (Figure 2.16).

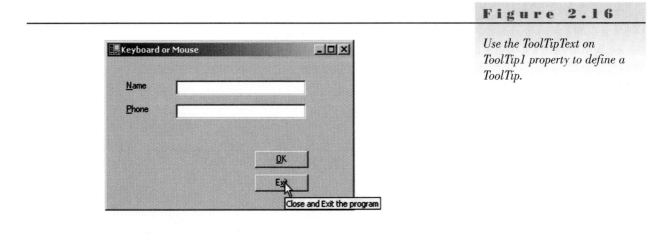

Figure   2.16

Use the ToolTipText on ToolTip1 property to define a ToolTip.

Coding for the Controls

You already know how to set initial properties for controls at design time. You may also want to set some properties in code, as your project executes. You can clear out the contents of text boxes and labels; reset the focus; and change the color of text.

Clearing Text Boxes and Labels

You can clear out the contents of a text box or label by setting the property to an **empty string.** Use "" (no space between the two quotation marks). This empty string is also called a *null string* or a *zero-length string*. You can also clear out a text box using the *Clear* method.

Examples

```
txtName.Text = ""        'Clear the contents
lblMessage.Text = ""     'Clear the contents
txtDataEntry.Clear()     'Clear the contents
```

Resetting the Focus

As your program runs, you want the insertion point to appear in the text box where the user is expected to type. The **focus** should therefore begin in the first text box. But what about later? If you clear the form's text boxes, you should reset the focus to the first text box. The *Focus* **method** handles this situation.

• The SetFocus method has been replaced by the Focus method.

Remember, the convention is Object.Method, so the statement to set the insertion point in the text box called txtName is as follows:

```
txtName.Focus()    'Make the insertion point appear here
```

Setting the Checked Property of Radio Buttons and Check Boxes

Of course, the purpose of radio buttons and check boxes is to allow the user to make selections. However, often you need to select or deselect a control in code. You can select or deselect radio buttons and check boxes at design time (to set initial status) or at run time (to respond to an event).

• The Value property has changed to the Checked property.

To make a radio button appear selected initially, set its Checked property to True in the Properties window. In code, assign True to its Checked property:

```
radRed.Checked = True        'Make button selected
chkDisplay.Checked = True     'Make box checked
chkDisplay.Checked = False    'Make box unchecked
```

Setting Visibility at Run Time

You can set the visibility of a control at run time.

```
lblMessage.Visible = False
```

You may want the visibility of a control to depend on the selection a user makes in a check box or radio button. This statement makes the visibility match the check box: When the check box is checked (Checked = True) the label is visible (Visible = True).

```
lblMessage.Visible = chkDisplay.Checked
```

▶ Feedback 2.2

1. Write the Basic statements to clear the text box called txtCompany and reset the insertion point into the box.
2. Write the Basic statements to clear the label called lblCustomer and place the insertion point into a text box called txtOrder.
3. What will be the effect of each of these Basic statements?
   (a) chkPrint.Checked = True
   (b) radColor.Checked = False
   (c) picDrawing.Visible = False
   (d) lblLocation.BorderStyle = BorderStyle.Fixed3D
   (e) lblCity.Text = txtCity.Text

Changing the Color of Text

You can change the color of text by changing the **ForeColor property** of a control. Actually, most controls have a ForeColor and a BackColor property. The ForeColor property changes the color of the text; the BackColor property controls the color around the text.

The Color Constants

Visual Basic provides an easy way to specify a large number of colors. These **color constants** are in the Color class. If you type the keyword Color and a period in the editor, you can see a full list of colors. Some of the colors are listed below.

• There are now many more named colors available; you must use the Color enumeration name as a prefix for color constants: Color.Green.

```
Color.AliceBlue
Color.AntiqueWhite
Color.Bisque
Color.BlanchedAlmond
Color.Blue
```

Examples

```
txtName.ForeColor = Color.Red
lblMessage.ForeColor = Color.White
```

Changing Multiple Properties of a Control

By now you can see that there are times when you will want to change several properties of a single control. In versions of Visual Basic previous to version 4, you had to write out the entire name (Object.Property) for each statement.

Examples

```
txtTitle.Visible = True
txtTitle.ForeColor = Color.White
txtTitle.Focus()
```

Of course, you can still specify the statements this way, but Visual Basic provides a better way: the With and End With statements.

The With and End With Statements—General Form

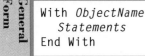

```
With ObjectName
    Statements
End With
```

You specify an object name in the With statement. All subsequent statements until the End With relate to that object.

The With and End With Statements—Example

```
With txtTitle
    .Visible = True
    .ForeColor = Color.White
    .Focus()
End With
```

The statements beginning with `With` and ending with `End With` are called a *With block*. The statements inside the block are indented for readability. Although indentation is not required by VB, it *is* required by good programming practices and aids in readability.

The real advantage of using the `With` statement, rather than spelling out the object for each statement, is that `With` is more efficient. Your Visual Basic projects will run a little faster if you use `With`. On a large, complicated project, the savings can be significant.

Concatenating Text

At times you need to join strings of text. For example, you may want to join a literal and a property. You can "tack" one string of characters to the end of another in the process called **concatenation**. Use an ampersand (&), preceded and followed by a space, between the two strings.

Examples

```
lblMessage.Text = "Your name is: " & txtName.Text
txtNameAndAddress.Text = txtName.Text & txtAddress.Text
```

TIP

Although in some situations Basic allows concatenation with the + operator, the practice is not advised. Depending on the contents of the text box, the compiler may interpret the + operator as an addition operator rather than as a concatenation operator, thereby giving unpredictable results. ■

Continuing Long Program Lines

Basic interprets the code on one line as one statement. You can type very long lines in the Editor window; the window scrolls sideways to allow you to keep typing. However, this method is inconvenient; it isn't easy to see the ends of the long lines.

When a Basic statement becomes too long for one line, use a **line-continuation character**. You can type a space and an underscore, press Enter, and continue the statement on the next line. It is OK to indent the continued lines. The only restriction is that the line-continuation character must appear between elements; you cannot place a continuation in the middle of a literal or split the name of an object or property.

Example

```
lblGreetings.Text = "Greetings " & txtName.Text & ": " & _
    "You have been selected to win a free prize. " & _
    "Just send us $100 for postage and handling."
```

Your Hands-On Programming Example

For this example you will write a program that uses many of the new controls and topics introduced in this chapter. The program will input the user's name and a message and display the two items concatenated in a label. The user can change the color of the label's text by selecting a color with radio buttons, and hide or display the output by checking a check box.

In your program you will include buttons to display the message in the label, clear the text boxes and label, and exit. Include keyboard access keys; make the Display button the default button, and make the Clear button the cancel button.

Place a logo on the form. Actually, you will place two picture boxes with different sizes for the logo on the form. Each time the user clicks on the logo, it will toggle the large and small versions of the logo.

Add a ToolTip to the logo that says "Click here".

Planning the Project

Sketch a form (Figure 2.17), which your users sign off as meeting their needs.

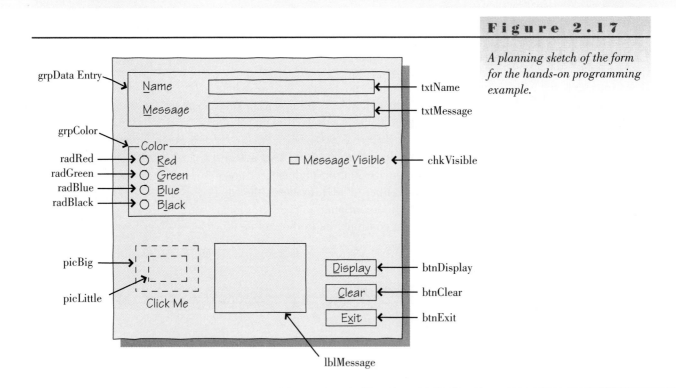

Figure 2.17

A planning sketch of the form for the hands-on programming example.

Note: Although this step may seem unnecessary, having your users sign off is standard programming practice and documents that your users have been involved and have approved the design.

Plan the Objects and Properties

Plan the property settings for the form and for each control.

Object	Property	Setting
Form1	Name	frmMessage
	Text	Message Formatter
	AcceptButton	btnDisplay
	CancelButton	btnClear
	StartPosition	CenterScreen
grpDataEntry	Name	grpDataEntry
	Text	(blank)
Label1	Text	&Name *Hint:* Do not change the name of this label.
txtName	Name	txtName
	Text	(blank)
Label2	Text	&Message
txtMessage	Name	txtMessage
	Text	(blank)
grpColor	Name	grpColor
	Text	Color
radRed	Name	radRed
	Text	&Red
radGreen	Name	radGreen
	Text	&Green
radBlue	Name	radBlue
	Text	&Blue
radBlack	Name	radBlack
	Text	B&lack
chkVisible	Name	chkVisible
	Text	Message &Visible
picBig	Name	picBig
	SizeMode	StretchImage
	Image	Microsoft Visual Studio .NET \ Common7 \ Graphics \ Icons \ Computer \ Cdrom01.ico
	ToolTip on ToolTip1	Click here
	Visible	True

Continued on page 84

Object	Property	Setting
picLittle	Name	picLittle (Note that the two picture boxes are in the same location, one on top of the other.)
	SizeMode	StretchImage
	Image	Microsoft Visual Studio .NET \ Common7 \ Graphics \ Icons \ Computer \ Cdrom02.ico
	ToolTip on ToolTip1	Click here
	Visible	False
Label3	Text	Click Me
ToolTip1	Name	ToolTip1
lblMessage	Name	lblMessage
	Text	(blank)
	TextAlign	MiddleCenter
	BorderStyle	Fixed Single
btnDisplay	Name	btnDisplay
	Text	&Display
btnClear	Name	btnClear
	Text	&Clear
btnExit	Name	btnExit
	Text	E&xit

Plan the Event Procedures

You will need event procedures for each button, radio button, check box, and picture box.

Procedure	Actions—Pseudocode
btnDisplay_Click	Set lblMessage to both the name and message from the text boxes (concatenate them).
btnClear_Click	Clear the two text boxes and label. Reset the focus in the first text box.
btnExit_Click	End the project.
radRed_CheckChanged	Make the ForeColor of lblMessage red.
radGreen_CheckChanged	Make the ForeColor of lblMessage green.
radBlue_CheckChanged	Make the ForeColor of lblMessage blue.

Continued on page 85

Procedure	Actions—Pseudocode
radBlack_CheckChanged	Make the ForeColor of lblMessage black.
picBig_Click	Make picBig invisible (Visible = False). Make picLittle visible (Visible = True).
picLittle_Click	Make picLittle invisible. Make picBig visible.
chkVisible_CheckChanged	Make label's visibility match that of check box.

Write the Project

Follow the sketch in Figure 2.17 to create the form. Figure 2.18 shows the completed form. The steps are as follows:

*   Set the properties of each object, as you have planned.

*   Working from the pseudocode, write each event procedure.

*   When you complete the code, thoroughly test the project.

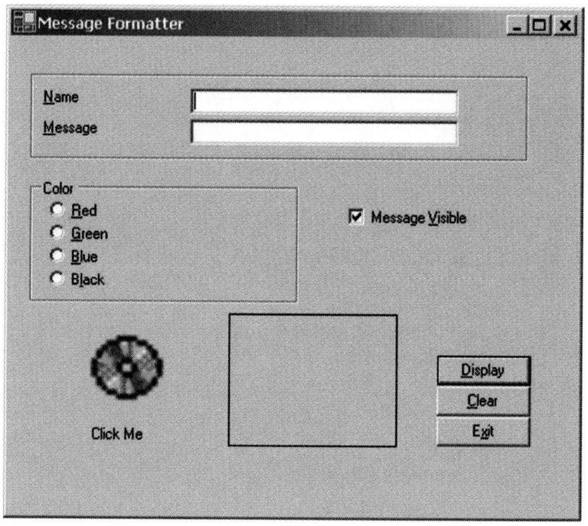

Figure 2.18

The form for the hands-on programming example.

The Project Coding Solution

```
'Project:        Ch0201
'Programmer:     Bradley/Millspaugh
'Date:           January 2002
'Description:    This project uses labels, text boxes, radio buttons,
'                a check box, images in picture boxes, and buttons
'                to change the display.

Public Class frmMessage
    Inherits System.Windows.Forms.Form
```

```vb
[Windows Form Designer generated code]
Private Sub btnDisplay_Click(ByVal sender As System.Object, ByVal e As _
        System.EventArgs) Handles btnDisplay.Click
    'Display the text in the message area

    lblMessage.Text = txtName.Text & ": " & txtMessage.Text
End Sub

Private Sub btnClear_Click(ByVal sender As System.Object, ByVal e As _
        System.EventArgs) Handles btnClear.Click
    'Clear the text controls

    With txtName
        .Clear()    'Clear the text box
        .Focus()    'Reset the insertion point
    End With
    txtMessage.Clear()
    lblMessage.Text = ""
End Sub

Private Sub btnExit_Click(ByVal sender As System.Object, ByVal e As _
        System.EventArgs) Handles btnExit.Click
    'Exit the project

    Me.Close()
End Sub

Private Sub radBlack_CheckedChanged(ByVal sender As System.Object, ByVal e As _
        System.EventArgs) Handles radBlack.CheckedChanged
    'Make label black

    lblMessage.ForeColor = Color.Black
End Sub

Private Sub radBlue_CheckedChanged(ByVal sender As System.Object, ByVal e As _
        System.EventArgs) Handles radBlue.CheckedChanged
    'Make label blue

    lblMessage.ForeColor = Color.Blue
End Sub

Private Sub radGreen_CheckedChanged(ByVal sender As System.Object, ByVal e As _
        System.EventArgs) Handles radGreen.CheckedChanged
    'Make label green

    lblMessage.ForeColor = Color.Green
End Sub

Private Sub radRed_CheckedChanged(ByVal sender As System.Object, ByVal e As _
        System.EventArgs) Handles radRed.CheckedChanged
    'Make label red

    lblMessage.ForeColor = Color.Red
End Sub
```

```
Private Sub picBig_Click(ByVal sender As System.Object, ByVal e As _
        System.EventArgs) Handles picBig.Click
    'Switch the icon

    picBig.Visible = False
    picLittle.Visible = True
End Sub

Private Sub picLittle_Click(ByVal sender As System.Object, ByVal e As _
        System.EventArgs) Handles picLittle.Click
    'Switch the icon

    picLittle.Visible = False
    picBig.Visible = True
End Sub

Private Sub chkVisible_CheckedChanged(ByVal sender As System.Object, ByVal e As _
        System.EventArgs) Handles chkVisible.CheckedChanged
    'Set Visibility for lblMessage

    lblMessage.Visible = chkVisible.Checked
End Sub

End Class
```

Good Programming Habits

1. To make the text in a text box right-justified or centered, set the TextAlign property.
2. You can use the Checked property of a check box to set other properties that must be True or False.
3. Always test the tab order on your forms. Fix it if necessary by changing the TabIndex properties.
4. You can create multiple controls of the same type without clicking on the tool in the toolbox every time. To create the first of a series, Ctrl-click on the tool; the tool will remain active and allow you to keep drawing more controls. Click on the pointer tool (the arrow) or press Esc when you are finished.
5. Use text boxes when you want the user to enter or change the text. Use label controls when you do not want the user to change the data. You can set the BorderStyle and BackColor properties of a label so that it looks just like a text box, but cannot be changed.

Summary

1. Text boxes are used primarily for user input. The Text property holds the value input by the user. You can also assign a literal to the text property during design time or run time.
2. Group boxes are used as containers for other controls and to group like items on a form.
3. Check boxes and radio buttons allow the user to make choices. In a group of radio buttons, only one can be selected; but in a group of check boxes, any number of the boxes may be selected.
4. The current state of check boxes and radio buttons is stored in the Checked property; the CheckChanged event occurs when the user clicks on one of the controls.
5. Picture box controls hold a graphic, which is assigned to the Image property. Set the SizeMode property to StretchImage to make the image fill the control.
6. The BorderStyle property of many controls can be set to None, Fixed-Single, or Fixed3D, to determine whether the control appears flat or three-dimensional.
7. Use a Label control to create a line on a form.
8. You can select multiple controls and treat them as a group, including setting common properties at once, moving them, or aligning them.
9. Make your programs easier to use by following Windows standard guidelines for colors, control size and placement, access keys, default and cancel buttons, and tab order.
10. Define keyboard access keys by including an ampersand in the Text property of buttons, radio buttons, and check boxes.
11. Set the AcceptButton property of the form to the desired button so that the user can press Enter to select the button. If you set the form's CancelButton property to a button, that button will be selected when the user presses the Esc key.
12. The focus moves from control to control as the user presses the Tab key. The sequence for tabbing is determined by the TabIndex properties of the controls. The Tab key stops only on controls that have their TabStop property set to True.
13. Add a ToolTip control to a form and then set the ToolTip on ToolTip1 property of a control to make a ToolTip appear when the user pauses the mouse pointer over the control.
14. Clear the Text property of a text box or a label by setting it to an empty string.
15. To place the insertion point into a text box as the program is running, use the Focus method.
16. You can set the Checked property of a radio button or check box at run time and also set the Visible property of controls in code.
17. Change the color of text in a control by changing its ForeColor property.
18. You can use the color constants to change colors during run time.
19. The With and End With statements provide an easy way to refer to an object multiple times without repeating the object's name.

20. Joining two strings of text is called *concatenation* and is accomplished by placing an ampersand between the two elements. (A space must precede and follow the ampersand.)

21. Use a space and an underscore to continue a long statement on another line.

Key Terms

AcceptButton property   *74*
access key   *73*
BorderStyle property   *68*
CancelButton property   *74*
check box   *66*
Checked property   *66*
color constant   *80*
component tray   *77*
concatenation   *81*
empty string   *78*
focus   *78*
Focus method   *78*
ForeColor property   *79*
group box   *65*
Image property   *67*
line-continuation character   *81*

PictureBox control   *67*
radio button   *66*
SizeMode property   *68*
StartPosition property   *76*
StretchImage   *68*
TabIndex property   *75*
TabStop property   *74*
text box   *65*
Text property   *65*
TextAlign property   *65*
ToolTip   *77*
ToolTip control   *77*
ToolTip on ToolTip1 property   *77*
Visible property   *68*
With and End With statements   *80*

Review Questions

1. You can display program output in a text box or a label. When should you use a text box? When is a label appropriate?

2. How does the behavior of radio buttons differ from the behavior of check boxes?

3. If you want two groups of radio buttons on a form, how can you make the groups operate independently?

4. Explain how to make a graphic appear in a picture box control.

5. Describe how to select several labels and set them all to 12-point font size at once.

6. What is the purpose of keyboard access keys? How can you define them in your project? How do they operate at run time?

7. Explain the purpose of the AcceptButton and CancelButton properties of the form. Give an example of a good use for each.

8. What is a ToolTip? How can you make a ToolTip appear?

9. What is the focus? How can you control which object has the focus?

10. Assume you are testing your project and don't like the initial position of the insertion point. Explain how to make the insertion point appear in a different text box when the program begins.

11. During program execution you want to return the insertion point to a text box called txtAddress. What Basic statement will you use to make that happen?

12. What Basic statements will clear the current contents of a text box and a label?
13. How are the `With` and `End With` statements used? Give an example.
14. What is concatenation and when would it be useful?
15. Explain how to continue a very long Basic statement onto another line.

Programming Exercises

2.1 Create a project that will switch a light bulb on and off, using the user interface shown below as a guide.

Form: Include a text box for the user to enter his or her name. Create two picture boxes, one on top of the other. Only one will be visible at a time. Use radio buttons to select the color of the text in the label beneath the light bulb picture box.

Include keyboard access keys for the radio buttons and the buttons. Make the Exit button the cancel button. Create ToolTips for both light bulb picture boxes; make the ToolTips say "Click here to turn the light on or off."

Project operation: The user will enter a name and click a radio button for the color (not necessarily in that order). When the light bulb is clicked, display the other picture box and change the message below it. Concatenate the user name to the end of the message.

The two icon files are Lightoff.ico and Lighton.ico and are found in the following folder by default: `Microsoft Visual Studio .NET\ Common7\Graphics\Icons\Misc.` (You will need to find the location of the Graphics folder on your system to find the icons.)

Coding: In the click event procedure for each Color radio button, change the color of the message below the light bulb.

2.2 Write a project to display the flags of four different countries, depending on the setting of the radio buttons. In addition, display the name of the country in the large label under the flag picture box. The user can also choose to display or hide the form's title, the country name, and the name of the programmer. Use check boxes for the display/hide choices.

Include keyboard access keys for all radio buttons, check boxes, and buttons. Make the Exit button the cancel button. Include ToolTips.

You can choose the countries and flags. You will find more than 20 flag icons in `Microsoft Visual Studio .NET\Common7\Graphics\ Icons\Flags`.

Hints: When a project begins running, the focus goes to the control with the lowest TabIndex. Because that control likely is a radio button, one button will appear selected. You must either display the first flag to match the radio button or make the focus begin in a different control. You might consider beginning the focus on the button.

Set the Visible property of a control to the Checked property of the corresponding check box. That way when the check box is selected, the control becomes visible.

Because all three selectable controls will be visible when the project begins, set the Checked property of the three check boxes to True at design time. Set the flag picture boxes to Visible = False so they won't appear at startup. (If you plan to display one picture box at startup, its Visible property must be set to True.)

Rather than stacking the picture boxes as was done in the chapter example, consider another method of setting up the four flag picture boxes. Try placing four small invisible flag icons near the bottom of the form. When the user selects a different country's flag, set the Image property of the large flag picture box to the Image property of one of the small, invisible picture boxes. For example,

```
picFlag.Image = picMexico.Image
```

Make sure to set the SizeMode property of the large picture box control to StretchImage.

2.3   Write a project to display a weather report. The user can choose one of the radio buttons and display an icon and a message. The message should give the weather report in words and include the person's name (taken from the text box at the top of the form). For example, if the user chooses the Sunny button, you might display "It looks like sunny weather today, John" (assuming that the user entered *John* in the text box).

Include keyboard access keys for the radio buttons and buttons. Make the Exit button the cancel button and include ToolTips.

You might consider the method of hiding and displaying picture boxes described in the hints for exercise 2. The four icons displayed are in the Microsoft Visual Studio .NET\Common7\Graphics\Icons\Elements folder and are called Cloud.ico, Rain.ico, Snow.ico, and Sun.ico.

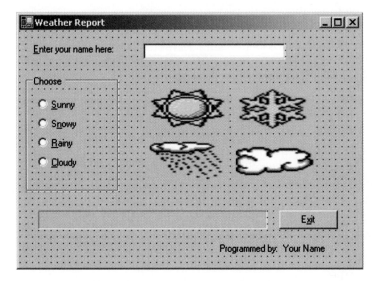

2.4   Write a project that will input the user name and display a message of the day in a label, along with the user's name. Include buttons (with keyboard access keys) for Display, Clear, and Exit. Make the Display button the accept button and the Clear button the cancel button. Include ToolTips where appropriate.

Include a group of radio buttons for users to select the color of the message. Give them a choice of three different colors.

Make your form display a changeable picture box. You can use the happy face icon files or any other images you have available (Microsoft Visual Studio .NET\Common7\Graphics\Icons\Misc\Face01.ico, Face02.ico, and Face03.ico).

You may choose to have only one message of the day, or you can have several that the user can select with radio buttons. You might want to choose messages that go with the different face icons.

2.5   Create a project that allows the user to input information and then display the lines of output for a mailing label.

Remember that fields to be input by the user require text boxes, but information to be displayed belongs in labels. Use text boxes for the first name, last name, street address, city, state, and ZIP code; give meaningful names to the text boxes and set the initial Text properties to blank. Add appropriate labels to each text box to tell the user which data will be entered into each box and also provide ToolTips.

Use buttons for Display Label Info, Clear, and Exit. Make the Display button the accept button and the Clear button the cancel button.

Use three labels for displaying the information for Line 1, Line 2, and Line 3.

A click event on the Display Label Info button will display the following:

Line 1—The first name and last name concatenated together.

Line 2—The street address.

Line 3—The city, state, and ZIP code concatenated together. (Make sure to concatenate a comma and a space between the city and state, using "," and two spaces between the state and ZIP code.)

Case Studies

VB Mail Order

Design and code a project that has shipping information.

Use an appropriate image in a picture box in the upper-left corner of the form.

Use text boxes with labels attached for Catalog Code, Page Number, and Part Number.

Use two groups of radio buttons on the form; enclose each group in a group box. The first group box should have a Text of Shipping and contain radio buttons for Express and Ground. Make the second group box have a Text property of Payment Type and include radio buttons for Charge, COD, and Money Order.

Use a check box for New Customer.

Add buttons for Clear and Exit. Make the Clear button the cancel button.

Add ToolTips as appropriate.

VB Auto Center

Modify the project from the VB Auto Center case study in Chapter 1, replacing the buttons with images in picture boxes. (See "Move and Copy Projects" in Appendix C for help in making a copy of the Chapter 1 project to use for this project.) Above each picture box place a label that indicates which department or command the graphic represents. A click on a picture box should produce the appropriate information in the special notices label.

Add an image in a picture box that clears the special notices label. Include a ToolTip for each picture box to help the user understand the purpose of the graphic.

Add radio buttons that will allow the user to view the special notices label in different colors.

Include a check box labeled "Hours." When the check box is selected, a new label will display the message "Open 24 Hours--7 days a week".

By default, the images are all stored in `Microsoft Visual Studio .NET \ Common7 \ Graphics \ Icons \ Industry`. You may have to locate the Graphics folder on your system.

Department/Command	Image for Picture box
Auto Sales	Cars.ico
Service Center	Wrench.ico
Detail Shop	Water.ico
Employment Opportunities	Mail12.ico
Exit	Msgbox1.ico

Video Bonanza

Design and code a project that displays the location of videos using radio buttons. Use a radio button for each of the movie categories and a label to display the aisle number. A check box will allow the user to display or hide a message for members. When the check box is selected, a message stating "All Members Receive a 10% Discount" will appear.

Include buttons (with keyboard access keys) for Clear and Exit. The Clear button should be set as the accept button and the Exit as the cancel button.

Place a label on the form in a 24-point font that reads "Video Bonanza." Use a line to separate the label from the rest of the interface. Include an image in a picture box.

Radio Button	Location
Comedy	Aisle 1
Drama	Aisle 2
Action	Aisle 3
Sci-Fi	Aisle 4
Horror	Aisle 5
New Releases	Back Wall

Very Very Boards

Create a project that will display an advertising screen for Very Very Boards. Include the company name, a slogan (use "The very best in boards," or make up your own slogan), and a graphic image for a logo. You may use the graphic included with the text materials (Skateboard.wmf) or one of your own.

Allow the user to select the color for the slogan text using radio buttons. Additionally, the user may choose to display or hide the company name, the slogan, and the logo. Use check boxes for the display options so that the user may select each option independently.

Include keyboard access keys for the radio buttons and the buttons. Make the Exit button the cancel

button. Create ToolTips for the company name ("Our company name"), the slogan ("Our slogan"), and the logo ("Our logo").

When the project begins execution, the slogan text should be red and the Red radio button selected. When the user selects a new color, the color of the slogan text should change to match.

Each of the check boxes must appear selected initially, since the company name, slogan, logo, and programmer name display when the form appears. Each time the user selects or deselects a check box, make the corresponding item display or hide.

Make the form appear in the center of the screen.

'Convert input values to numeric variables
intQuantity = CInt(txtQuantity.Text)
decPrice = CDec(txtPrice.Text)

CHAPTER

3

'Format and display answers for sale
lblExtended.Text = Format(decExtend
lblDiscount.Text = FormatNumber(decDiscount)
lblDiscountedPrice.Text = FormatCurrency(decDisc
'Handle exceptions
tch MyErr As InvalidCastException

Variables, Constants, and Calculations

at the completion of this chapter, you will be able to . . .

1. Distinguish between variables, constants, and controls.

2. Differentiate among the various data types.

3. Apply naming conventions incorporating standards and indicating scope and data type.

4. Declare variables using the Dim statement.

5. Select the appropriate scope for a variable.

6. Convert text input to numeric values.

7. Perform calculations using variables and constants.

8. Format values for output using the formatting functions.

9. Use Try/Catch blocks for error handling.

10. Display message boxes with error messages.

11. Accumulate sums and generate counts.

In this chapter you will learn to do calculations in Visual Basic. You will start with text values input by the user, convert them to numeric values, and perform calculations on them. You will also learn to format the results of your calculations and display them for the user.

Although the calculations themselves are quite simple (addition, subtraction, multiplication, and division), there are some important issues to discuss first. You must learn about variables and constants, the various types of data used by Visual Basic, and how and where to declare variables and constants. Variables are declared differently, depending on where you want to use them and how long you need to retain their values.

The code below is a small preview to show the calculation of the product of two text boxes. The first group of statements (the Dims) declares the variables and their data types. The second group of statements converts the text box contents to numeric and places the values into the variables. The last line performs the multiplication and places the result into a variable. The following sections of this chapter describe how to set up your code for calculations.

```
'Dimension the variables
Dim intQuantity          As Integer
Dim decPrice             As Decimal
Dim decExtendedPrice     As Decimal

'Convert input text to numeric and assign values to variables
intQuantity = CInt(txtQuantity.Text)
decPrice = CDec(txtPrice.Text)
'Calculate the product
decExtendedPrice = intQuantity * decPrice
```

- This chapter holds many changes. VB is now very strongly typed and some of the data types have changed. Students must pay very close attention to the data type of every variable and constant.

- Replace the Val conversion function with conversions to specific data type: CInt for Integer and CDec for Decimal.

Data: Variables and Constants

So far, all data you have used in your projects have been properties of objects. You have worked with the Text property of Text Boxes and Labels. Now you will work with values that are not properties. Basic allows you to set up locations in memory and give each location a name. You can visualize each memory location as a scratch pad; the contents of the scratch pad can change as the need arises. In this example, the memory location is called *intMaximum*.

intMaximum = 100

intMaximum
100

After executing this statement, the value of intMaximum is 100. You can change the value of intMaximum, use it in calculations, or display it in a control.

In the preceding example, the memory location called intMaximum is a variable. Memory locations that hold data that can be changed during project execution are called **variables;** locations that hold data that cannot change during execution are called **constants.** For example, the customer's name will vary as the information for each individual is processed. However, the name of the company and the sales tax rate will remain the same (at least for that day).

When you declare a variable or a **named constant,** Visual Basic reserves an area of memory and assigns it a name, called an **identifier.** You specify identifier names according to the rules of Basic as well as some recommended naming conventions.

The **declaration** statements establish your project's variables and constants, give them names, and specify the type of data they will hold. The statements are not considered executable; that is, they are not executed in the flow of instructions during program execution.

Here are some sample declaration statements:

```
Dim strName              As String        'Declare a string variable
Dim intCounter           As Integer       'Declare an integer variable
Const decDISCOUNT_RATE   As Decimal =0.15D 'Declare a named constant
```

The next few sections describe the data types, the rules for naming variables and constants, and the format of the declarations.

Data Types

The **data type** of a variable or constant indicates what type of information will be stored in the allocated memory space: perhaps a name, a dollar amount, a date, or a total. Table 3.1 shows the VB data types.

- Data types are significantly changed for interoperation with other .NET languages.

- Integer data type is a larger number; the former Integer type is now known as Short.

- Currency data type is no longer supported. The new Decimal data type replaces Currency for decimal numbers.

- The Variant data type is gone. The default data type now is Object.

The Visual Basic Data Types, the Kind of Data Each Type Holds, and the Amount of Memory Allocated for Each

Table 3.1

Data type	Use for	Storage size in bytes
Boolean	True or False values	2
Byte	0 to 255, binary data	1
Char	Single Unicode character	2
Date	1/1/0001 through 12/31/9999	8
Decimal	Decimal fractions, such as dollars and cents	16
Single	Single-precision floating point numbers with six digits of accuracy	4
Double	Double-precision floating-point numbers with 14 digits of accuracy	8
Short	Small integer in the range $-32,768$ to $32,767$	2
Integer	Whole numbers in the range $-2,147,483,648$ to $+2,147,483,647$	4
Long	Larger whole numbers	8
String	Alphanumeric data: letters, digits, and other characters	varies
Object	Any type of data	4

The most common types of variables and constants we will use are String, Integer, and Decimal. When deciding which data type to use, follow this guideline: If the data will be used in a calculation, then it must be numeric (usually Integer or Decimal); if it is not used in a calculation, it will be String. Use Decimal as the data type for any decimal fractions in business applications; Single and Double data types are generally used in scientific applications.

Consider the following examples:

Contents	Data type	Reason
Social Security number	String	Not used in a calculation.
Pay rate	Decimal	Used in a calculation, contains a decimal point.
Hours worked	Decimal	Used in a calculation, may contain a decimal point. (Decimal can be used for any decimal fraction, not just dollars.)
Phone number	String	Not used in a calculation.
Quantity	Integer	Used in a calculation; contains a whole number.

Naming Rules

A programmer has to name (identify) the variables and named constants that will be used in a project. Basic requires identifiers for variables and named constants to follow these rules: names may consist of letters, digits, and underscores; they must begin with a letter; they cannot contain any spaces or periods; and they may not be reserved words. (Reserved words, also called *keywords,* are words to which Basic has assigned some meaning, such as *print, name,* and *value.*)

Identifiers in VB are not case sensitive. Therefore, the names intSum, IntSum, intsum, and INTSUM all refer to the same variable.

Note: In earlier versions of VB, the maximum length of an identifier was 255 characters. In VB .NET, you can forget about the length limit, since the maximum is now 16,383.

• The maximum length for variable names has effectively been eliminated, since the limit is now 16,383 characters.

Naming Conventions

When naming variables and constants, you *must* follow the rules of Basic. In addition, you *should* follow some naming conventions. Conventions are the guidelines that separate good names from bad (or not-so-good) names. The meaning and use of all identifiers should always be clear.

Just as we established conventions for naming objects in Chapter 1, in this chapter we adopt conventions for naming variables and constants. The following conventions are widely used in the programming industry:

1. *Identifiers must be meaningful.* Choose a name that clearly indicates its purpose. Do not abbreviate unless the meaning is obvious, and do not use very short identifiers, such as *X* or *Y.*
2. *Precede each identifier with a lowercase prefix that specifies the data type.* This convention is similar to the convention we already adopted for naming objects and is widely used in the programming field.

3. *Capitalize each word of the name* (following the prefix). Always use mixed case for variables, uppercase for constants.

Here is a list of the most common data types and their prefixes:

Prefix	Data type
bln	Boolean
dat	Date
dec	Decimal
dbl	Double-precision floating point
int	Integer
lng	Long integer
sng	Single-precision floating point
str	String

• The prefix for Date variables has changed from "dtm" to "dat", since Microsoft changed the name of the data type from DateTime to Date. (Dates still can hold both the date and time.)

The following is a list of *sample identifiers:*

Field of data	Possible identifier
Social Security number	strSocialSecurityNumber
Pay rate	decPayRate
Hours worked	decHoursWorked
Phone number	strPhoneNumber
Quantity	intQuantity
Tax rate (constant)	decTAX_RATE
Quota (constant)	intQUOTA
Population	lngPopulation

▶ Feedback 3.1

Indicate whether each of the following identifiers conforms to the rules of Basic and to the naming conventions. If the identifier is invalid, give the reason. Remember, the answers to Feedback questions are found in Appendix A.

1. omitted
2. int#Sold
3. int Number Sold
4. int.Number.Sold
5. sng$Amount
6. Sub
7. strSub
8. Text
9. conMaximum
10. MinimumRate
11. decMaximumCheck
12. strCompanyName

Constants: Named and Intrinsic

Constants provide a way to use words to describe a value that doesn't change. In Chapter 2 you used the Visual Studio constants Color.Blue, Color.Red, Color.Yellow, and so on. Those constants are built into the environment and called *intrinsic constants;* you don't need to define them anywhere. The constants that you define for yourself are called *named constants.*

Named Constants

You declare named constants using the keyword `Const`. You give the constant a name, a data type, and a value. Once a value is declared as a constant, its value cannot be changed during the execution of the project. The data type that you declare and the data type of the value must match. For example, if you declare an integer constant, you must give it an integer value.

You will find two important advantages to using named constants rather than the actual values in code. The code is easier to read; for example, seeing the identifier decMAXIMUM_PAY is more meaningful than seeing a number, such as 1,000. In addition, if you need to change the value at a later time, you need to change the constant declaration only once; you do not have to change every reference to it throughout the code.

Const Statement—General Form

General Form
```Const Identifier [As Datatype] = Value```

Naming conventions for constants require a prefix that identifies the data type as well as the "As" clause that actually declares the data type.

This example sets the company name, address, and the sales tax rate as constants:

Const Statement—Examples

```
Const strCOMPANY_NAME As String = "R 'n R--for Reading 'n Refreshment"
Const strCOMPANY_ADDRESS As String = "101 S. Main Street"
Const decSALES_TAX_RATE As Decimal = .08D
```

Assigning Values to Constants

The values you assign to constants must follow certain rules. You have already seen that a text (string) value must be enclosed in quotation marks; numeric values are not enclosed. However, you must be aware of some additional rules.

Numeric constants may contain only the digits (0–9), a decimal point, and a sign (+ or –) at the left side. You cannot include a comma, dollar sign, any other special characters, or a sign at the right side. You can declare the data type of numeric constants by appending a type-declaration character. If you do not append a type-declaration character to a numeric constant, any whole number is assumed to be Integer and any fractional value is assumed to be Double. The type-declaration characters are

Decimal D
Double   R

• Use the type declaration characters for numeric constants and always make the constant the same data type as the variable to which you assign it.

Integer   I
Long   L
Short   S
Single   F

String literals (also called *string constants*) may contain letters, digits, and special characters, such as $#@%&*. You may have a problem when you want to include quotation marks inside a string literal, since quotation marks enclose the literal. The solution is to use two quotation marks together inside the literal. Visual Basic will interpret the pair as one symbol. For example, `"He said, ""I like it."""` produces this string: `He said, "I like it."`

Although you can use numeric digits inside a string literal, remember that these numbers are text and cannot be used for calculations.

The string values are referred to as **string literals** because they contain exactly (literally) whatever is inside the quotation marks.

The following table lists example constants.

Data type	Constant value example
Integer	5 125 2170 2000 −100 12345678I
Single	101.25F −5.0F
Decimal	850.50D −100D
Double	52875.8 52875.8R −52875.8R
Long	134257987L −8250758L
String literals	"Visual Basic" "ABC Incorporated" "1415 J Street" "102" "She said ""Hello."""

Intrinsic Constants

Intrinsic constants are system-defined constants. Many sets of intrinsic constants are declared in system class libraries and are available for use in your VB programs. For example, the color constants that you used in Chapter 2 are intrinsic constants.

You must specify the class name or group name as well as the constant name when you use intrinsic constants. For example, Color.Red is the constant "Red" in the class "Color." Later in this chapter you will learn to use constants from the MessageBox class for displaying message boxes to the user.

Declaring Variables

Although there are several ways to declare a variable, the most commonly used statement is the Dim statement.

● You can give a variable an initial value as you declare it:

```
Dim intMax As Integer = 100
```

Dim Statement—General Form

General Form
```
Dim Identifier [As Datatype]
```

If you omit the optional data type, the variable's type defaults to object. It is best to always declare the type, even when you intend to use objects.

Dim Statement—Examples

Examples
```
Dim strCustomerName      As String
Dim intTotalSold         As Integer
Dim sngTemperature       As Single
Dim decPrice             As Decimal
```

The reserved word Dim is really short for dimension, which means *size*. When you declare a variable, the amount of memory reserved depends on its data type. Refer to Table 3.1 (page 97) for the size of each data type.

● You can declare multiple variables on one statement and name the data type only once. In VB 6, the data type applied only to the one variable on which it was placed; in VB .NET, the data type applies to all variables named on the statement.

```
Dim intCount, intMax, _
  intNumber As Integer _
  'Creates 3 integer _
  variables
```

Entering Dim Statements

Visual Basic's IntelliSense feature helps you enter Dim statements. After you type the space that follows Dim VariableName As, a list pops up (Figure 3.1). This list shows the possible entries for data type to complete the statement. The easiest way to complete the statement is to begin typing the correct entry; the list automatically scrolls to the correct section (Figure 3.2). When the correct entry is highlighted, press Enter, Tab, or the spacebar to select the entry, or double-click if you prefer using the mouse.

Note: Some people find the IntelliSense feature annoying rather than helpful. You can turn off the feature by selecting *Tools / Options / Text Editor / All Languages* and deselecting *Auto list* members.

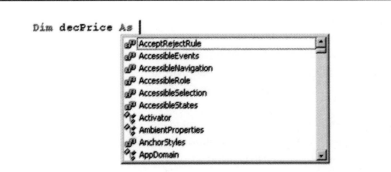

As soon as you type the space after "As," the IntelliSense menu pops up. You can make a selection from the list with your mouse or the keyboard.

Figure 3.2

```
Dim decPrice As dec|
```

DebuggableAttribute
Debugger
DebuggerHiddenAttribute
DebuggerStepThroughAttribute
Decimal
DefaultTraceListener
Delegate
DeletedRowInaccessibleException
{} Design
{} Diagnostics

Represents a decimal number.

Type the fist few characters of the data type and the IntelliSense list quickly scrolls to the correct section. When the correct word is highlighted, press Enter, Tab, or the Spacebar to select the entry.

Feedback 3.2

Write a declaration for the following situations. In your declaration, make up an appropriate variable identifier.

1. You need variables for payroll processing to store the following:
   (a) Number of hours, which can hold a decimal point.
   (b) String employee's name.
   (c) Department number (not used in calculations).
2. You need variables for inventory control to store the following:
   (a) Integer quantity.
   (b) Description of the item.
   (c) Part number.
   (d) Cost.
   (e) Selling price.

Scope and Lifetime of Variables

A variable may exist and be visible for an entire project, for only one form, or for only one procedure. The visibility of a variable is referred to as its **scope.** Visibility really means "this variable can be used or 'seen' in this location." The scope is said to be namespace, module level, local, or block. A **namespace variable** may be used in all procedures of the namespace, which is generally the entire project. **Module-level variables** are accessible from all procedures of a form. A **local variable** may be used only within the procedure in which it is declared, and a **block variable** is used only within a block of code inside a procedure.

You declare the scope of a variable by choosing where to place the Dim statement.

Note: Previous versions of VB and some other programming languages refer to namespace variables as a *global variables.*

Variable Lifetime

When you create a variable, you must be aware of its **lifetime**. The lifetime of a variable is the period of time that the variable exists. The lifetime of a local or block variable is normally one execution of a procedure. For example, each time you execute a sub procedure, the local Dim statements are executed. Each variable is created as a "fresh" new one, with an initial value of 0 for numeric variables and an empty string for string variables. When the procedure finishes, its variables disappear; that is, their memory locations are released.

- Microsoft has changed *global* scope to *namespace* scope. Any variable declared at the module level with the Public keyword is considered a namespace-level variable.

The lifetime of a module-level variable is the entire time the form is loaded, generally the lifetime of the entire project. If you want to maintain the value of a variable for multiple executions of a procedure, for example, to calculate a running total, you must use a module-level variable (or a variable declared as Static, which is discussed in Chapter 7).

Local Declarations

Any variable that you declare inside a procedure is local in scope which means it is known only to that procedure. A Dim statement can appear anywhere inside the procedure as long as it appears prior to the first use of the variable in a statement. However, good programming practices dictate that all Dims appear at the top of the procedure, prior to all other code statements (after the remarks).

```
'Module-level Declarations
Const mdecDISCOUNT_RATE      As Decimal = 0.15D

Private Sub btnCalculate_Click()
   'Calculate the price and discount

   Dim intQuantity          As Integer
   Dim decPrice             As Decimal
   Dim decExtendedPrice     As Decimal
   Dim decDiscount          As Decimal
   Dim decDiscountedPrice   As Decimal

   'Convert input values to numeric variables
   intQuantity = CInt(txtQuantity.Text)
   decPrice = CDec(txtPrice.Text)

   'Calculate values
   decExtendedPrice = intQuantity * decPrice
   decDiscount = decExtendedPrice * mdecDISCOUNT_RATE
   decDiscountedPrice = decExtendedPrice - decDiscount
```

Notice the Const statement in the preceding example. You can declare named constants to be local, block level, module level, or namespace in scope, just as you can variables. However, good programming practices say that constants should be declared at the module level. This technique places all constant declarations at the top of the code and makes them easy to find in case you need to make changes.

Module-Level Declarations

At times you need to be able to use a variable or constant in more than one procedure of a form. When you declare a variable or constant as module level, you can use it anywhere in that form. Place the declarations (Dim or Const) for module-level variables and constants in the Declarations section of the form. (Recall that you have been using the Declarations section for remarks since Chapter 1.) If you wish to accumulate a sum or count items for multiple executions of a procedure, you should declare the variable at the module level.

Figure 3.3 illustrates the locations for coding local variables and module-level variables.

Figure 3.3

The variables you dimension inside a procedure are local. Variables that you dimension in the Declarations section are module level.

```
(Declarations section)

Dim ModuleLevelVariables
Const NamedConstants

Private Sub btnCalculate_Click
    Dim LocalVariables

    ...
End Sub

Private Sub btnSummary_Click
    Dim LocalVariables

    ...
End Sub

Private Sub btnClear_Click
    Dim LocalVariables

    ...
End Sub
```

```
'Declarations section of a form

'Dimension module-level variables and constants
Dim mintQuantitySum        As Integer
Dim mdecDiscountSum        As Decimal
Dim mintSaleCount          As Integer
Const decMAXIMUM_DISCOUNT  As Decimal = 100.0D
```

Including the Scope in Identifiers

When you use variables, it is important to know their scope. For that reason you should include scope information in your naming conventions. To indicate a module-level variable, place a prefix of m before the identifier. Local variables do not have an additional prefix, so any variable without an initial m can be assumed to be local. For example,

```
Dim mdecTotalPay As Decimal
```

Note that the m stands for module level, and the dec stands for Decimal data type.

```
Const mintNUMBER_QUESTIONS As Integer = 50I
```

The m stands for module level, and the int stands for Integer data type.

Coding Module-Level Declarations

To enter module-level declarations, you must be in the Editor window at the top of your code (Figure 3.4). Place the `Dim` and `Const` statements after the Form Designer Generated Code section but before your first procedure.

Figure 3.4

Code module-level declarations in the Declarations section at the top of your code.

```
'                    Uses variables, constants, calculations, error
'                    handling, and a message box to the user.
'Folder:             Ch0302

Option Strict On

Public Class frmBooksale
    Inherits System.Windows.Forms.Form

Windows Form Designer generated code

    'Dimension module-level variables and constants
    Dim mintQuantitySum As Integer
    Dim mdecDiscountSum As Decimal
    Dim mdecDiscountedPriceSum As Decimal
    Dim mintSaleCount As Integer
    Const mdecDISCOUNT_RATE As Decimal = 0.15D


    Private Sub btnCalculate_Click(ByVal sender As System.Object,
```

Block-Level and Global Declarations

You won't use block-level or namespace-level declarations in this chapter. Block-level variables and constants have a scope of a block of code, such as `If / End If` or `Do / Loop`. These statements are covered later in this text.

Namespace-level variables and constants may be useful when a project has multiple forms and/or modules. Good programming practices exclude the use of namespace-level variables.

Feedback 3.3

Write the declarations (`Dim` or `Const` statements) for each of the following situations and indicate where each statement will appear.

1. The total of the payroll that will be needed in a Calculate event procedure and in a Summary event procedure.
2. The sales tax rate that cannot be changed during execution of the program but will be used by multiple procedures.
3. The number of participants that are being counted in the Calculate event procedure, but not displayed until the Summary event procedure.

Calculations

In programming you can perform calculations with variables, with constants, and with the properties of certain objects. The properties you will use, such as the Text property of a text box or a label, are usually strings of text characters. These character strings, such as "Howdy" or "12345", should not be used directly in calculations unless you first convert them to the correct data type.

Converting to the Correct Data Type

You will use functions to convert the property of a control to its numeric form before you use the value in a calculation. The function that you use depends on the data type of the variable to which you are assigning the value. For example, to convert text to an integer, use the CInt function; to convert to a decimal value, use CDec.

```
'Convert input values to numeric variables
intQuantity = CInt(txtQuantity.Text)
decPrice = CDec(txtPrice.Text)
'Calculate the extended price
decExtendedPrice = intQuantity * decPrice
```

Converting from one data type to another is sometimes called *casting*. In the preceding example, txtQuantity.Text is cast into an Integer data type and txtPrice.Text is cast into a Decimal data type.

Using Functions

Visual Basic supplies many functions that you can use in your programs. A **function** performs an action and returns a value. The expression to operate upon, called the *argument* (or multiple arguments, in some cases), must be enclosed in parentheses.

The first Basic functions we will use are the **conversion functions,** CInt and CDec. Both functions convert an argument into a numeric value of the correct data type. You will also use the CStr function to convert in the other direction—converting numeric values to strings for display purposes. And later in this chapter you use some formatting functions, which convert numeric values to formatted strings.

- The conversion functions, such as CInt and CDec, now parse some characters that would have been considered nonnumeric in VB 6. For example, the functions accept dollar signs, commas, parentheses, and signs on either end of a number.

- When CInt rounds to an integer, it rounds to the nearest *even number*, not the nearest whole number. Statisticians argue that this is a much better method of rounding, but we're not convinced.

The Conversion Functions—General Forms

<table>
<tr><td rowspan="3">General Form</td><td>

```
CInt(ExpressionToConvert)    'Convert to Integer
CDec(ExpressionToConvert)    'Convert to Decimal
CStr(ExpressionToConvert)    'Convert to String
```

</td></tr>
</table>

The expression you wish to convert can be the property of a control, a variable, or a constant.

A function cannot stand by itself. It returns (produces) a value that can be used as a part of a statement, such as the assignment statements in the following examples.

The Conversion Functions—Examples

<table>
<tr><td rowspan="5">Examples</td><td>

```
intQuantity = CInt(txtQuantity.Text)
decPrice = CDec(txtPrice.Text)
intWholeNumber = CInt(decFractionalValue)
decDollars = CDec(intDollars)
strValue = CStr(decValue)
```

</td></tr>
</table>

The numeric conversion functions examine the value stored in the argument and attempt to convert to a number in a process called *parsing*, which means to pick apart, character by character, and convert to another format. Although you can change the default parsing method based on the symbols you need to recognize, the defaults will probably serve you and your users very well.

The VB .NET conversion functions can recognize and convert many values that previous versions would have rejected as nonnumeric, such as dollar signs, commas, parentheses, and signs on either end of a number.

The CInt function first converts the argument to numeric and then rounds, if necessary, to produce an integer. The rounding method is different from what you might expect: It rounds to the nearest *even* number. For example, 1.5 rounds to 2, but 0.5 rounds to zero.

Here is a list of conversion examples:

Contents of string argument	CInt(Argument)	CDec(Argument)
123.45	123	123.45
$100	100	100.0
1,000.00	1000	1000.0
A123	(error)	(error)
−5	−5	−5.0
5−	−5	−5.0
(5)	−5	−5.0
1(5)	(error)	(error)
0.01	0	0.01
0.5	0	0.5
1.5	2	1.5
(blank)	(error)	(error)

When a conversion function encounters a value that it cannot parse to a number, such as a blank or a nonnumeric character, an error occurs. You will learn how to avoid those errors later in this chapter in the section titled "Handling Exceptions."

You will use the CInt and CDec functions most of the time. But in case you need to convert to Long, Single, or Double, VB also has conversion functions for those: CLng, CSng, and CDbl. These functions parse and convert values in the same manner as that described for the other functions.

- Excellent reference Help pages, perhaps for reading in class, include
  - Efficient Use of Data Types
  - + Operator
  - Option Strict Statement
  - Widening and Narrowing Conversions

Arithmetic Operations

The arithmetic operations you can perform in Visual Basic include addition, subtraction, multiplication, division, integer division, modulus, and exponentiation.

Operator	Operation
+	Addition
−	Subtraction
*	Multiplication
/	Division
\	Integer division
Mod	Modulus—Remainder of division
^	Exponentiation

The first four operations are self-explanatory, but you may not be familiar with \, Mod, or ^.

Integer Division (\)

Use integer division (\) to divide one integer by another giving an integer result, truncating (dropping) any remainder. For example, if intTotalMinutes = 150, then

```
intHours = intTotalMinutes\60
```

returns 2 for intHours.

Mod

The Mod operator returns the remainder of a division operation. For example, if intTotalMinutes = 150, then

```
intMinutes = intTotalMinutes Mod 60
```

returns 30 for intMinutes.

Exponentiation (^)

The exponentiation operator (^) raises a number to the power specified. The following are examples of exponentiation.

```
decSquared = decNumber ^ 2    'Square the number--Raise to the 2nd power
decCubed = decNumber ^ 3      'Cube the number--Raise to the 3rd power
```

Order of Operations

The order in which operations are performed determines the result. Consider the expression 3 + 4 * 2. What is the result? If the addition is done first, the result is 14. However, if the multiplication is done first, the result is 11.

The hierarchy of operations, or **order of precedence,** in arithmetic expressions from highest to lowest is

1. Any operation inside parentheses
2. Exponentiation
3. Multiplication and division
4. Integer division
5. Modulus
6. Addition and subtraction

In the previous example, the multiplication is performed before the addition, yielding a result of 11. To change the order of evaluation, use parentheses. The expression

$(3 + 4) * 2$

will yield 14 as the result. One set of parentheses may be used inside another set. In that case, the parentheses are said to be *nested.* The following is an example of nested parentheses:

```
((intScore1 + intScore2 + intScore3) / 3) * 1.2
```

Extra parentheses can always be used for clarity. The expressions

`2 * decCost * decRate` and `(2 * decCost) * decRate`

are equivalent, but the second is easier to understand.

Multiple operations at the same level (such as multiplication and division) are performed from left to right. The example 8 / 4 * 2 yields 4 as its result, not 1. The first operation is 8 / 4, and 2 * 2 is the second.

Evaluation of an expression occurs in this order:

1. All operations within parentheses. Multiple operations within the parentheses are performed according to the rules of precedence.
2. All exponentiation. Multiple exponentiation operations are performed from left to right.
3. All multiplication and division. Multiple operations are performed from left to right.
4. All integer division. Multiple operations are performed from left to right.
5. Mod operations. Multiple operations are performed from left to right.
6. All addition and subtraction are performed from left to right.

Although the precedence of operations in Basic is the same as in algebra, take note of one important difference: There are no implied operations in Basic. The following expressions would be valid in mathematics, but they are not valid in Basic:

> ☑**TIP**
>
> **U**se extra parentheses to make the precedence clearer. The operation will be easier to understand and the parentheses have no negative effect on execution. ■

Mathematical notation	Equivalent Basic function
2A	2 * A
3(X + Y)	3 * (X + Y)
(X + Y)(X − Y)	(X + Y) * (X − Y)

> ## Feedback 3.4

What will be the result of the following calculations using the order of precedence?

   Assume that intX = 2, intY = 4, intZ = 3

1. intX + intY ^ 2
2. 8 / intY / intX
3. intX * (intX + 1)
4. intX * intX + 1
5. intY ^ intX + intZ * 2
6. intY ^ (intX + intZ) * 2
7. (intY ^ intX) + intZ * 2
8. ((intY ^ intX) + intZ) * 2

Using Calculations in Code

You perform calculations in assignment statements. Recall that whatever appears on the right side of an = (assignment operator) is assigned to the item on the left. The left side may be the property of a control or a variable. It cannot be a constant.

Examples

```
decAverage = decSum/intCount
lblAmountDue.Text = CStr(decPrice - (decPrice * decDiscountRate))
txtCommission.Text = CStr(decSalesTotal * decCommissionRate)
```

   In the preceding examples, the results of the calculations were assigned to a variable, the Text property of a label, and the Text property of a text box. In most cases you will assign calculation results to variables or to the Text properties of labels. Text boxes are usually used for input from the user rather than for program output.

Assignment Operators

In addition to the equal sign (=) as an **assignment operator,** VB .NET has several operators that can perform a calculation and assign the result as one operation. The new assignment operators are +=, -=, *=, /=, \=, and &=. Each of these assignment operators is a shortcut for the standard method; you can use the standard (longer) form or the newer shortcut. The shortcuts allow you to type a variable name only once instead of requiring you to type it on both sides of the equal sign.

   For example, to add decSales to decTotalSales, the long version is

• New operators, similar to C++ and Java, are

```
+=   -+   *=   /=   \=   &=
(No ++ or --)
```

```
decTotalSales = decTotalSales + decSales    'Accumulate a total
```

Instead you can use the shortcut assignment operator:

```
decTotalSales += decSales                   'Accumulate a total
```

The two statements have the same effect.

   To subtract 1 from a variable, the long version is:

```
intCountDown = intCountDown - 1             'Subtract 1 from variable
```

And the shortcut, using the −= operator:

```
intCountDown -= 1                          'Subtract 1 from variable
```

Feedback 3.5

1. Write two statements to add 5 to intCount, using (*a*) the standard, long version and (*b*) the assignment operator.
2. Write two statements to subtract decWithdrawal from decBalance, using (*a*) the standard, long version and (*b*) the assignment operator.
3. Write two statements to multiply decPrice by intCount and place the result into decPrice. Use (*a*) the standard, long version and (*b*) the assignment operator.

Option Explicit and Option Strict

Visual Basic provides two options that can significantly change the behavior of the editor and compiler. These two options, **Option Explicit** and **Option Strict,** can make coding somewhat easier but provide opportunities for hard-to-find errors and very sloppy programming.

Option Explicit

When Option Explicit is turned off, you can use any variable name without first declaring it. The first time you use a variable name, VB allocates a new variable of Object data type. For example, you could write the line

```
Z = myTotal + 1
```

without first declaring either Z or myTotal. This is a throwback to very old versions of Basic that did not require variable declaration. In those days, programmers spent many hours debugging programs that had just a small misspelling or typo in a variable name.

You should always program with Option Explicit turned on. In VB .NET, the option is turned on by default for all new projects. If you need to turn it off, (not a recommended practice) place the line

```
Option Explicit Off
```

before the first line of code in a file.

Option Strict

Option Strict is a new option introduced in VB .NET. This option makes VB more like other strongly typed languages, such as C++, Java, and C#. When Option Strict is turned on, the editor and compiler try to help you keep from making hard-to-find mistakes. Specifically, Option Strict does not allow any implicit (automatic) conversions from a wider data type to a narrower one, or between String and numeric data types.

All of the code you have seen so far in this text has been written with Option Strict turned on. With this option, you must use the conversion functions, such as CInt and CDec, to convert to the desired data type from String or from a wider data type to a narrower type, such as from Decimal to Integer.

- Option Explicit is on by Default. The new Option Strict should be turned on. It is off by default.

- The statement Option Explicit actually turns *off* the option rather than turning it on. You must include the keyword On; omitting the keyword turns it off.

- With Option Strict turned on, VB becomes a "strongly typed" language, comparable to C++, Java, and C#. This forces programmers to be aware of the data type and explicitly convert, rather than rely on implicit conversions.

With Option Strict turned off, code such as this is legal:

```
intQuantity = txtQuantity.Text
```

and

```
intAmount = lngAmount
```

and

```
intTotal += decSaleAmount
```

With each of these legal (but dangerous) statements, the VB compiler makes assumptions about your data. And the majority of the time, the assumptions are correct. But bad input data or very large numbers can cause erroneous results or run-time errors.

The best practice is to always turn on Option Strict. This technique will save you from developing poor programming habits and will also likely save you hours of debugging time. For some reason, the developers at Microsoft elected to turn off Option Strict by default. In early beta trials of the software, the option was turned on by default, but in late betas, the option was turned off.

You can turn on Option Strict either in code or in the *Project Properties* dialog box. Place the line

```
Option Strict On
```

before the first line of code, after the general remarks at the top of a file.

Example

```
'Project:          MyProject
'Date:             Today
'Programmer:       Your Name
'Description:       This project calculates correctly.

Option Strict On

Public Class frmMyForm
    Inherits System.Windows.Forms.Form
```

To turn on Option Strict or Option Explicit for the entire project, open the *Project Properties* dialog box and select *Common Properties/Build*. There you will find settings for both Option Explicit and Option Strict. By default, Option Explicit is turned on and Option Strict is turned off. Setting *Option Strict On* in the project properties has one additional effect—any new files that you add to the project will have the option turned on automatically.

Note: Option Strict includes all of the requirements of Option Explicit. If Option Strict is turned on, variables must be declared, regardless of the setting of Option Explicit.

In another change from VB 6, you should always include the keyword On when setting an option. In VB 6, the statement

```
Option Explicit
```

turned *on* the option. In VB .NET, that same statement turns *off* the option, since the default is off.

Formatting Data

When you want to format data for display, use the **formatting functions.** To **format** means to control the way the output looks. For example, 12 is just a number, but $12.00 conveys more meaning for dollar amounts. When you use the formatting functions, you can choose to display a dollar sign, a percent sign, and commas. You can also specify the number of digits to appear to the right of the decimal point. VB rounds the value to return the requested number of decimal positions.

• Notice that you use the FormatCurrency function to format data of the Decimal data type.

The FormatCurrency Function—Simple Form

Simple Form
```FormatCurrency(NumericExpressionToFormat)```

The FormatCurrency function returns a string of characters formatted as dollars and cents. By default, the return value displays a dollar sign, commas, and two positions to the right of the decimal point. (*Note:* You can change the default format by changing your computer's regional settings.)

Usually, you will assign the formatted value to the Text property of a control for display.

The FormatCurrency Function—Simple Example

Example

```
lblBalance.Text = FormatCurrency(decBalance)
```

Examples			
Variable	**Value**	**Function**	**Returns**
decBalance	1275.675	FormatCurrency(decBalance)	$1,275.68
sngAmount	.9	FormatCurrency(sngAmount)	$0.90

Note that the formatted value returned by the FormatCurrency function is no longer purely numeric and cannot be used in further calculations. For example, consider the following lines of code:

```
decAmount += decCharges
lblAmount.Text = FormatCurrency(decAmount)
```

Assume that decAmount holds 1050 after the calculation and lblAmount.Text displays $1,050.00. If you want to do any further calculations with this amount, such as adding it to a total, you must use decAmount rather than lblAmount.Text. The variable decAmount holds a numeric value; lblAmount.Text holds a string of (nonnumeric) characters.

You can further customize the formatted value returned by the FormatCurrency function. You can specify the number of decimal positions to display, whether or not to display a leading zero for fractional values, whether to display negative numbers in parentheses, and whether to use the commas for grouping digits.

The FormatCurrency Function—General Form

General Form

```
FormatCurrency(ExpressionToFormat [, NumberOfDecimalPositions [, LeadingDigit _
    [, UseParenthesesForNegative [, GroupingForDigits]]]])
```

As you can see, the only required argument is the expression you want to format.

Examples

Variable	Value	Function	Returns
mdecTotal	1125.67	FormatCurrency(mdecTotal, 0)	$1,126
mdecTotal	1125.67	FormatCurrency(mdecTotal)	$1,126.67
mdecTotal	1125.67	FormatCurrency(mdecTotal, 2)	$1,126.67
decBalance	1234.567	FormatCurrency(decBalance, 0)	$1,235
decBalance	1234.567	FormatCurrency(decBalance)	$1,234.57
decBalance	1234.567	FormatCurrency(decBalance, 2)	$1,234.57

For an explanation of the other options of the FormatCurrency function, see Help.

The FormatNumber Function—Simple Form

Simple Form

```
FormatNumber(ExpressionToFormat)
```

The FormatNumber function is similar to the FormatCurrency function. The default format is determined by your computer's regional setting; it will generally display commas and two digits to the right of the decimal point.

The FormatNumber Function—Simple Examples

Examples

```
lblSum.Text = FormatNumber(decSum)
lblCount.Text = FormatNumber(intCount)
```

Both of these examples will display with commas and two digits to the right of the decimal point. You can specify the exact number of decimal digits, just as you can with the FormatCurrency function. The following example formats the number with commas and no digits to the right of the decimal point.

```
lblWholeNumber.Text = FormatNumber(intCount, 0)
```

The FormatNumber Function—General Form

```
FormatNumber(ExpressionToFormat [, NumberOfDecimalPositions [, LeadingDigit _
    [, UseParenthesesForNegative [, GroupingForDigits]]]])
```

See Help for an explanation of the optional arguments of the `FormatNumber` function.

Examples			
Variable	**Value**	**Function**	**Returns**
mdecTotal	1125.67	FormatNumber(mdecTotal, 0)	1,126
decBalance	1234.567	FormatNumber(decBalance)	1,234.57
decBalance	1234.567	FormatNumber(decBalance, 2)	1,234.57

The FormatPercent Function—Simple Form

```
FormatPercent(ExpressionToFormat)
```

To display numeric values as a percent, use the `FormatPercent` function. This function multiplies the argument by 100, adds a percent sign, and rounds to two decimal places. (As with the `FormatCurrency` and `FormatNumber` functions, the default number of decimal positions is determined by the computer's regional settings and can be changed.)

The FormatPercent Function—Simple Examples

```
lblPercentComplete.Text = FormatPercent(sngComplete)
lblInterestRate.Text = FormatPercent(decRate)
```

In the complete form of the `FormatPercent` function, you can select the number of digits to the right of the decimal point as well as customize other options, similar to the other formatting functions.

The FormatPercent Function—General Form

```
FormatPercent(ExpressionToFormat [, NumberOfDecimalPositions [, LeadingDigit _
    [, UseParenthesesForNegative [, GroupingForDigits]]]])
```

Variable	Value	Function	Returns
decCorrect	.75	FormatPercent(decCorrect)	75.00%
decCorrect	.75	FormatPercent(decCorrect, 1)	75.0%
decCorrect	.75	FormatPercent(decCorrect, 0)	75%
decRate	.734	FormatPercent(decRate)	73.40%
decRate	.734	FormatPercent(decRate, 0)	73%
decRate	.734	FormatPercent(decRate, 1)	73.4%
decRate	.734	FormatPercent(decRate, 2)	73.40%

The FormatDateTime Function—General Form

General Form

```
FormatDateTime(ExpressionToFormat [, NamedFormat])
```

You can format an expression as a date and/or time. The expression may be a string that holds a date or time value, a date type variable, or a function that returns a date. The named formats use your computer's regional settings. If you omit the optional named format, the function returns the date using the GeneralDate format.

The FormatDateTime Function—Examples

Examples

```
lblStartDate.Text = FormatDateTime(datStartDate, DateFormat.ShortDate)
lblStartTime.Text = FormatDateTime("1/1/00", DateFormat.LongDate)
lblDateAndTime.Text = FormatDateTime(datSomeDate)
```

The actual values returned by the FormatDateTime function depend on the regional settings on your computer. These are the return formats based on U.S. defaults.

Named format	Returns	Example
DateFormat.GeneralDate	A date and/or time	2/28/02 6:01:24 PM If the expression holds a date, returns a short date. If it holds a time, returns a long time. If it holds both, returns both a short date and long time.
DateFormat.LongDate	Day of week, Month Day, Year	Thursday, February 28, 2002
DateFormat.ShortDate	MM/DD/YY	2/28/02
DateFormat.LongTime	HH:MM:SS AM/PM	6:01:24 PM
DateFormat.ShortTime	HH:MM (24 hour clock)	18:01

Feedback 3.6

Give the line of code that assigns the formatted output and tell how the output will display for the specified value.

1. A calculated variable called *mdecAveragePay* has a value of 123.456 and should display in a label called *lblAveragePay*.
2. The variable sngCorrect, which contains 0.76, must be displayed as a percentage in the label called *lblPercentCorrect*.
3. The total amount collected in a fund drive is being accumulated in a variable called *mdecTotalCollected*. What statement will display the variable in a label called *lblTotal* with commas and two decimal positions but no dollar sign?

A Calculation Programming Example

R 'n R—for Reading 'n Refreshment needs to calculate prices and discounts for books sold. The company is currently having a big sale, offering a 15 percent discount on all books. In this project you will calculate the amount due for a quantity of books, determine the 15 percent discount, and deduct the discount, giving the new amount due—the discounted amount.

Planning the Project

Sketch a form (Figure 3.5) that meets the needs of your users.

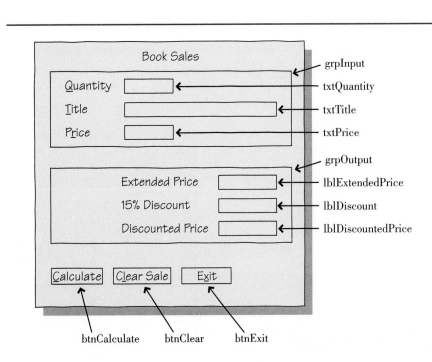

Figure 3.5

A planning sketch of the form for the calculation programming example.

Plan the Objects and Properties

Plan the property settings for the form and each of the controls.

Object	Property	Setting
Form	Name	frmBooksale
	Text	R 'n R for Reading 'n Refreshment
	AcceptButton	btnCalculate
	CancelButton	btnClear
Label1	Text	Book Sales
	Font	Bold, 12 point
grpInput	Name	grpInput
	Text	(blank)
Label2	Text	&Quantity
txtQuantity	Name	txtQuantity
	Text	(blank)
Label3	Text	&Title
txtTitle	Name	txtTitle
	Text	(blank)
Label4	Text	&Price
txtPrice	Name	txtPrice
	Text	(blank)
grpOutput	Name	grpOutput
	Text	(blank)
Label5	Text	Extended Price
lblExtendedPrice	Name	lblExtendedPrice
	Text	(blank)
	TextAlign	TopRight
	BorderStyle	Fixed3D
Label6	Text	15% Discount
lblDiscount	Name	lblDiscount
	Text	(blank)
	TextAlign	TopRight
	BorderStyle	Fixed3D
Label7	Text	Discounted Price
lblDiscountedPrice	Name	lblDiscountedPrice
	Text	(blank)
	TextAlign	TopRight
	BorderStyle	Fixed 3D

Continued on page 120

Object	Property	Setting
btnCalculate	Name	btnCalculate
	Text	&Calculate
btnClear	Name	btnClear
	Text	C&lear Sale
btnExit	Name	btnExit
	Text	E&xit

Plan the Event Procedures

Since you have three buttons, you need to plan the actions for three event procedures.

Event procedure	Actions—pseudocode
btnCalculate_Click	Dimension the variables and constants.
	Convert the input Quantity and Price to numeric.
	Calculate Extended Price = Quantity * Price.
	Calculate Discount = Extended Price * Discount Rate.
	Calculate Discounted Price = Extended Price − Discount.
	Format and display output in labels.
btnClear_Click	Set each text box and output label to blanks.
	Set the focus in the first text box.
btnExit_Click	Exit the project.

Write the Project

Follow the sketch in Figure 3.5 to create the form. Figure 3.6 shows the completed form.

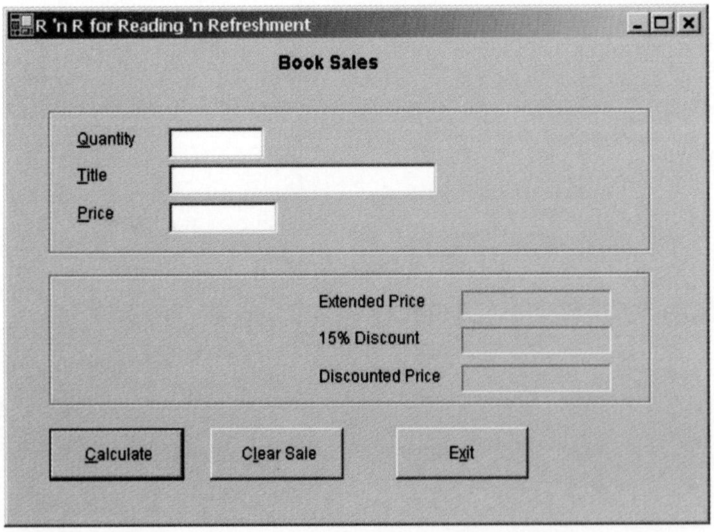

Figure 3.6

The form for the calculation programming example.

- Set the properties of each object, as you have planned.

- Write the code. Working from the pseudocode, write each event procedure.

- When you complete the code, use a variety of test data to thoroughly test the project.

Note: If the user enters nonnumeric data or leaves a numeric field blank, the program will cancel with a run-time error. In the "Handling Exceptions" section that follows this program, you will learn to handle the errors.

The Project Coding Solution

```
'Project:        Chapter Example 3.1
'Date:           January 2002
'Programmer:     Bradley/Millspaugh
'Description:    This project inputs sales information for books.
'                It calculates the extended price and discount for
'                a sale.
'                Uses variables, constants, and calculations.
'Folder:         Ch0301

Option Strict On

Public Class frmBooksale
    Inherits System.Windows.Forms.Form

[Windows Form Designer generated code]

    Const mdecDISCOUNT_RATE As Decimal = 0.15D

    Private Sub btnCalculate_Click(ByVal sender As System.Object, _
    ByVal e As System.EventArgs) Handles btnCalculate.Click
        'Calculate the price and discount

        Dim intQuantity As Integer
        Dim decPrice As Decimal
        Dim decExtendedPrice As Decimal
        Dim decDiscount As Decimal
        Dim decDiscountedPrice As Decimal

        'Convert input values to numeric variables
        intQuantity = CInt(txtQuantity.Text)
        decPrice = CDec(txtPrice.Text)

        'Calculate values
        decExtendedPrice = intQuantity * decPrice
        decDiscount = decExtendedPrice * mdecDISCOUNT_RATE
        decDiscountedPrice = decExtendedPrice - decDiscount

        'Format and display answers
        lblExtendedPrice.Text = FormatCurrency(decExtendedPrice)
        lblDiscount.Text = FormatNumber(decDiscount, 2)
        lblDiscountedPrice.Text = FormatCurrency(decDiscountedPrice)
    End Sub
```

```
Private Sub btnClear_Click(ByVal sender As System.Object, _
 ByVal e As System.EventArgs) Handles btnClear.Click
    'Clear previous amounts from the form

    txtTitle.Clear()
    txtPrice.Clear()
    lblExtendedPrice.Text = ""
    lblDiscount.Text = ""
    lblDiscountedPrice.Text = ""
    With txtQuantity
        .Clear()
        .Focus()
    End With
End Sub

Private Sub btnExit_Click(ByVal sender As System.Object, _
 ByVal e As System.EventArgs) Handles btnExit.Click
    'Exit the project

    Me.Close()
End Sub
End Class
```

Handling Exceptions

When you allow users to input numbers and use those numbers in calculations, lots of things can go wrong. The conversion functions, CInt and CDec, fail if the user enters nonnumeric data or leaves the text box blank. Or your user may enter a number that results in an attempt to divide by zero. Each of those situations causes an **exception** to occur, or as programmers like to say, *throws an exception.*

You can easily "catch" program exceptions by using VB .NET's new structured exception handling. You catch the exceptions before they can cause a run-time error and handle the situation, if possible, within the program. Catching exceptions as they happen is generally referred to as *error trapping,* and coding to take care of the problems is called *error handling.* The error handling in Visual Studio .NET is standardized for all of the languages using the Common Language Runtime, which greatly improves on the old error trapping in previous versions of VB.

• The all new structured exception handling uses Try/Catch blocks. We have elected to add the topic to this chapter and begin data validation here.

Try/Catch Blocks

To trap or catch exceptions, enclose any statement(s) that might cause an error in a Try/Catch **block.** If an exception occurs while the statements in the Try block are executing, then program control transfers to the Catch block; if a Finally statement is included, the code in that section executes last, whether or not an exception occurred.

The Try Block—General Form

```
Try
    statements that may cause error
Catch [VariableName As ExceptionType]
    statements for action when exception occurs
[Finally
    statements that always execute before exit of Try block]
End Try
```

The Try Block—Example

```
Try
    intQuantity = CInt(txtQuantity.Text)
    lblQuantity.Text = CStr(intQuantity)
Catch
    lblMessage.Text = "Error in input data."
End Try
```

The Catch as it appears in the preceding example will catch any exception. You can also specify the type of exception that you want to catch, and even write several Catch statements, each to catch a different type of exception. For example, you might want to display one message for bad input data and a different message for a calculation problem.

To specify a particular type of exception to catch, you use one of the predefined exception classes, which are all based on, or derived from, the System-Exception class. Table 3.2 shows some of the common exception classes.

To catch bad input data that cannot be converted to numeric, write this Catch statement:

```
Catch MyErr As InvalidCastException
      lblMessage.Text = "Error in input data."
```

Common Exception Classes   **Table 3.2**

Exception	Caused by
InvalidCastException	Failure of a conversion function, such as CInt or CDec. Usually blank or nonnumeric data.
ArithmeticException	A calculation error, such as division by zero or overflow of a variable.
System.IO.EndofStreamException	Failure of an input or output operation such as reading from a file.
OutOfMemoryException	Not enough memory to create an object.
Exception	Generic.

The Exception Class

Each exception is an instance of the Exception class. The properties of this class allow you to determine the code location of the error, the type of error, and the cause. The Message property contains a text message about the error, and the Source property contains the name of the object causing the error. The StackTrace property can identify the location in the code where the error occurred.

You can include the text message associated with the type of exception by specifying the Message property of the Exception object, as declared by the variable you named on the `Catch` statement. Be aware that the messages for exceptions are usually somewhat terse and not oriented to users, but they can sometimes be helpful.

```
Catch MyErr As InvalidCastException
    lblMessage.Text = "Error in input data: " & MyErr.Message
```

TIP

Display a list of all system exceptions by selecting *Debug/ Exceptions* ■

Handling Multiple Exceptions

If you want to trap for more than one type of exception, you can include multiple `Catch` blocks (handlers). When an exception occurs, the `Catch` statements are checked in sequence. The first one with a matching exception type is used.

```
Catch MyErr As InvalidCastException
    'statements for non numeric data
Catch MyErr As ArithmeticException
    'statements for calculation problem
Catch MyErr As Exception
    'statements for any other exception
```

The last `Catch` will handle any exceptions that do not match either of the first two exception types. Note that it is acceptable to use the same variable name for multiple `Catch` statements.

Displaying Messages in Message Boxes

You may want to display a message when the user has entered invalid data or neglected to enter a required data value. You can display a message to the user in a message box, which is a special type of window. You can specify the message, an optional icon, the title bar text, and button(s) for the message box (Figure 3.7).

- The MessageBox class replaces the MsgBox function (and moved to this chapter).

F i g u r e   3 . 7

Two sample message boxes created with the MessageBox class.

Invalid Data

⚠ You have entered an invalid amount. Try again

[OK]

Coffee Sales Summary

ⓘ Number Orders: 4
Average Sale: $10.94

[OK]

You use the Show **method** of the **MessageBox** object to display a message box. The MessageBox object is a predefined instance of the MessageBox class that you can use any time you need to display a message.

The MessageBox Object—General Form

There is more than one way to call the Show method. Each of the following statements is a valid call; you can choose the format you want to use. It's very important that the arguments you supply exactly match one of the formats. For example, you cannot reverse, transpose, or leave out any of the arguments. When there are multiple ways to call a method, the method is said to be *overloaded*. See the section "Using Overloaded Methods" later in this chapter.

• The MessageBox.Show method is overloaded, which gives the opportunity to cover that OOP concept.

General Form

```
MessageBox.Show(TextMessage)
MessageBox.Show(TextMessage, TitlebarText)
MessageBox.Show(TextMessage, TitlebarText, MessageBoxButtons)
MessageBox.Show(TextMessage, TitlebarText, MessageBoxButtons, MessageBoxIcon)
```

The TextMessage is the message you want to appear in the message box. The TitleBarText appears on the title bar of the MessageBox window. The MessageBoxButtons argument specifies the buttons to display. And the MessageBoxIcon determines the icon to display.

The MessageBox Statement—Examples

Examples

```
MessageBox.Show("Enter numeric data.")
MessageBox.Show("Try again.", "Data Entry Error")

MessageBox.Show("This is a message.", "This is a title bar", MessageBoxButtons.OK)

Try
    intQuantity = CInt(txtQuantity.Text)
    lblQuantity.Text = intQuantity
Catch err As InvalidCastException
    MessageBox.Show("Nonnumeric Data.", "Error", MessageBoxButtons.OK, _
        MessageBoxIcon.Exclamation)
End Try
```

The TextMessage String

The message string you display may be a string literal enclosed in quotes or it may be a string variable. You may also want to concatenate several items, for example, combining a literal with a value from a variable. If the message you specify is too long for one line, Visual Basic will wrap it to the next line.

The Title Bar Text

The string that you specify for TitlebarText will appear in the title bar of the message box. If you choose the first form of the Show method, without the TitlebarText, the title bar will appear empty.

MessageBox Buttons

When you show a message box, you can specify the button(s) to display. In Chapter 4, after you learn to make selections using the If statement, you will display more than one button and take alternate actions based on which button the user clicks. You specify the buttons using the MessageBoxButtons constants from the MessageBox class. The choices are OK, OKCancel, RetryCancel, YesNo, YesNoCancel, and AbortRetryIgnore. The default for the Show method is OK, so unless you specify otherwise, you will get only the OK button in your message box.

• New constants for buttons and icons are included in the Message-Box class.

MessageBox Icons

The easy way to select the icon to display is to type "MessageBoxIcon" and a period into the editor; the IntelliSense list pops up with the complete list. The actual appearance of the icons varies from one operating system to another. You can see a description of the icons in Help under "MessageBoxIcon Enumeration."

Constants for MessageBoxIcon

Asterisk

Error

Exclamation

Hand

Information

None

Question

Stop

Warning

Using Overloaded Methods

As you saw earlier, you can call the Show method with several different argument lists. This OOP feature, called **overloading,** allows the Show method to act differently for different arguments. Each argument list is called a **signature,** so you can say that the Show method has several signatures.

When you call the Show method, the arguments that you supply must exactly match one of the signatures provided by the method. You must supply the correct number of arguments of the correct data type and in the correct sequence.

Fortunately, the smart Visual Studio editor helps you enter the arguments; you don't have to memorize or look up the argument lists. Type "Message-Box.Show(" and IntelliSense pops up with the first of the signatures for the Show method (Figure 3.8). Notice in the figure that there are 12 possible forms

☑**TIP**

Use the keyboard Up and Down arrow keys rather than the mouse to view and select the signature. The on-screen arrows jump around from one signature to the next, making mouse selection difficult. ■

of the argument list, or 12 signatures for the Show method. (We only showed 4 of the 12 signatures in the previous example, to simplify the concept.)

To select the signature that you want to use, use the up or down arrows at the left end of the IntelliSense popup. For example, to select the signature that needs only the text of the message and the title bar caption, select the fifth format (Figure 3.9). The argument that you are expected to enter is shown in bold and a description of that argument appears in the last line of the pop-up. After you type the text of the message and a comma, the second argument appears in bold, and the description changes to tell you about that argument (Figure 3.10).

Figure 3.8

IntelliSense pops up the first of 12 signatures for the Show method. Use the up and down arrows to see the other possible argument lists.

```
Catch MyErr As InvalidCastException
        MessageBox.Show(
```
```
▲1 of 12▼   Show (text As String, caption As String, buttons As System.Windows.Forms.MessageBoxButtons, icon As System.Windows.Forms.MessageBoxIcon,
            defaultButton As System.Windows.Forms.MessageBoxDefaultButton, options As System.Windows.Forms.MessageBoxOptions) As System.Wind
text: The text to display in the message box.
```

Figure 3.9

```
Catch MyErr As InvalidCastException
        MessageBox.Show(
```
```
▲5 of 12▼   Show (text As String, caption As String) As System.Windows.Forms.DialogResult
text: The text to display in the message box.
```

Select the fifth signature to see the argument list. The currently selected argument is shown in bold and the description of the argument appears in the last line of the pop-up.

Figure 3.10

```
Catch MyErr As InvalidCastException
        MessageBox.Show("Error in Input Data",
```
```
▲5 of 12▼   Show (text As String, caption As String) As System.Windows.Forms.DialogResult
caption: The text to display in the title bar of the message box.
```

Type the first argument and a comma, and IntelliSense bolds the second argument and displays a description of the needed data.

Counting and Accumulating Sums

Programs often need to sum numbers. For example, in the previous programming exercise, each sale is displayed individually. If you want to accumulate totals of the sales amounts, of the discounts, or of the number of books sold, you need some new variables and new techniques.

As you know, the variables you declare inside a procedure are local to that procedure. They are re-created each time the procedure is called; that is, their lifetime is one time through the procedure. Each time the procedure is entered, you have a new fresh variable with an initial value of 0. If you want a variable to retain its value for multiple calls, in order to accumulate totals, you must de-clare the variable as module level. (Another approach, using Static variables, is discussed in Chapter 7.)

Summing Numbers

The technique for summing the sales amounts for multiple sales is to dimension a module-level variable for the total. Then in the btnCalculate_Click event for each sale, add the current amount to the total:

```
mdecDiscountedPriceSum += decDiscountedPrice
```

This assignment statement adds the current value for decDiscountedPrice into the sum held in mdecDiscountedPriceSum.

Counting

If you want to count something, such as the number of sales in the previous ex-ample, you need another module-level variable. Dimension a counter variable as integer:

```
Dim mintSaleCount as Integer
```

Then in the btnCalculate_Click event procedure, add one to the counter variable:

```
mintSaleCount += 1
```

This statement adds 1 to the current contents of mintSaleCount. The statement will execute once for each time the btnCalculate_Click event procedure exe-cutes. Therefore, mintSaleCount will always hold a running count of the num-ber of sales.

Calculating an Average

To calculate an average, divide the sum of the items by the count of the items. In the R 'n R book example, we can calculate the average sale by dividing the sum of the discounted prices by the count of the sales.

```
mdecAverageDiscountedSale = mdecDiscountedPriceSum / mintSaleCount
```

Your Hands-On Programming Example

In this project, R 'n R—for Reading 'n Refreshment needs to expand the book sale project done previously in this chapter. In addition to calculating individ-ual sales and discounts, management wants to know the total number of books sold, the total number of discounts given, the total discounted amount, and the average discount per sale. Help the user by adding ToolTips wherever you think they will be useful.

   Add error handling to the program, so that missing or nonnumeric data will not cause a run-time error.

Planning the Project

Sketch a form (Figure 3.11) that your users sign off as meeting their needs.

Figure 3.11

*A planning sketch of the form
for the hands-on programming
example.*

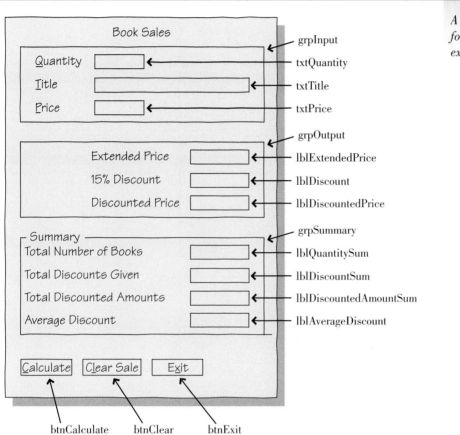

Plan the Objects and Properties

Plan the property settings for the form and each control. These objects and properties are the same as the previous example, with the addition of the summary information beginning with grpSummary.

Note: The ToolTips have not been added to the planning forms: Make up and add your own.

Object	Property	Setting
Form	Name	frmBooksale
	Text	R 'n R for Reading 'n Refreshment
	AcceptButton	btnCalculate
	CancelButton	btnClear
Label1	Text	Book Sales
	Font	Bold, 12 point
grpInput	Name	grpInput
	Text	(blank)

Continued on page 130

Object	Property	Setting
Label2	Text	&Quantity
txtQuantity	Name	txtQuantity
	Text	(blank)
Label3	Text	&Title
txtTitle	Name	txtTitle
	Text	(blank)
Label4	Text	&Price
txtPrice	Name	txtPrice
	Text	(blank)
grpOutput	Name	grpOutput
	Text	(blank)
Label5	Text	Extended Price
lblExtendedPrice	Name	lblExtendedPrice
	Text	(blank)
	BorderStyle	Fixed3D
	TextAlign	TopRight
Label6	Text	15% Discount
lblDiscount	Name	lblDiscount
	Text	(blank)
	BorderStyle	Fixed3D
	TextAlign	TopRight
Label7	Text	Discounted Price
lblDiscountedPrice	Name	lblDiscountedPrice
	BorderStyle	Fixed3D
	TextAlign	TopRight
	BorderStyle	Fixed3D
btnCalculate	Name	btnCalculate
	Text	&Calculate
btnClear	Name	btnClear
	Text	C&lear Sale
btnExit	Name	btnExit
	Text	E&xit
grpSummary	Name	grpSummary
	Text	Summary
Label8	Text	Total Number of Books
lblQuantitySum	Name	lblQuantitySum
	Text	(blank)
	BorderStyle	Fixed3D
	TextAlign	TopRight
Label9	Text	Total Discounts Given

Continued on page 131

Object	Property	Setting
lblDiscountSum	Name	lblDiscountSum
	Text	(blank)
	BorderStyle	Fixed3D
	TextAlign	TopRight
Label10	Text	Total Discounted Amounts
lblDiscountedAmountSum	Name	lblDiscountedAmountSum
	Text	(blank)
	BorderStyle	Fixed3D
	TextAlign	TopRight
Label11	Text	Average Discount
lblAverageDiscount	Name	lblAverageDiscount
	Text	(blank)
	BorderStyle	Fixed3D
	TextAlign	TopRight

Plan the Event Procedures

The planning that you did for the previous example will save you time now. The only procedure that requires more steps is the btnCalculate_Click event.

Event procedure	Actions—pseudocode
btnCalculate_Click	Dimension the variables.
	Try
	Convert the inputs Quantity and Price to numeric.
	Calculate Extended Price = Quantity * Price.
	Calculate Discount = Extended Price * Discount Rate.
	Calculate Discounted Price = Extended Price − Discount.
	Calculate the summary values:
	Add Quantity to Quantity Sum.
	Add Discount to Discount Sum.
	Add Discounted Price to Discounted Price Sum.
	Add 1 to Sale Count.
	Calculate Average Discount = Discount Sum / Sale Count.
	Format and display sale output in labels.
	Format and display summary values in labels.
	Catch
	Display error message.
btnClear_Click	Set each text box and label to blanks.
	Set the focus in the first text box.
btnExit_Click	Exit the project.

Write the Project

Following the sketch in Figure 3.11, create the form. Figure 3.12 shows the completed form.

- Set the properties of each of the objects, as you have planned.

- Write the code. Working from the pseudocode, write each event procedure.

- When you complete the code, use a variety of test data to thoroughly test the project.

Figure 3.12

The form for the hands-on programming example.

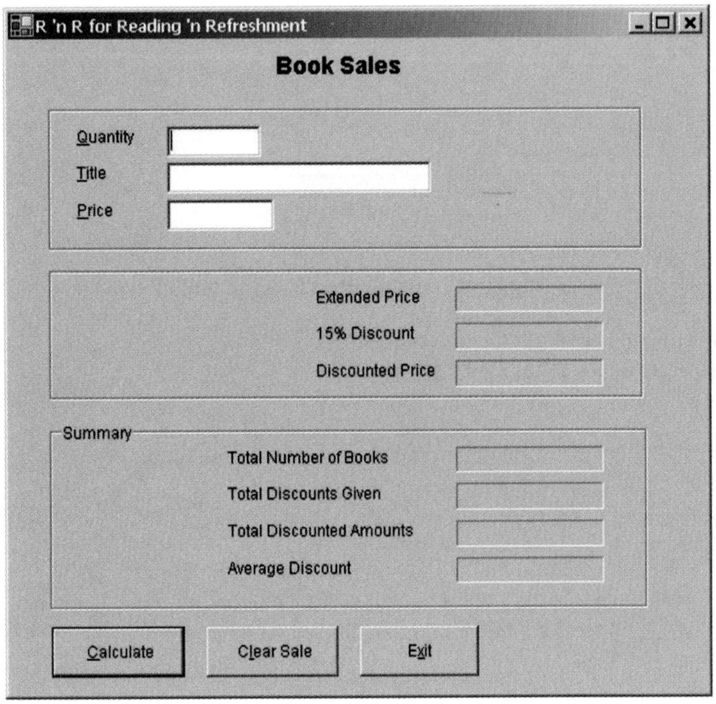

The Project Coding Solution

```
'Project:       Chapter Example 3.2
'Date:          January 2002
'Programmer:    Bradley/Millspaugh
'Description:   This project inputs sales information for books.
'               It calculates the extended price and discount for
'               a sale and maintains summary information for all
'               sales.
'               Uses variables, constants, calculations, error
'               handling, and a message box to the user.
'Folder:        Ch0302

Option Strict On

Public Class frmBooksale
    Inherits System.Windows.Forms.Form
```

```
[Windows Form Designer generated code ]

    'Dimension module-level variables and constants
    Dim mintQuantitySum As Integer
    Dim mdecDiscountSum As Decimal
    Dim mdecDiscountedPriceSum As Decimal
    Dim mintSaleCount As Integer
    Const mdecDISCOUNT_RATE As Decimal = 0.15D

    Private Sub btnCalculate_Click(ByVal sender As System.Object, _
     ByVal e As System.EventArgs) Handles btnCalculate.Click
        'Calculate the price and discount

        Dim intQuantity As Integer
        Dim decPrice As Decimal
        Dim decExtendedPrice As Decimal
        Dim decDiscount As Decimal
        Dim decDiscountedPrice As Decimal
        Dim decAverageDiscount As Decimal

        Try
            'Convert input values to numeric variables
            intQuantity = CInt(txtQuantity.Text)
            decPrice = CDec(txtPrice.Text)

            'Calculate values for sale
            decExtendedPrice = intQuantity * decPrice
            decDiscount = decExtendedPrice * mdecDISCOUNT_RATE
            decDiscountedPrice = decExtendedPrice - decDiscount

            'Calculate summary values
            mintQuantitySum += intQuantity
            mdecDiscountSum += decDiscount
            mdecDiscountedPriceSum += decDiscountedPrice
            mintSaleCount += 1
            decAverageDiscount = mdecDiscountSum / mintSaleCount

            'Format and display answers for sale
            lblExtendedPrice.Text = FormatCurrency(decExtendedPrice)
            lblDiscount.Text = FormatNumber(decDiscount)
            lblDiscountedPrice.Text = FormatCurrency(decDiscountedPrice)

            'Format and display summary values
            lblQuantitySum.Text = CStr(mintQuantitySum)
            lblDiscountSum.Text = FormatCurrency(mdecDiscountSum)
            lblDiscountedAmountSum.Text = FormatCurrency(mdecDiscountedPriceSum)
            lblAverageDiscount.Text = FormatCurrency(decAverageDiscount)

            'Handle exceptions
        Catch MyErr As InvalidCastException
            MessageBox.Show("Enter numeric data.", "Data Entry Error", _
                MessageBoxButtons.OK, MessageBoxIcon.Exclamation)
        Catch MyErr As Exception
            MessageBox.Show("Error: " & MyErr.Message)
        End Try

    End Sub
```

```
Private Sub btnClear_Click(ByVal sender As System.Object, _
 ByVal e As System.EventArgs) Handles btnClear.Click
    'Clear previous amounts from the form

    txtTitle.Clear()
    txtPrice.Clear()
    lblExtendedPrice.Text = ""
    lblDiscount.Text = ""
    lblDiscountedPrice.Text = ""
    With txtQuantity
        .Clear()
        .Focus()
    End With
End Sub

Private Sub btnExit_Click(ByVal sender As System.Object, _
 ByVal e As System.EventArgs) Handles btnExit.Click
    'Exit the project

    Me.Close()
End Sub

End Class
```

Summary

1. Variables and constants are temporary memory locations that have a name (called an *identifier*), a data type, and a scope. The value stored in a variable can be changed during the execution of the project; the values stored in constants cannot change.

2. The data type determines what type of values may be stored in a variable or constant. The most common data types are String, Integer, Decimal, Single Precision, and Boolean.

3. Identifiers for variables and constants must follow the Visual Basic naming rules and should follow good naming standards, called *conventions*. An identifier should be meaningful and have a lowercase prefix that indicates the data type and the scope. Variable and constant names should be mixed upper- and lowercase.

4. Intrinsic constants, such as Color.Red and Color.Blue, are predefined and built into Visual Studio. Named constants are programmer-defined constants and are declared using the Const statement. The location of the Const statement determines the scope of the constant.

5. Variables are declared using the Dim statement; the location of the statement determines the scope of the variable.

6. The scope of a variable may be namespace, module level, local, or block. Block and local variables are available only within the procedure in which they are declared; module-level variables are accessible in all procedures within a form; namespace variables are available in all procedures of all classes in a namespace, which is usually the entire project.

7. The lifetime of local and block variables is one execution of the procedure in which they are declared. The lifetime of module-level variables is the length of time that the form is loaded.

8. Identifiers should include a prefix that identifies the scope and the data type of the variable or constant.

9. A Visual Basic function performs an action and returns a value. The expressions named in parentheses are called *arguments.*

10. Use the conversion functions to convert text values to numeric before performing any calculations.

11. Calculations may be performed using the values of numeric variables, constants, and the properties of controls. The result of a calculation may be assigned to a numeric variable or to the property of a control.

12. A calculation operation with more than one operator follows the order of precedence in determining the result of the calculation. Parentheses alter the order of operations.

13. The formatting functions `FormatCurrency`, `FormatNumber`, `Format-Percent`, and `FormatDateTime` can be used to specify the appearance of values for display.

14. `Try / Catch / Finally` statements provide a method for checking for user errors such as blank or nonnumeric data or an entry that might result in a calculation error.

15. An error is called an *exception;* catching and taking care of exceptions is called *error trapping* and *error handling.*

16. You can trap for different types of errors by specifying the exception type on the `Catch` statement, and can have multiple `Catch` statements to catch more than one type of exception. Each exception is an instance of the Exception class; you can refer to the properties of the Exception object for further information.

17. A message box is a window for displaying information to the user.

18. The `Show` method of the MessageBox class is overloaded, which means that the method may be called with different argument lists.

19. You can calculate a sum by adding each transaction to a module-level variable. In a similar fashion, you can calculate a count by adding to a module-level variable.

Key Terms

Review Questions

1. Name and give the purpose of five types of data available in Visual Basic.
2. What does *declaring a variable* mean?
3. What effect does the location of a `Dim` statement have on the variable it declares?
4. Explain the difference between a constant and a variable.
5. What is the purpose of the `CInt` function? The `CDec` function?
6. Explain the order of precedence of operators for calculations.
7. What statement(s) can be used to declare a variable?
8. Explain how to make an interest rate stored in decRate display as a percentage with three decimal digits.
9. Should formatting functions be included for all display in a program? Justify your answer.
10. When should you use `Try/Catch` blocks? Why?
11. What is a message box and when should you use one?
12. Explain why the `MessageBox.Show` method has multiple signatures.
13. Why must you use module-level variables if you want to accumulate a running total of transactions?

Programming Exercises

3.1 Create a project that calculates the total of fat, carbohydrate, and protein calories. Allow the user to enter (in text boxes) the grams of fat, the grams of carbohydrate, and the grams of protein. Each gram of fat is nine calories; a gram of protein or carbohydrate is four calories.

Display the total calories for the current food item in a label. Use two other labels to display an accumulated sum of the calories and a count of the items entered.

Form: The form should have three text boxes for the user to enter the grams for each category. Include labels next to each text box indicating what the user is to enter.

Include buttons to Calculate, to Clear the text boxes, and to Exit.

Make the form's Text property "Calorie Counter".

Code: Write the code for each button. Make sure to catch any bad input data and display a message box to the user.

3.2 Lennie McPherson, proprietor of Lennie's Bail Bonds, needs to calculate the amount due for setting bail. Lennie requires something of value as collateral, and his fee is 10 percent of the bail amount. He wants the screen to provide boxes to enter the bail amount and the item being used for collateral. The program must calculate the fee.

Form: Include text boxes for entering in the amount of bail and the description of the collateral. Label each text box.

Include buttons for Calculate, Clear, and Exit.

The text property for the form should be "Lennie's Bail Bonds".

Code: Include event procedures for the click event of each button. Calculate the amount due as 10 percent of the bail amount and display it in a label, formatted as currency. Make sure to catch any bad input data and display a message to the user.

3.3   In retail sales, management needs to know the average inventory figure and the turnover of merchandise. Create a project that allows the user to enter the beginning inventory, the ending inventory, and the cost of goods sold.

Form: Include labeled text boxes for the beginning inventory, the ending inventory, and the cost of goods sold. After calculating the answers, display the average inventory and the turnover formatted in labels.

Include buttons for Calculate, Clear, and Exit. The formulas for the calculations are

$$\text{Average inventory} = \frac{\text{Beginning inventory} + \text{Ending inventory}}{2}$$

$$\text{Turnover} = \frac{\text{Cost of goods sold}}{\text{Average inventory}}$$

Note: The average inventory is expressed in dollars; the turnover is the number of times the inventory turns over.

Code: Include procedures for the click event of each button. Display the results in labels. Format the average inventory as currency and the turnover as a number with one digit to the right of the decimal. Make sure to catch any bad input data and display a message to the user.

Test data			Check figures	
Beginning	**Ending**	**Cost of goods sold**	**Average inventory**	**Turnover**
58500	47000	400000	$52,750.00	7.58
75300	13600	515400	44,450.00	11.60
3000	19600	48000	11,300.00	4.25

3.4   A local recording studio rents its facilities for $200 per hour. Management charges only for the number of minutes used. Create a project in which the input is the name of the group and the number of minutes it used the studio. Your program calculates the appropriate charges, accumulates the total charges for all groups, and computes the average charge and the number of groups that used the studio.

Form: Use labeled text boxes for the name of the group and the number of minutes used. The charges for the current group should be displayed and formatted in a label. Create a group box for the summary information. Inside the group box, display the total charges for all groups, the number of groups, and the average charge per group. Format all output appropriately. Include buttons for Calculate, Clear, and Exit.

Code: Use a constant for the rental rate per minute. Do not allow bad input data to cancel the program.

Test data	
Group	**Minutes**
Pooches	95
Hounds	5
Mutts	480

Check figures			
Total charges for group	**Total number of groups**	**Average charge**	**Total charges for all groups**
$ 316.67	1	$316.67	$ 316.67
$ 16.67	2	$166.67	$ 333.33
$1,600.00	3	$644.44	$1,933.33

3.5   Create a project that determines the future value of an investment at a given interest rate for a given number of years. The formula for the calculation is

$$\text{Future value} = \text{Investment amount} * (1 + \text{Interest rate}) \wedge \text{Years}$$

Form: Use labeled text boxes for the amount of investment, the interest rate (as a decimal fraction), and the number of years the investment will be held. Display the future value in a label formatted as Decimal.

Include buttons for Calculate, Clear, and Exit. Format all dollar amounts. Display a message to the user for nonnumeric or missing input data.

Test data			Check figures
Amount	**Rate**	**Years**	**Future value**
2000.00	.15	5	$4.022.71
1234.56	.075	3	$1,533.69

3.6   Write a project that calculates the shipping charge for a package if the shipping rate is $0.12 per ounce.

Form: Use labeled text boxes for the package-identification code (a six-digit code) and the weight of the package—one box for pounds and another one for ounces. Use a label to display the shipping charge.

Include buttons for Calculate, Clear, and Exit.

Code: Include event procedures for each button. Use a constant for the shipping rate, calculate the shipping charge, and display it formatted in a label. Display a message to the user for any bad input data.

Calculation hint: There are 16 ounces in a pound.

Shipping charge	ID	Weight
$0.60	L5496P	0 lb. 5 oz.
$3.84	J1955K	2 lb. 0 oz.
$2.04	Z0000Z	1 lb. 1 oz.

3.7   Create a project for the local car rental agency that calculates rental charges. The agency charges $15 per day plus $0.12 per mile.

       Form: Use text boxes for the customer name, address, city, state, ZIP code, beginning odometer reading, ending odometer reading, and the number of days the car was used. Use labels to display the miles driven and the total charge. Format the output appropriately.

       Include buttons for Calculate, Clear, and Exit.

       Code: Include an event procedure for each button. For the calculation, subtract the beginning odometer reading from the ending odometer reading to get the number of miles traveled. Use a constant for the $15 per day charge and the $0.12 mileage rate. Display a message to the user for any bad input data.

3.8   Create a project that will input an employee's sales and calculate the gross pay, deductions, and net pay. Each employee will receive a base pay of $900 plus a sales commission of 6 percent of sales.

       After calculating the net pay, calculate the budget amount for each category based on the percentages given.

Pay	
Base pay	$900; use a named constant
Commission	6% of sales
Gross pay	Sum of base pay and commission
Deductions	18% of gross pay
Net pay	Gross pay minus deductions

Budget	
Housing	30% of net pay
Food and clothing	15% of net pay
Entertainment	50% of net pay
Miscellaneous	5% of net pay

       Form: Use text boxes to input the employee's name and the dollar amount of the sales. Use labels to display the results of the calculations.

       Provide buttons for Calculate, Clear, and Exit. Display a message to the user for any bad input data.

Case Studies

VB Mail Order

The company has instituted a bonus program to give its employees an incentive to sell more. For every dollar the store makes in a four-week period, the employees receive 2 percent of sales. The amount of bonus each employee receives is based upon the percentage of hours he or she worked during the bonus period (a total of 160 hours).

The screen will allow the user to enter the employee's name, the total number of hours worked, and the amount of the store's total sales. The amount of sales should be entered only for the first employee. (*Hint:* Don't clear it.)

The Calculate button will determine the bonus earned by this employee, and the Clear button will clear only the name and hours-worked fields. Do not allow missing or bad input data to cancel the program; instead display a message to the user.

VB Auto Center

Salespeople for used cars are compensated using a commission system. The commission is based on the costs incurred for the vehicle.

Commission =
    Commission rate * (Sales price − Cost value)

The screen will allow the user to enter the sales-person's name, the selling price of the vehicle, and the cost value of the vehicle. Use a constant of 20 percent for the commission rate.

The Calculate button will determine the commission earned by the salesperson; the Clear button will clear the text boxes. Do not allow bad input data to cancel the program; instead display a message to the user.

Video Bonanza

Design and code a project to calculate the amount due and provide a summary of rentals. All movies rent for $1.80, and all customers receive a 10 percent discount.

The form should contain input for the member number and the number of movies rented. Inside a group box, display the rental amount, the 10 percent discount, and the amount due. Inside a second group box, display the number of customers served and the total rental income (after discount).

Include buttons for Calculate, Clear, and Exit. The Clear command clears the information for the current rental but does not clear the summary information. Do not allow bad input data to cancel the program; instead display a message to the user.

Very Very Boards

Very Very Boards rents snowboards during the snow season. A person can rent a snowboard without boots or with boots. Create a project that will calculate and print the information for each rental. In addition, calculate the summary information for each day's rentals.

For each rental, input the person's name, the driver's license or ID number, the number of snowboards, and the number of snowboards with boots. Snowboards without boots rent for $20; snowboards with boots rent for $30.

Calculate and display the charges for snowboards and snowboards with boots, and the rental total. In addition, maintain summary totals. Use constants for the snowboard rental rate and the snowboard with boots rental rate.

Create a summary group box with labels to indicate the day's totals for the number of snowboards and snowboards with boots rented, total charges, and average charge per customer.

Include buttons for Calculate Order, Clear, Clear All, and Exit. The Clear All command should clear the summary totals to begin a new day's summary. *Hint:* You must set each of the summary variables to zero as well as clear the summary labels.

Make your buttons easy to use for keyboard entry. Make the Calculate button the accept button and the Clear button the cancel button.

Do not allow bad input data to cancel the program; instead display a message to the user.

CHAPTER

4

Decisions and Conditions

at the completion of this chapter, you will be able to . . .

1. Use block Ifs to control the flow of logic.

2. Understand and use nested Ifs.

3. Read and create flowcharts indicating the logic in a selection process.

4. Evaluate conditions using the relational operators.

5. Combine conditions using And and Or.

6. Test the Checked property of radio buttons and check boxes.

7. Perform validation on numeric fields.

8. Call event procedures from other procedures.

9. Create message boxes with multiple buttons and choose alternate actions based on the user response.

10. Debug projects using breakpoints, stepping program execution, and displaying intermediate results.

In this chapter you will learn to write applications that can take one action or another, based on a condition. For example, you may need to keep track of sales separately for different classes of employees, different sections of the country, or different departments. You will also learn alternate techniques for checking the validity of input data and how to display multiple buttons on a message box and take different actions depending on the user response.

If Statements

A powerful capability of the computer is its ability to make decisions and to take alternate courses of action based on the outcome.

A decision made by the computer is formed as a question: Is a given condition true or false? If it is true, do one thing; if it is false, do something else.

If *the sun is shining* Then	(condition)
go to the beach	(action to take if condition is true)
Else	
go to class	(action to take if condition is false)
End If	(See Figure 4.1.)

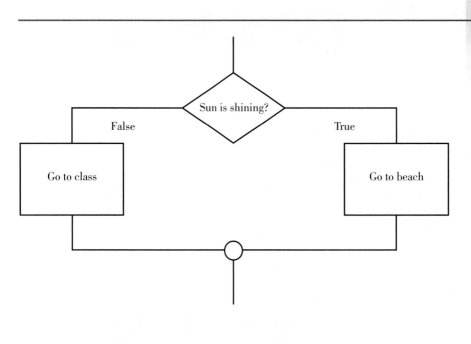

F i g u r e   4 . 1

The logic of an If . . . Then . . . Else *statement in flowchart form.*

or

If *you don't succeed* Then	(condition)
try, try again	(action)
End If	(See Figure 4.2.)

Figure 4.2

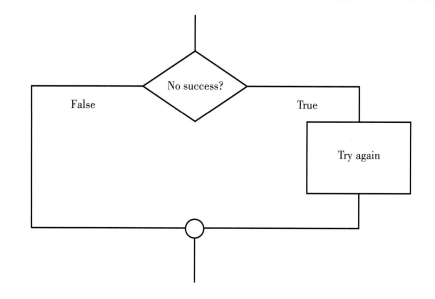

The logic of an If *statement without an* Else *action in flowchart from.*

Notice in the second example that no action is specified if the condition is not true.

In an If statement, when the condition is true, only the Then clause is executed. When the condition is false, only the Else clause, if present, is executed.

If . . . Then . . . Else Statement—General Form

General Form

```
If (condition) Then
  statement(s)
[ElseIf (condition) Then
  statement(s)]
[Else
  statements(s)]
End If
```

A block If...Then...Else must always conclude with End If. The word Then must appear on the same line as the If with nothing following Then (except a remark). End If and Else (if used) must appear alone on a line. The statements under the Then and Else clauses are indented for readability and clarity.

Notice that the keyword ElseIf is all one word but that End If is two words.

If . . . Then . . . Else Statement—Example

When the number of units in decUnits is less than 32, select the radio button for Freshman; otherwise, make sure the button is unselected (see Figure 4.3). Remember that when a radio button is selected, the Checked property has a Boolean value of True.

Example

```
decUnits = CDec(txtUnits.Text)
If decUnits < 32D Then
    radFreshman.Checked = True
Else
    radFreshman.Checked = False
End If
```

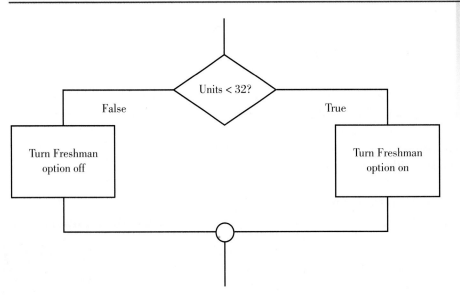

Figure 4.3

The If statement logic in flowchart form. If the number of units is fewer than 32, the Freshman radio button will be selected; otherwise the Freshman radio button will be selected.

Flowcharting If Statements

A flowchart is a useful tool for showing the logic of an If statement. It has been said that one picture is worth a thousand words. Many programmers find that a flowchart helps them organize their thoughts and design projects more quickly.

The symbols used in this text are a subset of the available flowcharting symbols. The diamond-shape symbol (called a *decision symbol*) represents a condition. The two branches from the symbol indicate which path to take when the condition evaluates True or False (see Figure 4.4).

Always take the time to indent properly as you enter an If statement. You will save yourself debugging time; the indentation helps to visualize the intended logic. The editor helps you indent your code. ■

Figure 4.4

The flowcharting symbols used for program decisions and processes.

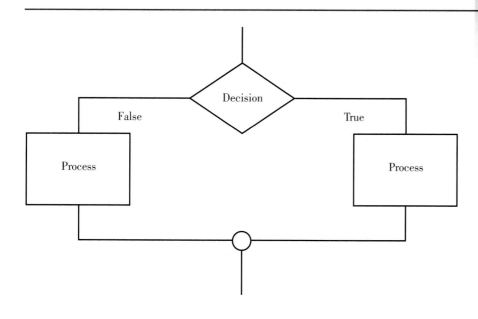

The Helpful Editor

You will find that the VS code editor is very helpful as you enter `If` statements. When you type an `If` statement and press Enter, the editor automatically adds the `End If` statement and places the insertion point on a blank line, indented from the `If`. And if you type `EndIf` without the space, the editor adds the space for you.

The editor also attempts to correct some errors for you. If you type the word `Else` and another statement on the same line, which is illegal syntax, the editor adds a colon. A colon is a statement terminator, which allows you to have multiple statements on one line. However, good programming practices dictate that you should have only one statement per line, so if you find an extra colon in your code, remove it and correct the syntax.

An example of illegal syntax is as follows:

```
If decUnits < 32D Then
    radFreshman.Checked.True
Else radFreshman.Checked = False
End If
```

The editor's solution, which you will fix, is

```
If decUnits < 32D Then
        radFreshman.Checked.True
Else: radFreshman.Checked = False
End If
```

Fix this poor solution by separating the two statements into two separate lines:

```
If decUnits < 32D Then
    radFreshman.Checked.True
Else
    radFreshman.Checked = False
End If
```

Conditions

The test in an `If` statement is based on a **condition.** To form conditions, six **relational operators** (Table 4.1) are used to compare values. The result of the comparison is either True or False.

The conditions to be tested can be formed with numeric variables and constants, string variables and constants, object properties, and arithmetic expressions. However, it is important to note that comparisons must be made on like types; that is, strings can be compared only to other strings, and numeric values can be compared only to other numeric values, whether a variable, constant, property, or arithmetic expression.

• Be much more careful to keep the data types the same in conditions.

The Six Relational Operators

T a b l e   4 . 1

Symbol	Relation tested	Examples
>	greater than	`CDec(txtAmount.Text) > mdecLimit` `intCorrect > 75`
<	less than	`CInt(txtSales.Text) < 10000` `txtName.Text < strName`
=	equal to	`txtPassword.Text = "101"`
<>	not equal to	`radFreshman.Checked <> True` `txtName.Text <> ""`
>=	greater than or equal to	`CInt(txtQuantity.Text) >= 500` `decInterestRate>= mdecMaxRate`
<=	less than or equal to	`txtName1.Text <= txtName2.Text`

Comparing Numeric Variables and Constants

When numeric values are involved in a test, an algebraic comparison is made; that is, the sign of the number is taken into account. Therefore, negative 20 is less than 10, and negative 2 is less than negative 1.

Even though an equal sign (=) means replacement in an assignment statement, in a relation test the equal sign is used to test for equality. For example, the condition

```
If CDec(txtPrice.Text) = decMaximum Then
```

means "Is the current numeric value stored in txtPrice.Text equal to the value stored in decMaximum?"

Sample Comparisons

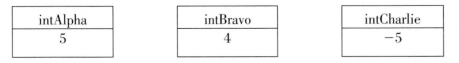

intAlpha
5

intBravo
4

intCharlie
−5

Condition	Evaluates
intAlpha = intBravo	False
intCharlie < 0	True
intBravo > intAlpha	False
intCharlie <= intBravo	True
intAlpha >= 5	True
intAlpha <> intCharlie	True

Comparing Strings

String variables can be compared to other string variables, string properties, or string literals enclosed in quotation marks. The comparison begins with the left-most character and proceeds one character at a time from left to right. As soon as a character in one string is not equal to the corresponding character in the second string, the comparison is terminated, and the string with the lower-ranking character is judged less than the other.

The determination of which character is less than another is based on the code used to store characters internally in the computer. The code, called the **ANSI code,** has an established order (called the *collating sequence*) for all letters, numbers, and special characters. (ANSI stands for American National Standards Institute.) In Table 4.2, A is less than B, L is greater than K, and all numeric digits are less than all letters. Some special symbols are lower than the numbers, some are higher, and the blank space is lower than the rest of the characters shown.

Note: VB actually stores string characters in Unicode, a coding system that uses 2 bytes to store every character. Using Unicode, all characters and symbols in foreign languages can be represented. For systems that do not use the foreign symbols, only the first byte of each character is used. And the first byte of Unicode is the same as the ANSI code. For comparison, Unicode can store 65,536 unique characters, ANSI code can store 256 unique characters, and ASCII, the earlier coding method, can store 128 unique characters. The first 128 characters of ANSI and Unicode are the same as the ASCII characters.

The ANSI Collating Sequence   **T a b l e   4 . 2**

Code	Character	Code	Character	Code	Character
32	Space (blank)	64	@	96	`
33	!	65	A	97	a
34	"	66	B	98	b
35	#	67	C	99	c
36	$	68	D	100	d
37	%	69	E	101	e
38	&	70	F	102	f
39	' (apostrophe)	71	G	103	g
40	(	72	H	104	h
41	)	73	I	105	i
42	*	74	J	106	j
43	+	75	K	107	k
44	, (comma)	76	L	108	l
45	–	77	M	109	m
46	.	78	N	110	n
47	/	79	O	111	o
48	0	80	P	112	p
49	1	81	Q	113	q
50	2	82	R	114	r
51	3	83	S	115	s
52	4	84	T	116	t
53	5	85	U	117	u
54	6	86	V	118	v
55	7	87	W	119	w
56	8	88	X	120	x
57	9	89	Y	121	y
58	:	90	Z	122	z
59	;	91	[	123	{
60	<	92	\	124		
61	=	93	]	125	}
62	>	94	^	126	~
63	?	95	_	127	Del

The condition txtPerson1.Text < txtPerson2.Text evaluates False. The *A* in *JOAN* is lower ranking than the *H* in *JOHN*.

The condition txtWord1.Text < txtWord2.Text evaluates True. When one string is shorter than the other, it compares as if the shorter string is padded with blanks to the right of the string, and the blank space is compared to a character in the longer string.

lblCar1.Text		lblCar2.Text
300ZX		Porsche

The condition lblCar1.Text < lblCar2.Text evaluates True. When the number *3* is compared to the letter *P,* the 3 is lower, since all numbers are lower ranking than all letters.

Feedback 4.1

intCountOne	intCountTwo	intCountThree	txtFour.Text	txtFive.Text
5	5	−5	"Bit"	"Bite"

Determine which conditions will evaluate True and which ones will evaluate False.

1. intCountOne >= intCountTwo
2. intCountThree < 0
3. intCountThree < intCountTwo
4. intCountOne <> intCountTwo
5. intCountOne + 2 > intCountTwo + 2
6. txtFour.Text < txtFive.Text
7. txtFour.Text <> txtFive.Text
8. txtFour.Text > "D"
9. "2" <> "Two"
10. "$" <= "?"

Testing for True or False

You can use shortcuts when testing for True or False. Visual Basic evaluates the condition in an If statement. If the condition is a Boolean variable name, it holds the values True or False.

For example:

```
If blnSuccessfulOperation = True Then . . .
```

is equivalent to

```
If blnSuccessfulOperation Then . . .
```

Comparing Uppercase and Lowercase Characters

When comparing strings, the case of the characters is important. An uppercase *Y* is not equal to a lowercase *y*. Because the user may type a name or word in uppercase, lowercase, or as a combination of cases, we must check all possibilities. The best way is to use ToUpper and ToLower **methods** of the String class, which return the uppercase or lowercase equivalent of a string, respectively.

● Use the ToUpper and ToLower methods of the String class in place of the UCase and LCase functions.

The ToUpper and ToLower Methods—General Form

General Form

```
TextString.ToUpper
TextString.ToLower
```

The ToUpper and ToLower Methods—Examples

Examples

txtOne.Text Value	txtOne.Text.ToUpper	txtOne.Text.ToLower
Basic	BASIC	basic
PROGRAMMING	PROGRAMMING	programming
Robert Jones	ROBERT JONES	robert jones
hello	HELLO	hello

An example of a condition using the ToUpper method follows.

```
If txtOne.Text.ToUpper = "BASIC" Then
    'Do something
End If
```

Note that when you convert txtOne.Text to uppercase, you must compare it to an uppercase literal ("BASIC") if you want it to evaluate as True.

Compound Conditions

You can use compound conditions to test more than one condition. Create **compound conditions** by joining conditions with **logical operators**. The logical operators are Or, And, and Not.

Logical operator	Meaning	Example	Explanation
Or	If one condition or both conditions are True, the entire condition is True.	CInt (lblNumber.Text) = 1 Or _ CInt (lblNumber.Text) = 2	Evaluates True when lblNumber.Text is either "1" or "2".
And	Both conditions must be True for the entire condition to be True.	CInt (txtNumber.Text) > 0 And _ CInt (txtNumber.Text) < 10	Evaluates True when lblNumber.Text is "1", "2", "3", "4", "5", "6", "7", "8", or "9".
Not	Reverses the condition so that a True condition will evaluate False and vice versa.	Not CInt (lblNumber.Text) = 0	Evaluates True when lblNumber.Text is any value other than "0".

Compound Condition Examples

Examples

```
If radMale.Checked = True And CInt(txtAge.Text) < 21 Then
    mintMinorMaleCount += 1
End If

If radJunior.Checked = True Or radSenior.Checked = True Then
    mintUpperClassmanCount += 1
End If
```

The first example requires that both the radio button test and the age test be True for the count to be incremented. In the second example, only one of the conditions must be True.

One caution when using compound conditions: Each side of the logical operator must be a complete condition. For example,

```
intCount > 10 or < 0
```

is incorrect. Instead, it must be

```
intCount > 10 or intCount < 0.
```

Combining And and Or

You can create compound conditions that combine multiple And and Or conditions. When you have both an And and an Or, the And is evaluated before the Or. However, you can change the order of evaluation by using parentheses; any condition inside parentheses will be evaluated first.

For example, will the following condition evaluate True or False? Try it with various values for decSale, radDiscount, and txtState.Text.

```
If decSale > 1000.0 Or radDiscount.Checked = True And txtState.Text.ToUpper <> "CA" Then
    '(Calculate the discount)
End If
```

decSale	radDiscount.Checked	txtState.Text.ToUpper	Evaluates
1500.0	False	CA	True
1000.0	True	OH	True
1000.0	True	CA	False
1500.0	True	NY	True
1000.0	False	CA	False

Nested If Statements

In many programs another If statement is one of the statements to be executed when a condition tests True or False. If statements that contain additional If statements are said to be ***nested*** If statements. The following example shows a nested If statement in which the second If occurs in the Then portion of the first If (Figure 4.5).

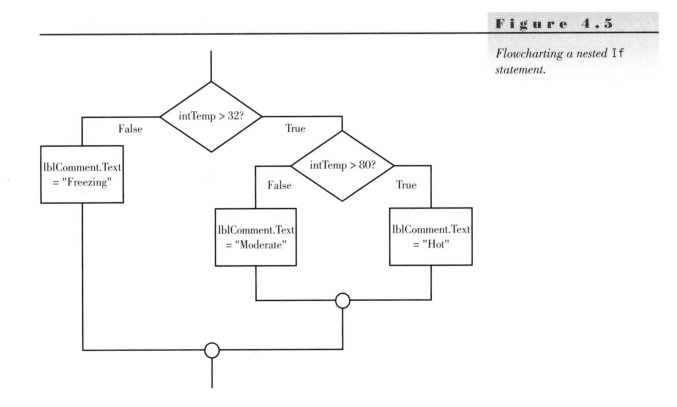

Figure 4.5

Flowcharting a nested If *statement.*

```
If intTemp > 32 Then
    If intTemp > 80 Then
        lblComment.Text = "Hot"
    Else
        lblComment.Text = "Moderate"
    End If
Else
    lblComment.Text = "Freezing"
End If
```

To nest If statements in the Else portion, you may use either of the following approaches; however, your code is simpler if you use the second method (using ElseIf . . . Then).

```
If intTemp <= 32 Then
    lblComment.Text = "Freezing"
Else
    If intTemp > 80 Then
        lblComment.Text = "Hot"
    Else
        lblComment.Text = "Moderate"
    End If
End If

If intTemp <= 32 Then
    lblComment.Text = "Freezing"
ElseIf intTemp > 80 Then
    lblComment.Text = "Hot"
Else
    lblComment.Text = "Moderate"
End If
```

You can nest Ifs in both the Then and Else. In fact, you may continue to nest Ifs within Ifs as long as each If has an End If. However, projects become very difficult to follow (and may not perform as intended) when Ifs become too deeply nested (Figure 4.6).

A flowchart of a nested If statement with Ifs nested on both sides of the original If.

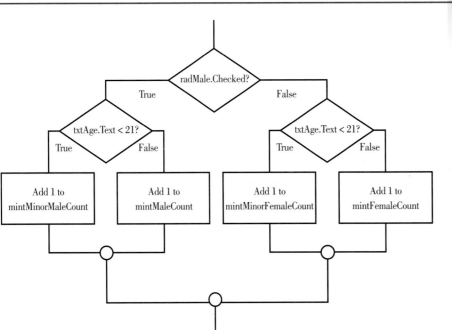

```
If radMale.Checked = True Then
    If CInt(txtAge.Text) < 21 Then
        mintMinorMaleCount += 1
    Else
        mintMaleCount += 1
    End If
Else
    If CInt(txtAge.Text) < 21 Then
        mintMinorFemaleCount += 1
    Else
        mintFemaleCount += 1
    End If
End If
```

Indentation can help you catch errors. Visual Basic always matches an Else with the last unmatched If, regardless of the indentation. ∎

Assume that `intFrogs = 10`, `intToads = 5`, and `intPolliwogs = 6`.
What will be displayed for each of the following statements?

1.
```
If intFrogs > intPolliwogs Then
    radFrogs.Checked = True
    radToads.Checked = False
Else
    radFrogs.Checked = False
    radToads.Checked = True
End If
```
2.
```
If intFrogs > intToads + intPolliwogs Then
    lblResult.Text = "It's the frogs"
Else
    lblResult.Text = "It's the toads and the polliwogs"
End If
```
3.
```
If intPolliwogs > intToads And intFrogs <> 0 Or intToads = 0 Then
    lblResult.Text = "It's true"
Else
    lblResult.Text = "It's false"
End If
```
4. Write the statements necessary to compare the numbers in txt-Apples.Text and txtOranges.Text. Display in lblMost.Text which has more, the apples or the oranges.
5. Write the Basic statements that will test the current value of decBalance. When decBalance is greater than zero, the check box for Funds Available called chkFunds should be selected, the decBalance set back to zero, and intCounter incremented by one. When decBalance is zero or less, chkFunds should not be selected (do not change the value of decBalance or increment the counter).

Using If Statements with Radio Buttons and Check Boxes

In Chapter 2 you used the Checkchanged event for radio buttons and check boxes to carry out the desired action. Now that you can use `If` statements, you should not take action in the Checkchanged events for these controls. Instead, use `If` statements to determine which options are selected.

To conform to good programming practice and make your programs consistent with standard Windows applications, place your code in the Click event of buttons, such as an OK button or an Apply button. For example, refer to the Visual Studio *Tools/Options* dialog box (Figure 4.7); no action will occur when you click on a radio button or check box. Instead, when you click on the OK button, VS checks to see which options are selected.

Figure 4.7

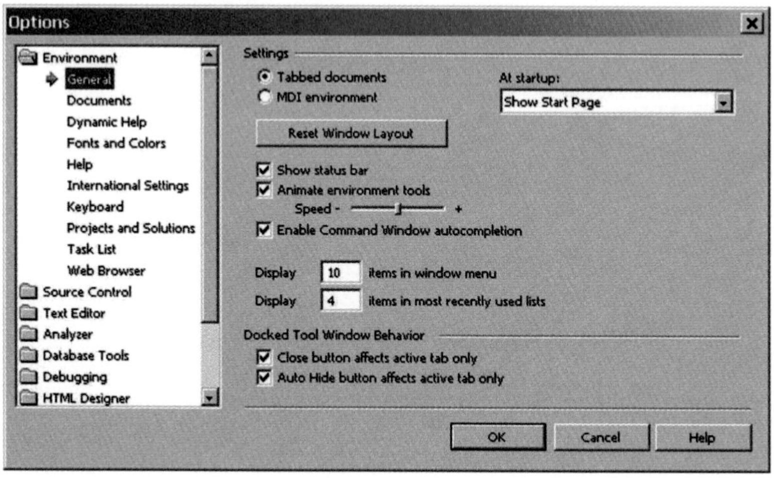

The Options dialog box. When the user clicks OK, the program checks the state of all radio buttons and check boxes.

In an application such as the message formatter project in Chapter 2 (refer to Figure 2.18), you could modify the code for the Display button to include code similar to the following:

```
If radBlue.Checked = True Then
    lblName.BackColor = Color.Blue
ElseIf radGreen.Checked = True Then
    lblName.BackColor = Color.Green
Else
    lblName.BackColor = Color.Black
End If

If chkFastShip.Checked = True Then
    decTotal += decFastShipRate
End If

If chkGiftWrap.Checked = True Then
    decTotal += decWrap
End If
```

A "Simple Sample"

Test your understanding of the use of the If statement by coding some short examples.

Test the Value of a Check Box

Create a small project that contains a check box, a label, and a button. Name the button btnTest, the check box chkTest, and the label lblMessage. In the Click event for btnTest, check the value of the check box. If the check box is currently checked, display "Check box is checked" in lblMessage.

• Test the Checked property of radio buttons and check boxes.

```
Private Sub btnTest_Click(ByVal sender As System.Object, ByVal e As System.EventArgs) _
  Handles btnTest.Click

    'Test the value of the check box

    If chkTest.Checked = True Then
        lblMessage.Text = "Check box is checked"
    End If
```

Test your project. When it works, add an `Else` to the code that displays "Check box is not checked".

Test the State of Radio Buttons

Remove the check box from the previous project and replace it with two radio buttons, named radFreshman and radSophomore and labeled "< 30 units" and ">= 30 units". Now change the `If` statement to display "Freshman" or "Sophomore" in the label.

```
If radFreshman.Checked = True Then
    lblMessage.Text = "Freshman"
Else
    lblMessage.Text = "Sophomore"
End If
```

Can you modify the sample to work for Freshman, Sophomore, Junior, and Senior? In the sections that follow, you will see code for testing multiple radio buttons and check boxes.

Checking the State of a Radio Button Group

Nested `If` statements work very well for determining which button of a radio button group is selected. Recall that in any group of radio buttons, only one button can be selected. Assume that your form has a group of radio buttons for Freshman, Sophomore, Junior, or Senior. In a calculation procedure, you want to add 1 to one of four counter variables, depending on which radio button is selected.

```
If radFreshman.Checked = True Then
    mintFreshmanCount += 1
ElseIf radSophomore.Checked = True Then
    mintSophomoreCount += 1
ElseIf radJunior.Checked = True Then
    mintJuniorCount += 1
ElseIf radSenior.Checked = True Then
    mintSeniorCount += 1
End If
```

Note that in most situations the final condition is unnecessary. You should be able to add to radSenior if the first three conditions are false. You might prefer to code the condition to make the statement more clear, or if no radio button is set initially, or if the program sets all radio buttons to False.

Checking the State of Multiple Check Boxes

Although nested `If` statements work very well for groups of radio buttons, the same is not true for a series of check boxes. Recall that if you have a series of check boxes, any number of the boxes may be selected. In this situation assume that you have check boxes for Discount, Taxable, and Delivery. You will need separate `If` statements for each condition.

```
If chkDiscount.Checked = True Then
    'Calculate the discount
End If
If chkTaxable.Checked = True Then
    'Calculate the tax
End If
If chkDelivery.Checked = True Then
    'Deliver it
End If
```

Enhancing Message Boxes

In Chapter 3 you learned to display a message box to the user. Now it's time to add such features as controlling the format of the message, displaying multiple buttons, checking which button the user clicks, and performing alternate actions depending on the user selection.

Displaying the Message String

The message string you display in a message box may be a string literal enclosed in quotes or it may be a string variable. You may also want to concatenate several items, for example, combining a literal with a value from a variable. It's usually a good idea to create a variable for the message and format the message before calling the `Show` method; if nothing else, it makes your code easier to read and follow.

✅**TIP**

Specify only the message for a "quick and dirty" message box for debugging purposes. It will display an OK button and an empty title bar:
`MessageBox.Show("I'm here.")` ■

Combining Values into a Message String

You can concatenate a literal such as "Total Sales: " with the value from a variable. You may need to include an extra space inside the literal to make sure that the value is separated from the literal.

```
Dim strMessage As String

strMessage = "Total Sales: " & CStr(mdecTotalSales)
MessageBox.Show(strMessage, "Sales Summary", MessageBoxButtons.OK)
```

This example does not format the number. To remedy this condition, consider formatting the number when you concatenate it to the string.

```
Dim strMessage As String

strMessage = "Total Sales: " & FormatDecimal(mdecTotalSales)
MessageBox.Show(strMessage, "Sales Summary", MessageBoxButtons.OK)
```

Creating Multiple Lines of Output

If your message is too long for one line, VB wraps it to a second line. But if you would like to control the line length and position of the split, you can insert a **NewLine character** into the string message. Use the Visual Studio constant `ControlChars.NewLine` to determine line endings. You can concatenate this constant into a message string to set up multiple lines.

In this example a second line is added to the MessageBox from the previous example.

• Replace vbCrLf with ControlChars. NewLine. Other ControlChars constants: Cr, CrLf, Tab, FormFeed, VerticalTab.

```
Dim strFormattedTotal    As String
Dim strFormattedAvg      As String
Dim strMessage           As String

strFormattedTotal = FormatDecimal(mdecTotalSales)
strFormattedAvg = FormatNumber(mdecAverageSale)
strMessage = "Total Sales: " & strFormattedTotal & ControlChars.NewLine & _
  "Average Sale: " & strFormattedAvg
MessageBox.Show(strMessage, "Sales Summary", MessageBoxButtons.OK)
```

You can even combine multiple NewLine constants to achieve double spacing and create multiple message lines (Figure 4.8).

Figure 4.8

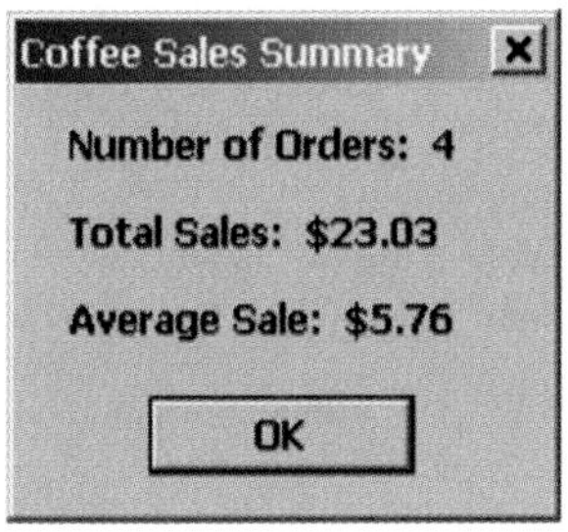

A message box with multiple lines of output, created by concatenating a NewLine character at the end of each line.

```
'Concatenate the message string
strMessageString = "Number of Orders: " & CStr(mintCustomerCount) _
    & ControlChars.NewLine & ControlChars.NewLine _
    & "Total Sales: " & FormatCurrency(mdecGrandTotal) _
    & ControlChars.NewLine & ControlChars.NewLine _
    & "Average Sale: " & FormatCurrency(decAverage)
'Display the message box
MessageBox.Show(strMessageString, "Coffee Sales Summary", MessageBoxButtons.OK)
```

Using the ControlChars Constants

You can use several other constants from the ControlChars list, in addition to the NewLine constant. Type "ControlChars" and a period into the editor to see the complete list.

ControlChar Constant	Description
CrLf	Carriage return/linefeed character combination
Cr	Carriage return
Lf	Line feed
NewLine	New line character; same effect as a carriage return/line feed character combination
NullChar	Character with a value of zero
Tab	Tab character
Back	Backspace character
FormFeed	Formfeed character (not useful in Microsoft Windows)
VerticalTab	VerticalTab character (not useful in Microsoft Windows)
Quote	Quotation mark character

Displaying Multiple Buttons

You can choose the buttons to display on the message box using the Message-BoxButtons constants (Figure 4.9). Figure 4.10 shows a MessageBox with two buttons using the `MessageBoxButtons.YesNo` constant. The `Show` method returns a **DialogResult object** that you can check to see which button the user clicked.

- In the MessageBox class, use the MessageBoxButtons constants to choose the buttons. Ex: `Message-BoxButtons.YesNo` rather than vbYesNo.

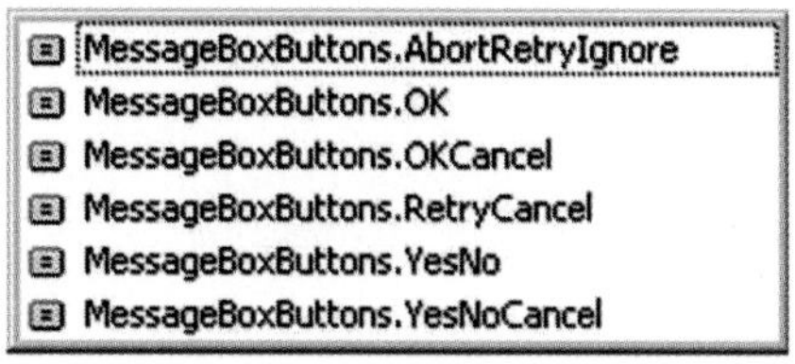

Figure 4.9

Choose the button(s) to display from the MessageBoxButtons constants.

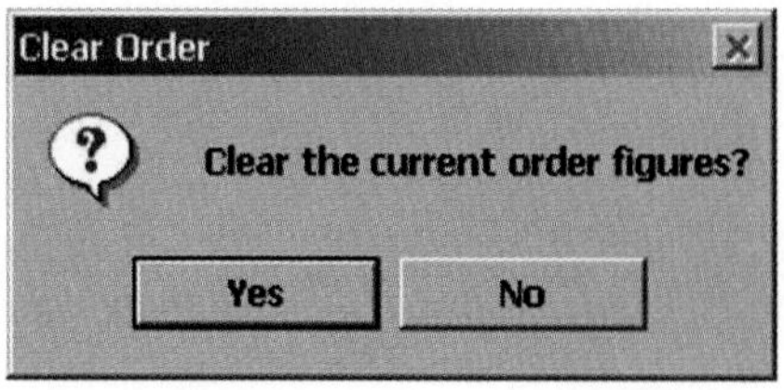

Figure 4.10

Display Yes and No buttons on a message box using `MessageBoxButtons.YesNo`.

Determining the Return Type of a Method

How do you know that the Show method returns an object of the DialogResult class? An easy way is to click in the word Show and press F1; Help will open to the correct page and show all of the possible argument lists along with the return type (Figure 4.11). Or, another easy way is to point to the Show keyword and pause; the argument list that you are using pops up (Figure 4.12).

- The MessageBox.Show method returns an object of the Dialog Result class. This is the first time students have declared an object of a different class.
- Compare the result of the MessageBox.Show method to the DialogResult constants: DialogResult.Yes, DialogResult.No, etc. Use these in place of vbYes, vbNo.

Figure 4.11

Click on the keyword Show *and press F1 to pop up the* Show *method's Help page. All possible argument lists appear along with the method's return type.*

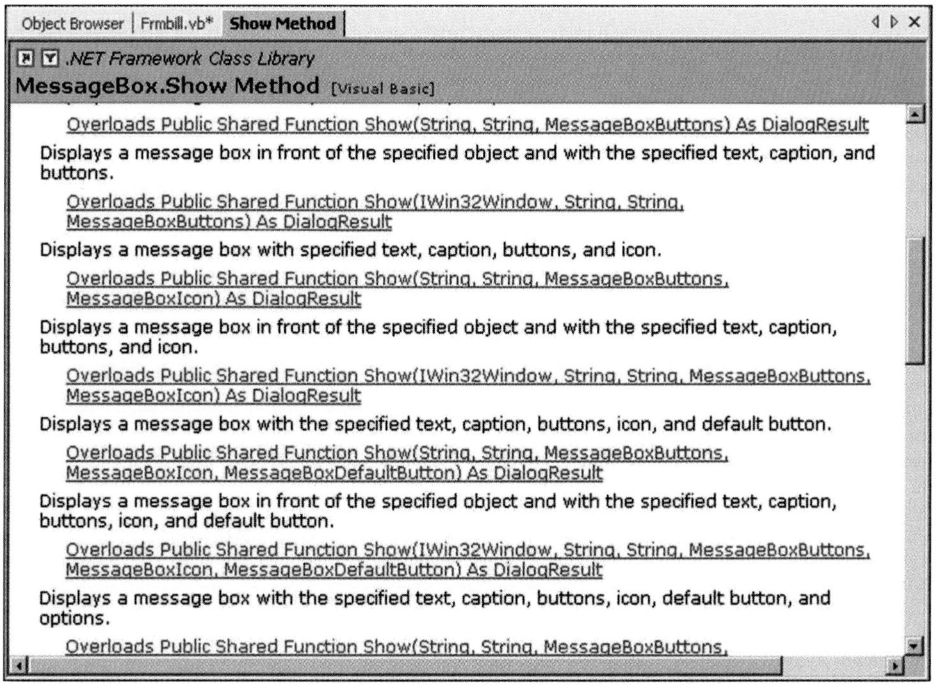
Object Browser | Frmbill.vb* | Show Method
.NET Framework Class Library
MessageBox.Show Method [Visual Basic]
Overloads Public Shared Function Show(String, String, MessageBoxButtons) As DialogResult
Displays a message box in front of the specified object and with the specified text, caption, and buttons.
Overloads Public Shared Function Show(IWin32Window, String, String, MessageBoxButtons) As DialogResult
Displays a message box with specified text, caption, buttons, and icon.
Overloads Public Shared Function Show(String, String, MessageBoxButtons, MessageBoxIcon) As DialogResult
Displays a message box in front of the specified object and with the specified text, caption, buttons, and icon.
Overloads Public Shared Function Show(IWin32Window, String, String, MessageBoxButtons, MessageBoxIcon) As DialogResult
Displays a message box with the specified text, caption, buttons, icon, and default button.
Overloads Public Shared Function Show(String, String, MessageBoxButtons, MessageBoxIcon, MessageBoxDefaultButton) As DialogResult
Displays a message box in front of the specified object and with the specified text, caption, buttons, icon, and default button.
Overloads Public Shared Function Show(IWin32Window, String, String, MessageBoxButtons, MessageBoxIcon, MessageBoxDefaultButton) As DialogResult
Displays a message box with the specified text, caption, buttons, icon, default button, and options.
Overloads Public Shared Function Show(String, String, MessageBoxButtons,

Figure 4.12

Pause the mouse pointer over the Show *keyword and IntelliSense pops up with the argument list you are using. It also shows the method's return type.*

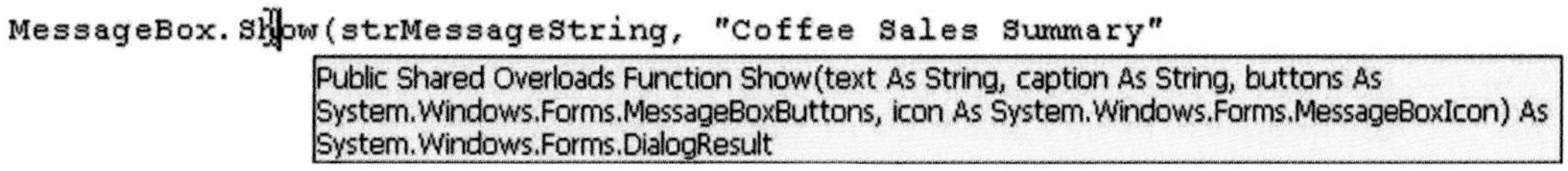
MessageBox.Show(strMessageString, "Coffee Sales Summary"
Public Shared Overloads Function Show(text As String, caption As String, buttons As System.Windows.Forms.MessageBoxButtons, icon As System.Windows.Forms.MessageBoxIcon) As System.Windows.Forms.DialogResult

Declaring an Object Variable for the Method Return

To capture the information about the outcome of the Show method, you must declare a variable that can hold an instance of the DialogResult type.

```
Dim dgrResult As DialogResult
```

Then you assign the return value of the Show method to the new variable.

```
dgrResult = MessageBox.Show("Clear the current order figures?", "Clear Order", _
    MessageBoxButtons.YesNo, MessageBoxIcon.Question)
```

The next step is to check the value of the return, comparing to the DialogResult constants, such as Yes, No, OK, Retry, Abort, and Cancel.

```
If dgrResult = DialogResult.Yes Then
    'Code to clear the order
End If
```

Specifying a Default Button and Options

Two additional signatures for the MessageBox.Show method are as follows:

```
MessageBox.Show(TextMessage, TitlebarText, MessageBoxButtons, MessageBoxIcons, _
    MessageBoxDefaultButton)
MessageBox.Show(TextMessage, TitlebarText, MessageBoxButtons, MessageBoxIcons, _
    MessageBoxDefaultButton, MessageBoxOptions)
```

When you display multiple buttons, you may want one of the buttons to be the default. For example, to make the second button (the No button) the default, use this statement:

```
dgrResult = MessageBox.Show("Clear the current order figures?", "Clear Order", _
    MessageBoxButtons.YesNo, MessageBoxIcon.Question, MessageBoxDefaultButton.Button2)
```

You can right-align the message in the message box by setting the MessageBoxOptions argument:

```
dgrResult = MessageBox.Show("Clear the current order figures?", "Clear Order", _
    MessageBoxButtons.YesNo, MessageBoxIcon.Question, MessageBoxDefaultButton.Button2, _
    MessageBoxOptions.RightAlign)
```

Input Validation

Careful programmers check the values entered into text boxes before beginning the calculations. Validation is a form of self-protection; it is better to reject bad data than to spend hours (and sometimes days) trying to find an error only to discover that the problem was caused by a "user error." Finding and correcting the error early can often keep the program from producing erroneous results or halting with a run-time error.

Checking to verify that appropriate values have been entered for a text box is called *validation.* The validation may include making sure that data is numeric, checking for specific values, checking a range of values, or making sure that required items are entered.

Checking for Numeric Values

You learned in Chapter 3 to use `Try/Catch` blocks to trap user errors. You also can make sure that input is truly numeric before attempting to convert it by using Visual Basic's `IsNumeric` **function.** The `IsNumeric` function returns True or False to indicate the result of the value checking.

• The `IsNumeric` function returns True for values that would fail in VB 6. Any value that can be successfully parsed using the conversion functions, such as `CInt` and `CDec`, will pass the `IsNumeric` test. Ex: "$1,234.56" returns True.

The IsNumeric Function—General Form

General Form

```
IsNumeric(expression)
```

The `IsNumeric` function tests whether the value is numeric and therefore can be used in a calculation. If numeric, the result will be True; if not, the result is False. This function can help avoid problems in procedures that contain calculations and also can help you to determine which input field is bad and display more helpful error messages to the user.

The `IsNumeric` function returns True for any value that can be converted correctly with the conversion functions, such as `CInt` and `CDec`. For example, `IsNumeric("$1,234.56")` returns True, since `CInt` and `CDec` can parse the value to a number. An empty string returns False; recall from Chapter 3 that the conversion functions throw an exception for a blank argument.

The IsNumeric Function—Example

Example

```
If IsNumeric(txtQuantity.Text) Then
    intQuantity = CInt(txtQuantity.Text)
    lblDue.Text = CStr(decPrice * intQuantity)
Else
    MessageBox.Show("Enter a numeric value for Quantity", "Invalid Data", _
    MessageBoxButtons.OK)
End If
```

Checking for a Range of Values

Data validation may also include checking the reasonableness of a value. Assume you are using a text box to input the number of hours worked in a day. Even with overtime, the company does not allow more than 10 work hours in a single day. You could check the input for reasonableness with this code:

```
If CInt(txtHours.Text) > 10 Then
    MessageBox.Show("Too many hours", "Invalid Data", MessageBoxButtons.OK)
End If
```

Checking for a Required Field

Sometimes you need to be certain that a value has been entered into a text box before proceeding. You can compare a text box value to an empty string literal.

```
If txtName.Text <> "" Then
      'Do Something
Else
    MessageBox.Show("Required Entry", "Sales Summary", MessageBoxButtons.OK)
End If
```

By checking separately for blank or nonnumeric data, you can display a better message to the user. Make sure to check for blanks first, since a blank field will also test nonnumeric. For example, if you reverse the order of the two If statements in the following example, blanks in txtQuantity will always produce the nonnumeric message.

```
If txtQuantity.Text <> "" Then            'Not blank
    If IsNumeric(txtQuantity.Text) Then    'Is numeric
        'Good Data - perform calculation
    Else                                   'Nonnumeric data
        strMessage = "Nonnumeric data entered for quantity."
        MessageBox.Show(strMessage, "Data Entry Error")
    End If
Else                                       'Missing data
    strMessage = "Enter the quantity."
    MessageBox.Show(strMessage, "Data entry error")
End If
```

Performing Multiple Validations

When you need to validate several input fields, how many message boxes do you want to display for the user? Assume that the user has neglected to fill in five text boxes and clicked on Calculate. You can avoid displaying five message boxes in a row by using a nested If statement. This way, you check the second value only if the first one passes, and you can exit the processing if a problem is found with a single field.

```
If txtName.Text <> "" Then
    If IsNumeric(txtUnits.Text) Then
        If radFreshman.Checked = True Or radSophomore. Checked = True _
            Or radJunior.Checked = True Or radSenior. Checked = True Then

            'Data valid -- Do calculations or processing here

        Else
            MessageBox.Show ("Please select a Grade Level.", "Data Entry Error", _
                MessageBoxButtons.OK)
        End If
    Else
        MessageBox.Show ("Enter number of units.", "Data Entry Error", _
          MessageBoxButtons.OK)
        txtUnits.Focus()
    End If
Else
    MessageBox.Show ("Please enter a name", "Data Entry Error", MessageBoxButtons.OK)
    txtName.Focus()
End If
```

Calling Event Procedures

If you wish to perform a set of instructions in more than one location, you don't have to duplicate the code. Write the instructions once in an event procedure, and "call" the procedure from another procedure. When you **call** an event procedure, the entire procedure is executed, and then execution returns to the statement following the call.

- Calling another procedure requires parentheses to indicate that it is a procedure.

- Event procedures require two arguments. We have elected to just pass the same two arguments as were passed to the calling procedure.

The Call Statement—General Form

General Form

```
[Call] ProcedureName()
```

Notice that the keyword `Call` is optional and rarely used. You must include the parentheses; if the procedure that you are calling requires arguments, then place the arguments within the parentheses, otherwise leave them empty.

The Call Statement—Examples

Examples

```
Call btnClear_Click(sender, e)
btnClear_Click(sender, e)          'Equivalent to previous statement
```

Notice the arguments for both of the example `Call` statements. In both cases, you are passing the same two arguments that were passed to the calling procedure. If you examine any of the editor-generated event procedure headers, you can see that every event procedure requires these two arguments, which can be used to track the object that generated the event.

```
Private Sub btnSummary_Click(ByVal sender As System.Object, ByVal e As _
    System.EventArgs) Handles btnSummary.Click

    ...

    btnNewOrder_Click(sender, e)    'Call the btnNewOrder_Click event procedure
```

In the programming example that follows, you will accumulate individual items for one customer. When that customer's order is complete, you need to clear the entire order and begin an order for the next customer. Refer to the interface in Figure 4.13; notice the two buttons: `Clear for Next Item` and `New Order`. The button for the next item clears the text boxes on the screen. The button for a new order must clear the screen text boxes and clear the subtotal fields. Rather than repeat the instructions to clear the individual screen text boxes, we can call the event procedure for btnClear_Click from the btnNewOrder_Click procedure.

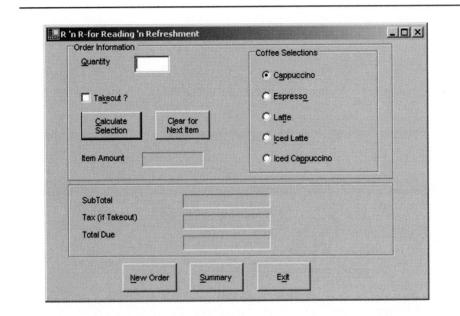

Figure 4.13

A form with buttons that perform overlapping functions. The `New Order` *button must do the same tasks as* `Clear for Next Item`.

```
Private Sub btnNewOrder_Click(ByVal sender As System.Object, ByVal e As _
  System.EventArgs) Handles btnNewOrder.Click
    'Clear the current order and add to totals

    btnClear_Click(sender, e)       'Call the btnClear_Click event procedure
    . . . 'Continue with statements to clear subtotals
```

In the btnNewOrder_Click procedure, all the instructions in btnClear_Click are executed. Then execution returns to the next statement following the call.

Your Hands-On Programming Example

Create a project for R 'n R—for Reading 'n Refreshment that calculates the amount due for individual orders and maintains accumulated totals for a summary. Have a check box for takeout items, which are taxable at 8 percent; all other orders are nontaxable. Include radio buttons for the five coffee selections: Cappuccino, Espresso, Latte, Iced Cappuccino, and Iced Latte. The prices for each will be assigned using these constants:

Cappuccino	2.00
Espresso	2.25
Latte	1.75
Iced (either)	2.50

Use a button for *Calculate Selection*, which will calculate and display the amount due for each item. Display appropriate error messages for missing or nonnumeric data.

A button for *Clear for Next Item* will clear the selections and the amount for the current item and set the focus back to the quantity. The *Clear* button should be disabled when the program begins and be enabled after the user begins an order.

Additional labels in a separate group box will display the summary information for the current order, including subtotal, tax, and total.

Buttons at the bottom of the form will be used for *New Order, Summary,* and *Exit.* The *New Order* button will confirm that the user wants to clear the current order. If the user agrees, clear the current order and add to the summary totals. The *Summary* button should display a message box with the number of orders, the total dollar amount, and the average sale amount per order.

Planning the Project

Sketch a form (Figure 4.14), which your users sign as meeting their needs.

Figure   4.14

The planning sketch of the form for the hands-on programming exercise.

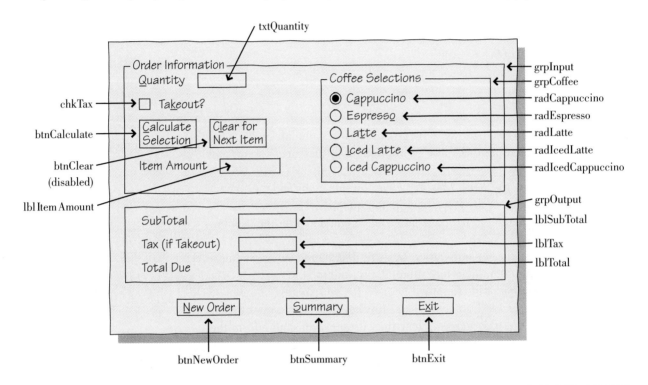

Plan the Objects and Properties

Plan the property settings for the form and each of the controls.

Object	Property	Setting
Form1	Name	frmBilling
	Text	R 'n R--for Reading 'n Refreshment
	AcceptButton	btnCalculate
	CancelButton	btnClear
grpInput	Text	Order Information
grpCoffee	Text	Coffee Selections
grpOutput	Text	(blank)

Continued on page 171

Object	Property	Setting
radCappuccino	Name Text Checked	radCappuccino C&appuccino True
radEspresso	Name Text	radEspresso Espress&o
radLatte	Name Text	radLatte La&tte
radIcedLatte	Name Text	radIcedLatte &Iced Latte
radIcedCappuccino	Name Text	radIcedCappuccino Iced Ca&ppuccino
Label1	Text	&Quantity
txtQuantity	Name Text	txtQuantity (blank)
chkTax	Name Text	chkTax Ta&keout ?
Label2	Text	Item Amount
Label3	Text	SubTotal
Label4	Text	Tax (if Takeout)
Label5	Text	Total Due
lblItemAmount	Name Text BorderStyle	lblItemAmount (blank) Fixed3D
lblSubTotal	Name Text BorderStyle	lblSubTotal (blank) Fixed3D
lblTax	Name Text BorderStyle	lblTax (blank) Fixed3D
lblTotal	Name Text BorderStyle	lblTotal (blank) Fixed3D
btnCalculate	Name Text	btnCalculate &Calculate Selection
btnClear	Name Text Enabled	btnClear C&lear for Next Item False

Continued on page 172

Object	Property	Setting
btnNewOrder	Name	btnNewOrder
	Text	&New Order
btnSummary	Name	btnSummary
	Text	&Summary
btnExit	Name	btnExit
	Text	E&xit

Plan the Event Procedures
You need to plan the actions for five event procedures.

Object	Procedure	Action
btnCalculate	Click	Validate for blank or nonnumeric amount.
		Find price of drink selection.
		Multiply price by quantity.
		Add amount to subtotal.
		Calculate tax if needed.
		Calculate total = subtotal + tax.
		Format and display the values.
		Disable the Takeout check box.
		Enable the Clear button.
btnClear	Click	Clear the coffee selections.
		Clear the quantity and the item price.
		Set the focus to the quantity.
		Disable the Clear button.
btnSummary	Click	If current order not added to totals
		call btnNewOrder_Click.
		Calculate the average.
		Display the summary totals in a message box.
btnNewOrder	Click	Confirm clearing current order.
		Clear the current order.
		Accumulate total sales and count.
		Set subtotal and total due to 0.
		Enable Takeout check box.
		Disable Clear button.
btnExit	Click	Terminate the project.

Write the Project   Follow the sketch in Figure 4.14 to create the form. Figure 4.15 shows the completed form.

- Set the properties of each object as you have planned.

- Write the code. Working from the pseudocode, write each event procedure.

- When you complete the code, use a variety of data to thoroughly test the project. Make sure the tab order is set correctly so that the insertion point begins in txtQuantity.

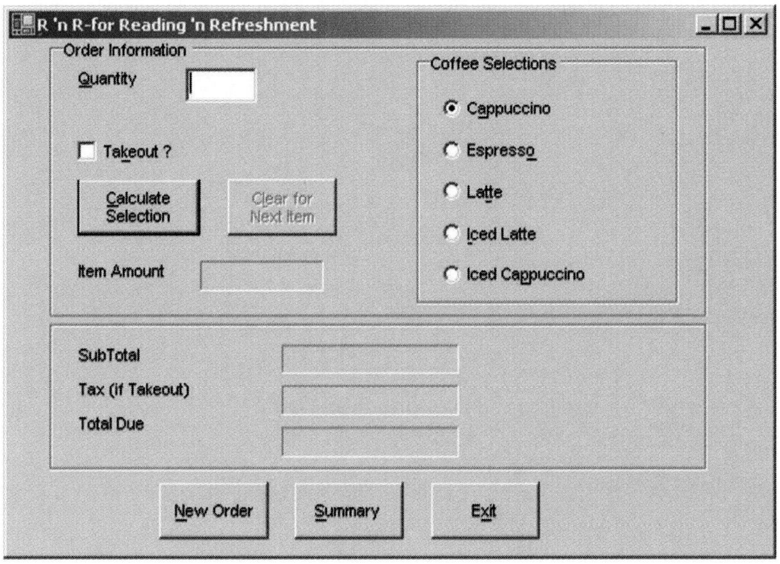

Figure 4.15

The form for the hands-on programming exercise.

The Project Coding Solution

```
'Program Name:    Billing
'Programmer:      Bradley/Millspaugh
'Date:            January 2002
'Description:     This project calculates the amount due
'                 based on the customer selection
'                 and accumulates summary data for the day.
'Folder:          Ch0401

Option Strict On

Public Class frmBilling
    Inherits System.Windows.Forms.Form

[Windows Form Designer generated code]
```

```
Dim mdecSubtotal As Decimal
Dim mdecTotal As Decimal
Dim mdecGrandTotal As Decimal
Dim mintCustomerCount As Integer
Const mdecTAX_RATE As Decimal = 0.08D
Const mdecCAPPUCCINO_PRICE As Decimal = 2D
Const mdecESPRESSO_PRICE As Decimal = 2.25D
Const mdecLATTE_PRICE As Decimal = 1.75D
Const mdecICED_PRICE As Decimal = 2.5D

Private Sub btnCalculate_Click(ByVal sender As System.Object, _
 ByVal e As System.EventArgs) Handles btnCalculate.Click
    'Calculate and display the current amounts, add to totals

    Dim decPrice As Decimal
    Dim intQuantity As Integer
    Dim decTax As Decimal
    Dim decItemAmount As Decimal
    Dim strMessage As String

    'Find the price
    If radCappuccino.Checked Then
        decPrice = mdecCAPPUCCINO_PRICE
    ElseIf radEspresso.Checked Then
        decPrice = mdecESPRESSO_PRICE
    ElseIf radLatte.Checked Then
        decPrice = mdecLATTE_PRICE
    ElseIf radIcedCappuccino.Checked Or radIcedLatte.Checked Then
        decPrice = mdecICED_PRICE
    Else
        MessageBox.Show("Please make a drink selection", "Selection Required", _
        MessageBoxButtons.OK, MessageBoxIcon.Information)
    End If

    'Calculate extended price and add to order total
    If txtQuantity.Text <> "" Then                 'Not blank
        If IsNumeric(txtQuantity.Text) Then        'Is numeric
            'Good Data - perform calculations
            Try
                intQuantity = CInt(txtQuantity.Text)
                decItemAmount = decPrice * intQuantity
                mdecSubtotal += decItemAmount
                If chkTax.Checked Then
                    decTax = mdecSubtotal * mdecTAX_RATE
                Else
                    decTax = 0
                End If
                mdecTotal = mdecSubtotal + decTax
                lblItemAmount.Text = FormatCurrency(decItemAmount)
                lblSubTotal.Text = FormatNumber(mdecSubtotal)
                lblTax.Text = FormatNumber(decTax)
                lblTotal.Text = FormatCurrency(mdecTotal)
                chkTax.Enabled = False             'Allow change for new order only
                btnClear.Enabled = True            'Allow Clear after an order is begun
            Catch
                strMessage = "Calculation error."
                MessageBox.Show(strMessage, "Error", _
                MessageBoxButtons.OK, MessageBoxIcon.Error)
            End Try
```

```
            Else            'Nonnumeric data
                strMessage = "Nonnumeric data entered for quantity."
                MessageBox.Show(strMessage, "Data Entry Error", _
                 MessageBoxButtons.OK, MessageBoxIcon.Information)
                txtQuantity.Focus()
            End If
        Else        'Missing data
            strMessage = "Enter the quantity."
            MessageBox.Show(strMessage, "Data entry error", _
             MessageBoxButtons.OK, MessageBoxIcon.Information)
            txtQuantity.Focus()
        End If
End Sub

Private Sub btnClear_Click(ByVal sender As System.Object, _
 ByVal e As System.EventArgs) Handles btnClear.Click
    'Clear appropriate controls

    radCappuccino.Checked = True
    radEspresso.Checked = False
    radLatte.Checked = False
    radIcedLatte.Checked = False
    radIcedCappuccino.Checked = False
    lblItemAmount.Text = ""
    With txtQuantity
        .Clear()
        .Focus()
    End With
End Sub

Private Sub btnExit_Click(ByVal sender As System.Object, _
 ByVal e As System.EventArgs) Handles btnExit.Click
    'Terminate the project

    Me.Close()
End Sub

Private Sub btnNewOrder_Click(ByVal sender As System.Object, _
 ByVal e As System.EventArgs) Handles btnNewOrder.Click
    'Clear the current order and add to totals

    Dim dgrResult As DialogResult
    Dim strMessage As String

    'Confirm clear of current order
    strMessage = "Clear the current order figures?"
    dgrResult = MessageBox.Show(strMessage, "Clear Order", _
     MessageBoxButtons.YesNo, MessageBoxIcon.Question, _
     MessageBoxDefaultButton.Button2)
    If dgrResult = DialogResult.Yes Then          'User said Yes
        btnClear_Click(sender, e)                 'Clear the screen fields
        lblSubTotal.Text = ""
        lblTax.Text = ""
        lblTotal.Text = ""

        Try
            'Add to Totals
            If mdecSubtotal <> 0 Then 'Should not be able to add to counts if no
                                      'new order/customer. Prevents accidental clicking.
```

```vb
                        mdecGrandTotal += mdecTotal
                        mintCustomerCount += 1
                        mdecSubtotal = 0
                        mdecTotal = 0     'Reset for next customer
                    End If
                Catch
                    strMessage = "Error in calculations."
                    MessageBox.Show(strMessage, "Error", MessageBoxButtons.OK, _
                      MessageBoxIcon.Error)
                End Try

                'Clear appropriate display items and enable check box
                With chkTax
                    .Enabled = True
                    .Checked = False
                End With
                btnClear.Enabled = False
            End If
        End Sub

        Private Sub btnSummary_Click(ByVal sender As System.Object, _
          ByVal e As System.EventArgs) Handles btnSummary.Click
            'Calculate the average and display the totals

            Dim decAverage As Decimal
            Dim strMessageString As String
            Dim strFormattedAvg As String

            If mdecTotal <> 0 Then
                'Make sure last order is counted
                btnNewOrder_Click(sender, e)
            End If

            If mintCustomerCount > 0 Then
                Try
                    'Calculate average
                    decAverage = mdecGrandTotal / mintCustomerCount

                    'Concatenate the message string
                    strMessageString = "Number of Orders: " & CStr(mintCustomerCount) _
                      & ControlChars.NewLine & ControlChars.NewLine _
                      & "Total Sales: " & FormatCurrency(mdecGrandTotal) _
                      & ControlChars.NewLine & ControlChars.NewLine _
                      & "Average Sale: " & FormatCurrency(decAverage)
                    MessageBox.Show(strMessageString, "Coffee Sales Summary", _
                      MessageBoxButtons.OK, MessageBoxIcon.Information)
                Catch
                    strMessageString = "Error in calculations."
                    MessageBox.Show(strMessageString, "Error", MessageBoxButtons.OK, _
                      MessageBoxIcon.Error)
                End Try
            Else
                strMessageString = "No sales data to summarize."
                MessageBox.Show(strMessageString, "Coffee Sales Summary", _
                  MessageBoxButtons.OK, MessageBoxIcon.Information)
            End If
        End Sub
    End Class
```

Debugging Visual Basic Projects

One of the advantages of programming in the Visual Studio environment is the availability of debugging tools. You can use these tools to help find and eliminate logic and run-time errors. The debugging tools can also help you to follow the logic of existing projects to better understand how they work.

Sometimes it's helpful to know the result of a condition, the value of a variable or property, or the sequence of execution of your program. You can follow program logic in Break mode by single-stepping through code; you also can get information about execution without breaking the program run, using the WriteLine method of the Debug class.

In the following sections you will learn to use many of the debugging tools on the Debug toolbar (Figure 4.16) and the *Debug* menu (Figure 4.17). Note that the Debug toolbar appears automatically when you choose the Start command; you can also make the toolbar display full-time by right-clicking on any toolbar and choosing *Debug* from the pop-up menu.

- You cannot make corrections to code and continue running as in VB 6. Code must be recompiled for the changes to take effect.

- You won't want to use the Immediate window, which is now Immediate mode in the Command window. It isn't available in Design time and has lost its usefulness for beginning programmers.

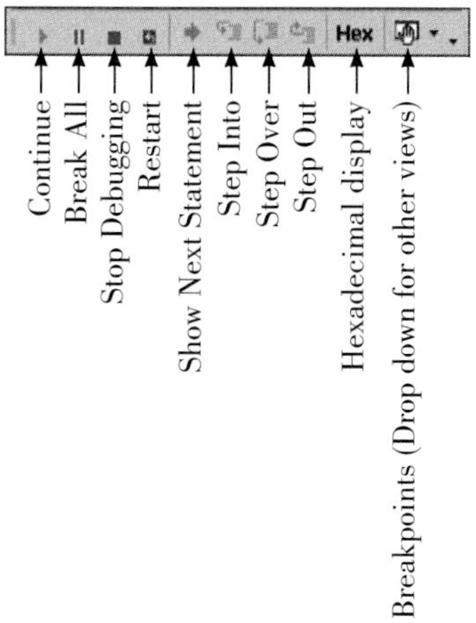

The labels pointing to the toolbar items read:
Continue
Break All
Stop Debugging
Restart
Show Next Statement
Step Into
Step Over
Step Out
Hexadecimal display
Breakpoints (Drop down for other views)

Figure 4.16

The Debug toolbar with its tools for debugging programs.

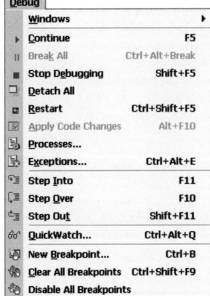

Writing to the Output Window

You can place a `Debug.WriteLine` **method** in your code. In the argument you can specify a message to write or an object that you want tracked.

• `Debug.WriteLine`, writes to the Output window. You can clear the Output window with *Right-click/Clear All.*

The Debug.WriteLine Method—General Form

```
Debug.WriteLine(TextString)
Debug.WriteLine(Object)
```

The `Debug.WriteLine` method is overloaded, so that you can pass it a string argument or the name of an object.

The Debug.WriteLine Method—Examples

```
Debug.WriteLine("btnCalculate procedure entered.")
Debug.WriteLine(txtQuantity)
```

When the `Debug.WriteLine` method executes, its output appears in the Output window. Figure 4.18 shows the output of the two example statements above. Notice the second line of output, for txtQuantity—the class of the object displays along with its current contents.

You may find it useful to place `WriteLine` methods in `If` statements, so that you can see which branch the logic followed.

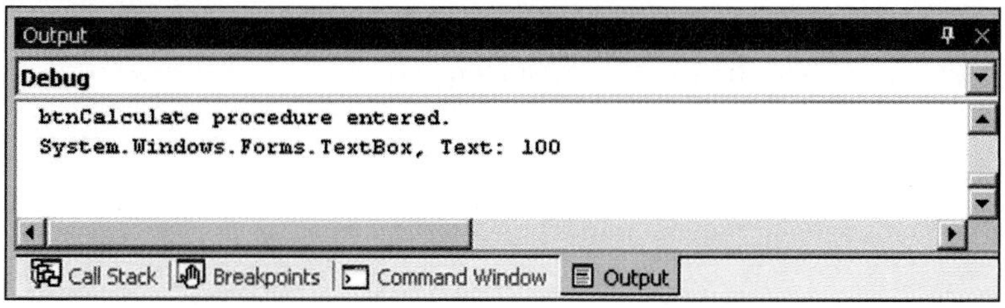

Figure 4.18

The Output window shows the output of the Debug.WriteLine method.

```
If intCount > 10 Then
    Debug.WriteLine("Count is greater than 10.")
    'Other processing
Else
    Debug.WriteLine("Count is not greater than 10.")
    'Other processing
End If
```

An advantage of using `WriteLine`, rather than the other debugging techniques that follow, is that you do not have to break program execution.

Clearing the Output Window

New to the VS IDE, you can clear the Output window. Right-click in the window and choose *Clear All*.

Pausing Execution with the Break Button

You can click on the Break button to pause execution. This step places the project into break time at the current line. However, you will generally prefer to break in the middle of a procedure. To choose the location of the break, you can force a break with a breakpoint.

• Setting breakpoints from the menu is more complicated. It's best to click in the editor's gray margin to set and clear breakpoints.

Forcing a Break

During the debugging process, often you want to stop at a particular location in code and watch what happens (e.g., which branch of an `If...Then...Else`; which procedures were executed; the value of a variable just before or just after a calculation). You can force the project to break by inserting a **breakpoint** in code.

```
If IsNumeric(txtQuantity.Text) Then
    lblDue.Text = CStr(decPrice * CDec(txtQuantity.Text))
Else
    MessageBox.Show("Please Enter a Numeric Value", "Error", MessageBoxButtons.OK)
End If
```

To set a breakpoint, place the mouse pointer in the gray margin indicator area at the left edge of the Editor window and click; the line will be highlighted in red and a large red dot will display in the margin indicator (Figure 4.19).

After setting a breakpoint, start execution. When the project reaches the breakpoint, it will halt, display the line, and go into break time.

You can remove a breakpoint by clicking again in the gray margin area, or clear all breakpoints from the *Debug* menu.

F i g u r e   4 . 1 9

A program statement with a breakpoint set appears highlighted, and a dot appears in the gray margin indicator area.

```
Booksale.vb*  Booksale.vb [Design]*                              ◀
Form1                                       ▼    btnCalculate_Click

    ●       If IsNumeric(txtQuantity.Text) Then
                lblExtendedPrice.Text = CStr(decPrice * CDec(txtQuantity.Text))
            Else
                MessageBox.Show("Please Enter a Numeric Value", "Error", MessageBoxButtons.OK)
            End If
```

Checking the Current Values of Expressions

You can quickly check the current value of an expression, such as a variable, a control, a condition, or an arithmetic expression. During break time, display the Editor window and point to the name of the expression that you want to view; a small label will pop up, similar to a ToolTip, which displays the current contents of the expression. If you want to view the contents of an expression of more than one word, such as a condition or arithmetic expression, highlight the entire expression and then point to the highlighted area; the current value will display.

The steps for viewing the contents of a variable during run time are as follows:

1. Break the execution using a breakpoint.
2. If the code does not appear in the editor, click on the editor's tab in the Document window.
3. Point to the variable or expression you wish to view.

The current contents of the expression will pop up in a label (Figure 4.20).

- The Debug toolbar appears when running a program in debug mode. You will find the Break and Stop buttons on the Debug toolbar, rather than the standard toolbar.

- The ToolTips that pop up with current values are somewhat more confusing because of the extra capabilities, such as displaying the class of objects and the definition of functions.

F i g u r e   4 . 2 0

Point to a variable name in code, and its current value displays.

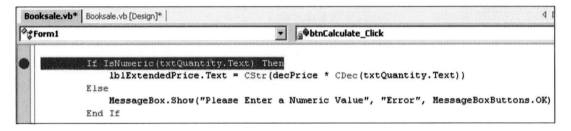

```
            'Calculate summary values
    ⇨       mintQuantitySum += intQuantity
            mdecDiscountSum += decDisc intQuantity = 10
            mdecDiscountedPriceSum += decDiscountedPrice
            mintSaleCount += 1
            decAverageDiscount = mdecDiscountSum / mintSaleCount
```

Stepping through Code

The best way to debug a project is to thoroughly understand what the project is doing every step of the way. Previously, this task was performed by following each line of code manually to understand its effect. You can now use the Visual Studio stepping tools to trace program execution line by line and see the progression of the program as it executes through your code.

You step through code at break time. You can use one of the techniques already mentioned to break execution or choose one of the stepping commands at design time; the program will begin running and immediately transfer to break time.

The three stepping commands on the *Debug* menu are *Step Into, Step Over,* and *Step Out.* You can also use the toolbar buttons for stepping or the keyboard shortcuts shown on the menu (refer to Figure 4.17).

These commands force the project to execute a single line at a time and to display the Editor window with the current statement highlighted. As you execute the project by pressing a command button, for example, the Click event occurs. Execution transfers to the Click event procedure, the Editor window for that procedure appears on the screen, and you can follow line-by-line execution.

Step Into

Most likely you will use the **Step Into** command more than the other two stepping commands. When you choose Step Into (from the menu, the toolbar button, or F11), the next line of code executes and the program pauses again in break time. If the line of code is a call to another procedure, the first line of code of the other procedure displays.

• The keyboard shortcut for Step Into is F11.

To continue stepping through your program execution, continue choosing the Step Into command. When a procedure is completed, your form will display again, awaiting an event. You can click on one of the form's buttons to continue stepping through code in an event procedure. If you want to continue execution without stepping, choose the Continue command (from the menu, the toolbar button, or F5).

Step Over

The **Step Over** command also executes one line of code at a time. The difference between Step Over and Step Into occurs when your code has calls to other procedures. Step Over displays only the lines of code in the current procedure being analyzed; it does not display lines of code in the called procedures.

You can choose *Step Over* from the menu, from the toolbar button, or by pressing F10. Each time you choose the command, one more program statement executes.

Step Out

You use the third stepping command when you are stepping through a called procedure. The **Step Out** command continues rapid execution until the called procedure completes, and then returns to break mode at the statement following the Call.

Continuing Program Execution

When you have seen what you want to see, continue rapid execution by pressing F5 or choosing Continue from the Debug toolbar or the *Debug* menu. If you want to restart execution from the beginning, choose the Restart command.

Stopping Execution

Once you have located a problem in the program's code, usually you want to stop execution, correct the error, and run again. Stop execution by selecting *Stop Debugging* from the *Debug* menu or the toolbar button, or press the keyboard shortcut: Shift + F5.

The Locals Window

Sometimes you may find that the **Locals window** displays just the information that you want (Figure 4.21). The Locals window displays all objects and variables that are within scope at break time. That means that if you break execution in the btnCalculate_Click event procedure, all variables local to that procedure display. You can also expand the Me entry to see the state of the form's controls.

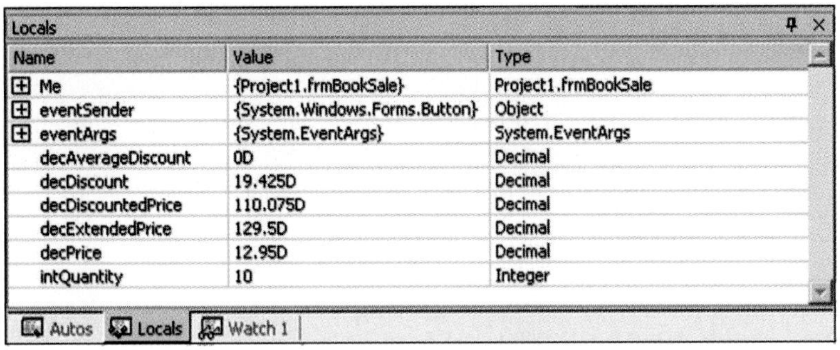

Figure 4.21

The Locals window shows the values of the local variables that are within scope of the current statement.

Locals			
Name	Value	Type	
⊞ Me	{Project1.frmBookSale}	Project1.frmBookSale	
⊞ eventSender	{System.Windows.Forms.Button}	Object	
⊞ eventArgs	{System.EventArgs}	System.EventArgs	
decAverageDiscount	0D	Decimal	
decDiscount	19.425D	Decimal	
decDiscountedPrice	110.075D	Decimal	
decExtendedPrice	129.5D	Decimal	
decPrice	12.95D	Decimal	
intQuantity	10	Integer	

Autos Locals Watch 1

The Autos Window

Another helpful debugging window is the Autos window. The **Autos window** "automatically" displays all variables and control contents that are referenced in the current statement and three statements on either side of the current one (Figure 4.22). Note that the highlighted line is about to execute next; the "current" statement is the one just before the highlighted one.

You can view the Autos window when your program stops at a breakpoint. Click on the Autos window tab (Figure 4.21) or open it from the *View* menu.

- The Autos window can be very useful to display the contents of variables and properties. Try it; you'll like it.

To use any of the debugging windows you must be in Break mode. ▪

Figure 4.22

The Autos window automatically adjusts to show the variables and properties that appear in the previous few lines and the next few lines.

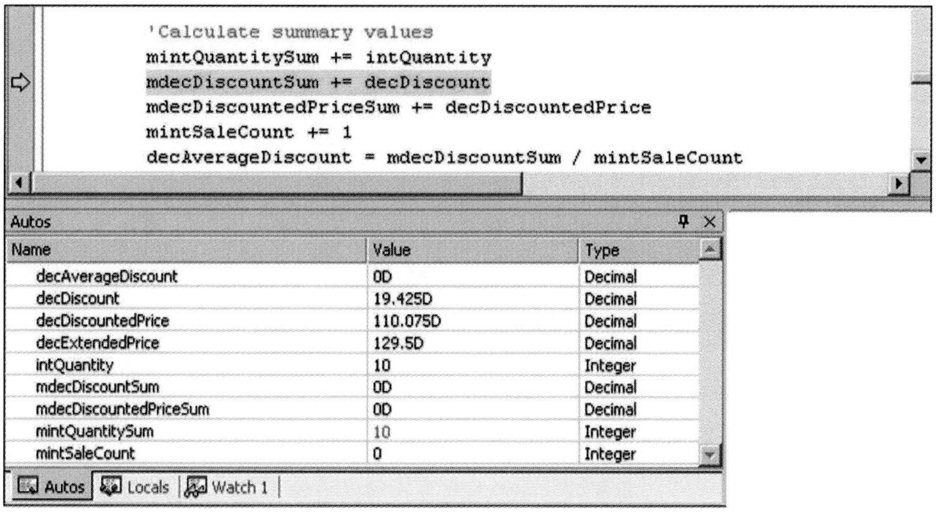

```
        'Calculate summary values
        mintQuantitySum += intQuantity
⇨       mdecDiscountSum += decDiscount
        mdecDiscountedPriceSum += decDiscountedPrice
        mintSaleCount += 1
        decAverageDiscount = mdecDiscountSum / mintSaleCount
```

Autos   ⊈ ✕

Name	Value	Type
decAverageDiscount	0D	Decimal
decDiscount	19.425D	Decimal
decDiscountedPrice	110.075D	Decimal
decExtendedPrice	129.5D	Decimal
intQuantity	10	Integer
mdecDiscountSum	0D	Decimal
mdecDiscountedPriceSum	0D	Decimal
mintQuantitySum	10	Integer
mintSaleCount	0	Integer

Autos | Locals | Watch 1

Debugging Step-by-Step Tutorial

In this exercise you will learn to set a breakpoint; pause program execution; single-step through program instructions; display the current values in properties, variables, and conditions; and debug a Visual Basic project.

Test the Project

STEP 1: Open the debugging project on your student diskette. The project is found in the Ch04Debug folder.

STEP 2: Run the program.

STEP 3: Enter color Blue, quantity 100, and press Enter or click on the Calculate button.

STEP 4: Enter another color Blue, quantity 50, and press Enter. Are the totals correct?

STEP 5: Enter color Red, quantity 30, and press Enter.

STEP 6: Enter color Red, quantity 10, and press Enter. Are the totals correct?

STEP 7: Enter color White, quantity 50, and press Enter.

STEP 8: Enter color White, quantity 100, and press Enter. Are the totals correct?

STEP 9: Exit the project. You are going to locate and correct the errors in the red and white totals.

Break and Step Program Execution

STEP 1: Display the program code. Scroll to locate this line, which is the first calculation line in the btnCalculate_Click event procedure:

```
decQuantity = CDec(txtQuantity.Text)
```

STEP 2: Click in the gray margin indicator area to set a breakpoint on the selected line. Your screen should look like Figure 4.23.

A program statement with a breakpoint set appears highlighted, and a dot appears in the gray margin indicator area.

```
Object Browser   Form1.vb [Design]   Form1.vb                          ◁ ▷ ✕
Form1                            ▼   btnCalculate_Click                      ▼
        Dim mdecBlueTotal As Decimal
        Dim mdecRedTotal As Decimal
        Dim mdecWhiteTotal As Decimal

        Private Sub btnCalculate_Click(ByVal sender As System.Object,
            'Calculate summary

            Dim decQuantity As Decimal
            Dim decTotal As Decimal

            'Convert input to numeric
●           decQuantity = CDec(txtQuantity.Text)

            'Add to correct total
            If radBlue.Checked Then
                mdecBlueTotal = mdecBlueTotal + decQuantity
            ElseIf radRed.Checked Then
                mdecRedTotal = decQuantity
            Else
                mdecWhiteTotal = mdecWhiteTotals + decQuantity
            End If
```

STEP 3: Run the project, enter Red, quantity 30, and press Enter. The project will transfer control to the btnCalculate_Click procedure, stop when the breakpoint is reached, highlight the current line, and enter break time (Figure 4.24).

Note: The highlighted line has not yet executed.

When a breakpoint is reached during project execution, Visual Basic enters break time, displays the Editor window, and the highlights the breakpoint line.

```
Form1                                          ▼   btnCalculate_C
        Dim mdecBlueTotal As Decimal
        Dim mdecRedTotal As Decimal
        Dim mdecWhiteTotal As Decimal

        Private Sub btnCalculate_Click(ByVal sender As System.Object,
            'Calculate summary

            Dim decQuantity As Decimal
            Dim decTotal As Decimal

            'Convert input to numeric
⇨           decQuantity = CDec(txtQuantity.Text)

            'Add to correct total
            If radBlue.Checked Then
                mdecBlueTotal = mdecBlueTotal + decQuantity
            ElseIf radRed.Checked Then
```

STEP 4: Press the F11 key, which causes VB to execute the current program statement (the assignment statement). (F11 is the keyboard shortcut for *Debug/Step Into*.) The statement is executed, and the highlight moves to the next statement (the If statement).

STEP 5: Press F11 again; the condition (radBlue.Checked) is tested and found to be False.

STEP 6: Continue pressing F11 a few more times and watch the order in which program statements execute.

View the Contents of Properties, Variables, and Conditions

STEP 1: Scroll up if necessary and point to the .Text portion of txtQuantity.Text in the breakpoint line; the contents of the Text property pops up (Figure 4.25). Note that if you instead point to the object name (txtQuantity), the class of the selected object pops up (txtQuantity = {System.Windows.Forms.TextBox}).

Point to a property reference in code, and the current content pops up.

```
'Convert input to numeric
decQuantity = CDec(txtQuantity.Text)
                              txtQuantity.Text = "30"
'Add to correct total
If radBlue.Checked Then
    mdecBlueTotal = mdecBlueTotal + decQuantity
ElseIf radRed.Checked Then
    mdecRedTotal = decQuantity
Else
    mdecWhiteTotal = mdecWhiteTotals + decQuantity
End If
```

STEP 2: Point to decQuantity and view the contents of that variable. Notice that the Text property is enclosed in quotes and the numeric variable is not. The 30D means 30 Decimal.

STEP 3: Point to radBlue.Checked in the If statement, taking care to point to the property name, not the object name. Then point to radRed.Checked. You can see the Boolean value for each of the radio buttons.

STEP 4: Point to mdecRedTotal to see the current value of that total variable. This value looks correct, since you just entered 30, which was added to the total.

Continue Program Execution

STEP 1: Press F5, the keyboard shortcut for the Continue command. The Continue command continues execution. If the current line is any line other than End Sub, execution continues and your form reappears. If the current line is End Sub, you may have to click on your project's Taskbar button to make the form reappear.

STEP 2: Enter color Red and quantity 10. When you press Enter, program execution will again break at the breakpoint.

The 10 you just entered should be added to the 30 previously entered for Red, producing 40 in the Red total.

Use the Step Into button on the Debug toolbar to step through execution. Keep pressing Step Into until the 10 is added to mdecRedTotal. Display the current contents of the total. Can you see what the problem is? *Hint:* mdecRedTotal has only the current amount, not the sum of the two amounts. The answer will appear a little later; try to find it yourself first.

You will fix this error soon, after testing the White total.

Test the White Total

STEP 1: Press F5 to continue execution. If the form does not reappear, click the project's Taskbar button.

STEP 2: Enter color White, quantity 100, and press Enter.

STEP 3: When execution halts at the breakpoint, press F5 to continue. This returns to rapid execution until the next breakpoint is reached.

STEP 4: Enter color White, quantity 50, and press Enter.

STEP 5: Press F11 several times when execution halts at the breakpoint until you execute the line that adds the 50 to the White total. Remember that the highlighted line has not yet executed; press Step Into one more time, if necessary, to execute the addition statement.

STEP 6: Point to each variable name to see the current values (Figure 4.26). Can you see the problem?

Figure 4.26

Point to the variable name in code and its current value displays as 50 Decimal.

```
'Add to correct total
If radBlue.Checked Then
    mdecBlueTotal = mdecBlueTotal + decQuantity
ElseIf radRed.Checked Then
    mdecRedTotal = decQuantity
Else
    mdecWhiteTotal = mdecWhiteTotals + decQuantity
End If    [mdecWhiteTotal = 50D]
```

STEP 7: Display the Autos window by clicking on its tab. Here you can see the current value of all properties and variables referred to by the previous two statements and the following three statements (Figure 4.27).

STEP 8: Identify all the errors. When you are ready to make the corrections, continue to the next step.

Figure 4.27

```
    End If

    'Format totals in labels
    lblTotalBlue.Text = FormatNumber(mdecBlueTotal, 0)
    lblTotalRed.Text = FormatNumber(mdecRedTotal, 0)
    lblTotalWhite.Text = FormatNumber(mdecWhiteTotal, 0)
```

Autos			
Name	Value	Type
decQuantity	50D	Decimal
lblTotalBlue.Text	"0"	String
lblTotalRed.Text	"10"	String
mdecBlueTotal	0D	Decimal
mdecRedTotal	10D	Decimal
mdecWhiteTotal	50D	Decimal
mdecWhiteTotals	Nothing	Object
radWhite.Checked	True	Boolean

Autos | Locals | Watch 1

The Autos window displays the current contents of variables and properties in the statements before and after the current statement.

Correct the Red Total Error

STEP 1: Stop program execution by clicking on the Stop Debugging toolbar button (Figure 4.28).

Figure 4.28

Object Browser | Form1.vb [Design]
Stop Debugging (Shift+F5)

Click on the Stop Debugging button on the Debug toolbar to halt program execution.

STEP 2: Locate this line:

```
mdecRedTotal = decQuantity
```

This statement replaces the value of mdecRedTotal with decQuantity rather than adding to the total.

STEP 3: Change the line to read:

```
mdecRedTotal += decQuantity
```

(*or* `mdecRedTotal = mdecRedTotal + decQuantity` *if you prefer.*)

> ✓TIP
>
> **D**isplay keyboard shortcuts on ToolTips, as in Figure 4.28, by selecting *Tools/Customize/Options/Other/Show shortcut keys in ScreenTips.* ■

Correct the White Total Error

STEP 1: Locate this line:

```
mdecWhiteTotal = mdecWhiteTotals + decQuantity
```

Have you found the problem with this line? Look carefully at the spelling of the variable names. The compiler would find this error if Option Explicit were turned on. Unfortunately, someone turned it off, which means that VB will allow you to use variables without first declaring them.

STEP 2: Scroll up to the top of the code and find this statement (just below the comments in the Declarations section).

```
Option Explicit Off
```

STEP 3: Change the statement to read

```
Option Explicit On
```

Note: Option Explicit defaults to the setting in Project Properties. If the option is turned on in Project Properties, you can just remove this line, if you prefer.

STEP 4: Run the project again. This time the compiler identifies the error in the variable name. Click No to the Continue question. The error appears in the Task List (Figure 4.29).

Display the Task List to view the error. Double-click on the error line to jump to that error in code.

```
Task List - 1 Build Error task shown (filtered)
!   ☑  Description
        Click here to add a new task
! ⬙     Name 'mdecWhiteTotals' is not declared.

☑ Task List | ▤ Output | 🎯 Find Symbol Results | 🔖 Index Results
```

STEP 5: Double-click on the error line in the Task List; the error line in code is highlighted.

STEP 6: Remove the *s* from mdecWhiteTotals. The line should read:

```
mdecWhiteTotal = mdecWhiteTotal + decQuantity
```

Or you can change it to read

```
mdecWhiteTotal += decQuantity
```

STEP 7: Press F5 to start program execution. Enter color White and 100 and press Enter.

STEP 8: Press F5 to continue when the project halts at the breakpoint.

STEP 9: Enter White, 50, and Enter.

STEP 10: At the breakpoint, clear the breakpoint by clicking on the red margin dot for the line.

STEP 11: Press F5 to continue and check the total on the form. It should now be correct.

STEP 12: Test the totals for all three colors carefully and then click Exit.

Force a Run-Time Error

STEP 1: Select *Clear All Breakpoints* from the *Debug* menu if the menu item is available. The item is available only when there are breakpoints set in the program.

STEP 2: Run the project. This time click the Calculate button without entering a quantity.

A run-time error will occur (Figure 4.30).

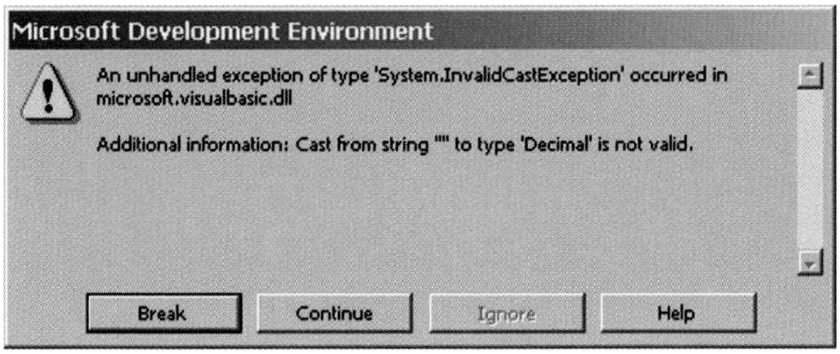

Figure 4.30

The missing data causes an exception and run-time error. Click on the Break button to correct the problem.

Microsoft Development Environment

⚠ An unhandled exception of type 'System.InvalidCastException' occurred in microsoft.visualbasic.dll

Additional information: Cast from string "" to type 'Decimal' is not valid.

| Break | Continue | Ignore | Help |

STEP 3: Click *Break* on the error dialog box, and the Editor window will display with the offending line highlighted in green (Figure 4.31). You can click on the tab for the Output window to see more description of the error.

You can click Stop Debugging or Continue, if you wish. Either will cancel execution.

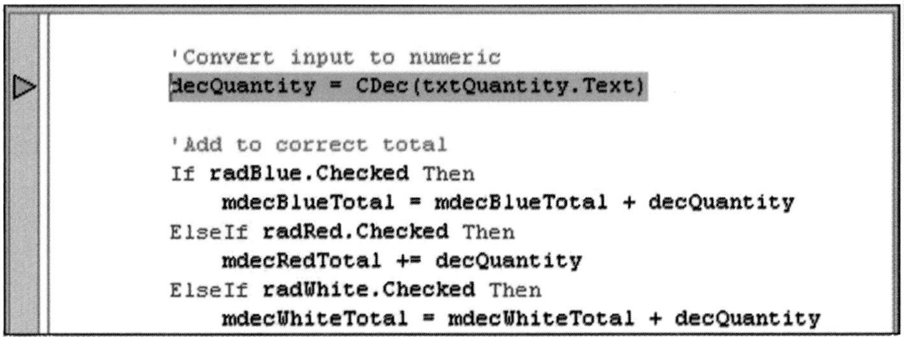

Figure 4.31

For a run-time error, the offending line is highlighted in green and the Output window shows a description of the error.

```
'Convert input to numeric
decQuantity = CDec(txtQuantity.Text)

'Add to correct total
If radBlue.Checked Then
    mdecBlueTotal = mdecBlueTotal + decQuantity
ElseIf radRed.Checked Then
    mdecRedTotal += decQuantity
ElseIf radWhite.Checked Then
    mdecWhiteTotal = mdecWhiteTotal + decQuantity
```

Summary

1. Visual Basic uses the If...Then...Else statement to make decisions. An Else clause is optional and specifies the action to be taken if the condition is false. An If...Then...Else statement must conclude with an End If.
2. Flowcharts can help visualize the logic of an If...Then...Else statement.
3. The conditions for an If statement are evaluated for True or False.
4. Conditions can be composed of the relational operators, which compare items for equality, greater than, or less than. The comparison of numeric

values is based on the quantity of the number, while string comparisons are based on the ANSI code table.

5. The `ToUpper` and `ToLower` methods of the String class can convert a text value to upper- or lowercase.

6. The `And` and `Or` logical operators may be used to combine multiple conditions. With the `And` operator, both conditions must be true for the entire condition to evaluate True. For the `Or` operator, if either or both conditions are true, the entire condition evaluates as True. When both `And` and `Or` are used in a condition, the `And` condition is evaluated before the `Or` condition.

7. A nested `If` statement contains an `If` statement within either the true or false actions of a previous `If` statement. Nesting an `If` statement inside of another requires the use of the `End If` clause. An `Else` clause always applies to the last unmatched `If` regardless of indentation.

8. The state of radio buttons and check boxes should be tested with `If` statements in the event procedure for a button, rather than coding event procedures for the radio button or check box.

9. The `MessageBox.Show` method can display a multiple-line message if you concatenate a NewLine character to determine a line break.

10. You can choose to display multiple buttons on a message box. The `MessageBox.Show` method returns an object of the DialogResult class, which you can check using the DialogResult constants.

11. Data validation checks the reasonableness or appropriateness of the value in a variable or property. Because an error will occur if the data placed in a text box are not numeric, a popular validation tool is the `IsNumeric` function.

12. One procedure can call another procedure.

13. A variety of debugging tools are available in Visual Basic. These include writing to the Output window, breaking program execution, displaying the current contents of variables, and stepping through code.

K e y   T e r m s

Review Questions

1. What is the general format of the statement used to code decisions in an application?
2. What is a condition?
3. Explain the purpose of relational operators and logical operators.
4. Differentiate between a comparison performed on numeric data and a comparison performed on string data.
5. How does Visual Basic compare the Text property of a text box?
6. Why would it be useful to include the ToUpper method in a comparison?
7. Name the types of items that can be used in a comparison.
8. Explain a Boolean variable test for True and False. Give an example.
9. Give an example of a situation where nested Ifs would be appropriate.
10. Define the term *validation*. When is it appropriate to do validation?
11. Define the term *checking a range*.
12. Explain the difference between Step Into and Step Over.
13. What steps are necessary to view the current contents of a variable during program execution?

Programming Exercises

4.1 Lynette Rifle owns an image consulting shop. Her clients can select from the following services at the specified regular prices: Makeover $125, Hair Styling $60, Manicure $35, and Permanent Makeup $200. She has distributed discount coupons that advertise discounts of 10 percent and 20 percent off the regular price. Create a project that will allow the receptionist to select a discount rate of 10 percent, 20 percent, or none, and then select a service. Display the price for the individual service in a label and have another label to display the total due after each visit is completed. A visit may include several services. Include command buttons for *Calculate, Clear,* and *Exit*.

4.2 Modify Programming Exercise 4.1 to allow for sales to additional patrons. Include buttons for *Next Patron* and *Summary*. When the receptionist clicks the *Summary* button, display the number of clients and the total dollar value for all services rendered in a summary message box. For *Next Patron*, confirm that the user wants to clear the totals for the current customer.

4.3 Create a project to compute your checking account balance.
Form: Include radio buttons to indicate the type of transaction: deposit, check, or service charge. A text box will allow the user to enter the amount of the transaction. Display the new balance in a label. Calculate the balance by adding deposits and subtracting service charges and checks. Include buttons for *Calculate, Clear,* and *Exit*.

4.4 Add validation to Programming Exercise 4.3. Display a message box if the new balance would be a negative number. If there is not enough money to cover a check, do not deduct the check amount. Instead, display a message box with the message "Insufficient Funds" and deduct a service charge of $10.

4.5 Modify Programming Exercise 4.3 or 4.4 by adding a *Summary* command button that will display the total number of deposits, the total dollar amount of deposits, the number of checks, and the dollar amount of the checks. Do not include checks that were returned for insufficient funds, but do include the service charges. Use a message box to display the Summary information.

4.6   Piecework workers are paid by the piece. Workers who produce a greater quantity of output are often paid at a higher rate.

Form: Use text boxes to obtain the person's name and the number of pieces completed. Include a *Calculate* button to display the dollar amount earned. You will need a *Summary* button to display the total number of pieces, the total pay, and the average pay per person. A *Clear* button should clear the name and the number of pieces for the current employee and a *Clear All* button should clear the summary totals after confirming the operation with the user.

Include validation to check for missing data. If the user clicks on the *Calculate* button without first entering a name and the number of pieces, display a message box. Also, you need to make sure to not display a summary before any data are entered; you cannot calculate an average when no items have been calculated. You can check the number of employees in the *Summary* event procedure or disable the *Summary* button until the first order has been calculated.

Pieces completed	Price paid per piece for all pieces
1–199	.50
200–399	.55
400–599	.60
600 or more	.65

4.7   Modify Programming Exercise 2.3 (the weather report) to treat radio buttons the proper way. Do not have an event procedure for each radio button; instead use an *OK* button to display the correct image and message.

Note: For help in basing a new project on an existing project, see "Copy and Move a Windows Project" in Appendix C.

4.8   Modify Programming Exercise 2.2 (the flag viewer) to treat radio buttons and check boxes in the proper way. Include a *Display* button and check the settings of the radio buttons and check boxes in the button's event procedure, rather than code event procedures for each radio button and check box.

Note: For help in basing a new project on an existing project, see "Copy and Move a Windows Project" in Appendix C.

Case Studies

Calculate the amount due for an order. For an order, the user should enter the following information into text boxes: customer name, address, city, state (two-letter abbreviation), and ZIP code. An order may consist of multiple items. For each item, the user will enter the product description, quantity, weight, and price into text boxes.

You will need buttons for *Next Item, Update Summary,* and *Exit.*

For the *Next Item* button, validate the quantity, weight, and price. Each must be present and numeric. For any bad data, display a message box. Calculate the charge for the current item and add the charge and weight into the appropriate totals. Do not calculate shipping and handling on individual items; rather, calculate shipping and handling on the entire order.

When the *Update Summary* button is clicked, calculate the sales tax, shipping and handling, and the total amount due for the order. Sales tax is 8 percent of the total charge and is charged only for shipments to a California address. Do not charge sales tax on the shipping and handling charges.

The shipping and handling charges depend on the weight of the products. Calculate the shipping charge as $0.25 per pound and add that amount to the handling charge (taken from the following table).

Weight	Handling
Less than 10 pounds	$1.00
10 to 100 pounds	$3.00
Over 100 pounds	$5.00

Display the entire amount of the bill in labels titled Dollar amount due, Sales tax, Shipping and handling, and Total amount due.

Test data

Description	Quantity	Weight	Price
Planter	2	3	19.95
Mailbox	1	2	24.95
Planter	2	3	19.95

Test data output for taxable

Dollar amount due	$104.75
Sales tax	8.38
Shipping and handling	6.50
Total amount due	119.63

Test data output for nontaxable

Dollar amount due	$104.75
Sales tax	0.00
Shipping and handling	6.50
Total amount due	111.25

VB Auto Center

Create a project that determines the total amount due for the purchase of a vehicle. Include text boxes for the base price and the trade-in allowance. Check boxes will indicate if the buyer wants additional accessories, such as a stereo system, leather interior, and/or computer navigation. A group box for the exterior finish will contain radio buttons for Standard, Pearlized, or Customized detailing.

Have the trade-in allowance default to zero; that is, if the user does not enter a trade-in value, use zero in your calculation. Validate the values from the text boxes, displaying a message box if necessary.

To calculate, add the price of selected accessories and finish to the base price. Calculate the sales tax on the calculated price and display the result in a *Subtotal* label. Then subtract any trade-in value from the total and display the result in an *Amount Due* label.

Include buttons for `Calculate`, `Clear`, and `Exit`. The `Calculate` button must display the total amount due after trade-in.

Item	Price
Stereo System	425.76
Leather Interior	987.41
Computer Navigation	1,741.23
Standard	No additional charge
Pearlized	345.72
Customized Detailing	599.99
Tax Rate	8%

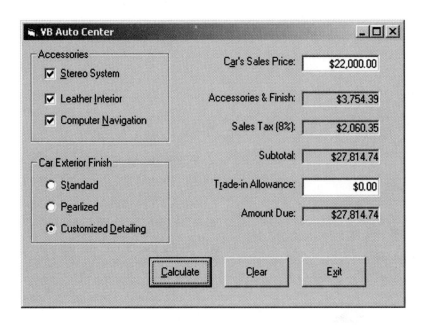

Video Bonanza

Design and code a project to calculate the amount due for rentals. Movies may be in VCR (videotape) format or DVD format. Videotapes rent for $1.80 each and DVDs rent for $2.50. New releases are $3 for DVD and $2 for videotape.

On the form include a text box to input the movie title and radio buttons to indicate whether the movie is in DVD or VCR format. Use one check box to indicate whether the person is a member; members receive a 10 percent discount. Another check box indicates a new release.

Use buttons for *Calculate, Clear for Next Item, Order Complete, Summary,* and *Exit.* The Calculate button should display the item amount and add to the subtotal. The *Clear for Next Item* clears the checkbox for new releases, the movie title, and the radio buttons; the member check box cannot be changed until the current order is complete. Include validation to check for missing data. If the user clicks on the *Calculate* button without first entering the movie title and selecting the movie format, display a message box.

For the *Order Complete* button, first confirm the operation with the user, and clear the controls on the form for a new customer.

The *Summary* button displays the number of customers and the sum of the rental amounts in a message box. Make sure to add to the customer count and rental sum for each customer order.

Very Very Boards

Very Very Boards does a big business in shirts, especially for groups and teams. They need a project that will calculate the price for individual orders, as well as a summary for all orders.

The store employee will enter the orders in an order form that has text boxes for customer name and order number. To specify the shirts, use a text box for the quantity, radio buttons to select the size (small, medium, large, extra large, and XXL), and check boxes to specify a monogram and/or a pocket. Display the shirt price for the current order and the order total in labels.

Include buttons to add a shirt to an order, clear the current item, complete the order, and display the summary of all orders. Do not allow the summary to display if the current order is not complete. Also, disable the text boxes for customer name and order number after an order is started; enable them again when the user clicks on the button to begin a new order. Confirm the operation before clearing the current order.

When the user adds shirts to an order, validate the quantity, which must be numeric and greater than zero. If the data does not pass the validation, do not perform any calculations but display a message box and allow the user to correct the value. Determine the price of the shirts from the radio buttons and check boxes for the monogram and pockets. Multiply the quantity by the price to determine the price, and add to the order total and summary total. Use constants for the shirt prices.

Prices for the shirts	
Small, medium, and large:	$10
Extra large	11
XXL	12
Monogram	Add $ 2
Pocket	Add $ 1

Display the order summary in a message box. Include the number of shirts, the number of orders, and the dollar total of the orders.

CHAPTER

5

Menus, Sub Procedures, and Functions

at the completion of this chapter, you will be able to . . .

1. Create menus and submenus for program control.

2. Display and use the Windows common dialog boxes.

3. Write reusable code in sub procedures and function procedures and call the procedures from other locations.

Menus

You have undoubtedly used menus quite extensively while working with the computer. **Menus** consist of a menu bar containing menus, each of which drops down to display a list of menu items. You can use menu items in place of or in addition to buttons to activate a procedure.

Menu items are actually controls; they have properties and events. Each menu item has a Name property, a Text property, and a Click event, similar to a button. When the user selects a menu item, either with the mouse or the keyboard, the menu item's Click event procedure executes.

It is easy to create menus for a Windows form using the Visual Studio environment's **Menu Designer**. Your menus will look like and behave like standard Windows menus.

Defining Menus

The Visual Studio Menu Designer allows you to add menus and menu items to your forms. You must add a MainMenu control from the toolbox (Figure 5.1), which appears in the component tray below the form. Once you have added the MainMenu control, it is extremely easy to create the menu items for your menu bar. The words *Type Here* appear at the top of the form, so that you can enter the text for your first menu (Figure 5.2). After you type the text for the first menu name, the words *Type Here* appear both below the menu name and to the right

- The all-new Menu Designer replaces the Menu Editor.

- To add menus, you add a MainMenu control to a form; the control goes in the component tray.

- To reactivate the Menu Designer, click again on the menu at the top of the form.

Figure 5.1

Add a MainMenu control to the form using the MainMenu tool from the toolbox.

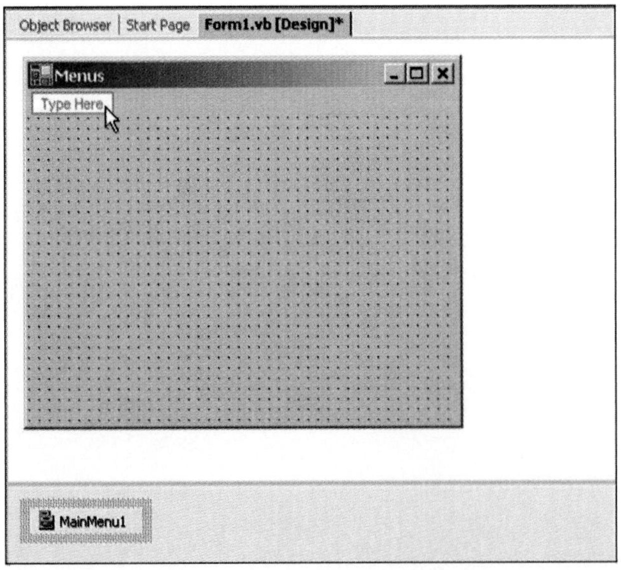

Figure 5.2

The MainMenu control appears in the component tray below the form and the Menu Designer allows you to begin typing the text for the menu items.

of the menu name. You can choose next to enter menu items for the first menu or to type the words for the second menu (Figure 5.3).

Figure 5.3

After typing the text for the first menu, you can add a second menu or add menu items below the menu name.

Note: If you click elsewhere on the form, you deactivate the Menu Designer. You can click on the menu at the top of the form to activate the Menu Designer again.

The Text Property

When you type the words for a menu or menu item, you are entering the Text property for a MenuItem object. The Text property holds the words that you want to appear on the screen (just like the Text property of a label or button). To conform to Windows standards, your first menu's Text property should be File, with a keyboard access key. Use the ampersand (&) in the text to specify the key to use for keyboard access, as you learned to do in Chapter 2. For example, for File, the Text property should be &File.

You can enter and change the Text property for each of your menu items using the Menu Designer. You can also change the Text property using the Properties window (Figure 5.4).

TIP

Do not use the same access key on a main menu name as you use on a form control. However, access keys on submenus do not conflict with menu or control access keys. ■

Figure 5.4

Modify the Text property of a menu item in the Properties window or the Menu Designer.

The Name

After you create menu items using the Menu Designer, you will find each MenuItem object listed in the Properties window, where you can view or change the properties. The Name property gives the MenuItem a name, similar to naming other controls.

Follow good consistent naming conventions for your menu items. The three-character prefix for a menu name is "mnu". Therefore, the name for the *File* menu should be *mnuFile*. For the items on a menu, use the prefix plus the name of the menu plus the name of the item. (You can abbreviate long names, if you do so consistently and clearly.) The name for the *Print* item on the *File* menu should be *mnuFilePrint*. The *Exit* item should be called *mnuFileExit*, which will trigger the mnuFileExit_Click event when the user selects it.

Submenus

The drop-down list of items below a menu name is called a *menu*. When an item on the menu has another list of items that pops up, the new list is called a **submenu.** A filled triangle to the right of the item indicates that a menu item has a submenu (Figure 5.5). You create a submenu by moving to the right of a menu item and typing the next item's text (Figure 5.6).

Figure 5.5

A filled triangle on a menu item indicates that a submenu will appear.

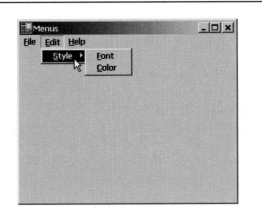

Figure 5.6

Create a submenu by typing to the right of the parent menu item.

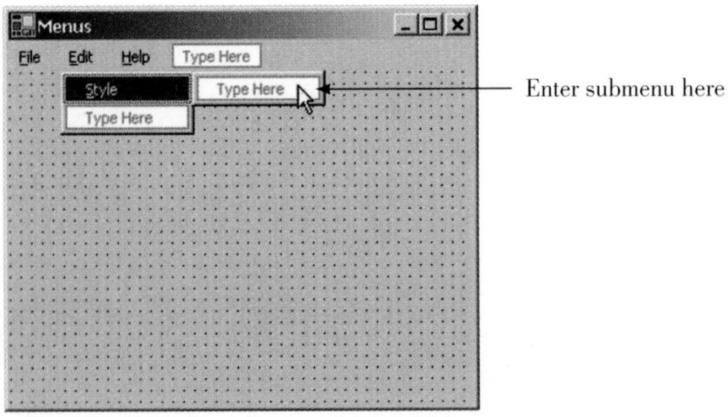

Enter submenu here

Separator Bars

When you have many items in a menu, you should group the items according to their purpose. You can create a **separator bar** in a menu, which draws a bar across the entire menu.

You can choose one of two ways to create a separator bar: 1) Type a single hyphen (-) for the text, or 2) right-click on the Menu Designer where you want the separator bar to appear and choose *Insert Separator* from the context menu. The Menu Designer will create a new MenuItem for the separator bar, which you can see in the Properties window. It isn't necessary to change the Name property of a separator bar control.

• It isn't necessary to create a named menu item for a separator bar.

Creating a Menu—Step-by-Step

You are going to create a project with one form and a menu bar that contains these menu items:

```
File       Help
    Exit       About
```

Create the Menu Items

STEP 1: Begin a new Windows Forms project (or open an existing one to which you want to add a menu).

STEP 2: Add a MainMenu control to the form. You can double-click or drag the tool to the form; the control will appear in the component tray at the bottom of the form (Figure 5.7).

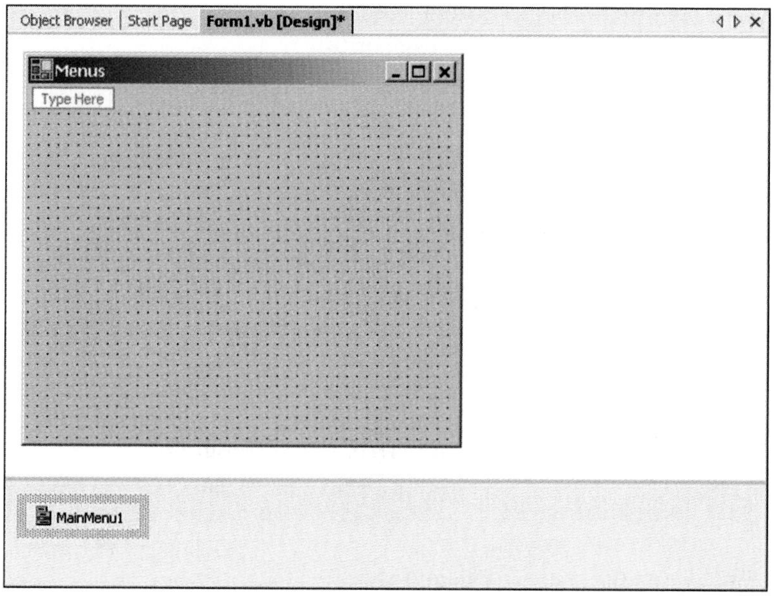

Figure 5.7

Add a MainMenu control to the form. It will appear in the component tray at the bottom of the form.

STEP 3: With the words "Type Here" selected, type "&File" over the words.

STEP 4: Move down to the "Type Here" words below the File menu and type "E&xit".

STEP 5: Move up and to the right and add the Help menu ("&Help").

STEP 6: Below the Help menu, add the About menu item ("&About").

     The menu bar is complete. Now we'll change the Name property of each of the controls.

Change the Properties of the Menu Items

STEP 1: Drop down the Object list in the Properties window (Figure 5.8). You can see a MainMenu object and a series of MenuItem objects.

TIP

Drag and drop a menu item to change the location and sequence of the items. Right-click the Menu Designer to insert an item. ■

Figure 5.8

The MenuItem controls are listed in the Object list of the Properties window.

Properties	🔲 ✕
Form1 System.Windows.Forms.Form	▾
Form1 System.Windows.Forms.Form	
MainMenu1 System.Windows.Forms.MainMenu	
MenuItem1 System.Windows.Forms.MenuItem	
MenuItem2 System.Windows.Forms.MenuItem	
MenuItem3 System.Windows.Forms.MenuItem	
MenuItem4 System.Windows.Forms.MenuItem	
AccessibleName	
AccessibleRole	Default
AllowDrop	False
AutoScale	True
AutoScroll	False
⊞ AutoScrollMargin	0, 0
⊞ AutoScrollMinSize	0, 0
BackColor	▢ Control

STEP 2: In the Properties window, select the MenuItem1 object. This should be the File menu; check the highlighted entry in the Menu Designer to make sure. Then change the Name property to *mnuFile*.

STEP 3: Next you will change the name of the Exit menu item. You can select the menu item on the form to make it appear in the Properties window, or select MenuItem2 in the Object list. Change the Name property to *mnuFileExit*.

STEP 4: Change the name of the Help menu item (MenuItem3) to mnuHelp.

STEP 5: Change the name of the About menu item (MenuItem4) to mnuHelpAbout.

     You also can use the Menu Designer to name your controls. Right-click on the Menu Designer and select the option *Edit Names*. The menu items display the Name properties, which you can change in place. Right-click again to see a check mark next to *Edit Names;* select the option a second time to switch back to displaying only the Text properties.

     Just as you always name buttons before writing the code, you should always name menu items before writing code, so that the event procedures are correctly named.

Coding for Menu Items

After you create your form's menu bar, it appears on the form in design time. Double-click any menu item and the Editor window opens in the control's Click event procedure where you can write the code. For example, in design time, open your form's *File* menu and double-click on *Exit*. The Editor window will open with the mnuFileExit_Click procedure displayed (assuming you have followed the suggested naming conventions and named the Exit item mnuFileExit).

Write the Code

STEP 1: Code the procedure for the Exit by pulling down the menu and double-clicking on the word *Exit*. Type in the remark and the Me.Close statement.

STEP 2: Open the mnuHelpAbout_Click event procedure. Use a Message-Box.Show statement to display the *About* box. The message string should say "Programmed by" followed by your name (Figure 5.9).

STEP 3: Test your menu items.

Figure 5.9

Display a message box for an About box.

Modifying Menu Items

You can use the Menu Designer to modify menu items. To add a new menu and menu items, right-click on the menu bar. Options include *Delete, Insert New, Insert Separator,* and *Edit Names.* The *Edit Names* option displays the names of the menu items instead of the Text properties.

You can also rearrange menu items: Drag and drop an item in its new location.

The Enabled Property

By default, all new menu items have their **Enabled property** set to True. An enabled menu item appears in black text and is available for selection, whereas the grayed out or **disabled** (Enabled = False) items are not available (Figure 5.10). You can set the Enabled property at design time or run time, in code:

```
mnuDisplayInstructions.Enabled = False
```

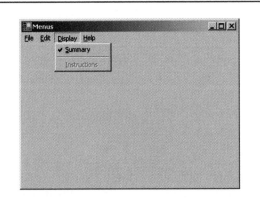

Menu commands can be disabled (grayed) or checked. A check mark usually indicates that the option is currently selected.

The Checked Property

A menu item may contain a check mark beside it, indicating that the item is **checked.** Usually a check mark next to a menu item indicates that the option is currently selected (refer to Figure 5.10). By default the **Checked property** is set to False; you can change it at design time or in code:

```
mnuDisplaySummary.Checked = True
```

Toggling Check Marks On and Off

If you create a menu item that can be turned on and off, you should include a check mark to indicate the current state. You set the initial state of the check mark in the Properties window. In code you can change its state by setting the menu item's Checked property. For example, for a menu item that displays or hides a summary, called *mnuDisplaySummary,* a check mark indicates that the summary is currently selected. Choosing the menu item a second time should remove the check mark and hide the summary.

TIP

You can toggle a Boolean value on and off using the Not operator:
mnuDisplaySummary.Checked _
= Not mnuDisplaySummary.Checked ■

```
Private Sub mnuDisplaySummary_Click(ByVal sender As System.Object, _
  ByVal e As System.EventArgs) Handles mnuDisplaySummary.Click
    'Hide or display the summary

    If mnuDisplaySummary.Checked Then
        'Hide the summary information
        mnuDisplaySummary.Checked = False
    Else
        'Show the summary information
        mnuDisplaySummary.Checked = True
    End If
End Sub
```

Standards for Windows Menus

When you write applications that run under Windows, your programs should follow the Windows standards. You should always include keyboard access keys; if you include keyboard shortcuts, such as Ctrl + key, stick with the standard keys, such as Ctrl + P for printing. Also, follow the Windows standards for placing the *File* menu on the left end of the menu bar and ending the menu with an *Exit* command. If you have a *Help* menu, it belongs at the right end of the menu bar.

Plan your menus so that they look like other Windows programs. Your users will thank you.

Common Dialog Boxes

You can use a set of predefined standard dialog boxes in your projects for such tasks as specifying colors and fonts, printing, opening, and saving. Use the **common dialog** controls to display the dialog boxes that are provided as part of the Windows environment. The common dialog controls provided with Visual Studio are OpenFileDialog, SaveFileDialog, FontDialog, ColorDialog, PrintDialog, and PrintPreviewDialog (Figure 5.11).

• The common dialog boxes are individual classes such as the ColorDialog and the FontDialog.

Figure 5.11

The common dialog tools in the toolbox.

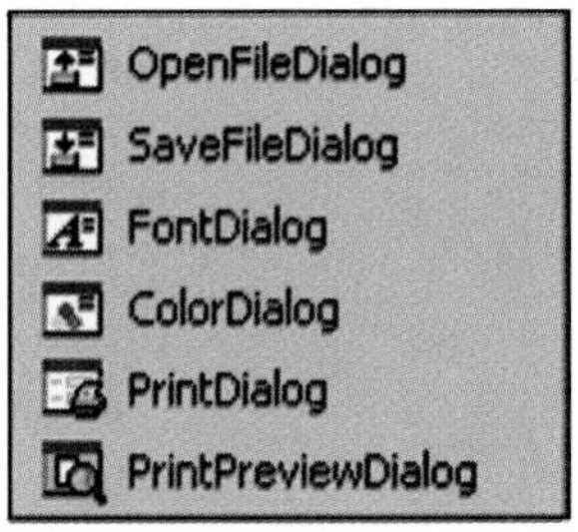

To use a common dialog control, you add the control to the form, placing it in the component tray. Name a common dialog control using "dlg" as its three-character prefix, such as dlgColor or dlgFont.

Displaying a Windows Common Dialog Box

After you place a common dialog control on your form, you can display the dialog box at run time using the *ShowDialog* **method.**

ShowDialog Method—General Form

General Form

```
DialogObject.ShowDialog()
```

The DialogObject is the name of the common dialog control that you placed on the form.

ShowDialog Method—Examples

```
dlgColor.ShowDialog()
dlgFont.ShowDialog()
```

Place the code to show the dialog in the event procedure for a menu item or button.

Using the Information from the Dialog Box

Displaying the *Color* dialog box (Figure 5.12) doesn't make the color of anything change. You must take care of that in your program code. When the user clicks on OK, the selected color is stored in a property that you can access. You can assign the value to the properties of controls in your project.

• Use the properties of the dialog box control to determine the values chosen by the user.

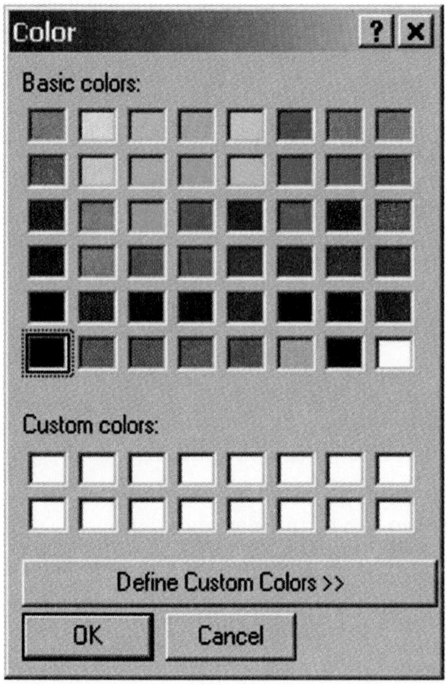

Figure 5.12

The Color common dialog box.

Using the Color Dialog Box

The color selected by the user is stored in the Color property. You can assign this property to another object, such as a control:

```
lblTitle.ForeColor = dlgColor.Color
```

Because Basic executes the statements in sequence, you would first display the dialog box with the ShowDialog method. (Execution then halts until the user responds to the dialog box.) Then you can use the Color property:

```
Public Sub mnuEditColor_Click(ByVal sender As System.Object, _
 ByVal e As System.EventArgs) Handles mnuEditColor.Click
    'Change the color of the total labels
    With dlgColor
        .ShowDialog()
        lblSubTotal.ForeColor = .Color
        lblTax.ForeColor = .Color
        lblTotal.ForeColor = .Color
    End With
End Sub
```

Using the Font Dialog Box

When you display the *Font* common dialog box (Figure 5.13), the available
fonts for the system display. After the user makes a selection, you can use the
Font property of the dialog box object. You may want to assign the Font property to the Font property of other objects on your form.

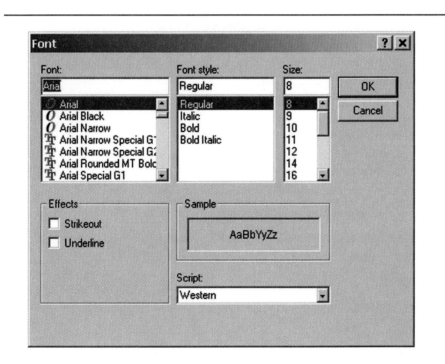

Figure 5.13

*The Font common dialog box.
The fonts that display are
those installed on the user's
system.*

• No flags are required for fonts.

```
Public Sub mnuEditFont_Click(ByVal sender As System.Object, _
 ByVal e As System.EventArgs) Handles mnuEditFont.Click
    'Change the font name for the subtotal labels

    With dlgFont
        .ShowDialog()
        lblSubTotal.Font = .Font
        lblTax.Font = .Font
        lblTotal.Font = .Font
    End With
End Sub
```

When the user clicks on the *Font* menu item, the *Font* dialog box appears on the screen. Execution halts until the user responds to the dialog box, either by clicking *OK* or *Cancel.*

Setting Initial Values

When a common dialog box for colors or fonts appears, what color or font do you want to display? It's best to assign initial values before showing the dialog box. Before executing the ShowDialog method, you should assign the existing values of the object's properties that will be altered. This step makes the current values selected when the dialog box appears. It also ensures that if the user selects the Cancel button, the property settings for the objects will remain unchanged:

```
dlgFont.Font = lblSubtotal.Font
```
or
```
dlgColor.Color = Me.BackColor
```

- Set the properties of the dialog box control before displaying the dialog to set the initial values.

Creating Context Menus

You can also add **context menus** to your applications. Context menus are the **shortcut menus** that pop up when you right-click. Generally the items in a context menu are specific to the component to which you are pointing, reflecting the options available for that component or that situation.

Creating a context menu is similar to creating a menu bar. You add a ContextMenu control, which appears in the component tray below the form. At the top of the form, in the Menu Designer, the words say *Context Menu* (Figure 5.14). A context menu does not have a top-level menu, only the menu items.

- Add a ContextMenu control to the form to create context menus. Then use the same Menu Designer as for main menus.

- Attach a context menu to a form or control by setting its ContextMenu property.

Figure 5.14

Add a ContextMenu control to the component tray and create the context menu using the Menu Designer.

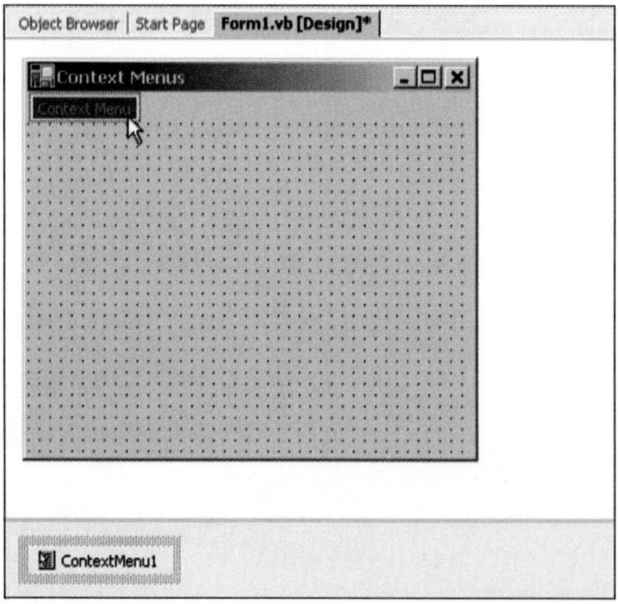

Click on the words *Context Menu* and the words *Type Here* appear underneath, where you can type the text of your first menu item (Figure 5.15).

Figure 5.15

Click on the words Context Menu *to add the first menu item for the new context menu.*

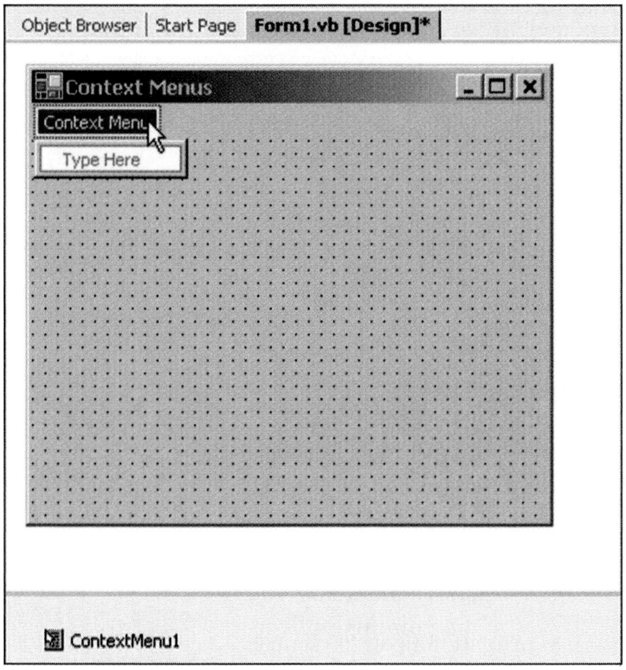

Your application can have more than one context menu. You assign the context menu to the form or control using the component's ContextMenu property. For example, a form has a ContextMenu property, a button has ContextMenu property, and all visible controls have ContextMenu properties. You can assign the same context menu control to each of the components, or a different context menu control to each. If you have only one context menu, attach it to the form; it will pop up if the user right-clicks anywhere on the form, including on a control.

Creating a Context Menu—Step-by-Step

You are going to create a context menu that contains these menu items:

Color
Font
Exit

Add the Context Menu to a Form

STEP 1: Begin a new Windows Forms project (or open an existing one to which you want to add a context menu). Change the form name and set the project's startup object to the new form name.

STEP 2: Add a ContextMenu control to the form; the control will appear in the component tray at the bottom of the form (refer to Figure 5.14).

STEP 3: Click on the words "*Context Menu*" in the Menu Designer to make a "Type Here" menu item appear.

STEP 4: Click on the words "*Type Here*" and type the text for the first menu item: "&Color".

STEP 5: Type the text for the second and third menu items: "&Font" and "E&xit".

STEP 6: Make sure that the Context Menu component in the component tray is selected and set the Name properties as follows:

- ContextMenu1   mnuContext

- Color   mnuContextColor

- Font   mnuContextFont

- Exit   mnuContextExit

STEP 7: Add a label named *lblMessage* to your form and set the Text property to "Right click for the Context Menu". Enlarge the label so that if the font is changed to something larger, the entire message can display.

STEP 8: Set the form's ContextMenu property to mnuContext. Notice that the property box has a drop-down list. If you have more than one context menu defined, you can choose from the list.

STEP 9: Add a ColorDialog control and name it *dlgColor*.

STEP 10: Add a FontDialog control and name it *dlgFont*.

In this example, right-clicking anywhere on the form allows you to change the foreground color or the font of the form. As you know, if you haven't set those properties for individual controls, the form's properties apply to all controls on the form.

TIP

Add a ContextMenu property to all controls and to the form. ■

STEP 11: Code the form as follows:

```
'Program:       Ch05ContextMenus
'Programmer:    Your Name
'Date:          Today's Date
'Description:   Create and apply a context menu.

Option Strict On

Public Class frmContext
    Inherits System.Windows.Forms.Form

[Windows Form Designer generated code]

    Private Sub mnuContextExit_Click(ByVal sender As Object, ByVal e As _
     System.EventArgs) Handles mnuContextExit.Click
    'Terminate the project

        Me.Close()
    End Sub

    Private Sub mnuContextColor_Click(ByVal sender As Object, ByVal e As _
     System.EventArgs) Handles mnuContextColor.Click
        'Change the form's ForeColor.
        'Applies to all controls on the form that haven't had their ForeColor changed
```

```
        With dlgColor
            .Color = Me.ForeColor          'Initialize the dialog box
            .ShowDialog()
            Me.ForeColor = .Color           'Assign the new color
        End With
    End Sub

    Private Sub mnuContextFont_Click(ByVal sender As System.Object, ByVal e As _
    System.EventArgs) Handles mnuContextFont.Click
        'Change the label's font.

        With dlgFont
            .Font = lblMessage.Font          'Initialize the dialog box
            .ShowDialog()
            lblMessage.Font = .Font           'Assign the new font
        End With
    End Sub
End Class
```

Test the Program

STEP 1: Experiment with right-clicking on the form and on the label. Test each of the options.

After you have the program working, experiment with adding more controls and setting the ContextMenu property of controls. You can determine which object the user right-clicked by referring to the context menu's SourceControl property.

```
mnuContext.SourceControl.ForeColor = dlgColor.Color    'Set the color of the selected control
```

Writing General Procedures

Often you will encounter programming situations in which multiple procedures perform the same operation. This condition can occur when the user can select either a button or a menu item to do the same thing. Rather than retyping the code, you can write reusable code in a **general procedure** and call it from both event procedures.

General procedures are also useful in breaking down large sections of code into smaller units that perform a specific task. By breaking down your calculations into smaller tasks, you simplify any maintenance that needs to be done in a program in the future. For example, bowling statistics for a league may require calculations for handicap and series total. If the formula for calculating handicaps changes, wouldn't it be nice to have a procedure that calculates handicaps only instead of one that performs all the calculations?

You can choose from two types of general procedures: sub procedures and function procedures:

- A **sub procedure** performs actions.

- A **function procedure** performs actions and returns a value (the **return value**).

You will likely use a sub procedure if you need to set property values for a series of objects. However, if you need to calculate a result, then a function procedure is the appropriate choice. Both sub procedures and function procedures are considered the **methods** of object-oriented programming.

Creating a New Sub Procedure

You can create a sub procedure in your code window by enclosing the desired lines of code within a set of Sub and End Sub statements.

Sub...End Sub Statements—General Form

```
Private Sub ProcedureName ()
    '... Statements in the procedure
End Sub
```

When you type the line
```
Private Sub ProcedureName
```
and press Enter, the editor automatically adds the parentheses to the Sub statement, adds the End Sub statement, and places the insertion point on the line between the two new lines.

Sub...End Sub Statements—Example

```
Private Sub SelectColor ()
    'Display the color dialog box

    dlgColor.ShowDialog()
End Sub
```

Note that VB .NET has choices other than Private for the access, such as Public, Friend, and Protected. In a later chapter you will learn about the other types of procedures; for now use Private for all general procedures.

The coding for the new procedure is similar to the other procedures we have been coding, but it is not yet attached to any event. Therefore, this code cannot be executed unless we specifically **call** the procedure from another procedure. To call a sub procedure, just give the procedure name, including the parentheses, which in this case is SelectColor( ).

```
Private Sub btnChangeMessage_Click(ByVal sender As System.Object, byVal e As _
  System.EventArgs) Handles btnChangeMessage.Click
    'Change the color of the message

    SelectColor()
    lblMessage.ForeColor = dlgColor.Color
End Sub

Private Sub btnChangeTitle_Click(ByVal sender As System.Object, byVal e As _
  System.EventArgs) Handles btnChangeTitle.Click
    'Change the color of the title

    SelectColor()
    lblTitle.ForeColor = dlgColor.Color
End Sub
```

Passing Arguments to Procedures

At times you may need to use the value of a variable in one procedure and then again in a second procedure that is called from the first. In this situation you could declare the variable as module level, but that approach makes the variable visible to all other procedures. To keep the scope of a variable as narrow as possible, consider declaring the variable as local and passing it to any called procedures.

As an example, we will expand the capabilities of the previous SelectColor sub procedure to display the original color when the dialog box appears. Because the SelectColor procedure can be called from various locations, the original color must be passed to the procedure.

```
Private Sub SelectColor(clrIncomingColor As Color)
    'Allow user to select a color

    With dlgColor
        .Color = clrIncomingColor  'Set the initial color
        .ShowDialog()
    End With
End Sub

Private Sub btnChangeMessage_Click()
    'Change the color of the message
    Dim clrOriginalColor As Color

    clrOriginalColor = lblMessage.ForeColor
    SelectColor(clrOriginalColor)
    lblMessage.ForeColor = dlgColor.Color
End Sub

Private Sub btnChangeTitle_Click()
    'Change the color of the title
    Dim clrOriginalColor As Color

    clrOriginalColor = lblTitle.ForeColor
    SelectColor(clrOriginalColor)
    lblTitle.ForeColor = dlgColor.Color
End Sub
```

Notice that in this example the SelectColor procedure now has an argument inside the parentheses. This syntax specifies that when called, an argument must be supplied.

When a sub procedure definition names an argument, any call to that procedure must supply the argument. In addition, the argument value must be the same data type in both locations. Notice that in the two calling procedures (btnChangeMessage_Click and btnChangeTitle_Click), the variable *clrOriginalColor* is declared as a Color data type.

Another important point is that the name of the argument does not have to be the same in both locations. The SelectColor sub procedure will take whatever Color value it is passed and refer to it as *clrIncomingColor* inside the procedure.

You may specify multiple arguments in both the sub procedure header and the call to the procedure. The number of arguments, their sequence, and their data types must match in both locations! You will see some examples of multiple arguments in the sections that follow.

Passing Arguments ByVal or ByRef

When you pass a value to a procedure you may pass it `ByVal` or `ByRef` (for by value or by reference). `ByVal` sends a copy of the argument's value to the procedure so that the procedure cannot alter the original value. `ByRef` sends a reference indicating where the value is stored in memory, allowing the called procedure to actually change the argument's original value. You can specify how you want to pass the argument by using the `ByVal` or `ByRef` keyword before the argument. If you don't specify `ByVal` or `ByRef`, arguments are passed by value.

• When passing variables to a procedure, the default is ByVal rather than ByRef.

```
Private Sub SelectColor(ByRef clrIncomingColor As Color)    'Argument passed by reference
Private Sub SelectColor(ByVal clrIncomingColor As Color)    'Argument passed by value
Private Sub SelectColor(clrIncomingColor As Color)          'Argument passed by value (the default)
```

Writing Function Procedures

In the past we have used predefined functions, such as the `FormatNumber` function and the `CInt` and `CDec` functions. The `FormatNumber` function returns the formatted characters; the conversion functions return the numeric value of the named argument.

As a programmer, you may need to calculate a value that will be needed in several different procedures or programs. You can write your own function that will calculate a value and call the function from the locations where it is needed. As an example, we will create a function procedure called *Commission,* which calculates and returns a salesperson's commission.

Typing in a block of code using the `Function...End Function` statements creates a function procedure. Since the procedure returns a value, you must specify a data type for the value.

Function...End Function Statements—General Form

General Form

```
Private Function ProcedureName() As Datatype

End Function
```

Functions can also be declared as `Public`, `Protected`, or `Friend`, which you will learn about later. `Private` is appropriate for all functions for now.

Function...End Function Statements—Example

Example

```
Private Function Commission() As Decimal
    'Statements in function
End Function
```

Notice that this procedure looks just like a sub procedure except that the word `Function` replaces the word `Sub` on both the first line and the last line. The procedure header also includes a data type, which is the type of the value returned by the function.

Remember that functions also have arguments. You supply arguments to a function when you call the function by placing a value or values inside the parentheses. You can choose to pass the arguments `ByVal` or `ByRef`.

When you write a function, you declare the argument(s) that the function needs. You give each argument an identifier and a data type. The name that you give an argument in the function procedure header is the identifier that you will use inside the function to refer to the value of the argument.

Examples

```
Private Function Commission(ByVal decSalesAmount As Decimal) As Decimal
Private Function Payment(decRate As Decimal, decTime As Decimal, _
   decAmount As Decimal) As Decimal
```

In the function procedure, the argument list you enter establishes the number of arguments, their type, and their sequence. When using multiple arguments, the sequence of the arguments is critical, just as when you use the predefined Visual Basic functions.

Returning the Result of a Function

The main difference between coding a function procedure and coding a sub procedure is that in a function procedure you must set up the return value. This return value is placed in a variable that Visual Basic names with the same name as the function name. In the first of the preceding examples, the variable name is Commission.

You can choose from two techniques for returning the result of the function:

- Somewhere inside the `Commission` function, set the function name to a value.

  Example: `Commission = 0.15D * decSalesAmount`

- Use the `Return` statement. If you use the `Return` statement, you do not use the function's name as a variable name.

  Example: `Return 0.15D * decSalesAmount`

• You can use the new *Return* statement rather than set the function name to the return value.

Writing a Commission Function

Here is the Commission function procedure coded using the first technique for returning a value.

```
Private Function Commission(ByVal decSalesAmount As Decimal) As Decimal
   'Calculate the sales commission

   If decSalesAmount < 1000D Then
      Commission = 0D
   ElseIf decSalesAmount <= 2000D Then
      Commission = 0.15D * decSalesAmount
   Else
      Commission = 0.2D * decSalesAmount
   End If
End Function
```

And here is the same Commission function procedure using the `Return` statement.

```
Private Function Commission(ByVal decSalesAmount As Decimal) As Decimal
    'Calculate the sales commission

    If decSalesAmount < 1000D Then
        Return 0D
    ElseIf decSalesAmount <= 2000D Then
        Return 0.15D * decSalesAmount
    Else
        Return 0.2D * decSalesAmount
    End If
End Function
```

Calling the Commission Function

In another procedure in the project, you can call your function by using it in an expression.

```
Dim decSales as Decimal
If IsNumeric(txtSales.Text) Then
    decSales = CDec(txtSales.Text)
    lblCommission.Text = FormatNumber(Commission(decSales))
End If
```

Notice in the preceding example that the argument named in the function call does not have the same name as the argument named in the function definition. When the function is called, a copy of decSales is passed to the function and is assigned to the named argument, in this case decSalesAmount. As the calculations are done (inside the function), for every reference to decSalesAmount, the value that was passed in for decSales is actually used.

You can nest the functions, if you wish:

```
lblCommission.Text = FormatNumber(Commission(CDec(txtSales.Text)))
```

To read this statement, begin with the inner parentheses: txtSales.Text is passed to `CDec` for conversion to Decimal; the result of that conversion is passed as an argument to the `Commission` function; the value returned by the `Commission` function is passed to the `FormatNumber` function; and the value returned from the `FormatNumber` function is assigned to lblCommission.Text.

Functions with Multiple Arguments

A function can have multiple arguments. The sequence and data type of the arguments in the `Call` must exactly match the arguments in the function procedure header.

Writing a Function with Multiple Arguments

When you create a function with multiple arguments such as a `Payment` function, you enclose the list of arguments within the parentheses. The following example indicates that three arguments are needed in the call: The first argument is the interest rate, the second is the time, and the third is the loan amount. All three argument values will have a data type of decimal, and the return value will be decimal. Look carefully at the following formula and notice how the identifiers in the parentheses are used.

```
Private Function Payment(decRate As Decimal, decTime As Decimal, _
    decAmt As Decimal) As Decimal
    'Calculate the monthly payment on an amortized loan

    'Set the return value of the function
    Payment = (decAmt * decRatePerMonth) _
        / ((1 - (1 / (1 + decRatePerMonth) ^ (decTime * 12D))))
End Function
```

Calling a Function with Multiple Arguments

To call this function from another procedure, use these statements:

```
decPrincipal = CDec(txtPrincipal.Text)
decRate = CDec(txtRate.Text)
decYears = CDec(txtYears.Text)
decPayment = Payment(decRate, decTime, decAmount)
```

You can format the result, as well as pass the value of the text boxes, by nesting functions:

```
lblPayment.Text = FormatDecimal(decPayment(CDec(txtRate.Text), _
    CDec(txtYears.Text), CDec(txtPrincipal.Text)))
```

When you call the function, the VS smart editor shows you the arguments of your function (Figure 5.16), just as it does for built-in functions (assuming that you have already entered the function procedure).

Figure 5.16

The Visual Studio IntelliSense feature pops up with the list of arguments for your own newly written procedure.

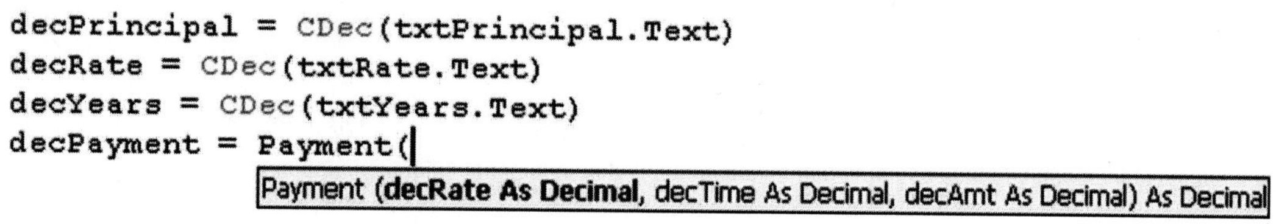

```
decPrincipal = CDec(txtPrincipal.Text)
decRate = CDec(txtRate.Text)
decYears = CDec(txtYears.Text)
decPayment = Payment(|
                Payment (decRate As Decimal, decTime As Decimal, decAmt As Decimal) As Decimal
```

Reusing Procedures

One of the big advantages of using a function is that you can call the procedure from more than one location, and even in more than one situation. The following example uses the CalculateBonus function to calculate a gift certificate bonus amount for a shopper and also to calculate a salesperson's commission. The amount and rate values are passed to the function procedure from the appropriate event procedures.

Notice also that a general sub procedure is used to clear the values on the interface.

```
'Project:        Chapter 5 reusable code example
'Programmer:     Theresa Berry
'Date:           January 2002
'Folder:         Ch05Shoppers
'Purpose:        This program inputs sales information and calculates
'                a bonus for shoppers and a commission for
'                salespeople. It demonstrates using a reusable function
'                procedure and a general sub

Option Strict On

Public Class frmMain
    Inherits System.Windows.Forms.Form

[Windows Form Designer generated code]

    'Declare module-level constants
    Const mdecBONUS_PERCENT As Decimal = 0.01D
    Const mdecCOMMISSION_LIMIT As Decimal = 500D
    Const mdecCOMMISSION_PERCENT As Decimal = 0.05D

    Public Sub mnuCalculateBonus_Click(ByVal sender As System.Object, _
     ByVal e As System.EventArgs) Handles mnuCalculateBonus.Click
        'Calculate and display the amount of the
        'bonus earned by the shopper.

        Dim decPurchase As Decimal
        Dim decBonus As Decimal

    If IsNumeric(txtPurchaseAmount.Text) Then
        decPurchase = CDec(txtPurchaseAmount.Text)
        decBonus = CalculateBonus(decPurchase, mdecBONUS_PERCENT) 'Call function procedure
        MessageBox.Show(txtName.Text & "has earned" & FormatCurrency(decBonus) _
         & "in gift certificates", "Congratulations", MessageBoxButtons.OK, _
         MessageBoxIcon.Information)
        txtName.Focus()
    Else
        MessageBox.Show("You must input a value for the amount of purchase", _
         "Input Requested", MessageBoxButtons.OK, MessageBoxIcon.Information)
        With txtPurchaseAmount
            .Text = ""
            .Focus()
        End With
    End If
End Sub

Public Sub mnuCalculateCommission_Click(ByVal sender As System.Object, ByVal e As _
 System.EventArgs) Handles mnuCalculateCommission.Click
    'Calculate and display the salesperson's commission

    Dim decPurchase As Decimal
    Dim decCommission As Decimal

    If IsNumeric(txtPurchaseAmount.Text) Then
        decPurchase = CDec(txtPurchaseAmount.Text)
        If decPurchase >= mdecCOMMISSION_LIMIT Then
            decCommission = CalculateBonus(decPurchase, mdecCOMMISSION_PERCENT)
            MessageBox.Show("Salesman" & txtSalespersonID.Text & "earns" _
             & FormatCurrency(decCommission) & "in commission for this sale.", _
             "Congratulations", MessageBoxButtons.OK, MessageBoxIcon.Information)
            txtName.Focus()
        Else
```

```
                    MessageBox.Show("No commission earned on this sale.", "Sorry", _
                        MessageBoxButtons.OK, MessageBoxIcon.Information)
            End If
        End If
    End Sub

    Public Sub mnuFileExit_Click(ByVal sender As System.Object, ByVal e As _
      System.EventArgs) Handles mnuFileExit.Click
        'End the project

        Me.Close()
    End Sub

    Public Sub mnuEditClear_Click(ByVal sender As System.Object, _
      ByVal e As System.EventArgs) Handles mnuEditClear.Click
        'Call the Clear procedure

        Clear()
    End Sub

    Public Sub mnuHelpAbout_Click(ByVal sender As System.Object, _
      ByVal e As System.EventArgs) Handles mnuHelpAbout.Click
        'Display the programmer information.

        MessageBox.Show("Programmer: Theresa Berry" & ControlChars.NewLine _
            & "July 1999", "Shoppers Paradise", MessageBoxButtons.OK, _
            MessageBoxIcon.Information)
    End Sub

    Private Function CalculateBonus(ByVal decAmount As Decimal, _
      ByVal decRate As Decimal) As Decimal
        'Calculate the amount of bonus earned based on the
        'sale amount and the percentage rate.

        CalculateBonus = decAmount * decRate
    End Function

    Private Sub Clear()
        'Clear the text boxes on the form.

        txtPurchaseAmount.Text = ""
        txtSalespersonID.Text = ""
        With txtName
            .Text = ""
            .Focus()
        End With
    End Sub
End Class
```

Breaking Calculations into Smaller Units

A project with many calculations can be easier to understand and to write if you break the calculations into small units. In this example that calculates bowling statistics, separate function procedures calculate the average, handicap, and series total, and find the high game.

```
'Project:          Chapter 5 Bowling Example
'Programmer:       Bradley/Millspaugh
'Date:             January 2002
'Folder:           Ch05Bowling
'Description:       This project calculates bowling statistics using
'                   multiple function procedures.

Option Strict On

Public Class frmBowling
    Inherits System.Windows.Forms.Form

[Windows Form Designer generated code]

Private Sub mnuEditClear_Click(ByVal sender As System.Object, _
 ByVal e As System.EventArgs) Handles mnuEditClear.Click
    'Clear the input area and individual bowler info

    With txtName
        .Text = ""
        .Focus()
    End With
    radMale.Checked = False
    radFemale.Checked = False
    txtScore1.Text = ""
    txtScore2.Text = ""
    txtScore3.Text = ""
    lblSeries.Text = ""
    lblAverage.Text = ""
    lblHighGame.Text = ""
    lblHandicap.Text = ""
End Sub

Private Sub mnuFileCalc_Click(ByVal sender As System.Object, _
 ByVal e As System.EventArgs) Handles mnuFileCalc.Click
    'Calculate individual and summary info
    Dim decAverage As Decimal
    Dim decHandicap As Decimal
    Dim intSeries As Integer
    Dim strHighGame As String
    Dim intGame1 As Integer
    Dim intGame2 As Integer
    Dim intGame3 As Integer

    If IsNumeric(txtScore1.Text) And IsNumeric(txtScore2.Text) _
     And IsNumeric(txtScore3.Text) Then
        intGame1 = CInt(txtScore1.Text)
        intGame2 = CInt(txtScore2.Text)
        intGame3 = CInt(txtScore3.Text)

        'Perform all calculations
        decAverage = FindAverage(intGame1, intGame2, intGame3)
        intSeries = FindSeries(intGame1, intGame2, intGame3)
        strHighGame = FindHighGame(intGame1, intGame2, intGame3)
        decHandicap = FindHandicap(decAverage)

        'Format the output
        lblAverage.Text = FormatNumber(decAverage, 1)
        lblHighGame.Text = strHighGame
        lblSeries.Text = CStr(intSeries)
        lblHandicap.Text = FormatNumber(decHandicap, 1)
    Else
```

```vb
        MessageBox.Show("Please Enter three scores", "Missing Data", _
            MessageBoxButtons.OK)
    End If
End Sub

Private Sub mnuFileExit_Click(ByVal sender As System.Object, _
 ByVal e As System.EventArgs) Handles mnuFileExit.Click
    'Terminate

    Me.Close()
End Sub

Private Function FindAverage(ByVal intScore1 As Integer, _
 ByVal intScore2 As Integer, ByVal intScore3 As Integer) As Decimal
    'Return the average of three games

    Return (intScore1 + intScore2 + intScore3) / 3D
End Function

Private Function FindHandicap(ByVal decAverage As Decimal) As Decimal
    'Calculate Handicap

    Return (200D - decAverage) * 0.8D
End Function

Private Function FindSeries(ByVal intGame1 As Integer, _
 ByVal intGame2 As Integer, ByVal intGame3 As Integer) As Integer
    'Calculate the series total

    Return intGame1 + intGame2 + intGame3
End Function

Private Function FindHighGame(ByVal intGame1 As Integer, _
 ByVal intGame2 As Integer, ByVal intGame3 As Integer) As String
    'Find the highest game in the series

    If intGame1 > intGame2 And intGame1 > intGame3 Then
        Return "1"
    ElseIf intGame2 > intGame1 And intGame2 > intGame3 Then
        Return "2"
    ElseIf intGame3 > intGame1 And intGame3 > intGame2 Then
        Return "3"
    Else
        Return "Tie"
    End If
 End Function
End Class
```

➤ **Feedback 5.1**

You need to write a procedure to calculate and return the average of three integer values.

1. Should you write a sub procedure or a function procedure?
2. Write the header line of the procedure.
3. Write the calculation.
4. How is the calculated average passed back to the calling procedure?

Your Hands-On Programming Example

Modify the hands-on programming example from Chapter 4 by replacing some of the buttons with menus. Use a function procedure to calculate the sales tax, and allow the user to select the font and color of the summary labels.

The project for R 'n R—for Reading 'n Refreshment calculates the amount due for individual orders and maintains accumulated totals for a summary. Use a check box for takeout items, which are taxable (8 percent); all other orders are nontaxable. Include option buttons for the five coffee selections: Cappuccino, Espresso, Latte, Iced Latte, and Iced Cappuccino. The prices for each will be assigned using these constants:

Cappuccino	2.00
Espresso	2.25
Latte	1.75
Iced (either)	2.50

Use a button for *Calculate Selection,* which will calculate and display the amount due for each item. A button for *Clear for Next Item* will clear the selections and amount for the single item. Additional labels in a separate frame will maintain the summary information for the current order to include subtotal, tax, and total.

The *Next Order* menu will clear the bill for the current customer and add to the totals for the summary. The menu for *Summary* should display the total of all orders, the average sale amount per customer, and the number of customers in a message box.

The *Edit* menu contains options that duplicate the Calculate and Clear button. The Font and Color options change the properties of the subtotal, tax, and total labels.

The *About* selection on the *Help* menu will display a message box with information about the programmer.

File	Edit	Help
New Order	Calculate Selection	About
Summary	Clear Item	
Exit		
	─────	
	Font	
	Color	

Planning the Project

Sketch a form (Figure 5.17), which your users sign off as meeting their needs.

Figure 5.17

A sketch of the form for the hands-on programming example.

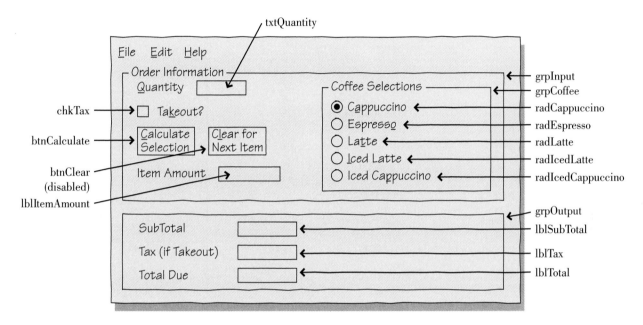

Plan the Objects and Properties

Plan the property settings for the form and each of the controls.

Object	Property	Setting
Form1	Name	frmBilling
	Text	R 'n R—for Reading 'n Refreshment
	AcceptButton	btnCalculate
	CancelButton	btnClear
grpInput	Text	Order Information
grpCoffee	Text	Coffee Selections
grpOutput	Text	(blank)
radCappuccino	Name	radCappuccino
	Text	C&appuccino
	Value	True
radEspresso	Name	radEspresso
	Text	Espress&o
radLatte	Name	radLatte
	Text	La&tte

Continued on page 224

Object	Property	Setting
radIcedLatte	Name	radIcedLatte
	Text	&Iced Latte
radIcedCappuccino	Name	radIcedCappuccino
	Text	Iced Ca&ppuccino
Label1	Text	&Quantity
txtQuantity	Name	txtQuantity
	Text	(blank)
chkTax	Name	chkTax
	Text	Ta&keout?
Label2	Text	Item Amount
Label3	Text	SubTotal
Label4	Text	Tax (if Takeout)
Label5	Text	Total Due
lblItemAmount	Name	lblItemAmount
	Text	(blank)
	BorderStyle	Fixed3D
lblSubTotal	Name	lblSubTotal
	Text	(blank)
	BorderStyle	Fixed3D
lblTax	Name	lblTax
	Text	(blank)
	BorderStyle	Fixed3D
lblTotal	Name	lblTotal
	Text	(blank)
	BorderStyle	Fixed3D
btnCalculate	Name	btnCalculate
	Text	&Calculate Selection
btnClear	Name	btnClear
	Text	C&lear for Next Item
mnuFile	Name	mnuFile
	Text	&File
mnuFileNew	Name	mnuFileNew
	Text	&New Order
mnuFileSummary	Name	mnuFileSummary
	Text	&Summary
mnuFileExit	Name	mnuFileExit
	Text	E&xit
mnuEdit	Name	mnuEdit
	Text	&Edit

Continued on page 225

Object	Property	Setting
mnuEditCalc	Name Text	mnuEditCalc Calculate &Selection
mnuEditClear	Name Text	mnuEditClear C&lear Item
mnuEditFont	Name Text	mnuEditFont &Font
mnuEditColor	Name Text	mnuEditColor &Color
mnuHelp	Name Text	mnuHelp &Help
mnuHelpAbout	Name Text	mnuHelpAbout &About
dlgColor	Name	dlgColor
dlgFont	Name	dlgFont

Plan the Event Procedures

You need to plan the actions for the buttons and the actions of the menu items, as well as the function for the sales tax.

Object	Procedure	Action
btnCalculate	Click	Validate for blank or nonnumeric amount. Find price of drink selection. Multiply price by quantity. Add amount to subtotal. Call tax function if needed. Calculate total = subtotal + tax. Format and display the values. Disable the Takeout check box. Enable the Clear button.
btnClear	Click	Clear the coffee selections. Clear the quantity and the item price. Set the focus to the quantity. Disable the Clear button.
mnuFileNew	Click	Confirm clearing current order. Clear the current order. Accumulate total sales and count. Set subtotal and total due to 0. Enable Takeout check box. Disable the Clear button.
mnuFileSummary	Click	If current order not added to totals call btnNewOrder_Click. Calculate the average. Display the summary totals in a message box.

Continued on page 226

Object	Procedure	Action
mnuFileExit	Click	Terminate the project.
mnuEditCalc	Click	Call calculate event procedure.
mnuEditClear	Click	Call clear event procedure.
mnuHelpAbout	Click	Display the About message box.
(Function procedure)	FindTax	Calculate the sales tax.

Write the Project

Follow the sketch in Figure 5.17 to create the form. Figure 5.18 shows the completed form.

- Set the properties of each object according to your plan. If you are modifying the project from Chapter 4, add the menus and the common dialog controls, and remove the extra buttons.

- Write the code. Working from the pseudocode, write each event procedure.

- When you complete the code, use a variety of data to thoroughly test the project.

Figure   5.18

The form for the hands-on programming example.

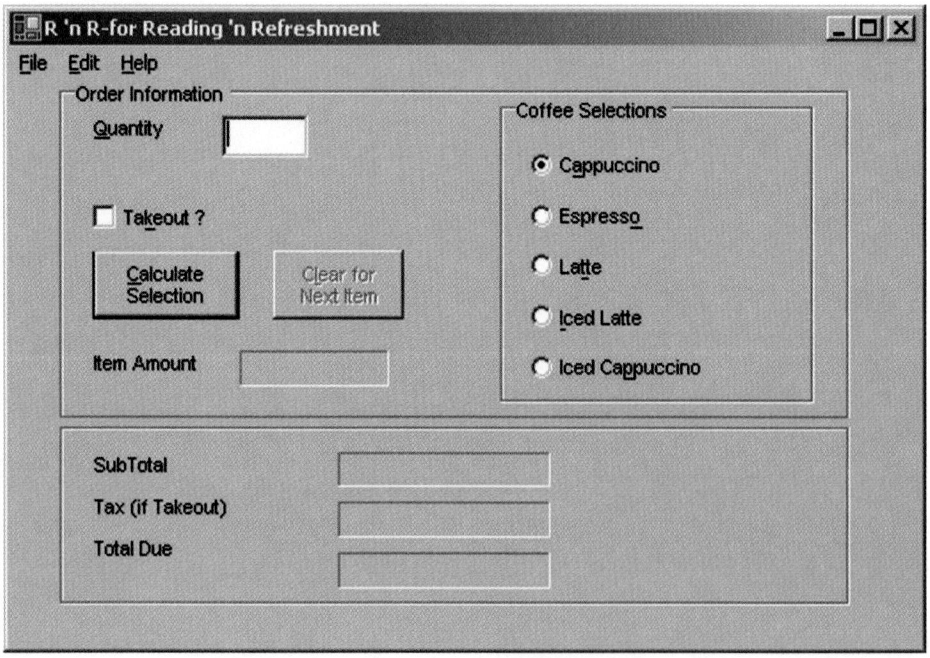

The Project Coding Solution

```
'Program Name:      Billing
'Programmer:        Bradley/Millspaugh
'Date:              Jan 2002
'Description:       This project calculates the amount due
'                   based on the customer selection
'                   and accumulates summary data for the day.
'                   Incorporates menus and common dialog boxes,
'                   which allow the user to change the font and
'                   color of labels.
'Folder:            Ch0501

Option Strict On

Public Class frmBilling
    Inherits System.Windows.Forms.Form

[Windows Form Designer generated code]

Dim mdecSubtotal As Decimal
    Dim mdecTotal As Decimal
    Dim mdecGrandTotal As Decimal
    Dim mintCustomerCount As Integer
    Const mdecTAX_RATE As Decimal = 0.08D
    Const mdecCAPPUCCINO_PRICE As Decimal = 2D
    Const mdecESPRESSO_PRICE As Decimal = 2.25D
    Const mdecLATTE_PRICE As Decimal = 1.75D
    Const mdecICED_PRICE As Decimal = 2.5D

    Private Sub btnCalculate_Click(ByVal sender As System.Object, _
    ByVal e As System.EventArgs) Handles btnCalculate.Click
        'Calculate and display the current amounts, add to totals

        Dim decPrice As Decimal
        Dim intQuantity As Integer
        Dim decTax As Decimal
        Dim decItemAmount As Decimal
        Dim strMessage As String

        'Find the price
        If radCappuccino.Checked Then
            decPrice = mdecCAPPUCCINO_PRICE
        ElseIf radEspresso.Checked Then
            decPrice = mdecESPRESSO_PRICE
        ElseIf radLatte.Checked Then
            decPrice = mdecLATTE_PRICE
        ElseIf radIcedCappuccino.Checked Or radIcedLatte.Checked Then
            decPrice = mdecICED_PRICE
        Else
            MessageBox.Show("Please make a drink selection", "Selection Required", _
                MessageBoxButtons.OK, MessageBoxIcon.Information)
        End If
```

```
                'Calculate extended price and add to order total
                If txtQuantity.Text <> "" Then 'Not blank
                    If IsNumeric(txtQuantity.Text) Then 'Is numeric
                        'Good Data - perform calculations
                        Try
                                intQuantity = CInt(txtQuantity.Text)
                                decItemAmount = decPrice * intQuantity
                                mdecSubtotal += decItemAmount
                                If chkTax.Checked Then
                                  decTax = FindTax(mdecSubtotal) 'Call function procedure
                                Else
                                  decTax = 0
                                End If
                                mdecTotal = mdecSubtotal + decTax
                                lblItemAmount.Text = FormatCurrency(decItemAmount)
                                lblSubTotal.Text = FormatNumber(mdecSubtotal)
                                lblTax.Text = FormatNumber(decTax)
                                lblTotal.Text = FormatCurrency(mdecTotal)
                                chkTax.Enabled = False     'Allow change for new order only
                                btnClear.Enabled = True    'Allow Clear after an order is begun
                        Catch
                                strMessage = "Calculation error."
                                MessageBox.Show(strMessage, "Error", _
                                    MessageBoxButtons.OK, MessageBoxIcon.Error)
                        End Try
                    Else 'Nonnumeric data
                        strMessage = "Nonnumeric data entered for quantity."
                        MessageBox.Show(strMessage, "Data Entry Error", _
                          MessageBoxButtons.OK, MessageBoxIcon.Information)
                        txtQuantity.Focus()
                    End If
                Else 'Missing data
                    strMessage = "Enter the quantity."
                    MessageBox.Show(strMessage, "Data entry error", _
                      MessageBoxButtons.OK, MessageBoxIcon.Information)
                    txtQuantity.Focus()
                End If
        End Sub

        Private Sub btnClear_Click(ByVal sender As System.Object, _
            ByVal e As System.EventArgs) Handles btnClear.Click
            'Clear appropriate controls

            radCappuccino.Checked = True
            lblItemAmount.Text = ""
            With txtQuantity
                .Clear()
                .Focus()
            End With
        End Sub
```

```vb
Private Sub mnuFileNew_Click(ByVal sender As System.Object, _
  ByVal e As System.EventArgs) Handles mnuFileNew.Click
    'Clear the current order and add to totals

    Dim dgrResult As DialogResult
    Dim strMessage As String

    'Confirm clear of current order
    strMessage = "Clear the current order figures?"
    dgrResult = MessageBox.Show(strMessage, "Clear Order", _
     MessageBoxButtons.YesNo, MessageBoxIcon.Question, _
     MessageBoxDefaultButton.Button2)

    If dgrResult = DialogResult.Yes Then 'User said Yes
        btnClear_Click(sender, e)           'Clear the screen fields
        lblSubTotal.Text = ""
        lblTax.Text = ""
        lblTotal.Text = ""

        Try
            'Add to Totals
            If mdecSubtotal <> 0 Then 'Should not be able to add to counts if no
                                      'new order/customer. Prevents accidental clicking.
                mdecGrandTotal += mdecTotal
                mintCustomerCount += 1
                mdecSubtotal = 0
                mdecTotal = 0          'Reset for next customer
            End If
        Catch
            strMessage = "Error in calculations."
            MessageBox.Show(strMessage, "Error", MessageBoxButtons.OK, _
            MessageBoxIcon.Error)
        End Try

        'Clear appropriate display items and enable check box
        With chkTax
            .Enabled = True
            .Checked = False
        End With
        btnClear.Enabled = False
    End If
End Sub

Private Sub mnuFileSummary_Click(ByVal sender As System.Object, _
  ByVal e As System.EventArgs) Handles mnuFileSummary.Click
    'Calculate the average and display the totals

    Dim decAverage As Decimal
    Dim strMessageString As String
    Dim strFormattedAvg As String

    If mdecTotal <> 0 Then
        'Make sure last order is counted
        mnuFileNew_Click(sender, e)    'Pass incoming arguments to called procedure
    End If
```

```vb
        If mintCustomerCount > 0 Then
            Try
                'Calculate average
                decAverage = mdecGrandTotal / mintCustomerCount

                'Concatenate the message string
                strMessageString = "Number of Orders: " & CStr(mintCustomerCount) _
                    & ControlChars.NewLine & ControlChars.NewLine _
                    & "Total Sales: " & FormatCurrency(mdecGrandTotal) _
                    & ControlChars.NewLine & ControlChars.NewLine _
                    & "Average Sale: " & FormatCurrency(decAverage)
                MessageBox.Show(strMessageString, "Coffee Sales Summary", MessageBoxButtons.OK, _
                    MessageBoxIcon.Information)
            Catch
                strMessageString = "Error in calculations."
                MessageBox.Show(strMessageString, "Error", MessageBoxButtons.OK, _
                    MessageBoxIcon.Error)
            End Try
        Else
            strMessageString = "No sales data to summarize."
            MessageBox.Show(strMessageString, "Coffee Sales Summary", MessageBoxButtons.OK, _
                MessageBoxIcon.Information)
        End If
End Sub

Private Sub mnuFileExit_Click(ByVal sender As System.Object, _
 ByVal e As System.EventArgs) Handles mnuFileExit.Click
    'Terminate the project

    Me.Close()
End Sub

Private Sub mnuEditCalc_Click(ByVal sender As System.Object, _
 ByVal e As System.EventArgs) Handles mnuEditCalc.Click
    'Call the Calculate event procedure

    btnCalculate_Click(sender, e)     'Pass incoming arguments to called procedure
End Sub

Private Sub mnuEditClear_Click(ByVal sender As System.Object, _
 ByVal e As System.EventArgs) Handles mnuEditClear.Click
    'Call the Clear event procedure

    btnClear_Click(sender, e)    'Pass incoming arguments to called procedure
End Sub

Private Sub mnuEditFont_Click(ByVal sender As System.Object, _
 ByVal e As System.EventArgs) Handles mnuEditFont.Click
    'Allow the user to select a new font for the summary totals

    With dlgFont
        .Font = lblSubTotal.Font
        .ShowDialog()
        lblSubTotal.Font = .Font
        lblTax.Font = .Font
        lblTotal.Font = .Font
    End With
End Sub
```

```
Private Sub mnuEditColor_Click(ByVal sender As System.Object, _
 ByVal e As System.EventArgs) Handles mnuEditColor.Click
    'Allow the user to select a new color for the summary totals

    With dlgColor
        .Color = lblSubTotal.ForeColor
        .ShowDialog()
        lblSubTotal.ForeColor = .Color
        lblTax.ForeColor = .Color
        lblTotal.ForeColor = .Color
    End With
End Sub

Private Sub mnuHelpAbout_Click(ByVal sender As Object, _
 ByVal e As System.EventArgs) Handles mnuHelpAbout.Click
    'Display the About message box
    Dim strMessage As String

    strMessage = "R 'n R Billing" & ControlChars.NewLine & ControlChars.NewLine _
     & "Programmed by Bradley and Millspaugh"

    MessageBox.Show(strMessage, "About R 'n R Billing", MessageBoxButtons.OK, _
     MessageBoxIcon.Information)
End Sub

Private Function FindTax(ByVal decAmount As Decimal) As Decimal
    'Calculate the sales tax

    Return decAmount * mdecTAX_RATE
End Function
End Class
```

Summary

1. The Visual Studio Menu Designer enables you to create menus, menu items, and submenus, each with keyboard access keys.
2. In the Menu Designer you can set and modify the order and level of menu items.
3. Each menu item has a Click event. The code to handle selection of a menu item belongs in the item's Click event procedure.
4. Common dialog boxes allow Visual Basic programs to display the predefined Windows dialog boxes for *Print, PrintPreview, File Open, File Save, Fonts,* and *Colors.* These dialog boxes are part of the operating environment; therefore, it is an unnecessary duplication of effort to have each programmer re-create them.
5. Context menus, or shortcut menus, are created using a ContextMenu control and the Menu Designer. Context menus pop up when the user right-clicks.
6. The programmer can write reusable code in general procedures. These procedures may be sub procedures or function procedures and may be called from any other procedure in the form module.
7. Both sub procedures and function procedures can perform an action. However, functions return a value, and sub procedures do not. The value returned by a function has a data type.

8. Arguments can be passed `ByRef` or `ByVal` (the default). `ByRef` passes a reference to the actual data item; `ByVal` passes a copy of the data.

9. A function procedure must return a value, which can be accomplished using the `Return` statement or by setting the name of the function to the result.

Key Terms

`ByRef` *214*	general procedure *211*
`ByVal` *214*	menu *198*
call (procedure call) *212*	Menu Designer *198*
checked *204*	method *212*
Checked property *204*	return value *211*
common dialog *205*	separator bar *201*
context menu *208*	shortcut menu *208*
disabled *204*	`ShowDialog` method *205*
Enabled property *204*	sub procedure *211*
function procedure *211*	submenu *200*

Review Questions

1. Explain the difference between a menu and a submenu.
2. How can the user know if a menu item contains a submenu?
3. What is a separator bar and how is it created?
4. Name at least three types of common dialog boxes.
5. What is a context menu? How would you attach a context menu to a control?
6. Why would you need procedures that are not attached to an event?
7. Code the necessary statements to produce a color dialog box and use it to change the background color of a label.
8. Explain the difference between a sub procedure and a function procedure.
9. What is a return value? How can it be used?
10. Explain the differences between `ByRef` and `ByVal`. When would each be used?

Programming Exercises

5.1 Modify Programming Exercise 4.6 (Piecework Pay) to replace buttons with menus and add a function procedure.

This project will input the number of pieces and calculate the pay for multiple employees. It also must display a summary of the total number of pieces, the total pay, and the average pay for all employees.

Menu: The menu bar must have these items:

File	Edit	Help
Calculate Pay	Clear	About
Summary	————	
Exit	Font	
	Color	

Piecework workers are paid by the piece. Workers who produce a greater quantity of output may be paid at a higher rate.

Use text boxes to obtain the name and the number of pieces completed. The *Calculate Pay* menu item calculates and displays the dollar amount earned. The *Summary* menu item displays the total number of pieces, the total pay, and the average pay per person in a message box. The *Clear* menu choice clears the name and the number of pieces for the current employee and resets the focus.

The *Color* and *Font* items should change the color and font of the information displayed in the amount earned label.

Use a message box to display the program name and your name for the *About* option on the *Help* menu.

Use a function procedure to find the pay rate and return a value to the proper event procedure.

Pieces completed	Price paid per piece for all pieces
1 to 199	.50
200 to 399	.55
400 to 599	.60
600 or more	.65

5.2 Redo the checking account programming exercises from Chapter 4 (4.3, 4.4, and 4.5), using menus and function procedures.

Menu:

File	Edit	Help
Transaction	Clear	About
Summary	————	
Exit	Font	
	Color	

Form: Use radio buttons to indicate the type of transaction: deposit, check, or service charge. Use a text box to allow the user to enter the amount of the transaction. Display the balance in a label.

Include validation that displays a message box if the amount of the transaction is a negative number. If there is not enough money to cover a check, display a message box with the message "Insufficient Funds." Do not pay the check, but deduct a service charge of $10.

Use function procedures for deposits, checks, and service charges. The deposit function adds the deposit to the balance; the check function subtracts the transaction amount from the balance; the service charge function subtracts $10 from the balance.

The *Summary* menu item displays the total number of deposits and the dollar amount of deposits, the number of checks, and the dollar amount of the checks in a message box.

The *Clear* menu item clears the radio buttons and the amount and resets the focus.

The *Color* and *Font* menu items change the color and font of the information displayed in the balance label.

Use a message box to display the program name and your name as the programmer for the *About* option on the *Help* menu.

Note: For help in basing a new project on an existing project, see "Copy and Move a Windows Project" in Appendix C.

5.3   A salesperson earns a weekly base salary plus a commission when sales are at or above quota. Create a project that allows the user to input the weekly sales and the salesperson name, calculates the commission, and displays summary information.

Form: The form should have text boxes for the salesperson name and his or her weekly sales.

Menu:

File	Edit	Help
Pay	Clear	About
Summary	————	
Exit	Font	
	Color	

Use constants to establish the base pay, the quota, and the commission rate.

The *Pay* menu item calculates and displays in labels the commission and the total pay for that person. However, if there is no commission, do not display the commission amount (do not display a zero commission amount).

Use a function procedure to calculate the commission. The function must compare sales to the quota. When the sales are equal to or greater than the quota, calculate the commission by multiplying sales by the commission rate.

Each salesperson receives the base pay plus the commission (if one has been earned). Format the dollar amounts to two decimal places; do not display a dollar sign.

The *Summary* menu item displays a message box containing total sales, total commissions, and total pay for all salespersons. Display the numbers with two decimal places and dollar signs.

The *Clear* menu item clears the name, sales, and pay for the current employee and then resets the focus.

The *Color* and *Font* menu items should change the color and font of the information displayed in the amount earned label.

Use a message box to display the program name and your name as programmer for the *About* option on the *Help* menu.

Test Data: Quota = 1000; Commission rate = .15; and Base pay = $250.

Name	Sales
Sandy Smug	1,000.00
Sam Sadness	999.99
Joe Whiz	2,000.00

Totals should be:

Sales	$3,999.99
Commissions	450.00
Pay	1,200.00

5.4 The local library has a summer reading program to encourage reading. The staff keeps a chart with readers' names and bonus points earned for the number of books read. Create a project using a menu and a function procedure that will determine the bonus points.

Menu:

File	Edit	Help
Points	Clear	About
Summary	———	
Exit	Font	
	Color	

Form: Use text boxes to obtain the reader's name and the number of books read. Use a label to display the number of bonus points.

The *Points* menu item should call a function procedure to calculate the points using this schedule: the first three books are worth 10 points each. The next three books are worth 15 points each. All books over six are worth 20 points each.

The *Summary* menu item displays the average number of books read for all readers that session.

The *Clear* menu item clears the name, the number of books read, and the bonus points and then resets the focus.

The *Color* and *Font* menu items change the color and font of the information displayed in the bonus points label.

Use a message box to display the program name and your name as programmer for the *About* option on the *Help* menu.

5.5   Modify Programming Exercise 2.2 (the flag viewer) to use a menu instead
       of radio buttons, check boxes, and buttons. Include check marks next to
       the name of the currently selected country and next to the selected dis-
       play options.

Menu:

<u>F</u>ile	<u>C</u>ountry	<u>D</u>isplay	<u>H</u>elp
E<u>x</u>it	<u>U</u>nited States	<u>T</u>itle	<u>A</u>bout
	<u>C</u>anada	C<u>o</u>untry Name	
	<u>J</u>apan	<u>P</u>rogrammer	
	<u>M</u>exico		

Case Studies

VB Mail Order

Modify the case study from Chapter 4 to use menus and
a function procedure. Refer to Chapter 4 for project
specifications. Use a function procedure to calculate
the shipping and handling based on the weight for an
entire order. (Do not calculate shipping and handling
on individual items—wait until the order is complete.)
Note: For help in basing a new project on an existing
project, see "Copy and Move a Windows Project" in
Appendix C.

Menu:

<u>F</u>ile	<u>E</u>dit	<u>H</u>elp
<u>S</u>ummary	<u>N</u>ext Item	<u>A</u>bout
E<u>x</u>it	Next <u>O</u>rder	
	———	
	<u>F</u>ont	
	<u>C</u>olor	

VB Auto Center

Modify the case study project from Chapter 4 to use
menus and a function procedure. Refer to Chapter 4
for project specifications. Use a function procedure to
calculate the sales tax.

Consider adding keyboard shortcuts to the menu
commands.

Note: For help in basing a new project on an existing
project, see "Copy and Move a Windows Project" in
Appendix C.

Menu:

<u>F</u>ile	<u>E</u>dit	<u>H</u>elp
E<u>x</u>it	<u>C</u>alculate	<u>A</u>bout
	C<u>l</u>ear	
	———	
	<u>F</u>ont	
	C<u>o</u>lor	

Video Bonanza

Modify the case study from Chapter 4 to use menus and a function procedure. Refer to Chapter 4 for project specifications. Use a function procedure to calculate the rental fee based on the type of video.

The *Help* menu *About* option should display a message box with information about the program and the programmer. The *Color* option should change the color of the total label.

Menu:

File	Edit	Help
Summary	Calculate Item	About
Exit	Next Item	
	Order Complete	
	———	
	Font	
	Color	

Optional extra: Set keyboard shortcuts for the menu commands.

Note: For help in basing a new project on an existing project, see "Copy and Move a Windows Project" in Appendix C.

Very Very Boards

Modify your project from Chapter 4 to add a menu and a function procedure. Refer to Chapter 4 for the project specifications.

Use a function procedure to calculate the price of shirts; display the *About* box in a message box.

Menu:

File	Sale	Display	Help
Summary	Add to Order	Font	About
———	Begin New Order	Color	
Exit	Clear for Next Item	———	
		Slogan	
		Logo	

Allow the user to change the font size and font color of the labels that display the company slogan.

Include keyboard shortcuts for the menu commands.

The Slogan and Logo: Make up a slogan for the company, such as "We're Number One" or "The Best in Boards." The logo should be a graphic; you can use an icon, any graphic you have available, or a graphic you create yourself with a draw or paint program. (Make sure to include the graphic on your project diskette.)

The *Slogan* and *Logo* menu choices must toggle and display a check mark when selected. For example, when the slogan is displayed, the *Slogan* menu command is checked. If the user selects the *Slogan* command again, hide the slogan and uncheck the menu command. The *Slogan* and *Logo* commands operate independently; that is, the user may select either, both, or neither item. When the project begins, the slogan and logo both must be displayed and their menu commands appear checked.

Note: For help in basing a new project on an existing project, see "Copy and Move a Windows Project" in Appendix C.

'Convert input values to numeric variables
intQuantity = CInt(txtQuantity.Text)
decPrice = CDec(txtPrice.Text)

CHAPTER

6

OOP: Creating Object-Oriented Programs

'Format and display answers for sale
lblExtended.Text = FormatCurrency(decExtende
lblDiscount.Text = FormatNumber(decDiscount)
lblDiscountedPrice.Text = FormatCurrency(decDisco
'Handle exceptions
ch MyErr As InvalidCastException

at the completion of this chapter, you will be able to . . .

1. Use object-oriented terminology correctly.

2. Create a two-tier application that separates the user interface from the business logic.

3. Differentiate between a class and an object.

4. Create a class that has properties and methods.

5. Use property procedures to set and retrieve properties of a class.

6. Declare object variables and assign values to the properties with a constructor or property procedures.

7. Instantiate an object in a project using your class.

8. Differentiate between shared members and instance members.

9. Understand the purpose of the constructor and destructor methods.

10. Inherit a new class from your own class.

11. Apply visual inheritance by deriving a form from another form.

Object-Oriented Programming

You have been using objects since Chapter 1. As you know quite well by now, **objects** have properties and methods and generate events that you can respond to (or ignore) if you choose. Up until now the classes for all objects in your projects have been predefined; that is, you could choose to create a new object of the form class, a button class, a text box class, or any other class of control in the toolbox. In this chapter you will learn to define your own new class and create objects based on that class.

Object-oriented programming (OOP) is currently the most accepted style of programming. Some computer languages, such as Java and SmallTalk, were designed to be object oriented (OO) from their inception. Other languages, such as Visual Basic, have been modified over the last few years to accommodate OOP. Visual Basic .NET is the first version of Visual Basic to be truly object oriented.

Writing object-oriented programs is a mind-set—a different way of looking at a problem. You must think in terms of using objects. As your projects become more complex, using objects becomes increasingly important.

- The OOP features are the biggest change to VB .NET.

- All new OOP constructs:
  - Inherits
  - Overloads
  - Overrides

Objects

Beyond the many built-in choices you have for objects to include in your projects, Visual Basic allows you to create your own new object type by creating a **class**. Just like other object types, your class may have both properties and methods. Remember: Properties are characteristics, and methods are actions that can be performed by a class of object.

An object is a *thing*, such as a button. You create a button object from the button tool in the toolbox. In other words, *Button* is a class, but *btnExit* is an actual occurrence or **instance** of the class; the instance is the object. Just as you may have multiple buttons in a project, you may have many objects of a new class type.

Defining your own class is like creating a new tool for the toolbox; the process does not create the object, only a definition of what that type of object looks like and how it behaves. You may then create as many instances of the class as you need. Your class may be a student, an employee, a product, or any other type of object that would be useful in a project.

Many people use a cookie analogy to describe the relationship of a class and an object. The cookie cutter is the class. You can't eat a cookie cutter, but you can use it to make cookies; the cookie is the object. When you make a cookie using a cookie cutter, you **instantiate** an object of the cookie class. You can use the same cookie cutter to make various kinds of cookies. Although all the cookies made will have the same shape, some may be chocolate, others are lemon or vanilla; some may be frosted or have colored sprinkles on top. The characteristics of the cookie, such as flavor and topping, are the properties of the object. You could refer to the properties of your cookie object as

```
Cookie1.Flavor = "Lemon"
Cookie1.Topping = "Cream Frosting"
```

What about methods? Recall that a method is an action or behavior—something the object can do or have done to it, such as Move, Clear, or Print. Possible methods for our cookie object might be Eat, Bake, or Crumble. Using object terminology, you can refer to Object.Method: `Cookie1.Crumble`.

Sometimes the distinction between a method and an event is somewhat fuzzy. Generally, anything you tell the object to do is a method; if the object does an action and needs to inform you, that's an event. So if you tell the cookie to crumble, that is a method; if the cookie crumbles on its own and needs to inform you of the fact, that's an event.

Object-Oriented Terminology

Key features of an object-oriented language are encapsulation, inheritance, and polymorphism.

Encapsulation

Encapsulation refers to the combination of characteristics of an object along with its behaviors. You have one "package" that holds the definition of all properties, methods, and events. For example, when you create a button, you can set or retrieve its properties, such as Text, Name, or BackColor. You can execute its methods, such as `Focus`, `Hide`, or `Show`, and you can write code for its events, such as Click or Double-click. But you cannot make up new properties or tell it to do anything that it doesn't already know how to do. It is a complete package; you can think of all of the parts of the package as being in a capsule.

You can witness encapsulation by looking at any program. The form is actually a class. All of the methods and events that you code are enclosed within the `Class` and `End Class` statements. The variables that you place in your code are actually properties of the specific form class that you are generating.

Encapsulation is sometimes referred to as data hiding. Each object keeps its data (properties) and procedures (methods) hidden. Through use of the `Public` and `Private` keywords, an object can "expose" only those data elements and procedures that it wishes to allow the outside world to see.

Inheritance

Inheritance is the ability to create a new class from an existing class. You can add enhancements to an existing class without modifying the original. By creating a new class that inherits from an existing class, you can add or change class variables and methods. For example, each of the forms that you create is inherited from, or derived from, the existing Form class. The original class is known as the **base class, superclass,** or the **parent class.** The inherited class is called a **subclass,** a **derived class,** or a **child class.** Of course, a new class can inherit from a subclass—that subclass becomes a superclass as well as a subclass.

Look closely at the first line of code for a form:

```
Public Class Form1
    Inherits System.Windows.Forms.Form
```

Inherited classes have an "is a" relationship with the base class. In the form example, the new Form1 "is a" Form.

The real purpose of inheritance is **reusability**. You may need to reuse or obtain the functionality from one class of object when you have another similar situation. The new Form1 class that you create has all of the characteristics and actions of the base class, System.Windows.Forms.Form. From there you can add the functionality for your own new form.

You can create your own hierarchy of classes. You place the code you want to be common in a base class. You then create other classes, the derived classes or subclasses, which can call the shared functions. This concept is very helpful if you have features that are similar in two classes. Rather than writing two classes that are almost identical, you can create a base class that contains the similar procedures.

An example of reusing classes could be a Person class, where you might have properties for name, address, and phone number. The Person class can be a base class, from which you derive an Employee class, a Customer class, or a Student class (Figure 6.1). The derived classes could call shared procedures from the base class and contain any procedures that are unique to the derived class. In inheritance, typically the classes go from general to the more specific.

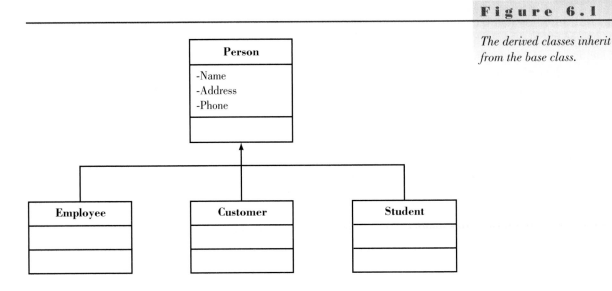

The derived classes inherit from the base class.

Polymorphism

The term *polymorphism* actually means the ability to take on many shapes or forms. As applied to OOP, polymorphism refers to methods having identical names but having different implementations, depending on the situation. For example, radio buttons, check boxes, and list boxes each have a `Select` method. In each case, the `Select` method operates appropriately for its class.

Polymorphism also allows a single class to have more than one method with the same name. When the method is called, the argument type determines which version of the method to use. Each of the identically named methods performs the same task in a slightly different way from the other methods.

Later in this chapter you will use both overloading a method and overriding a method to implement polymorphism. You have already seen examples of **overloading,** such as the `MessageBox.Show` method that gives you several argument lists for calling the method. **Overriding** refers to a method that has the same name as a method in its base class. The method in the subclass, or derived class, takes precedence, or overrides the identically named method in the base class.

Reusable Objects

A big advantage of object-oriented programming over traditional programming is the ability to reuse objects. When you create a new class, you can then use that class in multiple projects. Each object that you create from the class has its own set of properties. This process works just like the built-in VB controls you have been using all along. For example, you can create two PictureBox objects: picOne and picTwo. Each has its own Visible property and Image property, which will probably be set differently from each other.

As you begin creating classes in your projects, you will find many situations in which classes are useful. You might want to create your own class to provide database access. You could include methods for adding and deleting data members. If you work frequently with sales, you might create a Product class. The Product class would likely have properties such as description, quantity, and cost. The methods would probably include finding the current value of the product.

Multitier Applications

A common use of classes is to create applications in multiple "tiers" or layers. Each of the functions of a **multitier application** can be coded in a separate component and the components may be stored and run on different machines.

One of the most popular approaches is a three-tier application. The tiers in this model are the Presentation tier, Business tier, and Data tier (Figure 6.2). You also hear the term *n-tier application,* which is an expansion of the three-tier model. The middle tier, which contains all of the business logic, may be written in multiple classes that can be stored and run from multiple locations.

Figure 6.2

The three-tier model for application design.

Presentation Tier	Business Tier	Data Tier
User Interface Forms, controls, menus	**Business Objects** Validation Calculations Business logic Business rules	**Data Retrieval** Data storage

In a multitier application, the goal is to create components that can be combined and replaced. If one part of an application needs to change, such as a redesign of the user interface or a new database format, the other components do not need to be replaced. A developer can simply "plug in" a new user interface and continue using the rest of the components of the application.

The Presentation tier refers to the user interface, which in VB is the form. Consider that in the future the user interface could be redesigned or even converted to a Web page.

The Business tier is a class or classes that handle the data. This layer can include validation to enforce business rules as well as the calculations.

The Data tier includes retrieving and storing the data in a database. Occasionally an organization will decide to change database vendors or will need to retrieve data from several different sources. The Data tier retrieves the data and passes the results to the Business tier, or takes data from the Business tier and writes them in the appropriate location. Database handling is covered in Chapter 10.

Classes

The classes that you have worked with up until now have generated visual objects such as text boxes and labels. These were easily created from the toolbox at design time. You can also create objects at run time. One example of a class that you would instantiate at run time is the Font class.

Instantiating an Object

To create an object based on a class, you must create an instance of the class using the New **keyword.** This step is referred to as *instantiating an object*.

The New Keyword—General Form

General Form

```
New className()
```

You can give the new object a variable name if you will need to refer to it in the future, or you can instantiate and use the new object without naming it.

The New Keyword—Examples

Examples

```
dim fntMyFont = New Font("Arial", 12)
lblMessage.Font = fntMyFont

lblMessage.Font = New Font("Arial", 12)
```

Notice that when the object is created, two arguments are passed: the name of the font and the point size.

The New keyword creates a new instance of an object class. The object class can be a class that you create or a standard Visual Basic object such as a form or a control.

Specifying a Namespace

You may have noticed that when VB creates a new form class, the Inherits clause says

```
Inherits System.Windows.Forms.Form
```

The name of the class is Form; the **namespace** is System.Windows.Forms. Actually this is a bit of overkill; the entire namespace isn't needed for any classes

• Namespaces and *Inherits* are new features.

in the namespaces that are automatically included in a Windows Forms project, which include System, System.Windows.Forms, and System.Drawing.

When you refer to a class in a different namespace, you have two choices. You can write out the entire namespace and class, such as,

```
lblMessage.Font = New System.Drawing.Font("Arial", 12)
```

Or, you can add an Imports statement to include the namespace, and then refer only to the class name. For example,

```
Imports System.Drawing.Font
lblMessage.Font = New Font("Arial", 12)
```

For specifying fonts, both of these techniques are overkill, since the System.Drawing namespace is automatically imported into all Windows Forms projects. However, you will need to use these techniques for other classes and namespaces, and, if you examine the code generated by the Windows Form Designer, you will see examples with the namespaces spelled out.

✓ **TIP**

Before you can refer to properties or methods of a class, you must instantiate an object of the class. ∎

Designing Your Own Class

To design your own class, you need to analyze the characteristics and behaviors that your object needs. The characteristics or properties are defined as variables, and the behaviors (methods) are sub procedures or function procedures.

Creating Properties in a Class

Inside your class module you define variables, which are the properties of the class. Theoretically you could declare all variables as Public so that all other project code could set and retrieve their values. However, this approach violates the rules of encapsulation that require each object to be in charge of its own data. Remember that encapsulation is also called *data hiding*. To accomplish encapsulation, you will declare all variables in a class module as Private. As a private variable, the value is available only to the procedures within the class module, the same way that module-level variables are available only to procedures within the form module.

When your program creates objects from your class, you will need to assign values to the properties. Because the properties are private variables, you will use special property procedures to pass the values to the class module and to return values from the class module.

Property Procedures

The way that your class allows its properties to be accessed is through a **property procedure.** The procedure may contain a Get to retrieve a property value and/or a Set to assign a value to the property. The name that you use for the Property procedure becomes the name of the property to the outside world. Create "friendly" procedure names that describe the property without using a prefix, such as LastName or EmployeeNumber.

• New format for property procedures: A property procedure block has a *Get* section and a *Set* section.

• The *Property Let* is gone; it was changed to *Set*.

The Property Procedure—General Form

General Form

```
Private ClassVariable As DataType

[Public] Property PropertyName As DataType
    Get
        PropertyName = ClassVariable
    End Get

    Set(ByVal Value As DataType)

        [statements, such as validation]
        ClassVariable = Value
    End Set
End Property
```

The Set statement uses the Value **keyword** to refer to the incoming value for the property. Property procedures are public by default, so you can omit the optional Public keyword. Get blocks are similar to function procedures in at least one respect: Somewhere inside the procedure, before the End Get, you must assign a return value to the procedure name or use a Return statement to return a value. The data type of the incoming value for a Set must match the type of the return value of the corresponding Get.

The Property Procedure—Example

Example

```
Private mstrLastName As String

Property LastName As String
    Get
        LastName = mstrLastName
    End Get

    Set(ByVal Value As String)
        mstrLastName = Value
    End Set
End Property
```

Remember, the private module-level variable holds the value of the property. The Property Get and Set retrieve the current value and assign a new value to the property.

Read-Only Properties

In some instances you may wish to set a value for a property that can only be retrieved by an object but not changed. To create a read-only property, use the ReadOnly modifier and write only the Get portion of the property procedure.

• You can create read-only or write-only properties using the *Read-Only* and *WriteOnly* keywords.

```
Private mdecTotalPay As Decimal      'Define the property at the module level

ReadOnly Property SalesTotal() As Decimal     'Make the property read-only
    Get
        TotalPay = mdecTotalPay
    End Get
End Property
```

Creating a New Class—Step-by-Step

In this step-by-step tutorial you will create a new class to hold book sale information for R 'n R.

Begin the Project

A class is part of a Visual Basic project, so the first step is to create a new project.

STEP 1: Create a new Windows Form project called Ch06SBS.

Begin a New Class

STEP 1: Select *Add Class* from the *Project* menu. The *Add New Item* dialog box will appear (Figure 6.3).

Figure 6.3

Add a new class to a project in the Add New Item *dialog box.*

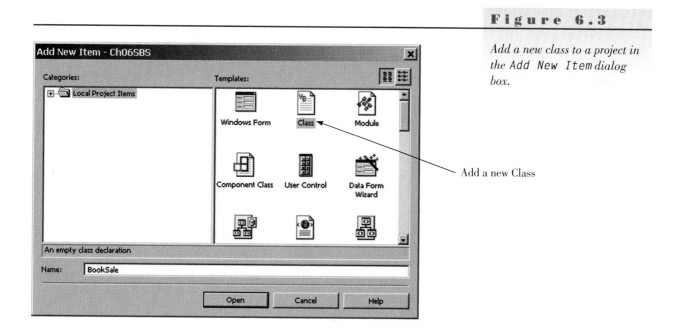

Add a new Class

STEP 2: From the *Add New Item* dialog choose *Class,* type "BookSale" for the class name and click on *Open.* You will see a new tab in the Editor window for the new class.

Define the Class Properties

STEP 1: In the declarations section of the Code window, right after the Class statement, declare the Private variables. These module-level variables become the properties of your new class.

```
Private mstrTitle As String
Private mintQuantity As Integer
Private mdecPrice As Decimal
```

TIP

Use prefixes on the module-level variable to hold the property value; use a friendly name without a prefix for the property names. ∎

This class has three private module-level variables: mstrTitle, mintQuantity, and mdecPrice (Figure 6.4). Because the variables are declared as private, they can be accessed only by procedures within the class module. To allow access from outside the class module, you must add property procedures.

Declare module-level variables for the class properties.

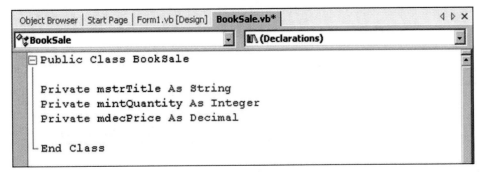

Add the Title Property Procedure

STEP 1: In the Editor window, after the property declarations, type "Property Title As String". Press Enter.

STEP 2: The Get and Set blocks will appear.

STEP 3: Write the code for the Property procedures, indenting as shown.

```
Property Title() As String
    Get
        Title = mstrTitle
    End Get

    Set(ByVal Value As String)
        mstrTitle = Value
    End Set
End Property
```

Add the Quantity Property Procedure

STEP 1: After the End Property for Title, type "Property Quantity As Integer". Press Enter.

STEP 2: The Get and Set blocks will appear.

STEP 3: Write the code for the Property procedure.

```
Property Quantity() As Integer
    Get
        Quantity = mintQuantity
    End Get

    Set(ByVal Value As Integer)
        If Value >= 0 Then
            mintQuantity = Value
        End If
    End Set
End Property
```

Notice that the incoming Value in the Set is being validated.

Add the Price Property Procedure

STEP 1: After the End Property for Quantity, add the property procedure for Price.

STEP 2: Write the code.

```
Property Price() As Decimal
    Get
        Price = mdecPrice
    End Get

    Set(ByVal Value As Decimal)
        If Value >= 0 Then
            mdecPrice = Value
        End If
    End Set
End Property
```

Code a Method

You can create methods by adding sub procedures and functions for the behaviors needed by the class. For this class, you will add a method as a function procedure to calculate the extended price, which is the price per book multiplied by the quantity.

STEP 1: After the property procedures, type in "Public Function Extended-Price As Decimal" and press Enter.

Notice that the editor adds the parentheses after the function name.

STEP 2: Type the code for the function.

```
Public Function ExtendedPrice() As Decimal
    'Calculate the extended price

    Return mintQuantity * mdecPrice
End Function
```

Add General Remarks

```
'Class Name: BookSale
'Programmer: Your Name
'Date:        Today's Date
'Description:       Handle book sale information.
'Folder:     Ch06SBS
```

Create Regions

Regions of code allow you to hide sections of code in the same way that the Editor window hides the Windows generated code. To add a region, place a #Region statement in your code followed by a string literal giving the name for the region. An End Region tag is automatically created.

- Create collapsible regions in code, similar to the Form Designer generated code section.

STEP 1: Type "#Region "Properties"" before your first property declaration. (Include the quotes around the literal "Properties".)

STEP 2: Move the #End Region to follow the end of the property procedures.

STEP 3: Create a region for your methods.

STEP 4: Check the indentation of your code. You can select a block of code and click the Increase Indent toolbar button or the Tab key.

STEP 5: Save your project.

The Complete Class Code

```
'Class Name:        BookSale
'Programmer:        Your Name
'Date:              Today's Date
'Description:       Handle book sale information.
'Folder:            Ch06SBS

Option Strict On

Public Class BookSale

#Region "Properties"

    Private mstrTitle As String
    Private mintQuantity As Integer
    Private mdecPrice As Decimal

    Property Title() As String
        Get
            Title = mstrTitle
        End Get

        Set(ByVal Value As String)
            mstrTitle = Value
        End Set
    End Property

    Property Quantity() As Integer
        Get
            Quantity = mintQuantity
        End Get

        Set(ByVal Value As Integer)
            If Value >= 0 Then
                mintQuantity = Value
            End If
        End Set
    End Property

    Property Price() As Decimal
        Get
            Price = mdecPrice
        End Get

        Set(ByVal Value As Decimal)
            If Value >= 0 Then
                mdecPrice = Value
            End If
        End Set
    End Property
#End Region

#Region "Methods"
    Public Function ExtendedPrice() As Decimal
        'Calculate the extended price
        Return mintQuantity * mdecPrice

    End Function
#End Region
End Class
```

► **Feedback 6.1**

1. What is the difference between an object and a class?
2. Write the property declarations for a class module for a Student class that will contain the properties: LastName, FirstName, StudentIDNumber, and GPA. Where will these statements appear?
3. Code the Property procedure to set and retrieve the value of the LastName property.
4. Code the Property procedure to retrieve the value of the ReadOnly GPA property.

Creating a New Object Using a Class

Creating a class does not create any objects. This is similar to creating a new tool for the toolbox but not yet creating an instance of the class.

Generally you will create new objects of your class in a two-step operation: first declare a variable for the new object and then instantiate the object using the New keyword. Use Dim, Public, or Private to declare the identifier and the class:

```
Private mBookSale As BookSale
```

This line merely states that the name mBookSale is associated with the Book-Sale class, but it does not create an instance of the object. You must use the New keyword to actually create the object:

```
mBookSale = New BookSale
```

In Visual Basic it is legal to declare and instantiate an object at the same time:

```
Dim mBookSale As New BookSale
```

However, the preferred method is to declare the statements separately where they are needed. This is a better approach for several reasons. The variable declarations generally belong in the Declarations section of code, which is at the top of the class and not inside a procedure. When you instantiate an object, you generally should include the New statement in a Try/Catch block for error checking, and a Try/Catch block *must* be inside a procedure. Also, if you place the New statement in the Declarations section, you have no control over when the object is actually created. It's best to use the New keyword inside of a procedure at the time the object is needed. And if the object is never needed, it won't be created needlessly.

If you *do* choose to declare the variable and instantiate it at the same time, these two statements are equivalent:

```
Dim mBookSale As BookSale = New BookSale
Dim mBookSale as New BookSale
```

The second statement is a coding shortcut for the first (more complete) statement. *Note:* The *m* prefix on the object variables indicates that the variables are declared at the module level.

Defining and Using a New Object—Step-by-Step

To continue the step-by-step tutorial for the BookSale class, the next step is to design the form for the user interface. The form has text boxes for the user to enter the title, quantity, and price, a menu choice to calculate the sale (the extended price), and another menu item to exit.

In the Calculate Sale event procedure, you will create an instance of the BookSale class and assign the input values for title, quantity, and price to the properties of the BookSale object. The ExtendedPrice method in the Book-Sale class calculates the amount of the sale, which appears in a label on the form. Figure 6.5 shows the completed form.

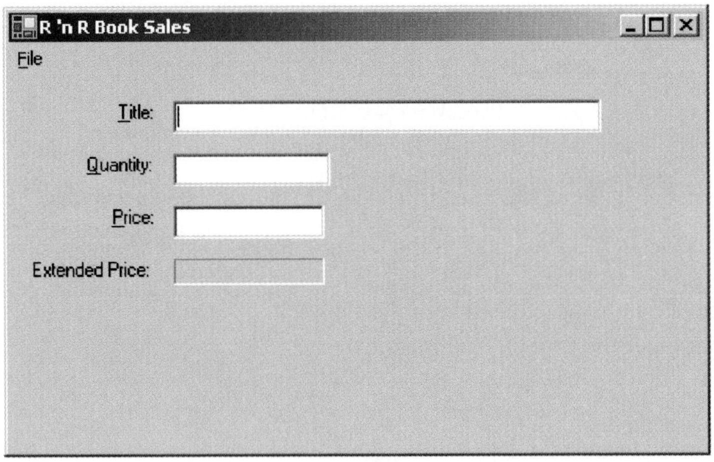

Figure 6.5

The user interface that uses the new BookSale class; the completed form for the step-by-step tutorial.

Placing all calculations in a separate class is a good thing. You are seeing your first example of dividing a program into a Presentation tier and a Business tier.

Create the Form

This is a continuation of the step-by-step tutorial for this chapter. If the project is not still open, open it now.

STEP 1: Open the form. Referring to Figure 6.5, create the user interface with text boxes for the title, quantity, and price, and a label for the extended price. Set appropriate properties for the form and the controls.

STEP 2: Change the form name to frmSales. Open the `Project Properties` dialog box and set the startup object to frmSales.

STEP 3: Create menu items on the `File` menu for `Calculate Sale` and `Exit`. Make sure to follow naming guidelines for the items, such as mnuFile-CalculateSale and mnuFileExit.

Add General Remarks

STEP 1: Type the remarks at the top of the code.

```
'Program:           Chapter 6 BookSale Step-by-Step
'Programmer:        Your Name
'Date:              Today's Date
'Description:       Calculate sales price using the BookSale class.
'                   Instantiate mBookSale as a new object of the BookSale class.
'Folder:            Ch06SBS
```

Declare the New Object

STEP 1: Declare the object variable in the Declarations section, right under the Windows Form Designer generated code.

```
Private mBookSale As BookSale          'Declare the new object
```

Write the Code

STEP 1: In the mnuFileCalculateSale event procedure, write the code to instantiate the BookSale object, assign the values to the properties, calculate the extended price, and assign the result to lblExtendedPrice. Notice that IntelliSense pops up with the properties and method of your new BookSale class.

```
Private Sub mnuFileCalculateSale_Click(ByVal sender As System.Object, _
  ByVal e As System.EventArgs) Handles mnuFileCalculateSale.Click
    'Calculate the extended price for the sale

    Try
        mBookSale = New BookSale()          'Instantiate the object

        mBookSale.Title = txtTitle.Text    'Set the properties
        mBookSale.Quantity = CInt(txtQuantity.Text)
        mBookSale.Price = CDec(txtPrice.Text)

        'Calculate and format the result
        lblExtendedPrice.Text = FormatNumber(mBookSale.ExtendedPrice)

    Catch
        MessageBox.Show("Error in quantity or price field.", "R 'n R Book Sales", _
          MessageBoxButtons.OK, MessageBoxIcon.Exclamation)
    End Try
End Sub
```

STEP 2: Code the mnuFileExit_Click procedure.

```
Me.Close()
```

Save Your Work

STEP 1: Click the Save All toolbar button to save the project, class, and form.

Run the Project

The next step is to watch the project run—hopefully without errors.

STEP 1: Run the program; your form should appear.
STEP 2: Fill in test values for the title, quantity, and price. Select the `Calculate Price` menu item. What did you get for the extended price? Is it correct?

Single-Step the Execution

If you get an error message or an incorrect answer in the output, you will need to debug the project. The quickest and easiest way to debug is to single-step program execution. Single-stepping is an interesting exercise, even if you *did* get the right answer.

To single-step, you need to be in break time. Place a breakpoint on the first line in the mnuFileCalculatePrice_Click procedure (the `Try` statement). Run the program, enter test values for quantity and price, and select `File/Calculate Price`. When the program stops at the breakpoint, press the F11 key repeatedly and watch each step; you will see execution transfer to the code for BookSale class for each property and for the `ExtendedPrice` method. If an error message halts program execution, point to the variable names and property names on the screen to see their current values.

When the click event procedure finishes, click on your project's task bar button, if necessary, to make the form reappear.

Instance Variables versus Shared Variables

The class properties that you have created up to this point belong to each instance of the class. Therefore, if you create two BookSale objects, each object has its own set of properties. This is exactly what you want for properties such as quantity and price, but what if you need to find a total or count for all of the BookSales objects? You don't want each new object to have its own count property; there would be nothing to increment.

The properties we have created thus far are called ***instance variables*** or ***instance properties.*** A separate memory location exists for each instance of the object. Now we will create **shared variables**, also called *shared properties*. A **shared property** is a single variable that exists, or is available, for all objects of a class.

Terminology varies from one OOP language to another. In some languages, shared members are called *class variables*. Microsoft documentation refers to *instance members* and *shared members*, which include both properties and methods. In general, a shared member has one copy for all objects of the class, and an instance member has one copy for *each* instance or object of the class. Methods can also be declared as shared and are considered shared members.

Another important point is that you can access shared members without instantiating an object of the class. When you display class documentation in MSDN Help, shared members display with a yellow *S* next to the name (Figure 6.6). You can reference these shared members with ClassName.Property or ClassName.Method, even though you have not instantiated an object from the class.

• Shared members provide the ability to have a single variable shared by all objects of a class.

Shared members display in MSDN Help with a yellow S.

| Object Browser | Payroll.vb | **String Members** | Form1.vb [Design]* | Form1.vb* | ◁ ▷ ✕ |

⊞ *.NET Framework Class Library*
String Members

Public Methods

➡◆Clone	Returns a reference to this instance of **String**.
➡◆ S Compare	Overloaded. Compares two specified **String** objects.
➡◆ S CompareOrdinal	Overloaded. Compares two **String** objects, without considering the local national language or culture.
➡◆CompareTo	Overloaded. Compares this instance with a specified object.
➡◆ S Concat	Overloaded. Concatenates one or more instances of **String**, or the **String** representations of the values of one or more instances of <u>Object</u>.
➡◆ S Copy	Creates a new instance of **String** with the same value as a specified instance of **String**.
➡◆CopyTo	Copies a specified number of characters from a specified position in this instance to a specified position in an array of Unicode characters.
➡◆EndsWith	Determines whether the end of this instance matches the specified **String**.

Creating Shared Members

Use the Shared keyword to create a shared member.

```
[Public|Private] Shared VariableName As Datatype

[Public|Private] Shared Function FunctionName(ArgumentList) As Datatype
```

If we want to accumulate a total of all sales and a count of the number of sales for our BookSale class, we need shared properties:

```
Private Shared mdecSalesTotal As Decimal       'Hold SalesTotal property
Private Shared mintSalesCount As Integer        'Hold SalesCount property
```

You will want to make these shared properties read-only, so that their values can be retrieved but not set directly. The values of the properties are accumulated inside the class; each time a new sale is calculated, the extended price is added to the total sales and the sales count is incremented by one.

```
Shared ReadOnly Property SalesTotal() As Decimal
    Get
        SalesTotal = mdecSalesTotal
    End Get
End Property

Shared ReadOnly Property SalesCount() As Integer
    Get
        SalesCount = mintSalesCount
    End Get
End Property
```

Note that the Shared keyword is optional in the property procedure. You need to use it if you plan to retrieve the property without first creating an instance of the class.

Adding Shared Properties to the Step-by-Step Tutorial

You will now make the BookSale class calculate the total of all sales and a count of the number of sales. You will need shared properties for the sales total and sales count in the class. Then on the form, you will add a menu option for *Summary* that displays the totals in a message box.

Add Shared Properties to the Class

STEP 1: In the BookSale class, add the declarations for mdecSalesTotal and mintSalesCount below the private variables at the top of the class.

```
Private Shared mdecSalesTotal As Decimal
Private Shared mintSalesCount As Integer
```

STEP 2: Add the property procedures for these two shared read-only properties inside the Properties region.

```
Shared ReadOnly Property SalesTotal() As Decimal
    Get
        SalesTotal = mdecSalesTotal
    End Get
End Property

Shared ReadOnly Property SalesCount() As Integer
    Get
        SalesCount = mintSalesCount
    End Get
End Property
```

STEP 3: Modify the ExtendedPrice method to add to the totals.

```
Public Function ExtendedPrice() As Decimal
    'Calculate the extended price and add to the totals
    Dim decExtendedPrice As Decimal

    decExtendedPrice = mintQuantity * mdecPrice
    mdecSalesTotal += decExtendedPrice
    mintSalesCount += 1
    Return decExtendedPrice
End Function
```

Modify the Form

STEP 1: Add a menu item for *File/Summary* to the form.
STEP 2: Write the event procedure for mnuFileSummary to display the sales total and sales count from the properties of the class. Format the sales total to display dollars and cents.

```
    Private Sub mnuFileSummary_Click(ByVal sender As System.Object, _
     ByVal e As System.EventArgs) Handles mnuFileSummary.Click
        'Display the sales summary information
        Dim strMessage As String

        strMessage = "Sales Total: " & FormatCurrency(mBookSale.SalesTotal) & _
          ControlChars.NewLine & "Sales Count: " & CStr(mBookSale.SalesCount)
        MessageBox.Show(strMessage, "R 'n R Book Sales Summary", _
          MessageBoxButtons.OK, MessageBoxIcon.Information)
    End Sub
```

STEP 3: Test the program. Try entering several sales and checking the totals. Also try selecting *Summary* without first calculating a sale. If the program throws an exception, it means that you left the Shared modifier off the property procedures for the two shared properties.

Constructors and Destructors

A **constructor** is a method that automatically executes when an object is instantiated. A **destructor** is a method that automatically executes when an object is destroyed.

Constructors

You can create a constructor for your class by writing a Sub New procedure. The constructor executes automatically when you instantiate an object of the class. Because the constructor method executes before any other code in the class, the constructor is an ideal location for any initialization tasks that you need to do, such as opening a database connection.

• A class constructor must be named New and may be overloaded. The old Class_Initialize and Class_Terminate procedures are gone.

The Sub New procedure must be Public, because the objects that you create must execute this method. Remember that the default is Public.

```
Sub New()
    'Constructor for class

    'Initialization statements
End sub
```

Overloading the Constructor

Recall from Chapter 3 that overloading means that two methods have the same name but a different list of arguments (the signature). You can create overloaded methods in your class by giving the same name to multiple procedures, each with a different argument list. The following example shows an empty constructor (one without arguments) and a constructor that passes arguments to the class.

```
Sub New()
    'Constructor with empty argument list
End Sub

Sub New(ByVal Title As String, ByVal Quantity As Integer, ByVal Price As Decimal)
    'Assign property values

    mstrTitle = Title
    mintQuantity = Quantity
    mdecPrice = Price
End Sub
```

Note: It isn't necessary to include the ByVal modifier, since ByVal is the default. However, the editor adds ByVal to the arguments if you leave it out.

Parameterized Constructor

The term **parameterized constructor** refers to a constructor that requires arguments. This popular technique allows you to pass arguments/properties as you create the new object. For example, in our previous BookSale example, the code in the form instantiated an object and then set properties:

- Parameterized constructors allow arguments to be passed when creating an object.

```
mBookSale = New BookSale() 'Instantiate the object
mBookSale.Title = txtTitle.Text 'Set the properties
mBookSale.Quantity = CInt(txtQuantity.Text)
mBookSale.Price = CDec(txtPrice.Text)
```

Using a parameterized constructor, the code in the form is shorter and cleaner:

```
'Instantiate the object and set the properties
mBookSale = New BookSale(txtTitle.Text, CInt(txtQuantity.Text), CDec(txtPrice.Text))
```

As a further improvement to the BookSale parameterized constructor, we will use the property procedures to assign initial property values. Within the class module, use the Me keyword to refer to the current class. So Me.Quantity refers to the Quantity property of the current class. This technique is preferable to just assigning the passed argument to the module-level property variables, since validation is performed in the Property Set procedures.

```
Sub New(ByVal Title As String, ByVal Quantity As Integer, ByVal Price As Decimal)
    'Assign property values

    Me.Title = Title
    Me.Quantity = Quantity
    Me.Price = Price
End Sub
```

When your class has both an empty constructor and a parameterized constructor, the program that creates the object can choose which method to use.

Adding Constructors to the Step-by-Step Tutorial

This optional continuation of the chapter step-by-step tutorial adds overloaded constructors to the BookSale class. You will add an empty constructor and a parameterized constructor, and modify the form to use the parameterized constructor.

Add the Constructors

STEP 1: Open the BookSale class and add the two constructor methods to the Methods region.

```
Sub New()
    'Empty argument list to create a new object
End Sub

Sub New(ByVal Title As String, ByVal Quantity As Integer, _
 ByVal Price As Decimal)
    'Assign property values

    Me.Title = Title
    Me.Quantity = Quantity
    Me.Price = Price
End Sub
```

Having the two overloaded constructors means that the program that creates objects from this class can use either method. Your program should still work correctly, but now we'll change the program to use the parameterized constructor.

Modify the Form

STEP 1: In the form's code, modify the mnuFileCalculateSale_Click event procedure to use the BookSale class parameterized constructor. Remove the four lines that instantiate the object and assign the properties and replace them with the single statement. Make sure to include the statement within the Try/Catch block.

```
'Instantiate the object and set the properties
mBookSale = New BookSale(txtTitle.Text, CInt(txtQuantity.Text), CDec(txtPrice.Text))
```

Test the Program

STEP 1: Run the program to test it. Everything should still work correctly.

STEP 2: Set a breakpoint at the top of the mnuFileCalculatePrice_Click procedure on the Try statement.

STEP 3: Run the program again, enter test values, and select *File/Calculate Sale*. When the program stops at the breakpoint, press F11 repeatedly and watch the steps that instantiate the object and assign property values. You will see each property procedure execute. When you are finished, stop execution.

Save this Version of the Program

STEP 1: This program will be used in Chapter 11. After you save and close the project, make a copy of the project folder. Name the folder copy Ch11SBS.

Destructors

If there is special processing that you need to do when an object goes out of scope, you can write a Finalize procedure, which is also called a *destructor*. However, Microsoft recommends against writing Finalize procedures unless you need to do something special that the system doesn't know how to handle, such as closing some types of database connections.

Garbage Collection

The **garbage collection** feature of the .NET Common Language Runtime (CLR) cleans up unused components. Periodically the garbage collector checks for unreferenced objects and releases all memory and system resources used by the objects. If you have written a Finalize procedure, it executes during garbage collection. Microsoft recommends that you rely on garbage collection to release resources and not try to finalize objects yourself. Using this technique, you don't know exactly when your objects will be finalized, since the CLR performs garbage collection on its own schedule, when it needs to recover the resources or has spare time.

- Microsoft advises against setting object variables to Nothing. Garbage collection periodically cleans up all nonreferenced objects.

Inheritance

When you create a class, the new class can be based on another class. You can make the new class inherit from one of the VB existing classes or from one of your own classes. Recall that a form uses inheritance using the statement

```
Public Class Form1
    Inherits System.Windows.Forms.Form.
```

The Inherits statement must follow the class header prior to any comments.

```
Public Class NewClass
    Inherits BaseClass
```

Inheriting Properties and Methods

All public data members and methods of the base class are inherited in the derived class. If you want a private member to be included, you must change the Private modifier in the base class to Protected. A protected class member acts like a private data member or method but is inherited by a derived class.

- The Protected qualifier allows a variable to act like a Private while still allowing for inheritance.

```
Protected mstrTitle As String                'Title property
Protected mintQuantity As Integer            'Quantity property
Protected mdecPrice As Decimal               'Price property
Protected Shared mdecSalesTotal As Decimal   'SalesTotal property
Protected Shared mintSalesCount As Integer   'SalesCount property
```

Inheriting Constructors

Although a derived class can inherit all public or protected methods, there is one exception. The subclass cannot inherit constructors from the base class. Each class must have its own constructors, unless the only constructor needed is an empty constructor. (Visual Basic automatically creates an empty constructor for all classes, so you don't need to write one if that's the only constructor that you need.)

Calling the Base Class Constructor

Often an inherited class needs to make sure that the constructor for the base class executes as well as the constructor for the inherited class. You can call the base class constructor with the statement

```
MyBase.New()
```

You generally place this code in the constructor for the inherited class, before any additional statements.

```
Sub New(ByVal Title As String, ByVal Quantity As Integer, ByVal Price As Decimal)
    'Assign property values

    MyBase.New()        'Call the base class constructor
    Me.Title = Title
    Me.Quantity = Quantity
    Me.Price = Price
End Sub
```

Overriding Methods

You can create a method with the same name and the same argument list as a method in the base class. The new method is said to override the base class method. The derived class will use the new method rather than the method in the base class.

To override a method in Visual Basic .NET, you must declare the original method with the `Overridable` keyword and declare the new method with the `Overrides` keyword.

• To override a method, the method in the base class must be declared with the `Overridable` keyword and the new method in the derived class must use the `Overrides` keyword.

Base Class

```
Public Overridable Function ExtendedPrice() As Decimal
```

Inherited Class

```
Overrides Function ExtendedPrice() As Decimal
```

Creating a Derived Class Based on BookSale

The BookSale class could be considered a generic class, which is appropriate for most sales. Now we want another similar class, but with some differences. The new class should have all of the same properties and methods of the Book-Sale class, but it should calculate sales with a student discount of 15 percent. We also want a new shared property in the new class to hold the total of the student discounts.

Our new derived class will be called *StudentBookSale;* the base class is *BookSale.* Figure 6.7 shows the diagram to indicate the inherited class. The inherited class automatically has all public properties and methods of the base class; in this case, StudentBookSale automatically has three properties and one method.

The diagram for a base class and a derived class.

Adding Inheritance to the Step-by-Step Tutorial

This continuation of the chapter step-by-step tutorial includes a new derived class, overriding a method, and adding a new property.

Add the New Class

STEP 1: Open your project, if necessary, and select *Add Class* from the *Project* menu.

STEP 2: In the *Add New Item* dialog choose *Class,* type "StudentBookSale" for the class name, and click on *Open.* You will see a new tab in the Editor window for the new class.

STEP 3: Add a new line after the class declaration and type the Inherits statement.

```
Public Class StudentBookSale
    Inherits BookSale
```

All of the public properties and methods of the base class will be inherited by the subclass.

Add the Constructors

STEP 1: The subclass must have its own constructors, since constructors are not inherited.

```
Sub New()
    'Constructor with empty argument list

    MyBase.New()    'Call the base class constructor
End Sub
```

```
Sub New(ByVal Title As String, ByVal Quantity As Integer, _
  ByVal Price As Decimal)
    'Assign property values

    MyBase.New()    'Call the base class constructor
    Me.Title = Title
    Me.Quantity = Quantity
    Me.Price = Price
End Sub
```

Add the New Property

STEP 1: Add a new read-only shared property in the Declarations section. This will hold the total of discounts.

```
Shared ReadOnly mdecDiscountTotal As Decimal
```

STEP 2: Add the property procedure for DiscountTotal.

```
Shared ReadOnly Property DiscountTotal() As Decimal
    Get
        DiscountTotal = mdecDiscountTotal
    End Get
End Property
```

Add a Constant

STEP 1: Add a constant in the Declarations section to hold the discount rate of 15 percent.

```
Const mdecDISCOUNT_RATE As Decimal = 0.15D
```

Override a Method

When you override a method from the base class in an inherited class, the method name and the argument list must exactly match.

STEP 1: Open the BookSale base class in the editor and modify the function header for ExtendedPrice.

```
Public Overridable Function ExtendedPrice() As Decimal
```

STEP 2: In the BookSale base class, change the Private modifier to Protected for the property variables. (See page 260 for an example.)

STEP 3: In the StudentBookSale inherited class, write the new ExtendedPrice function using the Overrides keyword. You can copy and paste the function from the base class and make the modifications, or type the entire function.

```
Overrides Function ExtendedPrice() As Decimal
    'Calculate the extended price and add to the totals
    Dim decExtendedPrice As Decimal
    Dim decDiscount As Decimal

    decDiscount = mintQuantity * mdecPrice * mdecDISCOUNT_RATE
    decExtendedPrice = mintQuantity * mdecPrice - decDiscount
    mdecSalesTotal += decExtendedPrice
    mintSalesCount += 1
    mdecDiscountTotal += decDiscount
    Return decExtendedPrice
End Function
```

Modify the Form to Use the Inherited Class

STEP 1: Add a check box to the form, named *chkStudent,* with the Text set to *Student.* You can set the RightToLeft property to Yes, if you want the text to appear to the left of the box (Figure 6.8). Rearrange the controls to keep the input fields together.

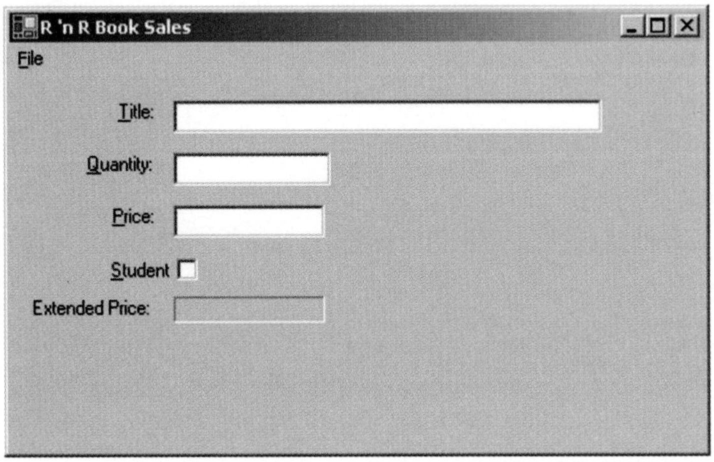

Figure 6.8

Add a Student check box to the form.

STEP 2: Add a module-level variable to the new StudentBookSale class.

```
Private mStudentBookSale As StudentBookSale
```

STEP 3: In the form, modify the mnuFileCalculateSale event procedure to create the correct object, depending on the state of chkStudent.

```
If chkStudent.Checked Then

    'Instantiate the StudentBookSale object and set the properties
    mStudentBookSale = New StudentBookSale(txtTitle.Text, _
        CInt(txtQuantity.Text), CDec(txtPrice.Text))
    'Calculate and format the result
    lblExtendedPrice.Text = FormatNumber(mStudentBookSale.ExtendedPrice)
Else

    'Instantiate the BookSale object and set the properties
    mBookSale = New BookSale(txtTitle.Text, CInt(txtQuantity.Text), _
        CDec(txtPrice.Text))
    'Calculate and format the result
    lblExtendedPrice.Text = FormatNumber(mBookSale.ExtendedPrice)
End If
```

Notice that the code calls the ExtendedPrice method in either case. But when chkStudent is checked, the ExtendedPrice function of the subclass is called; when the check box is not checked, the Extended-Price function of the base class is called. Both functions add to the shared SalesTotal and SalesCount properties, which will hold the totals for both classes.

STEP 4: In the form, modify the mnuFileSummary event procedure to include the discount total.

```
strMessage = "Sales Total: " & FormatCurrency(mBookSale.SalesTotal) & _
    ControlChars.NewLine & "Sales Count: " & CStr(mBookSale.SalesCount) & _
    ControlChars.NewLine & "Total of Student Discounts: " & _
    FormatCurrency(mStudentBookSale.DiscountTotal)
```

Creating a Base Class Strictly for Inheritance

Sometimes you may want to create a class solely for the purpose of inheritance by two or more similar classes. For example, you might create a Person class that you don't intend to instantiate. Instead you will create subclasses of the Person class, such as Employee, Customer, and Student.

For a base class that you intend to inherit, include the MustInherit modifier on the class declaration. In each of the methods in the base class that must be overridden, include the MustOverride modifier. The method that must be overridden does not contain any code in the base class.

- Use the MustOverride keyword in a base class method for a method that must have its implementation in the derived class.

```
MustInherit Class BaseClass
    Public MustOverride Sub SomeProcedure()
        'No code allowed here
    End Sub
End Class

Class DerivedClass
    Inherits BaseClass
    Public Overrides Sub SomeProcedure()
        'Code goes here
    End Sub
End Class
```

Inheriting Form Classes

Some projects require that you have several forms. You may want to use a similar design from one form to the next. You can use visual inheritance by designing one form and then inheriting any other forms from the first (Figure 6.9).

- Forms are classes that can be used for inheritance.

- You cannot just reference a form by name without creating an object variable and instantiating the object.

Figure 6.9

Create a base form and inherit the visual interface to new forms.

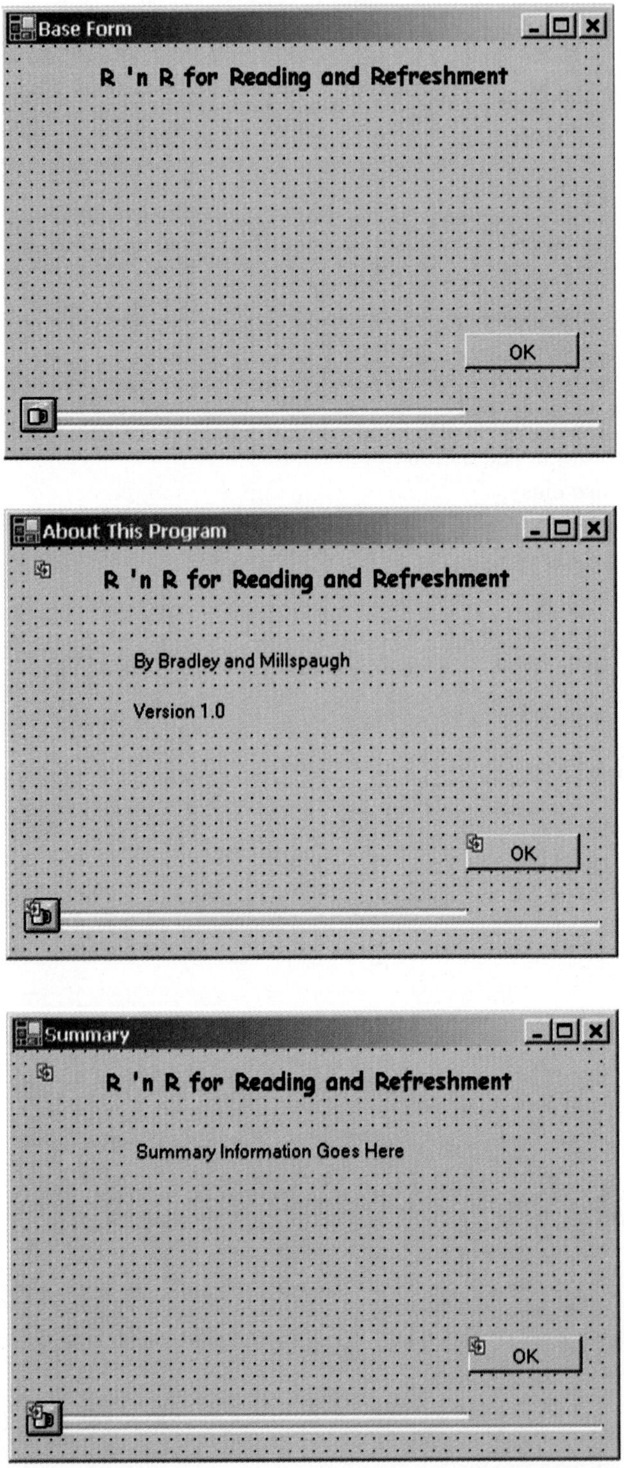

Once you have designed the form that you want to use for a pattern, you can add more forms that inherit from your design master, called your *base class*. Your base class inherits from System.Windows.Forms.Form, and your new forms inherit from your base class.

When you design the base class, you can include design elements and other controls, such as labels, text boxes, and buttons. You can also write procedures and declare variables in the base class. Just as you saw earlier, all public procedures and variables are inherited from the base class to the subclass. You can write procedures in the base class and specify Overridable or MustOverride, and then in the subclass write the identically named procedure with the Overrides clause.

You can create an inherited form class in two ways:

1. Select *Project/Add Windows Form* and type in a name for the new Windows form. Then modify the Inherits statement to inherit from your base form using your project name as the namespace.

```
Public Class MyDerivedForm
    Inherits ProjectName.BaseFormName
```

2. Select *Project/Add Inherited Form* and type the name of the new form. After naming your form, you are shown a dialog displaying the forms in the project from which to select.

Form Inheritance Example

This example has three forms that inherit from a base class. The base class has an OK button, a picture box, and labels. All forms that inherit from the base class will have all of these controls, but the Text property of the base class is not inherited. You cannot delete any of the controls on the inherited forms, but you can make a control invisible. For example, in frmMain, the OK button's Visible property is set to False.

The base class has a btnOK_Click event procedure, which can be overridden in the subclasses.

frmBase

```
Public Class frmBase
    Inherits System.Windows.Forms.Form

    Public Overridable Sub btnOK_Click(ByVal sender As System.Object, _
      ByVal e As System.EventArgs) Handles btnOK.Click
        'Allow inherited classes to override this method.

    End Sub
End Class
```

frmAbout

```
Public Class frmAbout
    Inherits Ch06Multiforms.frmBase

    Public Overrides Sub btnOK_Click(ByVal sender As System.Object, _
      ByVal e As System.EventArgs) Handles btnOK.Click
        'Override the base class method.

        Me.Close()
    End Sub
End Class
```

frmMain

```vb
Public Class frmMain
    Inherits Ch06Multiforms.frmBase

    Private Sub frmMain_Load(ByVal sender As System.Object, _
     ByVal e As System.EventArgs) Handles MyBase.Load
        'Hide the OK button for this form

        btnOK.Visible = False
    End Sub

    Private Sub mnuFileExit_Click(ByVal sender As Object, _
     ByVal e As System.EventArgs) Handles mnuFileExit.Click
        'Exit the application

        Me.Close()
    End Sub

    Private Sub mnuHelpAbout_Click(ByVal sender As Object, _
     ByVal e As System.EventArgs) Handles mnuHelpAbout.Click
        'Show the About form

        Dim frmAboutInstance As New frmAbout()
        frmAboutInstance.ShowDialog()
    End Sub

    Private Sub mnuFileSummary_Click(ByVal sender As Object, _
        ByVal e As System.EventArgs) Handles mnuFileSummary.Click
        'Show the Summary form

        Dim frmSummaryInstance As New frmSummary()
        frmSummaryInstance.ShowDialog()
    End Sub
End Class
```

frmSummary

```vb
Public Class frmSummary
    Inherits Ch06Multiforms.frmBase

    Public Overrides Sub btnOK_Click(ByVal sender As System.Object, _
     ByVal e As System.EventArgs) Handles btnOK.Click
        'Override the base class method.

        Me.Close()
    End Sub
End Class
```

Coding for Events of an Inherited Class

When you derive a new form class from an existing form, you often want to write code for events of inherited controls. Unfortunately, you can't double-click on an inherited control and have the event procedure open, like you can for most controls. In the previous example of form inheritance, for the btnOK_Click event procedure header, we copied the procedure from the base class into the derived class and made the modifications.

Displaying Values on a Different Form

When you have multiple forms in a project, you may want to reference controls on one form from another form. For example, maybe the code in the main form calculates information that you want to display on a summary form. Earlier you displayed summary information in a message box; in this chapter you will display the summary information on another form.

> • In OOP programming, you should avoid global variables if at all possible. Instead, create properties of a form's class and/or reference controls on another form. Global variables, now called namespace-level variables, are purposely omitted from this text.

You can easily refer to the controls on another form by using the identifier for the form instance. Write the reference as *FormInstance.ControlName. Property*.

```
Dim frmSummaryInstance As New frmSummary()
frmSummaryInstance.lblSalesTotal.Text = FormatCurrency(mBookSale.SalesTotal)
```

Using the Object Browser

The Object Browser is an important tool for working with objects. The Object Browser can show you the names of objects, properties, methods, events, and constants for VB objects, your own objects, and objects available from other applications.

> • The Object Browser is completely redesigned in the Visual Studio IDE.

If you don't see a tab for the Object Browser in the Editor window, you can open it easily. Choose *View/Other Windows/Object Browser,* or drop down the list of windows from the View toolbar button (Figure 6.10). In the Object Browser window (Figure 6.11), you can choose the libraries/namespaces in the *Browse* list. You can also search for specific items using the *Find Symbol* button.

Figure 6.10

Open the Object Browser from the toolbar button.

Class View	Ctrl+Shift+C
Server Explorer	Ctrl+Alt+S
Resource View	Ctrl+Shift+E
Macro Explorer	Alt+F8
Object Browser	Ctrl+Alt+J
Document Outline	Ctrl+Alt+T
Task List	Ctrl+Alt+K
Command Window	Ctrl+Alt+A
Output	Ctrl+Alt+O
Find Results 1	
Find Results 2	
Find Symbol Results	Ctrl+Alt+F12
Favorites	Ctrl+Alt+F

The Object Browser uses several icons to represent items. Notice in Figure 6.11 the icons that represent properties, methods, events, constants, classes, and namespaces. At the bottom of the window you can see a description of any item you select.

The Object Browser window; notice the icons to indicate the member type.

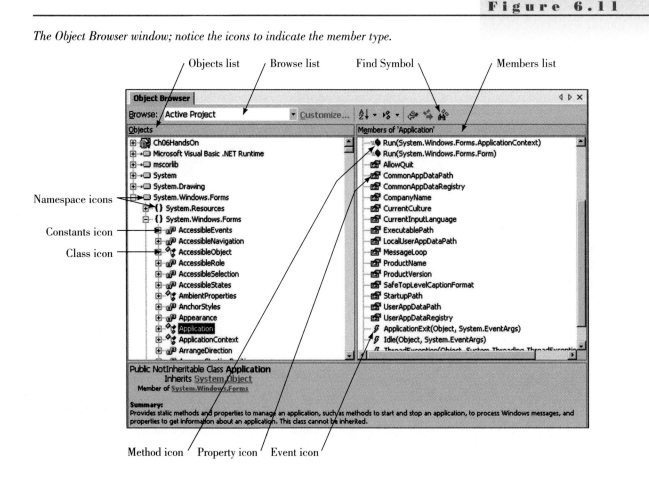

Examining VB Classes

You can look up the available properties, methods, events, or constants of a Visual Basic class. You can see which elements are defined in the class, what is the base class, and which properties, methods, and events are inherited. In Figure 6.12 notice the entries for System.Windows.Forms.MessageBox; the overloaded constructors appear in the *Members* list. And in Figure 6.13, you can see the constants for MessageBoxButtons.

Figure 6.12

Display the members of the System.Windows.Forms.MessageBox class.

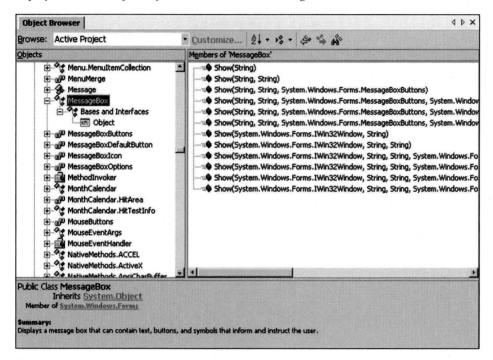

Figure 6.13

Display the MessageBoxButtons constants.

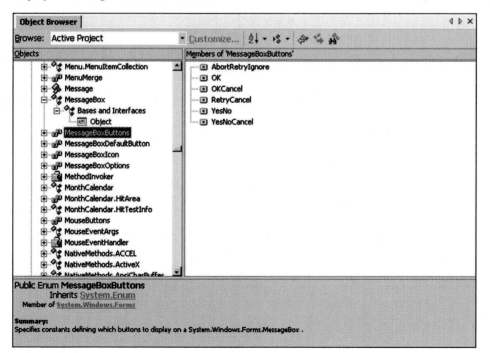

Examining Your Own Classes

You can see your own classes listed in the Object Browser. With the chapter step-by-step project open, select your project name in the Object Browser. Try clicking on each class name and viewing the list of properties and methods (Figure 6.14).

Figure 6.14

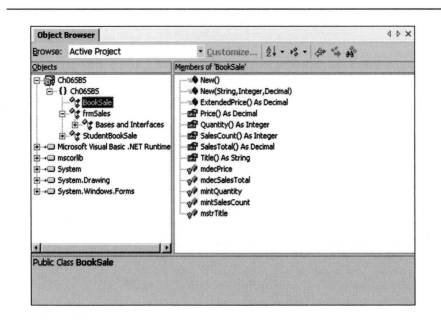

View the properties and methods for your own classes. Double-click on an item in the Members list to jump to its definition in code.

You can use the Object Browser to jump to the definition of any property or method by double-clicking on its name in the *Members* list. This technique is also a great way to jump to any of the procedures in your forms. Select your form name in the *Objects* list and double-click on the name of the procedure you want to view.

Your Hands-On Programming Example

This program must calculate book sales for R 'n R, with a discount of 15 percent for students. The project will use the BookSale and StudentBookSale classes developed in the chapter step-by-step.

Create a project with multiple forms that have a shared design element. Include a main form, an About form, and a Summary form that displays the sales summary information.

Design a base form to use for inheritance and make the other three forms inherit from the base form. The About form and Summary form must have an OK button, which closes the form. The main form will have menus and no OK button.

Main form menu:

F̲ile   H̲elp
  C̲alculate Sale   A̲bout
  C̲lear
  S̲ummary
  _____
  E̲xit

Planning the Project

Sketch a base form for inheritance, a main form, an About form, and a Summary form (Figure 6.15) for your users. The users approve and sign off the forms as meeting their needs.

Figure 6.15

The planning sketches of the forms for the hands-on programming example. a. the base form; b. the main form; c. the About form; and d. the Summary form.

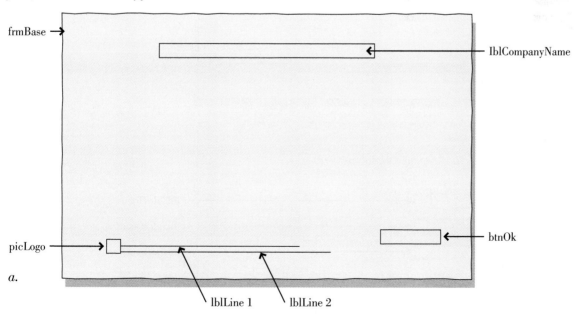

Figure continued on page 274

Figure 6.15

(continued from page 273)

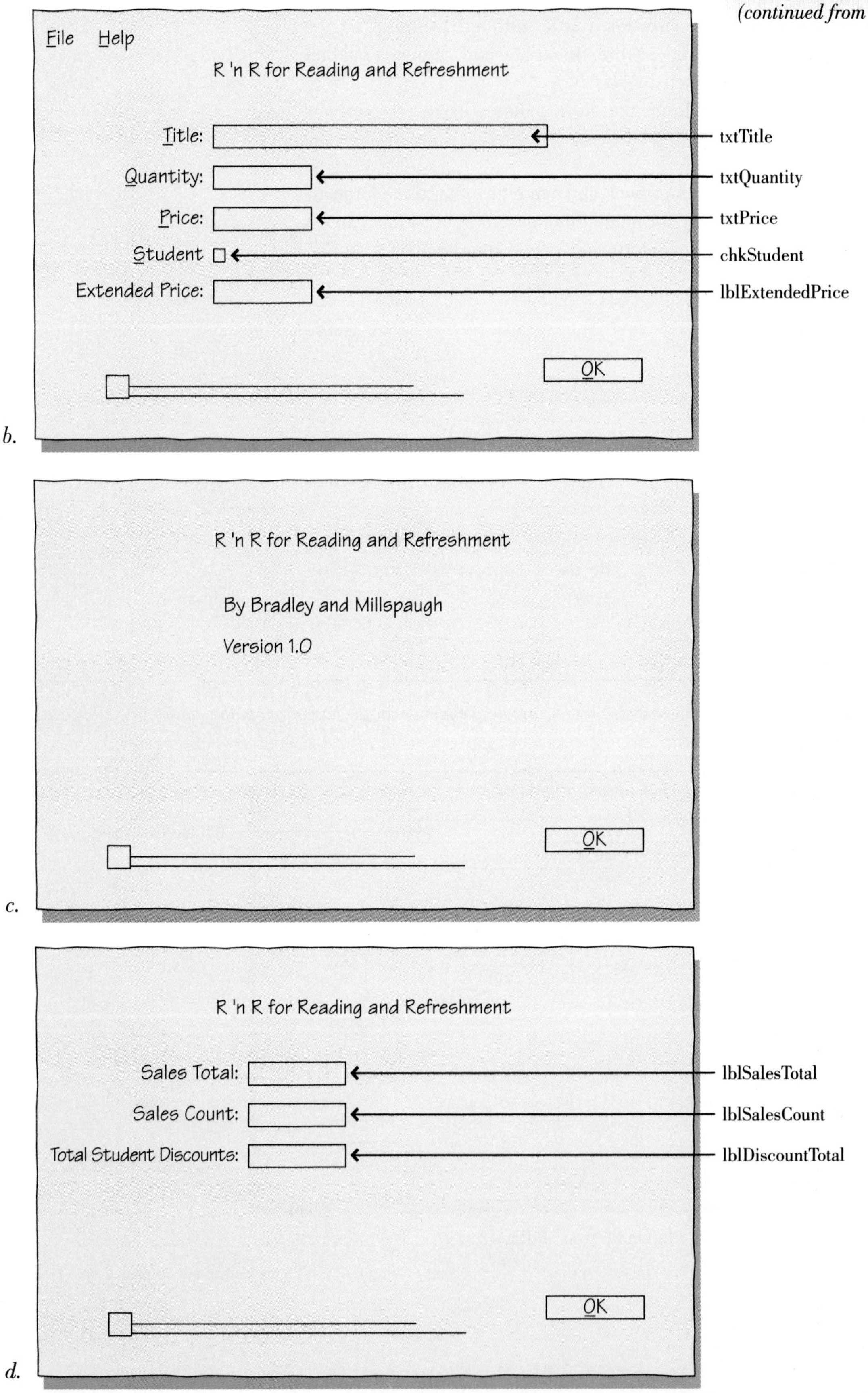

Plan the Objects and Properties for frmMain

Object	Property	Setting
frmMain	Name	frmMain
	Text	R 'n R Book Sales
	AcceptButton	btnOK
Label1	Name	Label1
	Text	&Title:
txtTitle	Name	txtTitle
	Text	(blank)
Label2	Name	Label2
	Text	&Quantity:
txtQuantity	Name	txtQuantity
	Text	(blank)
Label3	Name	Label3
	Text	&Price:
txtPrice	Name	txtPrice
	Text	(blank)
Label4	Name	Label4
	Text	Extended Price
chkStudent	Name	chkStudent
	Text	&Student
	RightToLeft	Yes
lblExtendedPrice	Name	lblExtendedPrice
	Text	(blank)
	BorderStyle	Fixed3D
mnuFile	Name	mnuFile
	Text	&File
mnuFileCalculateSale	Name	mnuFileCalculateSale
	Text	&Calculate Sale
mnuFileClear	Name	mnuFileClear
	Text	C&lear
mnuFileSummary	Name	mnuFileSummary
	Text	&Summary
mnuFileExit	Name	mnuFileExit
	Text	E&xit
mnuHelp	Name	mnuHelp
	Text	&Help
mnuHelpAbout	Name	mnuHelpAbout
	Text	&About

Plan the Procedures for frmMain

Procedure	Actions
Form_Load	Hide the inherited OK button.

mnuFileCalculateSale	If student sale then
	    Create a StudentBookSale object.
	    Calculate and format the extended price.
	Else
	    Create a BookSale object.
	    Calculate and format the extended price.
	End If

mnuFileClear	Clear text boxes and labels. Uncheck the check box. Set the focus on first text box.
mnuFileSummary	Declare an instance of the Summary form. Format and display the summary information on the Summary form. Show the Summary form.
mnuFileExit	End the project
mnuHelpAbout	Declare an instance of the About form. Show the About form.

Plan the Objects and Properties for frmAbout

Object	Property	Setting
frmAbout	Name Text	frmAbout About this Program
btnOK	Name Text	(Inherited) btnOK &OK

Plan the Procedures for frmAbout

Procedure	Actions
btnOK	Close this form.

Plan the Objects and Properties for frmSummary

Object	Property	Setting
frmSummary	Name	frmSummary
	Text	Summary
Label1	Name	Label1
	Text	Sales Total:
lblSalesTotal	Name	lblSalesTotal
	Text	(blank)
	BorderStyle	Fixed3D
Label2	Name	Label2
	Text	Sales Count:
lblSalesCount	Name	lblSalesCount
	Text	(blank)
	BorderStyle	Fixed3D
Label3	Name	Label3
	Text	Total Student Discounts:
lblDiscountTotal	Name	lblDiscountTotal
	Text	(blank)
	BorderStyle	Fixed3D
btnOK	Name	(Inherited) btnOK
	Text	&OK

Plan the Procedures for frmSummary

Procedure	Actions
btnOK	Close this form.

Plan the BookSale Object Class

Properties

Declare private module-level variables and write property procedures for all public properties:

    Instance:
        Title
        Quantity
        Price
    Shared:
        SalesTotal
        SalesCount

Methods

Procedure	Actions
ExtendedPrice	Calculate extended price = Quantity * Price. Add extended price to SalesTotal. Add 1 to SalesCount. Return extended price.

Plan the StudentBookSale Object Class

Inherit from BookSale.

Additional Properties

Shared:
    DiscountTotal

Methods

Procedure	Actions
ExtendedPrice	Calculate discount = price * quantity * discount rate. Calculate extended price = quantity * price − discount. Add extended price to SalesTotal. Add 1 to SalesCount. Add discount to DiscountTotal. Return extended price.

Write the Project

- Follow the sketches in Figure 6.15 to create the forms. Create the base form first and inherit the other three forms from the base form. Figure 6.16 shows the completed forms.

- Set the properties of each of the objects according to your plan.

- Write the code. Working from the pseudocode, write each procedure.

• When you complete the code, use a variety of data to thoroughly test the project.

Figure 6.16

The completed forms for the hands-on programming example. a. *the base form;* b. *the main form;* c. *the About form; and* d. *the Summary form.*

(Continued on page 280)

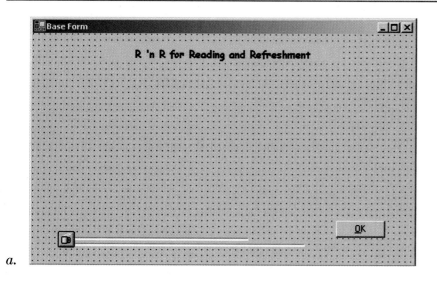

a.

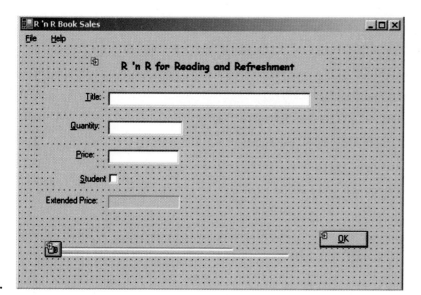

b.

Figure 6.16

(continued)

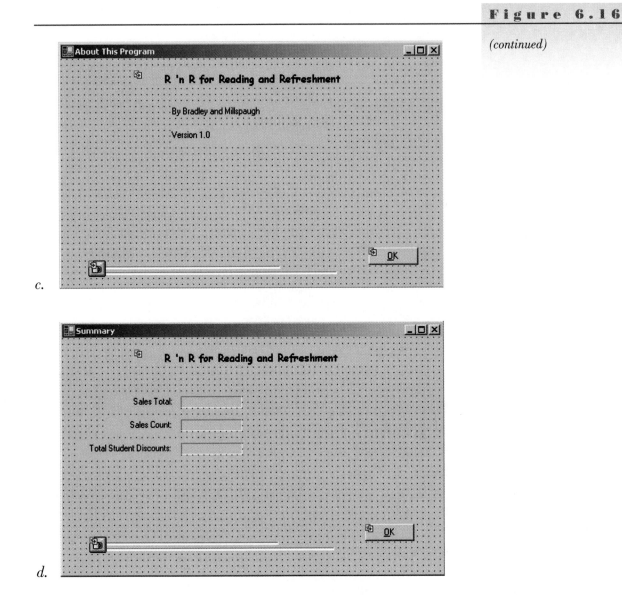

c.

d.

The Project Coding Solution

frmBase

```
'Program:          Chapter 6 BookSale Hands-On Program
'Programmer:       Bradley/Millspaugh
'Date:             January 2002
'Description:       Base form for hands-on project.
'Folder:           Ch06HandsOn

Option Strict On

Public Class frmBase
    Inherits System.Windows.Forms.Form

[Windows Form Designer generated code]
```

```vbnet
    Public Overridable Sub btnOK_Click(ByVal sender As System.Object, _
      ByVal e As System.EventArgs) Handles btnOK.Click
        'Allow inherited classes to override this method.

    End Sub
End Class
```

frmMain

```vbnet
'Program:           Chapter 6 BookSale Hands-On Program
'Programmer:        Bradley/Millspaugh
'Date:              January 2002
'Description:       Calculate sales price using the BookSale and StudentBookSale classes.
'                   Main form for hands-on project.
'Folder:            Ch06HandsOn

Option Strict On

Public Class frmMain
    Inherits Ch06HandsOn.frmBase

[Windows Form Designer generated code]

    Private mBookSale As BookSale          'Declare the new objects
    Private mStudentBookSale As StudentBookSale

    Private Sub frmMain_Load(ByVal sender As Object, _
      ByVal e As System.EventArgs) Handles MyBase.Load
        'Make the OK button invisible on this form

        btnOK.Visible = False
    End Sub

    Private Sub mnuFileCalculateSale_Click(ByVal sender As System.Object, _
      ByVal e As System.EventArgs) Handles mnuFileCalculateSale.Click
        'Calculate the extended price for the sale

        Try
            If chkStudent.Checked Then

                'Instantiate the StudentBookSale object and set the properties
                mStudentBookSale = New StudentBookSale(txtTitle.Text, _
                  CInt(txtQuantity.Text), CDec(txtPrice.Text))
                'Calculate and format the result
                lblExtendedPrice.Text = FormatNumber(mStudentBookSale.ExtendedPrice)
            Else

                'Instantiate the BookSale object and set the properties
                mBookSale = New BookSale(txtTitle.Text, CInt(txtQuantity.Text), _
                  CDec(txtPrice.Text))
                'Calculate and format the result
                lblExtendedPrice.Text = FormatNumber(mBookSale.ExtendedPrice)
            End If
        Catch
            MessageBox.Show("Error in quantity or price field.", "R 'n R Book Sales", _
              MessageBoxButtons.OK, MessageBoxIcon.Exclamation)
        End Try
    End Sub
```

```vb
    Private Sub mnuFileClear_Click(ByVal sender As System.Object, _
     ByVal e As System.EventArgs) Handles mnuFileClear.Click
        'Clear screen controls

        txtQuantity.Text = ""
        txtPrice.Text = ""
        lblExtendedPrice.Text = ""
        chkStudent.Checked = False
        With txtTitle
            .Text = ""
            .Focus()
        End With
    End Sub

    Private Sub mnuFileSummary_Click(ByVal sender As System.Object, _
     ByVal e As System.EventArgs) Handles mnuFileSummary.Click
        'Display the sales summary information
        Dim frmSummaryInstance As New frmSummary()

        With frmSummaryInstance
            .lblSalesTotal.Text = FormatCurrency(mBookSale.SalesTotal)
            .lblSalesCount.Text = CStr(mBookSale.SalesCount)
            .lblDiscountTotal.Text = FormatCurrency(mStudentBookSale.DiscountTotal)
            .ShowDialog()
        End With
    End Sub

    Private Sub mnuFileExit_Click(ByVal sender As Object, _
     ByVal e As System.EventArgs) Handles mnuFileExit.Click
        'Exit the application

        Me.Close()
    End Sub

    Private Sub mnuHelpAbout_Click(ByVal sender As System.Object, _
     ByVal e As System.EventArgs) Handles mnuHelpAbout.Click
        'Display the About form
        Dim frmAboutInstance As New frmAbout()
        frmAboutInstance.Show()
    End Sub
End Class
```

frmAbout

```vb
'Program:       Chapter 6 BookSale Hands-On Program
'Programmer:    Bradley/Millspaugh
'Date:          January 2002
'Description:   Calculate sales price using the BookSale class.
'               About form for hands-on project.
'Folder:        Ch06HandsOn

Option Strict On

Public Class frmAbout
    Inherits Ch06HandsOn.frmBase

[Windows Form Designer generated code]
```

```
        Public Overrides Sub btnOK_Click(ByVal sender As System.Object, _
        ByVal e As System.EventArgs) Handles btnOK.Click
            'Override the base class method.

            Me.Close()
        End Sub
End Class
```

frmSummary

```
'Program:           Chapter 6 BookSale Hands-On Program
'Programmer:        Bradley/Millspaugh
'Date:              January 2002
'Description:       Calculate sales price using the BookSale class.
'                   Summary form for hands-on project.
'Folder:            Ch06HandsOn

Option Strict On

Public Class frmSummary
    Inherits Ch06HandsOn.frmBase

[Windows Form Designer generated code]

    Public Overrides Sub btnOK_Click(ByVal sender As System.Object, _
    ByVal e As System.EventArgs) Handles btnOK.Click
        'Override the base class method.

        Me.Close()
    End Sub
End Class
```

BookSale Class

```
'Class Name:        BookSale
'Programmer:        Bradley/Millspaugh
'Date:              January 2002
'Description:       Handle book sale information.
'Folder:            Ch06HandsOn

Public Class BookSale

    Sub New()
        'Constructor with empty argument list

    End Sub

    Sub New(ByVal Title As String, ByVal Quantity As Integer, _
    ByVal Price As Decimal)
        'Assign property values

        Me.Title = Title
        Me.Quantity = Quantity
        Me.Price = Price
    End Sub

#Region "Properties"
    Protected mstrTitle As String            'Title property
    Protected mintQuantity As Integer        'Quantity property
    Protected mdecPrice As Decimal           'Price property
```

```vb
    Protected Shared mdecSalesTotal As Decimal          'SalesTotal property
    Protected Shared mintSalesCount As Integer          'SalesCount property

    Property Title() As String
        Get
            Title = mstrTitle
        End Get

        Set(ByVal Value As String)
            mstrTitle = Value
        End Set
    End Property

    Property Quantity() As Integer
        Get
            Quantity = mintQuantity
        End Get

        Set(ByVal Value As Integer)
            If Value >= 0 Then
                mintQuantity = Value
            End If
        End Set
    End Property

    Property Price() As Decimal
        Get
            Price = mdecPrice
        End Get

        Set(ByVal Value As Decimal)
            If Value >= 0 Then
                mdecPrice = Value
            End If
        End Set
    End Property

    Shared ReadOnly Property SalesTotal() As Decimal
        Get
            SalesTotal = mdecSalesTotal
        End Get
    End Property

    Shared ReadOnly Property SalesCount() As Integer
        Get
            SalesCount = mintSalesCount
        End Get
    End Property
#End Region

#Region "Methods"

    Public Overridable Function ExtendedPrice() As Decimal
        'Calculate the extended price and add to the totals
        Dim decExtendedPrice As Decimal
```

```
            decExtendedPrice = mintQuantity * mdecPrice
            mdecSalesTotal += decExtendedPrice
            mintSalesCount += 1
            Return decExtendedPrice
        End Function

#End Region

End Class
```

StudentBookSale Class

```
'Class Name:        StudentBookSale
'Programmer:        Bradley/Millspaugh
'Date:              January 2002
'Description:       Handle book sale information for student sales,
'                    which receive a discount.
'Folder:            Ch06HandsOn

Option Strict On

Public Class StudentBookSale
    Inherits BookSale

    Shared mdecDiscountTotal As Decimal
    Const mdecDISCOUNT_RATE As Decimal = 0.15D

    Sub New()
        'Constructor with empty argument list

        MyBase.New()
    End Sub

    Sub New(ByVal Title As String, ByVal Quantity As Integer, _
     ByVal Price As Decimal)
        'Assign property values

        MyBase.New()
        Me.Title = Title
        Me.Quantity = Quantity
        Me.Price = Price
    End Sub

    Shared ReadOnly Property DiscountTotal() As Decimal
        Get
            DiscountTotal = mdecDiscountTotal
        End Get
    End Property

    Overrides Function ExtendedPrice() As Decimal
        'Calculate the extended price and add to the totals
        Dim decExtendedPrice As Decimal
        Dim decDiscount As Decimal

        decDiscount = mintQuantity * mdecPrice * mdecDISCOUNT_RATE
        decExtendedPrice = mintQuantity * mdecPrice - decDiscount
        mdecSalesTotal += decExtendedPrice
        mintSalesCount += 1
        mdecDiscountTotal += decDiscount
        Return decExtendedPrice
    End Function
End Class
```

Summary

1. Objects have properties and methods, and can generate events.
2. You can create a new class that can then be used to create new objects.
3. Creating a new object is called *instantiating* the object; the object is called an *instance* of the class.
4. In object-oriented terminology, encapsulation refers to the combination of the characteristics and behaviors of an item into a single class definition.
5. Polymorphism allows different classes of objects to have similarly named methods that behave differently for that particular object.
6. Inheritance provides a means to derive a new object class based on an existing class. The existing class is called a *base class, superclass,* or *parent class.* The inherited class is called a *subclass, derived class,* or *child class.*
7. One of the biggest advantages of object-oriented programming is that objects that you create for one application may be reused in another application.
8. Multitier applications separate program functions into a Presentation tier (the user interface), Business tier (the logic of calculations and validation), and Data tier (accessing stored data).
9. The variables inside a class used to store the properties should be private, so that data values are accessible only by procedures within the class.
10. The way to make the properties of a class available to code outside the class is to use Property procedures. The Get portion returns the value of the property and the Set portion assigns a value to the property. Validation is often performed in the Set portion.
11. The public functions and sub procedures of a class module are its methods.
12. To instantiate an object of a class, you must use the New keyword either on the declaration statement or an assignment statement. The location of the New keyword determines when the object is created.
13. Shared members (properties and methods) have one copy that can be used by all objects of the class, generally used for totals and counts. Instance members have one copy for each instance of the object. Declare shared members with the Shared keyword.
14. A constructor is a method that automatically executes when an object is created; a destructor method is triggered when an object is destroyed.
15. A constructor method must be named New and may be overloaded.
16. A parameterized constructor requires arguments to create a new object.
17. The garbage collection feature periodically checks for unreferenced objects, destroys the object references, and releases resources.
18. A subclass inherits all public properties and methods of its base class, except for the constructor.
19. To override a method from a base class, the original method must be declared as overridable, and the new method must use the Overrides keyword.
20. A base class used strictly for inheritance cannot be instantiated. The class should be declared as MustInherit and the methods that must be overridden should be declared as MustOverride.
21. You can use visual inheritance to derive new forms from existing forms.
22. Refer to controls on a different form with the form instance name, control name, and property.

Key Terms

base class *241*
child class *241*
class *240*
constructor *257*
derived class *241*
destructor *257*
encapsulation *241*
garbage collection *260*
inheritance *241*
instance *240*
instance property *254*
instance variable *254*
instantiate *240*
multitier application *243*
MustInherit *265*
MustOverride *265*
namespace *244*

New keyword *244*
object *240*
overloading *242*
overriding *242*
parameterized constructor *258*
parent class *241*
polymorphism *242*
property procedure *245*
Protected *260*
ReadOnly *246*
reusability *241*
shared property *254*
shared variable *254*
subclass *241*
superclass *241*
Value keyword *246*

Review Questions

1. What is an object? a property? a method?
2. What is the purpose of a class?
3. Why should properties of a class be declared as private?
4. What are property procedures and what is their purpose?
5. Explain how to create a new object.
6. What steps are needed to assign property values to an object?
7. What actions trigger the constructor and destructor methods of an object?
8. How can you write methods for a new class?
9. What is a shared member? How is it created?
10. Explain the steps necessary to inherit a class from another class.
11. Differentiate between overriding and overloading.
12. What is a parameterized constructor?

Programming Exercises

Note: For help in basing a new project on an existing project, see "Copy and
      Move a Windows Project" in Appendix C.

6.1   Modify the program for Programming Exercise 5.1 (the piecework pay) to
       separate the business logic into a separate class. The class should have
       properties for Name and Pieces, as well as shared read-only properties to
       maintain the summary information.

6.2   Modify Programming Exercise 6.1 to include multiple forms. Create a
       base form that you can use for visual inheritance. Display the summary
       information and the About box on separate forms, rather than message
       boxes.

6.3   *Extra Challenge:* Modify Programming Exercise 6.2 to have an inherited class. Create a derived class for senior workers, who receive 10 percent higher pay for 600 or more pieces. Add a check box to the main form to indicate a senior worker.

6.4   Modify Programming Exercise 5.3 (the salesperson commissions) to separate the business logic into a separate class. The class should have properties for Name and Sales, as well as shared read-only properties to maintain the summary information.

6.5   Modify Programming Exercise 6.4 to include multiple forms. Create a base form that you can use for visual inheritance. Display the summary information and the About box on separate forms, rather than message boxes.

6.6   *Extra Challenge:* Modify Programming Exercise 6.5 to have an inherited class. Create a derived class for supervisors, who have a different pay scale. The supervisor quota is $2,000, the commission rate is 20 percent, and the base pay is $500. Include a check box on the main form to indicate a supervisor, and calculate separate totals for supervisors.

6.7   Modify Programming Exercise 5.5 (the check transactions) to separate the business logic from the user interface. Create a Transaction class and derived classes for Deposit, Check, and Service Charges. Display the summary information on a separate form rather than a message box.

          Optional extra: Use visual inheritance for the forms.

6.8   Modify Programming Exercise 5.4 (library reading program) to separate the business logic from the user interface. Create a class with properties for Name and Number of Books. Display the summary information and About box in separate forms rather than message boxes.

          Optional extra: Use visual inheritance for the forms.

6.9   *Extra Challenge:* Modify Programming Exercise 6.8 to have inherited classes. Have separate classes and separate totals for elementary, intermediate, and high school. Include radio buttons on the form to select the level; display totals for all three groups on the summary.

6.10   Create a project that contains a class for sandwich objects. Each sandwich object should have properties for Name, Bread, Meat, Cheese, and Condiments. Use a form for user input. Assign the input values to the properties of the object, and display the properties on a separate form.

6.11   Create a project containing a pet class. Each member will contain pet name, animal type, breed, and color. The form should contain text boxes to enter the information for the pets. A button or menu item should display the pet information on a separate form.

6.12   Modify your project from Chapter 3 to separate the user interface from the business logic (calculations) and return the results through a function method.

Case Studies

VB Mail Order

Modify your VB Mail Order project from Chapter 5 to separate the user interface from the business logic. Create two new classes: one for customer information and one for order items. The order item class should perform the calculations and maintain the summary information.

Add a menu option to display the customer information. Display the properties of the Customer object on a separate form.

Display the About box and the summary information on forms, rather than message boxes.

Optional extra: Use visual inheritance for the forms.

Need a bigger challenge? Create an inherited class for preferred customers. Preferred customers receive an automatic 5 percent discount on all purchases. Use a check box to determine if the customer is a preferred customer and instantiate the appropriate class. Maintain and display separate totals for preferred customers.

Note: For help in basing a new project on an existing project, see "Copy and Move a Windows Project" in Appendix C.

VB Auto Center

Modify your VB Auto Center project from Chapter 5 to separate the business logic from the user interface. Create a class for each purchase, with properties for each of the options. The methods of the class will calculate the subtotal, total, and amount due.

Make the About box display on a separate form, rather than a message box.

Need a bigger challenge? Add summary totals for

the number of sales, the total sales, and the total trade-ins. Maintain the totals as shared read-only properties of the class and display the summary information on a separate form.

Note: For help in basing a new project on an existing project, see "Copy and Move a Windows Project" in Appendix C.

Video Bonanza

Modify the Video Bonanza project from Chapter 5 to separate the user interface from the business logic. Create a class for each rental. Include a property for Title, and Boolean properties for Video Tape format and Members, and shared read-only properties for the summary information.

Display the summary information and the About box on forms, rather than message boxes.

Note: For help in basing a new project on an existing project, see "Copy and Move a Windows Project" in Appendix C.

Very Very Boards

Modify the Very Very Boards project from Chapter 5 to separate the user interface from the business logic. Create a class for each shirt sale with properties for Order Number, Quantity, and Size. Use Boolean properties for Monogram and Pocket, and a method to calculate the price. Maintain shared read-only properties for the summary information.

Display the summary information and the About box on forms, rather than message boxes.

Optional extra: Use visual inheritance for the forms.

Note: For help in basing a new project on an existing project, see "Copy and Move a Windows Project" in Appendix C.

7

Lists, Loops, and Printing

at the completion of this chapter, you will be able to . . .

1. Create and use list boxes and combo boxes.

2. Differentiate among the available types of combo boxes.

3. Enter items into list boxes using the Items collection in the Properties window.

4. Add and remove items in a list at run time.

5. Determine which item in a list is selected.

6. Use the Items.Count property to determine the number of items in a list.

7. Display a selected item from a list.

8. Use Do/Loops and For/Next statements to iterate through a loop.

9. Send information to the printer or the Print Preview window using the PrintDocument class.

Often you will want to offer the user a list of items from which to choose. You can use the Windows ListBox and ComboBox controls to display lists on a form. You may choose to add items to a list during design time, during run time, or perhaps during a combination of both. Several styles of list boxes are available; the style you use is determined by design and space considerations as well as by whether you will allow users to add items to the list.

List Boxes and Combo Boxes

Both list boxes and combo boxes allow you to have a list of items from which the user can make a selection. Figure 7.1 shows the toolbox tools for creating the controls; Figure 7.2 shows several types of list boxes and combo boxes, including **simple list boxes, simple combo boxes, drop-down combo boxes,** and **drop-down lists.** The list boxes on the left of the form in Figure 7.2 are all created with the ListBox tool; the boxes on the right of the form are created with the ComboBox tool. Notice the three distinct styles of combo boxes.

• List boxes and combo boxes are all new controls, but they are named the same as the old ones. There is also a new Checked list box control, which isn't covered in the text.

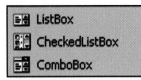

Figure   7.1

Use the ListBox tool and ComboBox tool to create list boxes and combo boxes on your forms.

ListBox controls and **ComboBox controls** have most of the same properties and operate in a similar fashion. One exception is that a combo box control has a DropDownStyle property, which determines whether or not the list box also has a text box for user entry and whether or not the list will drop down (refer to Figure 7.2).

Both list boxes and combo boxes have a great feature. If the box is too small to display all the items in the list at one time, VB automatically adds a scroll bar. You do not have to be concerned with the location of the scroll box in the scroll bar; the scrolling is handled automatically.

When you add a list control to a form, choose the style according to the space you have available and how you want the box to operate. Do you want the user to select from an existing list? If so, use a simple list box or a drop-down list (ComboBox DropDownStyle = DropDownList). Do you want the user to be able to type a new entry if necessary? In this case, use one of the two styles with an added text box: the drop-down combo box (DropDownStyle = DropDown) or the simple combo box (DropDownStyle = Simple).

• The old Style property changes to DropDownStyle.

At design time, the behavior of list boxes and combo boxes differs. For list boxes, Visual Basic displays the Name property in the control; for combo boxes, the Text property displays. Don't spend any time trying to make a list box appear empty during design time; the box will appear empty at run time. Combo boxes have a Text property, which you can set or remove at design time. List boxes also have a Text property, but you can only access it at run time.

When you name list boxes and combo boxes, use the prefixes "lst" and "cbo".

Figure 7.2

Various styles of list boxes and combo boxes.

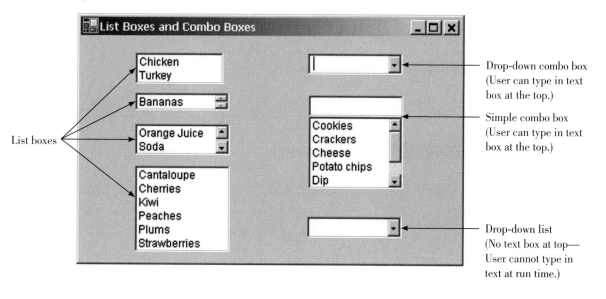

The Items Collection

The list of items that displays in a list box or combo box is a **collection.** VB collections are objects that have properties and methods to allow you to add items, remove items, refer to individual elements, count the items, and clear the collection. In the sections that follow, you will learn to maintain and refer to the Items collection.

You can refer to the items in a collection by an index, which is zero based. For example, if a collection holds 10 items, the indexes to refer to the items range from 0 to 9. To refer to the first item in the Items collection, use Items(0).

• The List property and ItemData properties are gone. Instead each control has an Items collection. The elements in the collection can be a string or an object, and the object can contain more than one field, replacing the function of ItemData. (ItemData was not covered in this chapter in the past and still isn't. It was covered in Chapter 8 of the VB 6 text.) We stick with strings in this chapter.

Filling a List

You can use several methods to fill the Items collection of a list box and combo box. If you know the list contents at design time and the list never changes, you can define the Items collection in the Properties window. If you must add items to the list during program execution, you will use the `Items.Add` or `Items.Insert` method in an event procedure. In Chapter 11 you will learn to fill a list from a data file on disk. This method allows the list contents to vary from one run to the next.

Using the Properties Window

The **Items property,** which is a collection, holds the list of items for a list box or combo box. To define the Items collection at design time, select the control and scroll the Properties window to the Items property (Figure 7.3). Click on the ellipses button to open the String Collection Editor (Figure 7.4) and type your list items, ending each line with the Enter key. Click OK when finished. You can open the editor again to modify the list, if you wish.

- Enter the Items collection in the Properties window at design time using the easier-to-use String Collection Editor.

- Press Enter at the end of each line rather than Ctrl + Enter as in old List property editor.

Figure 7.3

Select the Items property of a list box to enter the list items.

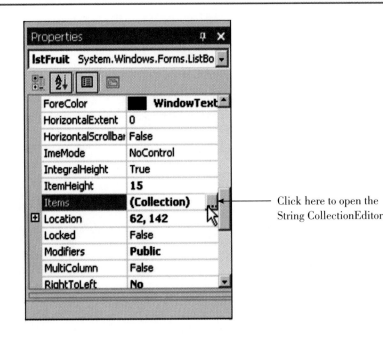

Click here to open the String CollectionEditor

Figure 7.4

In the String Collection Editor that opens, type each list item and press Enter to go to next line.

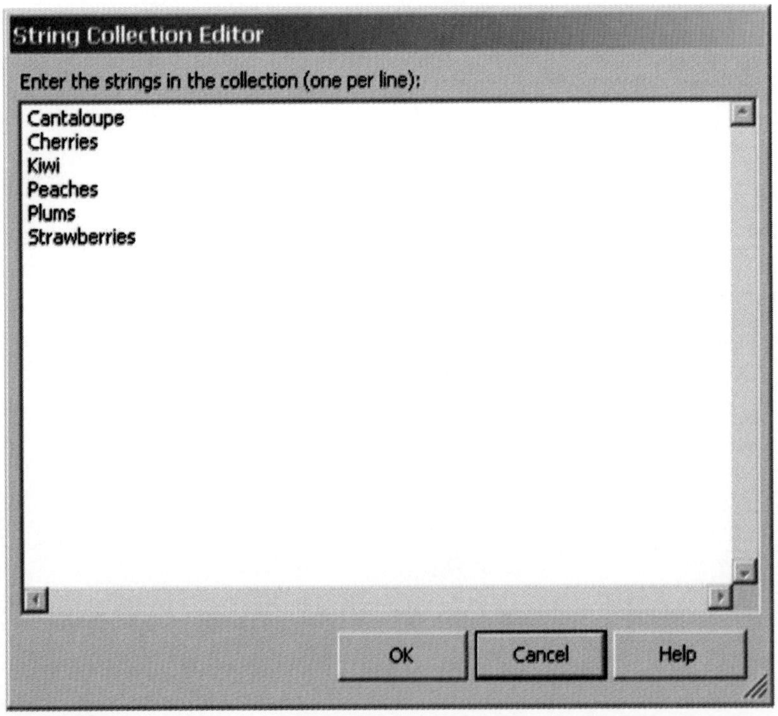

String Collection Editor

Enter the strings in the collection (one per line):

Cantaloupe
Cherries
Kiwi
Peaches
Plums
Strawberries

OK　　Cancel　　Help

Using the Items.Add Method

To add an item to a list at run time, use the `Items.Add` **method.** You can choose to add a variable, a constant, the contents of the text box at the top of a combo box, or the Text property of another control.

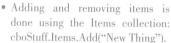
• Adding and removing items is done using the Items collection: cboStuff.Items.Add("New Thing").

The Items.Add Method—General Form

> **General Form**
>
> ```
> Object.Items.Add(ItemValue)
> ```

ItemValue is the string value to add to the list. If the value is a string literal, enclose it in quotation marks.

The new item generally goes at the end of the list. However, you can alter the placement by setting the control's **Sorted property** to True. Then the new item will be placed alphabetically in the list.

The Items.Add Method—Examples

> **Examples**
>
> ```
> lstSchools.Items.Add("Harvard")
> lstSchools.Items.Add("Stanford")
> lstSchools.Items.Add(txtSchools.Text)
> cboMajors.Items.Add(cboMajors.Text)
> cboMajors.Items.Add(strMajor)
> ```

When the user types a new value in the text box portion of a combo box, that item is not automatically added to the list. If you want to add the newly entered text to the list, use the `Items.Add` method:

```
cboCoffee.Items.Add(cboCoffee.Text)
```

or the preferable form:

```
With cboCoffee
    .Items.Add(.Text)
End With
```

Using the Items.Insert Method

You can choose the location for a new item added to the list. In the `Items.Insert` **method,** you specify the index position for the new item.

• Items collection methods: Add, Insert (give the location), Remove (by text string), RemoveAt (by index).

The Items.Insert Method—General Form

> **General Form**
>
> ```
> Object.Items.Insert(IndexPosition, ItemValue)
> ```

The index position is zero based. To insert a new item in the first position, use index position = 0.

The Items.Insert Method—Examples

> **Examples**
>
> ```
> lstSchools.Items.Insert(0, "Harvard")
> cboMajors.Items.Insert(1, cboMajors.Text)
> ```

If you choose the index position of an item using the Insert method, do not set the list control's Sorted property to True. A sorted list is always sorted into alphabetic order, regardless of any other order that you request.

The SelectedIndex Property

When a project is running and the user selects (highlights) an item from the list, the index number of that item is stored in the **SelectedIndex property** of the list box. Recall that the index of the first item in the list is 0. If no list item is selected, the SelectedIndex property is set to negative 1 (-1).

- The old ListIndex property becomes the SelectedIndex property.

You can use the SelectedIndex property to select an item in the list or deselect all items in code.

Examples

```
lstCoffeeTypes.SelectedIndex = 3      'Select the fourth item in list
lstCoffeeTypes.SelectedIndex = -1     'Deselect all items in list
```

The Items.Count Property

You can use the Count property of the Items collection to determine the number of items in the list. We will use the **Items.Count property** later in this chapter to process each element in the list. Items.Count is also handy when you need to display the count at some point in your project.

- Count is now a property of the Items collection: cboStuff. Items.Count.

Remember: Items.Count is always one more than the highest possible SelectedIndex, since the indexes begin with 0. For example, if there are five items in a list, Items.Count is 5 and the highest index is 4 (Figure 7.5).

Examples

```
intTotalItems = lstItem.Items.Count
MessageBox.Show("The number of items in the list is " & lstItem.Items.Count)
```

Items.SelectedIndex	Items.Count=5
(0)	Harvard
(1)	Stanford
(2)	University of California
(3)	Miami University
(4)	University of New York

Figure 7.5

For a list of five items, the indexes range from 0 to 4.

Referencing the Items Collection

If you need to display one item from a list, you can refer to one element of the Items collection. The Items collection of a list box or combo box holds the text of all list elements. You specify which element you want by including an index. This technique can be useful if you need to display a list item in a label or on another form. Later in this chapter we will use the Items property to send the contents of the list box to the printer.

- The old List property is now the Items collection.

Using the Items Collection—General Form

General Form	`Object.Items(IndexPosition) [ = Value]`

The index of the first list element is 0, so the highest index is Items.Count − 1.

You can retrieve the value of a list element or set an element to a new value.

Using the Items Collection—Examples

```
lstSchools.Items(5) = "University of California"
lblMyMajor.Text = cboMajors.Items(intIndex)
lblSelectedMajor.Text = cboMajors.Items(cboMajors.SelectedIndex)
lblSelectedMajor.Text = cboMajors.Text
```

To refer to the currently selected element of a list, you must combine the Items property and the SelectedIndex property:

```
strSelectedFlavor = lstFlavor.Items(lstFlavor.SelectedIndex)
```

Note that if you assign a value to a particular item, you replace the previous contents of that position. For example,

```
lstSchools.Items(0) = "My School"
```

places "My School" into the first position, replacing whatever was there already. It does not insert the item into the list or increase the value in Items.Count.

Removing an Item from a List

You can remove individual items from a list, either by specifying the index of the item or the text of the item. Use the `Items.RemoveAt` **method** to remove an item by index and the `Items.Remove` **method** to remove by specifying the text.

> • Remove (by text string) and RemoveAt (by index number) are both methods of the Items collection.

The Items.RemoveAt Method—General Form

General Form	`Object.Items.RemoveAt(IndexPosition)`

The index is required; it specifies which element to remove. The index of the first list element is 0, and the index of the last element is Items.Count − 1.

The Items.RemoveAt Method—Examples

```
lstNames.Items.RemoveAt(0)                            'Remove the first name from the list
cboSchools.Items.RemoveAt(intIndex)                   'Remove the item in position intIndex
cboCoffee.Items.RemoveAt(cboCoffee.SelectedIndex)     'Remove the currently selected item
```

The Items.Remove Method—General Form

General
Form
```
Object.Items.Remove(TextString)
```

The `Items.Remove` method looks for the named string in the Items collection. If the string is found, it is removed; however, if it is not found, no exception is generated.

The Items.Remove Method—Examples

```
lstNames.Items.Remove("My School")
cboSchools.Items.Remove(txtSchool.Text)          'Remove the matching item
cboCoffee.Items.Remove(cboCoffee.Text)           'Remove the currently selected item
```

If you remove the currently selected item using either the `RemoveAt` or `Remove` method, make your code more efficient and easier to read by using the `With` statement.

```
With cboCoffee
    If .SelectedIndex <> -1 Then
        .Items.RemoveAt(.SelectedIndex)          'Remove by Index
        '.Items.Remove(.Text)                     'Alternate -- remove by Text
    Else
        MessageBox.Show("First select the coffee to remove", "No selection made", _
            MessageBoxButtons.OK, MessageBoxIcon.Exclamation)
    End If
End With
```

Clearing a List

In addition to removing individual items at run time, you can also clear all items from a list. Use the `Items.Clear` **method** to empty a combo box or list box.

• The `Clear` method is a method of the Items collection: `cboStuff.Items.Clear`

The Items.Clear Method—General Form

General
Form
```
Object.Items.Clear()
```

The Clear Method—Examples

```
lstSchools.Items.Clear()
cboMajors.Items.Clear()
```

```
'Confirm clearing the majors list
Dim dgrResponse As DialogResult

dgrResponse = MessageBox.Show("Clear the majors list?", "Clear Majors List", _
    MessageBoxButtons.YesNo, MessageBoxIcon.Question)
If dgrResponse = DialogResult.Yes Then
    cboMajors.Items.Clear()
End If
```

List Box and Combo Box Events

Later in the chapter we will perform actions in event procedures for events of list boxes and combo boxes. Some useful events are the SelectedIndexChanged, TextChanged, Enter, and Leave. Note: Although we haven't used these events up until this point, many other controls have similar events. For example, you can code event procedures for the Enter, Leave, and TextChanged events of text boxes.

- The SelectedIndexChanged event occurs when the user makes a new selection.

The TextChanged Event

As the user types text into the text box portion of a combo box, the TextChanged event occurs. Each keystroke generates another TextChanged event. A list box does not have a TextChanged event, because list boxes do not have associated text boxes.

- The old Changed event becomes the TextChanged event.

The Enter Event

When a control receives the focus, an Enter event occurs. As the user tabs from control to control, an Enter event fires for each control. Later you will learn to make any existing text appear selected when the user tabs to a text box or the text portion of a combo box.

- The old GotFocus and LostFocus events are now the Enter and Leave events.

The Leave Event

You can also write code for the Leave event of a control. The Leave event fires when the control loses the focus. Programmers often use Leave event procedures to validate input data.

Feedback 7.1

Describe the purpose of each of the following methods or properties for a list box or combo box control.

1. Sorted
2. SelectedIndex
3. Items
4. DropDownStyle
5. Items.Count
6. `Items.Add`
7. `Items.Insert`
8. `Items.Clear`
9. `Items.RemoveAt`
10. `Items.Remove`

- List controls have new FindString and FindStringExact properties, which are not covered in this text, primarily to force students to use loops for searching.

- Saving the contents of a list into a disk file and reloading for the next run is covered in Chapter 11.

Do/Loops

Until now, there has been no way to repeat the same steps in a procedure without calling them a second time. The computer is capable of repeating a group of instructions many times without calling the procedure for each new set of data. The process of repeating a series of instructions is called *looping*. The group of repeated instructions is called a ***loop.*** An **iteration** is a single execution of the statement(s) in the loop. In this section you will learn about the

`Do/Loop`. Later in this chapter you will learn about another type of loop—a `For/Next` loop.

A `Do/Loop` terminates based on a condition that you specify. Execution of a `Do/Loop` continues *while* a condition is True or *until* a condition is True. You can choose to place the condition at the top or the bottom of the loop. Use a `Do/Loop` when the exact number of iterations is unknown.

Align the `Do` **and** `Loop` **statements** with each other and indent the lines of code to be repeated in between.

The Do and Loop Statements—General Form

General Form

```
Do {While | Until} Condition
    'statements in loop
Loop
```

or

General Form

```
Do
    'statements in loop
Loop {While | Until} Condition
```

The first form of the `Do/Loop` tests for completion at the top of the loop. With this type of loop, also called a ***pretest***, the statements inside the loop may never be executed if the terminating condition is True the first time it is tested.

Example

```
intTotal = 0
Do Until intTotal = 0
    'statements in loop
Loop
```

Because intTotal is 0 the first time the condition is tested, the condition is True and the statements inside the loop will not execute. Control will pass to the statement following the `Loop` statement.

The second form of the `Do/Loop` tests for completion at the bottom of the loop, which means that the statements in the loop will *always* be executed at least once. This form of loop is sometimes called a ***posttest***. Changing the example to a posttest, you can see the difference.

```
intTotal = 0
Do
    'statements in loop
Loop Until intTotal = 0
```

In this case the statements inside the loop will be executed at least once. Assuming the value for intTotal does not change inside the loop, the condition (intTotal = 0) will be True the first time it is tested, and control will pass to the first statement following the `Loop` statement. Figure 7.6 shows flowcharts of pretest and posttest loops, using both `While` and `Until`.

Figure 7.6

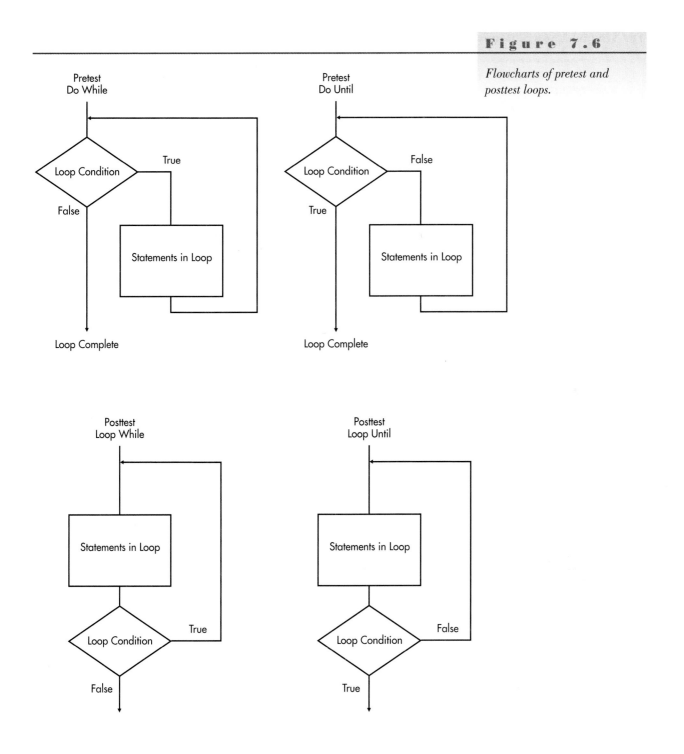

Flowcharts of pretest and posttest loops.

The Do and Loop Statements—Examples

```
Do Until intItemIndex = lstItems.Items.Count — 1
    'Statements in loop
Loop

Do While decAmount = 10D And decAmount >= 20D
    'Statements in loop
Loop

Do
    'Statements in loop
Loop Until intTotal < 0
```

The Boolean Data Type Revisited

In Chapter 2 you learned about the Boolean data type, which holds only the values True or False. You will find Boolean variables very useful when setting and testing conditions for a loop. You can set a Boolean variable to True when a specific circumstance occurs and then write a loop condition to continue until the variable is True.

An example of using a Boolean variable is when you want to search through a list for a specific value. The item may be found or not found, and you want to quit looking when a match is found.

Using a Boolean variable is usually a three-step process. First you must dimension a variable and set its initial value (or use the default VB setting of False). Then, when a particular situation occurs, you set the variable to True. A loop condition can then check for True.

```
Dim blnItemFound as Boolean = False
Do Until blnItemFound 'Checks for True
    . . .
```

A Boolean variable is always in one of two states—True or False. Many programmers refer to Boolean variables as *switches* or *flags*. Switches have two states—on or off; flags are considered either up or down.

Using a Do/Loop with a List Box

This small example combines a Boolean variable with a Do/Loop. Inside the loop each element of the list is compared to txtNewItem.Text for a match. The loop will terminate when a match is found or when all elements have been tested. Follow through the logic to see what happens when there is a match, when there isn't a match, when the match occurs on the first list element, and when the match occurs on the last list element.

```
Private Sub btnFind_Click(ByVal sender As System.Object, _
 ByVal e As System.EventArgs) Handles btnFind.Click

    'Look for a match between text box and list items
    Dim blnItemFound As Boolean = False
    Dim intItemIndex As Integer = 0
```

```
    Do Until blnItemFound Or intItemIndex = lstItems.Items.Count
        If txtNewItem.Text = lstItems.Items(intItemIndex) Then
            blnItemFound = True          'A match was found
        End If
        intItemIndex += 1
    Loop

    If blnItemFound Then
        MessageBox.Show("Item is in the list", "Item match", _
          MessageBoxButtons.OK, MessageBoxIcon.Information)
    Else
        MessageBox.Show("Item is not in the list", "No item match", _
          MessageBoxButtons.OK, MessageBoxIcon.Information)
    End If
End Sub
```

▶ **Feedback 7.2**

Explain the purpose of each line of the following code:

```
blnItemFound = False
intItemIndex = 0
Do Until blnItemFound Or intItemIndex = lstItems.Items.Count
    If txtNewItem.Text = lstItems.Items(intItemIndex) Then
        blnItemFound = True
    End If
    intItemIndex += 1
Loop
```

For/Next Loops

When you want to repeat the statements in a loop a specific number of times, the For/Next *loop* is ideal. The For/Next loop uses the For **and** Next **statements** and a counter variable, called the *loop index.* The loop index is tested to determine the number of times the statements inside the loop will execute.

```
Dim intLoopIndex As Integer
Dim intMaximum As Integer
intMaximum = lstSchools.Items.Count — 1

For intLoopIndex = 0 To intMaximum
    'The statements inside of the loop are indented
    'and referred to as the body of the loop
Next intLoopIndex
```

When the For statement is reached during program execution, several things occur. The loop index, intLoopIndex, is established as the loop counter and is initialized to 0 (the initial value). The final value for the loop index is set to the value of intMaximum, which was assigned the value of lstSchools.Items.Count −1 in the previous statement.

Execution is now "controlled by" the For statement. After the value of int-LoopIndex is set, it is tested to see whether intLoopIndex is greater than int-Maximum. If not, the statements in the body of the loop are executed. The Next statement causes the intLoopIndex to be incremented by 1. Then control passes back to the For statement. Is the value of intLoopIndex greater than intMaximum? If not, the loop is again executed. When the test is made and the loop index *is* greater than the final value, control passes to the statement immediately following the Next.

A counter-controlled loop generally has three elements (see Figure 7.7 for a flowchart of loop logic).

1. Initialize the counter.
2. Increment the counter.
3. Test the counter to determine when it is time to terminate the loop.

A flowchart of the logic of a For/Next loop.

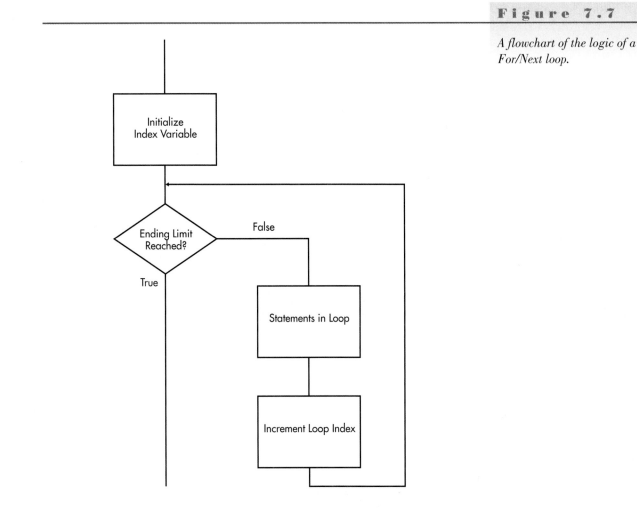

The For and Next Statements—General Form

```
For LoopIndex = InitialValue To TestValue [Step Increment]
    '
    '(Body of loop)
    '
Next [LoopIndex]
```

LoopIndex must be a numeric variable; InitialValue and TestValue may be constants, variables, numeric property values, or numeric expressions. The optional word `Step` may be included, along with the value to be added to the loop index for each iteration of the loop. When the `Step` is omitted, the increment is assumed to be 1.

The For and Next Statements—Examples

```
For intIndex = 2 To 100 Step 2
For intCount = intStart To intEnding Step intIncrement
For intCounter = 0 To cboCoffeeType.Items.Count - 1
For intNumber = (intNumberCorrect - 5) To intTotalPossible
For decRate = 0.05D To 0.25D Step 0.05D
For intCountDown = 10 To 0 Step -1
```

Each `For` statement has a corresponding `Next` statement, which must follow the `For`. All statements between the `For` and `Next` statements are considered to be the body of the loop and will be executed the specified number of times.

The first `For` statement example will count from 2 to 100 by 2. The statements in the body of the loop will be executed 50 times—first with intIndex = 2, next with intIndex = 4, next with intIndex = 6, and so forth.

When the comparison is done, the program checks for *greater than* the test value, not equal to. When intIndex = 100 in the preceding example, the body of the loop will be executed one more time. Then, at the `Next` statement, intIndex will be incremented to 102, the test will be made, and control will pass to the statement following the `Next`. If you were to display the value of intIndex after completion of the loop, its value would be 102.

> ☑ **TIP**
>
> Use a `For/Next` loop when you know the number of iterations needed for the loop. Use a `Do/Loop` when the loop should end based on a condition. ■

Negative Increment or Counting Backward

You can use a negative number for the `Step` increment to decrease the loop index rather than increase it. When the `Step` is negative, VB tests for *less than* the test value instead of *greater than*.

```
'Count Backwards
For intCount = 10 To 1 Step -1
    'Statements in body of loop
Next intCount
```

Conditions Satisfied before Entry

At times the final value will be reached before entry into the loop. In that case the statements in the body of the loop will not be executed at all.

```
'An unexecutable loop
intFinal = 5
For intIndex = 6 to intFinal
    'The execution will never reach here
Next intIndex
```

Altering the Values of the Loop Control Variables

Once a `For` loop has been entered, the values for InitialValue, TestValue, and Increment have already been set. Changing the value of these control variables within the loop will have no effect on the number of iterations of the loop. Many texts admonish against changing the values within the loop. However, Visual Basic just ignores you if you try.

```
'Bad Example--Changing the Control Variable
intFinal = 10
intIncrease = 2
For intIndex = 1 to intFinal Step intIncrease
    intFinal = 25
    intIncrease = 5
Next intIndex
```

If you tried this example and displayed the values of intIndex, you would find that the final value will remain 10 and the increment value will be 2.

The value that you *can* change within the loop is the loop index. However, this practice is considered poor programming.

```
'Poor Programming
For intIndex = 1 To 10 Step 1
    intIndex += 5
Next intIndex
```

Endless Loops

Changing the value of a loop index variable is not only considered a poor practice but also may lead to an endless loop. Your code could get into a loop that is impossible to exit. Consider the following example; when will the loop end?

```
'More Poor Programming
For intIndex = 1 To 10 Step 1
    intIndex = 1
Next intIndex
```

Exiting For/Next Loops

In the previous example of an endless loop, you will have to break the program execution manually. You can click on your form's close box or use the Visual Basic menu bar or toolbar to stop the program. If you can't see the menu bar or toolbar, you can usually move or resize your application's form to bring it into view. If you prefer, press Ctrl + Break to enter break time; you may want to step program execution to see what is causing the problem.

Usually For/Next loops should proceed to normal completion. However, on occasion you may need to terminate a loop before the loop index reaches its final value. Visual Basic provides an Exit For statement for this situation. Generally, the Exit For statement is part of an If statement.

The Exit For Statement—General Form

General Form	
`Exit For`	

The Exit For Statement—Example

Example

```
For intLoopIndex = 1 to 10
    If txtInput.Text = "" Then 'Nothing was entered into the input textbox
        MessageBox.Show("You must enter something")
        Exit For
    End If
    ... 'Statements in loop
Next intLoopIndex
```

Feedback 7.3

1. Identify the statements that are correctly formed and those that have errors. For those with errors, state what is wrong and how to correct it.

   (a) `For decIndex = 3.5D To 6.0D, Step 0.5D`
       `Next decIndex`

   (b) `For intIndex = intBegin To intEnd Step intIncrement`
       `Next intEnd`

   (c) `For 4 = 1 To 10 Step 2`
       `Next For`

   (d) `For intIndex = 100 To 0 Step -25`
       `Next intIndex`

   (e) `For intIndex = 0 To -10 Step -1`
       `Next intIndex`

   (f) `For intIndex = 10 To 1`
       `Next intIndex`

2. How many times will the body of the loop be executed for each of these examples? What will be the value of the loop index after normal completion of the loop?

   (a) `For intCounter = 1 To 3`

   (b) `For intCounter = 2 To 11 Step 3`

   (c) `For intCounter = 10 To 1 Step -1`

   (d) `For decCounter = 3.0D To 6.0D Step 0.5D`

   (e) `For intCounter = 5 To 1`

Making Entries Appear Selected

You can use several techniques to make the text in a text box or list appear selected.

Selecting the Entry in a Text Box

When the user tabs into a text box that already has an entry, how do you want the text to appear? Should the insertion point appear at either the left or right end of the text? Or should the entire entry appear selected? You can also apply this question to a text box that failed validation; shouldn't the entire entry be selected? The most user-friendly approach is to select the text, which you can do with the SelectAll method of the text box. A good location to do this is in

● Use the new SelectAll method to select the entire contents of a list box.

the text box's Enter event procedure, which occurs when the control receives the focus.

```
Private Sub txtName_Enter(ByVal sender As Object, _
 ByVal e As System.EventArgs) Handles txtName.Enter
    'Select any existing text

    txtName.SelectAll()
End Sub
```

Selecting an Entry in a List Box

You can make a single item in a list box appear selected by setting the SelectedIndex property.

- Set the SelectedIndex property of a list to make an entry appear selected.

```
lstCoffee.SelectedIndex = intIndex
```

When a list box has a very large number of entries, you can help users by selecting the matching entry as they type in a text box. This method is similar to the way the Help Topics list in Visual Basic works. For example, when you type *p*, the list quickly scrolls and displays words beginning with *p*. Then if you next type *r*, the list scrolls down to the words that begin with *pr* and the first such word is selected. If you type *i* next, the first word beginning with *pri* is selected. The following example implements this feature. See if you can tell what each statement does.

Notice that this is coded in the TextChanged event procedure for the control into which the user is typing; the event occurs once for every keystroke entered.

```
Private Sub txtCoffee_TextChanged(ByVal sender As System.Object, _
 ByVal e As System.EventArgs) Handles txtCoffee.TextChanged

    'Locate first matching occurrence in the list

    Dim intIndex As Integer = 0
    Dim blnFound As Boolean = False
    Dim strListCompare As String
    Dim strTextCompare As String

    Do While Not blnFound And intIndex < lstCoffee.Items.Count
        strListCompare = lstCoffee.Items(intIndex)
        strListCompare = strListCompare.ToUpper()
        strTextCompare = txtCoffee.Text.ToUpper()
        If strListCompare.StartsWith(strTextCompare) Then
            lstCoffee.SelectedIndex = intIndex
            blnFound = True
        End If
        intIndex += 1
    Loop
End Sub
```

Sending Information to the Printer

So far, all program output has been on the screen. You can use the new VB .NET PrintDocument and PrintPreviewDialog classes to produce output for the printer and also to preview the output on the screen.

Visual Basic was designed to run under Windows, which is a highly interactive environment. It is extremely easy to create forms for interactive programs, but it is not easy at all to print on the printer. Most professional programmers using Visual Basic use a separate utility program to format printer reports. Several companies sell utilities that do a nice job of designing and printing reports. The VB Professional Edition and Enterprise Edition include Crystal Reports for creating reports from database files.

- Printing is totally changed: No more Printer.Print, PictureBox. Print, Or Debug.Print. All references to Tab, Spc, and print zones are now gone.

The PrintDocument Control

You set up output for the printer using the methods and events of the new **PrintDocument control.** Add a PrintDocument control to a form; the control appears in the component tray below the form (Figure 7.8). Name your PrintDocument using "prt" as the prefix, for example, prtDocument.

- The PrintDocument control handles all printing in its PrintPage event. This event is considered a callback, because the control fires the event and the program responds by taking action in the event procedure.

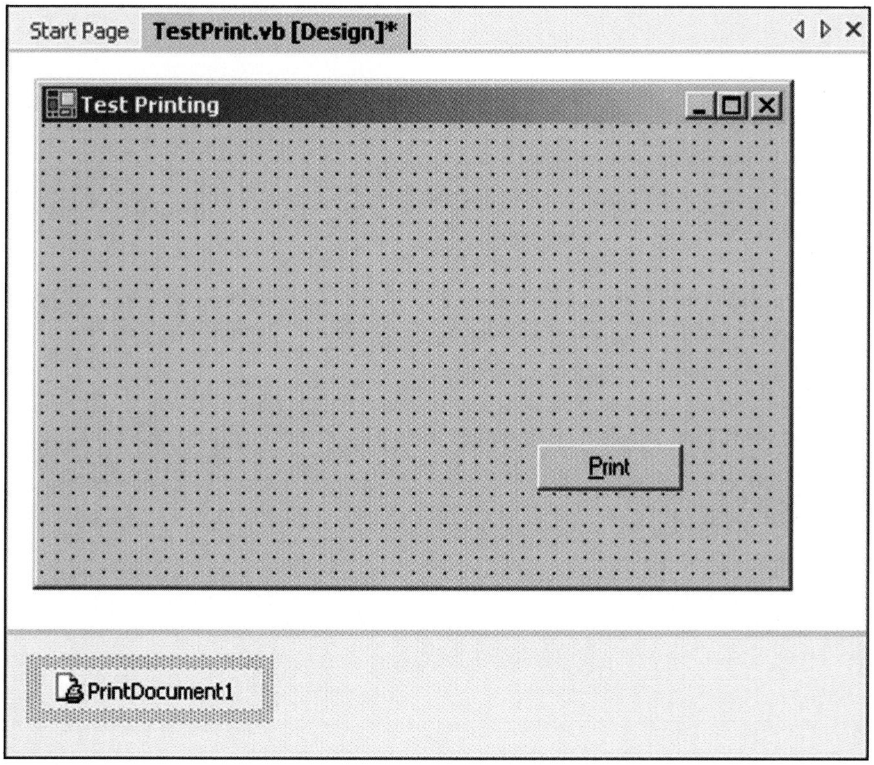

Figure 7.8

Add a PrintDocument control to your application. The control appears in the form's component tray.

Beginning the Print Operation

To start printing output, you execute the `Print` **method** of the PrintDocument control. This code belongs in the Click event procedure for the Print button or menu item that the user selects to begin printing.

```
Private Sub btnPrint_Click(ByVal sender As System.Object, _
  ByVal e As System.EventArgs) Handles btnPrint.Click
    'Print output on the printer

    prtDocument.Print()            'Start the print process
End Sub
```

Setting Up the Print Output

The logic for the actual printing belongs in the PrintDocument's **PrintPage event procedure.** The PrintPage event is fired once for each page to be printed. This technique is referred to as a ***callback,*** and is different from anything we have done so far. In a callback, the object notifies the program that it needs to do something or that a situation exists that the program needs to handle. The object notifies the program of the situation by firing an event.

The PrintDocument object is activated when you issue its `Print` method. It then fires a PrintPage event for each page to print. It also fires events for BeginPrint and EndPrint, for which you can write code if you wish.

```
Private Sub prtDocument_PrintPage(ByVal sender As Object, _
  ByVal e As System.Drawing.Printing.PrintPageEventArgs) _
  Handles prtDocument.PrintPage
    'Set up actual output to print

End Sub
```

Notice the argument:
`e As System.Drawing.Printing.PrintPageEventArgs`.
We will use some of the properties and methods of the PrintPageEventArgs argument for such things as determining the page margins and sending a string of text to the page.

The Graphics Page

You set up a graphics page in memory, and then the page is sent to the printer. The graphics page can contain strings of text as well as graphic elements.

You must specify the exact location on the graphics page for each element that you want to print. You can specify the upper-left corner of any element by giving its *X* and *Y* coordinates, or by using a Point structure or a Rectangle structure. We will stick with the *X* and *Y* coordinates in these examples (Figure 7.9).

- All logic for setting up the printed output appears in the PrintPage event procedure.

- The page is a Graphics object; you use the DrawString method of the Graphics class to place text; you must specify *X* and *Y* coordinates for every string of text, along with a font and a brush.

- Use properties of "e", which is the PrintPageEventArgs that is passed to the procedure. `e.graphics` refers to the page's graphic object, on which you can write and draw.

Figure 7.9

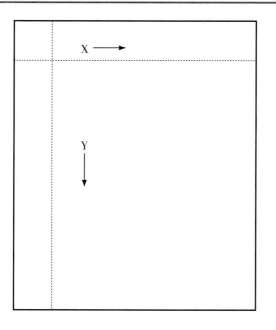

Using the DrawString Method

You use the `DrawString` **method** to send a line of text to the graphics page. The `DrawString` method belongs to the Graphics object of the PrintPageEventArgs argument. Refer back to the procedure header for the PrintPage event in "Setting Up the Print Output."

The DrawString Method—General Form

The `DrawString` method is overloaded, which means that there are several forms for calling the method. The form presented here is the least complicated and requires that page coordinates be given in X and Y format.

General Form

```
DrawString(StringToPrint, Font, Brush, Xcoordinate, Ycoordinate)
```

The DrawString Method—Examples

Examples

```
e.Graphics.DrawString(strPrintLine, fntPrintFont, Brushes.Black, sngPrintX, sngPrintY)
e.Graphics.DrawString("My text string", fntMyFont, Brushes.Black, 100.0, 100.0)
e.Graphics.DrawString(txtName.Text, New Font("Arial", 10), Brushes.Red, _
    sngLeftMargin,  sngCurrentLine)
```

Before you execute the `DrawString` method, you should set up the font that you want to use and the X and Y coordinates.

Setting the X and Y Coordinates

For each line that you want to print, you must specify the X and Y coordinates. It is helpful to set up some variables for setting these values, which should be declared as Single data type.

```
Dim sngPrintX As Single
Dim sngPrintY As Single
```

The PrintPageEventArgs argument has several useful properties (Figure 7.10), such as MarginBounds, PageBounds, and PageSettings. You can use these properties to determine present settings. For example, you may want to set the *X* coordinate to the current left margin and the *Y* coordinate to the top margin.

```
sngPrintX = e.MarginBounds.Left
sngPrintY = e.MarginBounds.Top
```

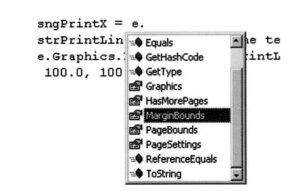

Use the properties of the PrintPageEventArgs argument to determine the current margin settings.

To send multiple lines to the print page, you must increment the Y coordinate. You can add the height of a line to the previous *Y* coordinate to calculate the next line's *Y* coordinate.

```
'Declarations at the top of the procedure
Dim fntPrintFont As New Font("Arial", 12)
'Make the line 2 pixels higher than the font
Dim sngLineHeight As Single = fntPrintFont.GetHeight + 2
' ... more declarations here


   'Print a line
   e.Graphics.DrawString(strPrintLine, fntPrintFont, Brushes.Black, sngPrintX, sngPrintY)
   'Increment the Y position for the next line
   sngPrintY += sngLineHeight
```

Printing the Contents of a List Box

You can combine the techniques for printing, a loop, and the list box properties to send the contents of a list box to the printer. You know how many iterations to make, using the Items.Count property. The Items collection allows you to print out the actual values from the list.

```
'Print out all items in the cboCoffee list

For intListIndex = 0 To cboCoffee.Items.Count - 1

    'Set up a line
    strPrintLine = CStr(cboCoffee.Items(intListIndex))
    'Send the line to the graphics page object
    e.Graphics.DrawString(strPrintLine, fntPrintFont, Brushes.Black, sngPrintX, sngPrintY)

    'Increment the Y position for the next line
    sngPrintY += sngLineHeight
Next
```

Printing the Selected Item from a List

When an item is selected in a list box or a combo box, the Text property holds
the selected item. You can use the Text property to print the selected item.

```
'Set up the line for the list selections
strPrintLine = "Coffee: " & cboCoffee.Text & "  Syrup: " & lstSyrup.Text
'Send the line to the graphics page object
e.Graphics.DrawString(strPrintLine, fntPrintFont, Brushes.Black, sngPrintX, sngPrintY)
```

Aligning Decimal Columns

When the output to the printer includes numeric data, the alignment of the
decimal points is important. Alignment can be tricky with proportional fonts,
where the width of each character varies. The best approach is to format each
number as you want it to print and then measure the length of the formatted
string. This technique requires a couple more elements: You need an object
declared as a SizeF structure, which has a Width property, and you need to use
the MeasureString method of the Graphics class. Both the SizeF structure
and MeasureString method work with pixels, which is what you want. It's the
same unit of measure as used for the *X* and *Y* coordinates of the DrawString
method.

> • Use the MeasureString method
> of the Graphics class to determine
> the width of a formatted string in
> pixels.

The following example prints a left-aligned literal at position 200 on the
line and right-aligns a formatted number at position 500. (Assume that all variables are properly declared.)

```
Dim stzStringSize As New SizeF() 'SizeF structure for font size info.

'Set X for left-aligned column
sngPrintX = 200F
'Set ending position for right-aligned column
sngColumnEnd = 500F

'Format the number
strFormattedOutput = FormatCurrency(decAmount)

'Calculate the X position of the amount
stzStringSize = e.Graphics.MeasureString(strFormattedOutput, fntPrintFont) 'Measure _
  string in this font
sngColumnX = sngColumnEnd - stzStringSize.Width 'Subtract width of string from the _
  column position
```

```
'Set up the line--each element separately
e.Graphics.DrawString("The Amount = ", fntPrintFont, Brushes.Black, sngPrintX, _
    sngPrintY)
e.Graphics.DrawString(strFormattedOutput, fntPrintFont, Brushes.Black, sngColumnX, _
    sngPrintY)
sngPrintY += sngLineHeight          'Increment line for next line
```

Displaying a Print Preview

A really great feature of the new VB .NET printing model is **print preview.** You can view the printer's output on the screen and then choose to print or cancel. This is especially helpful for testing and debugging a program, so that you don't have to keep sending pages to the printer and wasting paper.

The **PrintPreviewDialog control** is the key to print preview. You add the control to your form's component tray and name it "ppdSomething," such as ppdPrintPreview in the following example (Figure 7.11). Then you write two lines of code in the event procedure for the button or menu item where the user selects the print preview option. The PrintPreviewDialog class uses the same PrintDocument control that you declared for printer output. You assign the PrintDocument to the Document property of the PrintPreviewDialog and execute the ShowDialog method. The same PrintPage event procedure executes as for the PrintDocument.

- A great new feature of printing (to make up for all of the things they took away) is a Print Preview dialog box.

- Add a PrintPreviewDialog control and assign the PrintDocument object to it in code; the printed output appears in a Print Preview dialog. You and the students can then elect whether or not to send the output to the printer.

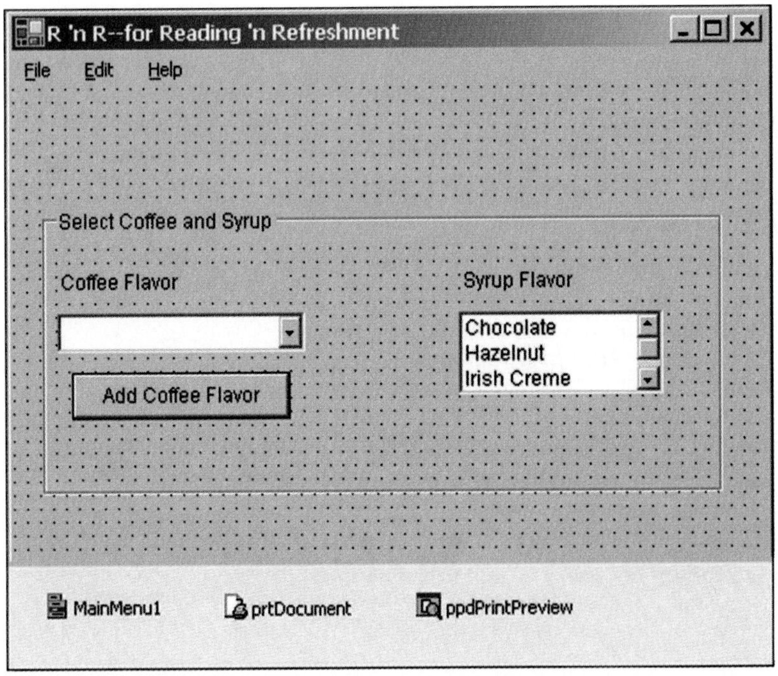

Figure 7.11

Add a PrintPreviewDialog control to your form's component tray and give it a name.

```
Private Sub mnuFilePrintPreview_Click(ByVal sender As Object, ByVal e As _
    System.EventArgs) Handles mnuFilePrintPreview.Click
    'Begin the process for print preview

    ppdPrintPreview.Document = prtDocument
    ppdPrintPreview.ShowDialog()
End Sub
```

Using Static Variables

Static local variables retain their value as long as the form is loaded, which is generally the life of the project, rather than being reinitialized for each call to the procedure. If you need to retain the value in a variable for multiple calls to a procedure, such as a running total, declare it as `Static`. (In the past we used module-level variables for this task. Using a static local variable is better than using a module-level variable because it is always best to keep the scope of a variable as narrow as possible.)

When printing multiple pages you want to know what page you are currently on. This variable can be declared at the local level, but it must retain the value from one execution of the procedure to the next. This is the perfect time to use a static local variable.

```
Static intPageCount As Integer = 1        'Count pages for multiple-page output
```

The format of the `Static` statement is the same as the format of the `Dim` statement. However, `Static` statements can appear only in procedures; `Static` statements never appear in the Declarations section of a module. Static variables do not require a scope prefix, since all static variables are local.

Printing Multiple Pages

You can easily print multiple pages, both to the printer and to the Print Preview dialog box. Recall that the PrintDocument's PrintPage event fires once for each page. You indicate that you have more pages to print by setting the HasMorePages property of the PrintPageEventArgs argument to True.

The following example prints four pages full of the same line, just to illustrate multiple-page output. Normally you will have a certain amount of data to print and stop when you run out.

```
Private Sub prtDocument_PrintPage(ByVal sender As Object, _
    ByVal e As System.Drawing.Printing.PrintPageEventArgs) Handles prtDocument.PrintPage

    'Print multiple-page output
    'Assume all declarations are here
    Static intPageCount As Integer = 1        'Count pages for multiple-page output

    sngPrintY = e.MarginBounds.Top
    strPrintLine = "This is a line of output"

    'Print the page number
    e.Graphics.DrawString("Page " & intPageCount, fntPrintFont, Brushes.Black, 600, _
      sngPrintY)
    sngPrintY += sngLineHeight * 2

    'Print a page full of the same line
    Do
        'Print a line
        e.Graphics.DrawString(strPrintLine, fntPrintFont, Brushes.Black, sngPrintX, _
          sngPrintY)
        sngPrintY += sngLineHeight
    Loop Until sngPrintY >= e.MarginBounds.Bottom 'Stop at the bottom margin
```

```
    intPageCount += 1           'Increment the page number

    'Indicate whether there are more pages to print
    If intPageCount <= 4 Then        'Print only 4 pages
        e.HasMorePages = True
    Else
        e.HasMorePages = False
    End If
End Sub
```

Feedback 7.4

What is the purpose of each of these elements? Where and how is each used?

1. The PrintDocument control
2. The `Print` method
3. The PrintPage event
4. The `DrawString` method
5. `System.Drawing.Printing.PrintPageEventArgs`
6. `MarginBounds.Left`
7. The PrintPreviewDialog control

Your Hands-On Programming Example

Create a project for R 'n R—for Reading 'n Refreshment that contains a drop-down combo box of the coffee flavors and a list box of the syrup flavors. Adjust the size of the boxes as needed when you test the project. The controls should have labels above them with the words *Coffee* and *Syrup*. Enter the initial values for the syrup flavors and coffee flavors in the Properties window. Set the Sorted property of both lists to True. The user will be able to add more coffee flavors to the list at run time.

Coffee flavors	Syrup flavors
Espresso Roast	(None)
Jamaica Blue Mountain	Chocolate
Kona Blend	Hazelnut
Chocolate Almond	Irish Cream
Vanilla Nut	Orange

Include one menu item to print all the flavors and another to print only a selected item from each list. Then include submenus for each of the print options to allow the user to send the output to the printer or the Print Preview window. These print commands belong on the *File* menu, along with the *Exit* command. Use a separator bar between the *Prints* and the *Exit*.

Include an *Edit* menu with commands to *Add coffee flavor*, *Remove coffee flavor*, *Clear coffee list*, and *Display coffee count*.

Add an About form into your project and add a *Help* menu with an *About* command.

After you have completed the project, try using different styles for the combo box and rerun the project. As an added challenge, modify the add coffee flavor routine so that no duplicates are allowed.

Planning the Project

Sketch a form (Figure 7.12), which your users sign off as meeting their needs.

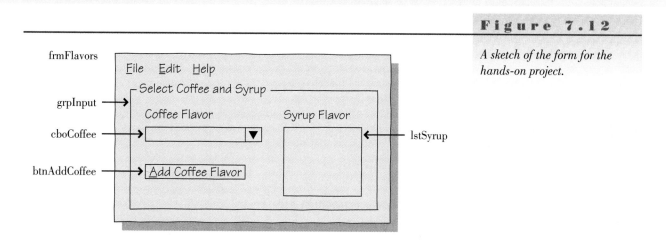

Figure 7.12

A sketch of the form for the hands-on project.

Plan the Objects and Properties

Object	Property	Setting
frmFlavors	Name	frmFlavors
	Text	R 'n R--for Reading 'n Refreshment
grpInput	Name	grpInput
	Text	Select Coffee and Syrup
Label1	Text	Coffee Flavor
Label2	Text	Syrup Flavor
cboCoffee	Name	cboCoffee
	DropDownStyle	DropDown
	Items	Chocolate Almond
		Espresso Roast
		Jamaica Blue Mtn.
		Kona Blend
		Vanilla Nut
	Sorted	True
	Text	(blank)

Continued on page 304

Object	Property	Setting
lstSyrup	Name	lstSyrup
	Items	Chocolate
		Hazelnut
		Irish Creme
		Orange
		(None)
	Sorted	True
btnAddCoffee	Name	btnAddCoffee
	Text	&Add Coffee Flavor
mnuFile	Name	mnuFile
	Text	&File
mnuFilePrintSelect	Name	mnuFilePrintSelect
	Text	Print &Selected Flavors
mnuFilePrintSelectPreview	Name	mnuFilePrintSelectPreview
	Text	Print Pre&view
mnuFilePrintSelectPrint	Name	mnuFilePrintSelectPrint
	Text	&Print
mnuFilePrintAll	Name	mnuFilePrintAll
	Text	Print &All Flavors
mnuFilePrintAllPreview	Name	mnuFilePrintAllPreview
	Text	Print Pre&view
mnuFilePrintAllPrint	Name	mnuFilePrintAllPrint
	Text	&Print
mnuFileExit	Name	mnuFileExit
	Text	E&xit
mnuEdit	Name	mnuEdit
	Text	&Edit
mnuEditAdd	Name	mnuEditAdd
	Text	&Add Coffee Flavor
mnuEditRemove	Name	mnuEditRemove
	Text	&Remove Coffee Flavor
mnuEditClear	Name	mnuEditClear
	Text	&Clear Coffee List
mnuEditCount	Name	mnuEditCount
	Text	Count Coffee &List
mnuHelp	Name	mnuHelp
	Text	&Help
mnuHelpAbout	Name	mnuHelpAbout
	Text	&About
prtDocument	Name	prtDocument
ppdPrintPreview	Name	ppdPrintPreview

Plan the Event Procedures

Main Form Procedure	Actions

btnAddCoffee	If text box in cboCoffee not empty then
	  Add contents of cboCoffee text box to items.
	  Clear the text box in cboCoffee.
	Else
	 Display error message.
	Set the focus to cboCoffee.

mnuFilePrintSelectPreview	If both coffee and syrup selected Set Boolean variable for selected item. Set the print preview document. Show the print preview dialog. Else Display error message.
mnuFilePrintSelectPrint	If both coffee and syrup selected Set Boolean variable for selected item. Start the print operation. Else Display error message.
mnuFilePrintAllPreview	Set the Boolean variable for entire list. Set the print preview document. Show the print preview dialog.
mnuFilePrintAllPrint	Set the Boolean variable for entire list. Start the print operation.
prtDocument_PrintPage	If Boolean variable set for entire list Use a loop to send all flavor names to the printer. Else Print selected items from both lists.
mnuFileExit	Terminate the project.
mnuEditAdd	Call btnAddCoffee_Click.

mnuEditRemove	If coffee flavor selected then
	 Remove selected item.
	Else
	 Display error message.

mnuEditClear	Display a message box to confirm the clear. If user clicks Yes Clear the coffee list
mnuEditCount	Display list count in message box.
mnuHelpAbout	Display the About box.

About Form	
Procedure	**Actions**
btnOK	Close the About box.

Write the Project

- Follow the sketch in Figure 7.12 to create the form. Figure 7.13 shows the completed form.

- Set the properties of each object as you have planned.

- Write the code. Working from the pseudocode, write each event procedure.

- When you complete the code, use a variety of data to thoroughly test the project.

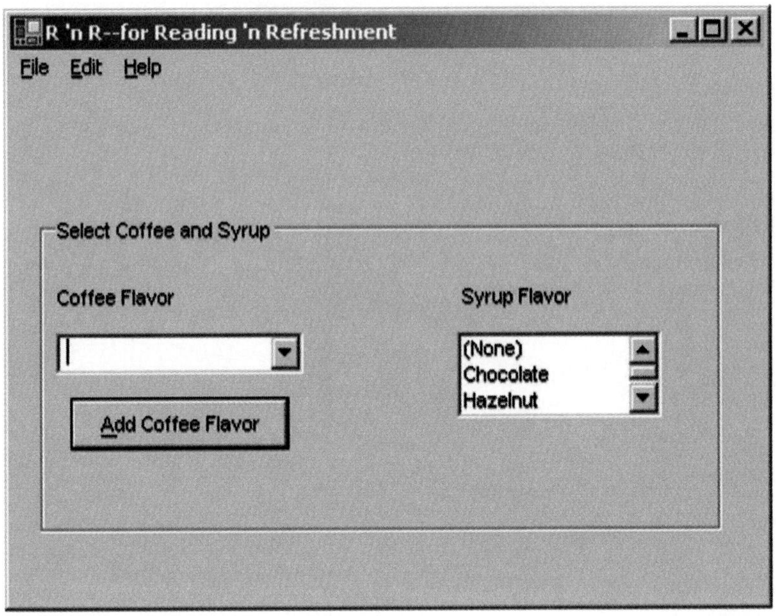

Figure 7.13

The form for the hands-on project.

The Project Coding Solution

Main Form

```
'Module:            frmFlavors
'Programmer:        Bradley/Millspaugh
'Date               January 2002
'Description:       Maintain a list of coffee flavors; print the selected flavor
'                      of coffee and syrup or print a list of all of the
'                      coffee flavors.
'Folder:            Ch0701

Public Class frmFlavors
    Inherits System.Windows.Forms.Form

[Windows Form Designer generated code]

'Declare module-level variables
    Private mblnPrintAll As Boolean        'Setting to select output to print

    Private Sub btnAddCoffee_Click(ByVal sender As System.Object, _
      ByVal e As System.EventArgs) Handles btnAddCoffee.Click
        'Add a new coffee flavor to the coffee list

        If cboCoffee.Text <> "" Then
            With cboCoffee
                .Items.Add(.Text)
                .Text = ""
            End With
        Else
            MessageBox.Show("Enter a coffee flavor to add", "Missing data", _
              MessageBoxButtons.OK, MessageBoxIcon.Exclamation)
        End If
        cboCoffee.Focus()
    End Sub

    Public Sub mnuEditAdd_Click(ByVal sender As System.Object, _
      ByVal e As System.EventArgs) Handles mnuEditAdd.Click
        'Add a new coffee to list

        btnAddCoffee_Click(sender, e)
    End Sub

    Public Sub mnuEditClear_Click(ByVal sender As System.Object, _
      ByVal e As System.EventArgs) Handles mnuEditClear.Click
        'Clear the coffee list
        Dim dgrResponse As DialogResult

        dgrResponse = MessageBox.Show("Clear the coffee flavor list?", _
          "Clear coffee list", MessageBoxButtons.YesNo, MessageBoxIcon.Question)
        If dgrResponse = DialogResult.Yes Then
            cboCoffee.Items.Clear()
        End If
    End Sub

    Public Sub mnuEditCount_Click(ByVal sender As System.Object, _
      ByVal e As System.EventArgs) Handles mnuEditCount.Click
        'Display a count of the coffee list

        MessageBox.Show("The number of coffee types is " & cboCoffee.Items.Count)
    End Sub
```

```vb
Public Sub mnuEditRemove_Click(ByVal sender As System.Object, _
  ByVal e As System.EventArgs) Handles mnuEditRemove.Click
    'Remove the selected coffee from list

    With cboCoffee
        If .SelectedIndex <> -1 Then
            .Items.RemoveAt(.SelectedIndex)
        Else
            MessageBox.Show("First select the coffee to remove", _
              "No selection made", MessageBoxButtons.OK, MessageBoxIcon.Exclamation)
        End If
    End With
End Sub

Public Sub mnuHelpAbout_Click(ByVal sender As System.Object, _
  ByVal e As System.EventArgs) Handles mnuHelpAbout.Click
    'Display frmAbout
    Dim AboutForm As New frmAbout()

    AboutForm.Show()
End Sub

Public Sub mnuFileExit_Click(ByVal sender As System.Object, _
  ByVal e As System.EventArgs) Handles mnuFileExit.Click
    'Terminate the project

    Me.Close()
End Sub

Private Sub mnuFilePrintAllPrint_Click(ByVal sender As System.Object, _
  ByVal e As System.EventArgs) Handles mnuFilePrintAllPrint.Click
    'Begin the print process to print all items

    mblnPrintAll = True
    prtDocument.Print()
End Sub

Private Sub mnuFilePrintAllPreview_Click(ByVal sender As System.Object, _
  ByVal e As System.EventArgs) Handles mnuFilePrintAllPreview.Click
    'Begin the process for print preview of all items

    mblnPrintAll = True
    ppdPrintPreview.Document = prtDocument
    ppdPrintPreview.ShowDialog()
End Sub

Private Sub mnuFilePrintSelectPrint_Click(ByVal sender As Object, _
  ByVal e As System.EventArgs) Handles mnuFilePrintSelectPrint.Click
    'Begin the print process to print the selected item

    If lstSyrup.SelectedIndex = -1 Then
        lstSyrup.SelectedIndex = 0                'Select (None) if nothing selected
    End If
    If cboCoffee.SelectedIndex <> -1 Then         'Items selected
        mblnPrintAll = False
        prtDocument.Print()
    Else                                          'No item selected
        MessageBox.Show("Select a flavor from the coffee list", "Print Selection", _
          MessageBoxButtons.OK, MessageBoxIcon.Exclamation)
    End If
End Sub
```

```
Private Sub mnuFilePrintSelectPreview_Click(ByVal sender As Object, _
 ByVal e As System.EventArgs) Handles mnuFilePrintSelectPreview.Click
    'Begin the process for print preview of the selected item

    If lstSyrup.SelectedIndex = -1 Then
        lstSyrup.SelectedIndex = 0                    'Select (None) if nothing selected
    End If
    If cboCoffee.SelectedIndex <> -1 Then        'Item selected
        mblnPrintAll = False
        ppdPrintPreview.Document = prtDocument
        ppdPrintPreview.ShowDialog()
    Else      'No item selected
        MessageBox.Show("Select a flavor from the coffee list", "Print Selection", _
            MessageBoxButtons.OK, MessageBoxIcon.Exclamation)
    End If
End Sub

Private Sub prtDocument_PrintPage(ByVal sender As Object, _
 ByVal e As System.Drawing.Printing.PrintPageEventArgs) _
 Handles prtDocument.PrintPage
    'Handle all printing and print previews

    Dim fntPrintFont As New Font("Arial", 12)
    Dim fntHeading As New Font("Arial", 14, FontStyle.Bold)
    Dim sngLineHeight As Single = fntPrintFont.GetHeight + 2
    Dim sngPrintX As Single = e.MarginBounds.Left
    Dim sngPrintY As Single = e.MarginBounds.Top
    Dim strPrintLine As String
    Dim intListIndex As Integer

    'Perform all printing and print preview
    If mblnPrintAll Then                              'Print or view all items
        'Loop through the entire list
        For intListIndex = 0 To cboCoffee.Items.Count - 1

            'Set up a line
            strPrintLine = CStr(cboCoffee.Items(intListIndex))
            'Send the line to the graphics page object
            e.Graphics.DrawString(strPrintLine, fntPrintFont, _
                Brushes.Black, sngPrintX, sngPrintY)
            'Increment the Y position for the next line
            sngPrintY += sngLineHeight
        Next intListIndex
    Else                                             'Print or view only selected items

        'Set up and display heading lines
        strPrintLine = "Print Selected Item"
        e.Graphics.DrawString(strPrintLine, fntHeading, _
            Brushes.Black, sngPrintX, sngPrintY)
        strPrintLine = "by Programmer Name"
        sngPrintY += sngLineHeight
        e.Graphics.DrawString(strPrintLine, fntHeading, _
            Brushes.Black, sngPrintX, sngPrintY)

        'Set up the selected line
        sngPrintY += sngLineHeight * 2    'Leave a blank line between heading and _
            detail line
        strPrintLine = "Coffee: " & cboCoffee.Text & _
            "  Syrup: " & lstSyrup.Text
```

```
            'Send the line to the graphics page object
            e.Graphics.DrawString(strPrintLine, fntPrintFont, _
            Brushes.Black, sngPrintX, sngPrintY)
        End If
    End Sub
End Class
```

About Form

```
'Module:          frmAbout
'Programmer:      Bradley/Millspaugh
'Date:            January 2002
'Description:     Display information about the program
'                  and the programmer.
'Folder:          Ch0701

Public Class frmAbout
    Inherits System.Windows.Forms.Form

[Windows Form Designer generated code]

    Private Sub btnOK_Click(ByVal sender As System.Object, ByVal e _
    As System.EventArgs) Handles btnOK.Click
        'Return to the main form

        Me.Close()
    End Sub
End Class
```

Summary

1. List boxes and combo boxes hold lists of values. The three styles of combo boxes are simple combo boxes, drop-down combo boxes, and drop-down lists.
2. The size of a list box or combo box is determined at design time. If all of the items will not fit into the box, VB automatically adds scroll bars.
3. The values for the items in a list are stored in the Items property, which is a collection. The items can be entered in the Items property in the Properties window. At run time, items are added to lists using the `Items.Add` or `Items.Insert` methods.
4. The SelectedIndex property can be used to select an item in the list or to determine which item is selected.
5. The Items.Count property holds the number of elements in the list.
6. The Items collection holds all elements of the list. The individual elements can be referenced by using an index.
7. The `Items.Remove` and `Items.RemoveAt` methods remove one element from a list.
8. The `Items.Clear` method may be used to remove the contents of a list box.
9. Code can be written for several events of list boxes and combo boxes. Combo boxes have a TextChanged event; both combo boxes and list boxes have Enter and Leave events.

10. A loop allows a statement or series of statements to be repeated. Do/Loops continue to execute the statements in the loop until a condition is met. Each pass through a loop is called an iteration.

11. Do/Loops can have the condition test at the top or the bottom of the loop and can use a While or Until to test the condition.

12. A Do/Loop can be used to locate a selected item in a combo box.

13. A loop index controls For/Next loops; the index is initialized to an initial value. After each iteration, the loop index is incremented by the Step value (the increment), which defaults to 1. The loop is terminated when the loop index is greater than the ending value.

14. The PrintDocument control and the PrintPreviewDialog control can be used to send program output to the printer or the screen.

15. The Print method of the PrintDocument control begins a print operation. The control's PrintPage event fires once for each page to print. All printing logic belongs in the PrintPage event procedure.

16. The page to print or display is a graphics object. Use the DrawString method to send a string of text to the page, specifying X and Y coordinates for the string.

17. Aligning columns of numbers is difficult using proportional fonts. Numbers can be right-aligned by formatting the number, measuring the length of the formatted string in pixels, and subtracting the length from the right end of the column for the X coordinate.

Key Terms

Review Questions

1. What is a list box? a combo box?
2. Name and describe the three styles of combo boxes.
3. How can you make scroll bars appear on a list box or combo box?
4. Explain the purpose of the SelectedIndex property and the Items.Count property.
5. When and how is information placed inside a list box or a combo box?
6. In what situation would a loop be used in a procedure?
7. Explain the difference between a pretest and a posttest in a `Do/Loop`.
8. Explain the differences between a `Do/Loop` and a `For/Next` loop.
9. What are the steps in processing a `For/Next` loop?
10. Discuss how and when the values of the loop index change throughout the processing of the loop.
11. What is the purpose of the PrintDocument control? the PrintPreviewDialog control?
12. In what procedure do you write the logic for sending output to the printer?
13. What is the purpose of the *X* and *Y* coordinates on a print page?

Programming Exercises

7.1   Create a project for obtaining student information.
Startup form controls are as follows:

- Text boxes for entering the name and units completed.

- Radio buttons for Freshman, Sophomore, Junior, and Senior.

- Check box for Dean's List.

- Use a list box for the following majors: Accounting, Business, Computer Information Systems, and Marketing.

- A simple combo for name of high school—initially loaded with Franklin, Highland, West Highland, and Midtown. If the user types in a new school name, it should be added to the list. *Hint:* Add the school in the combo boxes. Validate event procedure.

- Print button that prints the data from the form. Use the Print Preview dialog box.

- An OK button that clears the entries from the form and resets the focus. The button should be the Accept button for the form.

The Menus: The *File* menu should have an option for *Print Schools* and *Exit*. The *Help* menu should have an option for the *About* box.
    Note: Print your name at the top of the printer output for the schools. Display the printer output in the Print Preview dialog box.

7.2   R 'n R—for Reading 'n Refreshment needs a project that contains a form for entering book information.

The Form Controls:

- Text boxes for author and title.

- Radio buttons for type: fiction or nonfiction.

- DropDown list for Subject that will include Best-Seller, Fantasy, Religion, Romance, Humor, Science Fiction, Business, Philosophy, Education, Self-Help, and Mystery.

- List box for Shelf Number containing RC-1111, RC-1112, RC-1113, and RC-1114.

- Print button that prints the data from the form. Use the Print Preview dialog box.

- An OK button that clears the entries from the form and resets the focus. Make this the Accept button.

The Menu: The *File* menu will have an option for *Print Subjects* and *Exit*. The *Help* menu will have an option for the *About* box.

Note: Print your name at the top of the printer output for the subjects. Display the printer output in the Print Preview dialog box.

7.3 Create a project to input chartering information about yachts and print a summary report showing the total revenue and average hours per charter.

The Menus:

- The *File* menu will contain commands for *Print Summary, Print Yacht Types,* and *Exit.* Place a separator bar before *Exit.* The *Edit* menu should have commands for *Clear for Next Charter, Add Yacht Type, Remove Yacht Type,* and *Display Count of Yacht Types.* Include a separator bar after the *Clear* command. The *Help* menu will contain an *About* command that displays an About form.

The Form:

- The form should contain text boxes for responsible party and hours chartered. Include a label to show the calculated price of the charter.

- A drop-down combo box will contain the type of yacht: Ranger, Wavelength, Catalina, Coronado, Hobie, C & C, Hans Christian, and Excalibur. Any items that are added to the text box during processing must be added to the list.

- A drop-down list will contain size: 22, 24, 30, 32, 36, 38, 45. (No new sizes can be entered at run time.)

- An OK button will calculate and display the price and add to the totals. The calculations will require price per hour. Use the following chart:

Size	Hourly Rate
22	95.00
24	137.00
30	160.00
32	192.00
36	250.00
38	400.00
45	550.00

- A Clear button will clear the contents of the screen controls. The functions of the Clear button are the same as for the Clear for Next Charter menu item.

- Make the OK button the accept button and the Clear button the form's cancel button.

Summary Report:

The summary report will print the summary information and send the report to the printer and/or the Print Preview dialog box. The summary information will include Number of Charters, Total Revenue, and Average Hours Chartered. Include your name on the output and identifying labels for the summary information.

Yacht Types Report:

Display the yacht types in the combo box in the Print Preview dialog box. Include your name and a title at the top of the report.

7.4   Create a project that contains a list box with the names of all U.S. states and territories. When the user types the first letters of the state into a text box, set the SelectedIndex property of the list box to display the appropriate name. Include an `Exit` menu item.

Alabama	Kentucky	Oklahoma
Alaska	Louisiana	Oregon
American Samoa	Maine	Pennsylvania
Arizona	Maryland	Puerto Rico
Arkansas	Massachusetts	Rhode Island
California	Michigan	South Carolina
Colorado	Minnesota	South Dakota
Connecticut	Mississippi	Tennessee
Delaware	Missouri	Texas
District of Columbia	Montana	Trust Territories
Florida	Nebraska	Utah
Georgia	Nevada	Vermont
Guam	New Hampshire	Virgin Islands
Hawaii	New Jersey	Virginia
Idaho	New Mexico	Washington
Illinois	New York	West Virginia
Indiana	North Carolina	Wisconsin
Iowa	North Dakota	Wyoming
Kansas	Ohio	

7.5   Maintain a list of bagel types for Bradley's Bagels. Use a drop-down combo box to hold the bagel types and use buttons or menu choices to *Add Bagel Type, Remove Bagel Type, Clear Bagel List, Print Bagel List, Display Bagel Type Count,* and *Exit.* Keep the list sorted in alphabetic order.

Do not allow a blank type to be added to the list. Display an error message if the user selects *Remove* without first selecting a bagel type.

Before clearing the list, display a message box to confirm the operation.

Here are some suggested bagel types. You can make up your own list.

Plain	Poppy seed
Egg	Sesame seed
Rye	Banana nut
Salt	Blueberry

Case Studies

VB Mail Order

Create a project for VB Mail Order to maintain a list of catalogs. Use a drop-down combo box for the catalog names, and allow the user to enter new catalog names, delete catalog names, display a count of the number of catalogs, clear the catalog list, or print the catalog list.

Do not allow a blank catalog name to be added to the list. Display an error message if the user selects *Remove* without first selecting a catalog name. Before clearing the list, display a message box to confirm the operation.

To begin, the catalog list should hold these catalog names: Odds and Ends, Solutions, Camping Needs, ToolTime, Spiegel, The Outlet, and The Large Size.

Display the printed output in the Print Preview dialog box. Include your name and a heading at the top of the report.

VB Auto Center

Create an application for the car wash located at VB Auto Center.

The form will contain three list box or combo box controls that do not permit the user to type in items at run time. The first list will contain the names of the packages available for detailing a vehicle: Standard, Deluxe, Executive, or Luxury.

The contents of the other two lists will vary depending upon the package selected. Display one list for the interior work and one list for the exterior work. Store the descriptions of the items in string constants. You must clear the lists for the interior and exterior for each order and add new items to the lists each time the user makes a selection from the package list.

Use a drop-down list to allow the user to select a fragrance for deodorizing the interior. The choices are Hawaiian Mist, Baby Powder, Pine, Country Floral, Pina Colada, and Vanilla.

Include menu commands for *Print Order, Clear,* and *Exit.* The print option should send its output to the Print Preview window. Include your name and a heading at the top of the report.

The Order printout will contain the package name (Standard, Deluxe, Executive, or Luxury), the interior and exterior items included, and the fragrance selected. Use a For/Next loop when printing the interior and exterior lists.

	Item description	S	D	E	L
Exterior	Hand wash	✓	✓	✓	✓
	Hand wax		✓	✓	✓
	Check engine fluids			✓	✓
	Detail engine compartment				✓
	Detail under carriage				✓
Interior	Fragrance	✓	✓	✓	✓
	Shampoo carpets		✓	✓	✓
	Shampoo upholstery				✓
	Interior protection coat (dashboard and console)			✓	
	Scotchgard™				✓

Note: S-Standard; D-Deluxe; E-Executive; L-Luxury.

Video Bonanza

Maintain a list of movie categories. Use a drop-down combo box to hold the movie types and use buttons or menu choices to *Add a Category, Remove a Category, Clear all Categories, Print the Category List, Display the Movie Category Count,* and *Exit*. Keep the list sorted in alphabetic order.

Do not allow a blank type to be added to the list. Display an error message if the user selects *Remove* without first selecting a movie category. Before clearing the list, display a message box to confirm the operation.

The starting categories are

- Comedy

- Drama

- Action

- Sci-Fi

- Horror

Display the printed output in the Print Preview dialog box. Include your name and a heading at the top of the report.

Very Very Boards

Write a project to maintain a list of shirt styles. Keep the styles in a drop-down combo box, with styles such as crew, turtleneck, or crop top.

Add a *Style* menu with options to *Add Style, Remove Style, Clear Style List, Count Styles,* and *Print Style List.*

Display the printed output in the Print Preview dialog box. Include your name and a heading at the top of the report.

8

Arrays

'Convert input values to numeric variables
intQuantity = CInt(txtQuantity.Text)
decPrice = CDec(txtPrice.Text)

'Format and display answers for sale
lblExtendedPrice.Text = FormatCurrency(decExtende
lblDiscount.Text = FormatNumber(decDiscount)
lblDiscountedPrice.Text = FormatCurrency(decDisco

'Handle exceptions
ch MyErr As InvalidCastException

at the completion of this chapter, you will be able to . . .

1. Use the Select Case structure for multiple decisions.

2. Make one event procedure handle multiple controls and access the name of the control that caused the event.

3. Establish an array and refer to individual elements in the array with subscripts.

4. Use the For Each/Next to traverse the array.

5. Create a structure for multiple fields of related data.

6. Accumulate totals using arrays.

7. Distinguish between direct access and indirect access of a table.

8. Write a table lookup for matching an array element.

9. Combine the advantages of list box controls with arrays.

10. Store and look up data in multidimensional arrays.

The Case Structure

In Chapter 4 you used the If statement for testing conditions and making decisions. Whenever you want to test a single variable or expression for multiple values, the **Case structure** provides a flexible and powerful solution. Any decisions that you can code with a Case structure can also be coded with nested If statements, but usually the Case structure is simpler and clearer.

The Select Case Statement—General Form

```
Select Case expression
   Case ConstantList
      [Statement(s)]
   [Case ConstantList
      [Statement(s)]]
   .
   .
   .
   [Case Else]
      [Statement(s)]
End Select
```

The expression in a Case structure is usually a variable or property you wish to test.

The constant list is the value that you want to match; it may be a numeric or string constant or variable, a range of values, a relational condition, or a combination of these.

There is no limit to the number of statements that can follow a Case statement.

The Select Case Statement—Examples

```
Select Case intScore
   Case Is >= 100
      lblMessage1.Text = "Excellent Score"
      lblMessage2.Text = "Give yourself a pat on the back."
   Case 80 To 99
      lblMessage1.Text = "Very Good"
      lblMessage2.Text = "You should be proud."
   Case 60 To 79
      lblMessage1.Text = "Satisfactory Score"
      lblMessage2.Text = "You should have a nice warm feeling."
   Case Else
      lblMessage1.Text = "Your score shows room for improvement."
      lblMessage2.Text = ""
End Select

Select Case intListIndex
   Case 0
      HandleItemZero()
   Case 1, 2, 3
      HandleItems()
   Case Else
      HandleNoSelection()
End Select
```

The examples show a combination of relational operators, constant ranges, and multiple constants. Notice these points from the examples:

- When using a relational operator (e.g., Is >= 100) the word Is must be used.

- To indicate a range of constants, use the word To (e.g., 80 To 99).

- Multiple constants should be separated by commas.

The elements used for the constant list may have any of these forms:

```
constant [, constant...]          Case 2, 5, 9
constant To constant              Case 25 To 50
Is relational-operator constant   Case Is < 10
```

When you want to test for a string value, you must include quotation marks around the literals.

Example

```
Select Case txtTeamName.Text
    Case "Tigers"
        (Code for Tigers)
    Case "Leopards"
        (Code for Leopards)
    Case "Cougars", "Panthers"
        (Code for Cougars and Panthers)
    Case Else
        (Code for any nonmatch)
End Select
```

Note that in the previous example, the capitalization must also match exactly. A better solution would be

Example

```
Select Case txtTeamName.Text.ToUpper()
    Case "TIGERS"
        (Code for Tigers)
    Case "LEOPARDS"
        (Code for Leopards)
    Case "COUGARS", "PANTHERS"
        (Code for Cougars and Panthers)
    Case Else
        (Code for any nonmatch)
End Select
```

Although the Case Else clause is optional, generally you will want to include it in Select Case statements. The statements you code beneath Case Else execute only if none of the other Case conditions is matched. This clause provides checking for any invalid or unforeseen values of the expression being tested. If the Case Else clause is omitted and none of the Case conditions is True, the program continues execution at the statement following the End Select.

If more than one Case value is matched by the expression, only the statements in the *first* Case clause executes.

> ## Feedback 8.1
>
> Convert the following If statements to Select Case statements.
>
> 1.
> ```
> If intTemp <= 32 Then
>     lblComment.Text = "Freezing"
> ElseIf intTemp > 80 Then
>     lblComment.Text = "Hot"
> Else
>     lblComment.Text = "Moderate"
> End If
> ```
>
> 2.
> ```
> If intCount = 0 Then
>     MessageBox.Show("No items entered")
> ElseIf intCount < 11 Then
>     MessageBox.Show("1 — 10 items entered")
> ElseIf intCount < 21 Then
>     MessageBox.Show("11 — 20 items entered")
> Else
>     MessageBox.Show("More than 20 items entered")
> End If
> ```

Sharing an Event Procedure

A very handy feature of VB .NET is the ability to share an event procedure for several controls. For example, assume that you have a group of five radio buttons to allow the user to choose a color (Figure 8.1). Each of the radio buttons must have its own name and will ordinarily have its own event procedure. But you can add events to the Handles clause at the top of an event procedure to make the procedure respond to events of other controls.

• Control arrays are not supported in .NET. The new technique used is to write the Handles clause of an event procedure to handle the event for multiple controls.

Figure 8.1

The five radio buttons allow the user to choose the color.

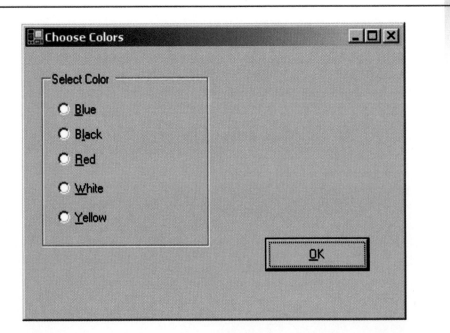

```
Private Sub radBlue_CheckedChanged(ByVal sender As System.Object, _
  ByVal e As System.EventArgs) _
  Handles radBlue.CheckedChanged, radBlack.CheckedChanged, _
  radRed.CheckedChanged, radWhite.CheckedChanged, radYellow.CheckedChanged
```

After you have added the additional events to the Handles clause, this event procedure will execute when the user selects *any* of the radio buttons.

A good, professional technique is to set up a module-level variable to hold the selection that the user makes. Then, in the OK button's event procedure you can take action based on which of the buttons was selected.

The key to using the shared event procedure is the sender argument that is passed to the CheckChanged event procedure. The sender is defined as an object, which has a Name property. However, if you refer to sender.Name with Option Strict turned on, you generate a compiler error telling you that late binding is not allowed. **Late binding** means that the type cannot be determined at compile time, but must be determined at run time. Late binding is allowed with Option Strict turned off, but should be avoided if possible for performance reasons.

You can use the properties of the sender arguments if you first cast (convert) sender to a specific object type, instead of the generic object. You can use the Ctype **function** to convert one object type to another:

```
CType(ValueToConvert, NewType)
```

The CType function returns an object of the new type. If the *ValueToConvert* is not in the range of legal values for *NewType*, an exception is generated at run time. Note that you could use CType rather than the conversion functions that you learned in Chapter 3, such as CInt, CDec, and CDbl.

For the radio button example, declare a variable as a RadioButton data type, cast the sender argument to a RadioButton object type, and assign it to the new variable:

```
Dim radSelected As RadioButtion
radSelected = CType(sender, RadioButton)
```

After these statements, you can refer to radSelected.Name to determine which radio button was selected:

```
Select Case radSelected.Name
    Case ''radBlue''
    ' . . .
```

You can declare a module-level variable as a Color data type, assign the chosen color in the shared event procedure, and then apply the color in the OK button's click event.

```
'Declare a module-level variable
Dim mcolorNew As Color

Private Sub radBlue_CheckedChanged(ByVal sender As System.Object, _
  ByVal e As System.EventArgs) _
  Handles radBlue.CheckedChanged, radBlack.CheckedChanged, _
  radRed.CheckedChanged, radWhite.CheckedChanged, radYellow.CheckedChanged
  'Save the name of the selected button
```

```
Dim radSelected As RadioButton

radSelected = CType(sender, RadioButton)
Select Case radSelected.Name
    Case "radBlue"
        mcolorNew = Color.Blue
    Case "radBlack"
        mcolorNew = Color.Black
    Case "radRed"
        mcolorNew = Color.Red
    Case "radWhite"
        mcolorNew = Color.White
    Case "radYellow"
        mcolorNew = Color.Yellow
    End Select
End Sub

Private Sub btnOK_Click(ByVal sender As Object, _
 ByVal e As System.EventArgs) Handles btnOK.Click
    'Change the color based on the selected radio button

    Me.BackColor = mcolorNew
End Sub
```

Single-Dimension Arrays

An **array** is a list or series of values, similar to a list box or a combo box. You can think of an array as a list box without the box—without the visual representation. Any time you need to keep a series of variables for later processing, such as reordering, calculating, or printing, you need to set up an array.

Consider an example that has a form for entering product information one product at a time. After the user has entered many products, you will need to calculate some statistics, perhaps use the information in different ways, or print it. Of course, each time the user enters the data for the next product, the previous contents of the text boxes are replaced. You could assign the previous values to variables, but they also would be replaced for each new product. Another approach might be to create multiple variables, such as strProduct1, strProduct2, strProduct3, and so on. This approach might be reasonable for a few entries, but what happens when you need to store 50 or 500 products?

When you need to store multiple values, use an array. An array is a series of individual variables, all referenced by the same name. Sometimes arrays are referred to as **tables** or **subscripted variables**. For an array for storing names, you may have strName(0), strName(1), strName(2), and so on.

Each individual variable is called an *element* of the array. The individual elements are treated the same as any other variable and may be used in any statement, such as an assignment statement. The **subscript** (which may also be called an *index*) inside the parentheses is the position of the element within the array. Figure 8.2 illustrates an array of 10 elements with subscripts from 0 to 9.

Figure 8.2

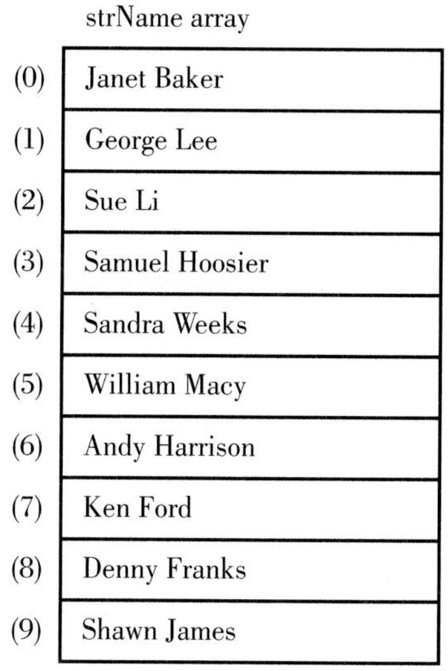

strName array

(0)	Janet Baker
(1)	George Lee
(2)	Sue Li
(3)	Samuel Hoosier
(4)	Sandra Weeks
(5)	William Macy
(6)	Andy Harrison
(7)	Ken Ford
(8)	Denny Franks
(9)	Shawn James

An array of string variables with 10 elements. Subscripts are 0 through 9.

Subscripts

The real advantage of using an array is not realized until you use variables for subscripts in place of the constants.

```
strName(intIndex) = ""

Debug.WriteLine(strName(intIndex))
```

Subscripts may be constants, variables, or numeric expressions. Although the subscripts must be integers, Visual Basic rounds any noninteger subscript.

A question has probably occurred to you by now—how many elements are there in the strName array? The answer is that you must specify the number of elements in a `Dim` statement.

The Dim Statement for Arrays—General Form

General Form

```
Dim ArrayName(UpperSubscript) As Datatype
Dim ArrayName() As Datatype = {InitialValueList}
```

The first form of the `Dim` statement allocates storage for the specified number of elements and initializes each numeric variable to 0. In the case of string arrays, each element is set to an empty string (zero characters).

In the second form of the `Dim` statement, you specify initial values for the array elements, which determines the number of elements. You cannot declare the upper subscript *and* initial values.

• You can assign initial values to an array declaration. If you assign initial values, you cannot specify the upper bound; the compiler figures out the number of elements based on the initial values.

The Dim Statement for Arrays—Examples

```
Dim strName(25) As String
Dim decBalance(10) As Decimal
Dim mstrProduct(99) As String
Dim mintValue() As Integer = {1, 5, 12, 18, 20}
Dim mstrDepartments() As String = {"Accounting", "Marketing", "Human Relations"}
Private mstrCategory(10) As String
Public mstrIDNumbers(5) As String
```

Array subscripts are zero based, so the first element is always element zero. The upper subscript is the highest subscript—1 less than the number of elements. For example, the statement

```
Dim mstrCategory(10) As String
```

creates an array of 11 elements with subscripts 0 through 10.

Notice that you declare a data type for the array. All of the array elements are the same data type. If you omit the data type, just as with single variables, the type defaults to Object.

> • All arrays are zero based. You can declare the upper subscript, which is the number of elements −1. You can no longer specify the lower bound, as in (1 To 10).

Valid Subscripts

A subscript must reference a valid element of the array. If a list contains 10 names, it wouldn't make sense to ask: What is the 15th name on the list? *or* What is the 2½th name on the list? Visual Basic rounds fractional subscripts and throws an exception for a subscript that is out of range.

Note: Arrays are derived from System.Array, which is a collection.

▶ Feedback 8.2

```
Dim strName(20) As String
Const intValue As Integer = 10
```

After execution of the preceding statements, which of the following are valid subscripts?

1. strName(20)
2. strName(intValue)
3. strName(intValue * 2)
4. strName(intValue * 3)
5. strName(0)
6. strName(intValue − 20)
7. strName(intValue / 3)
8. strName(intValue / 5 − 2)

For Each/Next Statements

When you use an array, you need a way to reference each element in the array. For/Next loops, which you learned to use in Chapter 7, work well to traverse the elements in an array. Another handy loop construct is the For Each and Next. The significant advantage of using the For Each and Next is that you don't have to manipulate the subscripts of the array.

• The variable used for a For Each statement should be the same data type as the elements of the array. VB 6 specified that the variable should be Variant; VB .NET will work using Object data type, but Option Strict requires the same type as the array elements.

The For Each and Next Statements—General Form

General Form

```
For Each ElementName In ArrayName
    'Statement(s) in loop
Next [ElementName]
```

Visual Basic automatically references each element of the array, assigns its value to ElementName, and makes one pass through the loop. If the array has 12 elements, for example, the loop will execute 12 times. The variable used for ElementName must be the same data type as the array elements or an Object data type.

In the following examples, assume that the arrays strName and intTotal have already been dimensioned and that they hold data.

The For Each and Next Statements—Examples

Examples

```
Dim strOneName As String
For Each strOneName In strName
    Debug.WriteLine(strOneName)        'Write one element of the array
Next strOneName

Dim intOneTotal As Integer
For Each intOneTotal In intTotal
    intOneTotal = 0                    'Set one element of the array to zero
Next intOneTotal
```

The For Each loop will execute if the array has at least one element. All the statements within the loop are executed for the first element. If the array has more elements, the loop continues to execute until all the elements are processed. When the loop finishes, execution of code continues with the line following the Next statement.

Note: You may use an Exit For statement within a loop to exit early.

Initializing an Array Using For Each

Although all numeric variables are initially set to 0, it is sometimes necessary to reinitialize variables. To zero out an array, each individual element must be set to 0.

```
'Reinitialize the intTotal array elements to zero

Dim intOneElement As Integer

For Each intOneElement In intTotal
    intOneElement = 0     'Set value of each element to 0
Next intOneElement
```

Structures

You have been using the VB data types, such as Integer, String, and Decimal, since Chapter 3. Now you will learn to combine multiple fields of related data to create a new **structure**. In many ways, a structure is similar to defining a new data type. For example, an Employee structure may contain last name, first name, Social Security number, street, city, state, ZIP code, date of hire, and pay code. A Product structure might contain a description, product number, quantity, and price. You can combine the fields into a structure using the Structure and End Structure statements.

- Structures are the replacement for user-defined types, which are gone.

- Structures have more capabilities than UDTs, such as allowing methods, but those are not covered in this text.

The Structure and End Structure Statements—General Form

General Form

```
[Public | Private] Structure NameOfStructure
    Dim FirstField As Datatype
    Dim SecondField As Datatype
    ...
End Structure
```

The Structure declaration cannot go inside a procedure. You generally place the Structure statement at the top of a file with the module-level declarations. You can also place a Structure in a separate file.

The Structure and End Structure Statements—Examples

```
Structure Employee
      Dim strLastName As String
      Dim strFirstName As String
      Dim strSSN As String
      Dim strStreet As String
      Dim strState As String
      Dim strZIP As String
      Dim datHireDate As Date
      Dim intPayCode As Integer
   End Structure

   Public Structure Product
      Dim strDescription As String
      Dim strID As String
      Dim intQuantity As Integer
      Dim decPrice As Decimal
   End Structure

   Structure SalesDetail
      Dim decSale() As Decimal
   End Structure
```

By default, a structure is public. You can declare the structure to be public or private, if you wish.

If you include an array inside a structure, you cannot specify the number of elements. You must use a ReDim statement in your code to declare the number of elements.

Declaring Variables Based on a Structure

Once you have created a structure, you can declare variables of the structure, just as if it were another data type. You can make up a prefix for the variable that helps to identify the structure, such as *prd* for Product or *sls* for Sales.

```
Dim empOffice As Employee
Dim empWarehouse As Employee
Dim prdWidget As Product
Dim prdInventory(100) As Product
Dim sdtHousewares As SalesDetail
Dim sdtHomeFurnishings As SalesDetail
```

Accessing the Elements in a Structure Variable

Each field of data in a variable declared as a structure is referred to as an *element* of the structure. To access elements, use the dot notation similar to that used for objects: Specify *Variable.Element*.

```
empOffice.strLastName
empOffice.datHireDate
empWarehouse.strLastName
prdWidget.strDescription
prdWidget.intQuantity
prdWidget.decPrice
prdInventory(intIndex).strDescription
prdInventory(intIndex).intQuantity
prdInventory(intIndex).decPrice
```

Notice the use of indexes in the preceding examples. Each example was taken from the preceding `Structure` and `Dim` statements. A variable that is not an array, such as prdWidget, does not need an index. However, for prdInventory, which was dimensioned as an array of 101 elements, you must specify not only the prdInventory item but also the element within the structure.

Including an Array in a Structure

The SalesDetail structure is a little more complicated than the other structures described above. In this structure we want to include an array of seven variables, one for each day of the week. However, VB does not allow you to declare the number of elements in the Structure declaration. You must use the `ReDim` statement inside a procedure to give the array a size.

```
'Module-level declarations
Structure SalesDetail
    Dim decSale() As Decimal
End Structure

Dim sdtHousewares As SalesDetail

'Inside a procedure:
ReDim sdtHousewares.decSale(6)    'Establish the number of elements in the array

'In processing
sdtHousewares.decSale(intDayIndex) = decTodaysSales
```

Because the decSale element of the SalesDetail structure is declared as an array, you must use a subscript to refer to each individual element within the structure.

Feedback 8.3

1. Write a `Structure` statement to hold student data containing last name, first name, student number, number of units completed, and GPA. The new structure should be called *StudentInfo*.
2. Declare an array of 100 students that will use the structure for student information.
3. Write the `Structure` statement for a structure called *Project* containing a project name, form name, and folder name.
4. Declare a variable called *prjMyProject* based on the Project structure.
5. Declare an array of 100 elements called *prjOurProjects*, based on the Project structure.

Using Array Elements for Accumulators

Array elements are regular variables and perform in the same ways as all variables used so far. You may use the subscripted variables in any way you choose, such as for counters or total accumulators.

To demonstrate the use of array elements as total accumulators, eight totals will be accumulated. For this example, eight scout troops are selling raffle tickets. A separate total must be accumulated for each of the eight groups. Each time a sale is made, the number of tickets must be added to the correct total. The statement

```
Dim mintTotal(7) As Integer
```

declares the eight accumulators with subscripts 0 to 7.

Adding to the Correct Total

Assume that your user inputs a group number into txtGroup.Text and the number of tickets sold into txtSale.Text. The sales may be input in any order with multiple sales for each group. Your problem is to add each ticket sale to the correct total, numbered 0 to 7, for groups numbered 1 to 8.

You can subtract one from the group number to use as the subscript to add to the correct total. For example, if the first sale of 10 tickets is for group 4, the 10 must be added to mintTotal(3). (Figure 8.3 shows the form and the variables used for this example.)

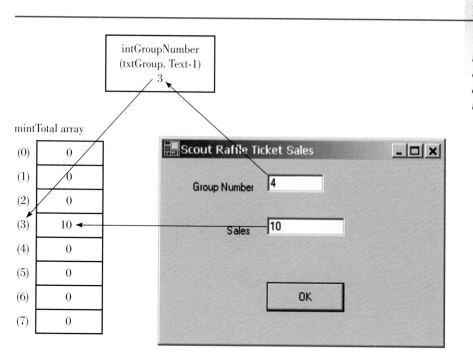

Figure 8.3

The group number entered in the txtGroup text box is used as a subscript to determine the correct intTotal array element to which to add.

```
'Convert input group number to subscript
intGroupNumber = CInt(txtGroup.Text) - 1
'Add sale to correct total
intSale = CInt(txtSale.Text)
mintTotal(intGroupNumber) += intSale
```

Of course, the user might enter an incorrect group number. Because you don't want the program to cancel with an exception, you must validate the group number.

```
Try
    'Convert input group number to subscript
    intGroupNumber = CInt(txtGroup.Text) - 1
    If intGroupNumber >= 0 And intGroupNumber <= 7 Then
        'Add sale to correct total
        intSale = CInt(txtSale.Text)
        mintTotal(intGroupNumber) += intSale
    Else
        MessageBox.Show("Enter a valid group number (1-8)", "Data Entry Error", _
            MessageBoxButtons.OK, MessageBoxIcon.Exclamation)
    End If
Catch
    MessageBox.Show("Numeric entries required for both group number and sales", _
        "Data Entry Error", MessageBoxButtons.OK, MessageBoxIcon.Exclamation)
End Try
```

Using the group number as an index to the array is a technique called **direct reference**. The groups are assigned numbers from 1 to 8. You can subtract 1 from the group number to create the subscripts, which are 0 to 7.

Debugging Array Programs

You can view the contents of array elements when your program is in break time. Set a breakpoint and view the Autos window (Figure 8.4). You will need to click on the plus sign to the left of the array name to view the individual array elements.

- You can view the contents of arrays during break time in either the Autos window or the Locals window.

Figure 8.4

View the contents of an array in the Autos window at break time.

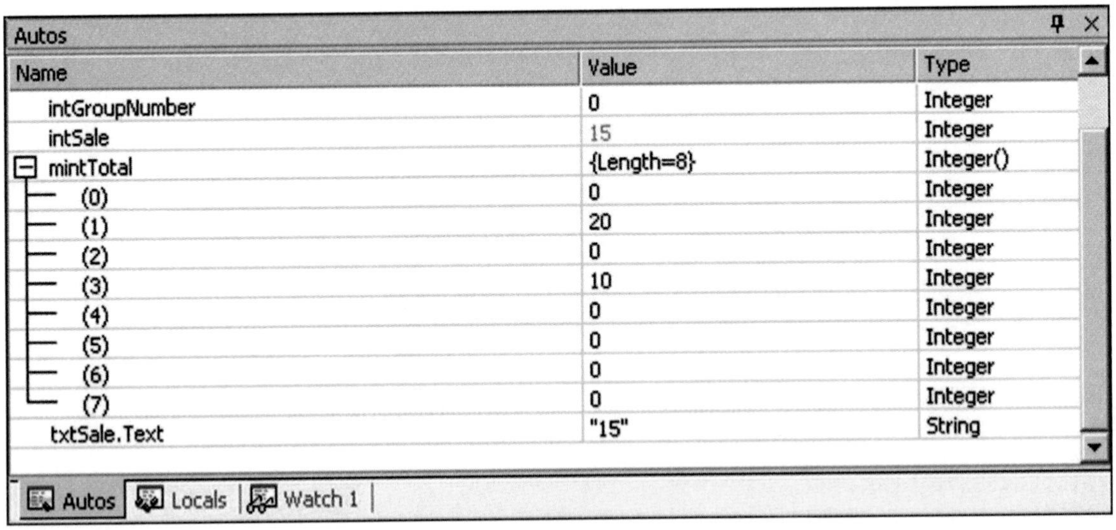

Autos		
Name	Value	Type
intGroupNumber	0	Integer
intSale	15	Integer
⊟ mintTotal	{Length=8}	Integer()
(0)	0	Integer
(1)	20	Integer
(2)	0	Integer
(3)	10	Integer
(4)	0	Integer
(5)	0	Integer
(6)	0	Integer
(7)	0	Integer
txtSale.Text	"15"	String

Autos   Locals   Watch 1

Table Lookup

Things don't always work out so neatly as having sequential group numbers that can be used to access the table directly. Sometimes you will have to do a little work to find (look up) the correct value. Reconsider the eight scout troops and their ticket sales. Now the groups are not numbered 1 to 8, but 101, 103, 110, 115, 121, 123, 130, and 145. The group number and the number of tickets sold are still input, and the number of tickets must be added to the correct total. But now you must do one more step—determine to which array element to add the ticket sales, using a **table lookup**.

The first step in the project is to establish a structure with the group numbers and totals and then dimension an array of the structure. Before any processing is done, you must load the group numbers into the table; the best place to do this is in the Form_Load event procedure, which is executed once as the form is loaded into memory.

Place the following statements in the declarations section of a form module:

```
'Declare structure and module-level variables
Structure GroupInfo
    Dim strGroupNumber As String
    Dim intTotal As Integer
End Structure

Dim mgiGroup(7) As GroupInfo      'Hold group number and total for 8 groups
```

Then initialize the values of the array elements by placing these statements into the Form_Load procedure:

```
Private Sub frmSales_Load(ByVal sender As System.Object, _
  ByVal e As System.EventArgs) Handles MyBase.Load
    'Initialize group numbers

    mgiGroup(0).strGroupNumber = "101"
    mgiGroup(1).strGroupNumber = "103"
    mgiGroup(2).strGroupNumber = "110"
    mgiGroup(3).strGroupNumber = "115"
    mgiGroup(4).strGroupNumber = "121"
    mgiGroup(5).strGroupNumber = "123"
    mgiGroup(6).strGroupNumber = "130"
    mgiGroup(7).strGroupNumber = "145"
End Sub
```

During program execution the user still enters the group number and the number of tickets sold into text boxes.

The technique used to find the subscript is called *a table lookup*. In this example the object is to find the element number (0 to 7) of the group number and add to the corresponding group total. If the user enters the third group number ("110"), the subscript is 2 and the sale is added to the total for subscript 2. If the seventh group number ("130") is entered, the sale is added to the total with the subscript 6, and so on. Hence, you need a way, given the group number in txtGroup.Text, to find the corresponding subscript of the mgiGroup array.

When Visual Basic executes the statement

`mgiGroup(intGroupNum).intTotal += intSale`

the value of intGroupNum must be a number in the range 0 to 7. The task for
the lookup operation is to find the number to place in intGroupNum, based on
the value of txtGroup.Text. Figure 8.5 shows the variables used for the lookup.
Figure 8.6 shows the flowchart of the lookup logic.

F i g u r e   8 . 5

*A lookup operation: The group number is looked up in the mgiGroup array; the correct subscript is found and used to add
the sale to the correct intTotal.*

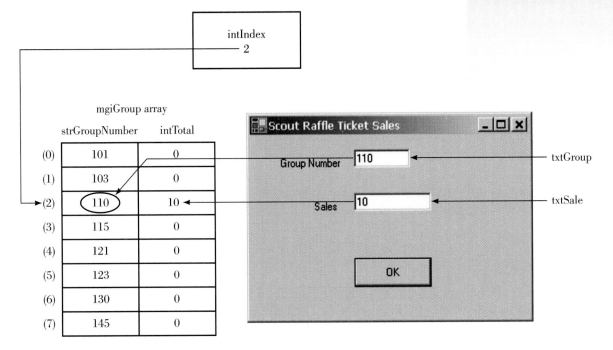

Figure 8.6

A flowchart of the logic of a lookup operation.

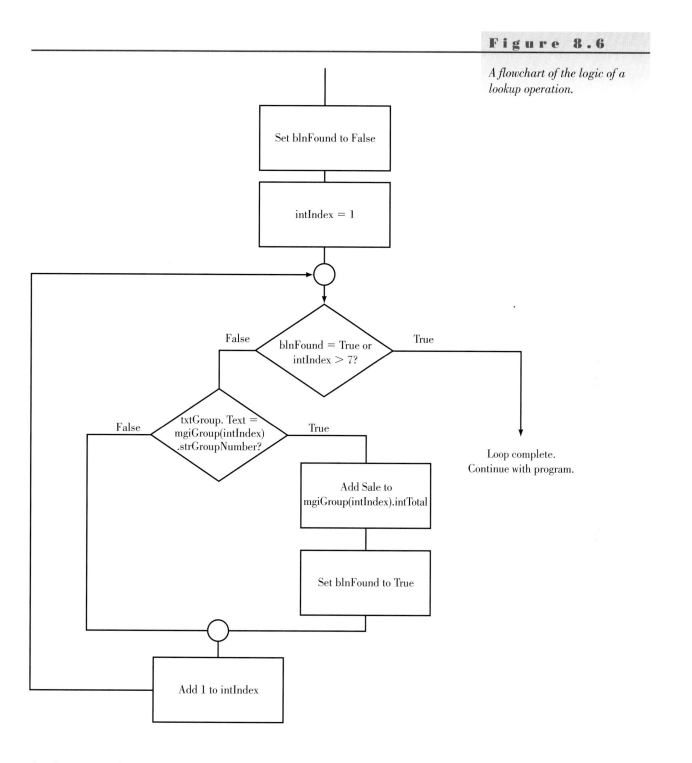

Coding a Table Lookup

For a table lookup, you will find that a Do/Loop works better than For Each. As you compare to each element in the array and eventually find a match, you need to know the subscript of the matching element.

```
'Accumulate the sales by group number
Dim intSale As Integer
Dim intIndex As Integer = 0
Dim blnFound As Boolean = False
```

```
'Look up input group number to find subscript
Do Until blnFound Or intIndex > 7
    If txtGroup.Text = mgiGroup(intIndex).strGroupNumber Then
        'Add sale to correct total
        intSale = CInt(txtSale.Text)
        mgiGroup(intIndex).intTotal += intSale
        blnFound = True
    End If
    intIndex += 1
Loop
```

Once again, you should do some form of validation. If the user enters an invalid group number, you should display a message box. You can check the value of the Boolean variable *blnFound* after completion of the loop to determine whether the loop terminated because of a match or without a match.

```
If Not blnFound Then
    MessageBox.Show("Enter a valid group number", "Data Entry Error", _
      MessageBoxButtons.OK, MessageBoxIcon.Exclamation)
    With txtGroup
        .Focus()
        .SelectAll()
    End With
End If
```

The table-lookup technique will work for any table, numeric or string. It isn't necessary to arrange the fields being searched in any particular sequence. The comparison is made to one item in the list, then the next, and the next—until a match is found. In fact, you can save processing time in a large table by arranging the elements with the most-often-used entries at the top so that fewer comparisons must be made.

Using List Boxes with Arrays

In the previous example of a lookup, the user had to type some information into a text box, which was used to look up the information in an array. A more efficient and friendly solution might be to substitute a list box for the text box. You can store the eight group numbers in a list box and allow the user to select from the list (Figure 8.7).

• List boxes and Combo boxes do not have an ItemData property. The substitute is to make the Items collection hold objects of a class that has multiple properties. We decided that presenting this technique would complicate and confuse the message of this chapter, which is primarily to introduce arrays.

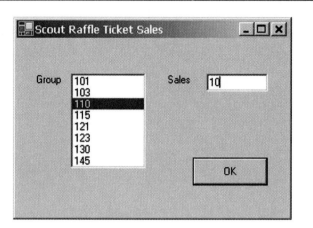

Figure 8.7

Allow the user to select from a list and you can use the list's SelectedIndex property as the subscript of the total array.

The initial Items collection can contain the values 101, 103, 110, 115, 121, 123, 130, and 145.

You have probably already realized that you can use the SelectedIndex property to determine the array subscript. Remember that the SelectedIndex property holds the position or index of the selected item from the list.

In place of the lookup operation, we can use this code:

```
'Declare module-level variables
Dim mintTotal(7) As Integer   'Hold totals for 8 groups

Private Sub btnOK_Click(ByVal sender As System.Object, ByVal e As System.EventArgs) _
Handles btnOK.Click
    'Accumulate the sales by group number
    Dim intSale As Integer
    Dim intGroupNumber As Integer

    If lstGroup.SelectedIndex <> -1 Then      'Selection made
        'Add to correct total
        intSale = CInt(txtSale.Text)
        intGroupNumber = lstGroup.SelectedIndex
        mintTotal(intGroupNumber) += intSale

        'Clear the screen fields
        lstGroup.SelectedIndex = -1
        txtSale.Text = ""
    Else
        MessageBox.Show("Select a group number from the list.", "Data Entry Error", _
        MessageBoxButtons.OK, MessageBoxIcon.Exclamation)
    End If
End Sub
```

Multidimensional Arrays

You may need to use two subscripts to identify tabular data, where data are arranged in **rows** and **columns**.

Many applications of two-dimensional tables quickly come to mind—insurance rate tables, tax tables, addition and multiplication tables, postage rates, foods and their nutritive value, population by region, rainfall by state.

To define a two-dimensional array or table, the `Dim` statement specifies the number of rows and columns in the array. The row is horizontal and the column is vertical. The following table has three rows and four columns:

The Dim Statement for Two-Dimensional Arrays—General Form

```
Dim ArrayName(RowHighestSubscript, ColumnHighestSubscript) As Datatype
Dim ArrayName( , ) As Datatype = {ListOfValues}
```

The Dim Statement for Two-Dimensional Arrays—Examples

```
Dim strName(2, 3) As String
Dim strName( , ) As String = { {"James", "Mary", "Sammie", "Sean"}, _
    {"Tom", "Lee", "Leon", "Larry"}, {"Maria", "Margaret", "Jill", "John"} }
```

Both of these two statements establish an array of 12 elements, with three rows and four columns. Just as with single-dimension arrays, you cannot specify the number of elements within parentheses *and* specify initial values.

Notice the parentheses in the second example: You must use a comma to specify that there are two dimensions to the array. Specify the initial values with the first dimension (the row) first and the second dimension (the column) second. The compiler determines the number of elements from the initial values that you supply. The second example above fills the table in this sequence:

(0, 0) James	(0, 1) Mary	(0, 2) Sammie	(0, 3) Sean
(1, 0) Tom	(1, 1) Lee	(1, 2) Leon	(1, 3) Larry
(2, 0) Maria	(2, 1) Margaret	(2, 2) Jill	(2, 3) John

You must always use two subscripts when referring to individual elements of the table. Specify the row with the first subscript and the column with the second subscript.

The elements of the array may be used in the same ways as any other variable—in accumulators, counts, and reference fields for lookup; in statements like assignment and printing; and as conditions. Some valid references to the table include:

```
strName(1, 2) = "New Name"
strName(intRowIndex, intColIndex) = "New Name"
lblDisplay.Text = strName(1, 2)
DrawString(strName(intRowIndex, intColIndex), fntMyFont, Brushes.Black, 100.0F, 100.0F)
```

Invalid references for the strName table would include any value greater than 2 for the first subscript or greater than 3 for the second subscript.

Initializing Two-Dimensional Arrays

Numeric array elements are initially set to 0 and string elements are set to empty strings. And of course you can assign initial values when you declare the array. But many situations require that you reinitialize arrays to 0 or some other value. You can use nested For/Next loops or For Each/Next to set each array element to an initial value.

Nested For/Next Example

The assignment statement in the inner loop will be executed 12 times, once for each element of strName.

```
Dim intRow As Integer
Dim intColumn As Integer

For intRow = 0 To 2
    For intColumn = 0 To 3
        strName(intRow, intColumn) = ""      'Initialize each element
    Next intColumn
Next intRow
```

For Each/Next Example

You can also perform the initialization with a For Each statement, which initializes all 12 elements.

```
Dim strElement As String

For Each strElement In strName
    strElement = ""                          'Initialize each element
Next strElement
```

Printing a Two-Dimensional Table

When you want to print the contents of a two-dimensional table, you can use a For Each/Next loop. This code prints one array element per line.

```
'Print one name per line
For Each strElement In strName
    'Set up a line
    e.Graphics.DrawString(strElement, fntPrintFont, _
    Brushes.Black, sngPrintX, sngPrintY)

    'Increment the Y position for the next line
    sngPrintY += sngLineHeight
Next strElement
```

If you wish to print an entire row in one line, use a For/Next loop and set up the *X* and *Y* coordinates to print multiple elements per line.

```
'Print one row per line
For intRowIndex = 0 To 2
   For intColIndex = 0 To 3
      e.Graphics.DrawString(strName(intRowIndex, intColIndex), fntPrintFont, _
      Brushes.Black, sngPrintX, sngPrintY)
      sngPrintX += 200                    'Move across the line
   Next intColIndex

   'Start next line
   sngPrintX = e.MarginBounds.Left        'Reset to left margin
   sngPrintY += sngLineHeight             'Move down to next line
Next intRowIndex
```

Summing a Two-Dimensional Table

You can find the sum of a table in various ways. You may sum either the columns or the rows of the table; or, as in a cross-foot, you can sum the figures in both directions and double-check the totals.

To sum the array in both directions, each column needs one total field and each row needs one total field. Two one-dimensional arrays will work well for the totals. Figure 8.8 illustrates the variables used in this example.

Figure 8.8

Two one-dimensional arrays hold totals for the two-dimensional array.

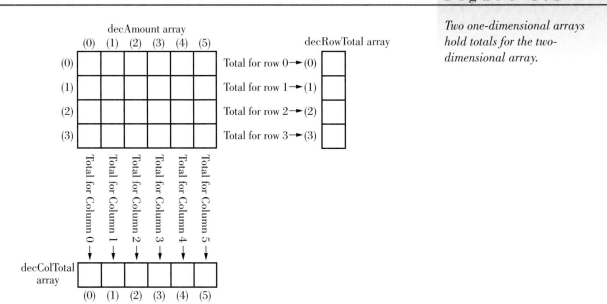

```
'Crossfoot total a 2D table
Dim decAmount(3, 5) As Decimal
Dim decRowTotal(3) As Decimal
Dim decColTotal(5) As Decimal
Dim intRowIndex As Integer
Dim intColIndex As Integer

For intRowIndex = 0 To 3
   For intColIndex = 0 To 5
      decRowTotal(intRowIndex) += decAmount(intRowIndex, intColIndex)
      decColTotal(intColIndex) += decAmount(intRowIndex, intColIndex)
   Next intColIndex
Next intRowIndex
```

▶ **Feedback 8.4**

Write VB statements to do the following:
1. Dimension a table called decTemperature with five columns and three rows.
2. Set each element in the first row to 0.
3. Set each element in the second row to 75.
4. For each column of the table, add together the elements in rows 1 and 2, placing the sum in row 3.
5. Print the entire table. (Write only the logic for printing inside the Print-Document_PrintPage event procedure.)

Lookup Operation for Two-Dimensional Tables

When you look up items in a two-dimensional table, you can use the same techniques discussed with single-dimensional arrays—direct reference and table lookup. The limitations are the same.

1. To use a direct reference, row and column subscripts must be readily available. For example, you can tally the hours used for each of five machines (identified by machine numbers 1 to 5) and each of four departments (identified by department numbers 1 to 4).

```
intRowIndex = CInt(txtMachine.Text) - 1
intColIndex = CInt(txtDepartment.Text) - 1
decHours = CDec(txtHours.Text)
decMachineTotal(intRowIndex, intColIndex) += decHours
```

2. A table lookup is the most common lookup technique.

Many two-dimensional tables used for lookup require additional one-dimensional arrays or lists to aid in the lookup process. For an example, use a shipping rate table (Figure 8.9) to look up the rate to ship a package. The shipping rate depends on the weight of the package and the zone to which it is being shipped. You could design the project with the weight and zones in list boxes, or you could use a text box and let the user input the data.

Figure 8.9

This shipping rate table in a two-dimensional array can be used to look up the correct shipping charge.

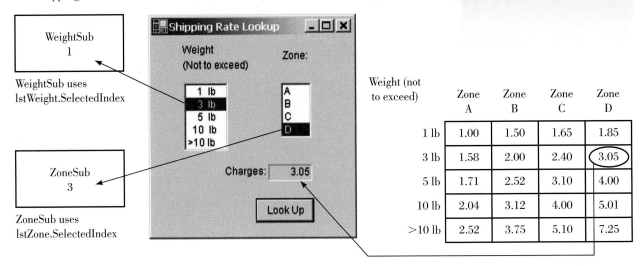

Weight (not to exceed)	Zone A	Zone B	Zone C	Zone D
1 lb	1.00	1.50	1.65	1.85
3 lb	1.58	2.00	2.40	3.05
5 lb	1.71	2.52	3.10	4.00
10 lb	2.04	3.12	4.00	5.01
>10 lb	2.52	3.75	5.10	7.25

Using List Boxes

In this example a list box holds the weight limits, and another list holds the zones. The values for the two lists are set with the Items properties at design time. The five-by-four rate table is two-dimensional, and the values are set when the table is declared.

```
'Look up values from list boxes

'Declare module-level variables
Dim mdecRate(,) As Decimal = {{1D, 1.5D, 1.65D, 1.85D}, {1.58D, 2D, 2.4D, 3.05D}, _
   {1.71D, 2.52D, 3.1D, 4D}, {2.04D, 3.12D, 4D, 5.01D}, {2.52D, 3.75D, 5.1D, 7.25D}}

Private Sub btnLookup_Click(ByVal sender As System.Object, _
ByVal e As System.EventArgs) Handles btnLookup.Click
    'Look up the shipping rate

    Dim intWeightSub As Integer
    Dim intZoneSub As Integer

    intWeightSub = lstWeight.SelectedIndex
    intZoneSub = lstZone.SelectedIndex
    If intWeightSub <> -1 And intZoneSub <> -1 Then
        lblCharges.Text = mdecRate(intWeightSub, intZoneSub)
    Else
        MessageBox.Show("Select the weight and zone.", "Information Missing", _
           MessageBoxButtons.OK, MessageBoxIcon.Exclamation)
    End If
End Sub
```

Using Text Boxes

If you are using text boxes rather than list boxes for data entry, the input requires more validation. You must look up both the weight and zone entries before you can determine the correct rate. The valid zones and weight ranges will be stored in two separate one-dimensional arrays. The first step in the project is to establish and fill the arrays. The five-by-four rate table is two-dimensional, and the values should be preloaded, as in the previous example.

Note that the Try/Catch blocks were omitted to clarify the logic. You should always use error trapping when converting input to numeric values.

```
'Look up values from text boxes

'Declare module-level variables
Dim mdecRate(,) As Decimal = {{1D, 1.5D, 1.65D, 1.85D}, {1.58D, 2D, 2.4D, 3.05D}, _
  {1.71D, 2.52D, 3.1D, 4D}, {2.04D, 3.12D, 4D, 5.01D}, {2.52D, 3.75D, 5.1D, 7.25D}}
Dim mintWeight() As Integer = {1, 3, 5, 10}
Dim mstrZone() As String = {"A", "B", "C", "D"}

Private Sub btnLookup_Click(ByVal sender As System.Object, _
 ByVal e As System.EventArgs) Handles btnLookup.Click
    'Look up the shipping rate

    Dim intWeightSub As Integer
    Dim intZoneSub As Integer
    Dim intIndex As Integer = 0
    Dim intWeightInput As Integer
    Dim blnWeightFound As Boolean = False
    Dim blnZoneFound As Boolean = False

    'Look up the weight to find the intWeightSub
    intWeightInput = CInt(txtWeight.Text)

    Do Until blnWeightFound Or intIndex > 3
        If intWeightInput <= mintWeight(intIndex) Then
            intWeightSub = intIndex
            blnWeightFound = True
        End If
        intIndex += 1
    Loop
    If Not blnWeightFound Then
        intWeightSub = 4
        blnWeightFound = True
    End If

    'Look up the zone to find the intZoneSub
    intIndex = 0
    Do Until blnZoneFound Or intIndex > 3
        If txtZone.Text.ToUpper = mstrZone(intIndex) Then
            intZoneSub = intIndex
            blnZoneFound = True
        End If
        intIndex += 1
    Loop
```

```
   'Display the appropriate rate
   If blnWeightFound And blnZoneFound Then
      lblCharges.Text = FormatNumber(mdecRate(intWeightSub, intZoneSub))
   Else
      MessageBox.Show("Select the weight and zone.", "Information Missing", _
        MessageBoxButtons.OK, MessageBoxIcon.Exclamation)
   End If
End Sub
```

Your Hands-On Programming Example

Create a project for R 'n R—for Reading 'n Refreshment that determines the price per pound for bulk coffee sales. The coffees are divided into categories: regular, decaf, and special blend. The prices are set by the quarter pound, half pound, and full pound. Use a Find Price button to search for the appropriate price based on the selections.

	Regular	Decaf	Blend
1/4 pound	2.60	2.90	3.25
1/2 pound	4.90	5.60	6.10
Full pound	8.75	9.75	11.25

Create a structure that contains the coffee type, amount, and price. Set up a module-level variable that is an array of 20 elements of your structure; this array will hold the transactions. Each time the Find Price button is pressed, look up and display the price of the coffee selection and add the data to the array.

Include a Clear button to clear the selections from the screen and a Print button that prints all of the transactions. Using Print Preview, print appropriate headings and the data from the transaction array.

When the Exit button is pressed, give the user another opportunity to print all the transactions.

Planning the Project

Sketch a form (Figure 8.10), which your users sign off as meeting their needs.

Figure 8.10

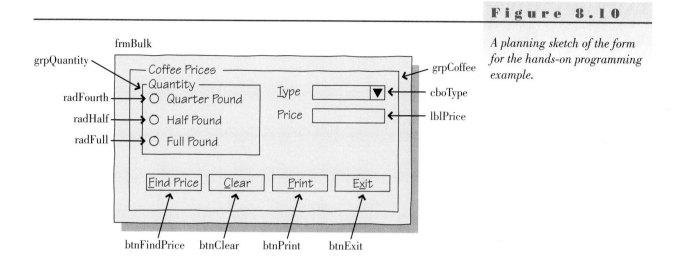

A planning sketch of the form for the hands-on programming example.

Plan the Objects and Properties

Object	Property	Setting
frmBulk	Name	frmBulk
	Text	R 'n R -- for Reading and Refreshment
	AcceptButton	btnFindPrice
grpCoffee	Text	Coffee Prices
grpQuantity	Text	Quantity
Label1	Text	&Type
Label2	Text	Price
cboType	Name	cboType
	Items	Regular
		Decaffeinated
		Special blend
	DropDownStyle	DropDownList
lblPrice	Name	lblPrice
	Text	(blank)
	BorderStyle	Fixed3D
	BackColor	Control
radFourth	Name	radFourth
	Text	Quarter Pound
	Checked	True
radHalf	Name	radHalf
	Text	Half Pound

Continued on page 360

Object	Property	Setting
radFull	Name	radFull
	Text	Full Pound
btnFindPrice	Name	btnFindPrice
	Text	&Find Price
btnClear	Name	btnClear
	Text	&Clear
btnPrint	Name	btnPrint
	Text	&Print
btnExit	Name	btnExit
	Text	E&xit
prtDocument	Name	prtDocument
ppdPreview	Name	ppdPreview

Plan the Event Procedures

You need to plan the actions for the event procedures.

Procedure	Actions
btnFindPrice_Click	Find the column from the list selection.
	Find the row from the radio button selection.
	Look up the price in the table.
	Display the price in the label.
	Store the type, quantity, and price in the transaction array.
btnClear_Click	Select the first radio button.
	Deselect the list entry.
	Clear the price label.
btnPrint_Click	Set up print preview.
	Print the report.
btnExit_Click	Display message box giving the user opportunity to print.
	If print selected
	Execute btnPrint_Click procedure.
	End If
	Terminate the project.
All radio buttons _Click	Save the name of the selected button.
prtDocument_PrintPage	Print title.
	Loop to print all of the stored transactions.

Write the Project

- Follow the sketch in Figure 8.10 to create the form. Figure 8.11 shows the completed form.

- Set the properties of each object, according to your plan.

- Write the code. Working from the pseudocode, write each event procedure.

- When you complete the code, use a variety of data to thoroughly test the project.

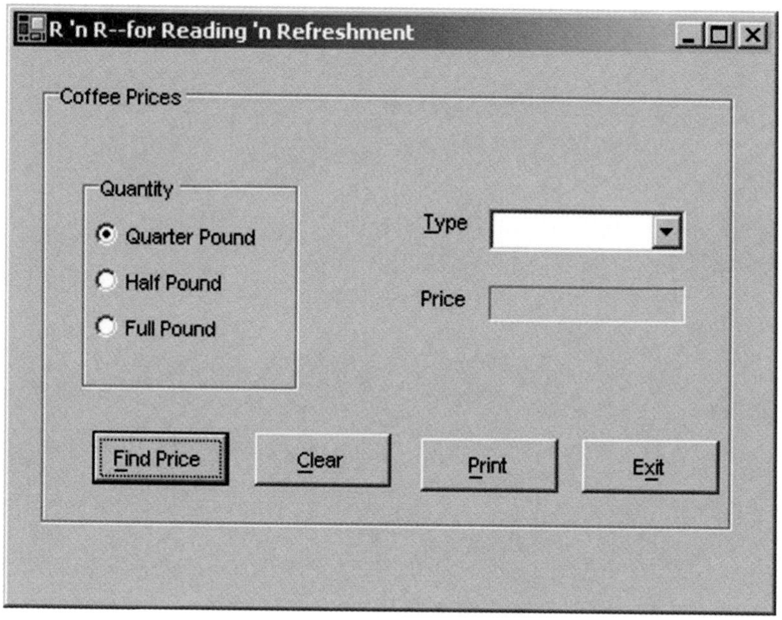

Figure 8.11

The form for the hands-on programming example.

The Project Coding Solution

```
'Module:          Ch0801
'Programmer:      Bradley/Millspaugh
'Date:            January 2002
'Description:     Look up the price for bulk coffee
'                   based upon quantity and type.
'                 Uses a structure and arrays, and prints a report
'                   of the transactions from the array.
'Folder:          Ch0801

Public Class frmBulk
    Inherits System.Windows.Forms.Form

[Windows Form Designer generated code]

'Declare structure and module-level variables
    Structure CoffeeSale
        Dim strType As String
        Dim strQuantity As String
        Dim decPrice As Decimal
    End Structure
```

```
Dim mcslTransaction(20) As CoffeeSale
Dim mintNumberTransactions As Integer
Dim mdecPrice(,) As Decimal = _
  {{2.6D, 2.9D, 3.25D}, {4.9D, 5.6D, 6.1D}, _
  {8.75D, 9.75D, 11.25D}}
Dim mstrSelectedButton As String

Private Sub btnClear_Click(ByVal sender As System.Object, _
 ByVal e As System.EventArgs) Handles btnClear.Click
    'Remove the selection from the list and
    ' clear the price

    radFourth.Select()              'Select first radio button
    cboType.SelectedIndex = -1      'Clear selection
    lblPrice.Text = ""
End Sub

Private Sub btnExit_Click(ByVal sender As System.Object, _
 ByVal e As System.EventArgs) Handles btnExit.Click
    'Terminate the project

    Dim dgrResponse As DialogResult
    dgrResponse = MessageBox.Show("Print the report?", _
     "Terminate the Application", MessageBoxButtons.YesNoCancel, MessageBoxIcon.Question)
    If dgrResponse = DialogResult.Yes Then
        btnPrint_Click(sender, e)
        Me.Close()
    ElseIf dgrResponse = DialogResult.No Then
        Me.Close()
    End If
    'For a response of Cancel, no action is taken.
End Sub

Private Sub btnFindPrice_Click(ByVal sender As System.Object, _
 ByVal e As System.EventArgs) Handles btnFindPrice.Click
    'Lookup the price using the quantity and type

    Dim intRow As Integer
    Dim intCol As Integer
    Dim decPrice As Decimal

    If mintNumberTransactions < 20 Then      'Allow only 20 transactions
        If cboType.SelectedIndex <> -1 Then 'Coffee selection made
            intCol = cboType.SelectedIndex
            'Determine quantity selected
            Select Case mstrSelectedButton
                Case "radFourth"
                    intRow = 0
                    mcslTransaction(mintNumberTransactions).strQuantity _
                     = "Quarter Pound"
                Case "radHalf"
                    intRow = 1
                    mcslTransaction(mintNumberTransactions).strQuantity _
                     = "Half Pound"
                Case "radFull"
                    intRow = 2
                    mcslTransaction(mintNumberTransactions).strQuantity _
                     = "Full Pound"
```

```
                Case Else 'No selection made; use quarter pound
                    intRow = 0
                    mcslTransaction(mintNumberTransactions).strQuantity _
                        = "Quarter Pound"
            End Select

            decPrice = mdecPrice(intRow, intCol)     'Retrieve price of selection
            lblPrice.Text = FormatCurrency(decPrice)
            'Save this transaction
            mcslTransaction(mintNumberTransactions).strType = cboType.Text
            mcslTransaction(mintNumberTransactions).decPrice = decPrice
            mintNumberTransactions += 1
        Else
            MessageBox.Show("Select the coffee type.", "Selection Incomplete", _
                MessageBoxButtons.OK, MessageBoxIcon.Exclamation)
        End If
    Else
        MessageBox.Show("Only 20 transactions allowed")
    End If
End Sub

Private Sub btnPrint_Click(ByVal sender As Object, _
 ByVal e As System.EventArgs) Handles btnPrint.Click
    'Print the report using Print Preview

    ppdPreview.Document = prtDocument
    ppdPreview.ShowDialog()
End Sub

Private Sub prtDocument_PrintPage(ByVal sender As Object, _
 ByVal e As System.Drawing.Printing.PrintPageEventArgs) _
 Handles prtDocument.PrintPage
    'Handle print and print previews

    Dim fntPrintFont As New Font("Arial", 12)
    Dim fntHeading As New Font("Arial", 14, FontStyle.Bold)
    Dim sngLineHeight As Single = fntPrintFont.GetHeight + 2
    Dim sngXCol1 As Single = e.MarginBounds.Left
    Dim sngPrintY As Single = e.MarginBounds.Top
    Dim sngXCol2 As Single = 300F
    Dim sngXCol3 As Single
    Dim strPrintLine As String
    Dim intListIndex As Integer
    Dim csaSale As CoffeeSale
    Dim stzStringSize As New SizeF()     'SizeF structure for font size info.
    Dim strFormattedPrice As String

    'Set up and display heading lines
    strPrintLine = "R 'n R Coffee Sales"
    e.Graphics.DrawString(strPrintLine, fntHeading, _
     Brushes.Black, sngXCol2, sngPrintY)
    strPrintLine = "by Programmer Name"
    sngPrintY += sngLineHeight
    e.Graphics.DrawString(strPrintLine, fntPrintFont, _
     Brushes.Black, sngXCol2, sngPrintY)
    sngPrintY += sngLineHeight * 2
```

```
            'Loop through the transactions
            For Each csaSale In mcslTransaction
                If csaSale.strQuantity <> "" Then    'Don't print if blank
                    'Set up a line
                    'Quantity
                    e.Graphics.DrawString(csaSale.strQuantity, fntPrintFont, _
                        Brushes.Black, sngXCol1, sngPrintY)

                    'Type
                    e.Graphics.DrawString(csaSale.strType, fntPrintFont, _
                        Brushes.Black, sngXCol2, sngPrintY)

                    'Right-align the price
                    strFormattedPrice = FormatNumber(csaSale.decPrice)
                    'Measure string in this font
                    stzStringSize = e.Graphics.MeasureString(strFormattedPrice, fntPrintFont)
                    'Subtract width of string from column position
                    sngXCol3 = 550 - stzStringSize.Width
                    e.Graphics.DrawString(strFormattedPrice, fntPrintFont, _
                        Brushes.Black, sngXCol3, sngPrintY)

                    'Increment the Y position for the next line
                    sngPrintY += sngLineHeight * 2    'Double space
                End If
            Next
        End Sub

    Private Sub radFourth_CheckedChanged(ByVal sender As System.Object, _
      ByVal e As System.EventArgs) _
      Handles radFourth.CheckedChanged, radHalf.CheckedChanged, radFull.CheckedChanged
        'Save the name of the selected radio button
        'This procedure is executed each time any radio button is selected

        Dim radButton As RadioButton
        radButton = CType(sender, RadioButton)
        mstrSelectedButton = radBotton.Name
    End Sub
End Class
```

S u m m a r y

1. A `Select Case` statement can be used when an expression is being tested for many different values or ranges of values. The statement also can include a `Case Else` for the situation that none of the values specified was a match.
2. A single event procedure can handle the Click event of multiple controls. The procedure's sender argument holds the name of the control that caused the event.
3. A series of variables with the same name is called an array. The individual values are referred to as elements, and each element is accessed by its subscript, which is a position number.
4. Array subscripts or indexes are zero based; they must be integers in the range of the array elements. VB rounds noninteger values.
5. You can assign initial values in the array declaration *or* specify the highest subscript allowed.

6. A special form of the `For` loop called `For Each` is available for working with arrays. The `For Each` eliminates the need for the programmer to manipulate the subscripts of the array.

7. You can declare a structure to combine related fields and then declare variables and arrays of the structure. `Structure` statements must appear in the declarations section at the top of a file.

8. Arrays can be used like any other variables; they can be used to accumulate a series of totals or to store values for a lookup procedure.

9. The information in arrays may be accessed directly by subscript, or a table lookup may be used to determine the correct table position.

10. You can use the SelectedIndex property of a list box as a subscript of an array.

11. Arrays may be multidimensional. A two-dimensional table contains rows and columns and is processed similarly to a one-dimensional array. Accessing a multidimensional array frequently requires the use of nested loops.

Key Terms

array *338*
case structure *334*
column *352*
`CType` function *337*
direct reference *346*
element *338*
`For Each` and `Next` *341*
index *338*

late binding *337*
row *352*
structure *342*
subscript *338*
subscripted variable *338*
table *338*
table lookup *347*

Review Questions

1. How can one event procedure be triggered for the Click event of multiple controls? Is there any way to tell which control caused the event?

2. Define the following terms:
   (a) Array
   (b) Element
   (c) Subscript
   (d) Index
   (e) Subscripted variable

3. What is a structure? When might a structure be useful?

4. Describe the logic of a table lookup.

5. Name some situations in which it is important to perform validation when working with subscripted variables.

6. Compare a two-dimensional table to an array of a structure.

7. How can you initialize values in a two-dimensional table?

Programming Exercises

8.1   *Array of a Structure*

Create a project to analyze an income survey. The statistics for each home include an identification code, the number of members in the household, and the yearly income. A menu will contain *File, Reports,* and *Help.* The *File* menu will contain *Exit.* As the data are entered, they should be assigned from the text boxes to the elements of a structure.

The reports for the project will be sent to the printer and include the following:

(a) A three-column report displaying the input data.
(b) A listing of the identification number and income for each household that exceeds the average income.
(c) The percentage of households having incomes below the poverty level.

Test Data

Poverty Level: 8,000 for a family of one or two, plus 2,000 for each additional member.

ID number	Annual income	Number of persons
2497	12500	2
3323	13000	5
4521	18210	4
6789	8000	2
5476	6000	1
4423	16400	3
6587	25000	4
3221	10500	4
5555	15000	2
0085	19700	3
3097	20000	8
4480	23400	5
0265	19700	2
8901	13000	3

Check Figures

Households exceeding average income: You should have seven entries on the list.

Households below poverty level: 21.43%

8.2   *Two-dimensional Table*

Modify Programming Exercise 8.1 to assign the data to a multidimensional array rather than use an array of a structure.

8.3   Create a project to keep track of concert ticket sales by your club. Ticket prices are based on seating location. Your program should calculate the price for each sale, accumulate the total number of tickets sold in each section, display the ticket price schedule, and print a summary of all sales.

The form should contain a list box of the sections for seating.

Section	Price
Orchestra	40.00
Mezzanine	27.50
General	15.00
Balcony	10.00

Do not allow the user to receive an exception for subscript out-of-range.

8.4   *Array of a Structure*

Create a project that will allow a user to look up state names and their two-letter abbreviations. The user will have the options to *Look up the Abbreviation* or to *Look up the State Name.* In the event that a match cannot be found for the input, print an appropriate error message.

Use radio buttons with a shared event procedure and a `Select Case` to determine which text box (state name or abbreviation) should have the focus and which should be disabled.

Data

AL	Alabama	HI	Hawaii
AK	Alaska	ID	Idaho
AS	American Samoa	IL	Illinois
AZ	Arizona	IN	Indiana
AR	Arkansas	IA	Iowa
CA	California	KS	Kansas
CO	Colorado	KY	Kentucky
CT	Connecticut	LA	Louisiana
DE	Delaware	ME	Maine
DC	District of Columbia	MD	Maryland
FL	Florida	MA	Massachusetts
GA	Georgia	MI	Michigan
GU	Guam	MN	Minnesota

Continued on page 368

MS	Mississippi		PR	Puerto Rico
MO	Missouri		RI	Rhode Island
MT	Montana		SC	South Carolina
NE	Nebraska		SD	South Dakota
NV	Nevada		TN	Tennessee
NH	New Hampshire		TX	Texas
NJ	New Jersey		TT	Trust Territories
NM	New Mexico		UT	Utah
NY	New York		VT	Vermont
NC	North Carolina		VA	Virginia
ND	North Dakota		VI	Virgin Islands
OH	Ohio		WA	Washington
OK	Oklahoma		WV	West Virginia
OR	Oregon		WI	Wisconsin
PA	Pennsylvania		WY	Wyoming

8.5   *Two-dimensional Table*

Create a project that looks up the driving distance between two cities. Use two drop-down lists that contain the names of the cities. Label one list "Departure" and the other "Destination". Use a *Look Up* button to calculate distance.

Store the distances in a two-dimensional table.

	Boston	Chicago	Dallas	Las Vegas	Los Angeles	Miami	New Orleans	Toronto	Vancouver	Washington DC
Boston	0	1004	1753	2752	3017	1520	1507	609	3155	448
Chicago	1004	0	921	1780	2048	1397	919	515	2176	709
Dallas	1753	921	0	1230	1399	1343	517	1435	2234	1307
Las Vegas	2752	1780	1230	0	272	2570	1732	2251	1322	2420
Los Angeles	3017	2048	1399	272	0	2716	1858	2523	1278	2646
Miami	1520	1397	1343	2570	2716	0	860	1494	3447	1057
New Orleans	1507	919	517	1732	1858	860	0	1307	2734	1099
Toronto	609	515	1435	2251	2523	1494	1307	0	2820	571
Vancouver	3155	2176	2234	1322	1278	3447	2734	2820	0	2887
Washington DC	448	709	1307	2420	2646	1057	1099	571	2887	0

8.6   *Two-dimensional Table*

Create a project in which the user will complete a 10-question survey.
Create a form containing labels with each of the questions and a group of
radio buttons for each question with the following responses: Always,
Usually, Sometimes, Seldom, and Never.

Use a two-dimensional array to accumulate the number of each response for each question.

Have a menu or button option that will print an item analysis on the
printer that shows the question number and the count for each response.

Sample of partial output:

Question	Always	Usually	Sometimes	Seldom	Never
1	5	2	10	4	6
2	2	2	10	2	1
3	17	0	10	0	0

Case Studies

VB Mail Order

Create a project that will calculate shipping charges
from a two-dimensional table of rates. The rate depends on the weight of the package and the zone to
which it will be shipped. The "Wt." column specifies
the maximum weight for that rate. All weights over 10
pounds use the last row.

Wt.	Zone			
	A	B	C	D
1	1.00	1.50	1.65	1.85
3	1.58	2.00	2.40	3.05
5	1.71	2.52	3.10	4.00
10	2.04	3.12	4.00	5.01
>10	2.52	3.75	5.10	7.25

VB Auto Center

VB Auto sells its own brand of spark plugs. To cross-reference to major brands, it keeps a table of equivalent part numbers. VB Auto wants to computerize the process of looking up part numbers in order to improve its customer service.

The user should be able to enter the part number and brand and look up the corresponding VB Auto part number. You may allow the user to select the brand (Brand A, Brand C, or Brand X) from a list or from radio buttons.

You can choose from two approaches for the look-up table. Either store the part numbers in a two-dimensional table or in an array of a structure. In either case, use the part number and brand entered by the user; look up and display the VB Auto part number.

VB Auto	Brand A	Brand C	Brand X
PR214	MR43T	RBL8	14K22
PR223	R43	RJ6	14K24
PR224	R43N	RN4	14K30
PR246	R46N	RN8	14K32
PR247	R46TS	RBL17Y	14K33
PR248	R46TX	RBL12-6	14K35
PR324	S46	J11	14K38
PR326	SR46E	XEJ8	14K40
PR444	47L	H12	14K44

Video Bonanza

Create a project that displays the aisle number of a movie category in a label. The movie categories will be in a list box. Store the aisle numbers and categories in an array.

A Search button should locate the correct location from the array and display it in a label. Make sure that the user has selected a category from the list and use the list box SelectedIndex property to find the appropriate aisle number.

Test Data	
Aisle 1	Comedy
Aisle 2	Drama
Aisle 3	Action
Aisle 4	Sci-Fi
Aisle 5	Horror
Back Wall	New Releases

Very Very Boards

Modify your project from Chapter 6 to keep track of each order in an array. You can then print out the entire order with detail lines for each type of shirt. Convert the event handling for the radio buttons to share an event procedure. Use a Case structure for selection.

Create an array of a structure, which holds the quantity, size, monogram (Boolean), pocket (Boolean), price, and extended price for each type of shirt ordered.

As each shirt type is added to an order, store the information in the array. Add a menu option to print out the order, which will have the customer name and order number at the top, and one line for each shirt type ordered. Use the following layout as a rough guide for your list. Make sure to align the numeric columns correctly. For the two Boolean fields (Monogram and Pocket), print Yes or No. Do not allow the user to print an invoice until the order is complete.

Very Very Boards Shirt Orders
By Your Name

Customer Name: xxxxxxxxxxxxxxxxxxxxx
Order Number: xxxxx

Quantity	Size	Monogram	Pocket	Price Each	Extended Price
========	====	========	======	==========	==============
xxx	xxx	xxx	xxx	xx	x,xxx

Order Total: xx,xxx

CHAPTER

9

Programming with Web Forms

at the completion of this chapter, you will be able to . . .

1. Explain the functions of the server and the client in Web programming.

2. Create a Web form and run it in a browser.

3. Describe the differences among the various types of Web controls and the relationship of Web controls to controls used on Windows forms.

4. Understand the event structure required for Web programs.

5. Design a Web Form using either a grid layout or a flow layout.

6. Validate Web input using the validator controls.

7. Define ASP, XML, WSDL, and SOAP.

Visual Basic and Web Programming

So far, all of your projects are based on Windows Forms and run stand-alone in the Windows environment. In this chapter you learn to program for the Internet. In Visual Basic .NET you use **Web Forms** to create the user interface for Web projects. A Web Form displays as a document in a **browser**, such as Netscape Navigator (NN) or Internet Explorer (IE). You also can use the Mobile Internet Toolkit and Mobile Web Forms to display documents on mobile devices such as cell phones and personal digital assistants (PDAs).

- This chapter is totally new.

- Web Forms are new to .NET. Previous versions had DHTML and IIS, which were very awkward to use.

- Make sure that students have installed IIS before installing VB .NET.

Client/Server Web Applications

Most Windows applications are stand-alone applications; Web applications require a server and a client. The server sends Web pages to the client, where the pages display inside a browser application (Figure 9.1).

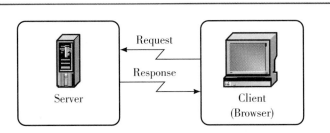

A server delivers Web pages to a client, where the pages display in a browser window. The server can be on a remote machine or on the same machine as the client.

Web Servers

To develop Web applications you must either use a remote Web server or make your local machine a Web server. The most common practice is to make the development machine a server by installing Internet Information Services (IIS). IIS handles the Web server functions and the browser acts as the client.
Note: You must install IIS *before* installing VB.

Web Clients

Browsers display pages written in hypertext markup language (HTML). The pages may also contain programming logic in the form of script, such as JavaScript, VBScript, or JScript, or Java applets. The browser renders the page and displays it on the local system.

You have likely seen Web pages that look different when displayed in different browsers or even in different versions of the same browser. Although many browser applications are available, the two most common are Internet Explorer and Netscape Navigator.

You may know which browser your users are using, such when you are programming for a network within a company, called an **intranet**. Or you may develop applications that run on the Internet and might display in any browser. If your projects will run on different browsers, you should test and check the output on multiple browsers.

Web Pages

One characteristic of HTML **Web pages** is that they are **stateless**. That is, a page does not store any information about its contents from one invocation to the next. Several techniques have been developed to get around this limitation, including storing cookies on the local machine and sending state information to the server as part of the page's address, called the uniform resource locator (URL). The server can then send the state information back with the next version of the page, if necessary.

When a user requests a Web page, the browser (client) sends a request to the server. The server may send a preformatted HTML file, or a program on the server may dynamically generate the necessary HTML to render the page. One Microsoft technology for dynamically generating HTML pages is dynamic HTML (DHTML); another more popular technique is active server pages (ASP).

ASP.NET

The latest Web programming technology from Microsoft is ASP.NET, which is their greatly improved and easier-to-use Web development tool that replaces ASP. ASP.NET provides libraries, controls, and programming support that allow you to write programs that interact with the user, maintain state, render controls, display data, and generate appropriate HTML. When you use Web Forms in Visual Basic .NET, you are using ASP.NET. Using VB and ASP.NET you can create object-oriented event-driven programs. These programs can have multiple classes and use inheritance.

Visual Basic and ASP.NET

Each Web Form that you design has two distinct pieces: 1) the HTML and instructions needed to render the page and 2) the Visual Basic code. This separation is new to ASP.NET and is a big improvement over the older methods that mix the HTML and programming logic (script or applets). A Web Form generates a file with an .aspx extension for the HTML and another file with an .aspx.vb extension for the Visual Basic code. Don't panic if you don't know HTML; the HTML is generated automatically by the Visual Studio IDE. This is similar to the automatically generated code in Windows Forms. You visually create the document using the IDE's designer, then you can view and modify the HTML tags in the Visual Studio editor.

The VB code contains the program logic to respond to events. This code module is called the "CodeBehind" module. The code looks just like the code you have been writing for Windows applications, but many of the events are different.

Creating Web Forms

You begin a Web Forms project in much the same way as a Windows Forms project. In the *New Project* dialog box, select *ASP.NET Web Application* (Figure 9.2). Notice that the project location is set to *http://localhost*, which is the folder on your machine set up by IIS. Also notice that the *Name* box is disabled; you name the project by modifying the location in the *Location* text box. Change the location to *http://localhost/ProjectName;* the ProjectName will become a new folder located in the Inetpub\wwwroot folder.

F i g u r e   9 . 2

Begin a new Web Forms project by selecting ASP.NET Web Application from the New Project dialog box.

Note: You must have correct Web Permissions settings to create Web projects. If the security on your campus network does not allow the proper permissions, you cannot create Web applications.

Web Forms in the Visual Studio IDE

As soon as you open a Visual Basic Web application, you notice many differences from working on a Windows application. As the project opens, a connection to the Web server is established (Figure 9.3). Instead of a Windows form, you see a Web document (Figure 9.4), also called a *Web page* or a *Web form*. A message appears on the form indicating the layout type, by default a grid layout. The message also tells how to change the layout. As soon as you add a control to the form, the message disappears.

If you look closely at Figure 9.4, you will notice several other differences from Windows Forms. The toolbar is different as is the list of files in the Solution Explorer. The toolbox has different controls, and even those that look the same, such as TextBoxes, Buttons, and Labels, are actually different from their Windows counterparts and have some different properties and events. For example, Web controls have an ID property rather than a Name property. When

- Web Forms are based on a completely different class than Windows Forms. The properties, methods, and events differ considerably.

- You use a completely different set of controls on Web Forms than on Windows Forms. Although many have the same names as those for Windows Forms, such as TextBox and Label, the properties and methods are very different.

you look at the code for a Web Form, you see that the form inherits from System.Web.UI.Page. And a Button control inherits from System.Web.UI.WebControls.Button.

Figure 9.3

The `Create New Web` *dialog box appears briefly to show the Web connection for the new project.*

Figure 9.4

The Visual Studio IDE with a new Web Form defined.

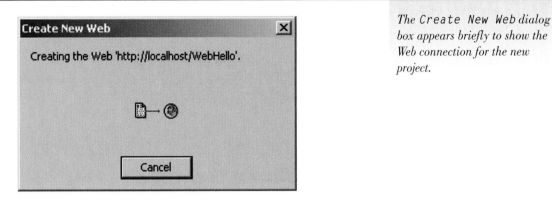

Creating Your First Web Form—Step-by-Step

This simple step-by-step tutorial creates a Web application that displays "Hello World" on a document in a browser window.

Begin the Project

STEP 1: From the *File* menu select *New* and then *Project*.

STEP 2: Select *Visual Basic Projects* as the project type and *ASP.NET Web Application* as the template.

STEP 3: Notice that the location defaults to *http://localhost/Project-Name*. Change only the project name to Ch09WebHello. The location should read *http://localhost/Ch09WebHello* (Figure 9.5).

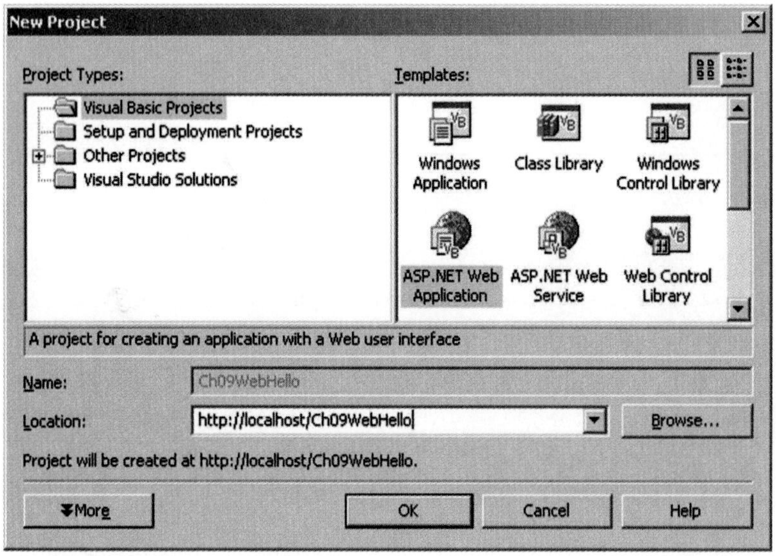

Figure 9.5

The New Project dialog box. Name the new Web application by changing the project name in the Location text box.

STEP 4: Click OK. A *Create New Web* dialog box appears briefly and then WebForm1.aspx appears.

Create the User Interface

STEP 1: Add a Label from the Web Forms section of the toolbox. Notice that the layout message disappears.

STEP 2: Change the Label's ID property to lblMessage and the Text property to "Hello World".

Run the Web Application

STEP 1: Run the project. The Internet Explorer browser should launch and open the page with your label showing.

STEP 2: Close the browser window to end execution. Or you can switch back to the VS IDE and click the Stop Debugging toolbar button (or select *Debug/Stop Debugging* or press Shift + F5).

Viewing the HTML Code

When you are viewing your Web form in the designer, you can see two tabs at the bottom of the form: *Design* and *HTML*. You can click on the *HTML* tab to see the static HTML code. Don't worry about reading the code; it is automatically generated like the Windows-generated code in a Windows Form.

Browser View

Sometimes you may want a preview of your Web page in a browser without actually running the project. Right-click on the form and select *View in Browser*. A new tab is added to the Editor window, which displays the Web page as it will appear in a browser.

Toolbars

When the Web form is open, the Design toolbar displays with some new buttons (Figure 9.6). These buttons include Display Borders, Show Details, Lock Element, Show Grid, and Snap-to Grid.

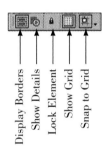

Display Borders | Show Details | Lock Element | Show Grid | Snap to Grid

Figure 9.6

The Design toolbar displays while you are creating the user interface for a Web Form.

Controls

Several types of controls are available for Web Forms. You can mix the control types on a single form.

- *HTML controls.* These are the standard HTML elements that operate only on the client. You cannot write any server-side programming logic for HTML controls. As you submit forms to the server, any HTML controls pass to the server and back as static text. You might want to use HTML controls if you have existing HTML pages that are working and you want to convert to ASP.NET for additional capabilities. In this chapter we won't use any HTML controls.

- *HTML server controls.* These controls match HTML controls on a one-for-one basis. They have all of the attributes of HTML (client) controls plus the added capability of object-oriented, event-driven, server-side programming. However, HTML server controls do not provide many of the features of Web server controls, such as type checking for data and customized rendering of the control based on the browser.

To change an HTML control to an HTML server control, right-click on the control and select *Run As Server Control.*

- *Web server controls*, also called *ASP.NET server controls*. These are the richest, most powerful controls provided by ASP.NET and the .NET framework. Web server controls do not directly correspond to HTML controls, but are rendered differently for different browsers in order to achieve the desired look and feel. Some of the special-purpose Web server controls are validation controls, Calendar, DataGrid, CheckBoxList, and RadioButtonList. In this chapter we will stick with Web server controls.

You can see the available controls in the toolbox when a Web Form is in Design view. Try clicking in the toolbox on *HTML, Web Forms,* and *Components.* The Web server controls on the *Components* list are nonvisual components that appear in the component tray of the Web Form. Keep your toolbox showing Web Forms controls.

In Design view, you can tell the difference between client-side HTML controls and server-side controls. The VS designer adds a small green arrow in the upper-left corner for all server controls (Figure 9.7), whether it is an HTML server control or an ASP.NET server control.

Figure 9.7

The small green arrow in the corner of a control indicates a server control.

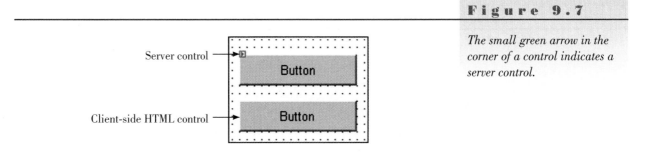

Event Handling

You write VB code for events of Web controls in the same way that you write for Windows controls. The events may actually occur on either the client or the server. The process of capturing an event, sending it to the server, and executing the required methods is all done for you automatically.

The events of Web Forms and controls are somewhat different from those of Windows Forms. For example, a Web Form has a Page_Load event rather than a Form_Load event. You can see the events of controls using the editor; drop down the Event list for a control such as a button. You will see that you still have a Click event, but the list of events is much shorter than it is for Windows Forms.

Files

The files that you find in a Web application differ greatly from those in a Windows application (Figure 9.8). Two files make up the form: the aspx file and the aspx.vb file. The aspx file holds the specifications for the user interface that are used by the server to render the page. The aspx.vb file holds the Visual Basic code that you write to respond to events. The aspx.vb file is the "code-behind"

file for the aspx file. When you are designing the user interface, you select the
FormName.aspx tab; when you are working on the code procedures, you select
the FormName.aspx.vb tab.

Figure 9.8

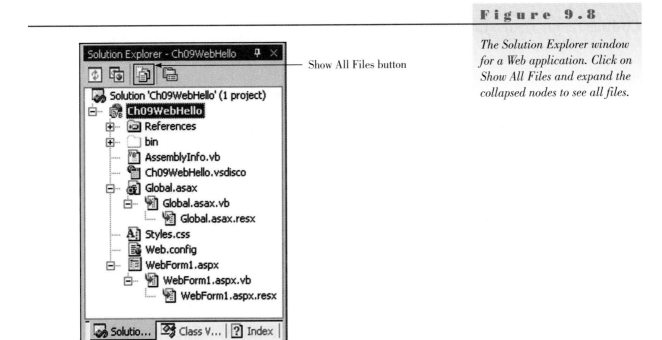

Show All Files button

*The Solution Explorer window
for a Web application. Click on
Show All Files and expand the
collapsed nodes to see all files.*

Several other files are generated for you, as listed in Table 9.1. One of
these is the Styles.css or Cascading Style Sheet for positioning and formatting
text and elements on a Web page. Another is the Web.config file, which may
appear in multiple directories on the server.

Files in a Web Project   **Table 9.1**

File	File type	Purpose
FormName.aspx	ASP.NET	Dynamically generates a Web user interface allowing for server-side code.
FormName.aspx.vb	Visual Basic Code	Supplies the code procedures for the form; the "code-behind" the aspx file.
AssemblyInfo.vb	Project information	Holds information about the project such as assembly names and versions.
ProjectName.vsdisco	XML discovery file	Holds links (URLs) to help locate the necessary Web services.
Global.asax	ASP.NET application file	Supplies any code needed to respond to Application- and Session-level events.
Styles.css	Cascading Style Sheet	Formats and positions Web page elements.
Web.config	Configuration	Contains configuration information about each URL resource used in the project.

When you compile a Web project, the compiler generates .dll (dynamic link library) files that hold the compiled code. When a request for the Web page is made by accessing the address (URL) of the Web page, the .dll file produces the HTML output for the page.

Coding Event Procedures—Step-by-Step

In this continuation of the earlier step-by-step tutorial, you will add a text box and a button, and code an event procedure for the button. When the user clicks the button, the page is submitted to the server. The event procedure executes on the server and the page is sent back to the client.

Add Controls and Code

STEP 1: If you closed your project, reopen it. You can choose from several methods to reopen the project:

- Switch to or display the Start page (*Help/Show Start Page*) and select your project.

- Open the *File* menu and select either *Recent Files* or *Recent Projects* and select your project.

- Select *File/Open/Project from Web* to locate your file under *localhost.*

STEP 2: Add a text box to the Web form and change its ID property to txtName.

STEP 3: Add a button called *btnSubmit* and change its Text property "Submit" (Figure 9.9).

Figure 9.9

Add a label and a button to the Web Form for the chapter step-by-step tutorial.

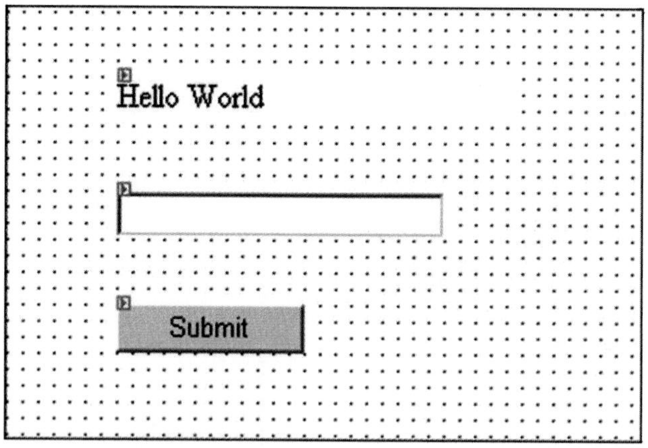

STEP 4: Double-click on the button to open the Editor window for the aspx.vb file. Write the code for the button:

```
'Display the name in the label
lblMessage.Text = "Hello " & txtName.Text
```

STEP 5: Run the program. Type your name into the text box and click the Submit button.

Watch the status bar of the browser after you click on Submit. First you should see a message *Web Site Found . . . Waiting for reply*. You can watch it send the information and then respond.

STEP 6: Close the browser window to stop execution.

Add Remarks

STEP 1: Finish up by adding remarks to the form's code.

```
'Project:          Ch09WebHello
'Programmer:       Your Name
'Date:             Today's Date
'Description:       Display the user name concatenated to a label.
'                  This is the step-by-step program for creating Web Forms.
```

Debugging

The Visual Studio IDE is designed to debug in many languages. You can set breakpoints, single-step execution, and display the contents of variables and properties. Try setting a breakpoint in the btnSubmit event procedure and re-run the program. The project compiles and displays in the browser. After you click on the button, the breakpoint halts execution and you can view the code and the values of properties, just as you can in Windows Forms. Single-step execution using the F11 key and view your objects and properties in the Autos or Locals window.

Testing in Other Browsers

You can test your project in another browser, such as Netscape Navigator. First launch the browser and then type the URL of your page into the Address bar. (As a shortcut, you can copy and paste the URL from the Address bar of Internet Explorer.) For the step-by-step tutorial, assuming that you called the project Ch09WebHello, the URL would be http://localhost/Ch09WebHello/WebForm1.aspx.

Feedback 9.1

1. How can you convert an HTML control to an HTML server control?
2. Why might a person *want* to convert an HTML control to an HTML server control?
3. What two files make up a Web Form? What is the purpose of each file?
4. How can you display a preview of how your Web Form will display in a browser without actually running the program?

Laying Out Web Forms

Using Web Forms, you have considerable control over the layout of a page. However, you must always be aware that users may have different browsers, different screen sizes, and different screen resolutions. ASP.NET generates appropriate HTML to render the page in various browsers but cannot be aware of the screen size, resolution, or window size on the target machine.

The Page Layout

The **pageLayout property** of a page determines how and where the controls on a Web page appear. The two choices for layout are **grid layout** (the default) or **flow layout.**

A flow layout works very much like adding text in a word processor. You have an insertion point and each control that you add appears immediately following the insertion point. You can add spaces and press the Enter key to set the location for each control. When the page is displayed in the browser, the user can resize the window and the controls will move to fit in the window, very much like changing the margins in a text file. The advantage of a flow layout is that your Web page can display on any size screen with any resolution; the disadvantage is that you have very little control over the exact placement of the controls.

The default grid layout allows you to determine the exact placement of controls, using an x and y grid. ASP.NET generates the correct HTML to display the controls in the correct location. However, if your page is large and the user's browser window is small, some controls may not be visible. You can expect a scroll bar to appear on the browser window, giving the user the opportunity to scroll sideways or down to see the rest of the page, but the effect may not be what you had in mind.

Using Tables for Layout

If you want to set up an area on your form with rows and columns, you can add a **table**. You can add controls and text to the table cells to align the columns as you want them. Although you can use tables in either a grid layout or a flow layout, you will find tables most useful in a flow layout. This is because a grid layout already gives you control of the placement of controls.

The table is an HTML control, which doesn't need any server-side programming. Although there is a Web server Table control, that is generally used when you want to write code to add rows, columns, or controls at run time. You can add a table from the HTML controls or from the *Table* menu, which appears when you are designing a Web form. The *Table/Insert/Table* menu item displays a dialog box (Figure 9.10) that allows you to select the number of rows and columns and set other properties, such as borders, alignment, and background color. Note that you can also set these properties in the Properties window when the table is selected.

Figure 9.10

In the Insert Table dialog box you can set the number of rows and columns and the properties for the table.

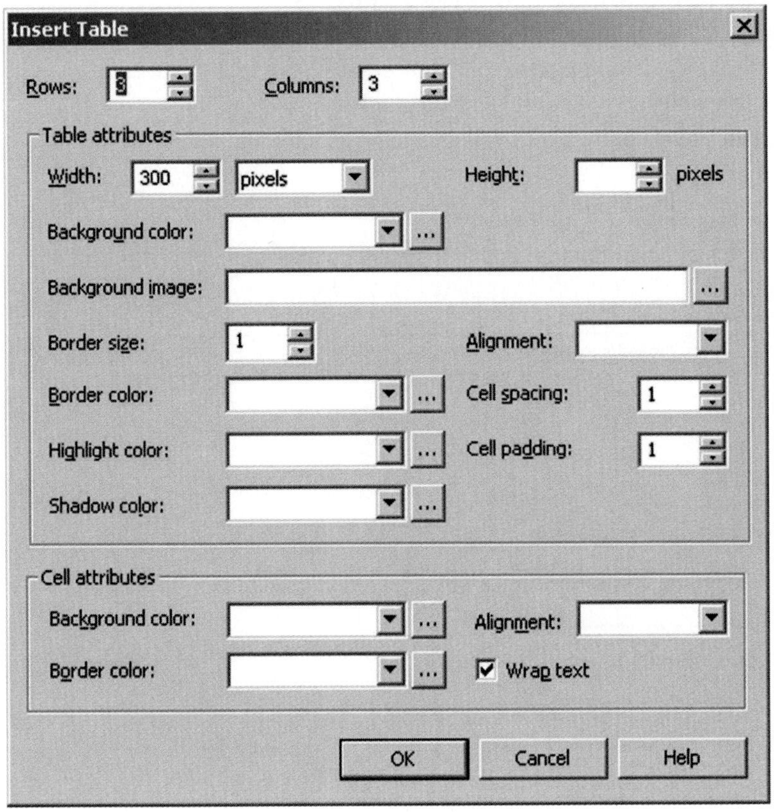

You can move a table to a new location. In a grid layout, select the table and move it as you would any other element. For a flow layout, you must insert spaces to move the table.

To add or delete a table row, first select a row. Then right-click and use the shortcut menu. You can use the same technique to add or delete a column.

Entering Data in a Table

You can add controls to any table cell or type text in a cell during Design time. If you want to be able to refer to the text in a cell at run time, add a label and give it an ID; otherwise, you can type text directly into the cell. Figure 9.11 shows a table in Design view. Although the table's Border is set to zero, the borders appear at Design time but not at Run time (Figure 9.12).

Figure 9.11

Add text and controls to the table cells. Although the Border property is set to zero, the borders still show at Design time.

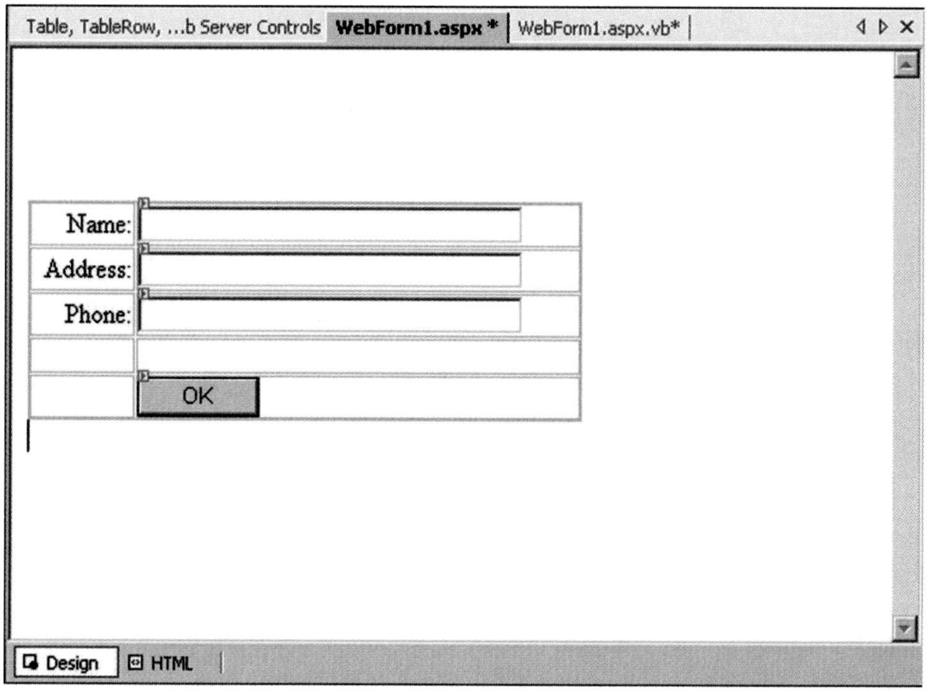

Figure 9.12

The table at run time. With the Border property set to zero, the borders do not appear.

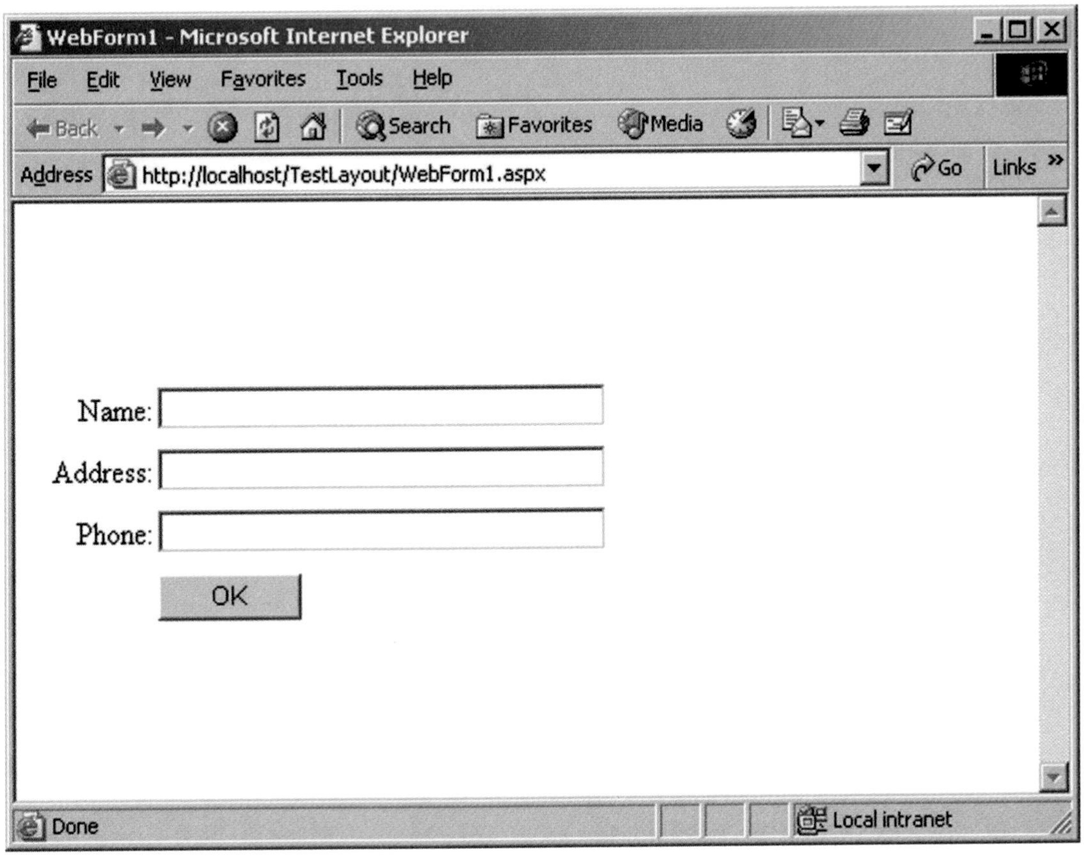

Feedback 9.2

1. List the differences between using a grid layout and a flow layout.
2. Name two ways to place a button at the bottom of a form using a flow layout.
3. What is the difference between an HTML Table control and a Web Table control?

Using the Validator Controls

ASP.NET provides several controls that can automatically validate input data. You add a **validator control**, attach it to an input control, such as a text box, and set the error message. At run time, when the user inputs data, the error message displays if the validation rule is violated. These validation controls run on the client-side, so the page does not have to be submitted to the server to view and clear the message. Table 9.2 lists the ASP.NET validator controls.

• These new validator controls run on the client side, so do not require an event to be sent to the server for each validation and error message.

Control	Purpose	Properties to set
RequiredFieldValidator	Requires that the user enter something into the field.	ControlToValidate ErrorMessage
CompareValidator	Compares the value in the field to the value in another control or to a constant value. You also can set the Type property to a numeric type and the CompareValidator will verify that the input value can be converted to the correct type.	ControlToValidate ControlToCompare *or* ValueToCompare Type (to force type checking) ErrorMessage
RangeValidator	Makes sure that the input value falls in the specified range	ControlToValidate MinimumValue MaximumValue Type (to force type checking) ErrorMessage
RegularExpressionValidator	Validates against a regular expression, such as a required number of digits or formatted value, such as a telephone number or Social Security number. Use the Regular Expression Editor to select or edit expressions; open by selecting the ellipses button on the ValidationExpression property.	ControlToValidate ValidationExpression ErrorMessage
ValidationSummary	Displays a summary of all of the messages from the other validation controls.	DisplayMode (can be set to a bulleted list, list, or message box)

Note that a blank entry passes the validation for each of the controls except the RequiredFieldValidator. If you want to ensure that the field is not blank *and* that it passes a range check, for example, attach both a RangeValidator and a RequiredFieldValidator control to a field.

Feedback 9.3

Describe how to validate a text box called txtNumber using validator controls. A numeric entry is required, in the range 0 to 1000. The field must not be blank.

Managing Web Projects

Managing the files for Web projects can be a challenge, especially if you need to move the project from one computer to another. Unless you are careful, your solution files (.sln and .suo) will be saved in a separate folder in a different location from the rest of your project.

• Successfully moving Web projects is not easy. If you find a good way, please notify the authors.

Location of Files

The Visual Studio IDE saves solution files in the default folder that you select in *Tools/Options/Environment.* In the *Projects and Solutions* section, the entry for Visual Studio projects location determines the location of the .sln and .suo files. This location is the same for Windows projects and for Web projects.

When you create a new Web project, all files *except the solution files* are stored in a new folder beneath Inetpub\wwwroot. For example, if you create a new Web project called *MyWebProject*, two folders called *MyWebProject* are created—one in your default project folder and one in wwwroot.

If you keep your project on a single development machine, the VS IDE can open either the project or solution file and keep track of the files. But if you need to move your project, the file arrangement can cause difficulties.

Recommendation: As soon as you open a new Web project, select the solution file in the Solution Explorer. Then select *File/Save SolutionName As*. Browse to find your folder name in Inetpub\wwwroot and save your solution file there. This will keep all of your files in the same folder.

Moving a Project

When you move a project folder from one computer to another, the project will not run until you take an extra step. To run a Web project from your local Web server (usually IIS), you must have a "virtual folder" defined. Fortunately, the VS IDE makes this happen when you create a new Web application. However, when you move the project to another computer, you must either create a virtual folder on that computer or declare the project folder to be Web-Shared.

To move a project, copy the project folder from Inetpub\wwwroot on the source computer to the same location on the target machine. Then either create a virtual directory or Web-Share the folder.

Creating a Virtual Directory

After you move a project to a new computer, you must open the Internet Services Manager to create a virtual directory. Select *Start/Settings/Control Panel/Administrative Tools/Internet Services Manager* and expand the node for the computer and for the default Web site to view the folders. Notice that the icon for the new folder is different from the existing virtual directories. You can select the icon for *Default Web Site* and choose *Action/New/Virtual Directory*, or right-click the icon and choose *New/Virtual Directory* from the shortcut menu. The Virtual Directory Creation Wizard opens, where you give an alias (use your project folder name) and enter the folder and path.

Open the project in the VS IDE, select the startup page in the Solution Explorer, right-click and choose *set as start page* from the shortcut menu. Your project should run after creating the IIS virtual directory and setting the start page.

Web Sharing the Project Folder

An alternative to creating an IIS virtual directory on the new computer is to declare the folder as Web-Shared. This procedure is a little easier than creating a virtual directory but can cause security problems on a network. On the target computer, select the folder name using Explorer or My Computer, right-click, and choose *Properties*. On the *Web Sharing* tab, select the radio button for *Share this folder*. An *Edit Alias* dialog box appears; click OK and OK again on the *Properties* dialog box. This makes the folder Web-Shared on the new machine.

Running the Relocated Project

After you create a virtual folder or Web-Share your project folder and set the start page, you should be able to open and run your project in the VS IDE using the path Inetpub/wwwroot, or enter the URL of your page in a browser to run it. The URL should be something like this:
`http://localhost/YourFolderName/YourFormName.aspx`.

Deleting a Web Project

You can delete a Web project; the procedure depends on how the project was created and whether its folder is an IIS virtual directory or a Web-Shared folder. If the project is still in the location created by the VS IDE, it is in an IIS virtual directory. If you have moved or renamed the project, you may have created an IIS virtual directory or a Web-Shared folder (see the previous section). You can easily delete an IIS virtual directory in Explorer or My Computer. When you try to delete a Web-Shared folder, you receive a message telling you that the folder is in use.

To delete a Web-Shared project folder, first unshare it: Right-click the folder name in My Computer or Explorer and select `Properties`. On the `Web Sharing` tab, select the button for `Do not share this folder` and answer `Yes` to the confirmation; then close the `Properties` dialog box. Although it seems like you should be able to delete the folder after this step, the folder is still marked as "In Use." You must either reboot or stop and restart IIS, then you can delete the folder.

Some Web Acronyms

You have seen many acronyms in this chapter, such as HTML, ASP, IIS, and URL. But we have only scratched the surface. As you read the Help files for VB .NET and begin developing Web applications, you will want to know the meaning of many more. These include the following:

XML   *Extensible Markup Language*. This popular tag-based notation is used to define data and its format, and transmit the data over the Web. XML is entirely text-based, does not follow any one manufacturer's specifications, and can pass through firewalls.
See the page "XML, Beginner's Guide" in Help for further information.

SOAP   *Simple Object Access Protocol*. An XML-based protocol for exchanging component information among distributed systems of many different types. Since it is based on XML, its messages can pass through network firewalls.
See `http://www.w3.org/TR/SOAP/`

HTTP	*HyperText Transfer Protocol.* The protocol used to send and receive Web pages over the Internet using standardized request and response messages.
Web Service	Code in classes used to provide middle-tier services over the Internet.
WSDL	*Web Services Description Language.* An XML document using specific syntax that defines how a Web service behaves and how clients interact with the service.

In the next chapter you learn to access data in a database. The XML for the transfer of data is automatically generated and you can view it in a manner similar to viewing HTML in this chapter.

Your Hands-On Programming Example

This project is a Web version of the Book Sales program for R 'n R from Chapter 3. The user enters the quantity, title, and price of a book, and the program calculates the extended price, a 15 percent discount, and the discounted price.

The input must be validated. The quantity and price are required fields, and the quantity must be an integer between 1 and 100.

Planning the Project

Sketch the Web form (Figure 9.13), which your users sign off as meeting their needs.

Figure 9.13

Sketch the form for the hands-on programming example.

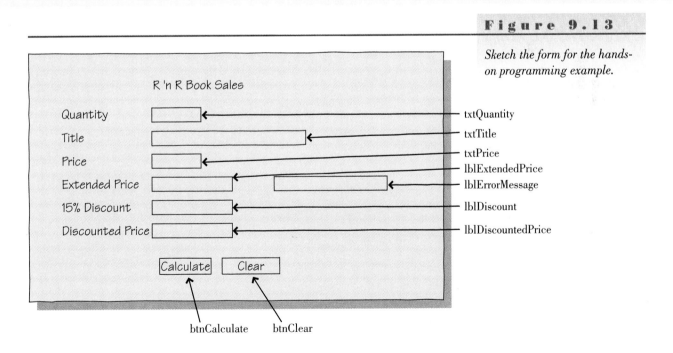

Plan the Objects and Properties

Object	Property	Setting
Label1	ID	Label1
	Text	R 'n R Book Sales
	Font	Bold, Arial, Medium
Label2	ID	Label2
	Text	Quantity
Label3	ID	Label3
	Text	Title
Label4	ID	Label4
	Text	Price
Label5	ID	Label5
	Text	Extended Price
Label6	ID	Label6
	Text	15% Discount
Label7	ID	Label7
	Text	Discounted Price
txtQuantity	ID	txtQuantity
txtTitle	ID	txtTitle
txtPrice	ID	txtPrice
lblExtendedPrice	ID	lblExtendedPrice
	Text	(blank)
	BorderStyle	Solid
	BorderWidth	1
lblDiscount	ID	lblDiscount
	Text	(blank)
	BorderStyle	Solid
	BorderWidth	1
lblDiscountedPrice	ID	lblDiscountedPrice
	Text	(blank)
	BorderStyle	Solid
	BorderWidth	1
btnCalculate	ID	btnCalculate
	Text	Calculate
btnClear	ID	btnClear
	Text	Clear
RequiredFieldValidator1	ID	RequiredFieldValidator1
	ControlToValidate	txtQuantity
	ErrorMessage	Required Field

Continued

Object	Property	Setting
RangeValidator1	ID	RangeValidator1
	ControlToValidate	txtQuantity
	Type	Integer
	MaximumValue	100
	MinimumValue	1
	ErrorMessage	Quantity must be 1-100.
RequiredFieldValidator2	ID	RequiredFieldValidator2
	ControlToValidate	txtPrice
	ErrorMessage	Required Field
lblErrorMessage	ID	lblErrorMessage
	Text	(blank)
	ForeColor	Red

Plan the Procedures

Procedure	Actions
btnCalculate_Click	Clear any text in lblErrorMessage.
	Convert input text values to numeric.
	Calculate the extended price = price * quantity.
	Calculate the discount = extended price * discount rate.
	Calculate the discounted price = extended price − discount.
	Format and display the results.
	Handle any conversion exceptions.
btnClear_Click	Clear all text boxes and labels.

Write the Project

- Follow the sketch in Figure 9.13 to create the Web page. Figure 9.14 shows the completed page and Figure 9.15 shows the page in Design view.

Figure 9.14

The finished Web application.

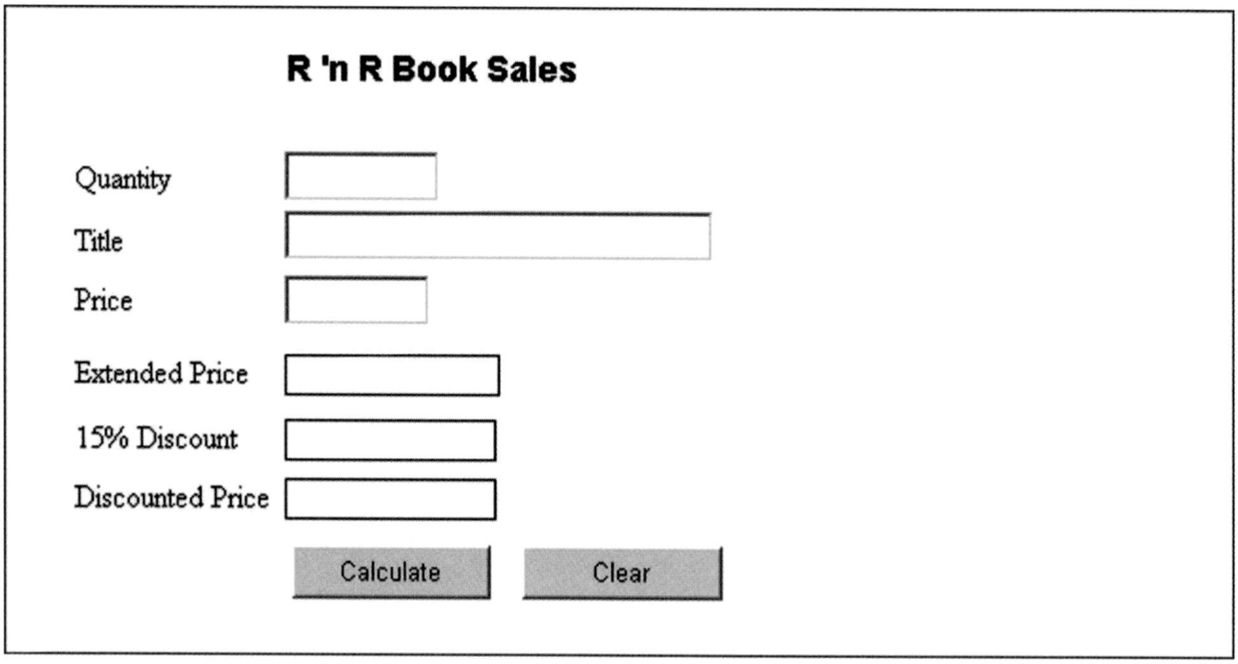

Figure 9.15

Lay out the controls in Design view.

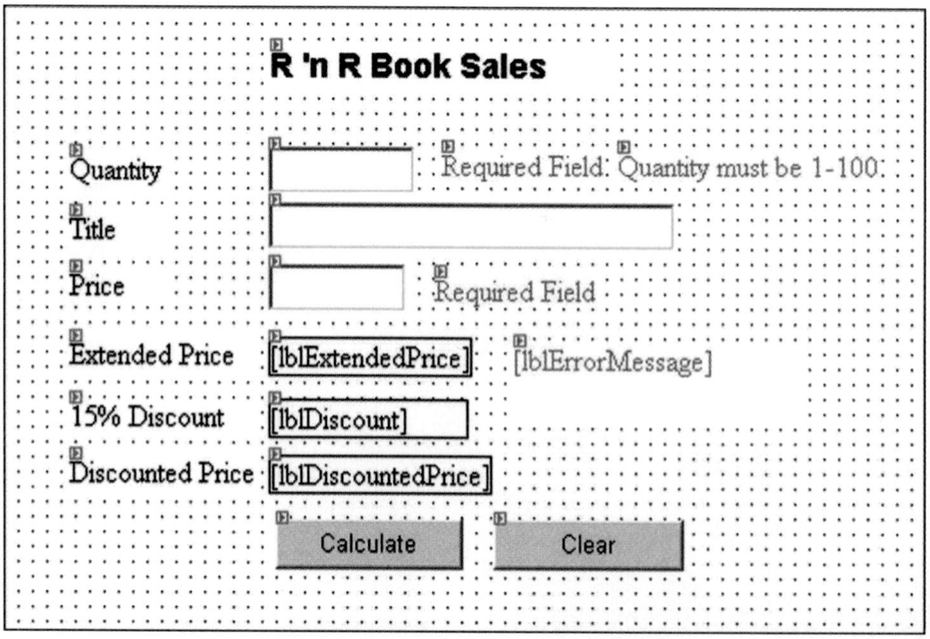

- Set the properties of each of the objects according to your plan.

- Write the code. Working from the pseudocode, write each procedure.

- When you complete the code, use a variety of data to thoroughly test the project. Make sure to test with empty fields, data out of range, and non-numeric data in the numeric fields.

The Project Coding Solution

```
'Program:        Chapter 9 Hands-on
'Programmer:     Bradley/Millspaugh
'Date:           January 2002
'Description:    A Web application to calculate the extended price for books sold,
'                a discount, and the discounted amount.
'                Uses validator controls for input validation.
'Folder:         Ch09HandsOn

Option Strict On

Public Class WebForm1
    Inherits System.Web.UI.Page

'... Automatically-generated code appears here.

    Const mdecDiscountRate As Decimal = 0.15D

    Private Sub Page_Load(ByVal sender As System.Object, ByVal e As System.EventArgs) _
    Handles MyBase.Load
        'Put user code to initialize the page here
    End Sub

    Private Sub btnCalculate_Click(ByVal sender As System.Object, _
    ByVal e As System.EventArgs) Handles btnCalculate.Click
        'Calculate the price and discount

        Dim intQuantity As Integer
        Dim decPrice As Decimal
        Dim decExtendedPrice As Decimal
        Dim decDiscount As Decimal
        Dim decDiscountedPrice As Decimal
        Dim decAverageDiscount As Decimal

        lblErrorMessage.Text = ""
        Try
            'Convert input values to numeric variables
            intQuantity = CInt(txtQuantity.Text)
            decPrice = CDec(txtPrice.Text)

            'Calculate values for sale
            decExtendedPrice = intQuantity * decPrice
            decDiscount = decExtendedPrice * mdecDiscountRate
            decDiscountedPrice = decExtendedPrice - decDiscount

            'Format and display answers for sale
            lblExtendedPrice.Text = FormatCurrency(decExtendedPrice)
            lblDiscount.Text = FormatNumber(decDiscount)
            'Right-align in the control using the PadLeft method
            lblDiscountedPrice.Text = FormatCurrency(decDiscountedPrice).PadLeft(15)
```

```
        'Handle exceptions
        Catch MyErr As InvalidCastException
            lblErrorMessage.Text = "Unable to calculate. Check for numeric values."
        End Try
    End Sub

    Private Sub btnClear_Click(ByVal sender As System.Object, _
     ByVal e As System.EventArgs) Handles btnClear.Click
        'Clear previous amounts from the form

        txtQuantity.Text = ""
        txtTitle.Text = ""
        txtPrice.Text = ""
        lblExtendedPrice.Text = ""
        lblDiscount.Text = ""
        lblDiscountedPrice.Text = ""
        lblErrorMessage.Text = ""
    End Sub
End Class
```

Summary

1. Web applications run in a browser whereas most Windows applications run stand-alone.
2. A Web application has a client, which is the system running the Web page in a browser; and a server, which is the location of the Web page files.
3. Different browsers may display Web pages differently. Web developers must test their applications on multiple browsers unless they know that all users will use the same browser, such as in a company intranet.
4. Web pages are static and stateless. They require processing to change the appearance of the page and cannot store variables on their own.
5. ASP.NET is the Web technology included in Visual Studio .NET. Web Forms in Visual Basic use ASP.NET.
6. Web projects running on the local machine are stored in a folder under Inetpub\wwwroot. The URL of the page is *http://localhost/Project-Name*.
7. The controls for Web pages are different from those used on Windows Forms.
8. In Design view, the HTML tab displays the HTML that is automatically generated.
9. You can display a page preview as it will appear in a browser.
10. Controls on Web pages may be HTML (client-side) controls, HTML server controls, or Web server controls, which are the controls provided by ASP.NET. Web server controls are rendered specifically for the browser being used.
11. Although the events of Web controls are somewhat different from those on Windows controls, coding for the events is the same.
12. A different set of files is generated for Web projects than for Windows projects.
13. A Web Form consists of two files: the .aspx file that holds the code to render the user interface, and the .aspx.vb file that holds the VB code.

14. A page may have a grid layout or a flow layout. In a flow layout, controls are placed one after another, from top to bottom, similar to a word processing document. In a grid layout, controls are placed in absolute *x* and *y* locations.
15. You can use an HTML table to lay out controls and text in rows and columns.
16. Validator controls allow testing for a required field, proper type of data, or a range of values.
17. XML is used to store and transfer data on the Internet. XML is tag-based and text-only and can be transmitted through network firewalls. SOAP and WSDL are based on XML.

Key Terms

browser *374*
flow layout *384*
grid layout *384*
intranet *374*
pageLayout property *384*

stateless *375*
table *384*
validator control *387*
Web Form *374*
Web page *375*

Review Questions

1. Explain the differences between the execution of a Windows application and a Web application.
2. Differentiate between the client and the server for a Web application.
3. What is meant by the statement that Web pages are stateless?
4. What is the localhost?
5. What are the differences between HTML controls and HTML server controls? Between HTML server controls and ASP.NET server controls?
6. How does event handling differ from Windows applications?
7. What functions are done by validator controls? How can you set up a validator control?
8. What is the purpose of XML? Of SOAP?

Programming Exercises

Hint: If you choose one of the projects that require a running total or count, you must maintain the variable yourself in an invisible control. Set the invisible control to the value of the module-level variable. Then in the Page_Load event procedure, add this code:

```
IfIsPostBack And txtInvisible.Text <> "" Then
  mdecTotal = CDec(txtInvisible.Text)
End If
```

9.1 Rewrite your project from Chapter 3 to be a Web project.
9.2 Rewrite any of your previous projects to be a Web project.

9.3   Write Programming Exercise 3.1, the calorie counter, as a Web project. Include validation to make sure that the user does not leave any input fields blank. See the hint before Programming Exercise 9.1.

9.4   Write Programming Exercise 3.3, the inventory turnover, as a Web project. Include validation to make sure that amounts are numeric and not left blank.

9.5   Write Programming Exercise 3.5, the future value of an annuity, as a Web project. Validate the input fields.

9.6   Create a Web page for entering new customer information. The fields include name, email, username, and password. Include a second text box to confirm the password. Set the TextMode property of the two password fields to "Password". Use a table to lay out your controls in a flow layout.

   Validate that all fields contain information. Display appropriate messages for any empty fields. Include a Submit button.

   When all information is entered and the Submit button is pressed, compare the two password fields to see if they are equal. If not, clear both text boxes and display a message to reenter the password information. When the passwords match, display a message that says "Welcome" and the name of the customer.

Case Studies

VB Mail Order

Write the VB Mail Order project from Chapter 3 as a Web project. Use validator controls for the validation.

VB Auto Center

Write the VB Auto Center project from Chapter 3 as a Web project. Use validator controls for the validation.

Video Bonanza

Write the Video Bonanza project from Chapter 3 as a Web project. Use validator controls for the validation. See the hint before Programming Exercise 9.1.

Very Very Boards

Write the Very Very Boards project from Chapter 3 as a Web project. Use validator controls for the validation. See the hint before Programming Exercise 9.1.

10

Accessing Database Files

at the completion of this chapter, you will be able to . . .

1. Use database terminology correctly.

2. Create Windows and Web projects to display database data.

3. Display data in a DataGrid control.

4. Bind data to text boxes and labels.

5. Navigate through the records in a dataset.

6. Display the record number.

7. Create a parameterized query.

8. Allow the user to select from a combo box or list box and display the corresponding record in data-bound controls.

Database Files

Most data handling today is done with relational database files. Many manufacturers produce database management systems (DBMS), each with its own proprietary format. One challenge for software developers has been accessing data from multiple sources that are stored in different formats. Most of the new tools available to developers, including Microsoft's Visual Studio .NET, attempt to handle data from multiple locations (servers) and data stored in different formats.

Visual Basic and Database Files

You can use Visual Basic to write projects that display and update the data from database files. Visual Basic .NET uses ADO.NET, which is the next generation of database technology, based on Microsoft's previous version called *ActiveX Data Objects (ADO)*. One big advantage of ADO.NET is that data is stored and transferred in Extensible Markup Language (XML). You will find more information about XML in the section "XML Data" later in this chapter.

> • Despite the names, there is little similarity between ADO and ADO .NET. The dialogs for the connections are similar.

ADO.NET allows you to access database data in many formats. The two basic types of connections are SQLClient for SQL Server (Microsoft's DBMS) and OLEDB for all other database formats. Using OLEDB you can obtain data from sources such as Access, Oracle, Sybase, or DB2. The examples in this text use an Access database.

Database Terminology

To use database files, you must understand the standard terminology of relational databases. Although there are various definitions of standard database terms, we will stick with those used by Access.

An Access file (with an .mdb extension) can hold multiple tables. Each **table** can be viewed like a spreadsheet, with rows and columns. Each **row** in a table represents the data for one item, person, or transaction and is called a **record**. Each **column** in a table is used to store a different element of data, such as an account number, a name, an address, or a numeric amount. The elements represented in columns are called **fields**. You can think of the table in Figure 10.1 as consisting of rows and columns or of records and fields.

Most tables use a **key field** (or combination of fields) to identify each record. The key field is often a number, such as employee number, account number, identification number, or Social Security number; or it may be a text field, such as last name; or a combination, such as last name and first name.

A relational database generally contains multiple tables and relationships between the tables. For example, an Employee table may have an Employee ID field and the Payroll table will also have an Employee ID field. The two tables are related by Employee ID. You can find the employee information for one payroll record by retrieving the record for the corresponding Employee ID.

Any time a database table is open, one record is considered the current record. As you move from one record to the next, the current record changes.

Figure 10.1

A database table consists of rows (records) and columns (fields).

ISBN	Title	Author	Publisher
0-111-11111-1	89 Years in a Sand Trap	Beck, Fred	Hill and Wang
0-15-500139-6	Business Programming in C	Millspaugh, A. C.	The Dryden Press
0-394-75843-9	Cultural Literacy	Hirsch, E. D. Jr.	Vintage
0-440-22284-2	Five Days in Paris	Steel, Daniell	Dell Publishing
0-446-51251-6	Megatrends	Naisbitt, John	Warner Books
0-446-51652-X	Bridges of Madison County	Waller, Robert James	Warner Books
0-446-60274-4	The Rules	Fein/Schneider	Warner Books
0-451-16095-9	The Stand	King, Stephen	Signet
0-452-26011-6	Song of Solomon	Morrison, Toni	Plume/Penguin
0-517-59905-8	How to Talk to Anyone, Anytime, Anywhere	King, Larry	Crown
0-534-26076-4	A Quick Guide to the Internet	Bradley, Julia Case	Integrated Media Group

Record or row

Field or column

XML Data

XML is an industry-standard format for storing and transferring data. You can find the specifications for XML at http://www.w3.org/XML, which is the site for the World Wide Web Consortium (W3C).

You don't need to know any XML to write database applications in VB. The necessary XML is generated for you automatically, like the automatically generated VB code and HTML. However, a few facts about XML can help you understand what is happening in your programs.

Most proprietary database formats store data in binary, which cannot be accessed by other systems or pass through Internet firewalls. Data stored in XML is all text, identified by tags, similar to HTML tags. An XML file can be edited by any text editor program, such as Notepad.

If you have seen or written any HTML, you know that opening and closing tags define elements and attributes. For example, any text between <b> and </b> is rendered in bold by the browser.

```
<b>This text is bold.</b> <i>This is italic.</i>
```

The tags in XML are not predefined as they are in HTML. The tags can identify fields by name. For example, following are three records of the RnR-Books database file exported from Access to XML. (Later in this chapter you will be using the RnRBooks Access database for VB projects.)

• Visual Studio automatically generates XML code for the transfer of data. You can view the schema from the Solution Explorer.

```
<?xml version="1.0" encoding = "UTF-8"?>
<dataroot xmlns:od = "urn:schemas-microsoft-com:officedata">
    <Books>
        <ISBN>0-07-248819-0</ISBN>
        <Title>Programming with Java</Title>
        <Author>Bradley/Millspaugh</Author>
        <Publisher>McGraw-Hill/Irwin</Publisher>
    </Books>
    <Books>
        <ISBN>0-446-51652-X</ISBN>
        <Title>Bridges of Madison County</Title>
        <Author>Waller, Robert James</Author>
        <Publisher>Warner Books</Publisher>
    </Books>
    <Books>
        <ISBN>0-451-16095-9</ISBN>
        <Title>The Stand</Title>
        <Author>King, Stephen</Author>
        <Publisher>Signet</Publisher>
    </Books>
</dataroot>
```

In addition to an XML data file, you usually also have an XML schema file. The schema describes the fields, data types, and any constraints, such as required fields. ADO.NET validates the data against the schema and checks for constraint violations. The schema also is defined with XML tags and can be viewed or edited in a text editor. You will be able to see the schema for your data files in a VB project by viewing the .xsd file shown in the Solution Explorer.

The format of XML data offers several advantages for programming. Because an XML schema provides for strong data typing, the various data types can be handled properly. And ADO.NET can treat the XML data as objects, allowing the IntelliSense feature of the VS .NET environment to provide information for the programmer. In addition, data handling in XML and ADO.NET executes faster than earlier forms of ADO.

► Feedback 10.1

1. Assume you have a database containing the names and phone numbers of your friends. Describe how the terms *file, table, row, column, record, field,* and *key field* apply to your database.
2. What is an advantage of transferring data as XML, rather than a proprietary format, such as Access or SQLServer?

Using ADO.NET and Visual Basic

In Visual Basic, you can display data from a database on a Windows Form or a Web Form. You add controls to the form and bind data to the controls. The controls may be labels or text boxes or one of the special controls designed just for data, such as the DataGrid or DataList. However, just as you found in Chapter 9, the controls for a Windows application are different from the controls for a Web application and have different properties and events. In this chapter you will write database applications using both Windows Forms and Web Forms. Figure 10.2 shows a data table displaying in a DataGrid on a Web Form.

• There is no data control to bind to controls and provide navigation. You must define a connection, a data adapter, and a dataset. You can bind the dataset to a control such as a DataGrid, and the individual fields of the dataset to controls such as labels and text boxes. If you want navigation, you must write code to do it.

The DataGrid control is bound to a table in a dataset. The data fields display automatically in the cells of the grid.

Setting up data access in Visual Basic requires several steps. This list is an overview—each of the steps is further described in the sections that follow.

- Set up a connection. A **connection** establishes a link to a data source, which is a specific file and/or server.

- Set up a data adapter. A **data adapter** handles retrieving and updating the data. In the programs in this chapter, the data adapter retrieves the records from the database and creates a dataset.

- Add controls to your form and set properties to bind the controls to the fields in the dataset.

- Write some VB code, primarily to fill the dataset. You'll be amazed at how little code it takes to display the data.

Figure 10.3 shows a visual representation of the required steps.

Figure 10.3

To display database data in bound controls on a form, you need to define a connection, a data adapter, and a dataset.

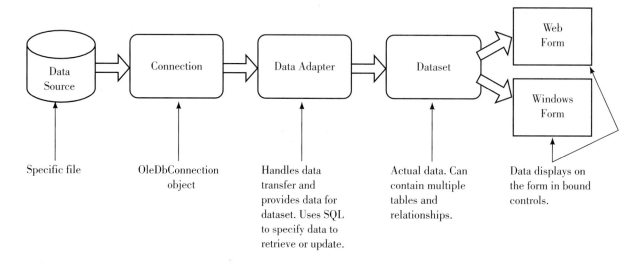

Specific file	OleDbConnection object	Handles data transfer and provides data for dataset. Uses SQL to specify data to retrieve or update.	Actual data. Can contain multiple tables and relationships.	Data displays on the form in bound controls.

Creating a Connection

A Connection object establishes a link from a specific file or database to your program. ADO.NET provides two types of Connection objects: an OleDbConnection and an SqlConnection (Figure 10.4). You use the SqlConnection only for a Microsoft SQLServer database; for all others you use the OleDbConnection.

Figure 10.4

The Data controls in the toolbox. The OleDbConnection and SqlConnection provide connections to a data source.

The Server Explorer is a great help for working with connections (Figure 10.5). If the Server Explorer is closed, choose *View/Server Explorer.*

Figure 10.5

Connect to Database button

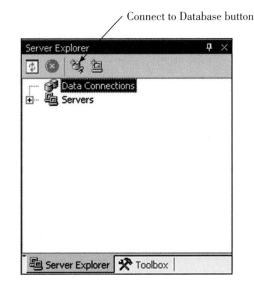

Use the Server Explorer to manage database connections.

You can choose from several techniques for creating a new connection:
1. Right-click on *Data Connections* in the Server Explorer and select *Add Connection* from the shortcut menu.
2. Click on the *Connect to Database* button in the Server Explorer.
3. In the toolbox, click on Data to see the set of Data components, and drag an OleDbConnection object from the toolbox to the form. Select *ConnectionString* in the Properties window, and click on *New Connection.*
4. Wait until you create the data adapter; the Data Adapter Configuration Wizard provides a button to create a new connection.

No matter which method you use to begin a connection, the `Data Link Properties` dialog box appears (Figure 10.6). Click on the `Provider` tab and notice the possible data providers. For an Access database, select `Microsoft Jet 4.0 OLE DB Provider` and click `Next`. On the `Connection` tab that appears (Figure 10.7) you can enter or browse to the actual database file. Then click the `Test Connection` button to make sure the connection succeeds.

Select the data provider on the `Data Link Properties` *dialog box.*

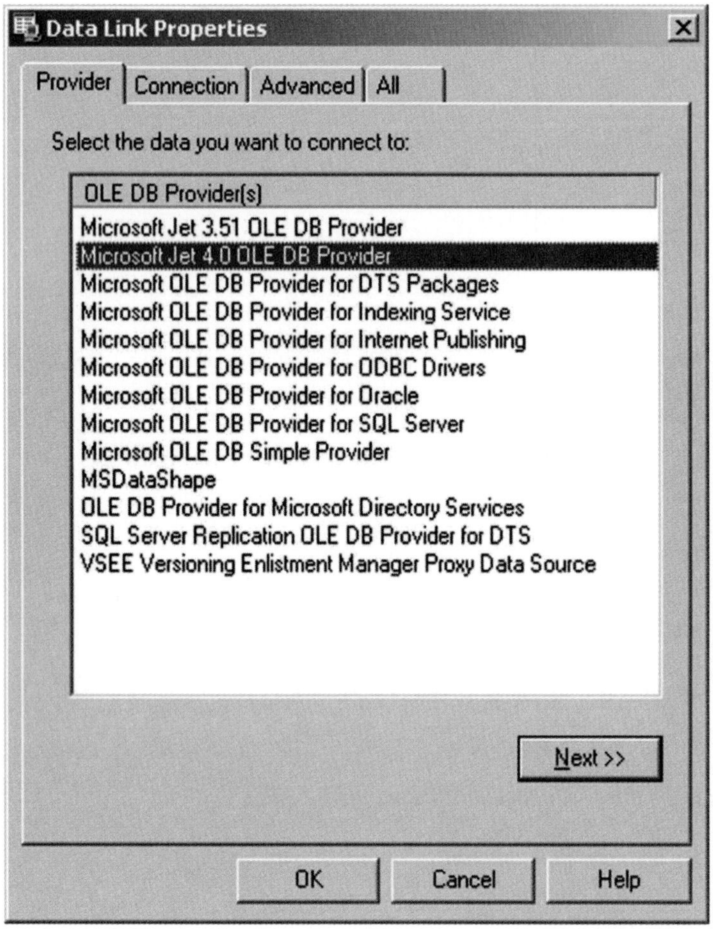

Figure 10.7

Browse to find the database filename on the `Connection` *tab of the* `DataLink  Properties` *dialog box.*

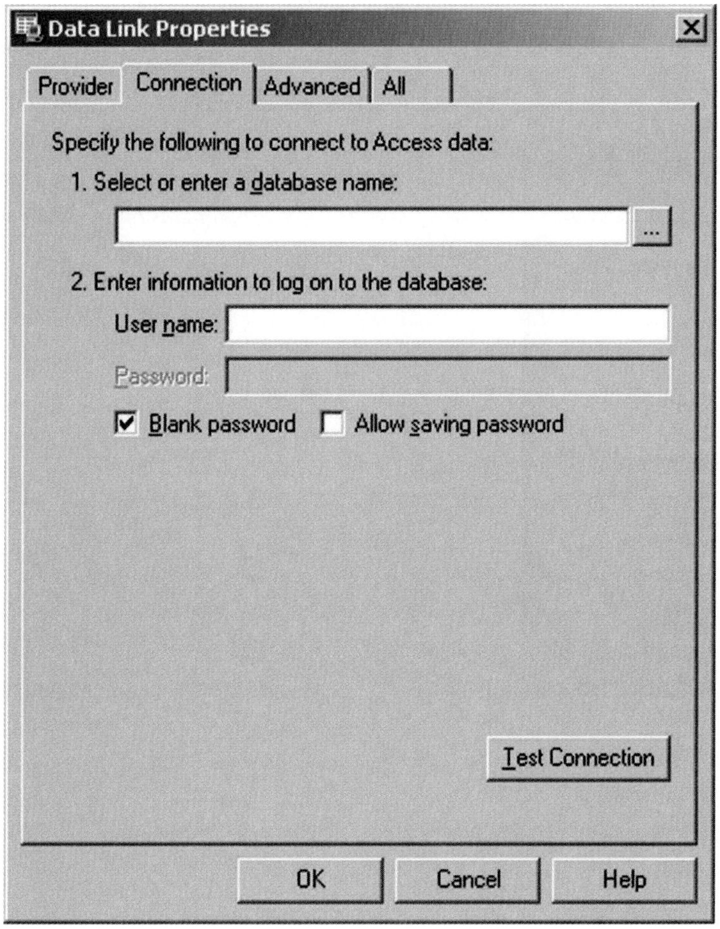

Once you create a connection to a database file on a computer, that connection appears in the Server Explorer for all projects. You can use the same connection for multiple projects. And you can expand the nodes for the connection to view the tables and fields in the database file (Figure 10.8).

Figure 10.8

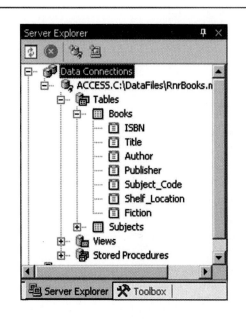

Expand the nodes for the connection to see the tables and fields in the database.

Setting Up a Data Adapter

A data adapter does all of the work of passing data back and forth between a data source and a program. The data source for a data adapter does not have to be a database; it can also be a text file, an object, or even an array.

The data adapters available for ADO.NET are the OleDbDataAdapter and the SqlDataAdapter (refer to Figure 10.4). Note that the type of data adapter must match that of the connection: Use the OleDbDataAdapter for any data from an OLE DB provider. The SqlDataAdapter is faster but works only with Microsoft's SQL Server 7.0 and later.

You can add a new data adapter in several ways:

1. Drag a table name from the Server Explorer to the form. This technique adds both a new connection and a new data adapter to the project. To view or modify the configuration of the data adapter, select *Configure Data Adapter* from the *Data* menu or right-click and select the option from the shortcut menu.
2. Ctrl + click on the field names that you want to include; then drag the selected fields as a group to the form. This technique, like the previous one, creates both a new connection and a new data adapter.
3. Add an OleDbDataAdapter control from the Data tools in the toolbox. The Data Adapter Configuration Wizard opens automatically.

• Two adapters for connections are available: one for SQL Server and the generic OleDb adapter.

• For database access, you can either use a data adapter and disconnected dataset, or use data commands that send SQL and DDL directly to the database. When working directly with a database, you use a data command object with either an SQL statement or a stored procedure.

• If you use data commands to return a result set, you set up and use a data reader to retrieve the data in the program.

• This text does not cover using data commands; the topic is covered in the advanced text.

The Data Adapter Configuration Wizard walks you through the steps for selecting the fields in a database (Figure 10.9). Note that you need to use the Configuration wizard only if you add the OleDbDataAdapter from the toolbox; if you use either method 1 or method 2 above, the data adapter is configured automatically. You can always select the control and check or modify the configuration using the wizard.

Figure 10.9

The first screen of the Data Adapter Configuration Wizard. Click Next to configure the data adapter.

You select the connection for the data adapter on the second screen of the wizard (Figure 10.10). If you already have connections defined, they appear in the drop-down list. Notice that you can click the `New Connection` button to create a new connection at this point.

Figure 10.10

Select the connection or click `New Connection` *to create a new one.*

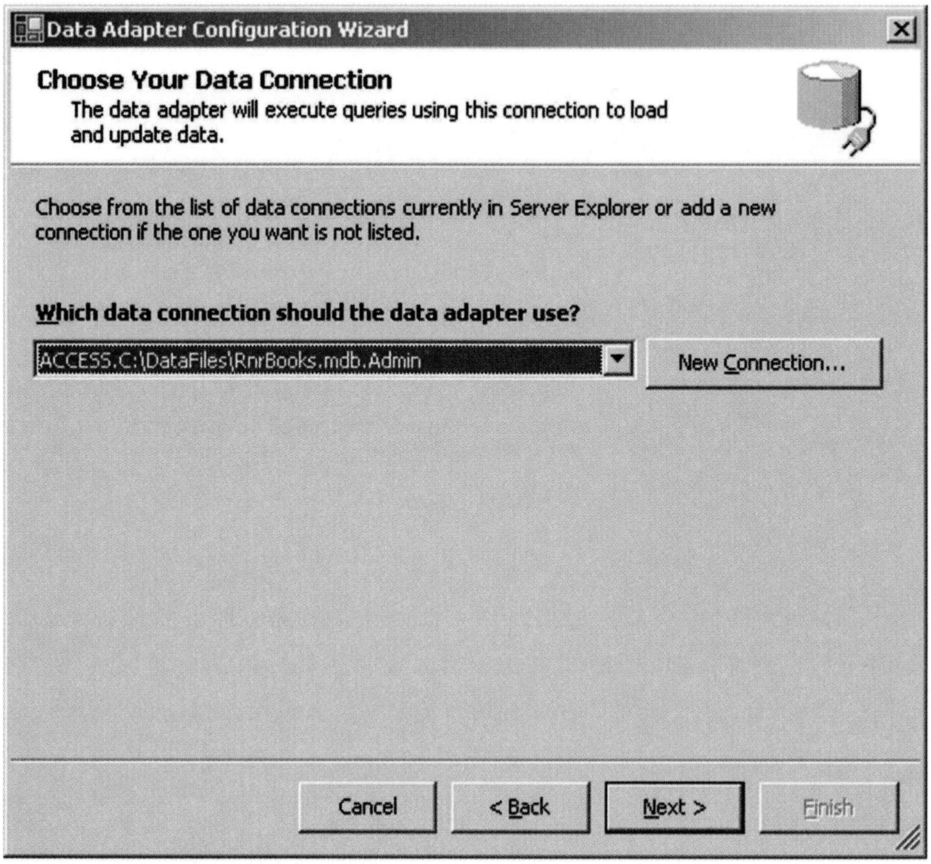

On the next screen of the wizard you have only one choice (Figure 10.11) unless you are using an SQLServer database. A data adapter can select the data from a database using an SQL statement or stored procedures. Stored procedures are prewritten SQL statements stored in the database and are not available in an Access database. Notice that the wizard screen tells you that you create the SQL statement to load the data and that the wizard will create SQL statements to perform the updates.

Figure 10.11

The third screen of the wizard provides only one choice when you are configuring a data adapter for an Access database.

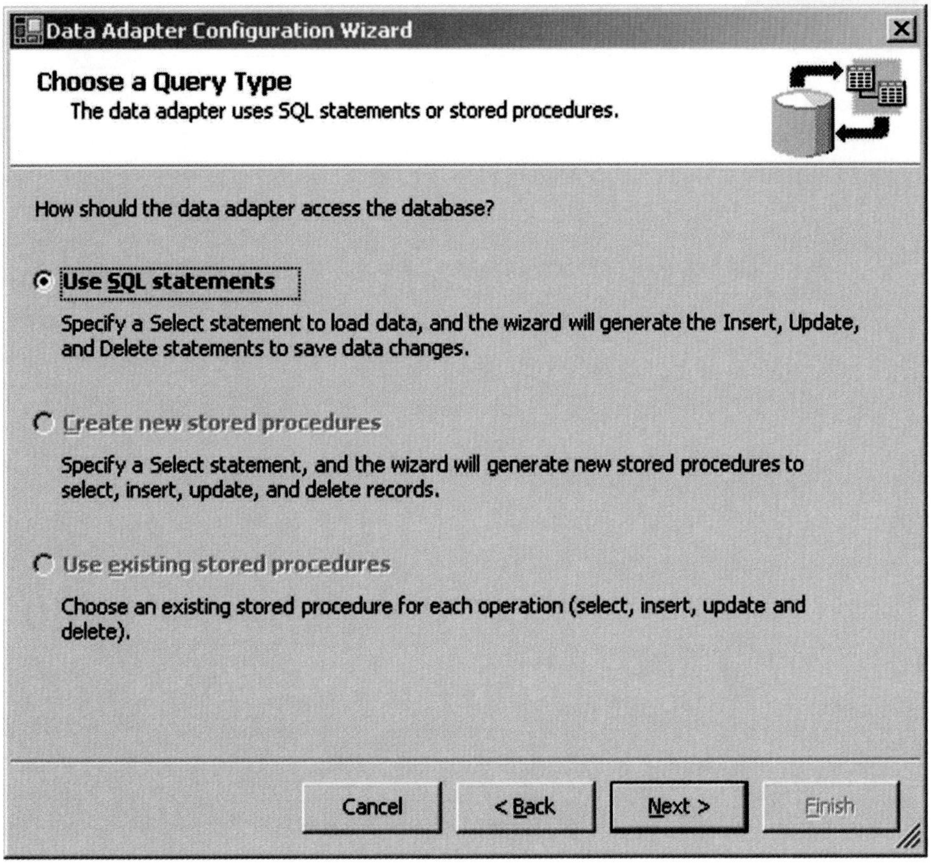

What appears on the next screen of the wizard depends on how you created the data adapter. If you dragged a table name or field names from the Server Explorer, an SQL Select statement appears in the window (Figure 10.12). If you created the data adapter by adding a control from the toolbox, you will have to write the SQL Select statement.

Figure 10.12

If the SQL Select statement does not appear automatically, you can enter it directly or click on Query Builder *to build the statement.*

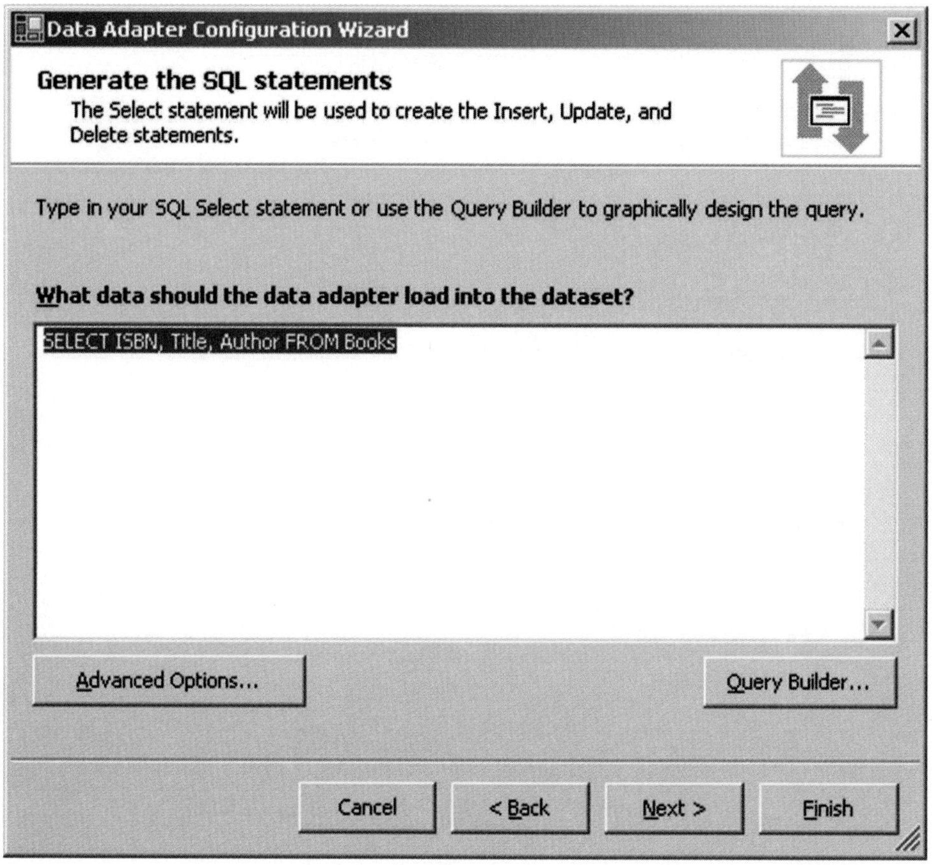

SQL, or Structured Query Language, is an industry-standard language that is used to select and update data in a relational database. But don't worry if you don't know SQL: You can use the built-in Query Builder to write the statement for you.

If you need help with the SQL Select statement, click on the Query Builder button. The Query Builder resembles the Query Builder in Access. Select the table(s) that you want and then select the fields that you want (Figure 10.13). The Query Builder generates the necessary SQL to select the data.

Figure 10.13

The Query Builder can generate an SQL Select statement for you. Select the table(s) and field(s) that you want to include.

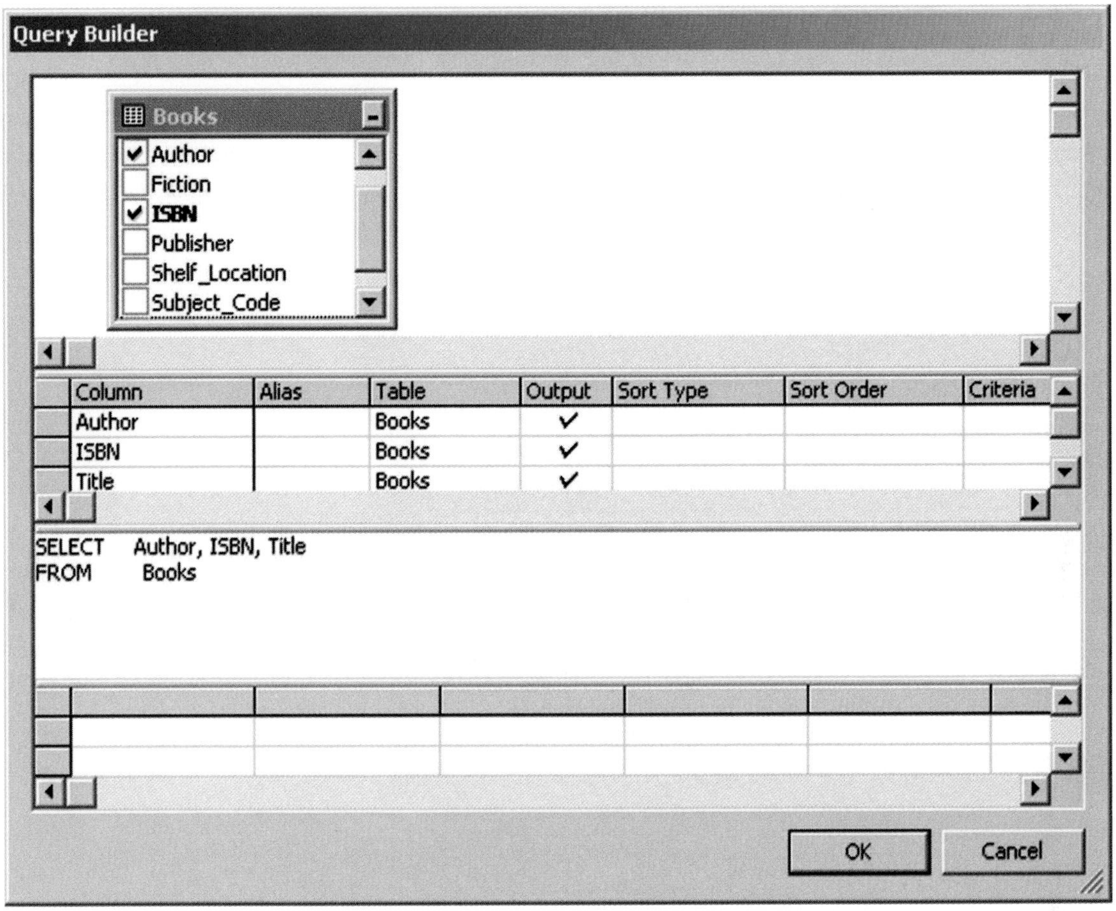

After you enter the SQL Select statement, you are finished configuring the data adapter. The next step is to set up the dataset.

Defining a Dataset

A **dataset** is a temporary set of data stored in the memory of the computer. In ADO.NET, datasets are disconnected, which means that the copy of data in memory does not keep an active connection to the data source. This technique is a big improvement from the recordsets in previous versions of ADO, which maintain open connections to the data source. A dataset may contain multiple tables; however, the examples in this chapter use only one table per dataset.

- ADO.NET uses datasets rather than recordsets. A dataset can hold multiple tables and relationships. The old recordset is more like one of the tables inside a dataset than like the dataset itself.

- Datasets are disconnected. After the dataset is retrieved from the database, the connection is no longer active. However, if you explicitly opened the connection, you should close it to release the resources.

- You don't generally create a dataset with an SQL Join statement, which creates one complete record for each of the detail records (the *many* side of the relationship). Instead the dataset holds each of the tables and the relationships and can display hierarchical data. Note that this introductory text uses only a single table for a dataset; the advanced text will work with related tables.

To define a dataset, select the OleDbAdapter control. Then select *Gener-ate Dataset* from the *Data* menu or right-click and select from the shortcut menu. In the *Generate Dataset* dialog that opens, name the dataset using "ds" as the prefix (Figure 10.14).

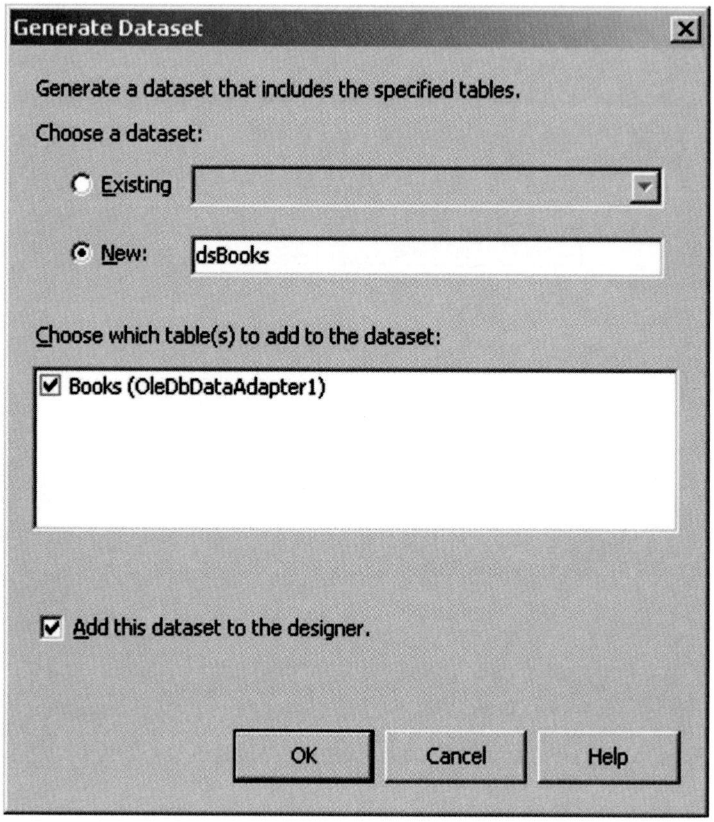

Figure 10.14

In the Generate Dataset dialog box, name the dataset.

When your program runs, you must write code to fill the dataset. This actually opens the connection to the data source and retrieves the data into the dataset. Any controls that you have bound to the dataset will automatically fill with data. Figure 10.15 shows how data passes from the data source to the dataset to the user interface.

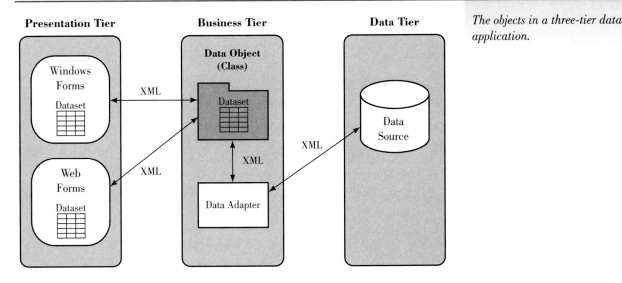

Figure 10.15

The objects in a three-tier data application.

The Fill Method

To fill the dataset at run time, you must execute the `Fill` method of the data adapter. You will generally add this method to the Form_Load event procedure or Page_Load for Web projects. There are several formats for the `Fill` method; we are going to use one that specifies only the dataset name.

The Fill Method—General Form

> **General Form**
>
> ```
> DataAdapterName.Fill(DataSetName)
> ```

The Fill Method—Example

> **Example**
>
> ```
> dbRnR.Fill(DsBooks1)
> ```

Binding Data to Controls

To bind a dataset to controls, you just set a few properties of the controls. If you are binding to a grid, as in our first step-by-step example, you set the grid's DataSource property to the name of the dataset and the DataMember property to the name of the table. Later in the chapter you'll bind individual fields to controls, such as labels and text boxes. In this case, you will set the DataBindings property of each control to the correct dataset field.

- You can display data in bound controls on a Windows Form simply by setting properties of the controls and calling the *Fill* method of the data adapter.

- Web Forms can display data in bound fields or grids. You must use the *BindData* method in code to actually bind the controls.

- Web Forms are static pages and do not retain data. Each time a page is displayed the dataset is re-created.

➤ **Feedback 10.2**

Explain the purpose of and the differences between *connections*, *data adapters*, and *datasets*.

Creating a Database Application

In the following step-by-step tutorial, you will create a Web application that displays data from the Books table of the RnRBooks.mdb Access database file. You will select only a few of the fields from the table and display them in a DataGrid control on a Web Form. With only a couple of exceptions, the same procedures work for a Windows application; in those cases the differences are noted.

Creating a Bound DataGrid Control—Step-by-Step

Make sure that you have the RnRBooks.mdb file available before you begin the step-by-step tutorial. If you copy the file from CD to disk, make sure to remove the ReadOnly attribute from the file.

• The DataGrid control is all new in VB .NET.

Begin the Project

STEP 1: Begin a new Visual Basic project using the ASP.NET Web Application template. Name your application *Ch10SBS* by changing the location to http://localhost/Ch10SBS.

Note: You can also create a Windows application following most of these same instructions.

STEP 2: Select the solution in the Project Explorer (the top line labeled `Solution`) and select `File/Save Ch10SBS.sln As`. Browse to find the folder `C:\Inetpub\wwwroot\Ch10SBS` and save your solution file. Note that this step is necessary only if you want to successfully move your project from one computer to another at a later time.

Set Up the Connection

• The Server Explorer is a great help in managing database connections.

STEP 1: Display the Server Explorer, if necessary, by selecting `View/Server Explorer`.

STEP 2: Click on the `Connect to Database` button in the Server Explorer.

STEP 3: In the `Data Link Properties` dialog, click on the `Provider` tab and select `Microsoft Jet 4.0 OLE DB Provider` (Figure 10.16). Then click `Next`.

Figure 10.16

Select the data provider for an Access database file.

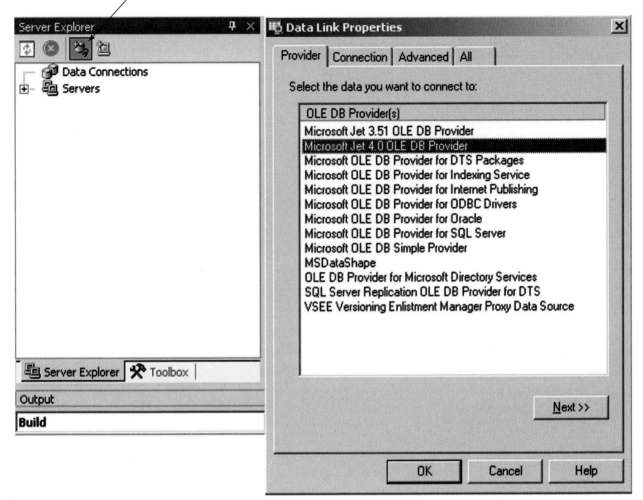

STEP 4: On the *Connection* tab, click the build button (...) and navigate to the folder with your RnRBooks.mdb file. Select the file and click on the *Open* button.

STEP 5: Click on *Test Connection* and you should see a message box indicating "Test connection succeeded." Click OK on the message box and also on the *DataLink Properties* dialog box.

STEP 6: In the Server Explorer, expand the nodes for the connection, the tables, and the Books table. You should see the fields in the Books table.

Add the Connection and Data Adapter to the Form

STEP 1: In the Server Explorer, hold down the Ctrl key and click to select the ISBN, Title, and Author fields (Figure 10.17).

Figure 10.17

Select the three desired fields in the Server Explorer.

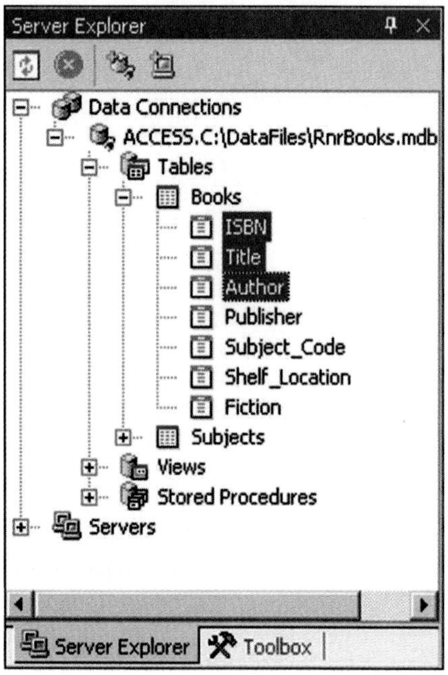

STEP 2: Drag the three selected fields from the Server Explorer to the form. A new connection and data adapter will appear in the component tray.

Check and/or Modify the Data Adapter's SQL

STEP 1: Click somewhere away from the two new controls in the component tray to deselect them. Then right-click on the OleDbDataAdapter1 control and select *Configure Data Adapter* (or select the option from the *Data* menu). Note that the option does not appear if the connection object is also selected.

　　　The Data Adapter Configuration Wizard appears. Read the first screen and click *Next*.

STEP 2: Check out the wizard's Connection page. The connection that you just created should be selected. If more than one connection appears on the list, make sure the correct one is selected. Then click *Next*.

STEP 3: Click *Next* on the wizard's Choose a Query Type page. You can only choose *Use SQL statements* for an Access database.

STEP 4: Look at the Generate the SQL Statements page. Your SQL statement should be similar to Figure 10.18. You can change the SQL statement here or click on the *Query Builder* button to visually select the fields and build the SQL statement.

• The Query Builder is very similar to the Query Designer in Access.

Figure 10.18

You can enter or modify the SQL Select statement using the Data Adapter Configuration Wizard.

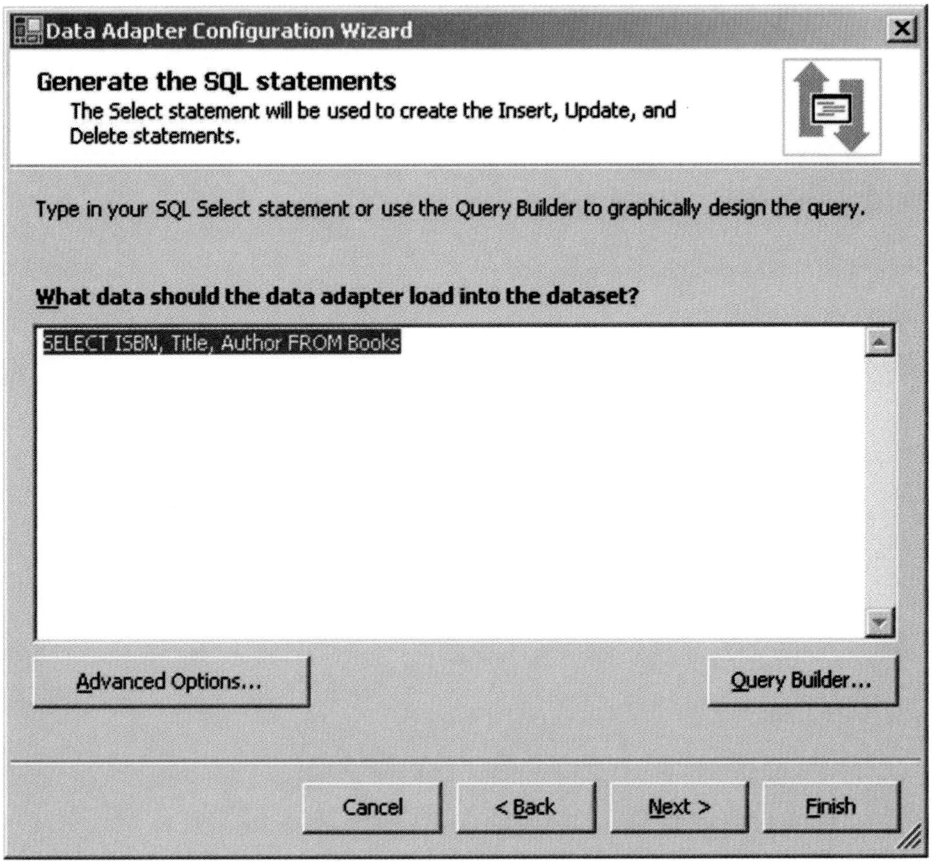

Note: In an SQL statement, the order of the selected fields, the capitalization, and the spacing are unimportant.

STEP 5: Click *Finish* when you are done.

Name the Adapter

At the bottom of your form you should have OleDbConnection1 and OleDbDataAdapter1. Since we are going to use the data adapter in code, it should have a nicer name. Use "db" as the prefix.

STEP 1: Select the OleDbDataAdapter1 control and in the properties window change the name to dbRnR.

STEP 2: Press Enter or Tab and make sure the change was made on the control.

Generate a Dataset

STEP 1: Select the dbRnR data adapter control and choose *Generate Dataset* from the *Data* menu or right-click and choose the item from the short-cut menu. In the *Generate Dataset* dialog box (Figure 10.19), name the new dataset *dsBooks* and click OK.

Name the new dataset in the Generate Dataset *dialog box.*

A new DataSet control is added to the component tray. Note in the Properties window that the control name is *DsBooks1*.

STEP 2: Watch the Solution Explorer as dsBooks.xsd is added. This is the schema for the new dataset.

STEP 3: Double-click on *dsBooks.xsd* to see the schema of the data.

STEP 4: The bottom of the window shows two tabs, one for DataSet and one for XML. Go ahead and take a peek at the XML tab and be grateful that it's all generated automatically. You can close the dsBooks.xsd window or click back on your Web Form.

Add a Data Grid

STEP 1: Make sure the Web Form is showing and display the toolbox with the Web Forms controls. Add a large DataGrid control to your form.

STEP 2: Set the ID property to *dbgBooks*.

STEP 3: Set the DataSource property to *DsBooks1*.

STEP 4: Set the DataMember to *Books*.

STEP 5: Set the DataKeyField to *ISBN*.

Write the Code

STEP 1: Double-click on the form to display the Editor window.

STEP 2: Type the following code in the Page_Load event procedure:

```
'Fill the dataset and bind the grid

dbRnR.Fill(DsBooks1)
dbgBooks.DataBind()
```

Note that in a Windows application, the second statement isn't necessary. The Windows DataGrid control is automatically bound when you set the design-time properties.

Run the Project

STEP 1: Run the project. The grid should fill with data from the database file.

STEP 2: Close the browser window to stop the application.

Modify the Grid Format

STEP 1: Switch back to your form in design view.

STEP 2: Right-click the grid and choose *Auto Format* from the shortcut menu. Select one of the formats and click OK.

STEP 3: Run the project again and admire your work. Not too bad for two lines of code, right? (The corresponding Windows application requires only one line of code.)

STEP 4: Stop the application.

Displaying a Data Preview

Sometimes it is helpful to see what your data looks like while you are designing the user interface. The .NET environment provides a `Data Adapter Preview` dialog to display a preview of a dataset. Select the data adapter control in the Design window and select `Data/Preview Data` (or right-click and select from the shortcut menu). In the dialog box make sure that your data adapter name displays in the Data Adapters list and click `Fill Dataset`. The data selected by the data adapter's SQL Select statement appears in the window (Figure 10.20). Note that you can resize the columns and scroll the window to see all of the data.

- You can preview the actual data in the database file.

TIP

You can change the data adapter's SQL Select statement by redisplaying the wizard. Select the data adapter and select `Configure Data Adapter` from the `Data` menu or the shortcut menu. ■

Figure 10.20

Display a preview of the dataset in the `Data Adapter Preview` *dialog box.*

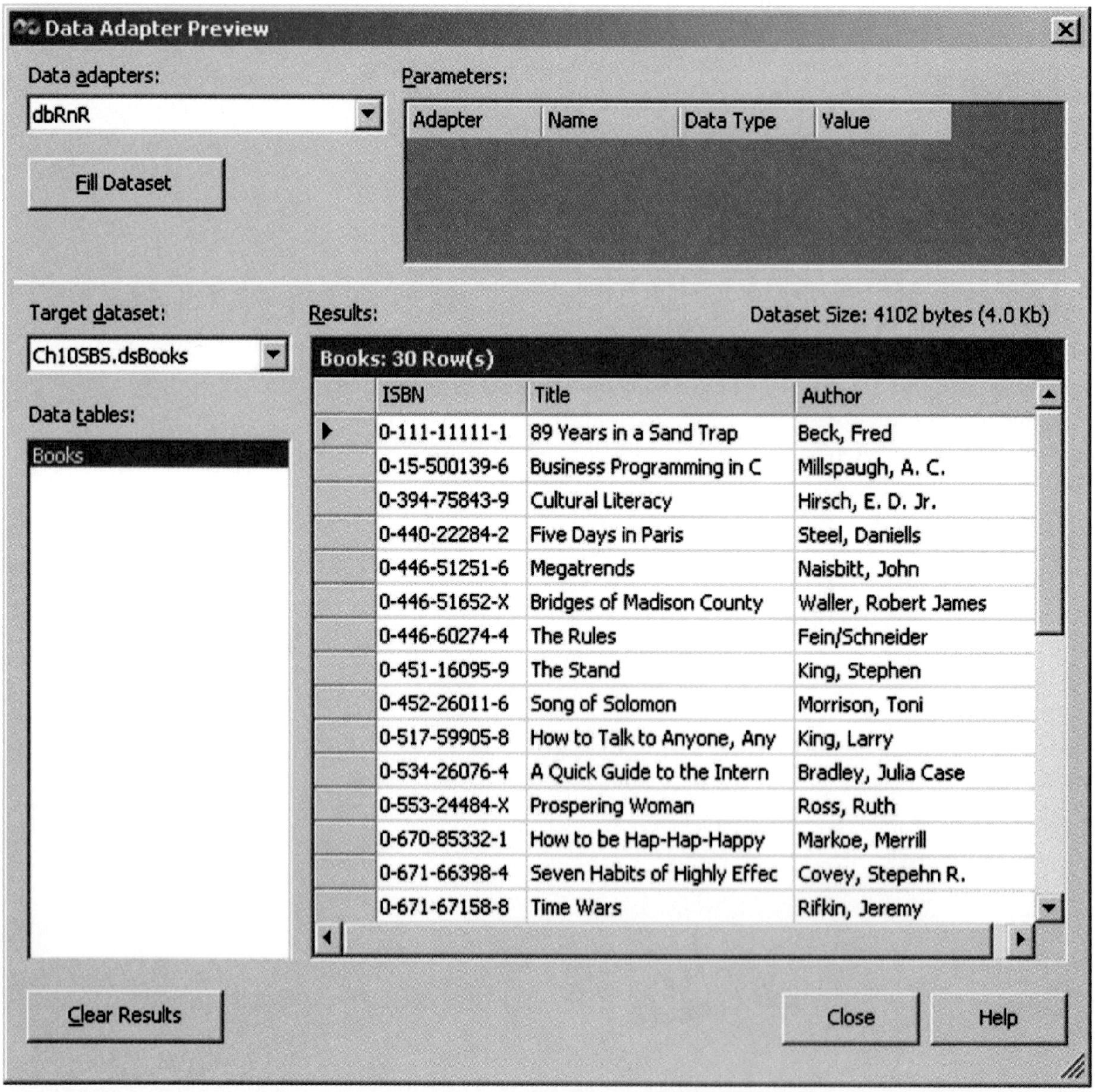

Data Adapter Preview
Data adapters:
dbRnR
Fill Dataset
Parameters:
Adapter
Name
Data Type
Value
Target dataset:
Ch10SBS.dsBooks
Data tables:
Books
Results:
Dataset Size: 4102 bytes (4.0 Kb)
Books: 30 Row(s)
ISBN
Title
Author
0-111-11111-1 89 Years in a Sand Trap Beck, Fred
0-15-500139-6 Business Programming in C Millspaugh, A. C.
0-394-75843-9 Cultural Literacy Hirsch, E. D. Jr.
0-440-22284-2 Five Days in Paris Steel, Daniells
0-446-51251-6 Megatrends Naisbitt, John
0-446-51652-X Bridges of Madison County Waller, Robert James
0-446-60274-4 The Rules Fein/Schneider
0-451-16095-9 The Stand King, Stephen
0-452-26011-6 Song of Solomon Morrison, Toni
0-517-59905-8 How to Talk to Anyone, Any King, Larry
0-534-26076-4 A Quick Guide to the Intern Bradley, Julia Case
0-553-24484-X Prospering Woman Ross, Ruth
0-670-85332-1 How to be Hap-Hap-Happy Markoe, Merrill
0-671-66398-4 Seven Habits of Highly Effec Covey, Stepehn R.
0-671-67158-8 Time Wars Rifkin, Jeremy
Clear Results
Close
Help

Binding Data

When you connect a control or property to one or more data elements, that is called *data binding*. ADO .NET has two forms of data bindings: simple binding and complex binding. You set the bindings in the form's Properties window.

Simple Data Binding

Simple binding connects one control to one data element. Use simple binding to display a field value in a control such as a text box or a label. You can also bind data elements to buttons, check boxes, radio buttons, picture boxes, and any other control that shows (*Data Bindings*) in the Properties window. In the next step-by-step example you will bind data elements to labels.

Complex Data Binding

If you need to bind more than one data element to a control, you need to use **complex binding**. This technique is used for the data grid control and for list boxes. Using complex binding, you set the control's DataSource and DataMember properties; and depending on the control-type, you may need to set more properties.

Using Data-Bound Labels

As mentioned previously, you can display data elements in individual controls. Using this technique you can display one record at a time. Each label or text box control is connected to a single field in a dataset. You can also add buttons for navigation, to display the previous or next record. Figure 10.21 shows the Windows form for the next step-by-step example.

• To bind a database field to a control, use the DataBindings property, which appears on the top of the Properties window. (You have to scroll the list up, above the Name property.)

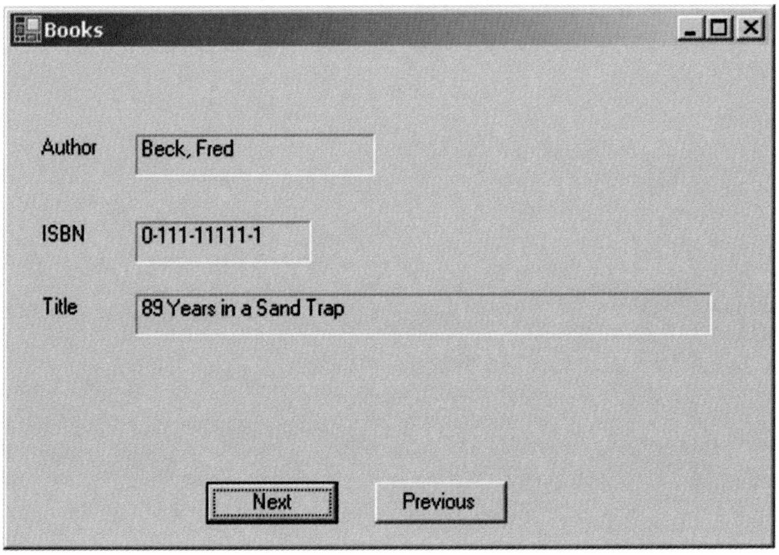

Figure   1 0 . 2 1

This Windows form displays fields for one record. Navigation buttons allow the user to move from one record to the next.

The process of binding labels and text boxes is similar for Web Forms and for Windows Forms. The differences are covered later in the chapter.

The following example demonstrates bound data with a Windows Form. One advantage of the Windows Form is that you can allow the user to scroll through the records without making another round-trip to the server.

Navigating through a Dataset

When you are using bound data on a Windows Form, you can refer to properties of the form's **BindingContext**. The current record position within the dataset is stored in the Position property. You can check the value of the Position property or change its value to move to a different record within the dataset. Adding 1 to the Position property makes the next record current; subtracting 1 from Position moves to the previous record. To move to the next record, the code is

```
Me.BindingContext(DsBooks1, "Books").Position + = 1
```

Similarly, to move the previous record use this code:

```
Me.BindingContext(DsBooks1, "Books").Position - = 1
```

The Position property is zero based. If you plan to use the Position as a record number, you will need to add 1:

```
intRecordPosition = Me.BindingContext(DsBooks1, _
  "Books").Position + 1
```

• There are no MoveNext, Move Previous methods. For navigation, use Me.BindingContext in a Windows Form. It's a bad idea to use navigation in a Web Form; the dataset is re-created for every post-back, and only the data for the selected record is sent with the page.

Retrieving the Record Count

You can retrieve the count of the number of records in the current dataset. You specify the dataset, name of the table, Rows collection, and Count property:

```
intRecordCount = DsBooks1.Tables("Books").Rows.Count
```

Each dataset has a Tables collection. You can specify the name of the table, as in the previous line of code, or specify the table by its index position. A single table is index zero:

```
intRecordCount = DsBooks1.Tables(0).Rows.Count
```

• You can still display record numbers and counts, but the numbers are not very meaningful since the dataset can be filtered and sorted.

Binding Data to Labels—Step-by-Step

This example creates the form shown in Figure 10.21. Each data element is bound to a label.

Begin a New Project

STEP 1: Begin a new project using the Windows Application template. Name the project *Ch10WindowsDataBoundControls*.

Set Up the Data Adapter and Dataset

STEP 1: If you are using the same computer as for the previous example, the Server Explorer should still show the connection. If no connection appears in the Server Explorer, click on the `Connect to Database` button and set up the connection, following the instructions in the DataGrid step-by-step.

STEP 2: In the Server Explorer, expand the nodes to see the fields in the Books table. Select ISBN, Title, and Author.

STEP 3: Drag the selected fields to the form to create the connection and data adapter controls.

STEP 4: Select the data adapter control and generate the dataset, calling it *dsBooks*.

STEP 5: Name the data adapter control *dbRnR*.

Add the Label and Button Controls

STEP 1: Referring to Figure 10.21, add three labels to the form. Set the Text property values to *Author*, *ISBN*, and *Title*.

STEP 2: Add three labels next to the previous ones, naming them *lblAuthor*, *lblISBN*, and *lblTitle*. Change the BorderStyle property of the labels to *Fixed3D*.

STEP 3: Add two buttons named *btnPrevious* and *btnNext*. Use Next and Previous for the Text values or use > and <.

STEP 4: Change the Text Property of the form to *Books*.

Bind the Data Fields

STEP 1: Select *lblAuthor* and expand the DataBindings property at the top of the Properties window. Select *Text* and then expand *DsBooks1* until you see a list of fields. Double-click on *Author*. (Or you can select *Author* and press Enter.)

STEP 2: Set the DataBindings Text property to *ISBN* for *lblISBN*.

STEP 3: Set the DataBindings Text property to *Title* for *lblTitle*.

• It's easy to miss the Data Bindings properties. Scroll all the way to the top of the Properties list.

Write the Code

STEP 1: Code the Form_Load event procedure.

```
'Fill the data set

dbRnR.Fill(DsBooks1)
```

STEP 2: Code the btnNext_Click event procedure.

```
'Display next record

Me.BindingContext(DsBooks1, "Books").Position + = 1
```

STEP 3: Code the btnPrevious_Click event.

```
'Display previous record

Me.BindingContext(DsBooks1, "Books").Position - = 1
```

Run the Project

STEP 1: Run the project. Try the Next and Previous buttons. What happens when you get to the last record?

STEP 2: Stop execution by closing the form.

STEP 3: Adjust the label sizes if necessary.

Question: How many lines of code did it take to write an application to browse through a database?

Display the Record Position

Another nice touch is to display the record number. However, you must be aware that the records in a dataset may be filtered or sorted, so the record numbers are subject to change.

STEP 1: Add a label named *lblRecordNumber* to the Form.

STEP 2: Code a procedure for displaying the record number.

```
Private Sub DisplayRecordPosition()
    'Display the record position and number of records
    Dim intRecordCount As Integer
    Dim intRecordPosition As Integer

    intRecordCount = DsBooks1.Tables("Books").Rows.Count
    If intRecordCount = 0 Then
        lblRecordNumber.Text = "(No records)"
    Else
        intRecordPosition = Me.BindingContext(DsBooks1, "Books").Position + 1
        lblRecordNumber.Text = "Record " & intRecordPosition.ToString _
         & " of " & intRecordCount.ToString
    End If
End Sub
```

STEP 3: Call the new procedure from the Form_Load and the click events for btnNext and btnPrevious.

```
'Program:        Ch10WindowsBoundControls
'Programmer:     Bradley/Millspaugh
'Date:           Jan 2002
'Description:    Display book information in labels; includes navigation and a record
                     count.
'Folder:         Ch10WindowsBoundControls

Option Strict On

Private Sub frmBooks_Load(ByVal sender As System.Object, _
 ByVal e As System.EventArgs) Handles MyBase.Load
    'Fill the dataset

    dbRnR.Fill(DsBooks1, "Books")
    DisplayRecordPosition()
End Sub

Private Sub DisplayRecordPosition()
    'Display the record number and number of records
    Dim intRecordCount As Integer
    Dim intRecordPosition As Integer

    intRecordCount = DsBooks1.Tables("Books").Rows.Count
    If intRecordCount = 0 Then
        lblRecordNumber.Text = "(No records)"
    Else
        intRecordPosition = Me.BindingContext(DsBooks1, "Books").Position + 1
        lblRecordNumber.Text = "Record " & intRecordPosition.ToString _
            & " of " & intRecordCount.ToString
    End If
End Sub
```

```
Private Sub btnPrevious_Click(ByVal sender As System.Object, _
 ByVal e As System.EventArgs) Handles btnPrevious.Click
    'Display previous record

    Me.BindingContext(DsBooks1, "Books").Position -= 1
    DisplayRecordPosition()
End Sub

Private Sub btnNext_Click(ByVal sender As System.Object, _
 ByVal e As System.EventArgs) Handles btnNext.Click
    'Display next record

    Me.BindingContext(DsBooks1, "Books").Position += 1
    DisplayRecordPosition()
End Sub
```

STEP 4: Run the program and test the record number code.

▶ Feedback 10.3

What properties of a Label control must be set to bind the control to a data field?

Populating Combo Boxes with Data

Many applications allow the user to select an item to display from a list. You can fill a list box or combo box with values from a database. Consider the previous example with book titles. A better approach might be to display the list of titles in a drop-down list and allow the user to make a selection. Then, after the title is selected, the corresponding data elements fill the Author and ISBN fields.

You can use any of the toolbox list controls to automatically fill with values. For Windows Forms, use the ListBox or ComboBox control; for Web Forms, use the ListBox or DropDownList. These controls have the necessary properties to bind to a data source. However, the programming for Windows controls differs from that of Web controls. First we will cover the Windows version, and then show the techniques required for the Web version.

Filling a List—Windows Forms

To automatically fill a list box or combo box with data from a dataset (Figure 10.22), you must set two properties: the DataSource and DisplayMember properties. The DataSource connects to the data adapter. The DisplayMember connects to the specific field name for the data that you want to display in the list.

• The properties for binding to a list are changed. The DisplayMember property determines the data to display in the list.

Figure 10.22

Automatically fill a drop-down list with the field values from a dataset.

Book Lookup

Title: 89 Years in a Sand Trap

- 89 Years in a Sand Trap
- Business Programming in C
- Cultural Literacy
- Five Days in Paris
- Megatrends
- Bridges of Madison County
- The Rules
- The Stand

ISBN

Author

After you add a list box to a form that has a dataset defined, drop down the Properties list for the DataSource and select the data adapter name. Then drop down the list for the DisplayMember property; it will show the field names in the dataset so that you can select. For example, for the combo box shown in Figure 10.22, the DataSource is set to *DsTitles1* (the data adapter) and the DisplayMember property is set to *Books.Title* (the table and field name). That's all there is to it. When you run your program, the list automatically fills with the values from the selected field.

You must still use the `Fill` method for the dataset, just as you do for filling grids and individual fields.

```
'Fill the dataset for the list box

dbTitles.Fill(DsTitles1)
```

TIP

If you have duplicate entries in a list box, modify the SQL Select statement to include the keyword DISTINCT, such as SELECT DISTINCT Author FROM Books. ■

Using Multiple Data Adapters

When you need more than one dataset or more than one table in a dataset, you can use multiple data adapters. A single Connection object can supply the connections for multiple data adapters.

For the list box example (Figure 10.23), you will likely need two data adapters: one for the elements in the list box and a second to generate a dataset with only the selected record. The information for the second dataset is unknown until run time; that is, which element the user selects from the list.

• Although a dataset can hold multiple tables and their relationships, Microsoft recommends one dataset (and one data adapter) per table.

Figure 10.23

Allow the user to select a book title from the drop-down list; then display the corresponding Author and ISBN for the selected title.

Creating a Parameterized Query

When you want your dataset to contain only selected record(s), you can modify the SQL Select statement used by the data adapter. A Where clause in an SQL query specifies which records to select.

Examples:

```
SELECT Title, Author, ISBN FROM Books
    WHERE Title = "A Midsummer Night's Dream"
SELECT Name, AmountDue FROM OverdueAccounts
    WHERE AmountDue > 100
```

Usually you don't know until run time the value that you want to include in the Where clause. In that case, you can use a question mark in place of the actual value and supply the value as a parameter in code. This type of query is called a ***parameterized query***.

```
SELECT Title, Author, ISBN FROM Books
    WHERE Title = ?
```

Recall that the SQL Select statement is part of the data adapter configuration. You can either type the Select statement yourself or use the Query Builder to create it for you. Select the data adapter and choose *Data/Configure Data Adapter* to open the wizard. On the fourth page of the wizard, select *Query Builder*. If necessary, add the Books table and click to select the desired fields (Author, ISBN, and Title, in this case). For the Title, type " = ?" in the **Criteria** column (Figure 10.24). The Query Builder creates the correct SQL for you. Note that the Query Builder adds the optional parentheses around "(Title = ?)", even when you leave them out.

F i g u r e   1 0 . 2 4

Using the Query Designer, enter " =?" as the criterion for Title to create a parameterized query.

Displaying the Data for a Selected Item

You supply the value for a parameterized query at run time. The user may enter a value in a text box or, better yet, select an item from a list, as in the previous list box example. For a list box selection, write your code in the control's SelectedIndexChanged event procedure.

> • Use the new SelectedIndexChanged event of list boxes and combo boxes to indicate that a selection was made from the list.

Specify the parameter value using the Parameters collection of the data adapter's SelectCommand property. You assign the value from the combo box or list box to a specific parameter.

```
dbRnR.SelectCommand.Parameters("Title").Value = cboTitles.Text
```

You must assign the parameter value before executing the Fill method. Notice also in the following code example that you clear out any previous contents of the dataset when you create the new dataset.

```
Private Sub cboTitles_SelectedIndexChanged(ByVal sender As System.Object, _
  ByVal e As System.EventArgs) Handles cboTitles.SelectedIndexChanged
    'Get the record to match the selected title

    DsBooks1.Clear()
    dbRnR.SelectCommand.Parameters("Title").Value = cboTitles.Text
    dbRnR.Fill(DsBooks1)
End Sub
```

If you have the user enter a value into a text box instead of selecting from a list, you must watch out for entries that don't exist in the dataset. Include a button for the event such as "Find". Then in the Find button's event procedure, check for an empty dataset after the Fill method.

```
Private Sub btnFind_Click(ByVal sender As System.Object, _
  ByVal e As System.EventArgs) Handles btnFind.Click
    'Get record to match the selected title

    DsBooks1.Clear()
    dbRnR.SelectCommand.Parameters("Title").Value = txtTitle.Text
    dbRnR.Fill(DsBooks1)
    If DsBooks1.Tables("Books").Rows.Count = 0 Then
        MessageBox.Show("Title not found.")
    End If
End Sub
```

You don't need to check for an unmatched value when the user selects from a combo box because all elements are known to be in the database.

Using Web Forms

You must take a few more steps when programming for the Web. This is mostly due to the nature of Web pages in a client/server environment. Remember that a Web page is stateless. Each time a page displays, it is a "new fresh page." The page's Load event occurs for every round-trip to the server, which happens more often than you might think.

In the Web version of the list selection program (see Figure 10.23), each time the user makes a selection from the list, a postback occurs. A **postback** is a round-trip to the server. After a postback, the Web page redisplays and the Page_Load event occurs. You must modify the logic in the Page_Load event procedure; otherwise the dataset for the list elements will be re-created and the selection that the user made will be lost. The page's IsPostBack property is set to False the first time the page displays and True every time after the first.

- Web Forms work completely differently from Windows Forms. Unless you check for postback, you will regenerate the same dataset and lose the user's list selection.

```
Private Sub Page_Load(ByVal sender As System.Object, _
  ByVal e As System.EventArgs) Handles MyBase.Load
    'Create the dataset and fill the drop-down list

    If Not IsPostBack Then          'Fill list only the first time the page displays
        dbTitles.Fill(DsTitles1)
        cboTitles.DataBind()
    End If
End Sub
```

The Web version of the list-selection program requires one more change. In the Windows version, as soon as the user makes a selection from the list, the list control's SelectedIndexChanged event occurs. But in the Web version, making a selection from the list does not cause a postback (and an immediate event) to occur unless you set another property. At design time, change the list control's AutoPostBack property to True. Then when the user selects from the list, a postback occurs and the SelectedIndexChanged event procedure executes.

Notice that you must also write code to bind the labels to the newly created dataset.

Web Version

```
Private Sub cboTitles_SelectedIndexChanged(ByVal sender As System.Object, _
  ByVal e As System.EventArgs) Handles cboTitles.SelectedIndexChanged
    'Display related information for ISBN and Author

    If cboTitles.SelectedIndex <> -1 Then       'A selection is made
        dbRnR.SelectCommand.Parameters("Title").Value = cboTitles.SelectedItem.Text
        dbRnR.Fill(DsBooks1)                     'Retrieve dataset for matching record
        lblISBN.DataBind()                       'Bind labels to data fields
        lblAuthor.DataBind()
    End If
End Sub
```

Feedback 10.4

1. What properties of a ListBox or ComboBox control must be set to fill the list with data automatically?
2. In what event procedure do you write the code to find the selected item and fill the bound controls?

Making a Database Project Portable

If you need to move database projects from one computer to another, you must modify the connection information. Of course, you must have the database file available on the new computer, and you must create a connection to the file.

When you know that you must move a project, store the database file in the same folder with your project. Then when you copy the project folder, you will also have the data file.

For a Windows Project

- Move the project folder, including the solution file and the database file, to the new computer.
- Open the project and the Server Explorer.
- In the Server Explorer, click on the *Connect to Database* button and create a new connection for the database file in your project folder.
- Display your form in Design view and select the icon for your OleDbConnection1 component in the component tray.
- Select the ConnectionString property in the Properties window and drop down the list in the Settings box. All of the connections on that machine will appear, including the new one you just added. Select your new connection.

- If you have more than one connection component, modify each to use the new connection.

For a Web Project

- Follow the steps from Chapter 9 (p. 389) for moving a Web project. That is, place the project folder in Inetpub\wwwroot and either create a virtual directory or Web-Share the folder.

- Set the ConnectionString property of the connection object as shown in the steps above for a Windows project.

Advanced Topic—Updating a Dataset

With some extra programming, you can allow the user to add records, edit records, and delete records from a dataset. You will need to display the dataset fields in bound text boxes, rather than labels, so that the user can type in changes.

Remember that a dataset is a temporary set of data in memory, disconnected from the original data source. The user can make changes to the data in the dataset, but those changes are not transferred to the original data source until you execute the Update method of the data adapter. You can choose to execute the Update method after every change, or once when the program terminates, which is the technique used in the example program that follows. Figure 10.25 shows the form for the update example.

- In ADO.Net you can work with a database in two ways, using a dataset or writing code and a DataReader to work directly with the database.

- With a data adapter you can make the changes in the dataset and then write the changes back to the data source.

- The SQL statements for the data adapter are automatically generated and executed when the Update method for the dataset is executed. For the OleDbDataAdapters, the parameters are determined by sequence; for SQLDataAdapters, the parameters are by name.

Figure 10.25

The form for the update program. The Save button is enabled when an Add or an Edit is in progress. In both of those procedures, the text on the Add button changes to "Cancel" and the navigation buttons are disabled.

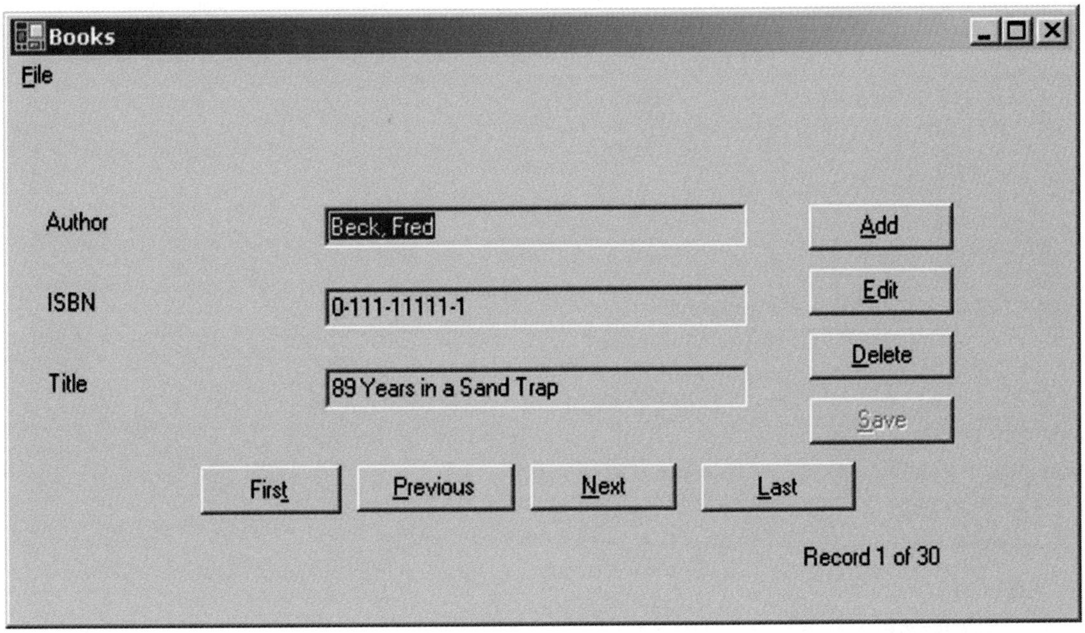

The Update Method

The Update method of the data adapter saves the changes from the dataset to the original data source.

The Update Method—General Form

General Form
`DataAdapter.Update(dataset, "table")`

The Update Method—Example

Example
`dbRnR.Update(DsBooks1, "Books")`

- When the user makes changes to the values in bound controls, the changes transfer to the dataset automatically. However, the dataset is disconnected from the original data source. You must execute the Update method to write the changes back to the data source.

- The Update method automatically loops through the records in a table to determine what update is needed (update, insert or delete) and then performs the appropriate SQL command.

- If no change has been made to a row (determined by the DataRow.RowState), then no SQL statement is sent.

- The return value of the Update is the number of records affected by the operation; if the operation fails a zero is returned.

The best place to code the Update method is in the form's Closing event procedure. The Closing event occurs when Me.Close executes, which happens whether the user closes using a menu command or clicks the form's Close button.

We want to ask the user whether to save the dataset only when changes have been made, so we will add a module-level Boolean variable to indicate that at least one change has been made. The industry-standard term for data that has been modified is *dirty*. Place the following statement in the declarations section at the top of the code and then set the variable to True in each procedure that allows changes.

```
'Declarations section
Dim mblnIsDirty As Boolean 'Indicate whether changes have been made to the dataset

    Private Sub frmBooks_Closing(ByVal sender As Object, _
      ByVal e As System.ComponentModel.CancelEventArgs) Handles MyBase.Closing
        'Save the changes
        If mblnIsDirty Then
            If MessageBox.Show("Do you want to save the changes?", "Books", _
              MessageBoxButtons.YesNo, MessageBoxIcon.Question) = DialogResult.Yes Then
                Try
                    dbRnR.Update(DsBooks1, "Books")
                Catch
                    MessageBox.Show("Error saving the file", "Books")
                End Try
            End If
        End If
    End Sub
```

The Logic of an Update Program

An update program needs procedures to modify existing records (called *editing records*), delete records, and add new records. As mentioned earlier, these procedures modify the dataset in memory; the changes are saved in the original data source only when the Update method executes.

Make sure to enclose all statements that access the dataset in Try/Catch blocks. You don't want to allow the program to cancel with an exception.

Editing Records

You display the data fields in bound text boxes. An easy way to allow changes to the data would be to just allow the user to type in changes in the text boxes. Any changes made to bound fields are automatically saved in the dataset. However, this is considered a dangerous practice. Instead, set the ReadOnly property of each text box to True, which locks the text box.

When the user clicks the Edit button, set the ReadOnly property of each text box to False. You also should disable the navigation buttons so that the user cannot move off the record and automatically save any changes. The only choices the user should have during an edit should be Save or Cancel. Enable the Save button and change the Text property of the Add button to "Cancel".

If the user clicks Save, all you have to do is reverse the actions taken for Edit: Set the ReadOnly property of the text boxes to True, enable the navigation buttons, disable the Save button, set the Text property of the Add button back to "Add". Also set mblnIsDirty to True, indicating that a change has been made to a record.

• The Locked property of text boxes changes to the ReadOnly property.

Pseudocode to Begin an Edit

Unlock the text boxes.
Disable the navigation buttons.
Enable the Save button.
Change the Text property of the Add button to "Cancel".

Pseudocode to Save after an Edit

Lock the text boxes.
Enable the navigation buttons.
Disable the Save button.
Change the Text property of the Add button back to "Add".
Set blnIsDirty to True to indicate that a change has been made.

Canceling an Edit Operation

If the user clicks Cancel during an Edit operation, you are faced with a problem. In addition to all of the actions that you take for a Save, you must also replace the original values into the text boxes. Otherwise, any changes entered into the bound text boxes will be automatically saved to the dataset, even though the user selected Cancel. See the RejectChanges procedure in the program listing on page 441 for the code to replace the Text property of the text boxes with their original values.

Pseudocode to Cancel an Edit Operation

Lock the text boxes.
Enable the navigation buttons.
Disable the Save button.
Change the Text property of the Add button back to "Add".
Replace the Text property of the text boxes with their original values.

Deleting Records

To delete the current record, you execute the Delete method of the table's Rows collection. Also set mblnIsDirty to True, indicating that a change has been made to the dataset.

```
Dim intCurrentRecordNumber As Integer = Me.BindingContext(DsBooks1, "Books").Position
DsBooks1.Books.Rows(intCurrentRecordNumber).Delete()
mblnIsDirty = True
```

Pseudocode for a Delete Operation

Delete the current record.
Set mblnIsDirty to True to indicate that a change has been made.
Display the current record position (which has changed due to the delete).

Adding Records

The logic of an Add operation is more complicated than editing or deleting. The user must click an Add button to begin an Add operation. The program must clear the text boxes, unlock them, and allow the user to enter the data for the new record. Just as with an Edit, the user should have the choices Save and Cancel.

All records are added to the end of the table. You can modify the data adapter's SQL Select statement if you want the records to appear in ISBN order the next time the program runs:

```
SELECT Author, ISBN, Title FROM Books
    ORDER BY ISBN
```

The Add Button

The btnAdd_Click event procedure must perform the actions to begin an Add. And since we're changing the Text property of the Add button to "Cancel" during an Add or Edit, the procedure must also include the Cancel logic. Another module-level Boolean variable will be helpful, to indicate that an Add is in progress.

```
'Declarations section
Dim mblnAdding As Boolean          'Indicate that an Add is in progress
```

Pseudocode for the btnAdd_Click Event Procedure

If the button's Text is "Cancel" then

Lock the text boxes.
Enable the navigation buttons.
Disable the Save button.
Change the Text of the Add button back to "Add".
Reject changes (replace the text boxes with their previous contents).
Set mblnAdding to False

Else (the button's Text is "Add")

Unlock the text boxes.
Clear the text boxes.
Set the focus to the first text box.

Disable the navigation buttons.
Enable the Save button.
Change the Text of the Add button to "Cancel".
Set mblnAdding to True.

Saving an Added Record

After the user has entered the data for a new record and clicks the Save button, you must create a new row, set the row's fields to the text box values, and add the row to the table by using the Add method:

```
Dim newRow As DataRow = DsBooks1.Books.NewRow
newRow("Author") = txtAuthor.Text
newRow("ISBN") = txtISBN.Text
newRow("Title") = txtTitle.Text
DsBooks1.Books.Rows.Add(newRow)
```

The Save Button

The Save button is enabled for both Adds and Edits, so the logic of the Save button must determine which operation is in progress by checking the Boolean variable *mblnAdding*.

Pseudocode for the Save Button

If an Add is in progress
    Set up a new row.
    Add the new row to the dataset.
End If
'For saving both Adds and Edits
Lock the text fields.
Enable the navigation buttons.
Disable the Save button.
Set the Text of the Add button back to "Add".
Set mblnIsDirty to True, indicating that a change has been made.
Set mblnAdding to False, indicating that an Add is not in progress.

The Full Program

Remember that you should include error trapping in every procedure that accesses the dataset.

```
'File:          Ch10WindowsUpdate
'Programmer:    Bradley/Millspaugh
'Date:          Jan 2002
'Description:   Update book information in bound text boxes;
'               includes navigation, add, delete, and edit.
'Folder:        Ch10WindowsUpdate

Option Strict On

Public Class frmBooks
    Inherits System.Windows.Forms.Form

[Windows Form Designer generated code]
```

```vb
Dim mblnAdding As Boolean        'Indicate that an Add is in progress
Dim mblnIsDirty As Boolean       'Indicate whether changes have been made to the dataset

'**Form Event Procedures **

Private Sub frmBooks_Load(ByVal sender As System.Object, _
 ByVal e As System.EventArgs) Handles MyBase.Load
    'Fill the dataset

    dbRnR.Fill(DsBooks1)
    DisplayRecordPosition()
End Sub

Private Sub frmBooks_Closing(ByVal sender As Object, _
 ByVal e As System.ComponentModel.CancelEventArgs) Handles MyBase.Closing
    'Save the changes

    If mblnIsDirty Then
        If MessageBox.Show("Do you want to save the changes?", "Books", _
          MessageBoxButtons.YesNo, MessageBoxIcon.Question) = DialogResult.Yes Then
            Try
                    dbRnR.Update(DsBooks1, "Books")
            Catch
                    MessageBox.Show("Error saving the file", "Books")
            End Try
        End If
    End If
End Sub

Private Sub btnAdd_Click(ByVal sender As System.Object, _
 ByVal e As System.EventArgs) Handles btnAdd.Click
    'Begin an Add operation or cancel the current operation

    If btnAdd.Text = "&Cancel" Then        'Cancel an Add or Edit
        LockTextBoxes()
        EnableNavigation()
        btnSave.Enabled = False
        btnAdd.Text = "&Add"
        RejectChanges()
        mblnAdding = False
    Else        'Begin an Add operation
        UnlockTextBoxes()
        ClearText()
        txtAuthor.Focus()
        DisableNavigation()
        btnSave.Enabled = True
        btnAdd.Text = "&Cancel"
        lblRecordNumber.Text = ""
        mblnAdding = True
    End If
End Sub

Private Sub btnDelete_Click(ByVal sender As System.Object, _
 ByVal e As System.EventArgs) Handles btnDelete.Click
    'Delete the current row

    Try
        Dim intCurrentRecordNumber As Integer = Me.BindingContext(DsBooks1, _
          "Books").Position
```

```
            DsBooks1.Books.Rows(intCurrentRecordNumber).Delete()
            mblnIsDirty = True
            DisplayRecordPosition()
        Catch
            MessageBox.Show("Unable to delete the record", "Books")
        End Try
End Sub

Private Sub btnEdit_Click(ByVal sender As System.Object, _
 ByVal e As System.EventArgs) Handles btnEdit.Click
    'Allow editing to current record

    UnlockTextBoxes()
    DisableNavigation()
    btnSave.Enabled = True
    btnAdd.Text = "&Cancel"
End Sub

Private Sub btnFirst_Click(ByVal sender As System.Object, _
 ByVal e As System.EventArgs) Handles btnFirst.Click
    'Move to the first record

    Try
        Me.BindingContext(DsBooks1, "Books").Position = 0
        DisplayRecordPosition()
    Catch
        'Ignore any errors during navigation
    End Try
End Sub

Private Sub btnLast_Click(ByVal sender As Object, _
 ByVal e As System.EventArgs) Handles btnLast.Click
    'Move to the last record

    Try
        With Me.BindingContext(DsBooks1, "Books")
            .Position = .Count - 1
            DisplayRecordPosition()
        End With
    Catch
        'Ignore any errors during navigation
    End Try
End Sub

Private Sub btnNext_Click(ByVal sender As System.Object, _
 ByVal e As System.EventArgs) Handles btnNext.Click
    'Display the next record

    Try
        Me.BindingContext(DsBooks1, "Books").Position += 1
        DisplayRecordPosition()
    Catch
        'Ignore any errors during navigation
    End Try
End Sub

Private Sub btnPrevious_Click(ByVal sender As System.Object, _
 ByVal e As System.EventArgs) Handles btnPrevious.Click
    'Display the previous record
```

```
        Try
            Me.BindingContext(DsBooks1, "Books").Position -= 1
            DisplayRecordPosition()
        Catch
            'Ignore any errors during navigation
        End Try
End Sub

Private Sub btnSave_Click(ByVal sender As System.Object, _
 ByVal e As System.EventArgs) Handles btnSave.Click
    'Save the new record for an Add or Edit

    If mblnAdding Then        'Add in progress
        Try
            Dim newRow As DataRow = DsBooks1.Books.NewRow
            newRow("Author") = txtAuthor.Text
            newRow("ISBN") = txtISBN.Text
            newRow("Title") = txtTitle.Text
            DsBooks1.Books.Rows.Add(newRow)
        Catch exc As Exception
            MessageBox.Show("Unable to add the record." & _
              ControlChars.NewLine & exc.Message, "Books")
        End Try
        mblnAdding = False
        lblRecordNumber.Text = "Record added at the end of the table"
    End If

    'Actions to take to complete an Add or an Edit
    LockTextBoxes()
    EnableNavigation()
    btnSave.Enabled = False
    btnAdd.Text = "&Add"
    mblnIsDirty = True
End Sub

Private Sub mnuFileExit_Click(ByVal sender As System.Object, _
 ByVal e As System.EventArgs) Handles mnuFileExit.Click
    'End the program

    Me.Close()
End Sub

'*** General Procedures ***

Private Sub ClearText()
    'Clear text fields

    txtAuthor.Clear()
    txtISBN.Clear()
    txtTitle.Clear()
End Sub

Private Sub DisableNavigation()
    'Disable navigation buttons

    btnNext.Enabled = False
    btnPrevious.Enabled = False
    btnFirst.Enabled = False
    btnLast.Enabled = False
End Sub
```

```
    Private Sub DisplayRecordPosition()
        'Display the current record position and count
        Dim intRecordCount As Integer
        Dim intRecordPosition As Integer

        intRecordCount = DsBooks1.Tables("Books").Rows.Count
        intRecordPosition = Me.BindingContext(DsBooks1, "Books").Position + 1

        If intRecordCount = 0 Then
            lblRecordNumber.Text = "(No records)"
        Else
            lblRecordNumber.Text = "Record " & intRecordPosition.ToString & _
            " of " & intRecordCount.ToString
        End If
    End Sub

    Private Sub EnableNavigation()
        'Enable navigation buttons

        btnNext.Enabled = True
        btnPrevious.Enabled = True
        btnFirst.Enabled = True
        btnLast.Enabled = True
    End Sub

    Private Sub LockTextBoxes()
        'Change to ReadOnly

        txtAuthor.ReadOnly = True
        txtISBN.ReadOnly = True
        txtTitle.ReadOnly = True
    End Sub

    Private Sub RejectChanges()
        'Replace original value into bound screen fields
        Dim intRecordPosition As Integer = Me.BindingContext(DsBooks1, "Books").Position
        Dim curRow As DataRow = DsBooks1.Books.Rows(intRecordPosition)     'Current row

        Try
            txtAuthor.Text = curRow("Author", DataRowVersion.Original).ToString
            txtISBN.Text = curRow("ISBN", DataRowVersion.Original).ToString
            txtTitle.Text = curRow("Title", DataRowVersion.Original).ToString
        Catch
        End Try
    End Sub

    Private Sub UnlockTextBoxes()
        'Change the ReadOnly property

        txtAuthor.ReadOnly = False
        txtISBN.ReadOnly = False
        txtTitle.ReadOnly = False
    End Sub
End Class
```

Your Hands-On Programming Example

Create a Windows application that contains a drop-down list of titles from the RnRBooks.mdb database file. When the user selects a title, display the corresponding ISBN and author in labels. Include additional labels to identify the contents of the list box and the data fields.

Make the ISBN and Author labels appear empty until the user selects a title from the drop-down list.

Planning the Project

Sketch the form (Figure 10.26), which your users sign off as meeting their needs. Figure 10.27 shows the form in Design mode.

Figure 10.26

A planning sketch of the form for the hands-on programming example.

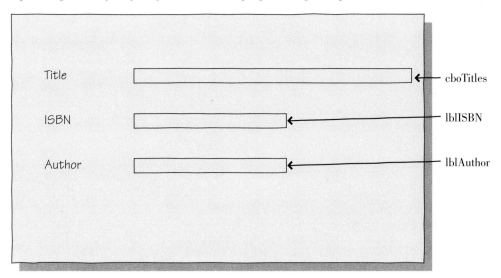

Figure 10.27

The form for the hands-on programming example in Design mode, showing the component tray.

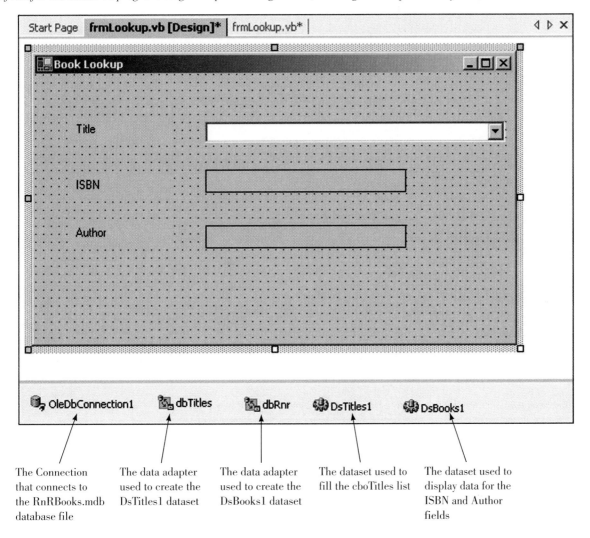

Plan the Objects and Properties

Object	Property	Setting
dbTitles (data adapter)	Name SelectCommand.CommandText	dbTitles SELECT Title, ISBN FROM Books
DsTitles1 (dataset)	Name	DsTitles1
dbRnR (data adapter)	Name SelectCommand.CommandText	dbRnR SELECT Author, ISBN, Title FROM Books WHERE (Title = ?)
DsBooks1 (dataset)	Name	DsBooks1

Continued on page 444

Object	Property	Setting
Label1	Text	Title
Label2	Text	ISBN
Label3	Text	Author
cboTitles	Name DataSource DisplayMember	cboTitles DsTitles1 (Fills list with the DsTitles1 dataset.) Books.Title (Displays field from the DsBooks1 dataset.)
lblISBN	Name Text DataBindings.Text	lblISBN (blank) Books.ISBN (Displays field from the DsBooks1 dataset.)
lblAuthor	Name Text DataBindings.Text	lblAuthor (blank) Books.Author (Displays field from the DsBooks1 dataset.)

Plan the Procedures

Procedure	Actions
Form_Load	Load the combo box with the Titles.
cboTitles_SelectedIndexChanged	Display the data related to the selected item.

Write the Project

- Create a new Windows project and move a copy of the data file to the project folder. Make sure that the data file is not ReadOnly.

- Create a connection to the data file and create two data adapters for the two datasets.

- Follow the sketch in Figure 10.26 and Figure 10.27 to create the form. Figure 10.28 shows the completed form.

- Set the properties of each of the objects according to your plan.

- Write the code. Working from the pseudocode, write each procedure.

- When you complete the code, thoroughly test the project.

Figure 10.28

The form for the hands-on programming example.

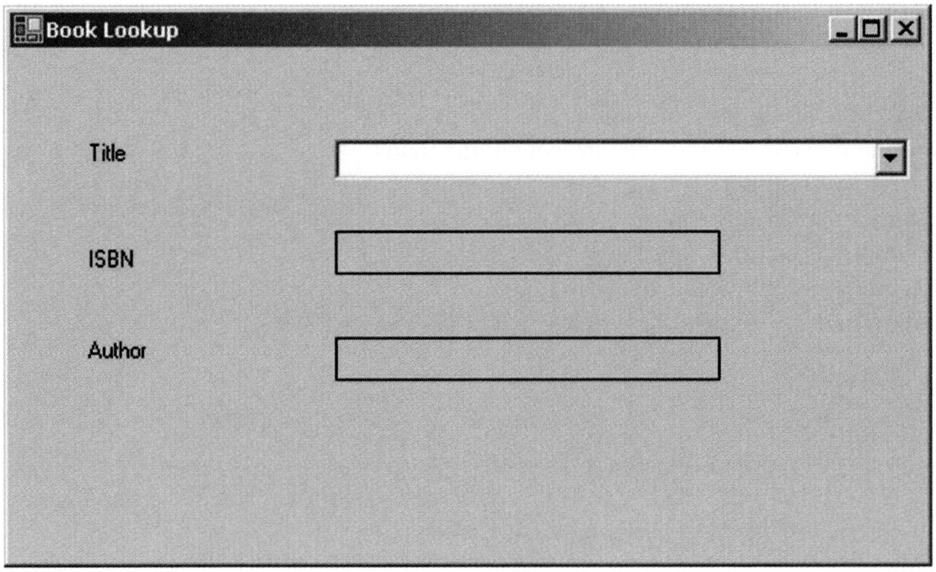

The Project Coding Solution

```
'Program:          Ch10HandsOnWindows
'Programmer:       Bradley/Millspaugh
'Date:             Jan 2002
'Description:       Display book information for the title selected from a list.
'Folder:           Ch10HandsOnWindowsForms

Option Strict On

Public Class frmLookup
    Inherits System.Windows.Forms.Form

[Windows Form Designer generated code]

    Private Sub cboTitles_SelectedIndexChanged(ByVal sender As System.Object, _
    ByVal e As System.EventArgs) Handles cboTitles.SelectedIndexChanged
        'Get record to match selected title

        DsBooks1.Clear()
        dbRnr.SelectCommand.Parameters("Title").Value = cboTitles.Text
        dbRnr.Fill(DsBooks1)
    End Sub

    Private Sub frmLookup_Load(ByVal sender As System.Object, _
    ByVal e As System.EventArgs) Handles MyBase.Load
        'Fill the list box

        dbTitles.Fill(DsTitles1)
    End Sub
End Class
```

Summary

1. Visual Studio .NET uses Microsoft's ADO.NET technology to access databases in many different formats.
2. ADO.NET provides two types of connections for databases: OLEDB and SQL Server.
3. Access databases are composed of tables of related information. Each table is organized into rows representing records and columns containing fields of data.
4. The key field uniquely identifies a row or record.
5. ADO.NET stores and transfers data using a format called *XML (Extensible Markup Language)*, which can be used by many different platforms.
6. Many controls can be bound to a database including labels, text boxes, list boxes, or a DataGrid.
7. A connection establishes a link to a data source, which is a specific data file or server.
8. A data adapter handles the transfer of data between a data source and a dataset.
9. A dataset stores information from the database in the memory of the computer. A dataset can contain multiple tables and their relationships.
10. You can create connections and data adapters by dragging table names or field names from the Server Explorer to the form.
11. A data adapter uses an SQL Select statement to specify the data to retrieve. You can write your own SQL Select statement or use the Query Designer in the Data Adapter Configuration Wizard.
12. The `Fill` method of the data adapter retrieves the data from the data source and fills the dataset.
13. Simple data binding connects one control to one data element while complex binding is needed for data lists and data grids.
14. To bind a grid to a data source, set the grid's DataSource property to the data adapter, the DataMember property to the name of the table, and the DataKeyField to the key field of the table.
15. For a Web Form application, you must execute the data adapter's `Fill` method and the grid's `DataBind` method. A Windows application does not use the `DataBind` method.
16. Use the form's BindingContext object to retrieve or change the current record number.
17. To bind a single control to a database field, set the control's DataBindings.Text field to the name of the field.
18. You can automatically fill a list box or combo box with the field values from a dataset. Set the DataSource property to the data adapter and the DisplayMember property to the name of the field that should display in the list.
19. A common approach is to allow the user to select a value from a list and then display the data values for the selected item in bound labels.
20. Multiple data adapters are needed when filling a list box and displaying data in bound controls.
21. A parameterized query is an SQL statement that contains a value to be supplied at run time.
22. When the user selects a value from a list box, display the data in the SelectedIndexChanged event procedure.

23. If the user enters a selection in a text box rather than selecting from a list for a parameterized query, code should be included to test for no records matching the criteria.

24. In Web applications, a list will be refilled automatically for every postback unless code is included in the Page_Load event procedure. Also, the AutoPostBack property of the list control must be set to True so that the SelectedIndexChanged event will fire when the user makes a selection.

25. When you move a database project to another computer, you must reset the connection used by the data adapter.

Key Terms

BindingContext   *424*
column   *400*
complex binding   *423*
connection   *403*
criteria   *430*
data adapter   *403*
data binding   *423*
dataset   *413*
field   *400*

key field   *400*
parameterized query   *429*
postback   *431*
record   *400*
row   *400*
simple binding   *423*
table   *400*
XML   *401*

Review Questions

1. Explain the purpose of a connection.
2. Explain the purpose of the data adapter control. How does a data adapter differ from a connection?
3. What is a dataset?
4. How is a data grid used?
5. Explain the steps to bind a single control, such as a label, to a field in a dataset.
6. Describe the steps necessary to display the position and record count for a single record.
7. Which properties must be set to bind a combo box to a field in a database and display a drop-down list of the choices for that field?
8. What is a parameterized query? When would it be used?
9. When would you need multiple data adapters on a form?
10. What is a postback? When does it occur?
11. How can you keep a Web application from re-creating the list data when a postback occurs?

Programming Exercises

Note: Each of these exercises can be written as a Windows application or a Web application. It isn't recommended to include record navigation in Web applications, however.

10.1 The Rnrbooks.mdb database file holds two tables: the Books table used in this chapter and the Subjects table. The Subjects table has only two fields: the Subject Code (the key) and the Subject Name. Write a project that displays the Subjects table in a grid.

10.2 Write a project to display the two fields in the Subjects table described in Programming Exercise 10.1. Display the field values in labels and include buttons for record navigation. Also display the record number and record count.

10.3 Write a project to display a list of the subject names in the Subjects table described in Programming Exercise 10.1. Use a drop-down combo box. Display the subject code for the name selected from the list in a label.

10.4 Write a project to display the Publishers table from the Biblio.mdb database from your StudentData folder on the text CD. The Publishers table has the following fields: PubID (the key field), Name, Company Name, Address, City, State, ZIP, Telephone, and Fax.

Display the data in labels and include buttons for record navigation.

10.5 Write a project using the Publishers table described in Programming Exercise 10.4. Display the Name field in a drop-down list. When the user selects a name, display the data for the rest of the fields in bound labels.

10.6 Complete one of the Programming Exercises 10.1, 10.3, or 10.5 as a Windows application. Then convert the project to a Web application.

Case Studies

VB Mail Order

1. Create a Windows application to display the VB Mail Order Customer table from the VbMail.mdb database on your student CD. Include buttons for Next and Previous, and display the record number and count.

2. Create a Web application to display the Customer table in a grid on a Web Form.

Fields
Customer ID
LastName
FirstName
Address
City
State
ZipCode

VB Auto Center

Create a Windows application or a Web application to display the VB Auto Center Vehicle table from the VbAuto.mdb database on your student CD. Create a drop-down combo box of manufacturers. Be sure to include each manufacturer only once. (*Hint*: Add DISTINCT to the SQL Select statement.)

Display the remaining fields in labels for the selected element.

Fields
InventoryID
Manufacturer
ModelName
Year
VehicleID
CostValue

Video Bonanza

1. Create a Windows application to display the information from the Studio table in the VBVideo.mdb database. Display the data in labels and include record navigation and the record number.

The Studio table contains these fields:

Studio ID
Studio Name
Contact Person
Phone

2. Create a Web application to display Studio table in a grid on a Web Form.

Very Very Boards

1. Create a Windows application to display the Product table from the VeryBoards.mdb database file on your student CD. Display the data in labels and include record navigation and the record number.

The Product table contains these fields:

ProductID
Description
MfgID
Unit
Cost
LastOrderDate
LastOrderQuantity

2. Create a Web application to display Product table in a grid on a Web Form.

11

Saving Data and Objects in Files

at the completion of this chapter, you will be able to . . .

1. Store and retrieve data in files using streams.

2. Save the values from a list box and reload for the next program run.

3. Check for the end of file.

4. Test whether a file exists.

5. Display the standard *Open File* dialog box to allow the user to choose the file.

6. Use serialization to store and retrieve objects.

Data Files

Many computer applications require that data be saved from one run to the next. Although the most common technique is to use a database, many times a database is overkill. Perhaps you just need to store a small amount of data, such as the date of the last program run, the highest ID number assigned, a user preference, or the property values of an object to transfer to another application. This chapter deals with techniques to store and retrieve **data files** on disk.

Note that default security policy for the Internet and for intranets does not allow access to disk files. This chapter presents only basic file input and output (I/O) for Windows applications.

- Data file handling is completely different from the old VB methods.

- Use streams for transfer of data.

- Microsoft is recommending strongly that applications not use the registry to store program state but instead have their own .ini or config file. You could use streams to create and read these files.

Data Files and Project Files

In computer terminology anything that you store on a diskette or hard disk is given its own unique name and called a *file*. Each of your Visual Basic projects requires multiple files—for the forms, code modules, assembly information, and project information. However, the files you will create now are different; they contain actual data, such as names and addresses, inventory amounts, and account balances.

Data File Terminology

The entire collection of data is called a ***file***. The file is made up of **records**— one record for each entity in the file. Each record can be broken down further into **fields** (also called data elements). For example, in an employee file, the data for one employee are one record. In a name and address file, the data for one person are a record.

In the name and address file, each person has a last name field, a first name field, address fields, and a phone number field. Each field in a record pertains to the same person. Figure 11.1 illustrates a name and address file.

Figure 11.1

The rows in this data file represent records; the columns represent fields.

Last Name	First Name	Street	City	State	Zip	Phone	Email
Maxwell	Harry	795 W. J Street	Ontario	CA	91764	909-555-1234	
Helm	Jennifer	201 Cortez Way	Pomona	CA	91766	818-555-2222	JHelm@ms.org
Colton	Craig	1632 Granada Place	Pomona	CA	91766	909-555-3333	

A record   A field

File Handling Using Streams

Visual Studio handles data files using streams. A **stream** is designed to transfer a series of bytes from one location to another. Streams are objects that have methods and properties, just like any other object. The stream objects are found in the **System.IO namespace.** Your file-handling project must contain an Imports statement before the statement declaring the form's class.

```
Imports System.IO

Public Class frmMyFileIO
    Inherits System.Windows.Forms.Form
```

• StreamReader and StreamWriter can easily handle lists of data; they work well for maintaining the contents of a list box.

File I/O

You can read and write data in a disk file. You may have the user enter data into text boxes that you want to store in a file; that is called *writing* or *output*. At a later time, when you want to retrieve the data from the file, that is *reading* or *input* (Figure 11.2).

Figure 11.2

Write output from a program to a file; read input from the file into a program.

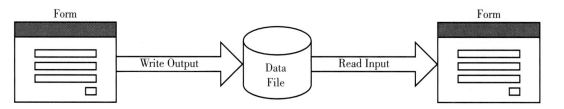

In VB, the simplest way to read and write small amounts of data is to use the **StreamReader** and **StreamWriter** objects. Generally, you write the StreamWriter code first, to create the data file. Then you can write the StreamReader code to read the file that you just created.

Writing Data

To write data to a file, you first have the user input the data into text boxes and then write the data to the disk. The steps for writing data are:

• Declare a new StreamWriter object, which also declares the name of the data file.

• Use the StreamWriter's WriteLine method to copy the data to a buffer in memory. (A buffer is just a temporary storage location.)

• Call the StreamWriter's Close method, which transfers the data from the buffer to the file and releases the system resources used by the stream.

Instantiating a StreamWriter Object—General Form

```
Dim ObjectName As New StreamWriter("FileName")
Dim ObjectName As New StreamWriter("FileName", BooleanAppend)
```

You declare a new StreamWriter object for writing data to a file. The first argument in the constructor specifies the name of the file. The default location for the file is the bin directory beneath the folder for the current project. You can also specify the complete path of the file.

In the second version of the StreamWriter constructor, you can specify that you want to append data to an existing file. Specify True to append.

Declaring a new StreamWriter object opens the file. The file must be open before you can write in the file. If the file does not already exist, a new one is created. Because no exception occurs whether or not the file exists, you can declare the StreamWriter object in the declarations section of your program or in a procedure.

TIP

Use .txt as your extension to allow easy viewing of the file in Notepad. ■

Declaring a StreamWriter Object—Examples

```
Dim datPhone As New StreamWriter("Phone.txt")
Dim datNames As New StreamWriter("C:\MyFiles\Names.txt")
Dim datLogFile As New StreamWriter("C:\MyFiles\LogFile.txt", True)
```

The StreamWriter object has both a `Write` and a `WriteLine` **method.** The difference between the two is a carriage-return character. The `Write` method places items consecutively in the file with no delimiter (separator). The `WriteLine` method places an Enter (carriage return) between items. We will use the `WriteLine` in this chapter because we want to easily retrieve the data elements later.

The WriteLine Method—General Form

```
ObjectName.WriteLine(DataToWrite)
```

The DataToWrite argument may be string or numeric. The `WriteLine` method converts any numeric data to string and actually writes string data in the file.

The WriteLine Method—Examples

```
datPhone.WriteLine(txtName.Text)
datPhone.WriteLine(txtPhone.Text)

datNames.WriteLine("Sammy")

datBankBalance.WriteLine(decBalance)
```

If you are inputting data from the user and writing in a file, you generally place the `WriteLine` in a button click event procedure. That way you can write one record at a time. Figure 11.3 shows the form for this phone list example.

Figure 11.3

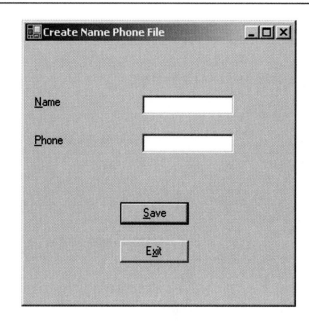

The user enters data into the text boxes and clicks the Save button, which writes this record in the stream's buffer.

```
Private Sub btnSave_Click(ByVal sender As System.Object, _
 ByVal e As System.EventArgs) Handles btnSave.Click
    'Save the record to the file

    datPhone.WriteLine(txtName.Text)
    datPhone.WriteLine(txtPhone.Text)

    With txtName
       .Text = ""
       .Focus()
    End With
    txtPhone.Text = ""
End Sub
```

The Save button writes the data from the screen to the StreamWriter object and then clears the screen.

Closing a File

After you finish writing data in a file, you must close the file. Closing a file is good housekeeping; it finishes writing all data from the stream's buffer to the disk and releases the system resources. Use the StreamWriter's `Close` **method,** which is similar to closing a form. A common location for the `Close` method is in your program's Exit command or the form's closing event procedure (see page 466).

```
Private Sub btnExit_Click(ByVal sender As System.Object, _
 ByVal e As System.EventArgs) Handles btnExit.Click
    'Close the file and the form

    datPhone.Close()
    Me.Close()
End Sub
```

Viewing the Contents of a File

After you run your project, you can view the new file using a text editor, such as Notepad. You can also view the file in the Visual Studio IDE. In the Solution Explorer, select the project name. If you don't see the Bin and Obj folders listed, click on the *Show All Files* button at the top of the window. Then you can expand the Bin folder, find the data file name, and select it. The contents of the file should appear in the Editor window (Figure 11.4).

- It's very easy to view the contents of a text file in the VS IDE.

- The default location for files is the project's bin folder. You must select *Show All Files* to make the file appear in the Solution Explorer.

F i g u r e   1 1 . 4

View the contents of your new file in the VS IDE.

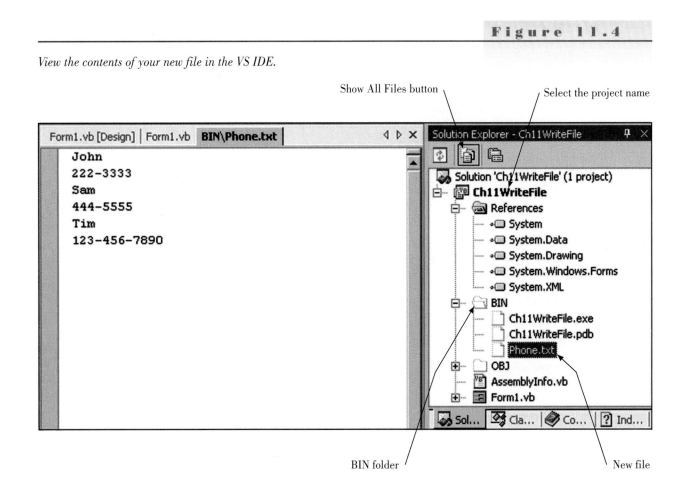

Show All Files button

Select the project name

BIN folder

New file

Reading Files

You use the StreamReader class to read the data from a file that you created with a StreamWriter.

The steps for reading the data from a file are the following:

- Declare an object of the StreamReader class. The constructor declares the file name and optional path. This statement opens the file so that you can read from it.

- Use the ReadLine method to read the data. You may need to use a loop to retrieve multiple records.

- When finished, close the stream using the StreamReader's Close method.

Instantiating a StreamReader Object—General Form

| General Form | ```
Dim ObjectName As New StreamReader("FileName")
``` |
|---|---|

The StreamReader class works in much the same way as the StreamWriter. However, the file must exist in the location that the application expects it. If no such file exists, an exception occurs. For this reason, you must declare the StreamReader object in a procedure, so that you can enclose it in a `Try/Catch` block.

Instantiating a StreamReader Object—Examples

```
Try
    Dim datNames As New StreamReader("C:\MyFiles\Names.txt")
Catch
    MessageBox.Show("File does not exist")
End Try

'In declarations section, to create a module-level variable name
Dim datPhone As StreamReader
...
'In a procedure, to catch an exception for a missing file
Try
    datPhone = New StreamReader("Phone.txt")
Catch
    MessageBox.Show("File does not exist")
End Try
```

Using the ReadLine Method

Use the StreamReader's `ReadLine` **method** to read the previously saved data. Each time you execute the method, it reads the next line from the file. Assign the value from the read to the desired location, such as a label, a text box, or a string variable. The `ReadLine` method has no arguments.

```
lblName.Text = datPhone.ReadLine()
```

Checking for the End of the File

How can you tell when there is no more data in the file? One way is to use the StreamReader's `Peek` **method.** The Peek method looks at the next element without really reading it. The value returned when you peek beyond the last element is negative 1 (-1).

```
If datPhone.Peek <> -1 Then
    lblName.Text = datPhone.ReadLine()
    lblPhone.Text = datPhone.ReadLine()
End If
```

Note that the `ReadLine` method does not throw an exception when you attempt to read past the end of the file.

You must always make sure to read the data elements in the same order in which they were written. Otherwise your output will display the wrong values. For example, if you reversed the two lines in the program segment above, the phone number would display for the name and vice versa. The `ReadLine` method just reads the next line and assigns it to the variable or property that you specify.
```

The File Read Program

Here is the completed program that reads the name and phone numbers from a file and displays them on the form (Figure 11.5). Each time the user clicks *Next,* the program reads and displays the next record.

Figure 11.5

Each time the user clicks Next, the next record is read from the file and displayed in the labels.

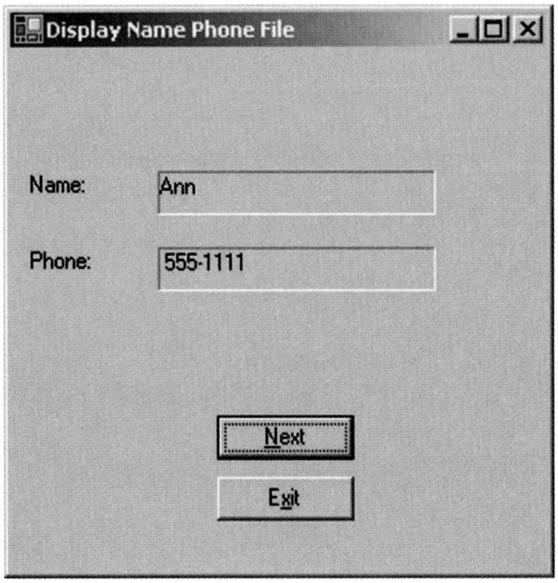

```
'Program:        Ch11ReadFile
'Programmer:     Bradley/Millspaugh
'Date:           Jan 2002
'Description:    Retrieve the information stored in a data file
'                and display it on the screen.
'                Uses a StreamReader.

Option Strict On
Imports System.IO

Public Class frmDisplay
    Inherits System.Windows.Forms.Form

[Windows Form Designer generated code]

    Private datPhone As StreamReader

    Private Sub frmDisplay_Load(ByVal sender As System.Object, _
      ByVal e As System.EventArgs) Handles MyBase.Load
        'Open the file and display the first record

        Try
            datPhone = New StreamReader("Phone.txt")
            DisplayRecord()
        Catch
            'File is not found
            MessageBox.Show("File does not exist")
        End Try
    End Sub
End Sub
```

```
    Private Sub btnNext_Click(ByVal sender As System.Object, _
     ByVal e As System.EventArgs) Handles btnNext.Click
        'Read the next record

        DisplayRecord()
    End Sub

    Private Sub btnExit_Click(ByVal sender As System.Object, _
     ByVal e As System.EventArgs) Handles btnExit.Click
        'End the project

        datPhone.Close()
        Me.Close()
    End Sub

    Private Sub DisplayRecord()
        'Read and display the next record

        If datPhone.Peek <> -1 Then
            lblName.Text = datPhone.ReadLine()
            lblPhone.Text = datPhone.ReadLine()
        End If
    End Sub
End Class
```

Feedback 11.1

1. Write the statement to create a datInventory object that will write data to a file called "Inventory.txt".
2. Code the statement to write the contents of txtDescription into datInventory.
3. Why should the declaration statement for a StreamReader object be in a Try/Catch block? Does the declaration statement for a StreamWriter object need to be in a Try/Catch block? Why or why not?
4. Write the statement(s) to read a description and a product number from datInventory assuming it has been opened as a StreamReader object. Make sure to test for the end of the file.

Using the File Common Dialog Boxes

In the preceding file read and write programs, the file names are hard-coded into the programs. You may prefer to allow the user to browse and enter the file-name at run time. You can display the standard Windows *Open File* dialog box, in which the user can browse for a folder and filename and/or enter a new filename. Use the **OpenFileDialog** common dialog control to display the dialog box, and then use the control's FileName property to open the selected file.

• The common dialog controls are all new for VB .NET. You can use the OpenFileDialog control for both opening existing files and saving new files.

OpenFileDialog Control Properties

You will find the following properties of the OpenFileDialog control very useful:

Property	Description
Name	Name of control. Use "dlg" for the prefix.
CheckFileExists	Display an error message if the file does not exist. Set to False for saving a file, since you want to create a new file if the file does not exist. Leave at the default True to read an existing file.
CheckPathExists	Display an error message if the path does not exist. Set to False for saving a file, since you want it to create the new folder if necessary.
FileName	The name of the file selected or entered by the user, which includes the file path. Access this property after displaying the dialog box to determine which file to open. You can also give this property an initial value, which places a default filename in the dialog box when it appears.
Filter	Filter file extensions to display. Example: `.txt|*.txt|All files|*.*`
InitialDirectory	Directory to display when the dialog box opens. Set this in code to Application.StartupPath to begin in the same folder as your application.
Title	Title bar of the dialog box.

Displaying the Open File Dialog Box

To display an *Open File* dialog box (Figure 11.6), you must first add an Open-FileDialog control to your form. The control appears in the component tray. At design time set initial properties for Name, CheckFileExists, CheckPathExists, Filter, and Title (see the preceding table for the values). In code, set the Initial-Directory property to **Application.StartupPath,** display the dialog box using the ShowDialog method, and retrieve the FileName property.

Figure 11.6

Display the Windows Open File *dialog box using the OpenFileDialog control. The Filter property determines the entries for* Files of type.

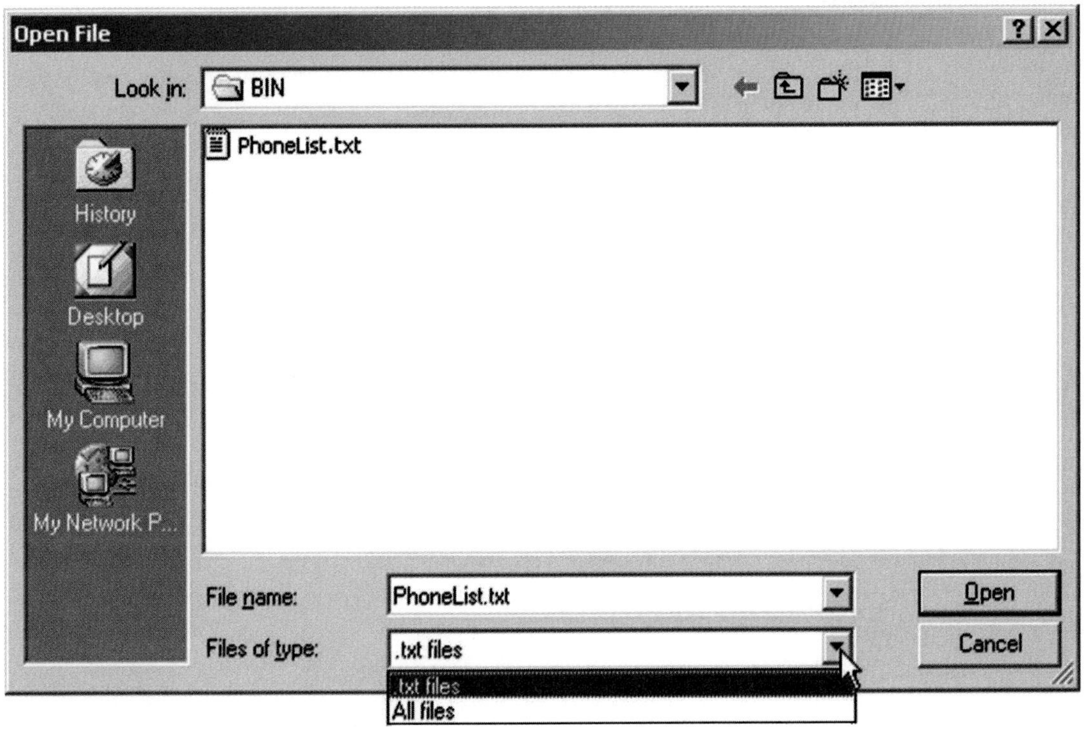

```
Private Sub mnuFileOpen_Click(ByVal sender As System.Object, _
  ByVal e As System.EventArgs) Handles mnuFileOpen.Click
    'Open the file
    Dim dgrResult As DialogResult

    dlgOpen.InitialDirectory = Application.StartupPath    'Begin in the project folder
    dgrResult = dlgOpen.ShowDialog()                      'Display the File Open dialog box
    If dgrResult <> DialogResult.Cancel Then              'User didn't click the Cancel button
        datPhone = New StreamWriter(dlgOpen.FileName)     'Open the output file
    End If
End Sub
```

Notice that the user may click on the Cancel button of the *Open File* dialog box. Check the DialogResult for Cancel. And if the user *does* click Cancel, that presents one more problem for the program: You cannot close a StreamWriter object that isn't open.

Checking for Successful File Open

In the preceding file-open procedure, the statement
`datPhone = New StreamWriter(dlgOpen.FileName)`
may not execute. In that case, the StreamReader is not instantiated. You can
check for instantiation using the VB keyword `Nothing`. An object variable that
has not been instantiated has a value of `Nothing`. Notice the syntax: You must
use the keyword `Is` rather than the equal sign (=).

```
If Not datPhone Is Nothing Then   'Is the file open?
    datPhone.Close()
End If
```

* Any object variable that has been
declared but not instantiated is =
Nothing.

The Write File Program

Here is the complete listing of the Write File program, which allows the user to
select the file name. The user can select the *Open* command from the *File*
menu. But if the Save button is clicked and the file is not yet open, the *Open
File* dialog box displays automatically.

```
'Program:        Ch11 Open and Write File
'Programmer:     Bradley/Millspaugh
'Date:           Jan 2002
'Description:    Create a file using a StreamWriter.
'                Displays the File Open dialog box for the user to
'                enter the file and path.
'Folder:         Ch11OpenAndWriteFile

Option Strict On
Imports System.IO

Public Class frmPhone
    Inherits System.Windows.Forms.Form

[Windows Form Designer generated code]

    Dim datPhone As StreamWriter

    Private Sub btnSave_Click(ByVal sender As System.Object, _
      ByVal e As System.EventArgs) Handles btnSave.Click
        'Save the record to the file

        If Not datPhone Is Nothing Then        'Is the file open?
            datPhone.WriteLine(txtName.Text)
            datPhone.WriteLine(txtPhone.Text)
            With txtName
                .Text = ""
                .Focus()
            End With
            txtPhone.Text = ""
        Else                                   'File is not open
            MessageBox.Show("You must open the file before you can save a record", _
            "File Not Open", MessageBoxButtons.OK, MessageBoxIcon.Information)
            mnuFileOpen_Click(sender, e)       'Display the File Open dialog box
        End If
    End Sub
```

```
Private Sub mnuFileExit_Click(ByVal sender As System.Object, _
 ByVal e As System.EventArgs) Handles mnuFileExit.Click
    'Close the file and the form

    If Not datPhone Is Nothing Then                    'Is the file open?
        datPhone.Close()
    End If
    Me.Close()
End Sub

Private Sub mnuFileOpen_Click(ByVal sender As System.Object, _
 ByVal e As System.EventArgs) Handles mnuFileOpen.Click
    'Open the file
    Dim dgrResult As DialogResult

    dlgOpen.InitialDirectory = Application.StartupPath    'Begin in the project folder
    dgrResult = dlgOpen.ShowDialog()                'Display the File Open dialog box
    If dgrResult <> DialogResult.Cancel Then    'User didn't click the Cancel button
        datPhone = New StreamWriter(dlgOpen.FileName)    'Open the output file
    End If
    txtName.Focus()
End Sub
End Class
```

► Feedback 11.2

1. What Filter property setting displays only .txt files?
2. Write the statement to set dlgOpen to begin in the same folder as the application.
3. Write the statement to close the StreamWriter datPhone; make sure to allow for the possibility that the file is not open.

Saving the Contents of a List Box

In Chapter 7 you wrote a program to maintain a list. The user was allowed to add items and remove items, but the next time the program ran, the list changes were gone. The changes were not saved from one execution to the next.

Now that you know how to save data in a file, you can save the contents of a list when the program exits and reload the list when the program reopens. The techniques that you need to use for this project are:

* Do not give any values to the list's Items collection at design time. Instead, when the program begins, open the data file and read the items into the list elements.

* If the user makes any changes to the list, ask whether to save the list when the program ends.

* Include a menu option to save the list.

* If the file holding the list elements does not exist when the program begins, give the user the option of creating a new list by adding the items.

The examples in this section use the hands-on example from Chapter 7, which allows the user to make changes to the Coffee Flavor list (Figure 11.7). We will load the list from a file in the Form_Load procedure and query the user to save the list if any changes are made.

The form for the list save program, taken from Chapter 7.

Loading the List Box

Assuming that the list items are stored in a data file, you can read the file into the list in the Form_Load procedure. Loop through the file until all elements are read, placing each item in the list with the Items.Add method.

```
Do Until datFlavors.Peek = -1
    cboCoffee.Items.Add(datFlavors.ReadLine())
Loop
```

Checking for Existence of the File

When you create a StreamReader object, the constructor checks to make sure the file exists. If the file does not exist, what do you want to do? Maybe the user wants to exit the program, locate the file, and try again. Or maybe the user prefers to begin with an empty list, add the list items, and create a new file. This technique is a good way to create the file in the first place.

You can catch the exception for a missing file and display a message box asking if the user wants to create a new file.

```
dgrResponse = MessageBox.Show("Create a new file?", "File not Found", _
  MessageBoxButtons.YesNo, MessageBoxIcon.Question)
```

If the user says Yes, allow the program to begin running with an empty list; the file will be created when the program exits or the user saves the list. If the user says No, exit the program immediately.

```
Private Sub frmFlavors_Load(ByVal sender As System.Object, _
  ByVal e As System.EventArgs) Handles MyBase.Load
    'Load the items in the cboCoffee list
    Dim dgrResponse As DialogResult

    Try
        'Open the file
        Dim datFlavors As New StreamReader("Coffees.txt")
        'Read all elements into the list
        Do Until datFlavors.Peek = -1
            cboCoffee.Items.Add(datFlavors.ReadLine())
        Loop
        'Close the file
        datFlavors.Close()
    Catch        'File missing
        dgrResponse = MessageBox.Show("Create a new file?", "File not Found", _
          MessageBoxButtons.YesNo, MessageBoxIcon.Question)
        If dgrResponse = DialogResult.No Then
            mnuFileExit_Click(sender, e)          'Exit the program
        End If
    End Try
End Sub
```

Saving the File

In this program the user can choose a menu option to save the file. Open a StreamWriter object and loop through the Items collection of the list box, saving each element with a WriteLine method.

```
Private Sub mnuFileSave_Click(ByVal sender As System.Object, _
  ByVal e As System.EventArgs) Handles mnuFileSave.Click
    'Save the list box contents in a file
    Dim datFlavors As New StreamWriter("Coffees.txt")          'Open the file
    Dim intIndex As Integer
    Dim intMaximum As Integer

    intMaximum = cboCoffee.Items.Count - 1
    For intIndex = 0 To intMaximum
        datFlavors.WriteLine(cboCoffee.Items(intIndex))
    Next intIndex
    datFlavors.Close()          'Close the file
    mblnIsDirty = False
End Sub
```

The last line in this procedure needs some explanation. The next section explains the reason for mblnIsDirty = False.

Querying the User to Save

If your program allows users to make changes to data during program execution, it's a good idea to ask them if they want to save the changes before the program ends. This is similar to working in a word processing program or the VB editor. If you close the file after making changes, you receive a message asking if you want to save the file. But if you haven't made any changes since the last save, no message appears.

To keep track of data changes during execution, you need a module-level Boolean variable. Because the standard practice in programming is to refer to the data as *dirty* if changes have been made, we will call the variable mblnIsDirty. In each procedure that allows changes (Add, Remove, Clear), you must set mblnIsDirty to True. After saving the file, set the variable to False.

Just before the project ends, you must check the value of mblnIsDirty—if True, ask the user if he or she wants to save; if False, you can just exit without a message.

> • The concept of dirty data is covered here and in Chapter 10, to allow you to cover the chapters in any order.

The Form_Closing Procedure

If you want to do something before the project ends, such as ask the user to save the file, the best location is the form's **Closing event** procedure. This is a much better place for such a question than your exit procedure because the user can quit the program in more than one way. The Form_Closing event procedure executes before the Unload when the user clicks on your Exit button or menu command, clicks on the window's Close button, or even exits Windows.

```
Private Sub frmFlavors_Closing(ByVal sender As Object, _
 ByVal e As System.ComponentModel.CancelEventArgs) Handles MyBase.Closing
    'Ask user to save the file
    Dim dgrResponse As DialogResult

    If mblnIsDirty = True Then
       dgrResponse = MessageBox.Show("Coffee list has changed. Save the list?", _
         "Coffee List Changed", MessageBoxButtons.YesNo, MessageBoxIcon.Question)
       If dgrResponse = DialogResult.Yes Then
          mnuFileSave_Click(sender, e)
       End If
    End If
End Sub
```

Programming Example

This programming example puts together the routines in the previous section. The form, based on the hands-on example in Chapter 7, is shown in Figure 11.7. The user can add new flavors to the list, remove items from the list, or clear the list. Any changes can be saved in a file; the next program run retrieves the elements from the file, so the changes carry through from one run to the next.

```
'Program:           Ch11 List Save and Reload
'Programmer:        Bradley/Millspaugh
'Date:              January 2002
'Description:       Maintain a list of coffee flavors. The flavors are stored to disk
'                   and reloaded for the next program run.
'Folder:            Ch11ListSave

Option Strict On
Imports System.IO

Public Class frmFlavors
    Inherits System.Windows.Forms.Form

[Windows Form Designer generated code]

    'Declare module-level variables
    Private mblnIsDirty As Boolean

    Private Sub btnAddCoffee_Click(ByVal sender As System.Object, _
     ByVal e As System.EventArgs) Handles btnAddCoffee.Click
        'Add a new coffee flavor to the coffee list

        If cboCoffee.Text <> "" Then
            With cboCoffee
                .Items.Add(.Text)
                .Text = ""
                mblnIsDirty = True
            End With
        Else
            MessageBox.Show("Enter a coffee flavor to add", "Missing data", _
              MessageBoxButtons.OK, MessageBoxIcon.Exclamation)
        End If
        cboCoffee.Focus()
    End Sub

    Public Sub mnuEditAdd_Click(ByVal sender As System.Object, _
     ByVal e As System.EventArgs) Handles mnuEditAdd.Click
        'Add a new coffee to list

        btnAddCoffee_Click(sender, e)
    End Sub

    Public Sub mnuEditClear_Click(ByVal sender As System.Object, _
     ByVal e As System.EventArgs) Handles mnuEditClear.Click
        'Clear the coffee list
        Dim dgrResponse As DialogResult

        dgrResponse = MessageBox.Show("Clear the coffee flavor list?", _
          "Clear coffee list", MessageBoxButtons.YesNo, MessageBoxIcon.Question)
        If dgrResponse = DialogResult.Yes Then
            cboCoffee.Items.Clear()
            mblnIsDirty = True
        End If
    End Sub

    Public Sub mnuEditCount_Click(ByVal sender As System.Object, _
     ByVal e As System.EventArgs) Handles mnuEditCount.Click
        'Display a count of the coffee list

        MessageBox.Show("The number of coffee types is" & cboCoffee.Items.Count)
    End Sub
```

```
Public Sub mnuEditRemove_Click(ByVal sender As System.Object, _
 ByVal e As System.EventArgs) Handles mnuEditRemove.Click
    'Remove the selected coffee from list

    With cboCoffee
        If .SelectedIndex <> -1 Then
            .Items.RemoveAt(.SelectedIndex)
            mblnIsDirty = True
        Else
            MessageBox.Show("First select the coffee to remove", "No selection made", _
                MessageBoxButtons.OK, MessageBoxIcon.Exclamation)
        End If
    End With
End Sub

Public Sub mnuFileExit_Click(ByVal sender As System.Object, _
 ByVal e As System.EventArgs) Handles mnuFileExit.Click
    'Terminate the project

    Me.Close()
End Sub

Private Sub frmFlavors_Load(ByVal sender As System.Object, _
 ByVal e As System.EventArgs) Handles MyBase.Load
    'Load the items in the cboCoffee list
    Dim dgrResponse As DialogResult

    Try
        'Open the file
        Dim datFlavors As New StreamReader("Coffees.txt")
        'Read all elements into the list
        Do Until datFlavors.Peek = -1
            cboCoffee.Items.Add(datFlavors.ReadLine())
        Loop
        'Close the file
        datFlavors.Close()
    Catch 'File missing
        dgrResponse = MessageBox.Show("Create a new file?", "File not Found", _
            MessageBoxButtons.YesNo, MessageBoxIcon.Question)
        If dgrResponse = DialogResult.No Then
            mnuFileExit_Click(sender, e)        'Exit the program
        End If
    End Try
End Sub

Private Sub frmFlavors_Closing(ByVal sender As Object, _
 ByVal e As System.ComponentModel.CancelEventArgs) Handles MyBase.Closing
    'Ask user to save the file
    Dim dgrResponse As DialogResult

    If mblnIsDirty = True Then
        dgrResponse = MessageBox.Show("Coffee list has changed. Save the list?", _
            "Coffee List Changed", MessageBoxButtons.YesNo, MessageBoxIcon.Question)
        If dgrResponse = DialogResult.Yes Then
            mnuFileSave_Click(sender, e)
        End If
    End If
End Sub
```

```
Private Sub mnuFileSave_Click(ByVal sender As System.Object, _
 ByVal e As System.EventArgs) Handles mnuFileSave.Click
    'Save the list box contents in a file
    Dim datFlavors As New StreamWriter("Coffees.txt") 'Open the file
    Dim intIndex As Integer
    Dim intMaximum As Integer

    intMaximum = cboCoffee.Items.Count - 1
    For intIndex = 0 To intMaximum
        datFlavors.WriteLine(cboCoffee.Items(intIndex))
    Next intIndex
    datFlavors.Close()          'Close the file
    mblnIsDirty = False
    End Sub
End Class
```

> ## Feedback 11.3

1. Write the loop to save all of the elements from lstNames using dat-Names, a StreamWriter already opened and connected to Names.txt.
2. In what procedure should the code from question 1 be placed?
3. Write the statements in the Form_Load event procedure to load the list of names into lstNames.

Serialization

Sometimes you may need to store an object. You can save an object and the current value of all of its properties using serialization. The term **serialization** is used in many programming languages and refers to a series or stream of bits. An object's state is converted to a series of bits that can be saved and later used to re-create the object. Reading the saved data back and re-creating the object is called **deserialization.**

The .NET framework uses serialization when performing functions such as marshalling (transferring) an object to another application.

If you want to be able to save an object, the class must be declared as Serializable and you must have a formatter. Two types of formatters are available: Binary and SOAP. The **Binary formatter** stores data in a binary form. Simple Object Access Protocol (SOAP) is a specification for storing data for transfer across platforms. The data from a **SOAP formatter** is actually stored in an XML format.

You can make any of your projects that contain a class module serializable, allowing the properties of an object to be saved. To accomplish this you must:

- Declare the class as Serializable.

In the form's code:

- Declare a Formatter object.
- Declare a FileStream object that includes the name of the file.
- Use the Formatter object's Serialize method to save the object's properties.
- Close the FileStream.

• Store the state of an object using serialization. The class must be declared as Serializable. You deserialize to re-create the object.

Making a Class Serializable

Before you can **serialize** an object, you must modify the class header to include the Serializable attribute.

```
<Serializable()> Public Class BookSale
    (body of the class)
End Class
```

All that you need to do is to add `<Serializable()>` in front of the class header.

Adding a Formatter Object

You write the code to actually store (serialize) the object in your form's code, not in the serializable class. You declare a new formatter object using either the BinaryFormatter or SoapFormatter class.

```
Dim FormatObject As SoapFormatter = New SoapFormatter
Dim FormatObject As BinaryFormatter = New BinaryFormatter
```

A formatter object requires an import for the formatter class. This brings the number of import statements for saving an object to three: one for the System.IO for saving files, one for serialization, and one for the formatter.

```
Imports System.IO
Imports System.Runtime.Serialization
Imports System.Runtime.Serialization.Formatters.Binary
```

Using a FileStream

Serialization uses the **FileStream** class, rather than the StreamReader and StreamWriter classes we used earlier. Declaring a FileStream is similar to declaring the other stream classes, but also requires a file mode in addition to the path for the file.

- A FileStream object is needed to serialize (save) and deserialize (restore) objects.

- A FileStream has different modes: Create can be used to first write the file and Open to retrieve the objects.

Declaring a FileStream Object—Constructor

General Form

```
Dim ObjectName As FileStream = New FileStream("file name", FileMode.Open | Create)
```

We will use only the Open and Create modes. Use FileMode.Create when you open the file for output and FileMode.Open when you want to retrieve the record. Note that there is also an OpenOrCreate mode that can be used if the stream is instantiated at the module level and you want to be able to both read and write.

Declaring a FileStream Object—Example

```
Dim datBooks As FileStream = New FileStream("Books", FileMode.Create)
```

Saving an Object

After you open the file by declaring an object of the FileStream class and declare the Formatter object, you save your object using the `Serialize` method of the Formatter.

The Serialize Method—General Form

<table>
<tr><td>General Form</td><td><code>FormatterObject.Serialize(StreamObject, ObjectToSave)</code></td></tr>
</table>

The Serialize Method—Example

<table>
<tr><td>Example</td><td><code>MyFormatter.Serialize(datBooks, mBookSale)</code></td></tr>
</table>

The `Serialize` method actually writes the data to the buffer. You must code a `Close` method to complete the save operation to disk.

```
Private Sub mnuFileSave_Click(ByVal sender As System.Object, _
  ByVal e As System.EventArgs) Handles mnuFileSave.Click
    'Save the contents of the object
    Dim datBooks As FileStream = New FileStream("Books", FileMode.Create)
    Dim BookFormatter As BinaryFormatter = New BinaryFormatter()

    BookFormatter.Serialize(datBooks, mBookSale)
    datBooks.Close()
End Sub
```

Re-creating an Object

You read an object back in with the `Deserialize` method of the formatter. The necessary steps are the following:

* Create a FileStream object in the Open mode.

* Declare a Formatter object.

* Use the Formatter's `Deserialize` method, converting the input to the desired object type.

* Transfer the fields from the object to the screen.

* Close the stream.

When you are deserializing an object you must be sure to convert the input data to the correct type:

```
mBookSale = CType(BookFormatter.Deserialize(datbooks), BookSale)
```

Following is the complete method to retrieve an object.

```
Private Sub mnuFileRetrieve_Click(ByVal sender As System.Object, _
  ByVal e As System.EventArgs) Handles mnuFileRetrieve.Click
    'Retrieve an object from disk
      Dim BookFormatter As BinaryFormatter = New BinaryFormatter()

      Try
          'Read the data and convert it to the BookSale class
          Dim datBooks As FileStream = New FileStream("Books", FileMode.Open)
          mBookSale = CType(BookFormatter.Deserialize(datBooks), BookSale)
          datBooks.Close()

          'Transfer data to the screen
          txtTitle.Text = mBookSale.Title
          txtQuantity.Text = FormatNumber(mBookSale.Quantity, 0)
          txtPrice.Text = FormatNumber(mBookSale.Price)
          lblExtendedPrice.Text = FormatNumber(mBookSale.ExtendedPrice)
      Catch
          MessageBox.Show("No saved object found", "File Error", _
            MessageBoxButtons.OK, MessageBoxIcon.Exclamation)
      End Try
End Sub
```

Your Hands-On Programming Example

Modify the step-by-step example program from Chapter 6 to store and retrieve a book object using serialization. Note that this program is based on the step-by-step example as it appears on page 259, before adding the inherited class. This folder should be called *Ch11SBS*.

The user enters book sale information, which is assigned to the properties of a BookSale object. The ExtendedPrice method of the BookSale object calculates the extended price that displays on the screen.

Include menu options to save the record (the BookSale object), clear the screen, and retrieve the record. The Clear method clears the screen so that you can see the data disappear and then redisplay.

Planning the Project

Begin with the Chapter 6 SBS project, which contains a form (Figure 11.8) and a BookSale class. Add the new menu items to the *File* menu:

Save Record
Clear
Retrieve Record

Figure 11.8

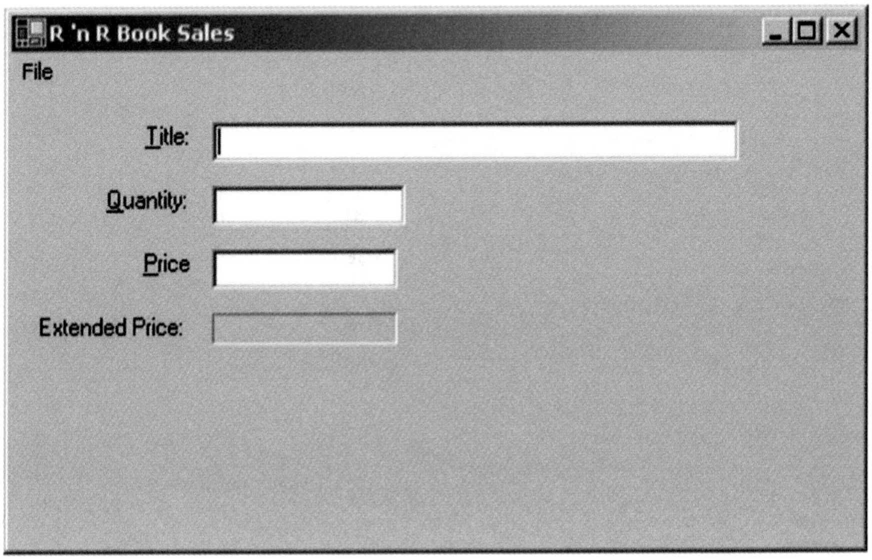

The completed form for the hands-on programming example. Note that this form is based on the step-by-step example in Chapter 6.

Plan the Objects and Properties

Object	Property	Setting
mnuFileSave	Name	mnuFileSave
mnuFileClear	Name	mnuFileClear
mnuFileRetrieve	Name	mnuFileRetrieve

Plan the Procedures

Procedure	Actions
mnuFileSave	Declare an instance of a file stream and a formatter.
	Call the Serialize method of the formatter.
	Close the file stream.
mnuFileClear	Clear text boxes and labels.
	Set the focus on first text box.
mnuFileRetrieve	Declare an instance of a file stream and a formatter.
	Call the Deserialize method of the formatter.
	Transfer data to the text boxes.
	Close the file stream.

Write the Project

Begin with the step-by-step procedure in Chapter 6 through page 259.

- Add the menu items and set the properties according to your plan.

- Write the code for the new menu items. Working from the pseudocode, write each procedure.

- When you complete the code, thoroughly test the project.

The Project Coding Solution

```
'Program:        Chapter 11 Serialization Hands-On
'Programmer:     Bradley/Millspaugh
'Date:           Jan 2002
'Description:    Calculate sales price using the BookSale class.
'                Instantiate mBookSale as a new object of the BookSale class.
'                Store the object to disk using serialization and
'                retrieve and recreate the object using deserialization.
'Folder:         Ch11SerializationHandsOn

Option Strict On
Imports System.IO
Imports System.Runtime.Serialization
Imports System.Runtime.Serialization.Formatters.Binary

Public Class frmSales
    Inherits System.Windows.Forms.Form

[Windows Form Designer generated code]

    Private mBookSale As BookSale 'Declare the new object

    Private Sub mnuFileCalculateSale_Click(ByVal sender As System.Object, _
      ByVal e As System.EventArgs) Handles mnuFileCalculateSale.Click
        'Calculate the extended price for the sale
```

```vb
    Try
        'Instantiate the object and set the properties
        mBookSale = New BookSale(txtTitle.Text, CInt(txtQuantity.Text), _
          CDec(txtPrice.Text))

        'Calculate and format the result
        lblExtendedPrice.Text = FormatNumber(mBookSale.ExtendedPrice)

    Catch
        MessageBox.Show("Error in quantity or price field", "R 'n R Book Sales", _
          MessageBoxButtons.OK, MessageBoxIcon.Exclamation)
    End Try
End Sub

Private Sub mnuFileExit_Click(ByVal sender As Object, _
 ByVal e As System.EventArgs) Handles mnuFileExit.Click
    'Exit the application

    Me.Close()
End Sub

Private Sub mnuFileSummary_Click(ByVal sender As System.Object, _
 ByVal e As System.EventArgs) Handles mnuFileSummary.Click
    'Display the sales summary information
    Dim strMessage As String

    strMessage = "Sales Total: " & FormatCurrency(mBookSale.SalesTotal) & _
      ControlChars.NewLine & "Sales Count: " & CStr(mBookSale.SalesCount)
    MessageBox.Show(strMessage, "R 'n R Book Sales Summary", _
      MessageBoxButtons.OK, MessageBoxIcon.Information)
End Sub

Private Sub mnuFileSave_Click(ByVal sender As System.Object, _
 ByVal e As System.EventArgs) Handles mnuFileSave.Click
    'Save the contents of the object
    Dim datBooks As FileStream = New FileStream("Books", FileMode.Create)
    Dim BookFormatter As BinaryFormatter = New BinaryFormatter()

    BookFormatter.Serialize(datBooks, mBookSale)
    datBooks.Close()
End Sub

Private Sub mnuFileClear_Click(ByVal sender As System.Object, _
 ByVal e As System.EventArgs) Handles mnuFileClear.Click
    'Clear the text boxes

    txtQuantity.Text = ""
    txtPrice.Text = ""
    lblExtendedPrice.Text = ""
    With txtTitle
        .Text = ""
        .Focus()
    End With
End Sub

Private Sub mnuFileRetrieve_Click(ByVal sender As System.Object, _
 ByVal e As System.EventArgs) Handles mnuFileRetrieve.Click
    'Retrieve the record from disk
    Dim BookFormatter As BinaryFormatter = New BinaryFormatter()
```

```
        Try
            'Read the data and convert it to the BookSale class
            Dim datBooks As FileStream = New FileStream("Books", FileMode.Open)
            mBookSale = CType(BookFormatter.Deserialize(datBooks), BookSale)
            datBooks.Close()

            'Transfer data to the screen
            With mBookSale
                txtTitle.Text = .Title
                txtQuantity.Text = FormatNumber(.Quantity, 0)
                txtPrice.Text = FormatNumber(.Price)
                lblExtendedPrice.Text = FormatNumber(.ExtendedPrice)
            End With
        Catch
            MessageBox.Show("No saved object found", "File Error", _
                MessageBoxButtons.OK, MessageBoxIcon.Exclamation)
        End Try
    End Sub
End Class

'Class Name:        BookSale
'Programmer:        Bradley/Millspaugh
'Date:              Jan 2002
'Description:       Handle book sale information.
'Folder:            Ch11SerializationHandsOn

<Serializable()> Public Class BookSale
    Sub New()
        'Constructor with empty argument list
    End Sub

    Sub New(ByVal Title As String, ByVal Quantity As Integer, _
     ByVal Price As Decimal)
        'Assign property values

        Me.Title = Title
        Me.Quantity = Quantity
        Me.Price = Price
    End Sub
#Region "Properties "

    Protected mstrTitle As String                    'Title property
    Protected mintQuantity As Integer                'Quantity property
    Protected mdecPrice As Decimal                   'Price property
    Protected Shared mdecSalesTotal As Decimal       'SalesTotal property
    Protected Shared mintSalesCount As Integer       'SalesCount property

    Property Title() As String
        Get
            Title = mstrTitle
        End Get

        Set(ByVal Value As String)
            mstrTitle = Value
        End Set
    End Property
```

```
    Property Quantity() As Integer
        Get
            Quanitity = mintQuantity
        End Get

        Set(ByVal Value As Integer)
            If IsNumeric(Value) Then
                mintQuantity = CInt(Value)
            End If
        End Set
    End Property

    Property Price() As Decimal
        Get
            Price = mdecPrice
        End Get

        Set(ByVal Value As Decimal)
            If IsNumeric(Value) Then
                mdecPrice = CDec(Value)
            End If
        End Set
    End Property

    Shared ReadOnly Property SalesTotal() As Decimal
        Get
            SalesTotal = mdecSalesTotal
        End Get
    End Property

    Shared ReadOnly Property SalesCount() As Integer
        Get
            SalesCount = mintSalesCount
        End Get
    End Property
#End Region

#Region "Methods "
    Public Overridable Function ExtendedPrice() As Decimal
        'Calculate the extended price and add to the totals
        Dim decExtendedPrice As Decimal

        decExtendedPrice = mintQuantity * mdecPrice
        mdecSalesTotal += decExtendedPrice
        mintSalesCount += 1
        Return decExtendedPrice
    End Function
#End Region
End Class
```

Summary

1. A data file is made up of records, which can be further broken down into fields or data elements. The field used for organizing the file is the key field.

2. A stream object is used to transfer data to and from a data file. The StreamWriter outputs (writes) the data and the StreamReader inputs (reads) data.

3. The constructors for a StreamWriter and StreamReader take the name of the file, with an optional path, as a parameter.

4. The `WriteLine` method writes a field to disk.

5. A `Close` method should be used prior to the termination of a program that uses streams.

6. The `Peek` method looks at the next element which allows testing for the end of the file.

7. List box data may be saved to a stream. The Items collection should be filled in the Form_Load if the file exists. Any changes are saved back to the file when the program terminates.

8. A boolean variable is used to track whether changes are made to the data.

9. The form's Closing event procedure is a good place to put the code to prompt the users if they wish to save any changes.

10. The OpenFileDialog common dialog control can be used to display the *Open File* dialog and allow the user to select the file name.

11. Saving the state of an object is called *serialization;* retrieving and re-creating the object is called *deserialization.*

12. The FileStream class provides the ability to use different modes for saving files.

13. An object can be saved to a file stream if the class is declared as Serializable.

14. Serialization has two formatters for determining the way the data is stored: binary or SOAP.

Key Terms

Application.StartupPath   *461*
Binary formatter   *469*
`Close` method   *455*
Closing event   *466*
data file   *452*
deserialization   *469*
field   *452*
file   *452*
FileStream   *470*
`Nothing`   *462*
OpenFileDialog   *459*
`Peek` method   *457*

`ReadLine` method   *457*
record   *452*
serialization   *469*
serialize   *470*
SOAP formatter   *469*
stream   *453*
StreamReader   *453*
StreamWriter   *453*
System.IO namespace   *453*
`Write` method   *454*
`WriteLine` method   *454*

Review Questions

1. What is the difference between a Visual Basic project file and a data file?
2. Explain what occurs when a stream object is instantiated.
3. Name two types of stream classes. What is the difference between the two?
4. What is the difference between a `Write` method and a `WriteLine` method?
5. What steps are necessary for storing the list items from a list box into a disk file?
6. What is the format for the statements to read and write streams?
7. What method can be used to determine the end of file?
8. When is exception handling necessary for stream handling?
9. Explain when a form's Closing event occurs and what code might be included in the Closing event procedure.
10. What is serialization and when would it be used?
11. What statement must be included in a class if you want to serialize objects of the class?
12. What is a SOAP formatter?

Programming Exercises

11.1 Rewrite Programming Exercise 8.4 using a file to store the state names and abbreviations. You need two projects: The first will allow the typist to enter the state name and the abbreviation in text boxes and store them in a file. The second project will perform the functions specified in Programming Exercise 8.4.

11.2 Create a file for employee information and call it Employee.txt. Each record will contain fields for first name, last name, Social Security number, and hourly pay rate.

Write a second project to process payroll. The application will load the employee data into an array of structures from the file with an extra field for the pay. The form will contain labels for the information from the array (display one record at a time) and a text box for the hours worked.

A button called *FindPay* will use a For Next loop to process the array. You will calculate the pay and add the pay to the totals. Then display the labels for the next employee. (Place the pay into the extra field in the array.)

The Exit button will print a report on the printer and terminate the project. (Print the array.)

Processing: Hours over 40 receive time-and-a-half pay. Accumulate the total number of hours worked, the total number of hours of overtime, and the total amount of pay.

Sample Report

Ace Industries

Employee Name	Hours Worked	Hours Overtime	Pay Rate	Amount Earned
Janice Jones	40	0	$5.25	$210.00
Chris O'Connel	35	0	5.35	187.25
Karen Fisk	45	5	6.00	285.00
Tom Winn	42	2	5.75	247.25
Totals	162	7		$929.50

11.3 Modify Programming Exercise 7.5 to store the list box for Bradley's Bagels in a data file. Load the list during the Form Load and then close the file. Be sure to use error checking in case the file does not exist.

In the exit procedure prompt the user to save the bagel list back to the disk.

Note: For help in basing a new project on an existing project, see "Copy and Move a Windows Project" in Appendix C.

11.4 Create a simple text editor that has one large text box (with its Multiline property set to True) or a RichTextBox control. Set the text control to fill the form and set its Anchor property to all four edges, so that the control fills the form even when it is resized.

Allow the user to save the contents of the text box in a data file and load a data file into the text box using the *Open File* dialog box.

11.5 Create a project that stores personal information for a little electronic "black book." The fields in the file should include name, phone number, pager number, cell phone number, voice mail number, and email address. Create an object containing the appropriate fields and text boxes to enter the data.

Create a second project to load the names into a list box. Perform a "look up" and display the appropriate information for the selected name.

Case Studies

VB Mail Order

Modify your project from Chapter 7 to save the changes to the catalog name combo box from one run to the next. When the program begins, load the list from the data file. If the file does not exist, display a message asking the user if he or she wants to create it.

Allow the user to save changes from a *Save* menu.

When the program terminates, check to see if there are any unsaved changes. If so, prompt the user to save the changes.

Note: For help in basing a new project on an existing project, see "Copy and Move a Windows Project" in Appendix C.

VB Auto Center

Write a project to store vehicle information including model, manufacturer, year, and vehicle identification number (VIN).

Create a second project that reads the data from the file and loads a drop-down combo box with the VINs. When a number is selected from the combo box the appropriate information regarding the vehicle should display in labels.

Video Bonanza

Modify your project from Chapter 7 to save the changes to the movie combo box from one run to the next. When the program begins, load the list from the data file. If the file does not exist, display a message asking the user if he or she wants to create it.

Allow the user to save changes from a *Save* menu.

When the program terminates, check to see if there are any unsaved changes. If so, prompt the user to save the changes.

Note: For help in basing a new project on an existing project, see "Copy and Move a Windows Project" in Appendix C.

Very Very Boards

Modify your project from Chapter 7 to save the changes to the shirt style combo box from one run to the next. When the program begins, load the list from the data file. If the file does not exist, display a message asking if the user wants to create it.

Allow the user to save changes from a *Save* menu.

When the program terminates check to see if there are any unsaved changes. If so, prompt the user to save the changes.

Note: For help in basing a new project on an existing project, see "Copy and Move a Windows Project" in Appendix C.

12

Graphics and Animation

at the completion of this chapter, you will be able to . . .

1. Use graphics methods to draw shapes, lines, and filled shapes.

2. Create a drawing surface with a Graphics object.

3. Instantiate Pen and Brush objects as needed for drawing.

4. Create animation by changing pictures at run time.

5. Create simple animation by moving images.

6. Use the Timer component to automate animation.

7. Use scroll bars to move an image.

8. Draw a pie chart using the methods of the Graphics object.

You had your first introduction to graphics when you learned to print documents in Chapter 7. In this chapter you will learn to draw shapes, such as lines, rectangles, and ellipses, using the methods of the Graphics object. You can use the Graphics methods to draw pictures and charts in a business application.

You will do simple animation by replacing and moving graphics. You also will use a Timer component to cause events to fire, so that you can create your own animation.

Graphics in Windows and the Web

The term ***graphics*** refers to any text, drawing, image, or icon that you display on the screen. You have placed a graphic image in a picture box control to display pictures on your forms. A picture box can also display animated .gif files, so you can easily produce animation on the screen.

You can display a graphics file on either a Web Form or a Windows Form. Recall that the Web control is an Image control whereas the Windows control is a PictureBox. Both display graphics files, but the Windows control accepts a few more file formats.

Using Windows Forms, you can draw graphics shapes, such as circles, lines, and rectangles on a form or control. The Graphics methods work only on Windows Forms, not Web Forms. Therefore, the programs in the next section use Windows Forms only.

The Graphics Environment

The .NET Framework uses a technology called *GDI+* for drawing graphics. GDI+ is an advancement and improvement over the previous Graphics Device Interface (GDI) used in previous versions of VB. GDI+ is designed to be device-independent, so that the programmer doesn't have to be concerned about the physical characteristics of the output device. For example, the code to draw a circle is the same whether the output goes to a large-screen monitor, a low-resolution monitor, or the printer.

- Graphics use the new GDI+, which is not compatible with the VB 6 GDI (Graphics Device Interface). Graphics are now more device-independent.

- Graphics are based on the System.Drawing namespace.

- A Graphics object must be created as a drawing space; it may be on the form or on a control.

Steps for Drawing Graphics

When you draw a picture, you follow these general steps. The sections that follow describe the steps in more detail.

- Create a Graphics object to use as a drawing surface.

- Instantiate a Pen or Brush object to draw with.

- Call the drawing methods from the Graphics object.

Looking over the steps, you realize that this is what you did for creating printer output in Chapter 7. In that chapter you used the `DrawString` method to place text on the Graphics object; in this chapter you will use methods that draw shapes.

The Paint Event Procedure

You draw lines and shapes on a form or control by drawing on a Graphics object. And where do you place the code for the drawing methods? In the Paint event procedure for the form or the control on which you are drawing.

Each time a window is displayed, resized, moved, maximized, restored, or uncovered, the form's Paint event executes. In the Paint event, the form and its controls are redrawn. If you draw some graphics on the form, in say the Form_Load event procedure or the click event of a button, the graphics are not automatically redrawn when the form is repainted. The only way to make sure that the graphics appear is to create them in the Paint event procedure. Then they are redrawn every time the form is rendered.

So far we have ignored the Paint event and allowed the repainting to proceed automatically. Now we will place code in that event procedure. You can write code in the form's Paint event procedure to draw on the form, or code in a control's Paint event procedure to draw graphics on the control.

In the Paint event procedure, you must declare a Graphics object. You assign the Graphics property of the procedure's PaintEventArgs argument to the new Graphics object.

> **☑ TIP**
>
> To write code for the form's Paint method, select (*Base class Events*) from the Object list and then drop down the Method list in the Editor window. ■

```
Private Sub frmGraphics_Paint(ByVal sender As Object, _
  ByVal e As System.Windows.Forms.PaintEventArgs) Handles MyBase.Paint
    'Create a graphics object
    Dim gr As Graphics = e.Graphics
```

You can also create a graphic object by calling the `CreateGraphics` method of a form or control. You would use this method when you want to display a graphic from a procedure other than the Paint event.

```
Me.CreateGraphics.MethodName          'Draw on the form
myGroupBox.CreateGraphics.MethodName  'Draw on a control
```

Pen and Brush Objects

Using a **Pen object** you can draw lines or outlined shapes such as rectangles or circles. A **Brush object** creates filled shapes. You can set the width of a Pen and the color for both a Pen and a Brush. Figure 12.1 shows some lines and shapes created with Pen and Brush objects.

- Pen objects are used to draw lines and shapes.

- Filled shapes are created with a Brush object.

F i g u r e   1 2 . 1

Graphic shapes created by drawing with Pen and Brush objects and the methods of the Graphics class.

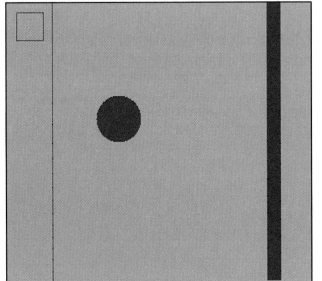

When you create a new Pen object, you set the color using the Color constants, such as Color.Red, Color.Blue, and Color.Aquamarine. You can also set the pen's width, which is measured in pixels. The term **pixel** is an abbreviation of *picture element*—a dot that makes up a picture. You are probably most familiar with pixels in the determination of the resolution of a monitor. A display of 1,280 by 1,024 is a reference to the number of pixels horizontally and vertically.

The Pen Class—Constructors

General Form

```
Pen(Color)
Pen(Color, Width)
```

If you don't set the width of the pen, it defaults to 1 pixel.

The Pen Class—Examples

Examples

```
Dim penRed As New Pen(Color.Red)
Dim penWide As New Pen(Color.Black, 10)
```

You may find that you want several different pens. For each different color or line width, you can create another Pen object or redefine an already dimensioned Pen variable if you are finished with it.

If you want to create filled figures, declare Brush objects. Create one for each different color that you want to use.

The SolidBrush Class—Constructor

General Form

```
SolidBrush(Color)
```

Use the Color constants to assign a color to your Brush objects.

The SolidBrush Class—Example

Example

```
Dim brushBlue As New SolidBrush(Color.Blue)
```

You may have deduced from the name of the SolidBrush class that other types of brushes exist. See Help if you are interested in using a TextureBrush, HatchBrush, LinearGradientBrush, or PathGradientBrush.

The Coordinate System

Graphics are measured from a starting point of 0,0 for the x and y coordinates beginning in the upper-left corner. The x is the horizontal position, and the y is the vertical measurement. The starting point depends on where the graphic is being placed. If the graphic is going directly on a form, the 0,0 coordinates are the upper-left corner of the form. You can also draw graphics in a container, such as a PictureBox, GroupBox, or Button. In this case, the container has its own 0,0 coordinates to be used as the starting point for measuring the location of items inside the container (Figure 12.2).

- Measurement for graphics is in pixels.

- The Scale methods are gone. You can no longer define a custom coordinate system for graphics. All graphics use pixels.

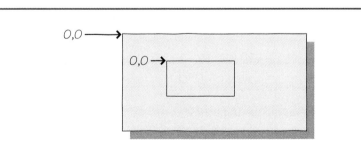

Figure 12.2

The coordinates for graphics begin with 0,0 in the upper-left corner of a form or container.

Each of the drawing methods allows you to specify the starting position using x and y coordinates. Most of the methods also allow you to specify the position using a Point structure. In some methods it is useful to use a Rectangle structure, and in others a Size structure comes in handy.

The Point Structure

A **Point structure** is designed to hold the *x* and *y* coordinates as a single unit. You can create a Point object, giving it values for the *x* and *y*. Then you can use the object anywhere that accepts a Point as an argument.

```
Dim myStartingPoint As New Point(20, 10)
```

You can see an example of a Point in the design of any of your forms. Examine the Location property of any control; the Location is assigned a Point object, with *x* and *y* properties.

The Size Structure

A **Size structure** has two components, the width and height. Both are integers that specify the size in pixels. Some Graphics methods accept a Size structure as an argument.

```
Dim myPictureSize As New Size(100, 20) 'Width is 100, height is 20
```

You can also see an example of a Size structure by examining the design of any of your forms. Each of the controls has a Size property, which has width and height properties.

For an interesting exercise, examine the Windows-generated code for a Button control. The Location is set to a new Point object and the size is set to a new Size object.

The Rectangle Structure

A **Rectangle structure** defines a rectangular region, specified by its upper-left corner and its size.

```
Dim myRegion As New Rectangle(myStartingPoint, myPictureSize)
```

The overloaded constructor also allows you to declare a new Rectangle by specifying its location in *x* and *y* coordinates and its width and height.

```
Dim myOtherRegion As New Rectangle(intX, intY, intWidth, intHeight)
```

Note that you also can create Point, Size, and Rectangle structures for single-precision floating-point values. Specify the PointF, SizeF, and RectangleF structures.

Graphics Methods

The drawing methods fall into two basic categories: draw and fill. The draw methods create an outline shape and the fill methods are solid shapes. The first argument in a draw method is a Pen object whereas the fill methods use Brush objects. Each of the methods also requires the location for the upper-left corner, which you can specify as *x* and *y* coordinates or as a Point object. Some of the methods require the size, which you may supply as width and height, or as a Rectangle object.

Graphics Methods—General Form

General
Form

```
DrawLine(Pen, intX1, intY1, intX2, intY2)
DrawLine(Pen, Point1, Point2)

DrawRectangle(Pen, intX, intY, intWidth, intHeight)
DrawRectangle(Pen, Rectangle)

FillRectangle(Brush, intX, intY, intWidth, intHeight)
FillRectangle(Brush, Rectangle)

FillEllipse(Brush, intX, intY, intWidth, intHeight)
FillEllipse(Brush, Rectangle)
```

The following code draws the outline of a rectangle in red using the DrawRectangle **method** and draws a line with the DrawLine **method.** The FillEllipse **method** is used to draw a filled circle.

```
Private Sub frmGraphics_Paint(ByVal sender As Object, _
 ByVal e As System.Windows.Forms.PaintEventArgs) Handles MyBase.Paint
    'Create a graphics object
    Dim gr As Graphics = e.Graphics
    Dim penRed As New Pen(Color.Red)

    'Draw a red rectangle
    gr.DrawRectangle(penRed, 10, 10, 30, 30)

    'Draw a red line
    gr.DrawLine(penRed, 50, 0, 50, 300)

    'Draw a blue filled circle
    Dim brushBlue As New SolidBrush(Color.Blue)
    gr.FillEllipse(brushBlue, 100, 100, 50, 50)

    'Draw a fat blue line
    Dim penWide As New Pen(Color.Blue, 15)
    gr.DrawLine(penWide, 300, 0, 300, 300)
End Sub
```

Code the form's Paint event procedure by selecting *BaseClass events* from the editor's Class list and *Paint* from the Method list. ■

Table 12.1 shows some of the methods in the Graphics class. For excellent help in using the methods, see the MSDN Help page.

```
Contents
   Visual Studio .NET
      .NET Framework
         Programming with the .NET Framework
            Drawing and Editing Images
               About GDI+ Managed Code
                  Lines, Curves, and Shapes
```

Selected Methods from the Graphics Class   **T a b l e   1 2 . 1**

Method	Purpose
Clear()	Clear the drawing surface by setting it to the container's background color.
Dispose()	Releases the memory used by a Graphics object.
DrawArc(*Pen, intX1, intY1, intX2, intY2, intWidth, intHeight*) DrawArc(*Pen, Rectangle, sngStartAngle, sngAngleLength*)	Draw an arc (segment of an ellipse).
DrawLine(*Pen, intX1, intY1, intX2, intY2*) DrawLine(*Pen, Point1, Point2*)	Draw a line from one point to another.
DrawEllipse(*Pen, intX, intY, intWidth, intHeight*) DrawEllipse(*Pen, Rectangle*)	Draw an oval shape. A circle has equal width and height.
DrawRectangle(*Pen, intX, intY, intWidth, intHeight*) DrawRectangle(*Pen, Rectangle*)	Draw a rectangle.
DrawPie(*Pen, intX, intY, intWidth, intHeight, _ intAngleStart, intAngleLength*) DrawPie(*Pen, Rectangle, sngAngleStart, sngAngleLength*)	Draw a partial circle (segment of a pie).
DrawString(*strText, Font, Brush, sngX, sngY*) DrawString(*strText, Font, Brush, PointF*)	Draw a string of text. Note that coordinates are single-precision.
FillEllipse(*SolidBrush, intX, intY, intWidth, intHeight*) FillEllipse(*SolidBrush, Rectangle*)	Draw a filled oval; a circle for equal width and height.
FillPie(*Brush, intX, intY, intWidth, intHeight, _ intAngleStart, intAngleLength*) FillPie(*Brush, Rectangle, sngAngleStart, sngAngleLength*)	Draw a partial filled oval (segment of a pie).
FillRectangle(*SolidBrush, intX, intY, intWidth, intHeight*) FillRectangle(*SolidBrush, Rectangle*)	Draw a filled rectangle.

Random Numbers

Often it is useful to be able to generate random numbers. The Rnd **function** returns a number between 0 and 1. This means that any number from 0 to 1 (excluding 1) is just as likely to come up as any other. Rnd is popular for use in games, as well as in problems in probability and queuing theory.

The Rnd Function—General Form

General Form	
	`Rnd()`

You can use the Rnd function to generate integer values in the range 1 through a given number using this formula:

`Int(Rnd * Upperbound + 1)`

Note that the Rnd function generates a single-precision value, so you should use the CInt function to convert the value to integer.

The Rnd Function—Examples

Examples

```
'Generate integers in the range 1 - 10
intRandom = CInt(Int(Rnd() * 10 + 1))

'Generate integers in the range 1 to the width of the form
intRandom = CInt(Int(Rnd() * Me.Width + 1))
```

Unfortunately, the computer can't really generate random numbers. Each time you run an application, the Rnd function produces the identical sequence of "random" numbers. To generate a different series for each run, include the Randomize **statement** (once) in the program initialization. This is called *seeding* the random number generator. The Randomize statement uses the current value of the system clock to produce a different value each time.

A Random Number Example

This example program draws graphics using the Graphics methods and generates snowflakes using the Rnd function. Figure 12.3 shows the screen generated by this code.

Figure 12.3

This output is produced by the Ch12RandomNumbers example program. The program draws the figure and generates random snowflakes in the form's Paint event procedure.

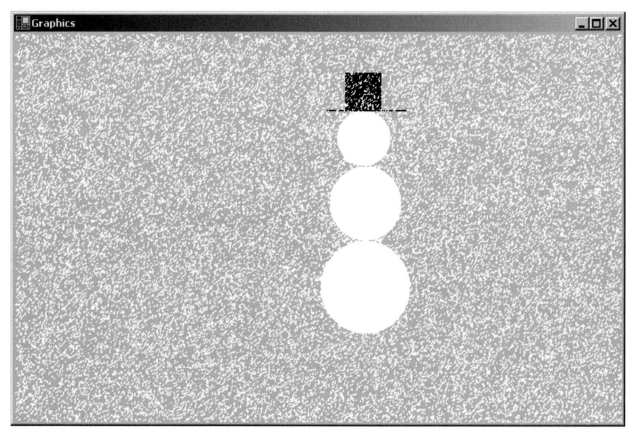

```
'Program                Chapter 12 Random Numbers
'Programmer:            Bradley/Millspaugh
'Date:                  Jan 2002
'Description:           Draw a snowman using filled ellipses and then snow using
'                       random locations.
'Folder:                Ch12RandomFunction

Option Strict On

Public Class frmGraphics
    Inherits System.Windows.Forms.Form

[Windows Form Designer generated code]

    Private Sub frmGraphics_Load(ByVal sender As Object, _
     ByVal e As System.EventArgs) Handles MyBase.Load
        'Seed the random number generator

        Randomize()
    End Sub

    Private Sub frmGraphics_Paint(ByVal sender As Object, _
     ByVal e As System.Windows.Forms.PaintEventArgs) Handles MyBase.Paint
        'Generate dots (snowflakes) in random locations
        'Draw a snowman at the bottom center of the screen
        Dim intX As Integer = CInt(Me.Width/2)
        Dim intY As Integer = CInt(Me.Height/2)
        Dim intIndex As Integer
        Dim gr As Graphics = e.Graphics
        Dim penWhite As New Pen(Color.White, 2)
        Dim brushWhite As New SolidBrush(Color.White)
        Dim penBlack As New Pen(Color.Black)
        Dim brushBlack As New SolidBrush(Color.Black)

        'Draw the snowman
        gr.FillEllipse(brushWhite, intX, intY, 100, 100)
        intY -= 80               'Top of last circle
        intX += 10               'Offset for smaller circle
        gr.FillEllipse(brushWhite, intX, intY, 80, 80)
        intY -= 60
        intX += 8
        gr.FillEllipse(brushWhite, intX, intY, 60, 60)

        'Add a top hat
        gr.DrawLine(penBlack, intX - 10, intY, intX + 80, intY)
        gr.FillRectangle(brushBlack, intX + 10, intY - 40, 40, 40)

        'Make it snow in random locations
        For intIndex = 1 To 40000
            intX = CInt(Int((Rnd() * Me.Width + 1)))
            intY = CInt(Int((Rnd() * Me.Height + 1)))
            gr.DrawLine(penWhite, intX, intY, intX + 1, intY + 1)
        Next
    End Sub
End Class
```

☑ TIP

Use the Randomize statement prior to a Rnd function to generate different random numbers for each execution of the program. ■

> ### Feedback 12.1
>
> 1. Write the statements necessary to draw a green vertical line down the center of a form.
> 2. Write the statements to draw one circle inside another one.
> 3. Write the statements to define three points and draw lines between the points.

Simple Animation

There are several ways to create animation on a form. The simplest way is to display an animated .gif file in a PictureBox control. The animation is already built into the graphic. Other simple ways to create animation are to replace one graphic with another, move a picture, or rotate through a series of pictures. You can also create graphics with the various graphics methods.

If you want to create animation on a Web page, displaying an animated .gif file is the best way. Another way is to embed a Java applet, which creates the animation on the client side. It doesn't make any sense to create animation using server-side controls, since each movement would require a round-trip to the server.

Displaying an Animated Graphic

You can achieve animation on either a Windows Form or a Web Form by displaying an animated .gif file (Figure 12.4). Use a PictureBox control on a Windows Form and an Image control on a Web Form.
Note: You can find the graphics for the programs in this chapter in the Graphics folder of your text CD.

Figure 12.4

Create animation by displaying an animated .gif file on either a Windows Form or a Web Form.

Controlling Pictures at Run Time

You can add or change a picture at run time. To speed execution, it is usually best to have the pictures loaded into controls that you can make invisible until you are ready to display them. But you can also use the `FromFile` **method** to load a picture at run time.

If you store a picture in an invisible control, you can change the Visible property to True at run time; or you may decide to copy the picture to another control.

```
picLogo.Visible = True
picLogo.Image = picHold.Image
```

You can use the `Fromfile` method to retrieve a file during run time. One problem with this method is that the path must be known. When you are running an application on multiple systems, the path names may vary.

```
picLogo.Image = Image.FromFile("C:\VB\LOGO.BMP")
```

If you store your image file in your project's Bin folder, you can omit the path. The Bin folder is the default folder for the application's executable file.

To remove a picture from the display, either hide it or use the `Nothing` constant.

```
picLogo.Visible = False
picLogo.Picture = Nothing
```

Switching Images

An easy way to show some animation is to replace one picture with another. Many of the icons in the Visual Studio icon library have similar sizes but opposite states, such as a closed file cabinet and an open file cabinet; a mail box with the flag up and with the flag down; a closed envelope and an open envelope; or a traffic light in red, yellow, or green. (Recall that in Chapter 2 you used the two light bulbs: LightOn and LightOff.)

This sample program demonstrates switching between two phone icons: a phone and a phone being held. The program has three PictureBox controls: one to display the selected image and two, with their Visible property set to false, to hold the two images. The two icons are Phone12.ico and Phone13.ico in the Graphics\Icons\Comm folder. When the user clicks the Change button, the icon is switched to the opposite one. (See Figure 12.5.)

Figure 12.5

Create animation by switching from one icon to another. Each of these graphics is placed into the upper picture box when the user clicks the Change button.

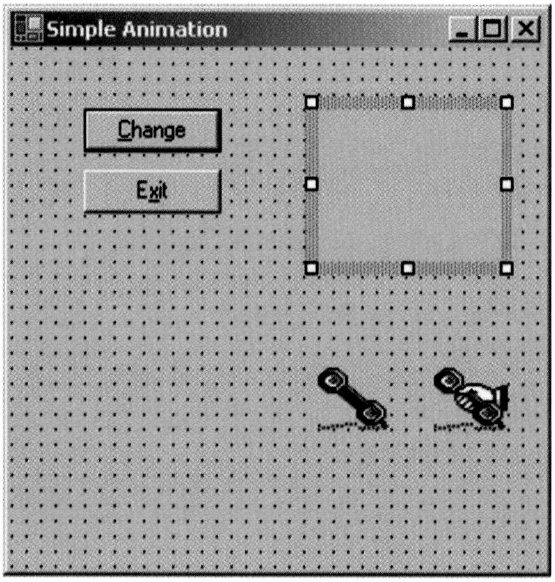

```
'Program:          Chapter 12 Simple Animation
'Programmer:       Bradley/Millspaugh
'Date:             Jan 2002
'Description:       Change a picture of a phone to show someone holding it.
'Folder:           Ch12SimpleAnimation

Option Strict On

Public Class frmAnimation
    Inherits System.Windows.Forms.Form

    Private Sub btnExit_Click(ByVal sender As System.Object, _
      ByVal e As System.EventArgs) Handles btnExit.Click
        'End the program

        Me.Close()
    End Sub

    Private Sub btnChange_Click(ByVal sender As System.Object, _
      ByVal e As System.EventArgs) Handles btnChange.Click
        'Toggle the image from one to the other
        Static blnSwitch As Boolean = True
```

```
        If blnSwitch Then
            picDisplay.Image = picWithHand.Image
            blnSwitch = False
        Else
            picDisplay.Image = picPhone.Image
            blnSwitch = True
        End If
    End Sub

    Private Sub frmAnimation_Load(ByVal sender As Object, _
     ByVal e As System.EventArgs) Handles MyBase.Load
        'Set the initial image

        picDisplay.Image = picPhone.Image
    End Sub
End Class
```

Moving a Picture

The best way to move a control is to use the control's SetBounds **method. The**
SetBounds method produces a smoother-appearing move than the move that is
produced by changing the Left and Top properties of controls.

- The Move method of a control has been replaced with the SetBounds method.

The SetBounds Method—General Form

General Form	`SetBounds(intX, intY, intWidth, intHeight)`

You can use a control's SetBounds method to move it to a new location and/or
to change its size.

The SetBounds Method—Examples

Examples	`picPlane.SetBounds(intX, intY, planeWidth, planeHeight)` `picEngine.SetBounds(intX, intY, intWidth, intHeight)`

The program example in the next section uses a timer and the SetBounds
method to move a graphic across the screen.

The Timer Component

Generally events occur when the user takes an action. But what if you want to
make events occur at some interval without user action? You can cause events
to occur at a set interval using the **Timer component** and its **Tick event.**
Timers are very useful for animation; you can move or change an image each
time the Tick event occurs.

When you have a timer component on a form, it "fires" each time an interval elapses. You can place any desired code in the Tick event procedure; the

- The Timer component is placed in the component tray.

- A Timer has a Tick event.

code executes each time the event occurs. You choose the interval for the timer by setting its **Interval property,** which can have a value of 0 to 65,535. This value specifies the number of milliseconds between the calls to the Tick event. One second is equivalent to 1,000 milliseconds. Therefore, for a 3-second delay, set the timer's Interval property to 3,000. You can set the value at run time or at design time.

You can keep the Tick event from occurring by setting the Timer's Enabled property to False. The default value is False, so you must set it to True when you want to enable the Timer. You can set the Enabled property at design time or run time.

When you add a timer to your form it goes into the component tray. The tool for the timer is represented by the little stopwatch in the toolbox (Figure 12.6). The three-character prefix for naming a timer is "tmr".

Figure 12.6

⏱ Timer

The tool for the Timer component.

This Timer example program achieves animation in two ways: it moves an animated .gif file for a steam engine across the screen. When the steam engine moves off the left edge of the form, it reappears at the right edge, so it comes around again. Figure 12.7 shows the form. You'll have to use your imagination for the animation.

Figure 12.7

Each time the Timer fires, the train moves 10 pixels to the left.

```
'Program           Ch12 Timer Animation
'Programmer:       Bradley/Millspaugh
'Date:             Jan 2002
'Description:       Move a steam engine across the screen.
'                  It reappears on the other side after leaving the screen.
'Folder:            Ch12TimerAnimation

Option Strict On

Public Class frmTimer
    Inherits System.Windows.Forms.Form

    Private Sub tmrTrain_Tick(ByVal sender As System.Object, _
    ByVal e As System.EventArgs) Handles tmrTrain.Tick
        'Move the graphic across the form
        Static intX As Integer = picEngine.Left
        Static intY As Integer = picEngine.Top
        Static intWidth As Integer = picEngine.Width
        Static intHeight As Integer = picEngine.Height

        'Set new X coordinate
        intX -= 10
        If intX <= -picEngine.Width Then        'Graphic entirely off edge of form
            intX = Me.Width
        End If
        'Move image
        picEngine.SetBounds(intX, intY, intWidth, intHeight)
    End Sub
End Class
```

► **Feedback 12.2**

1. Write the statement(s) to move btnCommand 10 pixels to the left using the SetBounds method.
2. How long is an interval of 450?
3. What fires a Timer's Tick event?

The Scroll Bar Controls

You can add **horizontal scroll bars** and **vertical scroll bars** to your form (Figure 12.8). These scroll bar controls are similar to the scroll bars in Windows that can be used to scroll through a document or window. Often scroll bars are used to control sound level, color, size, and other values that can be changed in small amounts or large increments. The HScrollBar control and VScrollBar control operate independently of other controls and have their own methods, events, and properties.

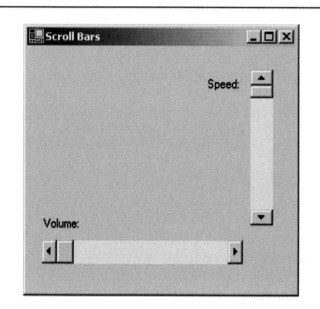

Scroll Bar Properties

Properties for scroll bars are somewhat different from the controls we have worked with previously. Because the scroll bars represent a range of values, they have the following properties: **Minimum** for the minimum value, **Maximum** for the maximum value, **SmallChange** for the distance to move when the user clicks on the scroll arrows, and **LargeChange** for the distance to move when the user clicks on the gray area of the scroll bar or presses the Page Up or Page Down keys (Figure 12.9). Each of these properties has a default value (Table 12.2).

• The scroll bar Change event is replaced by the ValueChanged event. Min and Max properties are now Minimum and Maximum.

Figure   12.9

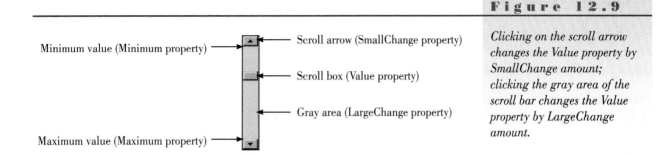

Minimum value (Minimum property) ——————

Maximum value (Maximum property) ——————

Scroll arrow (SmallChange property)

Scroll box (Value property)

Gray area (LargeChange property)

Default Values for Scroll Bar Properties

Table   12.2

Property	Default value
Minimum	0
Maximum	100
SmallChange	1
LargeChange	10
Value	0

The **Value property** indicates the current position of the scroll box (also called the *thumb*) and its corresponding value within the scroll bar. When the user clicks the up arrow of a vertical scroll bar, the Value property decreases by the amount of SmallChange (if the Minimum value has not been reached) and moves the scroll box up. Clicking the down arrow causes the Value property to increase by the amount of SmallChange and moves the thumb down until it reaches the bottom or Maximum value.

When naming scroll bars, use a prefix of "hsb" for horizontal scroll bars and "vsb" for vertical scroll bars. Figure 12.10 shows the horizontal scroll bar tool and vertical scroll bar tool from the toolbox.

Figure   12.10

Scroll Bar Events

The events that occur for scroll bars differ from the ones used for other controls. Although a user might click on the scroll bar, there is no Click event; rather there are two events: a **ValueChanged event** and a **Scroll event.** The ValueChanged event occurs anytime that the Value property changes, whether it's changed by the user or by the code.

If the user drags the scroll box, a Scroll event occurs. In fact, multiple scroll events occur, as long as the user continues to drag the scroll box. As soon as the user releases the mouse button, the Scroll events cease and a ValueChanged event occurs. When you write code for a scroll bar, usually you will want to code both a ValueChanged event procedure and a Scroll event procedure.

A Programming Example

This little program uses scroll bars to move an image of a car around inside a container (Figure 12.11). The image is in a PictureBox, and a GroupBox is the container. By placing the image inside a container, you use the container's co-ordinates rather than those of the form.

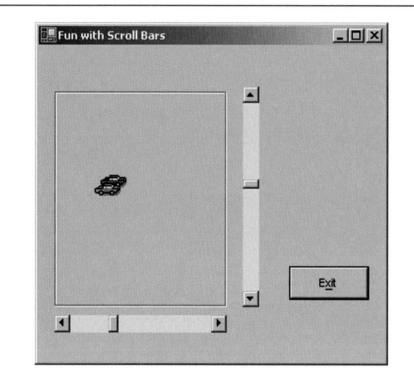

The form for the scroll bar programming example. Move the car around inside the container using the scroll bars.

A horizontal scroll bar will make the image move sideways in the container, and the vertical scroll bar will make it move up and down. Although you want the Maximum properties of the scroll bars to reflect the height and width of the container, due to the shape of the image, you may need to set the properties using trial and error. For example, the width of the GroupBox is 176 pixels, but the Maximum property of the horizontal scroll bar is set to 150; that's the point at which the car's bumper touches the edge of the container.

```
'Program:        Scroll
'Programmer:     Bradley/Millspaugh
'Date:           Jan 2002
'Description:    Use scroll bars to move an image
'                horizontally and vertically within the
'                limits of a group box.
'Folder:         Ch12ScrollBars

Option Strict On

Public Class frmScroll
    Inherits System.Windows.Forms.Form

[Windows Form Designer generated code]

    Private Sub btnExit_Click(ByVal sender As System.Object, _
      ByVal e As System.EventArgs) Handles btnExit.Click
        'Terminate the project

        Me.Close()
    End Sub

    Private Sub hsbMoveCar_Scroll(ByVal sender As System.Object, _
      ByVal e As System.Windows.Forms.ScrollEventArgs) Handles hsbMoveCar.Scroll
        'Control the side-to-side movement
        'Used when the scroll box is moved

        picCar.Left = hsbMoveCar.Value
    End Sub

    Private Sub vsbMoveCar_Scroll(ByVal sender As System.Object, _
      ByVal e As System.Windows.Forms.ScrollEventArgs) Handles vsbMoveCar.Scroll
        'Position the up and down movement
        'Used when the scroll box is moved

        picCar.Top = vsbMoveCar.Value
    End Sub

    Private Sub vsbMoveCar_ValueChanged(ByVal sender As Object, _
      ByVal e As System.EventArgs) Handles vsbMoveCar.ValueChanged
        'Position the up and down movement
        'Used for arrow clicks

        picCar.Top = vsbMoveCar.Value
    End Sub

    Private Sub hsbMoveCar_ValueChanged(ByVal sender As Object, _
      ByVal e As System.EventArgs) Handles hsbMoveCar.ValueChanged
        'Control the side-to-side movement
        'Used for arrow clicks

        picCar.Left = hsbMoveCar.Value
    End Sub
End Class
```

Your Hands-On Programming Example

Create a project that will draw a pie chart showing the relative amount of sales for Books, Periodicals, and Food for RnR—for Reading and Refreshment.

Include text boxes for the user to enter the sales amount for Books, Periodicals, and Food. Include buttons for Display Chart, Clear, and Exit.

Draw the pie chart in the Display Chart button's Click event procedure and use the `CreateGraphics.FillPie` method to draw each of the pie segments.

```
Me.CreateGraphics.FillPie(Brush, intX, intY, intWidth, intHeight, intBeginAngle, intLength)
```

Planning the Project

Sketch a form (Figure 12.12) that your users sign off as meeting their needs.

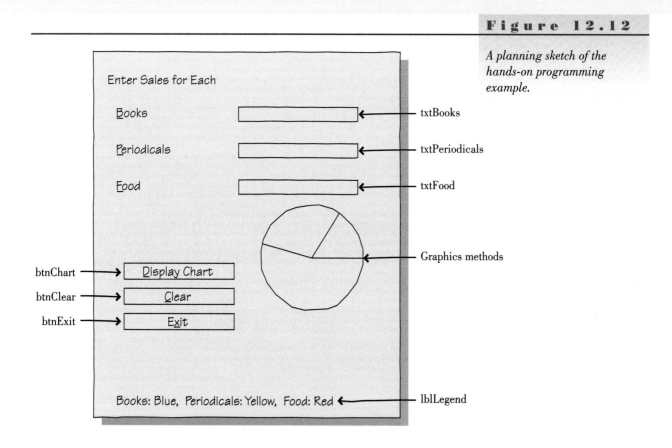

Figure 12.12

A planning sketch of the hands-on programming example.

Plan the Objects and Properties
Plan the property settings for the form and each control.

Object	Property	Setting
Form	Name	frmPieChart
	Text	R 'n R Sales Pie Chart
	AcceptButton	btnDisplayChart
	CancelButton	btnClear
Label1	Name	Label1
	Text	Enter Sales for Each
Label2	Name	Label2
	Text	&Books
txtBooks	Name	txtBooks
	Text	(blank)
Label3	Name	Label3
	Text	&Periodicals
txtPeriodicals	Name	txtPeriodicals
	Text	(blank)
Label4	Name	Label4
	Text	&Food
txtFood	Name	txtFood
	Text	(blank)
lblLegend	Name	lblLegend
	Text	Books: Blue, Periodicals: Yellow, Food: Red
	Visible	False
btnChart	Name	btnChart
	Text	&Display Chart
btnClear	Name	btnClear
	Text	C&lear
btnExit	Name	btnExit
	Text	E&xit

Plan the Event Procedures

Event procedure	Actions—pseudocode

btnChart_Click	If text fields are numeric
	    Create Graphic object.
	    Find total sales.
	    Calculate ratio of each department to total sales.
	    Draw portions of the pie for each department.

btnClear_Click	Set each text box and label to blanks. Clear the chart. Set the focus in the first text box.
btnExit_Click	Exit the project.

Write the Project

Following the sketch in Figure 12.12, create the form. Figure 12.13 shows the completed form.

- Set the properties of each of the objects, as you have planned.

- Write the code. Working from the pseudocode, write each event procedure.

- When you complete the code, use a variety of test data to thoroughly test the project.

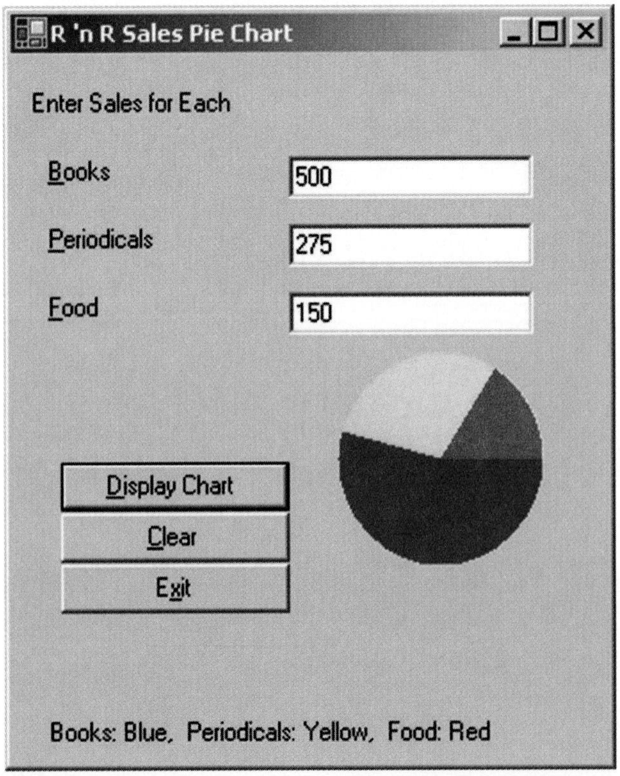

Figure 12.13

The form for the hands-on programming example.

The Project Coding Solution

```
'Program:           Chapter 12 Pie chart
'Programmer:        Bradley/Millspaugh
'Date:              Jan 2002
'Description:       Draw a chart for relative sales amounts.
'Folder:            Ch12PieChart

Option Strict On

Public Class frmPieChart
    Inherits System.Windows.Forms.Form

[Windows Form Designer generated code]

    Private Sub btnChart_Click(ByVal sender As System.Object, _
      ByVal e As System.EventArgs) Handles btnChart.Click
        'Display a pie chart showing relative sales by department
        'Need total sales amount
        Dim decTotalSales As Decimal
        Dim decBookSales As Decimal
        Dim decPeriodicalSales As Decimal
        Dim decFoodSales As Decimal

        If IsNumeric(txtBooks.Text) Then
            decBookSales = CDec(txtBooks.Text)
            If IsNumeric(txtPeriodicals.Text) Then
                decPeriodicalSales = CDec(txtPeriodicals.Text)
                If IsNumeric(txtFood.Text) Then
                    decFoodSales = CDec(txtFood.Text)
                    decTotalSales = decBookSales + decPeriodicalSales + decFoodSales

                    'Create the pie chart
                    Dim brushBooks As New SolidBrush(Color.Blue)
                    Dim brushPeriodicals As New SolidBrush(Color.Yellow)
                    Dim brushFood As New SolidBrush(Color.Red)
                    'Draw the chart
                    'Amounts are a portion of the total circle of 360 degrees
                    'The pie graphic includes a start angle and end angle
                    If decTotalSales <> 0 Then
                        lblLegend.Visible = True
                        'Find the end of the book portion of 360 degrees
                        Dim intEndBooks As Integer = CInt(decBookSales/decTotalSales * 360)
                        Me.CreateGraphics.FillPie(brushBooks, 160, 140, 100, 100, 0, intEndBooks)
                        'Find the end of the Periodicals portion
                        Dim intEndPeriodicals As Integer = CInt(decPeriodicalSales/ _
                          decTotalSales * 360)
                        Me.CreateGraphics.FillPie(brushPeriodicals, 160, 140, 100, 100, _
                          intEndBooks, intEndPeriodicals)
                        Dim intEndFood As Integer = CInt(decFoodSales/decTotalSales * 360)
                        Me.CreateGraphics.FillPie(brushFood, 160, 140, 100, 100, _
                          intEndPeriodicals + intEndBooks, intEndFood)
                    End If
                Else
                    MessageBox.Show("Invalid Food Sales")
                    txtFood.Focus()
                End If
```

```
            Else
                MessageBox.Show("Invalid Periodical Sales")
                txtPeriodicals.Focus()
            End If
        Else
            MessageBox.Show("Invalid Book Sales")
            txtBooks.Focus()
        End If
    End Sub

    Private Sub btnExit_Click(ByVal sender As System.Object, _
      ByVal e As System.EventArgs) Handles btnExit.Click
        'End the project

        Me.Close()
    End Sub

    Private Sub btnClear_Click(ByVal sender As System.Object, _
      ByVal e As System.EventArgs) Handles btnClear.Click
        'Clear the screen controls
        Dim brushClear As New SolidBrush(frmPieChart.DefaultBackColor)

        txtFood.Text = ""
        txtPeriodicals.Text = ""
        With txtBooks
            .Text = ""
            .Focus()
        End With
        Me.CreateGraphics.FillEllipse(brushClear, 160, 140, 100, 100)
        lblLegend.Visible = False
    End Sub
End Class
```

Summary

1. A drawing surface is created with a Graphics object.
2. The graphics methods should appear in the form's Paint event procedure, so that the graphics are redrawn every time the form is repainted.
3. Pen objects are used for lines and the outline of shapes; brushes are used for filled shapes.
4. Measurements in drawings are in pixels.
5. The coordinate system begins with 0,0 at the upper-left corner of the container object.
6. You can declare a Point structure, a Size structure, or a Rectangle structure to use as arguments in the graphics methods.
7. The Rnd function returns "random" numbers in the range 0 – 1. Use the Randomize statement to seed the random number generator, so that a different series of numbers is generated for each program run.
8. An animated .gif file can be displayed in a PictureBox or Image control to display animation on a Windows Form or a Web Form.
9. Animation effects can be created by using similar pictures and by controlling the location and visibility of controls.
10. Pictures can be loaded, moved, and resized at run time.

11. The Timer component can fire a Tick event that occurs at specified intervals.

12. Scroll bar controls are available for both horizontal and vertical directions. Properties include Minimum, Maximum, SmallChange, LargeChange, and Value. Scroll and ValueChanged events are used to respond to the action.

Key Terms

Brush object   *486*
DrawLine method   *489*
DrawRectangle method   *489*
FillEllipse method   *489*
FromFile method   *495*
graphics   *484*
horizontal scroll bar   *500*
Interval property   *498*
LargeChange property   *500*
Maximum property   *500*
Minimum property   *500*
Pen object   *486*
pixel   *486*

Point structure   *488*
Randomize statement   *491*
Rectangle structure   *488*
Rnd function   *491*
Scroll event   *501*
SetBounds method   *497*
Size structure   *488*
SmallChange property   *500*
Tick event   *497*
Timer component   *497*
Value property   *501*
ValueChanged event   *501*
vertical scroll bar   *500*

Review Questions

1. What is a pixel?
2. What class contains the graphics methods?
3. Describe two ways to add a Graphics object to a form.
4. Name three methods available for drawing graphics.
5. How is a pie-shaped wedge created?
6. Differentiate between using a Brush and Pen object.
7. Which function loads a picture at run time?
8. How is a picture removed at run time?
9. What steps are necessary to change an image that contains a turned-off light bulb to a turned-on light bulb?
10. What is the purpose of the Timer component?
11. Explain the purpose of these scroll bar properties: Minimum, Maximum, SmallChange, LargeChange, Value.

Programming Exercises

12.1   Create a project that contains two buttons labeled Smile and Frown. The Smile button will display a happy face; Frown will display a sad face. Use graphics methods to draw the two faces.

12.2   Use graphics methods to create the background of a form. Draw a picture of a house, including a front door, a window, and a chimney.

12.3   Use a PictureBox control with a .bmp file from Windows. Set the Size-Mode property to StretchImage. Use a scroll bar to change the size of the image.

12.4 Use graphics from any clip art collection to create a project that has a button for each month of the year. Have an appropriate image display in a PictureBox for each month.

12.5 Use the bicycle icon from Visual Basic and a Timer component to move the bicycle around the screen. Add a Start button and a Stop button. The Stop button will return the bicycle to its original position. (The bicycle icon is stored as Graphics\Icons\Industry\Bicycle.ico.)

12.6 Modify the snowman project (Ch 12 Random Numbers) from the chapter by adding eyes, a mouth, and buttons.

12.7 Modify the chapter hands-on example to add two more categories: Drinks and Gifts. Allow the user to enter the additional values and make the pie chart reflect all five categories. Make sure to set the legend label at the bottom of the form to include the new categories.

Case Studies

VB Mail Order

Create a logo for VB Mail Order using graphics methods. Place the logo in the startup form for the project from Chapter 6. Add appropriate images and graphics to enhance each form. The graphics may come from .bmp files, .gif files, clip art, or your own creation from Paintbrush.

VB Auto Center

Have the startup screen initially fill with random dots in your choice of colors. Use graphics methods to draw an Auto Center advertisement that will appear on the screen. Have various appropriate images (icons) appear in different locations, remain momentarily, and then disappear.

Video Bonanza

Use the timer component and the random number generator to create a promotional game for Video Bonanza customers. Create three PictureBox controls that will display an image selected from five possible choices. When the user clicks on the Start button, a randomly selected image will display in each of the PictureBox controls and continue to change for a few seconds (like a slot machine) until the user presses the Stop button. If all three images are the same, the customer receives a free video rental.

Display a message that says "Congratulations" or "Better Luck Next Visit."

Very Very Boards

Modify your Very Very Boards project from Chapter 6 or 8 to add a moving graphic to the About form. Use the graphic Skateboard.gif or other graphic of your choice. Include a timer component to move the graphic across the form. When the graphic reaches the edge of the form, reset it so that the graphic will ap-pear at the opposite edge of the screen and begin the trip again.

Note: For help in basing a new project on an existing project, see "Copy and Move a Windows Project" in Appendix C.

CHAPTER

13

Additional Topics in Visual Basic

rmat and display answers for sale.
ExtendedPrice.Text = FormatCurrency(decExtend
Discount.Text = FormatNumber(decDiscount)
DiscountedPrice.Text = FormatCurrency(decDisc
ndle exceptions
MyErr As InvalidCastException

at the completion of this chapter, you will be able to . . .

1. Create a multiple document project with parent and child forms.

2. Arrange the child forms vertically, horizontally, or cascaded.

3. Store images in an image list.

4. Add toolbars and status bars to your forms.

5. Use calendar controls and date functions.

6. Create data reports using Crystal Reports.

This chapter introduces some topics that can make your programs a bit more professional. You can improve the operation of multiple-form applications by using a multiple document interface (MDI), which allows you to set up parent and child forms. Most professional applications have toolbars and status bars, which you learn to create in this chapter. Also, Visual Studio .NET includes Crystal Reports to provide an easy method to produce data reports directly from your applications.

Multiple Document Interface

All of the projects so far have been **single document interface (SDI).** Using SDI, each form in the project acts independently from the other forms. However, VB also allows you to create a **multiple document interface (MDI).** For an example of MDI, consider an application such as Microsoft Word. Word has a **parent form** (the main window) and **child forms** (each document window). You can open multiple child windows, and you can maximize, minimize, restore, or close each child window, which always stays within the boundaries of the parent window. When you close the parent window, all child windows close automatically. Figure 13.1 shows an MDI parent window with two open child windows.

- MDI now allows multiple parent forms.

- An MDI parent is set with the IsMdiContainer property of a regular form. It isn't necessary to create a separate class of form.

- Child forms are set at run time after the form is instantiated.

Figure 13.1

The main form is the parent and the smaller forms are the child forms in an MDI application.

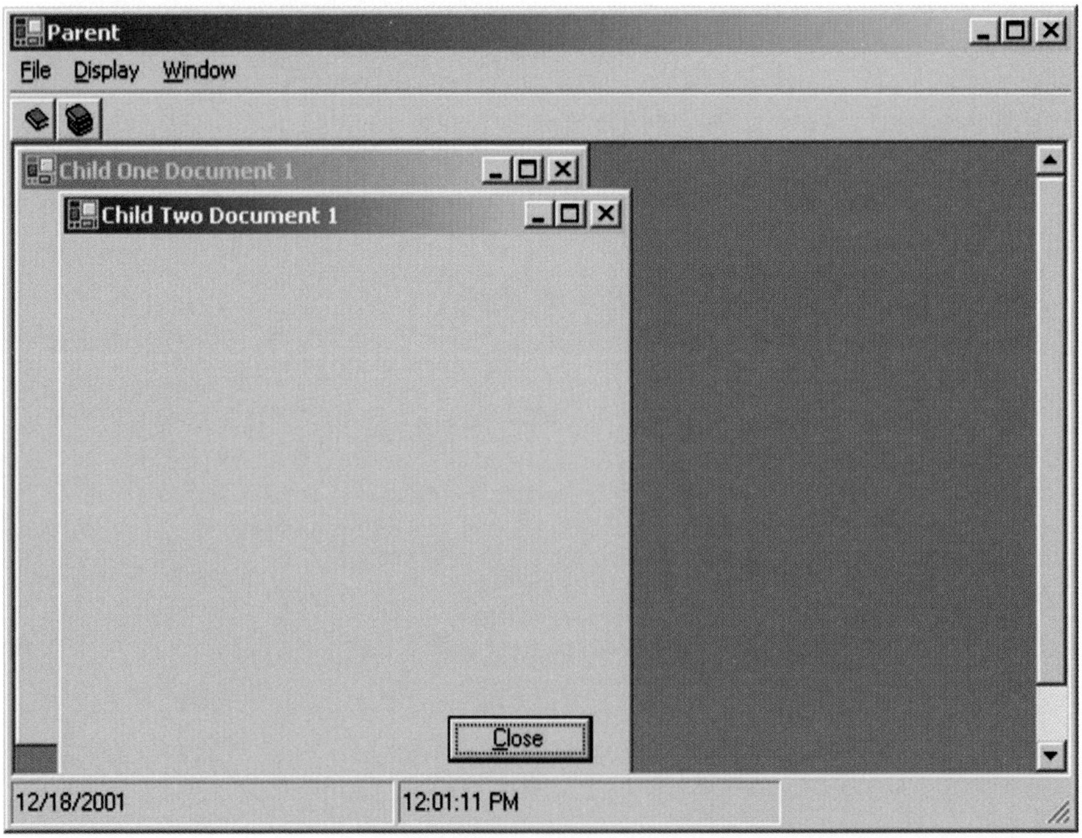

With MDI, a parent and child relationship exists between the main form and the child forms. One of the rules for MDI is that if a parent form closes, all of its children leave with it. Pretty good rule. Another rule is that children cannot wander out of the parent's area; the child form always appears inside the parent's area.

VB allows you to combine MDI and SDI. For example, you may have a parent form and several child forms *and* some forms that operate independently. For example, a splash form likely should remain SDI.

One feature of MDI is that you can have several documents open at the same time. The menu bar generally contains a *Window* menu that allows you to display a list of open windows and move from one active document to another.

Creating an MDI Project

You can make any form a parent. Simply change its **IsMdiContainer property** to True. In a VB .NET project you can have multiple parent forms.

Creating a child is almost as easy. Of course, your project must contain more than one form. You make a form into a child window in code at run time. Before displaying the child form from the parent, set the child's MdiParent property to the current (parent) form.

```
Private Sub mnuDisplayChildOne_Click(ByVal sender As System.Object, _
  ByVal e As System.EventArgs) Handles mnuDisplayChildOne.Click
    'Display Child One

    Dim frmChildOne As New frmChildOne()
    frmChildOne.MdiParent = Me
    frmChildOne.Show()
End Sub
```

Our example application allows the user to display multiple child windows. Therefore, the title bar of each child window should be unique. We can accomplish this by appending a number to the title bar before displaying the form. This is very much like Microsoft Word, with its Document1, Document2, and so forth.

```
'Module-level declarations
Dim mintChildOneCount As Integer

Private Sub mnuDisplayChildOne_Click(ByVal sender As System.Object, _
  ByVal e As System.EventArgs) Handles mnuDisplayChildOne.Click
    'Display Child One

    Dim frmChildOne As New frmChildOne()
    frmChildOne.MdiParent = Me
    mintChildOneCount += 1
    frmChildOne.Text = "Child One Document " & mintChildOneCount.ToString
    frmChildOne.Show()
End Sub
```

Adding a Window Menu

A parent form should have a *Window* menu (Figure 13.2). The *Window* menu lists the open child windows and allows the user to switch between windows and arrange multiple child windows. Take a look at the *Window* menu in an application such as Word or Excel: You will see a list of the open documents as well as options for arranging the windows.

• The Arrange methods have been replaced with enumerations used with the LayoutMdi Method of the parent form:

```
Me.LayoutMdi(MdiLayout.
Cascade)
```

F i g u r e   1 3 . 2

The Window *menu in an MDI application lists the open child windows and allows the user to select the arrangement of the windows.*

After you create a *Window* menu on your parent form, it's very easy to make it display the list of open child windows. Just set the menu's **MdiList property** to True. To arrange the windows requires a little code.

Layout Options

When several child windows are open, the windows may be arranged in several different layouts: tiled vertically, tiled horizontally, or cascaded. You set the type of layout with an argument of the LayoutMdi **method.**

```
Me.LayoutMdi(MdiLayout.TileHorizontal)
```

You can use one of the three constants: TileHorizontal, TileVertical, and Cascade.

```
Private Sub mnuWindowHorizontal_Click(ByVal sender As System.Object, _
  ByVal e As System.EventArgs) Handles mnuWindowHorizontal.Click
    'Arrange the child forms

    Me.LayoutMdi(MdiLayout.TileHorizontal)
End Sub

Private Sub mnuWindowVertical_Click(ByVal sender As System.Object, _
  ByVal e As System.EventArgs) Handles mnuWindowVertical.Click
    'Arrange the child forms

    Me.LayoutMdi(MdiLayout.TileVertical)
End Sub

Private Sub mnuWindowCascade_Click(ByVal sender As System.Object, _
  ByVal e As System.EventArgs) Handles mnuWindowCascade.Click
    'Arrange the child forms

    Me.LayoutMdi(MdiLayout.Cascade)
End Sub
```

Toolbars and Status Bars

You can enhance the usability of your programs by adding features such as a toolbar and/or status bar. You probably find that you use the toolbars in applications as an easy shortcut for menu items. Status bars normally appear at the bottom of the screen to display information for the user.

To create a toolbar, you need a **toolbar control** and an **image list component,** which holds the graphics that appear on the toolbar buttons.

Image Lists

When you need several images to display in an application, you can store them in an image list component. Then you can assign the individual images to other controls, as needed. The toolbar control requires that its images be stored in an image list.

You add an image list to a form in the same way as any other component: Simply drag the ImageList control (Figure 13.3) from the toolbox and a new object appears in the component tray. Name your image list using "ils" for the prefix.

- The image list contains a collection of images. You can now add images after connecting the image list to a toolbar.

- The buttons collection of the toolbar control displays the images from the attached image list.

Figure   13.3

The ImageList control in the toolbox.

After adding the image list to the form, you add images to the component's Images collection. In the Properties window, locate the Images property and click the Builder (ellipses) button to open the Image Collection Editor (Figure 13.4). Click on the Add button in the left pane to add images to the collection. An index is automatically assigned to each image in the collection. You use the index of each image to assign the pictures to the toolbar buttons, but you will be able to see a preview of each image.

Figure 13.4

Add images to the ImageList control using the Image Collection Editor.

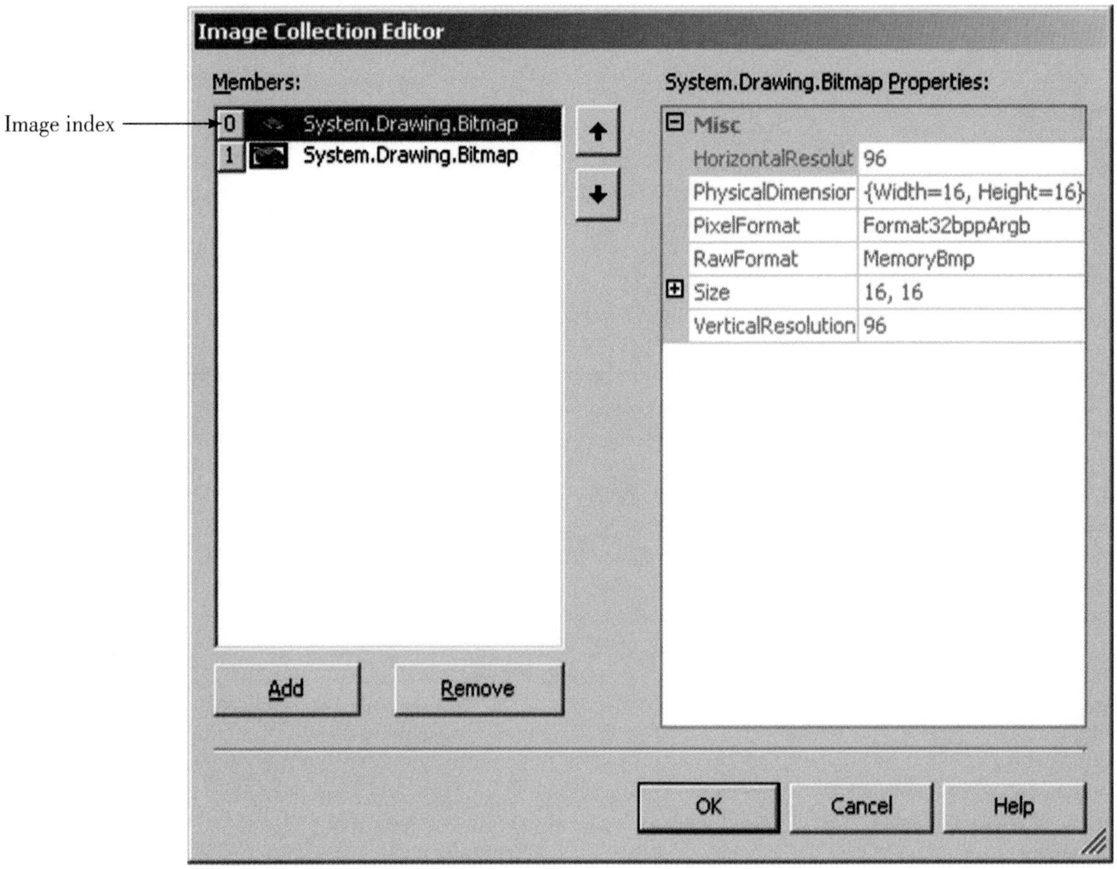

Toolbars

You use the ToolBar tool (Figure 13.5) in the toolbox to create a Toolbar object for your project. The new toolbar does not yet contain any buttons. You add the buttons using the Buttons collection in the Properties window. Name your Toolbar object with "tlb" for the prefix. Refer to Figure 13.1 to see a toolbar.

• You can give each toolbar button its own name. But there is only one Click event for the entire toolbar.

Figure 13.5

The ToolBar control in the toolbox.

Setting Up the Buttons

Before you add buttons to the new toolbar, assign your image list component to the ImageList property of the toolbar. Then simply click on the Builder (ellipses) button for the Buttons collection to open the ToolBarButton Collection Editor (Figure 13.6). Click the *Add* button, which adds a new button to the collection. Then you set the properties for the new button in the right pane of the window. When you drop down the list for the ImageIndex property, the index and images from the image list appear (Figure 13.7).

Figure   13.6

Add buttons to the new toolbar by clicking the Add button in the left pane of the ToolBarButton Collection Editor.

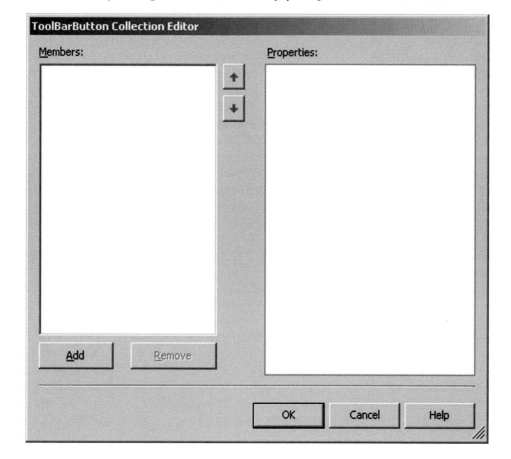

Figure 13.7

Set the properties of each toolbar button in the right pane of the ToolBarButton Collection Editor. Drop down the list for the ImageIndex property to view the images and select the correct index.

A big improvement in VB .NET over previous versions is that you can add images to the image list after you attach the image list to the toolbar.

Coding for the Toolbar

The toolbar has a single ButtonClick event that occurs when the user clicks on any of the buttons. You can use the event arguments to determine which button was clicked. For example, assuming that the toolbar is named tlbParent, you can find the index of the selected button with this code:

`tlbParent.Buttons.IndexOf(e.Button)`

You can use the index of the selected button in a `Select Case` statement to send the user to the appropriate menu procedure.

> **✓TIP**
>
> **S**et the ToolTipText property of each toolbar button to aid the user, in case the meaning of each graphic is not perfectly clear. ∎

```
Private Sub tlbParent_ButtonClick(ByVal sender As System.Object, _
  ByVal e As System.Windows.Forms.ToolBarButtonClickEventArgs) Handles _
  tlbParent.ButtonClick
    'Execute appropriate procedure for button clicked

    Select Case tlbParent.Buttons.IndexOf(e.Button)
       Case 0
           mnuDisplayChildOne_Click(sender, e)
       Case 1
           mnuDisplayChildTwo_Click(sender, e)
    End Select

End Sub
```

Status Bars

A **status bar** is usually located at the bottom of a form (refer to Figure 13.1). A status bar displays information such as date, time, status of the Caps Lock or Num Lock key, or error or informational messages. If you want a status bar on your form you need to take two steps: add a **StatusBar control** (Figure 13.8) to your form and add **StatusBarPanel objects** to the status bar.

• You can give each status bar panel its own name and refer to the panel by name in code. It isn't necessary to use indexes.

Figure 13.8

The StatusBar control in the toolbox.

After adding a status bar to your form, you need to set a few properties. Name the control using "sbr" as the prefix. By default, the **ShowPanels property** is set to False; change this to True. The status bar can display either the Text property of the control or the Text properties of the panels, but not both.

You add panels to the status bar by selecting the Panels collection. Click the *Add* button in the StatusBarPanel Collection Editor, add a panel, and set its properties in the right pane of the window (Figure 13.9). Name the panels using "sbp" as the prefix. You may find that you need to adjust the panel width to display the information completely.

Figure 13.9

Add panels to a status bar using the StatusBarPanel Collection Editor. Add the panel in the left side of the window and set the panel's properties in the right side.

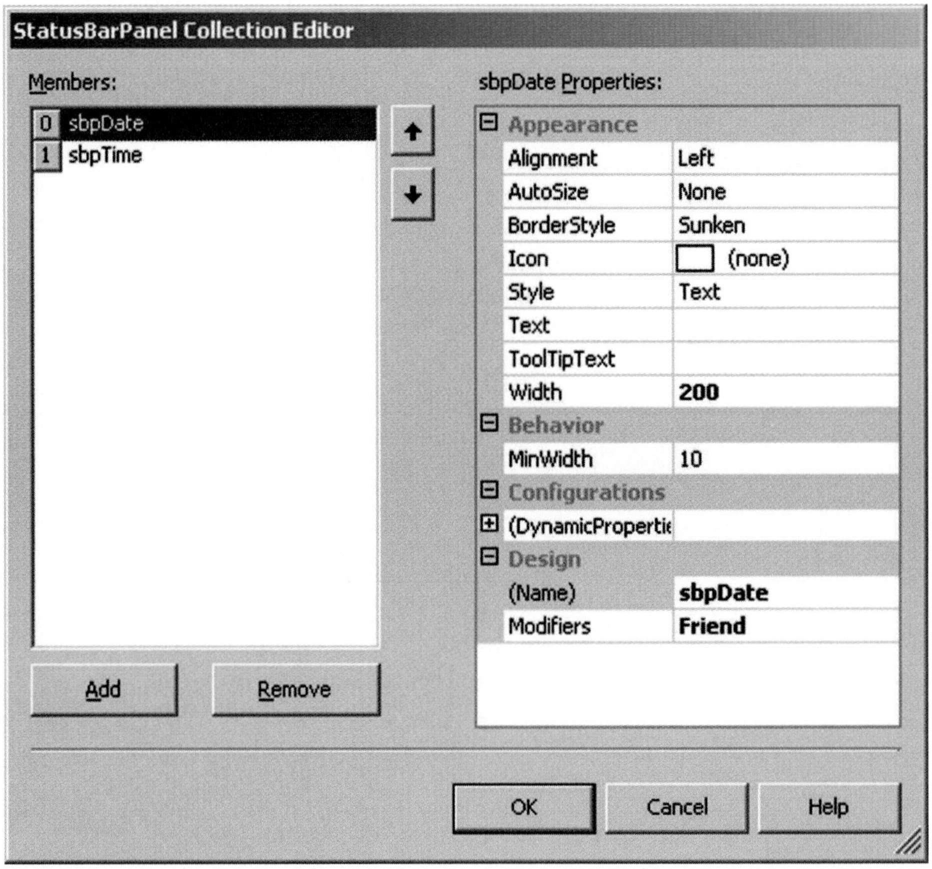

Assigning Values to Panels

You assign values to the Text property of panels at run time:

```
sbpDate.Text = Now.ToShortDateString
sbpTime.Text = Now.ToShortTimeString
sbpInformation.Text = "It's very late."
```

Displaying the Date and Time

You use the properties and methods of the **DateTime structure** to retrieve and format the current date and time. The **Now property** holds the system date and time in a numeric format that can be used for calculations. You can format the date for display using one of the methods: `ToShortDateString`, `ToLongDateString`, `ToShortTimeString`, or `ToLongTimeString`. The actual display format of each method depends on the local system settings.

You can set the display value of status bar panels in any procedure; however, the display does not update automatically. Generally you will set initial values in the Form_Load event procedure and use a Timer component to update the time.

- You must write code to display any item(s) on the status bar; none are displayed automatically.

- Status bars require a Timer component and code to update the time.

```
Private Sub frmParent_Load(ByVal sender As Object, _
  ByVal e As System.EventArgs) Handles MyBase.Load
    'Display the date and time in the status bar

    sbpDate.Text = Now.ToShortDateString
    sbpTime.Text = Now.ToLongTimeString
End Sub

Private Sub tmrClock_Tick(ByVal sender As System.Object, _
  ByVal e As System.EventArgs) Handles tmrClock.Tick
    'Update the date and time on the status bar
    'Interval = 1000 milliseconds (one second)

    sbpDate.Text = Now.ToShortDateString
    sbpTime.Text = Now.ToLongTimeString
End Sub
```

Don't forget to set the Enabled and Interval properties of your timer.

Feedback 13.1

1. Write the statements to display frmAbout as a child form.
2. Assume that you have a toolbar called tlbMain that has buttons for *Exit* and *About* with indexes of 0 and 1. Write the code to execute the correct procedure when the user clicks one of the buttons.
3. What steps are necessary to display the current time in a status bar panel called sbpCurrentTime?

Some More Controls

There are many other controls in the toolbox. You may want to play with some of them to see how they work. This section demonstrates two more controls: the DateTimePicker and MonthCalendar controls.

The Calendar Controls

The DateTimePicker and the MonthCalendar controls (Figure 13.10) provide the ability to display calendars on your form. One advantage of the Date-TimePicker is that it takes less screen space; it displays only the day and date unless the user drops down the calendar. You can use either control to allow the user to select a date, display the current date, or set a date in code and display the calendar with that date showing.

Figure 13.10

The calendar controls: The DateTimePicker drops down a calendar when selected and shows the current day and date when not dropped down; the MonthCalendar control displays the calendar.

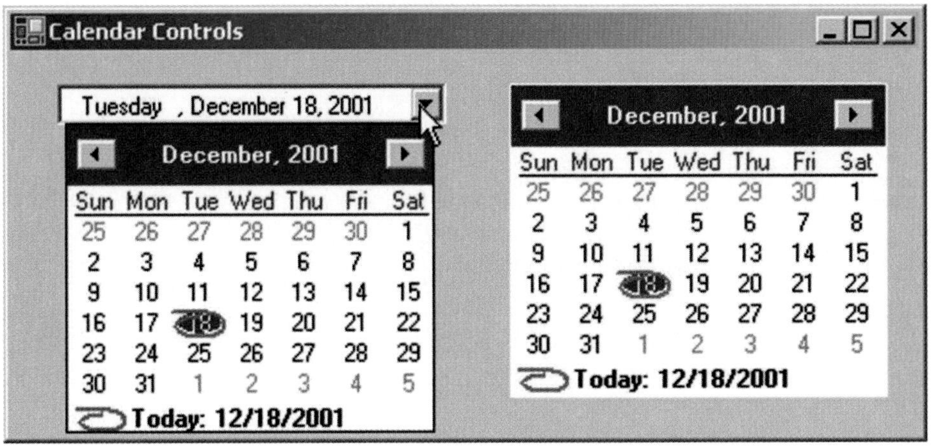

The DateTimePicker control contains a Value property for the date. When the control initially displays, the Value is set to the current date. You can let the user select a date and then use the Value property or you can assign a Date value to the property.

The following example allows the user to enter a birthdate in a text box, validates the text box entry with the IsDate function, and converts the text box value to a date using the CDate function.

```
If IsDate(txtBirthdate.Text) Then
    dtmBirthdate.Value = CDate(txtBirthdate.Text)
End If
```

This example program demonstrates the use of the calendar, date functions, and some interesting features of Visual Basic. Figure 13.11 shows the form for the project.

Figure 13.11

The birthday form with the calendar for the DateTimePicker dropped down.

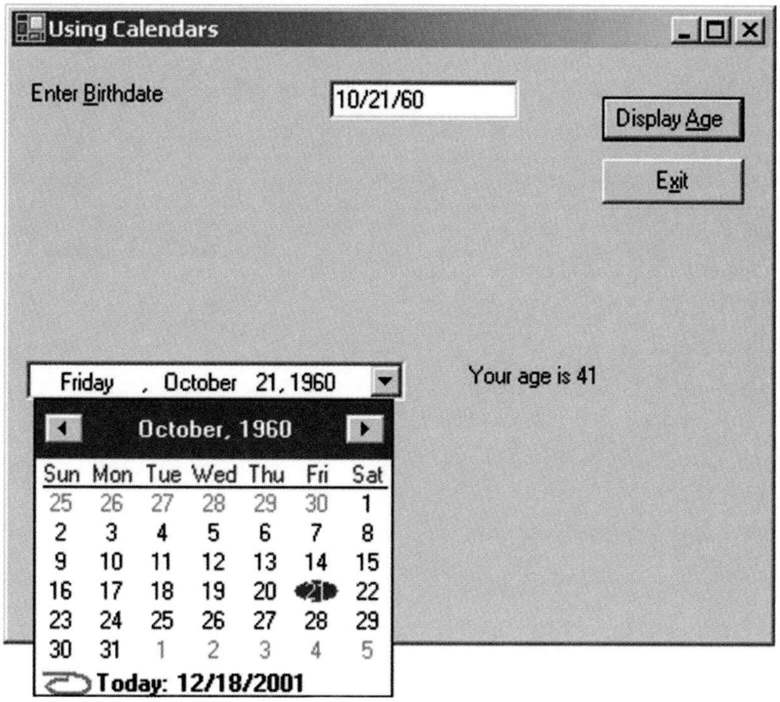

```
'Program         Chapter 13 Calendar control
'Programmer:     Bradley/Millspaugh
'Date:           January 2002
'Description:     Enters and tests a date, displays a calendar and uses
'                 Date functions
'Folder:         Ch13Calendar

Option Strict On

Public Class frmCalendar
    Inherits System.Windows.Forms.Form

[Windows Form Designer generated code]

Private Sub btnDisplay_Click(ByVal sender As System.Object, _
 ByVal e As System.EventArgs) Handles btnDisplay.Click
    'If valid date, set calendar and display
```

```
        If IsDate(txtBirthdate.Text) Then
            With dtmBirthdate
                .Value = CDate(txtBirthdate.Text)
                .Visible = True
            End With
        Else
            MessageBox.Show("Invalid Date")
        End If
    End Sub

    Private Sub dtmBirthdate_ValueChanged(ByVal sender As System.Object, _
     ByVal e As System.EventArgs) Handles dtmBirthdate.ValueChanged
        'Calculate the age when the calendar value changes
        Dim intYears As Integer

        With dtmBirthdate.Value
            'If birthday already passed this year
            If .DayOfYear <= Now.DayOfYear Then
                intYears = Now.Year - .Year
            Else        'Birthday yet to come this year
                intYears = Now.Year - .Year - 1
            End If
        End With

        With lblAge
            .Text = "Your age is " & intYears.ToString
            .Visible = True
        End With
    End Sub

    Private Sub cmdExit_Click(ByVal sender As System.Object, _
     ByVal e As System.EventArgs) Handles cmdExit.Click
        'Terminate the project

        Me.Close()
    End Sub
End Class
```

Notice the ValueChanged event procedure for the DatePicker. It contains a few surprises. The date Value has all of the methods and properties available for the system time:

```
intYears = dtmBirthdate.Value.Year - Now.Year
```

You can see all of the methods and properties using Visual Studio's IntelliSense feature.

▶ **Feedback 13.2**

1. Write the code to assign the date from dtmAppointment to the field txtAppointment.
2. Use the IntelliSense or Help to list five properties of the Value property for a calendar control.
3. Which of the five properties listed in question 2 are also available for the Now property?

Crystal Reports

One of the powerful features of the new version of Visual Basic is the report designer by Crystal Decisions called **Crystal Reports.** The Crystal Report Gallery contains "experts" to guide you in creating standard reports, forms, and even mailing labels, or you can use an existing report or generate a new one. Using Crystal Reports you can publish reports on Windows Forms or on Web Forms.

It takes two steps to create and display a report:

1. Add a Report Designer and design the report template. The template includes the settings for connection to the database and the layout of the report.
2. Add a **CrystalReportViewer control** to a form and connect it to the report template.

Once you have added the report to a project and run the project, you can view the report and send the report to the printer, if you wish.

- Crystal Reports are back and more powerful. The Report Designer of VB 6 is gone.

- No code is required to write a report, design the template, and add a CrystalReportViewer object to the form.

Adding a Report Designer

You add a new Report Designer to a project by selecting *Add New Item* from the *Project* menu and choosing the *Crystal Report* icon. Give the report a name before pressing the Enter key (Figure 13.12).

Figure 13.12

Add a new Crystal Report item and give it a name on the Add New Item dialog box.

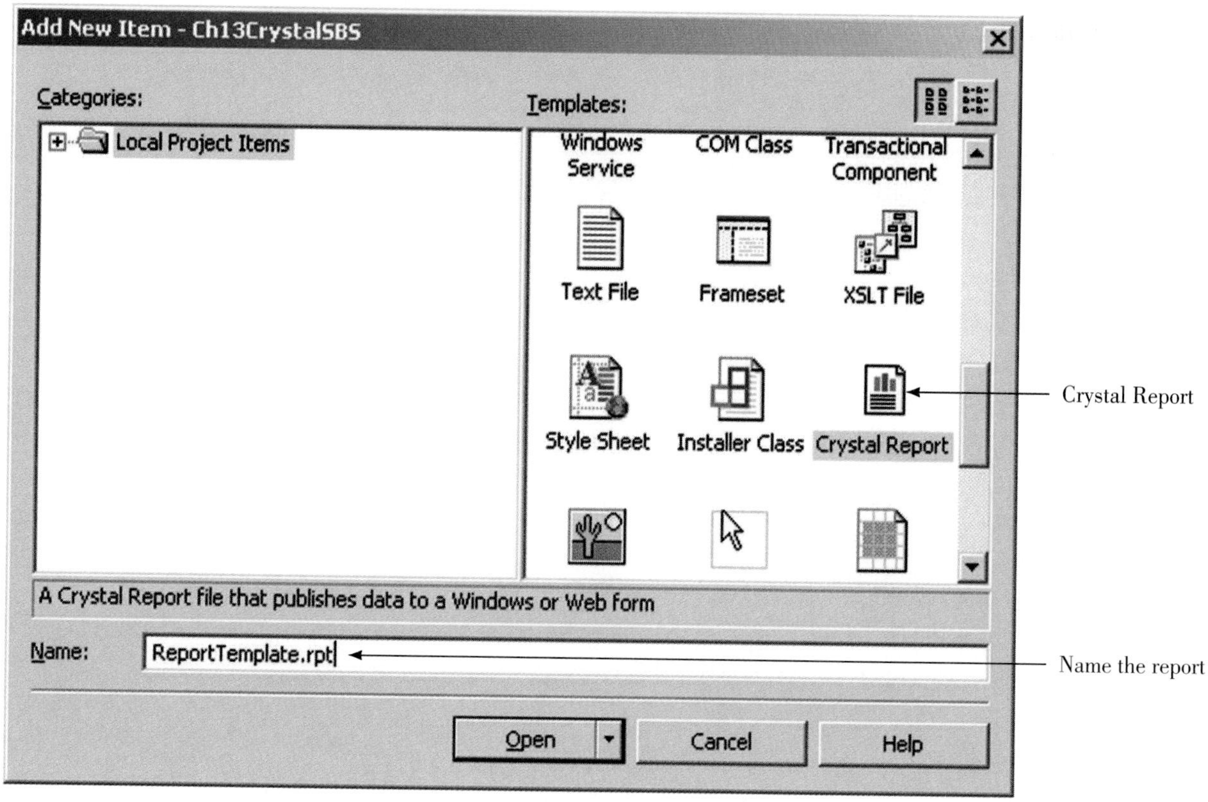

Next you are given a choice of the type of report to create (Figure 13.13). You can choose *Using the Report Expert* to open a wizard that steps you through the report creation process. Or you can choose *As a Blank Report* to create your own report from scratch. The third choice, *From an Existing Report,* allows you to create a modification of a report you have already created. The example in this chapter uses the wizard.

F i g u r e   1 3 . 1 3

Select the type of new report for the Crystal Reports Designer.

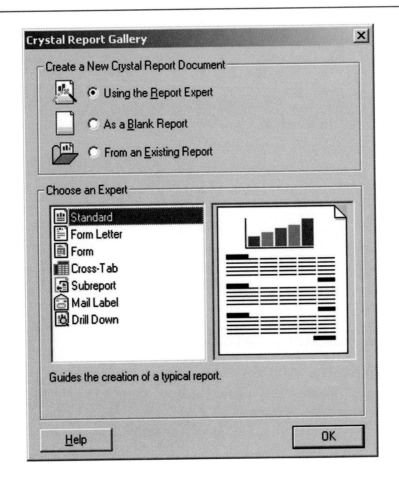

Creating a Report—Step-by-Step

The following tutorial walks you through the steps for creating a Crystal Report for R 'n R. Figure 13.14 shows the completed report.

Figure 13.14

The completed report from the step-by-step example.

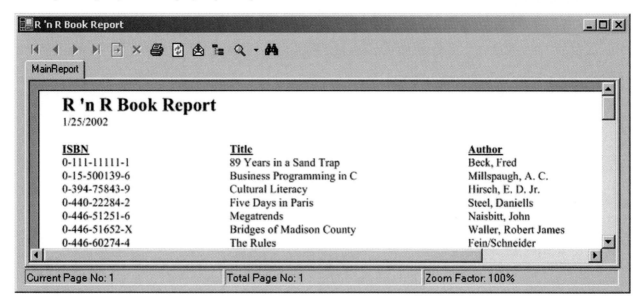

Create the Project

STEP 1: Create a new Windows Applications project called *Ch13CrystalSBS*.

STEP 2: Change the form's Text property to "R 'n R Book Report".

STEP 3: Change the form's Name property to frmReport, display the project properties, and set the project's startup object to frmReport.

STEP 4: Using Windows Explorer or My Computer, copy RnRBooks.mdb into your Ch13CrystalSBS folder. (You can find RnRBooks.mdb on the text CD.) Make sure that the file is not ReadOnly.

Design the Report

STEP 1: Select *Add New Item* from the *Project* menu and click on the *Crystal Report* icon.

STEP 2: Type the name "ReportTemplate" and press Enter (refer to Figure 13.12). The Registration Wizard may appear; click "Register Later".

STEP 3: Make sure the option for *Using the Report Expert* and the standard report type are selected (refer to Figure 13.13). Click OK.

STEP 4: On the first screen of the Standard Report Expert (the wizard), click on the plus sign to expand the node for Database Files (Figure 13.15). An *Open* dialog box appears; browse to find RnRBooks.mdb in your project folder, select the file name, and click *Open*. The names of the tables in the database should appear.

Figure 13.15

The first screen of the Standard Report Expert wizard. Expand the node for Database Files to connect to your database file.

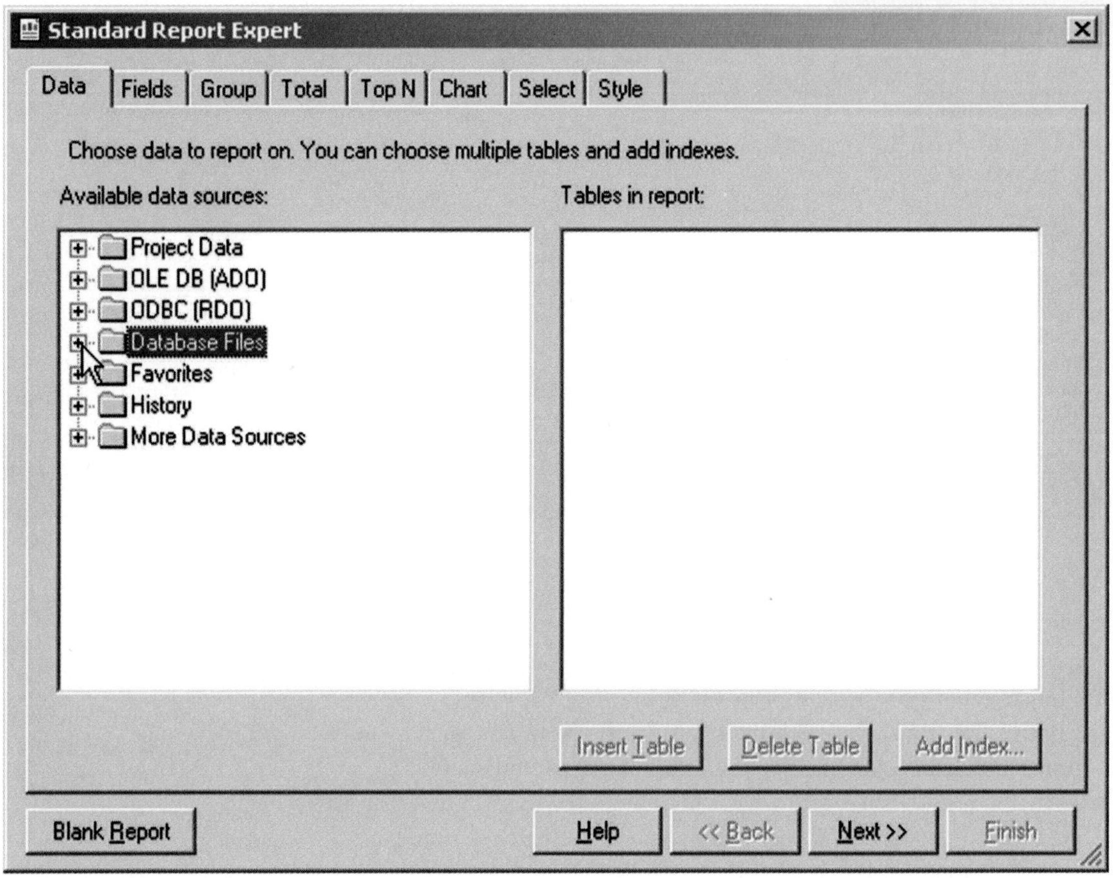

STEP 5: Select the Books table and click *Insert Table* (or double-click the Books table). The table name will appear in the right pane (Figure 13.16).

Figure 13.16

Select the Books table and add it to the right pane.

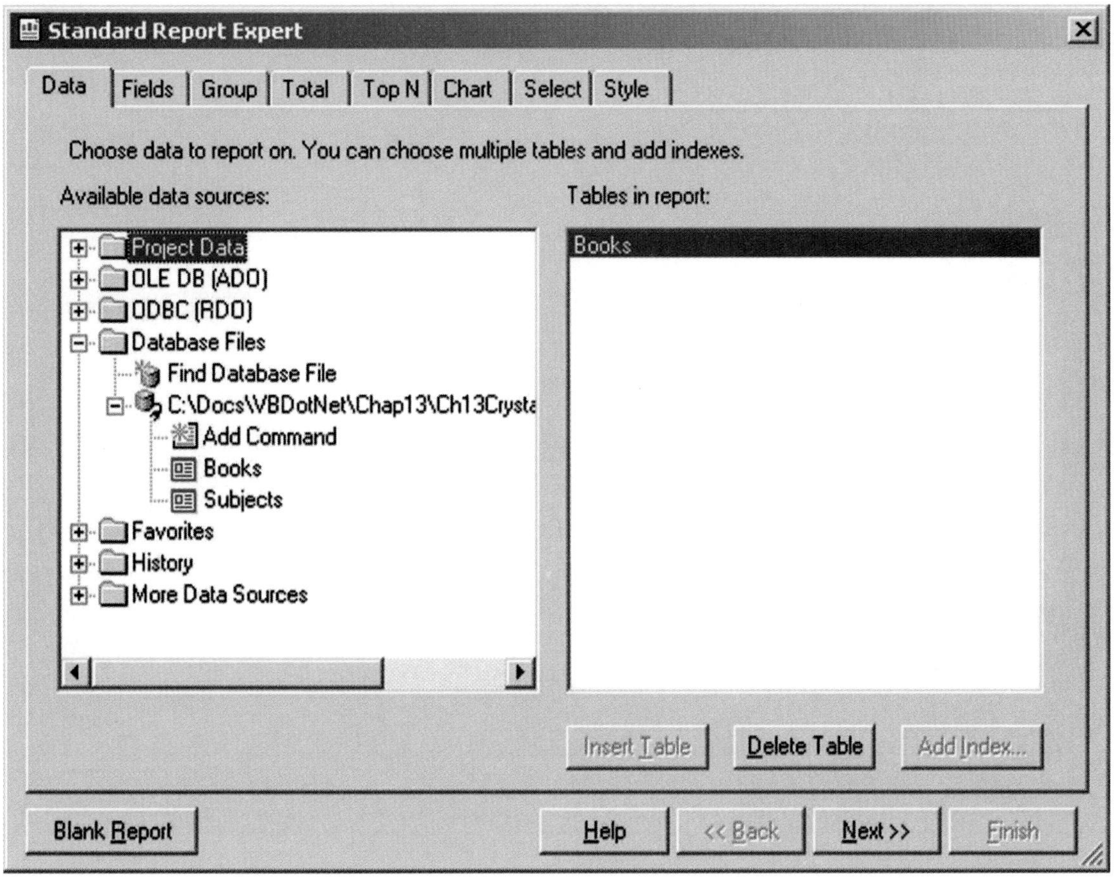

You can click through every tabbed page of the wizard, or use the tabs to go directly to the pages that you want to use.

STEP 6: Click *Next,* which takes you to the *Fields* page of the wizard.

On this screen you select the fields that you want to include on the report. Select the field names from the list on the left and add them to the list on the right. You can either click the field name and click *Add,* or double-click the field name.

STEP 7: Add ISBN, Title, and Author to the *Fields to Display* list (Figure 13.17).

Figure 13.17

Double-click on each field name to add it to the Fields to Display list.

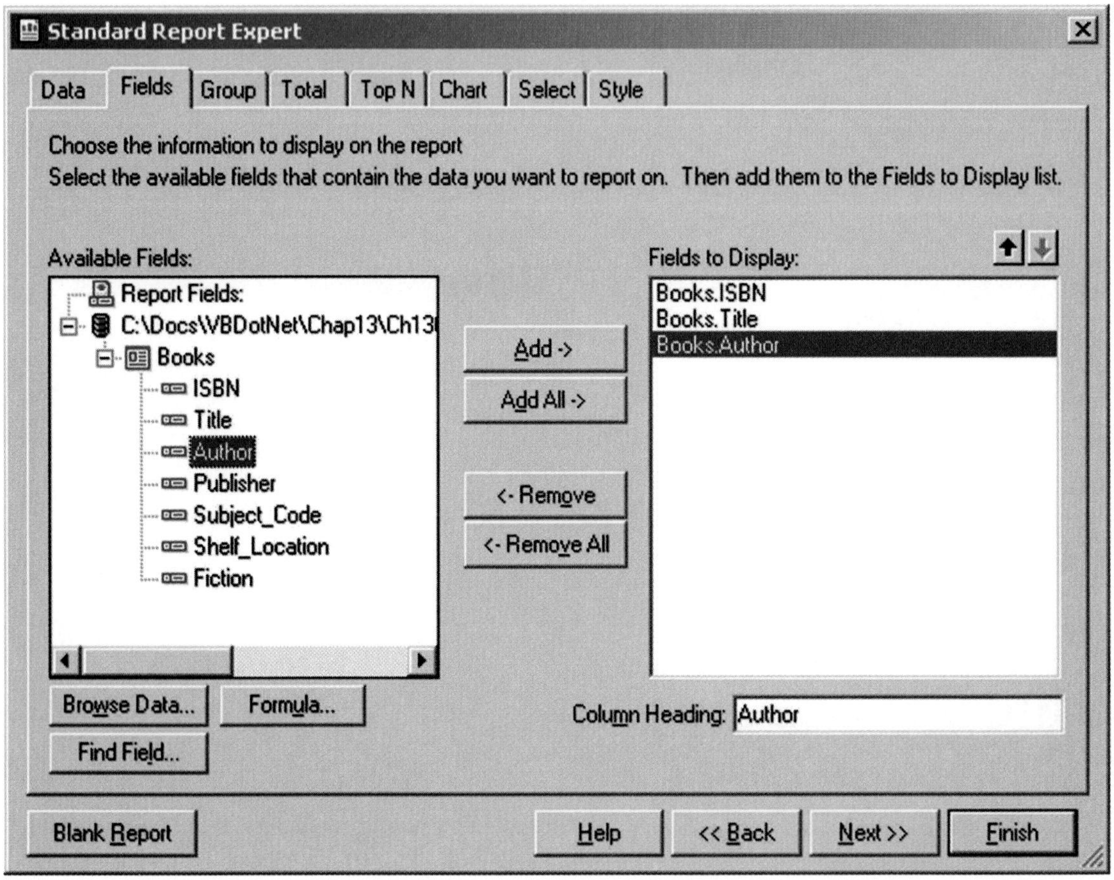

STEP 8: Click on the *Style* tab at the top of the wizard. (If you want to view the other tabs, you can click *Next* through each page. For this report, you only need the *Style* tab.)

TIP

Click on a field in the Available Fields list and select *Browse Data* to see the actual data in the table. ■

STEP 9: For *Title*, type "R 'n R Book Report". Click on each of the entries in the *Style* box to see the possibilities. Then click on *Standard* and click *Finish*. The report designer appears with the entries that you selected (Figure 13.18).

Figure 13.18

The Crystal Reports report designer with the layout created by the wizard.

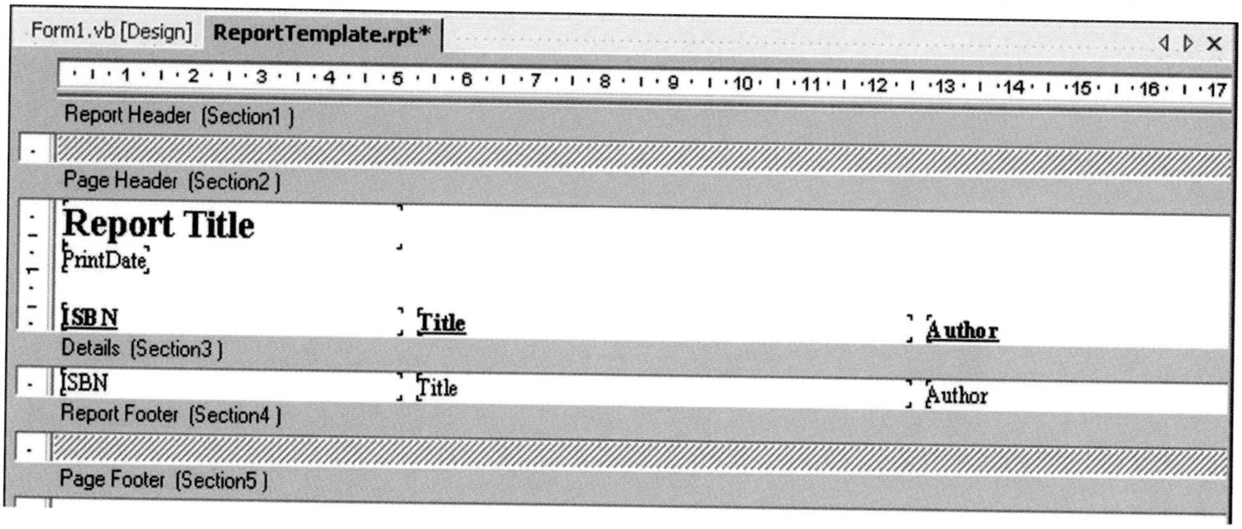

At this point, the report template is complete. However, you can make lots of adjustments and changes to the content and format. The various parts of the report layout screen are covered later in "The Report Designer" section (page 532).

Display the Report

STEP 1: Return to the Form Designer window.
STEP 2: Drag a CrystalReportsViewer tool to the form. It's the last tool in the list.
STEP 3: Increase the size of the form and of the viewer.
STEP 4: Change the Name property of the viewer to rptRnR.
STEP 5: Set the ReportSource property to ReportTemplate.rpt by using the *Browse* option and finding the file in the Ch13CrystalSBS folder.

STEP 6: Change the DisplayGroupTree property to False. Figure 13.19 shows the form at this point.

Figure 13.19

The form with the Crystal Reports report viewer control. Expand the form and the control to allow space for the report to display.

STEP 7: Set the Anchor property of the control to anchor to all four edges (top, bottom, left, and right). This will make the control resize if you resize the form.

Run the Project

STEP 1: Run the project. The report should appear with the data you selected. Take note of the spacing and formatting, to see if there is anything you'd like to change. You'll have a chance to make adjustments in a minute. Also try resizing and/or maximizing the form.

STEP 2: Close the form to return to design mode. You can make any desired adjustments to the report layout or to the form. See the section "Modifying Report Design" (page 534) for some help.

The Report Designer

When the Crystal Reports Report Designer displays, you have many options. You can see two new toolbars, a separate section in the toolbox, and a **Field Explorer** window (Figure 13.20), which appears as a separate tab in the Toolbox window (Figure 13.21). You can use the Field Explorer to add new fields to your report. Use the items in the toolbox to add elements such as lines, boxes, or additional text that is not bound to a data field, such as explanations or additional title lines.

Figure 13.20

The Crystal Reports section →

The toolbox section for Crystal Reports.

Field Explorer tab

Figure 13.21

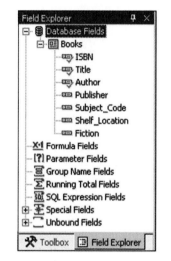

The Crystal Reports Field Explorer.

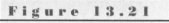

The report template contains several bands for information. Refer to Figure 13.18.

- The Report Header appears one time at the beginning of the report. You can place any item in this section that you want to appear on only the first page of a multipage report.

- The Page Header appears at the top of each page. Generally the Page Header section holds the report title and column headings.

- The Details section holds the data for the body of the report. Here you place the fields that you want to appear on each line of the report. Generally, this is the data from each record.

- The Report footer appears once at the end of the report.

- The Page footer appears at the bottom of each page.

Modifying Report Design

You can move, resize, and reformat the fields in the designer. Click on any field and resize it using the sizing handles, or drag the control to move it. To reformat a field, right-click and select *Format* from the shortcut menu.

If you want to recall the Report Expert (the wizard) or change the style of the report, right-click on the report design. On the shortcut menu, select *Report* (Figure 13.22). From the pop-up menu, you can choose *Report Expert* to open the wizard or *Style Expert* to select a new report style.

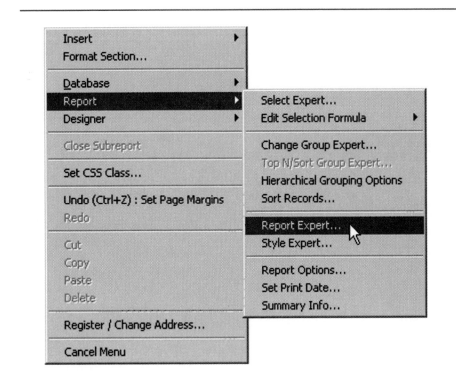

Figure 13.22

Make changes to the report design by selecting Report Expert from the shortcut menu. Or select Style Expert to choose a new report style.

Do you want to change the page margins? If so, right-click on the designer, select *Designer* and *Page Setup* (Figure 13.23).

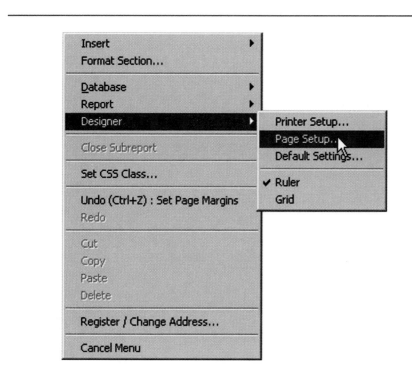

Adding a Report to a Web Form

You can display reports from Web Forms, but there are a few differences from Windows Forms. Just as with all controls, you use a different CrystalReportsViewer control on your Web form. You will find the correct control in the Web Forms section of the toolbox. The Web version of the report viewer does not have a printer option; you can only display the report on the screen.

You must set the viewer's ReportSource property in code, rather than the Properties window. Add this code to the Web Form's Page_Load event procedure, substituting the path and report designer name for the actual name on your system.

```
Private Sub Page_Load(ByVal sender As System.Object, _
  ByVal e As System.EventArgs) Handles MyBase.Load
      'Put user code to initialize the page here

      CrystalReportViewer1.ReportSource = _
      "C:\inetpub\wwwroot\CrystalReports\CrystalReport1.rpt"
End Sub
```

Moving a Crystal Reports Project

When you move a project that has a Crystal Report, you must make two changes:

1. Change the data source for the report template. In the Field Explorer, right-click on the Database Fields icon and choose *Set Location* from the shortcut menu. In the *Set Location* dialog box you can browse to find the current location of the database file.
2. Change the ReportSource property of the CrystalReportViewer control on the form. You can browse to locate the project's current folder.

Summary

1. A multiple document interface (MDI) contains parent and child forms. Closing the parent also closes all child forms. The child forms stay within the bounds of the parent form.
2. To create an MDI parent form, set a form's IsMdiContainer property to True. To create a child form, set the form's MdiParent property to the parent form in code.
3. MDI applications generally have a *Window* menu, which displays a list of open child windows and provides choices for arranging the child windows.
4. An image list component contains a collection of the images for other controls, such as the buttons on a toolbar.
5. To create a toolbar, add the control, attach the image list, and add buttons to the Buttons collection. Set each button to one of the images in the image list.
6. A toolbar provides shortcuts to menu options. A `Select Case` statement can be used in the toolbar's ButtonClick event procedure to determine which button was clicked and take appropriate action.
7. A status bar contains information for the user along the bottom of a form. After adding a status bar to a project, add panels to its Panels collection.
8. The date can be assigned to the Text property of a panel during the Form_Load event procedure, but the time display requires an update routine using a Timer component.
9. The DateTimePicker and MonthCalendar tools have accurate calendars for displaying and inputting dates.
10. Variables in Visual Studio contain properties and methods associated with the data type. In other words, even Integers are classes and variables are objects.
11. Crystal Reports make it easy to generate reports for database applications.
12. The Crystal Report Designer is used to create a report template.
13. The CrystalReportViewer control is placed on a form to display the data.

Key Terms

Review Questions

1. What is meant by *MDI?*
2. What are the advantages of having parent and child forms?
3. What are the layouts available for arranging child windows?
4. How can a child form be created? A parent form?
5. What steps are necessary to create a toolbar and have its buttons execute menu procedures?
6. What must be done to create a status bar? To display a panel with the current time? To keep the time display current?
7. Describe two controls that you can use for displaying dates on a form.
8. Describe the steps necessary to add a database report to a form.

Programming Exercises

13.1 Write an MDI project that is a simple text editor. Allow the user to open multiple documents, each in a separate child form. For the text editor, use one big TextBox control with its Multiline property set to True or a RichTextBox control. Set the control's Anchor property to all four edges so the control fills its form.

Each form should have its own Load File and Save file functions. Use the FileStreams that you learned about in Chapter 11.

13.2 Add a toolbar to a previous project to provide shortcuts to the menu items.

13.3 Add a toolbar to the calendar program from this chapter.

13.4 Add a report to your database project from Chapter 10. You can add a form to display the report.

Answers to Feedback Questions

Feedback 1.1

These exercises are designed to become familiar with the Help system. There are no "correct" answers.

 Feedback 2.1

Property	Setting
Name	picIcon
BorderStyle	Fixed3D
SizeMode	StretchImage
Visible	True

 Feedback 2.2

1. ```
   txtCompany.Text = ""
   txtCompany.Focus()
   ```

2. ```
   lblCustomer.Text = ""
   txtOrder.Focus()
   ```

3. (a) Places a check in the checkbox.
   (b) Radio button is deselected.
   (c) Makes the picture invisible.
   (d) Makes the label appear sunken.
   (e) Assigns the text value in txtCity.Text to the text value of lblCity.Text.

 Feedback 3.1

1. Does not have a prefix indicating a data type.
2. Identifiers cannot contain special characters such as #.
3. An identifier cannot contain blank spaces.
4. Periods are used to separate items such as Object.Property.
5. Identifiers cannot contain special characters such as $.
6. *Sub* is a reserved word.
7. The name is valid; however, it does not indicate anything about what the variable is used for.
8. *Text* is a property name, and, therefore, it is a reserved word.
9. The name is valid; however, the prefix used should clearly indicate the data type.
10. A prefix indicating the data type should be used.
11. Valid.
12. Valid.

▶ Feedback 3.2

Note: Answers may vary; make sure the prefix indicates the data type.

1. (a) decHours
   (b) strEmployeeName
   (c) strDepartmentNumber
2. (a) intQuantity
   (b) strDescription
   (c) strPartNumber
   (d) decCost
   (e) decSellingPrice

▶ Feedback 3.3

Note: Answers may vary; make sure the prefix indicates the data type.

1. `Dim mdecPayroll As Decimal`
   Declared at the module level.

2. `Const mdecSALES_TAX As Decimal = .08`
   Declared at the module level.

3. `Dim mintParticipantCount As Integer`
   Declared at the module level.

▶ Feedback 3.4

1. 18
2. 1
3. 6
4. 5
5. 22
6. 2,048
7. 22
8. 38

▶ Feedback 3.5

1. (a) `intCount = intCount + 5`
   (b) `intCount += 5`
2. (a) `decBalance = decBalance − decWithdrawal`
   (b) `decBalance −= decWithdrawal`
3. (a) `decPrice = decPrice * intCount`
   (b) `decPrice *= intCount`

► Feedback 3.6

1. `lblAveragePay.Text = FormatCurrency(mdecAveragePay)`
   $123.46

2. `lblPercentCorrect.Text = FormatPercent(sngCorrect, 0)`
   or
   `lblPercentCorrect.Text = FormatPercent(sngCorrect)`

3. `lblTotal.Text = FormatNumber(mdecTotalCollected)`
   or
   `lblTotal.Text = FormatNumber(mdecTotalCollected, 2)`

► Feedback 4.1

1. True
2. True
3. True
4. False
5. False
6. True
7. True
8. False
9. True
10. True

► Feedback 4.2

1. radFrogs will be checked.
   radToads will be unchecked.
2. "It's the toads and the polliwogs"
3. "It's true"

4.
```
If CInt(txtOranges.Text) > CInt(txtApples.Text) Then
    lblMost.Text = "Oranges"
Else
    lblMost.Text = "Apples"
End If
```

5.
```
If decBalance > 0 Then
    chkFunds.Checked = True
    decBalance = 0
    intCounter += 1
Else
    chkFunds.Checked = False
End If
```

► Feedback 5.1

1. Function procedure; a value will be returned.

2.
```
Private Function Average(intValueOne As Integer, _
  intValueTwo As Integer, intValueThree As Integer) _
  As Integer
```

3.
```
Average = (intValueOne + intValueTwo + intValueThree)/3
```

4. The answer is assigned to the field with the same name as the function, or the answer appears on a Return statement.

► Feedback 6.1

1. An object is an instance of a class. A class defines an item type (like the cookie cutter defines the shape), whereas the object is an actual instance of the class (as the cookie made from the cookie cutter).

2.
```
Private mstrLastName As String
Private mstrFirstName As String
Private mstrStudentID As String
Private mdecGPA As Decimal
```
These statements will appear at the module level.

3.
```
Property LastName() As String
    Get
        LastName = mstrLastName
    End Get
    Set(ByVal Value As String)
        mstrLastName = Value
    End Set
End Property
```

4.
```
ReadOnly Property GPA() As Decimal
    Get
        GPA = mdecGPA
    End Get
End Property
```

▶ Feedback 7.1

1. Alphabetizes the items in a list box or combo box.
2. Stores the index number of the currently selected (highlighted) item; has a value of −1 if nothing is selected.
3. Is a collection that holds the text of all list elements in a list box or combo box.
4. Determines whether or not a list box will also have a text box for user input. It also determines whether or not the list will drop down.
5. Stores the number of elements in a list box or combo box.
6. Adds an element to a list at run time.
7. Adds an element to a list and inserts the element in the chosen position (index).
8. Clears all elements from a list box or combo box.
9. Removes an element from the list by referring to its index.
10. Removes an element from a list by looking for a given string.

▶ Feedback 7.2

```
blnItemFound = False        'Set the initial value of the found switch to False
intItemIndex = 0            'Initialize the counter for the item index
'Loop through the items until the requested item is found or the end of the list is reached
Do Until blnItemFound Or intItemIndex = lstItems.Items.Count
    'Check if the text box entry matches the item in the list
    If txtNewItem.Text = lstItems.Items(intItemIndex) Then
        blnItemFound = True          'Set the found switch to True
    End If
    intItemIndex += 1        'Increment the counter for the item index
Loop
```

▶ Feedback 7.3

1. (a) There should not be a comma after the test value.
   (b) The Next statement must contain the same variable that follows the For statement, intIndex in this case.
   (c) The item following the word For must be a variable and the same variable must be used on the Next statement. 4 is not a proper variable name and For is a reserved word.
   (d) Valid.
   (e) Valid.
   (f) This loop will never be executed; needs to have a negative Step argument.
2. (a) Will be executed 3 times; intCounter will have an ending value of 4.
   (b) Will be executed 4 times; have an ending value of 14 in intCounter.
   (c) Will be executed 10 times; intCounter will have an ending value of 0.
   (d) Will be executed 7 times; intCounter will have an ending value of 6.5.
   (e) Will never be executed because the starting value is already greater than the test value; intCounter will have an ending value of 5.

▶ Feedback 7.4

1. A control used to set up output for the printer. Add the control to the form's component tray at design time. Begin the printing process by executing the `Print` method of the control; the control's PrintPage event occurs.

2. Starts the printing process. Belongs in the Click event procedure for the Print button.

3. The PrintPage event is a callback that occurs once for each page to print. The PrintPage event procedure contains all the logic for printing the page.

4. Sends a line of text to the graphics object. The `DrawString` method is used in the PrintPage event procedure.

5. An argument passed to the PrintPage event procedure. Holds items of information such as the page margins.

6. MarginBounds.Left is one of the properties of the PrintPageEventArgs argument passed to the PrintPage event procedure. The property holds the left margin and can be used to set the x coordinate to the left margin.

7. A control that allows the user to view the document in Print Preview. The control is added to the component tray at design time. In the event procedure where the user selects Print Preview, the print document is assigned to this control.

▶ Feedback 8.1

Convert the following `If` statements to `Select Case` statements:

1.
```
Select Case intTemp
    Case Is > 80
        lblComment.Text = "Hot"
    Case Is > 32
        lblComment.Text = "Moderate"
    Case Else
        lblComment.Text = "Freezing"
End Select
```

2.
```
Select Case intCount
    Case 0
        MessageBox.Show("No items entered.")
    Case 1 To 10
        MessageBox.Show("1 - 10 items entered.")
    Case 11 To 20
        MessageBox.Show("11 - 20 items entered.")
    Case Else
        MessageBox.Show("More than 20 items entered.")
End Select
```

► Feedback 8.2

1. Valid.
2. Valid.
3. Valid.
4. Invalid, beyond the range of the array.
5. Valid.
6. Invalid; negative number.
7. Gives a decimal number but Visual Basic will round the fraction and use that integer.
8. Valid.

► Feedback 8.3

1. ```
Structure StudentInfo
    Dim strLastName As String
    Dim strFirstName As String
    Dim strStudentNumber As String
    Dim decUnitsCompleted As Decimal
    Dim decGPA As Decimal
End Structure
```

2. ```
Dim stuInformation(99) As StudentInfo
```

3. ```
Structure Project
    Dim strProjectName As String
    Dim strFormName As String
    Dim strFolderName As String
End Structure
```

4. ```
Dim prjMyProject As Project
```

5. ```
Dim prjOurProjects(99) As Project
```
```

▶ Feedback 8.4

1. ```
Dim decTemperature(2, 4) As Decimal
```

2. ```
For intColumn = 0 To 4
    decTemperature(0, intColumn) = 0
Next intColumn
```

3. ```
For intColumn = 0 To 4
    decTemperature(1, intColumn) = 75D
Next intColumn
```

4. ```
For intColumn = 0 To 4
    decTemperature(2, intColumn) = decTemperature(0, _
      intColumn) + decTemperature(1, intColumn)
Next intColumn
```

5. ```
For intRowIndex = 0 To 2
    For intColumnIndex = 0 To 4
        e.Graphics.DrawString(CStr(decTemperature _
          (intRowIndex, intColumnIndex)), fntPrintFont, _
          Brushes.Black, sngPrintX, sngPrintY)
        sngPrintX += 200
    Next intColumnIndex

    'Begin a new line
    sngPrintX = e.MarginBounds.Left
    sngPrintY += sngLineHeight
Next intRowIndex
```

## ▶ Feedback 9.1

1. Right-click on the control and choose *Run As Server Control*.
2. So that the control will respond to events and can execute an event procedure when clicked.
3. .aspx; Holds the information about the user interface.
   .aspx.vb; Holds the code that runs behind the .aspx file.
4. Right-click on the form and select *View in Browser*.

## ▶ Feedback 9.2

1. Grid Layout allows you to determine the exact placement of controls. Flow Layout places each control immediately following the insertion point.
2. (a) Press the Enter key until the insertion point is at the bottom of the form.
   (b) Add a table to the form and place the button in a cell at the bottom of the table.
3. An HTML table works on the client side only; the data must be added at design time. A Web Table can be changed dynamically at run time.
```

Feedback 9.3

Attach a RequiredFieldValidator control so that the field cannot be left blank. Attach a CompareValidator to make sure that the entry can be converted to numeric. Attach a RangeValidator to check if the input falls within the specified range by setting the MinimumValue = 0 and the MaximumValue = 1000.

Feedback 10.1

1. The *file* is the database.
   The *table* contains the *rows* and *columns*, which hold the information about your friends.
   Each *row/record* contains information about an individual friend.
   A *column* or *field* contains an element of data, such as the name or phone number.
   The *key field* is the field used to organize the file; it contains a unique value that identifies a particular record, for example, the name field.
2. XML is stored as text, which can pass through Internet firewalls and can be edited using any text editor.

Feedback 10.2

The connection object creates a link between the data source and the program. The data adapter passes information back and forth between the data source and the dataset. The dataset holds a copy of the data that was retrieved from the data source and is used in your program to access the data, either field by field (for labels and text boxes) or by connecting it to a grid.

Feedback 10.3

Set the DataBindings.Text property to the field in the table from which you want to display information.

 Feedback 10.4

1. The DataSource and DisplayMember properties must be set.
2. The code is written in that control's SelectedIndexChanged event procedure.

▶ Feedback 11.1

1. ```
Dim datInventory As New StreamWriter("Inventory.txt")
```

2. ```
datInventory.WriteLine(txtDescription.Text)
```

3. The declaration for the StreamReader object needs to be in a `Try/Catch` block in case the file does not exist. The declaration for the StreamWriter object does not need to be in a `Try/Catch` block because in this case, the program is generating a file, not trying to locate one.

4. ```
If datInventory.Peek <> −1 Then
    lblDescription.Text = datInventory.ReadLine()
    lblProductNumber.Text = datInventory.ReadLine()
End If
```

## ▶ Feedback 11.2

1. ```
.txt files|*.txt
```

2. ```
dlgOpen.InitialDirectory = Application.StartupPath
```

3. ```
If Not datPhone Is Nothing Then
    datPhone.Close()
End If
```

▶ Feedback 11.3

1. ```
intCount = lstNames.Items.Count − 1
For intIndex = 0 To intCount
    datNames.WriteLine(lstNames.Items(intIndex))
Next intIndex
```

2. The above code should be placed in a Save procedure, which should be called from the form's Closing event procedure.

3. ```
Dim datNames As New StreamReader("Names.txt")
Do Until datNames.Peek = −1
    lstNames.Items.Add(datNames.ReadLine())
Loop
```

▶ Feedback 12.1

1.
```
Dim gr As Graphics = e.Graphics
Dim penGreen As New Pen(Color.Green)
Dim intX As Integer
Dim intY As Integer
intY = CInt(Me.Top + Me.Height)
intX = CInt(Me.Width/2)
gr.DrawLine(penGreen, intX, 0, intX, intY)
```

2.
```
gr.DrawEllipse(penGreen, intX, intY, 100F, 100F)
gr.DrawEllipse(penBlue, intX + 25, intY + 25, 50F, 50F)
```

3.
```
Dim pntPoint1 As New Point(20, 20)
Dim pntPoint2 As New Point(100, 100)
Dim pntPoint3 As New Point(200, 50)
gr.DrawLine(penGreen, pntPoint1, pntPoint2)
gr.DrawLine(penGreen, pntPoint2, pntPoint3)
gr.DrawLine(penGreen, pntPoint3, pntPoint1)
```

▶ Feedback 12.2

1.
```
Static intX As Integer = btnCommand.Left - 10
Static intY As Integer = btnCommand.Top
Static intWidth As Integer = btnCommand.Width
Static intHeight As Integer = btnCommand.Height
btnCommand.SetBounds(intX, intY, intWidth, intHeight)
```

2. A little less than half a second.
3. The Tick event fires each time the specified interval has elapsed.

▶ Feedback 13.1

1. Write the statements to display frmAbout as a child form.

```
Dim frmAboutMe As New frmAbout()
frmAboutMe.MdiParent = Me
frmAboutMe.Show()
```

2.
```
Select Case tlbMain.Buttons.IndexOf(e.Button)
    Case 0
        CloseMe()        'Make up your own procedure names
    Case 1
        ShowAboutForm()
End Select
```

3. In the Form_Load event procedure:

```
sbpCurrentTime.Text = Now.ToLongTimeString
```

Add a timer control; set the Interval property and include this statement
in the timer's Tick event procedure:

```
sbpCurrentTime.Text = Now.ToLongTimeString
```

▶ Feedback 13.2

1. `txtAppointment.Text = dtmAppointment.ToString`

2. Hour; Millisecond; Minute; Second; Month; Day; Year; Now
3. All of the above properties are available for the Now property.

Functions for Working with Dates, Financial Calculations, Mathematics, and String Operations

Visual Basic includes many functions and methods you can use in your projects. In Chapter 3 you were introduced to functions where you used the conversion functions: `CInt`, `CDec`, `CStr`, and the formatting functions: `FormatCurrency`, `FormatNumber`, `FormatPercent`, and `FormatDateTime`. This appendix introduces some additional functions and methods for handling dates, for performing financial calculations and mathematical operations, for converting between data types, and for performing string operations.

Working with Dates

Chapter 13 has a section introducing dates and the Calendar control. You can use the date functions and the methods of the DateTime structure to retrieve the system date, break down a date into component parts, test whether the contents of a field are compatible with the Date data type, and convert other data types to a Date.

The DateTime Structure

When you declare a variable of Date data type in VB, the .NET Common Language Runtime uses the DateTime structure, which has an extensive list of properties and methods. You can use the shared members of the DateTime structure (identified by a yellow *S* in the MSDN Help lists) without declaring an instance of Date or DateTime. For example, to use the Now property:

`datToday = Now`

To use the nonshared members, you must reference an instance of a DateTime structure, such as a variable of Date type. For example:

`lblTime.Text = datToday.ToShortTimeString`

Following is a partial list of some useful properties and methods of the DateTime structure:

Property or Method	Purpose
Date	Date component
Day	Integer day of month; 1–31
DayOfWeek	Integer day; 0 = Sunday
DayOfYear	Integer day; 1–366
Hour	Integer hour; 0–23
Minute	Integer minutes; 0–59
Second	Integer seconds; 0–59
Month	Integer month; 1 = January
Now (Shared)	Retrieve system date and time
Today (Shared)	Retrieve system date
Year	Year component
ToLongDateString	Date formatted as long date
ToLongTimeString	Date formatted as long time
ToShortDateString	Date formatted as short date
ToShortTimeString	Date formatted as short time

Retrieving the System Date and Time

You can retrieve the system date and time from your computer's clock using the Now property or the Today property. *Now* retrieves both the date and time; *Today* retrieves only the date.

Examples

```
Dim datDateAndTime As Date
datDateAndTime = Now

Dim datDate As Date
datDate = Today
```

To display the values formatted:

```
lblDateAndTime.Text = datDateAndTime.ToLongDateString
lblDate.Text = datDate.ToShortDateString
```

Date Variables

The Date data type may hold values of many forms that represent a date. Examples could be May 22, 2002 or 5/22/02 or 5-22-2002. When you assign a literal value to a Date variable, enclose it in # signs:

```
Dim datMyDate as Date
datMyDate = #5-22-02#
```

You can also use the `FormatDateTime` function to format dates and times (see Chapter 3).

Converting Values to a Date Format

If you want to store values in a Date data type, you usually need to convert the value to a Date type. The *CDate* function converts a value to Date type, but throws an exception if unable to create a valid date from the argument. Use the *IsDate* function first to make sure you have a valid date value, or catch the exception.

```
If IsDate(txtDate.Text) Then          Try
   datMyDate = CDate(txtDate.Text)        datMyDate = CDate(txtDate.Text)
Else                                  Catch
   MessageBox.Show("Invalid date")        MessageBox.Show("Invalid date")
End If                                 End Try
```

Financial Functions

Visual Basic provides functions for many types of financial and accounting calculations, such as payment amount, depreciation, future value, and present value. When you use these functions, you eliminate the need to know and code the actual formulas yourself. Each financial function returns a value that you can assign to a variable, or to a property of a control.

Category	Purpose	Function
Depreciation	Double-declining balance	DDB
	Straight line	SLN
	Sum-of-the-years digits	SYD
Payments	Payment	Pmt
	Interest payment	IPmt
	Principal payment	PPmt
Return	Internal rate of return	IRR
	Rate of return when payments and receipts are at different rates	MIRR
Rate	Interest rate	Rate
Future value	Future value of an annuity	FV
Present value	Present value	PV
	Present value when values are not constant	NPV
Number of periods	Number of periods for an annuity (Number of payments)	NPer

You must supply each function with the necessary arguments. You specify the name of the function, followed by parentheses that enclose the arguments.

IntelliSense helps you type the arguments of functions. When you type the parentheses, the arguments appear in order. The one to be entered next is in bold. The order of the arguments is important because the function uses the values in the formula based on their position in the argument list. For example, the following Pmt function has three arguments: the interest rate, the number of periods, and the amount of loan. If you supply the values in a different order, the Pmt function will calculate with the wrong numbers.

The PMT Function

You can use the Pmt function to find the amount of each payment on a loan if the interest rate, the number of periods, and the amount borrowed are known.

The Pmt Function—General Form

General Form

```
Pmt(dblInterestRatePerPeriod, dblNumberOfPeriods, dblAmountOfLoan)
```

The interest rate must be specified as Double and adjusted to the interest rate per period. For example, if the loan is made with an annual rate of 12 percent and monthly payments, the interest rate must be converted to the monthly rate of 1 percent. Convert the annual rate to the monthly rate by dividing by the number of months in a year (AnnualPercentageRate/12).

The number of periods for the loan is the total number of payments. If you want to know the monthly payment for a five-year loan, you must convert the number of years to the number of months. Multiply the number of years by 12 months per year (NumberOfYears * 12).

The Pmt function requires Double arguments and returns a Double value.

The Rate Function—Example

```
Try
    dblMonthlyRate = CDbl(txtRate.Text)/12
    dblMonths = CDbl(txtYears.Text) * 12
    dblAmount = CDbl(txtAmount.Text)
    dblMonthlyPayment = -Pmt(dblMonthlyRate, dblMonths, dblAmount)
    lblMonthlyPayment.Text = FormatCurrency(dblMonthlyPayment)
Catch
    MessageBox.Show("Invalid data")
End Try
```

Notice in the example that the fields used in the payment function are from text boxes that the user can enter, and the answer is displayed formatted in a label.

Also notice the minus sign when using the Pmt function. When an amount is borrowed or payments are made, that is considered a negative amount. You need the minus sign to reverse the sign and make a positive answer.

The Rate Function

You can use the Rate function to determine the interest rate per period when the number of periods, the payment per period, and the original amount of the loan are known.

The Rate Function—General Form

```
Rate(dblNumberOfPeriods, dblPaymentPerPeriod, dblLoanAmount)
```

The Rate function requires Double arguments and returns a Double value.

The Rate Function—Example

```
Try
    dblMonths = CDbl(txtYears.Text) * 12
    dblPayment = CDbl(txtPayment.Text)
    dblAmount = CDbl(txtLoanAmt.Text)
    dblPeriodicRate = Rate(dblMonths, -dblPayment, dblAmount)
    dblAnnualRate = dblPeriodicRate * 12
    lblYearlyRate.Text = FormatPercent(dblAnnualRate)
Catch
    MessageBox.Show("Invalid data")
End Try
```

Notice that the Rate function, like the Pmt function, needs a minus sign to produce a positive result.

Functions to Calculate Depreciation

If you need to calculate the depreciation of an asset in a business, Visual Basic provides three functions: the double-declining balance (DDB) method, the straight-line method, and the sum-of-the-years digits method.

The DDB function calculates the depreciation for a specific period within the life of the asset, using the double-declining balance method formula. Once again, you do not need to know the formula but only in what order to enter the arguments. Incidentally, the salvage value is the value of the item when it is worn out.

The DDB (Double-Declining Balance) Function—General Form

General Form

```
DDB(dblOriginalCost, dblSalvageValue, dblLifeOfTheAsset, dblPeriod)
```

The DDB function returns a Double value and requires Double arguments.

The DDB Function—Example

Example

```
dblCost = CDbl(txtCost.Text)
dblSalvage = CDbl(txtSalvage.Text)
dblYears = CDbl(txtYears.Text)
dblPeriod = CDbl(txtPeriod.Text)
lblDepreciation.Text = FormatCurrency(DDB(dblCost, dblSalvage, dblYears, dblPeriod))
```

The other financial functions work in a similar manner. You can use Help to find the argument list, an explanation, and an example.

Mathematical Functions

In Visual Basic .NET, the mathematical functions are included as methods in the System.Math class. To use the methods, you must either import System.Math or refer to each method with the Math namespace.

For example, to use the Abs (absolute value) method, you can use either of these techniques:

```
dblAnswer = Math.Abs(dblArgument)
```

or

```
Imports System.Math        'At the top of the module
dblAnswer = Abs(dblArgument)    'In a procedure
```

A few functions are not methods of the Math class but are Visual Basic functions. These functions, such as Fix and Int, cannot specify the Math namespace.

A good way to see the list of math functions is to type "Math." in the Editor; IntelliSense will pop up with the complete list. The following table presents a partial list of the Math methods:

Method	Returns	Argument data type	Return data type
Abs(x)	The absolute value of x. $\lvert x \rvert = x$ if $x \geq 0$ $\lvert x \rvert = -x$ if $x \leq 0$	Overloaded: All types allowed.	Return matches argument type.
Atan(x)	The angle in radians whose tangent is x.	Double	Double
Cos(x)	The cosine of x where x is in radians.	Double	Double
Exp(x)	The value of e raised to the power of x.	Double	Double
Log(x)	The natural logarithm of x, where $x \geq 0$.	Double	Double
Max(x1, x2)	The larger of the two arguments.	Overloaded: All types allowed. Both arguments must be the same type.	Return matches argument type.
Min(x1, x2)	The smaller of the two arguments.	Overloaded: All types allowed. Both arguments must be the same type.	Return matches argument type.
Round(x) Round(x, *DecimalPlaces*)	The rounded value of x, rounded to the specified number of decimal positions. *Note:* .5 rounds to the nearest even number.	Overloaded: Double or Decimal; Integer DecimalPlaces	Return matches argument type.
Sign(x)	The sign of x. –1 if $x < 0$ 0 if $x = 0$ 1 if $x > 0$	Overloaded: All types allowed.	Return matches argument type.
Sin(x)	The sine of x where x is in radians.	Double	Double
Sqrt(x)	The square root of x where x must be ≥ 0.	Double	Double
Tan(x)	The tangent of x where x is in radians.	Double	Double

Here are some useful VB functions:

Method	Returns	Argument data type	Return data type
Fix(x)	The integer portion of x (truncated).	Any numeric expression.	Integer
Int(x)	The largest integer $\leq x$.	Any numeric expression.	Integer
Rnd( )	A random number in the range 0–1 (exclusive).		Single

Working with Strings

Visual Basic provides many methods for working with text strings. Although several of the methods are covered in this text, many more are available.

Strings in Visual Studio are **immutable,** which means that once a string is created, it cannot be changed. Although many programs in this text seem to modify a string, actually a new string is created and the old string is discarded.

For string handling, you can use any of the many methods of the String class. You can also use the StringBuilder class, which is more efficient if you are building or modifying strings, since the string can be changed in memory. In other words, a StringBuilder is *mutable* (changeable) and a String is *immutable*.

Here is a partial list of the methods in the String class. For shared methods, you don't need to specify a String instance; for nonshared methods, you must attach the method to the String instance. Examples of shared method and nonshared method follow.

Shared method:

```
If Compare(strA, strB) > 0 Then
    '...
```

Nonshared method:

```
If strMyString.EndsWith("ed") Then
    '...
```

Method	Returns

Compare(*strA, strB*)
(Shared)
	Integer:
	    Negative if *strA* < *strB*
	    Zero if *strA* = *strB*
	    Positive if *strA* > *strB*

Compare(*strA, strB,*
blnIgnoreCase)
(Shared)
	Case insensitive if blnIgnoreCase is True.
	Integer:
	    Negative if *strA* < *strB*
	    Zero if *strA* = *strB*
	    Positive if *strA* > *strB*

Compare(*strA, intStartA, strB,*
intStartB, intLength)
(Shared)
	Compare substrings, start position indicates beginning character to compare for a length of intLength.
	Integer:
	    Negative if *strA* < *strB*
	    Zero if *strA* = *strB*
	    Positive if *strA* > *strB*

Compare(*strA, intStartA, strB,*
intStartB, intLength,
blnIgnoreCase)
(Shared)
	Case insensitive if blnIgnoreCase is True.
	Compare substrings, start position indicates beginning character to compare for a length of intLength.
	Integer:
	    Negative if *strA* < *strB*
	    Zero if *strA* = *strB*
	    Positive if *strA* > *strB*

Continued on page 562

Method	Returns
EndsWith(*strA*)	Boolean. True if the String instance ends with strA. Case sensitive.
Equals(*strA*)	Boolean. True if the String instance has the same value as strA. Case sensitive.

IndexOf(*strA*)	Integer. Index position in String instance that strA is found.
	    Positive: String found at this position.
	    Negative: String not found.

IndexOf(*strA, intStartPosition*)	Integer. Index position in String instance that strA is found, starting at intStartPosition.
	    Positive: String found at this position.
	    Negative: String not found.

IndexOf(*strA, intStartPosition, intNumberCharacters*)	Integer. Index position in String instance that strA is found, starting at intStartPosition, for a length of intNumberCharacters.
	    Positive: String found at this position.
	    Negative: String not found.

Insert(*intStartIndex, strA*)	New string with strA inserted in the String instance, beginning at intStartIndex.
LastIndexOf(*strA*)	Integer: Index position of strA within String instance, searching from the right end.
LastIndexOf(*strA, intStartPosition*)	Integer: Index position of strA within String instance, searching leftward, beginning at intStartPosition.
LastIndexOf(*strA, intStartPosition, intNumberCharacters*)	Integer: Index position of strA within String instance, searching leftward, beginning at intStartPosition, for a length of intNumberCharacters.
PadLeft(*intTotalLength*)	New String with String instance right justified; padded on left with spaces for a total length of intTotalLength.
PadLeft(*intTotalLength, chrPad*)	New String with String instance right justified; padded on left with the specified character for a total length of intTotalLength.
PadRight(*intTotalLength*)	New String with String instance left justified; padded on right with spaces for a total length of intTotalLength.
PadRight(*intTotalLength, chrPad*)	New String with String instance left justified; padded on right with the specified character for a total length of intTotalLength.

Continued on page 563

Method	Returns
Remove(*intStartPosition,* *intNumberCharacters*)	New String with characters removed from String instance, beginning with intStartPosition for a length of intNumberCharacters.
Replace(*strOldValue,* *strNewValue*)	New String with all occurrences of the old value replaced by the new value.
StartsWith(*strA*)	Boolean. True if the String instance starts with strA. Case sensitive.
Substring(*intStartPosition*)	New String that is a substring of String instance; beginning at intStartPosition, including all characters to the right.
Substring(*intStartPosition,* *intNumberCharacters*)	New String; a substring of String instance, beginning at intStartPosition for a length of intNumberCharacters.
ToLower()	New String; the String instance converted to lowercase.
ToUpper()	New String; the String instance converted to uppercase.
Trim()	New String; the String instance with all white-space characters removed from the left and right ends.
TrimEnd()	New String; the String instance with all white-space characters removed from the right end.
TrimStart()	New String; the String instance with all white-space characters removed from the left end.

Functions for Converting between Data Types

Each of the following functions converts an expression to the named data type.

Function	Return Type
CBool(*Expression*)	Boolean
CDate(*Expression*)	Date
CDbl(*Expression*)	Double
CDec(*Expression*)	Decimal
CInt(*Expression*)	Integer
CLng(*Expression*)	Long
CObj(*Expression*)	Object
CShort(*Expression*)	Short
CSng(*Expression*)	Single
CStr(*Expression*)	String
CType(*Object, type*)	Specific type

C

Tips and Shortcuts for Mastering the Environment

Set Up the Screen for Your Convenience

As you work in the Visual Studio integrated development environment (IDE), you will find many ways to save time. Here are some tips and shortcuts that you can use to become more proficient in using the IDE to design, code, and run your projects.

Close or Hide Extra Windows

Arrange your screen for best advantage. While you are entering and editing code in the Editor window, you don't need the toolbox, the Solution Explorer window, the Properties window, or any other extra windows. You can hide or close the extra windows and quickly and easily redisplay each window when you need it.

Hiding and Displaying Windows

You can use AutoHide on each of the windows in the IDE. Each window except the Document window in the center of the screen has a push-pin icon that you can use to AutoHide the window or "tack" it into place.

You can AutoHide each window separately, or select *Window/Auto Hide All*. In this screen, all extra windows are hidden.

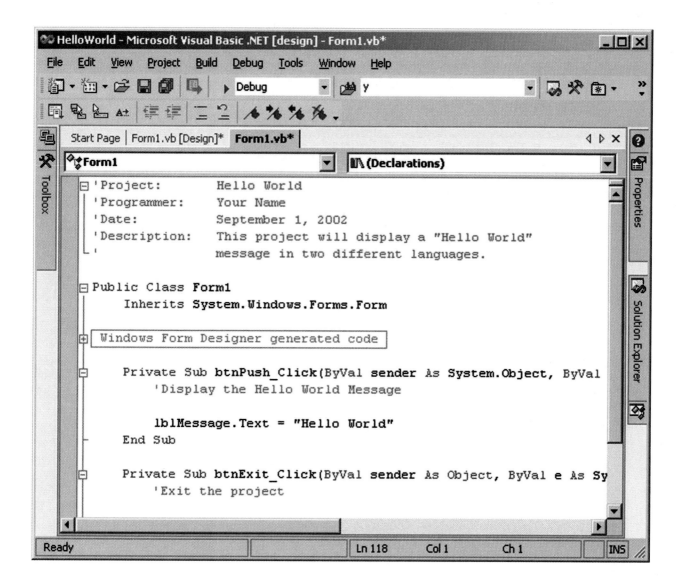

Point to the icon for one of the hidden windows to display it. Notice the mouse pointer on the Solution Explorer icon, which opens the Solution Explorer window temporarily. When you move the mouse pointer out of the window, it hides again.

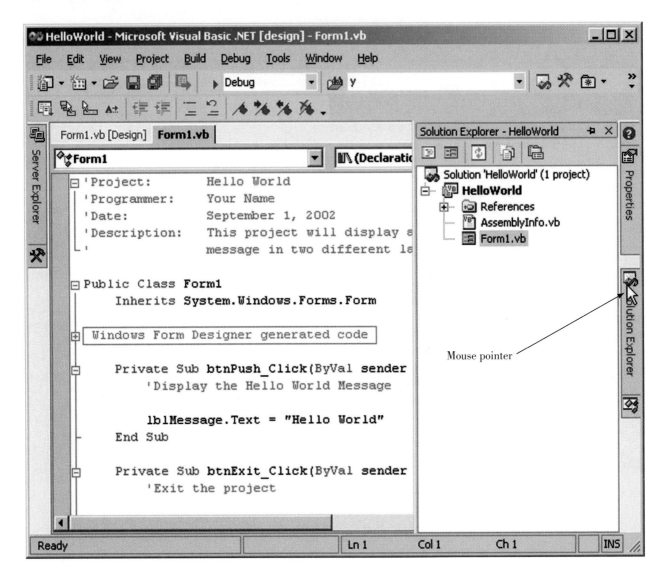

Mouse pointer

To undo the AutoHide feature, display a window and click its push-pin icon.

Closing Windows

You can close any window by clicking its close button. You can also close any extra tabs in the Document window; each document has its own close button.

Displaying Windows

You can quickly and easily open each window when you need it. Each window is listed on the *View* menu, or use the buttons on the standard toolbar.

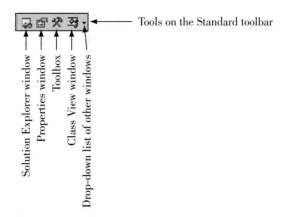

Tools on the Standard toolbar

Solution Explorer window
Properties window
Toolbox
Class View window
Drop-down list of other windows

Display Windows Using Keyboard Shortcuts

Solution Explorer window	Ctrl + Alt + L
Properties window	F4
Toolbox	Ctrl + Alt + X

Switch between Documents

When you have several tabs open in the Document window, you can switch by clicking on their tabs or use keyboard shortcuts.

Editor window for form's code	F7
Form Designer	Shift + F7
Cycle through open document tabs	Ctrl + Tab *or* Ctrl + F6
Navigate backward (to previous Help page)	Backspace key *or* Ctrl + – (minus sign)
Navigate forward (after navigating backward)	Ctrl + Shift + – (minus sign)

Use the Full Screen

When you are designing a form or editing code, you can work in full-screen mode. This gives you maximum screen space by getting rid of all extra windows. Unfortunately, it also hides all toolbars (the Edit toolbar can be a great timesaver while editing code). Select *View/Full Screen* to display in full-screen mode. A small *Full Screen* button appears, which you can use to switch back to regular display. You can also press Shift + Alt + Enter or select *View/Full Screen* a second time to toggle back.

Modify the Screen Layout

For most operations, the new Visual Studio tabbed Document window layout is an improvement over the VB 6 environment. However, if you prefer, you can switch to MDI (multiple document interface), which is similar to the style used in VB 6. Set this option in the `Tools/Options/Environment/General Settings.`

Each of the windows in the IDE is considered either a Tool window or a Document window. The Document windows generally display in the center of the screen with tabs. The rest of the windows—Solution Explorer, Properties window, Task List, Output, Server Explorer, etc.—are Tool windows and share many characteristics. You can float each of the windows, tab-dock them in groups, and move and resize individual windows or groups of windows. For example, you can point to a window's title bar and drag it on top of another window to tab-dock them together. Drag on a tab to separate a window from its tabbed group. The following floating window has the Properties window, toolbox, Solution Explorer, Server Explorer, Class View, Help Contents, and Help Index all docked together. The window was also resized to make the tabs more readable.

This combined window is *not* a recommended layout. It is intended only to show the possibilities. You may want to experiment with moving and resizing windows for your own convenience. You can also float a window, which makes it appear on top of the other windows, or dock the window along the top, bottom, left, or right. Experiment!

If you want to return to the default layout, choose `Tools/Options/Environment/General/Reset Window Layout.`

Set Options for Your Work

You can change many options in the VS IDE. Choose *Tools/Options* to display the *Options* dialog box. You may want to click on each of the categories to see the options that you can select.

Note: If you are working in a shared lab, check with the instructor or lab technician before changing options.

Environment

General:	If it isn't already set, you may want to set the *At startup* option to *Show Start Page*.
Dynamic Help:	Set categories and topic types to limit the help available. See note below.
Projects and Solutions:	Set the default folder for your projects. It's best to leave the *Build* and *Run* options to automatically save changes, but you may prefer to have a prompt or save them yourself.

Text Editor

You can set options for all languages or for Basic, which is Visual Basic. The following presumes that you first select Basic.

General:	Make sure that *Auto list members* is selected and *Hide advanced members* is deselected. You may want to turn on *Word wrap,* so that long lines wrap to the next line instead of extending beyond the right edge of the screen.
Tabs:	Choose *Smart indenting.* *Tab size* and *Indent size* should both be set to 4.
VB Specific:	All three options should be selected.

Windows Forms Designer

Grid Settings:	Notice that you can change the spacing of the grid dots, turn the grid on or off, and set the snap-to-grid option.

Turn Off Dynamic Help

Dynamic Help can be very useful; it displays a series of links that relate to the current operation. However, unless you have a very fast computer with lots of memory, the option can slow the IDE response time considerably. Try creating a project with Dynamic Help turned on and then again with it turned off to see which way works best for you.

Turn off Dynamic Help by closing its window; display it again by selecting *Help/Dynamic Help.* You can also adjust the number and types of links displayed in *Tools/Options/Environment/Dynamic Help.*

Use Shortcuts in the Form Designer

You can save time while creating the user interface in the Form Designer by using shortcuts.

Create Multiple Controls of the Same Type

When you want to create several controls of the same class, you must select the toolbox tool each time you draw a new control. That is, unless you use this method: When you select the toolbox tool for the first control, hold down the Ctrl key as you click. After you create the first new control, the tool stays selected so that you can create as many more controls of that class as you wish.

When you are finished, click on the Pointer to deselect the tool, or click on another toolbox tool.

Use the Layout Toolbar

The Layout toolbar is great for working with multiple controls. You must have more than one control selected to enable many of the buttons. The same options are available from the *Format* menu.

The Layout toolbar buttons (left to right): Align to Grid, Align Lefts, Align Centers, Align Rights, Align Tops, Align Middles, Align Bottoms, Make Same Width, Size to Grid, Make Same Height, Make Same Size, Make Horizontal Spacing Equal, Increase Horizontal Spacing, Decrease Horizontal Spacing, Remove Horizontal Spacing, Make Vertical Spacing Equal, Increase Vertical Spacing, Decrease Vertical Spacing, Remove Vertical Spacing, Center Horizontally, Center Vertically, Bring to Front, Send to Back

Nudge Controls into Place

Sometimes it is difficult to place controls exactly where you want them. Of course, you can use the alignment options of the *Format* menu or the Layout toolbar. You can also nudge controls in any direction by holding down the Ctrl key and pressing one of the arrow keys. Nudging moves a control one pixel in the direction you specify. For example, Ctrl + right arrow moves a selected control one pixel to the right.

Use Shortcuts in the Editor

Several features of the Editor can save you time while editing code. These are summarized in the following sections.

Use the Text Editor Toolbar

By default the Text Editor toolbar displays when the Editor window is open.

You can save yourself considerable time and trouble if you become familiar with and use some of these shortcuts.

- *Comment Selected Lines* Use this command when you want to convert some code to comments, especially while you are testing and debugging projects. You can remove some lines from execution, to test the effect, without actually removing them. Select the lines and click the `Comment Selected Lines` button; each line will have an apostrophe appended at the left end.

- *Uncomment Selected Lines* This command undoes the `Comment Selected Lines` command. Select some comment lines and click the button; the apostrophes at the beginning of the lines are deleted.

- *Increase Indent* and *Decrease Indent* You can use these buttons to indent or outdent single lines or blocks of code. The buttons work the same as the Tab and Shift + Tab keys.

- *Toggle Bookmark* This button sets and unsets individual bookmarks. Bookmarks are useful when you are jumping around in the Editor window. Set a bookmark on any line by clicking in the line and clicking the Toggle Bookmark button; you will see a mark in the gray margin area to the left of the marked line. You may want to set bookmarks in several procedures where you are editing and testing code.

- *Jump to Next Bookmark* and *Jump to Previous Bookmark* Use these buttons to quickly jump to the next or previous bookmark in the code.

- *Clear All Bookmarks* You can clear individual bookmarks with the `Toggle Bookmark` button or clear all bookmarks using this button.

- *Object Member List, Parameter Info,* and *Quick Info* Generally these Intelli-Sense options are turned on and the information pops up automatically. You might prefer to keep these options turned off (`Tools/Options/Text Editor`) and click the buttons when you actually want the lists to appear.

- *Word Completion* This is an especially useful one! Try clicking the Word Completion button as you are typing the name of an object or a variable. If you have typed enough for the editor to identify the word, it will automatically fill in the rest when you press Enter or another character such as a space bar or equal sign. Or better yet, use one of the keyboard shortcuts: Ctrl + Spacebar or Alt + right arrow.

Use Keyboard Shortcuts When Editing Code

While you are editing code, save yourself time by using keyboard shortcuts.

Task	Shortcut
Delete the current line (insertion point anywhere in the line).	Ctrl + L
Delete from the insertion point left to the beginning of the word.	Ctrl + Backspace
Delete from the insertion point right to the end of the word.	Ctrl + Delete
Complete the word.	Ctrl + Spacebar *or* Alt + right arrow
Jump to a procedure (insertion point on procedure name). Use this shortcut while working on the sub procedures and functions that you write. For example, when writing a call to a function, you might want to check the coding in the function. Point to the procedure name in the `Call` and press F12. If you want to return to the original position, set a bookmark before the jump.	F12
Jump to the top of the current code file.	Ctrl + Home
Jump to the bottom of the current file.	Ctrl + End
Indent a block of code.	Select the lines and use the Tab key or the Increase Indent toolbar button
Outdent (decrease indent) a block of code.	Select the lines and use the Shift + Tab keys or the Decrease Indent toolbar button
View the form's Designer window.	Shift + F7
Return to the Editor window.	F7

You will find that most of the editing and selecting keyboard shortcuts for Microsoft Word also work in the Editor window.

Split the Editor Window

You can view more than one section of code at a time by splitting the Editor window. Point to the Split bar at the top of the vertical scroll bar and drag the bar down to the desired location. To remove the split, you can either drag the split bar back to the top or double-click the split bar.

```
Form1                           (Declarations)
                                                              ◄—— Split bar
    Private Sub btnPush_Click(ByVal sender As System.Object, ByVa
         'Display the Hello World Message

         lblMessage.Text = "Hello World"
    End Sub

    Private Sub btnExit_Click(ByVal sender As Object, ByVal e As
         'Exit the project

         Me.Close()
    End Sub
```

Use Drag-and-Drop Editing

You can use drag-and-drop to move or copy text to another location in the Editor window or to another project. To move code, select the text, point to the selection, and drag it to a new location. You can copy text (rather than move it) by holding down the Ctrl key as you drag.

Use the Task List

The Task List displays error messages after your program is compiled. This makes sense—your tasks are to fix each of the errors. You can also add items to the task list as a reminder to yourself, so that you don't forget to do something. A very easy way to add items to the Task List is to write a comment in your code with the TODO keyword.

```
'TODO Come back here and write this code.
'TODO Check on this.
```

You can also add tasks to the Task List by clicking at the top of the list; this creates a new line where you can enter text. If the Task List is filtered, as shown in its title bar, select *View/Show Task* and choose *All*.

Use the Class View Window

The Class View window shows your project in a hierarchical tree view. You can view the classes, objects, event procedures, general procedures, and variables in your projects. You can view the declaration of the various symbols and jump directly to locations in your code.

Each type of object displays with a different symbol. In addition, the symbols may display signal icons that indicate the object's accessibility, such as Public, Private, Protected, or Friend.

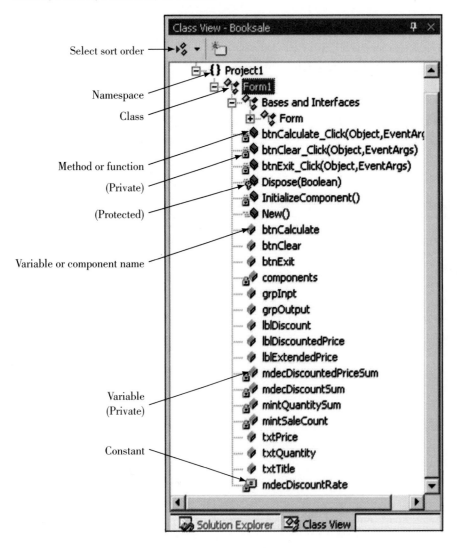

You can jump to the definition of any symbol in the Editor window. This is especially helpful for jumping to procedures in a large project. Point to the name of an event procedure, such as btnCalculate_Click; then double-click, or right-click and select *Go To Definition* from the shortcut menu. If you choose to go to a definition that is in your code, the Editor window opens (if necessary), and the insertion point appears on the selected line. If you choose to go to a definition that is in another class, the Object Browser opens with that symbol selected.

Use the Object Browser

The Visual Studio Object Browser can be a valuable source of information. You can use the Object Browser to examine namespaces, objects, properties, methods, events, and constants for your project and for all Visual Studio namespaces. Use the *Find Symbol* button to look up any symbol that you want to examine.

The Object Browser and the Class View window use the same symbols and signal icons.

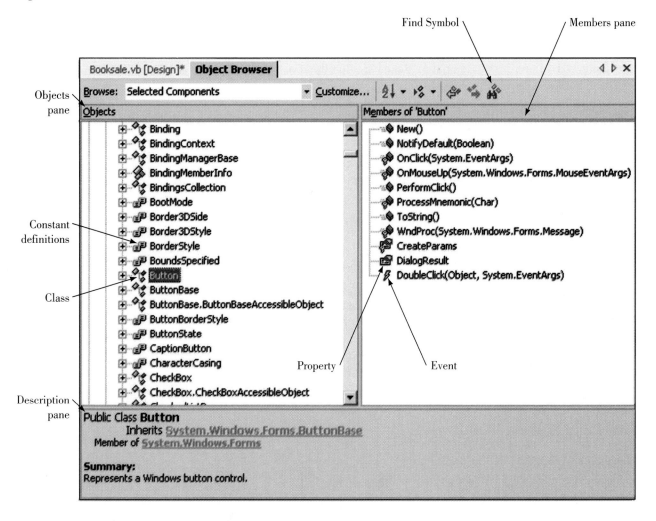

Use Context-Sensitive Help

The quickest way to get Help is to use context-sensitive Help. Click on a control or a line of code and press F1; Help displays the closest matching item it can locate. You can also get help on the IDE elements: Click in any area of the IDE and press Shift + F1; the Help explanation will be about using the current window or IDE element rather than about the objects and language.

Copy and Move Projects

In a programming class, you often must move projects from one computer to another, and must base one project on another one. To create a new project based on a previous one, you should copy the project. Then you can move it as necessary.

Windows projects that do not connect to a database file are very easy to copy and move. The problems occur for Web projects and database projects.

Copy and Move a Windows Project

You can copy an entire Windows project folder from one location to another using Windows Explorer or My Computer. Make sure that the project is not open in Visual Studio and copy the entire folder.

To base one project on a previous project, take the following steps:

- Make sure the project is not open.

- Copy the folder to a new location using Windows Explorer or My Computer.

- Rename the new folder for the new project name, still using Windows Explorer or My Computer.

- Open the new project (the copy) in the Visual Studio IDE.

- In the IDE's Solution Explorer, rename the solution and the project. The best way to do this is to right-click on the name and choose the *Rename* command from the shortcut menu.

- Rename the forms, if desired. If you rename the startup form, you must open the *Project Properties* dialog box and set the Startup Object.

Warning: Do not try to copy a project that is open using the *Save As* command, attempting to place a copy in a new location. The original solution and project files are modified, and you won't be able to open the original project.

Copy and Move a Web Project

If you plan to copy and/or move a Web project, make sure to explicitly save the solution file in the same folder as the project. By default, VB creates two folders for your Web projects: one in Inetpub\wwwroot and one in your default location for project files. If you save the solution file in the same folder as the rest of the project (in Inetpub\wwwroot), then you can delete or ignore the second project folder.

You can make a copy of a Web project by copying the entire folder using Windows Explorer or My Computer. To make a project in a copied or moved project run in IIS, see "Moving a Project" in Chapter 9 (p. 389).

Copy and Move a Database Project

The problem with moving a database project is that the Connection object is tied to a physical file that includes the file's path. When you copy or move a project folder, you must open the project and modify the connection for the database file. See "Making a Database Project Portable" in Chapter 10 (p. 432).

Glossary

A

AcceptButton property Form property that sets the default button, which is activated with the Enter key.

access key Underlined character that allows the user to select using the keyboard rather than the mouse, also called a *hot key*.

ANSI code A coding method used to represent characters on a microcomputer (American National Standards Institute).

argument The expression to operate upon in a function or method; a value being passed to or from a procedure.

array A series of variables; each individual element can be referenced by its index position. Also called a *list*.

assignment operator An equal sign (=); assigns a value to the variable or property named on the left side of the sign.

assignment statement Assigns a value to a variable or property using an assignment operator.

Autos window Window that opens in IDE during execution; automatically displays all variables and control contents that are referenced in the current statement and three statements on either side of the current one.

B

base class Class that is inherited from; also called a *super class* or *parent class*.

Binary formatter Object serialization format that stores the data in binary form.

BindingContext The current record position of the dataset is stored in the Position property of the binding context.

block variable A variable declared inside a block of code; only accessible within that block.

BorderStyle property Property of a control that allows the control to appear flat or three-dimensional.

breakpoint Indicated point in project code where execution should break; used for debugging.

break time Temporary break in execution of a program used for debugging.

browser An application used to render and display HTML code; used to display Web pages; in VB used to execute Web Forms.

Brush object Graphical object for drawing filled shapes.

Button Control used to activate a procedure.

ByRef Declares that an argument passed to a procedure should be passed as the address of the data so that both calling and called procedures have access to the same memory location.

ByVal Declares that an argument passed to a procedure should be passed as a copy of the data. The calling and called procedures do not have access to each other's variables.

C

call (procedure call) Execute a procedure.

callback An object notifies the program that it needs to do something or that a situation exists that the program needs to handle. The object notifies the program of the situation by firing an event.

CancelButton property Form property that sets the cancel button, which is activated with the Esc key.

Case structure Selection structure; can be used in place of an If statement.

check box A control used to indicate a value that may be True or False. In any group of check boxes, any number may be selected.

Checked property Determines if a checkbox is checked or not.

child class A class inherited from another class called the *parent*. Also called a *derived class* or *subclass*.

child form Multiple Document Interface. A child form belongs to a parent form. It is displayed inside the parent, and closes when the parent does.

class A prototype or blueprint for an object; includes specifications for the properties and methods.

clean compile Code compiles to Common Language Runtime without errors.

Close method Closes forms or files; releases resources used by the object.

Closing event Occurs before a form unloads. A good location to place the code to prompt the users if they wish to save any changes.

code Programming statements in the Basic language.

collection An object that can contain a series of objects; has properties and methods.

color constant Values assigned in the Color class. Examples: Color.Red and Color.Blue.

column A vertical section of a grid control.

ComboBox control A control that is a combination of a list box and a text box.

common dialog A set of Windows dialog boxes available to Visual Basic programmers for Open, Save, Fonts, Print, and Color.

complex binding Connects multiple fields in a dataset to a control, such as a grid.

compound condition Multiple conditions combined with the use of the logical operators And or Or.

concatenation Joining string (text) fields. The ampersand (&) is used to concatenate text.

condition An expression that will evaluate True or False. May be a comparison of two values (variables, properties, constants) using relational operators.

connection Object that establishes a link to a data source.

constant A value that cannot change during program execution.

constructor A procedure that runs automatically when an object is instantiated from that class. In VB, a constructor is coded with Sub New.

context menu A pop-up menu, sometimes referred to as a *shortcut menu* or a *right-mouse menu*.

context-sensitive Help Use of the F1 function key to directly access the Help topic related to the code or object containing the cursor.

control An object used on a graphical interface, such as a radio button, text box, button, or label.

conversion functions Convert an argument into a different data type; often used to convert text input data to numeric data for calculations.

criteria Conditions for selection.

Crystal Reports A robust report generator for database files.

CrystalReportViewer control Provides application the ability to display reports generated through Crystal Reports.

D

data adapter An object that handles retrieving and updating of the data in a dataset.

data binding Connecting a control or property to one or more data elements.

data file A file used to store small amounts of information such as the contents of a list box.

dataset A temporary set of data stored in the memory of the computer.

data type Specifies the type of data a variable or constant can hold, such as Integer, Decimal, or String.

DateTime structure Used to retrieve and format the current date and time.

Debug.WriteLine method Statement to write a line in the Debug window; used to write a message for debugging.

debugging Finding and eliminating computer program errors.

declaration Statements to establish a project's variables and constants, give them names, and specify the type of data they will hold.

Declaration section Code outside of a procedure, used to declare module-level variables.

derived class A subclass inherited from a base class.

deserialization Reads an object that has been serialized or saved to a file. Re-creates the saved object.

design time The status of the Visual Studio environment while a project is being developed, as opposed to run time or break time.

destructor A method that is called as an object goes out of scope.

DialogResult object   Used to determine which button the user clicked on a message box.

direct reference   Accessing an element of an array by a subscript when the value of the subscript is known.

disabled   Enabled property set to false; user can see the control but cannot access it.

Do and Loop statements Statements to indicate the beginning and ending of a loop. A condition can appear on the Do or on the Loop.

Document window   IDE window that displays the Form Designer, the Code Editor, the Object Browser, and the pages of Help that you request.

DrawLine method   Method of the Graphics object.

DrawRectangle method Method of the Graphics object; used to draw squares and rectangles.

DrawString method   Method of the Graphics object; sends a line of text to the graphics page.

drop-down combo box   A combo box control with a down-pointing arrow that allows the user to drop down the list. Allows efficient use of space on a form.

drop-down list   A list box with a down-pointing arrow that allows the user to drop down the list. Allows efficient use of space on a form.

E

element   Single item within a table, array, list, or grid.

empty string   A string containing no characters; also called a *null string* or *zero-length string*.

Enabled property   Determines if the control is available to the user.

encapsulation   OOP feature that specifies that all methods and properties of a class be coded within the class. The class can hide or expose the methods and properties, as needed.

End If   Terminates a block If statement.

Enterprise Architect Edition The version of Visual Studio with the most features.

Enterprise Developer Edition A version of Visual Studio more robust than the Professional Edition but with fewer features than the Enterprise Architect Edition.

event   An action that may be caused by the user, such as a click, drag, key press, or scroll. Events can also be triggered by an internal action, such as repainting the form or validating user input.

event procedure   A procedure written to execute when an event occurs.

exception   An error that occurs at run time.

F

field   A group of related characters used to represent one characteristic or attribute of an entity in a data file or database.

Field Explorer   Window for adding fields to a Crystal Report layout.

FileStream   Class used for object serialization; used to

transfer a series of characters to or from a file.

FillEllipse method   Method of the Graphics object; used to draw circles and ovals.

flow layout   Design for Web Forms; each element follows the previous one, similar to a word-processing document.

focus   The currently selected control on the user interface. For controls such as buttons, the focus appears as a light dotted line. For text boxes, the insertion point (also called the *cursor*) appears inside the box.

Focus method   Sets the focus to a control.

ForeColor property   Property that determines the color of the text.

form   An object that acts as a container for the controls in a graphical interface.

format   A specification for the way information will be displayed, including dollar signs, percent signs, and number of decimal positions.

formatting functions Functions used to make output easier to read. Numeric data can be formatted as currency or percent.

Form Designer   The IDE window for creating the user interface.

For/Next loop   A loop structure; usually used when the number of iterations is known.

FromFile method   Retrieves an image from a file.

function   Performs an action and returns a value.

function procedure   A procedure that returns a value.

G

garbage collection   Automatic deletion of objects from memory after they are out of scope.

general procedure   A procedure not attached to an event; may be a sub procedure or a function procedure.

graphical user interface (GUI) Program application containing icons, buttons, and menu bars.

graphics   An image file assigned to a PictureBox control; methods of the Graphics class, such as `DrawString`, `DrawLine`, and `DrawEllipse`.

grid layout   Default layout for Web Forms; controls may be placed anywhere on the form; location specified with *x* and *y* coordinates.

group box   A control used as a container for other controls, such as a group of radio buttons.

H

handle   A small square on a selected control at design time; used to resize a control. Also called a *resizing handle*.

I

IDE   See *integrated development environment*.

identifier   A name for a variable, procedure, and named constant; supplied by the programmer.

`If...Then...Else`   Statement block for testing a condition and taking alternate actions based on the outcome of the test.

image list component Contains a collection of images to use for other controls, such as a toolbar.

Image property   A graphic file with an extension of .bmp, .gif, .jpg, .png, .ico, .emf, or .wmf.

immutable   The inability of a string to be modified once it is created. A new string must be created for any modifications.

increment operator   Shortcut operator for increasing the value of a variable by 1 (+=).

index   Position within a list or array.

inheritance   Ability to create a new class based on an existing class.

instance   An object created from a class.

instance property   See *instance variable*.

instance variable   Each object created from the class has a separate occurrence of the variable.

instantiate   Create an object using the `New` keyword.

integrated development environment (IDE)   Tool for writing projects and solutions, includes an editor, tools, debugger, and other features for faster development.

Interval property   Determines the amount of time until a Timer component fires a Tick event; measured in milliseconds.

intranet   Network within a company.

intrinsic constant   Constants supplied with a language or application such as Color.Blue.

IsMdiContainer property Used to create a parent form for MDI.

`IsNumeric` **function**   Tests a variable to determine if the value contains only numeric characters.

`Items.Add` **method**   Adds elements to the Items collection of a list box.

`Items.Clear` **method**   Clears all elements from a list box.

Items.Count property Property that holds the number of elements in a list box.

`Items.Insert` **method**   Inserts an element in a list for a list box.

Items property   Collection of elements for a list box or combo box control.

`Items.Remove` **method** Removes the currently selected item from a list.

`Items.RemoveAt` **method** Removes the specified item from a list.

iteration   A single pass through the statements in a loop.

K

key field   The field (or fields) on which a data file is organized; used to search for a record.

L

Label   A control that displays text; cannot be altered by the user.

`LayoutMdi` **method**   Arranges MDI child windows vertically, horizontally, or cascaded.

lifetime   The period of time that a variable exists.

line-continuation character   A space and underscore; used in program code to indicate that a

Basic statement continues on the next line.

ListBox control A control that holds a list of values; the user cannot add new values at run time.

Locals window Window that opens in IDE during execution; displays all objects and variables that are within scope at break time.

local variable The scope of a variable or constant that limits its visibility to the current procedure.

logical operator The operators `And`, `Or`, and `Not`; used to construct compound conditions and to reverse the truth of a condition.

logic error An error in a project that does not halt execution but causes erroneous results in the output.

loop A control structure that provides for the repetition of statements.

loop index A counter variable used in a `For/Next` loop.

M

Maximum property Scrollbar property for highest possible value.

MdiList property Determines whether the menu will display a list of open MDI child windows; used on the `Window` menu.

menu A list of choices; the available commands displayed in a menu bar.

Menu Designer Feature of the development environment for creating menus, accessed by adding a Main Menu component to the component tray.

MessageBox A dialog box that displays a message to the user.

method Predefined actions (procedures) provided with objects.

Minimum property Scrollbar property for lowest possible value.

module-level variable A variable that can be used in any procedure within the current class or module.

multiple document interface (MDI) Multiple form project that has parent and child forms.

multitier application A program designed in components or services, where each segment performs part of the necessary actions. Each of the functions of a multitier application can be coded in a separate component and the components may be stored and run on different machines.

`MustInherit` Modifier on a class definition. The class cannot be instantiated, but instead must be used for inheritance.

`MustOverride` Modifier on a procedure definition; requires that the procedure be overridden in an inherited class.

N

named constant Constant created and named by the developer.

namespace Used to organize a group of classes in the language library; the hierarchy used to locate the class. No two classes may have the same name within a namespace.

namespace-level variable A variable that can be used in any procedure within the currrent namespace, which is generally the current project.

nested `If` An If statement completely contained within another If statement.

`New` **keyword** Used to instantiate an object; creates an object and assigns memory for property values.

`NewLine` The Visual Studio constant `ControlChars.NewLine` used to determine line endings.

Nothing An object variable that does not have an instance of an object assigned. Formerly used to destroy an object.

Now property Current date and time from the DateTime structure.

O

object An occurrence of a class type that has properties and methods; a specific instance of a control type, form, or other class.

object-oriented programming (OOP) An approach to programming that uses classes to define the properties and methods for objects. Classes may inherit from other classes.

OpenFileDialog Common dialog component used to display the Windows *Open File* dialog box; allows the user to view files and select the file to open.

Option Explicit Setting this option On forces variables and objects to be declared before they can be used.

Option Strict Setting this option On enforces strong data typing.

order of precedence Hierarchy of mathematical operations; the order in which operations are performed.

overloading   Allows a method to act differently for different arguments; multiple procedures in the same class with the same name but with different argument lists.

overriding   A method in a derived (inherited) class with the same name and argument list as a method in the parent (base) class. The method in the derived class overrides (supersedes) the one in the parent class for objects of the derived class.

P

parameterized constructor A constructor (`Sub New`) that contains an argument list; as opposed to an empty constructor.

parameterized query   Allows a value for a query to be supplied at run time.

parent class   The base class for inheritance, also called a *super class*.

parent form   MDI container for child forms.

Peek method   Used to look ahead to determine if records remain in a file stream.

Pen object   Graphical object for drawing lines and shapes.

PictureBox control   A control used to display an image.

pixel   Picture element; a single dot on the screen; a unit of measurement for displaying graphics.

Point structure   Holds *x* and *y* coordinates as a single unit.

polymorphism   OOP feature that allows methods to take different actions depending on the situation. Methods may have the same name but different argument

lists; also refers to the naming convention of keeping method names consistent.

postback   A round-trip to the server.

posttest   A loop that has its test condition after the body of the loop; the statements within the loop will always be executed at least once; also called an *exit test*.

pretest   A loop that has its test condition at the top; the statements inside the loop may never be executed; also called an *entry test*.

PrintDocument control Contains methods and events to set up output for the printer.

Print method   A method of the PrintDocument class to begin executing code for printing.

PrintPage event procedure Contains the logic for printing.

print preview   View the printer's output on the screen and then choose to print or cancel.

PrintPreviewDialog control Used to allow print previews for an application.

procedure   A unit of code; may be a sub procedure, function procedure, or property procedure.

Professional Edition   A version of Visual Basic that includes fewer features than the Enterprise editions.

Properties window   A window in the IDE used to set values for properties at design time.

property   Characteristic or attribute of an object; control properties may be set at design time or run time depending on the specific property.

property procedure   Procedure written with `Set` and `Get` keywords

to pass values to and from private variables in a class.

Protected   Access modifier for a variable or procedure; behaves as private but allows inheritance.

pseudocode   Planning tool for code using an English expression or comment that describes the action.

R

radio button   A control used to indicate a value that may be True or False (selected or not selected). In any group of radio buttons, only one button may be selected.

Randomize statement   Starts (seeds) the random function at different points.

ReadLine method   Reads one record from a file; reads to the end of the line.

ReadOnly   A property that can be retrieved but not set by objects; indicates that only a `Get` method exists for the property.

record   A group of related fields; relates to data files and database tables.

Rectangle structure   Defines a rectangular region, specified by its upper-left corner and its size.

relational operator   Used to compare two fields for greater than >, less than <, or equal to =.

remark   A Basic statement used for documentation; not interpreted by the compiler; also called a *comment*.

return value   Value returned from a function.

reusability   Code modules that can be used in multiple projects.

Rnd **function** Returns a number from a random number list. The numbers are in the range 0 to 1.

row A horizontal section of a grid control or one record in a file.

run time During the time a project is executing.

run-time error An error that occurs as a program executes; causes execution to break.

S

scope The extent of visibility of a variable or constant. The scope may be namespace, module level, block, or local.

Scroll event Scrollbar event that occurs as the user moves the scroll box.

SelectedIndex property Index of the item currently selected in a list box or combo box.

separator bar A horizontal line used to separate groups of menu commands.

serialization A series of bits used to save the state of an object's properties so that the object can be re-created at a later time.

SetBounds **method** Set the location of a control; used to move a control.

shared property A property that can be used by all objects of the class; generally used for totals and counts. Only one copy exists for all objects of the class.

shared variable See *shared property.*

shortcut menu The menu that pops up when the right mouse button is clicked. Also called a *pop-up menu, context menu,* or *right-mouse menu.*

ShowDialog **method** Displays a common dialog box.

Show **method** Displays a form or message box.

ShowPanels property Determines whether the panels in a status bar display or not.

signature The argument list of a method or procedure.

simple binding Connecting a single data field to a single control, such as a label or text box.

simple combo box Fixed size combo box.

simple list box Fixed size list box.

single document interface (SDI) Forms act independently in a multiple form project.

SizeMode property Allows the size of an image in a picture box to stretch or shrink.

Size structure A size specified by width and height; measured in pixels.

SmallChange property Scrollbar property for amount of move by a click on an arrow.

SOAP formatter Format for storing objects following the standards for simple object access protocol (SOAP).

solution A Visual Basic application; can consist of one or more projects.

Solution Explorer window An IDE window that holds the filenames for the files included in your project and a list of the classes it references.

solution file A text file that holds information about the solution and the projects it contains.

StartPosition property Determines the screen location of the first form in a project when execution begins.

stateless Does not store any information about its contents from one invocation to the next.

Static local variable A local variable with a lifetime that matches the module. The variable retains its value as long as the form is loaded.

status bar An area along the lower edge of a window used to display information for the user.

StatusBar control A control to create a status bar at the bottom of a form.

StatusBarPanel object Individual item on a StatusBar control.

Step Into Debugging command; executes each statement, including those in called procedures.

Step Out Debugging command; continues rapid execution until the called procedure completes, and then returns to break mode at the statement following the call.

Step Over Debugging command; executes each statement in main procedure but does not show statements in called procedures.

stream An object used to transfer a series of bytes from one location to another.

StreamReader Object used to input small amounts of information stored in a disk file.

StreamWriter Object used to write small amounts of information to disk.

StretchImage Setting for the value of the SizeMode property of a PictureBox control.

string literal A constant enclosed in quotation marks.

strongly typed A feature of VB that requires the programmer to always be aware of the data type. If you assign data to a wider type, VB can implicitly (automatically) convert for you; if you are assigning data to a narrower type, where precision or accuracy might be lost, VB will generate a compiler error.

structure A grouping that combines multiple fields of related data.

style Formatting for a Web Form.

Style Builder An IDE feature for adding styles to HTML pages.

subclass A derived class; also called a *child class*.

submenu A menu within a menu.

sub procedure A procedure that performs actions but does not return a value.

subscript The position of an element within an array; also called an *index*.

subscripted variable An element of an array.

superclass A base class for inheritance, also called a *parent class*.

syntax error An error caused by failure to follow the syntax rules of the language; often caused by typographical errors. The Editor informs you of syntax errors.

System.IO namespace Holds the stream objects for persistence and serialization.

T

TabIndex property Determines the order the focus moves as the Tab key is pressed.

table A two-dimensional array.

table lookup Logic to find an element within an array.

TabStop property Determines if a control can receive focus.

TextAlign property Used to change the alignment of text within the control.

text box A control for data entry; its value can be entered and changed by the user.

Text property The value that displays on a control such as the words in a text box or label.

Tick event One firing of a Timer component; each time the interval passes, another Tick event occurs.

Timer component Fires Tick events at a specified time interval.

`ToLower` **method** Converts text to all lowercase letters.

toolbar The bar beneath the menu bar that holds buttons; used as shortcuts for menu commands.

toolbar control Displays buttons for shortcuts to menu items.

toolbox A window that holds icons for tools; used to create controls and components on a form.

ToolTip Small label that pops up when the mouse pointer pauses over a toolbar button or control.

ToolTip component Placed on a form to allow the individual controls to display ToolTips. A ToolTip property is added to each control.

ToolTip on ToolTip1 property The new property added to each control when a ToolTip component is added to the form.

`ToUpper` **method** Converts text to all uppercase letters.

`Try/Catch` **block** Traps user errors or program errors.

U

user interface The display and commands seen by a user; how the user interacts with an application. In Windows, the graphical display of an application containing controls and menus.

V

validation Checking to verify that appropriate values have been entered.

validator controls Controls that can automatically validate input data; used on Web Forms.

`Value` **keyword** Incoming value for a Set clause in a property procedure.

variable Memory location that holds data that can be changed during project execution.

Visible property Determines if a control can be seen or not.

Visual Studio environment The development environment including tools for designing the interface, editing program code, running and debugging applications; also called the *IDE*.

W

Web Form Form in Visual Studio for creating pages that display in a browser.

Web page   A static page consisting of HTML elements; displayed in a browser application.

`With` **and** `End With` **statements** A block of code that refers to the same object. The object name appears in the `With` statement; all subsequent statements until the `End With` relate to that object.

`WriteLine` **method**   Writes one record to a stream object; includes a carriage return character at the end.

`Write` **method**   Writes one record to a stream object; does not include a carriage return.

X

XML   Extensible Markup Language. A format for data; popular for data storage and transfer on the Internet.

Index